AN ENCYCLOPEDIA
OF
CHINESE FOOD AND
COOKING

AN ENCYCLOPEDIA

OF CHINESE FOOD AND COOKING

Wonona W. and Irving B. Chang
Helene W. and Austin H. Kutscher

Edited by LILLIAN G. KUTSCHER

CHARLOTTE ADAMS, *Consulting Editor*

CROWN PUBLISHERS, INC. · NEW YORK

To Our Children

Amos Chang
Mei-Ming Chang
Mei-Chuin Chang
Harlan Kutscher
Ken Kutscher
Martin Kutscher
Michael Goldberg
Bob Goldberg
Carol Goldberg
Richard Goldberg

who shared our enjoyment and
increased the pleasure of our adventure
in Chinese cuisine and culture.

Library of Congress Catalog Card Number: 78-93402
ISBN: 0-517-506610
Manufactured in the United States of America
Published simultaneously in Canada by
  General Publishing Company Limited
Design by Shari de Miskey

20   19   18

CONTENTS

PREFACE

SOME PEOPLE SEEM TO EAT ONLY TO LIVE. BUT, FOR THE FORTUNATE INDIvidual, eating can be a perpetual adventure into a world of new flavors and delights. This book is addressed not to the hunger stiflers but to those who unabashedly enjoy food. Truly, the enjoyment of food is not only a great pleasure at workday's end (unfortunately, often only a main dish), it is frequently a prime source of enjoyment at recreation, celebration, and vacation times. Some people even consider the enjoyment of good food a sign of culture, and measure a civilization by its cuisine.

As for the Chinese chef, he is prepared to try, fail, try again—and learn. The *Tai See Foo* innovates, invents, and eliminates, creating new combinations of available foodstuffs; the Chinese menu thrives on endless variety. Consider the innumerable English-language Chinese cookbooks published in the United States. Their collection constitutes a fascinating hobby.

Ours is an encyclopedia of Chinese foods that includes a broad range of recipes. Also, we have tried to assemble in one book all the information rarely included, and never as a whole, in other cookbooks. It is intended not only for the connoisseur of Chinese cooking who would like to know more about the food he prepares at home (or is served in a restaurant), but also for the novice who would like to know why certain foods are employed, their characteristics, and their contributions to the recipes.

One of the most important functions we have undertaken is to anticipate the innumerable questions of someone attempting to prepare a meal from an esoteric recipe. Among many other practical details, we have included a uniform romanization of the names of Chinese foodstuffs, their English equivalents, and pertinent descriptive information, with detailed photographs of each ingredient, as well as advice on where and what foods to purchase and how to store and prepare them for cooking. In this way, we hope to teach the reader not only how to cook but what he is cooking; not only how but what to buy. This arrangement has never appeared elsewhere, nor has our compilation of "instant" dishes. Similarly, foods and their preparation suitable for low-sodium or no-sodium diets, diabetic diets, and ulcer diets are unique to this volume.

While nearly every section contains more complete details than in any book of its kind previously published in the English language, every attempt has been made to keep the work concise, simple, and practical.

However, before getting on with the business of cooking, it is vital that prior to attempting the recipes, all introductory matter be read as often as necessary (including a review of the Ingredients chapter and Shopping List) to acquaint oneself with certain particularly important aspects of Chinese cooking. Also, this material should be regarded as procedural directions to be reread at the *time* of cooking.

Each recipe, unless otherwise noted, serves four people when a soup and four entrees are included in the meal. (An exception are the dietetic recipes, which serve two.) If a larger quantity of food is needed, the recipes may be doubled (but rarely cooked in any larger quantity). Conversely, because it may be difficult for the beginning cook to make four entrees for one dinner, it is perfectly feasible to start out preparing double the quantities of only two entrees (or to make a single Chinese dish daily and serve it as an adjunct to the usual fare). Four recipes, of course, each with a different dominant ingredient, provide greater variety.

As for serving, the traditional style is for everyone to have his own bowl of rice and to help himself with his chopsticks from the several entrees placed in the center of the table. Obviously, it is not necessary to abandon the Western style of serving to enjoy Chinese food, but, if preferred, it might be wiser to provide serving spoons or chopsticks with each entree.

ACKNOWLEDGMENTS

WE WISH TO EXPRESS OUR DEEP GRATITUDE TO OUR CHINESE FRIENDS AND family members who for years patiently assisted us in compiling the contents of this book. Among them are Dr. and Mrs. Ian Hu, Miss Marguerite Kwok, Dr. and Mrs. Fu-liang P. Chang, Dr. and Mrs. Daniel Yang, Mrs. Irene Chu, Mrs. Katherine C. Wang, and, of course, our children, Amos, Mei-Ming, and Mei-Chuin.

Also we wish to thank the efficient New York Chinatown grocery clerks and shop managers who helped us to obtain the proper food supplies. We particularly appreciate the kindness, cooperation, and courtesy of owners and maître d's of restaurants that became our favorites; these people tried to satisfy our every request, assigning the preparation of our meals to their master chefs. We especially acknowledge the assistance of the gracious and charming Mrs. H. H. Li, General Li, and Jimmy Lee of General Li's China Garden Restaurant, White Plains, New York; Jack Yee, formerly of Sun Luck Gourmet, New York, New York; Henry Lam of The New York Tea Garden Restaurant, Morristown, New Jersey; the proprietor of Lin's Garden in Chinatown, New York; and the staffs of Ark's Jade Room Restaurant, Fort Lee, New Jersey, and Chinaland, Atlantic City, New Jersey.

Much of the philosophy associated with Chinese cuisine, its symbolism and lore—which have added so much pleasure to our adventures—were imparted by our dear friends C. S. Chan and Barbara Bonanno of the Wing Fat Oriental Art Store, Atlantic City, New Jersey.

We are also grateful to Mrs. H. H. Li for the colored pictures of dishes prepared from our recipes and to Mr. Henrik Malpica for his photographs of the uncooked ingredients.

We are particularly indebted to Hsi-chin Tsai, M.D., of National Taiwan University for his cooperation in evaluating the Chinese ingredients for the chapters on diet ingredients, guides, and recipes, and to George Hyman, M.D., for his cooperation in evaluating the suitability of the American ingredients.

A final note of thanks is due Harlan Kutscher for his research on the history of Chinese teas and to Ken and Martin Kutscher especially for their efforts these past five years.

W.W.C.
I.B.C.
H.W.K.
A.H.K.

AUTHORS' NOTE

AN ENCYCLOPEDIA OF CHINESE FOOD AND COOKING IS THE RESULT OF A COL-
laboration of at least twenty-five years of appreciation, enjoyment, and preparation of Chinese foods and dishes: Austin H. Kutscher has concentrated on
Chinese cooking; Helene W. Kutscher on Cantonese and Mandarin dialects
pertaining to foods; Wonona W. Chang has spent a lifetime in the kitchen
and in marketing for family meals; and Irving B. Chang has devoted years to
studying the characteristics and background of Chinese foods.

Though we have pooled our resources to prepare a book on the general
subject of Chinese foods, each has employed a different and individual ap-
proach. HWK pursued her studies of the Chinese language for the explicit
purpose of finding, obtaining, and learning the "how" of preparing the many
ingredients among the sixty-odd Chinese cookbooks we accumulated, and for
attaining the skill to order properly and effectively any of the innumerable
dishes available to the Chinese in the countless restaurants we have visited
throughout the country. Because of her superior knowledge, we were able to
enjoy being served in a truly native rather than Americanized fashion. It had
been our experience that without her knowledge of the intrinsic details of
Chinese cuisine, we could not purchase the requisite foodstuffs; salesfolk were
frequently unwilling to sell characteristic merchandise and/or could not understand what we wanted because of the language barrier, despite our dili-
gence in communicating our needs. If we did succeed in purchasing any
items, often we did not really know what to do with them.

Once we were familiar with our materials, together with a significant vo-
cabulary of pertinent Chinese words and phrases, we set to work to produce
a book that would include not only a vast number of detailed illustrative recipes but that would be devoted to making Chinese marketing and cooking
more feasible, practicable, and correct, and render dining out more pleasur-
able and authentic.

Throughout we have kept in mind the discipline of the *Tai See Foo*, or master chef. Traditionally, the *Tai See Foo* begins his career as an assistant.
When he has acquired a sufficient number of the tricks of the trade, after at
least three years, two and a half just learning and practicing to cut properly,
apprenticeship is completed. By these men and in this manner have recipes
and cooking techniques been passed from one generation of chefs to the next.
The true *Tai See Foo* achieves his knowledge not only from cookbooks and
written notes but also from a lifetime of experience with the taste, feel, smell,
and appearance of food. As with French chefs, who may have learned many

of their skills from the *Tai See Foo*, a chef in China has come of age when he is able to prepare an appetizing meal on short notice from "everyday" material.

Although chefs of great skill and experience are prized throughout the world, nowhere is the *Tai See Foo* held in such importance (esteem as is reserved only for scholars!) as in China, where, in relation to the Chinese philosophy of life, his profession over the centuries has been looked upon with the greatest respect in the community.

CHINESE CUISINE: BACKGROUND

CHINESE COOKERY IS LEARNED NOT ONLY FROM STUDYING A RECIPE BUT FROM attention to theory, by practice, and by care. As a culinary art, it has been developed over centuries.

The raisons d'être of Chinese cooking are the country's centuries-old agricultural background; food preservation techniques that had to substitute for refrigeration; nutritional requirements; and, perhaps most important, esthetic considerations of color, texture, fragrance, and palatability. In the absence of refrigeration, the Chinese demonstrated their ingenuity in preserving meats and vegetables: by drying, the most popular method; by salting; by candying, as of fruits; by blanching (vegetables); and, with eggs, by their encasement in a mixture of lime, clay, and wheat chaff, curing them for forty days or longer, depending on the period of preservation.

The Chinese value food highly, and rarely waste any—many recipes require the use of leftovers, and cooking ahead is standard practice.

The basic flavors are six: sweet, sour, bitter, spicy (sharp), pungent, salty. Their distribution, proportion, and employment must be controlled for proper blending.

A study of three thousand years of recipes reveals that meat has always been a major item in the Chinese diet. However, the meat ration per person was small, except among the well off. Efficient utilization, proper color arrangements, and palatability often required highly imaginative combinations. Often the meat could be only a flavoring for a dish rather than the main ingredient. Hence, many recipes were devised to make small amounts of meat go as far as possible.

China's economy has seldom been able to afford such animals as the cow and the lamb; inadequate pastureland for cattle has made raising these animals difficult. Moreover, each farmer was likely to have an ox for plowing his fields, and because of the long and faithful service of the animals, oxen were spared. Pork is therefore China's most common meat; pigs forage for their food and grow fat on almost anything. Since these animals just eat and sleep, their slaughter causes few qualms. In the north, mutton is commonly used, particularly by the Chinese Mohammedans (in the northwest) who believe pork is profane and should not be consumed by man. Beliefs vary with the animal. The Chinese believe that the sheep is symbolic of retired life and of filial piety—the lamb kneels respectfully before its mother while feeding. The cock is supposed to be the incarnation of the *yang*, which represents all the warm, positive elements of universal life. It also symbolizes six virtues: literary spirit, warlike disposition, courage (willingness to fight), the ability to chase away ghosts, punctuality (crowing to announce each new day), and benevolence (sharing food with its mate). Ducks symbolize felicity and are emblems of conjugal fidelity; one of a pair will die soon after being separated from its mate. The pigeon and dove represent longevity, faithfulness, benevolence, and filial duty. Fish symbolize wealth and abundance; because they usually swim in pairs within schools they represent the joys and harmony of union and fecundity (for their immense reproductive powers).

The egg represents both the positive (white) and negative (yolk): *yin* and *yang*, the principles of universal life. *Yang*, the positive life force, in the heavens stands for sun and light; among humans, for vigor, male potency, penetration, and the monad. *Yin* relates to the negative forces of the earth, and is identified with the moon, darkness, quiescence, the female qualities.

This has nothing to do with the scarcity of meat. Many Chinese Buddhists, for religious reasons, will eat only vegetables, the cooking of which this group developed to a high degree. The scientific study of vegetables became a part of Taoism, and its devotees devised a highly nutritional vegetable diet, an art so refined that their vegetable dishes resemble meats in taste as well as texture.

REGIONAL CHINESE COOKING

China is divided into distinctive schools of cooking—each distinguished primarily by a varied combination of spices and sauces—that are defined geographically. The four most important are Peking, Canton, Shanghai, and Szechuan, all tending toward mutual exclusivity (the Cantonese customarily do not serve foods from Peking).

For our purposes, Peking will represent the North, and incorporates the varieties of Tientsin, Shantung (outstanding), Tsingtao, and Tungchow. Canton will represent the South, and incorporates the varieties of Kwangtung, Kwangsi, Fukien (outstanding), Tsaochow, Kweilin, and Nannien. Shanghai will represent the East, and incorporates the varieties of Yangchow, Hangchow, Nanking, Suchow, Ninpo, Tsenkiang, and Hweiyang. Szechuan (though actually in the Southwest) will represent the West, and incorporates the varieties of Chunking, Kweichow, Kweiyang, Hunnan, Hupeh, Yunnan, Chentu, and Kunming.

Other regions no doubt have contributed greatly to the overall Chinese cuisine, but these may represent only one or a few characteristic dishes, and therefore cannot be considered representative of a specific school. However, where possible, such individual regions have been identified for a unique dish.

Two further designations regarding origin are assigned to the recipes in this book: adapted and general, the former derived from authentic, formerly untranslated Chinese texts. Because the original Chinese text provided no quantities for ingredients, and gave no sources, these adapted recipes had to be perfected in the author's kitchen; the general recipes are so designated because their principal ingredients, as well as their auxiliary vegetables, seasonings, spices, and sauces, are found and used throughout China.

Peking, for centuries the capital of China (as it is again), was inhabited by China's emperors and aristocrats. Since the twelfth century, it has been the seat of government and China's intellectual and cultural center. It was natural in such an environment for many elegant, imaginative dishes to be created, or imported. Peking's essential character always resisted change, its many barbarian conquests and subsequent occupations notwithstanding. It was the same with regard to cooking. Many chefs from other areas migrated to the capital, and it became the home of some of the finest restaurants in the world. Peking became the center of Chinese culinary culture to such an extent that all other schools of cooking established themselves and set up restaurants there. Some, centuries old, still use the ancient cooking techniques. The finest of Canton, Fukien, Honan, Shantung, and Szechuan dishes for example were to be found in Peking restaurants. Peking had become (before the advent of Chinese Communism) for Chinese food what Paris is for French food—the representative of a nation's cuisine.

Peking cooking exhibits the greatest ingenuity and inventiveness. The school is known for its steam breads, noodles (made from wheat flour), fish, duck, sweet bean sauce, scallions, leeks, and many other foods. Anyone who has ever tasted Peking Duck, Mu Shu Pork, Mandarin Duck, Mandarin Fish, Rice Crust Soup, and Mongolian Roast Beef will never forget Peking's contribution.

Fruits such as pears, persimmons, apples, oranges, plums, apricots, peaches, and melons are common—as in the South.

Cantonese cooking is undoubtedly the best-known school, partly because the Cantonese emigrated to many countries, including the United States, Australia, England, France, Indonesia, Thailand, and Burma. Canton became rich through foreign trade, and from such wealth and leisure grew the desire for good food and its subsequent indulgence. Cantonese dishes are easily characterized by their reliance on color; their spices are not very unusual or hot, though they do like hoisin sauce, as well as plum sauce and soy sauce. Cooking techniques rely heavily on stir-fried dishes—prepared in oil over high heat—and steaming. Specialties are Shark Fin Soup, Sea Bass with Black Beans, Beef and Salted Cabbage, Pork and Salted Egg, Won Ton, Meat Patties in Rice Dough. Suckling pig and roast pork are also favorites.

Shanghai is China's largest, most famous seaport. Surprisingly, it is not as inventive in its cooking as Peking and Canton. In Shanghai, there is more dependence on soy sauce, and a great deal more sugar is used. Popular dishes are Lion's Head, Drunken Chicken, Preserved Mustard Green Soup, Scallion Fish, Honey Ham, and Salt Cured Chicken. Much seafood is used (cooked alive), fresh-water shrimp, bamboo shoots, and pork. Rice is the staple.

Szechuan is the largest of China's provinces, and the most populous. Of the major schools, Szechuan cooking is probably the least known here, though its rice is shipped all over the world. The Szechuan restaurants in the large Chinese cities are famous for their dishes. This region's cooking is enriched by the availability of many spices. The use of Szechuan anise pepper most distinguishes the style of cooking from that of other regions. Other spicy foods include various herbs and preserved kohlrabi. Naturally, hot and sour dishes prevail, and specialties are Szechuan Duck, Sliced Hoisin Pork, Bean Curd, Spicy Chicken, Spiced Turnip, and Hot and Sour Soup.

Foochow dishes from the province of Fukien along the southern coast are ingenious, with outstanding seafood and mushroom dishes and excellent teas. Their dishes are characteristically soupy and light, though they do have their spicy red fermented bean sauce. Their soy sauce is also excellent. Some specialty foods are suckling pig, spring rolls, seaweeds, green teas, paper-thin pancakes, rice noodles, and dried cuttlefish, with rice as a staple.

Hunan Province is in the mid-Yangtze Valley, in southeast central China. Its most famous cities are Changsha and Hengyang. These are known for their peppery dishes and freshwater fish dishes. Hunan dishes, spicy, hot, sweet and sour, are less varied and less colorful than Canton's. Some favorites are Sweet and Sour Fish, Sweet and Sour Kidneys, and Pork in Cream of Rice. Its carp from the Yellow River is well known throughout China.

Shantung, in the north, has the highest density population of China's provinces. Shantung is the birthplace of Confucius. It is well known for its inventiveness in cooking—and has exchanged recipes with Peking over the years. Meats cooked in wine, smoked meats, sweet and sour dishes, Chinese cabbage, chicken, noodles, and steamed bread are favorites. Rice runs second to bread, noodles, corn, and barley.

UTENSILS FOR COOKING, SERVING, AND EATING

IT IS ENTIRELY POSSIBLE TO COOK CHINESE DISHES WITH AVAILABLE AMERICAN utensils, however desirable the authentic Chinese variety. Particularly useful are the American thermostatically regulated electric frying pans. These come in a wide range of sizes, shapes, and depths, and maintain heat at constant temperatures not possible with Chinese utensils. These electric pans achieve heat that rivals the better Chinese cooking utensils as well as high-heat ranges, and are preferable to ordinary American utensils used on an electric range; quite possibly, many will find them preferable to the Chinese sort. They are capable of producing dishes that equal the traditional methods when slow, even cooking is required. The same results also can be achieved by a heavy aluminum pot on a gas range. Ranges in American and Chinese kitchens and restaurants differ markedly. American kitchen ranges are divided between gas and electric types; the former are far preferable for cooking Chinese food. With electric ranges, if the pot is not removed after the heating element is turned off, further cooking, perhaps overcooking, occurs.

Preparations for cooking require twelve tools, three primary: a large sharp knife (often a cleaver), a hardwood cutting board (or chopping block), and a heavy smooth skillet (often the *wok*) or electric frying pan. The knife and cutting board are essential because knives are not set at the table; hence, practically all foods are served bite-size whether meat or vegetable, cooked sufficiently tender to be grasped by the chopsticks and eaten without further ado. Exceptions are for special dishes, such as whole fish, duck, or chicken, favored at banquets. These are cut in small portions at the table, and served. All the implements are as follows:

Cleaver (dai doh; tsoi doh)

The blade of the cleaver is rectangular, approximately 3⅓ inches wide and 8 inches long; its back tapers from a thickness of ⅛ inch to a thinner, sharper, cutting edge; a cylindrically shaped wooden or bamboo handle about 4 inches long is attached at the end along the back. It handles easily, is well balanced, and should be kept extremely sharp. Once the cleaver's versatility and safety are discovered, one can understand why it is employed constantly by chefs.

It is used for chopping through bones (using powerful strokes, as when splitting poultry into halves, quarters, or smaller segments); chopping through the shells of lobsters and crabs; mincing all kinds of meats; scaling large whole fish and chopping the bones; pounding foods flat; tenderizing abalone or beef steaks; crushing, peeling, and pounding garlic, ginger, or onion; mashing; slicing vegetables; crushing Chinese condiments, such as black beans and garlic, into a paste; tearing and slicing ingredients, then scooping and transferring them from the chopping block to a pan or storage utensil. A thin-bladed cleaver is used for light-duty cutting; a heavier one for heavy-duty cutting.

The weight of the blade should be permitted to do the work—it is comparatively infrequent that any sawing back and forth is necessary if the food is cut cleanly and sharply.

Because it is made of carbon steel, a highly rustable metal, it should not be left to dry after washing but dried immediately and put away. Carbon steel is preferable to stainless steel because it takes an edge readily and consequently is sharpened easily.

Chopping Block (jum baahn)

Actually, this is a smooth-surfaced tree cross section, 12 to 15 inches in diameter and 6 to 8 inches thick. It is used for heavy chopping, mincing, and boning, and gets constant use. Often a small auxiliary block is useful. A chopping block should never be soaked in water. It should be wiped clean with a wet sponge or rubbed with steel wool. When foods must be minced to a pulp or light slicing is to be performed, an ordinary cutting board similar to a breadboard may be used.

Rolling Pin (mein jong)

This is no more than a simple wooden roller, about 1½ inches in diameter and anywhere from 8 to 30 inches long. It is used for rolling dough thin or crushing nuts, and is very popular in China. A roller should never be soaked in water. It should be wiped clean with a moist sponge.

Pastry Board (an baahn)

This smooth-surfaced board is a rectangle about 22 by 28 inches, usually with two projections: a "stop" at each end, one to keep the board steady while dough is being formed into noodles, won-ton, etc., and another to prevent any flour from spilling out over the table and floor. It is also popular in China.

Wok

This is an iron pot that is much like a French frying pan. Its round bottom usually requires a metal ring to hold it steady on modern ranges. The ring sits on or straddles the top-of-the-range burner, permitting the heat to radiate over the wok's entire bottom surface. The ring is perforated with air holes all around to feed the flame and is an essential piece of equipment to be purchased with the wok.

Some woks are made of aluminum or copper. The round bottom provides flexibility in exposing portions to be cooked; also, the sauce and oil drain to the center where the heat is concentrated.

The wok's combined thinness and rounded bottom permit the quick cooking and concentrated heat employed in most Chinese recipes. Stirring is extremely simple. Heat is radiated quickly and is evenly distributed, and the wok's large cooking area is convenient for toss-cooking (in which ingredients are actually tossed), or cooking odd-shaped foods (a whole fish with head).

The wok's size depends upon the amount of food to be cooked (sizes range for from one to ten servings). Diameters range from 10 to 24 inches (the latter commonly used in restaurants). A 14-inch wok most often is recommended for the American kitchen. The 12-incher features an innovation—a frying-pan-type handle, but much handier and less cumbersome. Woks are available at Chinese groceries and at American hardware stores. Attachments include a cover (usually aluminum) and a deep cup for steaming or long cooking. It is one of the most practical utensils devised by man. It is an all-purpose cooking pan, with which many foods can be easily prepared—from stir-frying to braising, stewing, deep frying (tsa), steaming (jing), smother-cooking (munn), red-cooking (hung shu), casserole steaming (dun), poaching (chung), toss-cooking (chao), boiling (bo), and light frying (jeen).

When purchased, the wok should be seasoned before it is used. Otherwise the food content will stick to it. It should be washed with hot water and soap, greased over the entire inside surface with peanut oil or any other kind of cooking oil, placed on its special ring over a high heat for about a minute, then rinsed with hot water, and the process repeated several times. Seasoning the wok with peanut oil seals the pores of the metal. This prevents the ingredients from sticking and avoids a metallic flavor in the food. After seasoning it should be washed carefully with hot water only. Any excess oil on the inside should be scraped or scoured, without soap. Scouring here is defined as rubbing with salt on a paper towel. Most often, residual gravy is scraped with a stiff brush and washed away in hot water. Gradually, as it becomes seasoned, the appearance of the wok changes from that of a shiny metal to black. It is then ready for use, after which, because it is made of iron, it should be dried immediately over heat, after rinsing, to prevent rusting.

Though for authenticity a wok is as desirable as a cleaver and chopsticks, the kitchen knife, fork, and electric skillet can replace them quite satisfactorily. The electric frying pan, thermostatically controlled, can for the most part do the work of the wok, especially large woks (their cooking temperatures may be difficult to control in the average home). A cast-iron wok is preferable to any other. A skillet with a copper-lined bottom, though it is a rapid conductor does not distribute heat evenly, and, hence, is inferior to the cast-iron wok—whose counterpart in American kitchens is the heavy frying pan. Some people might consider the wok an impractical luxury but doing without one means a considerable diminution of pleasure, if not a decrease in cooking effectiveness.

Ladle and Turner (tong piu and wok chan)

The ladle is curved and the turner is flat. These are especially useful for stirring and turning quickly to prevent ingredients from burning. The ladle is held in the left hand and the turner in the right as the food is stirred with a circular motion, lifting and dropping it as in a tossed salad, but with care to avoid bruising the ingredients. A large metal spoon and a pancake turner are good substitutes.

Steaming Utensils

Improvised: An inverted flat-bottomed strainer is frequently used, or a small pan or pot perforated with many holes and inverted over a larger pot of boiling water—the water level kept to about three-fourths of the height of the perforated pan or pot. A round rack with legs about 3 inches high is also available, on which the steaming platter (able to withstand steam heat) may be placed.

The platter containing the ingredients to be steamed should be placed upon the inverted pot or strainer and the lid of the steamer placed tightly over. There must be adequate room for steam to circulate freely between food and cover. Additional boiling water may be added during prolonged steaming to avoid total evaporation (and burning of the pot). At the conclusion of steaming, the heat is turned off, and after allowing a moment for the hot steam to dissipate itself the cover should be removed gently (with a kitchen glove to avoid scalding the hand). The pyrex or aluminum pan (or the food itself, such as a bun) is then removed, using a kitchen glove or a special three-pronged holder.

An electric frying pan may be substituted if it is deep enough to permit the placement of a rack, with two to three inches of boiling water coming up almost to the top level. A flat dish or bowl containing the ingredients to be cooked is placed on top of the rack.

Chinese steam racks, bamboo or aluminum (jing loong): These are layers or tiers of bamboo mesh or aluminum, perforated trays—porous in construction—designed to permit full steam penetration from a large pot underneath. Water is boiled in the pot. The trays rest on the pot of boiling water and are covered with a large metal lid during the steaming process. The trays can also be stacked on a wok.

The dish containing the food for steaming should be placed on the steam tray. When the water is reboiled, the heat is turned down since rapid boiling does not provide more heat than slow boiling. The cautions and other comments on the improvised methods apply here as well.

As for the bamboo steamers, they are cumbersome and present a storage problem. Also, they have no handles for hanging. Steamers commonly found in this country are aluminum.

Strainers (lo dou)

These are flatter than the standard American variety and consequently better for maneuvering large objects in and out of a vessel of cooking fat. They are not essential.

Fire Pot or Mongolian Stove (ho go)

This stove is made of brass or aluminum. It is about 15 inches or more in diameter, and features a metal "chimney" in its center in which charcoal is placed and burned. These central coals heat soup and other ingredients that are placed in the bowl surrounding the chimney.

A central stove is used much like a charcoal broiler, employing about six chunks of charcoal (lighter fluid may be used to help start the fire). When the coals are red hot, ingredients are added to the hot soup in the surrounding bowl or container. A cover fits around the chimney and over the bowl. Ingredients to be cooked should be placed on separate dishes about the firepot; also soup bowls, plates, and spoons. Everyone helps himself by picking up a slice of meat or vegetable, placing it in the boiling broth until cooked, and then extracting and eating it. Because the soup is boiling hot and the meat and vegetables are sliced thin, it takes no more than a few seconds' to a few minutes' cooking time; later the soup is served in the bowls, its flavor enhanced by the foods cooked in it.

This stove is essential for all fire-pot cooking, and, of course, it must be kept clean. It derives from the ancient Asian steppes, where nomadic tribes, gathered around a fire, cooked their food in a primitive cauldron by immersing chunks of meat on skewers. Today gourmets use the Mongolian stove in authentic festive fashions. A convenient substitute would be a deep thermostatically controlled electric frying pan.

Pressure Cooker (gow op gor)

For red-cooking and other dishes requiring long cooking time and the tenderizing of tougher meat cuts, we have the pressure cooker. The general rules for its use are the same as those for American cooking. Fifteen pounds of pressure and about 20 minutes' cooking time are necessary.

Chopsticks (phai-tzi)

Gold, silver, ivory, coral, wood, and even twentieth-century plastics are available, but plain bamboo chopsticks are cheapest and perhaps best. Generally the top half is squared, the bottom half rounded and slightly tapered; average length is about 10 inches, with a $\frac{1}{4}$-inch thickness at the top. Most chopsticks are durable and rarely break in use. Bamboo and wooden types are used in the kitchen since they can withstand high temperatures and do not alter the taste of the food. They are used as eggbeaters, cooking forks, mixing spoons, draining spoons, etc. Ivory chopsticks are equivalent to sterling silver. They must not become overheated or they will warp and turn yellow or brown. They should be washed in sudsy, lukewarm water and dried thoroughly.

To be eaten with chopsticks, food must be fragile enough to be easily broken into dainty pieces by these instruments or precut or presliced into segments that can be picked up easily. Noodles and rice in particular are eaten with chopsticks. Of the two, the rice is more readily picked up or, more properly, gently shoved into the mouth directly from the bowl.

Chopsticks are not difficult to manage. They are grasped a little below their midpoint, with the smaller ends toward the plate, or bowl. The upper chopstick is held between the pads of the thumb, index, and middle fingers. The lower chopstick remains stationery between the middle of the thumb and index finger and on the pad of the third finger, which supports it. Food is manipulated by the spreading movement of the upper chopstick to encompass the food and then the food is grasped with the aid of the lower chopstick. Firm and steady pressure will hold the food between the tips until it reaches the mouth. Too firm a pressure will cause the food-laden ends of the chopsticks to slip past each other, scattering the food on the plate.

A learner should not attempt to pick up everything without first discriminating between dull-surfaced objects, elusive, slippery objects, or indefinite loose particles. Dull-surfaced objects can be picked up directly with the chopsticks, whereas loose objects must be lifted by sliding the chopsticks under them and more or less scooping them up. The bowl should be held in the fingers or palm. This shortens the distance the food travels from bowl to mouth. To master the skill takes only a little practice and perseverance; an early clumsiness should not discourage one. As with any manual skill, it takes time to learn.

When a diner has finished eating, the chopsticks should be placed together —pointing away from him—on his bowl, thus indicating that, although he has finished eating, other guests should continue enjoying their food.

Eating with chopsticks is the best way to enjoy Chinese food since it permits just the right amount of sauce on a morsel.

COOKING
PREPARATIONS

ALTHOUGH NATIVE-BORN CHINESE IN AMERICA WOULD PREFER TO FOLLOW the methods of food preparation in just the same way as their forefathers did, even to using the authentic utensils, it is totally impractical. Even the orthodox Chinese compromise with traditional techniques, techniques that are laborious and cumbersome here.

Cutting

However, most Chinese still insist that their foods be brought to the table cut to uniform size and shape, preferably bite-size, which of course derives from Chinese cooking techniques. Several methods are used to achieve this end: straight cutting, diagonal cutting, mincing, dicing, shredding, and strip-and-roll diagonal cutting.

In straight cutting, the knife should enter the meat or vegetable at right angles to the board. The middle fingers of the left hand act as a protective surface and guide; they are at right angles to the food. Slices should be approximately 1 inch long and ⅛ inch thick. Meats that are slightly frozen are easiest to cut. All are straight cut against the grain.

In diagonal cutting, the knife enters at a 45° angle. This method reduces cooking time because more surface is exposed to the heat, ensuring tenderness and an attractive shape. The left hand (the guiding, protective surface) should be relaxed and assume a 45° angle. The cutting motion is a smooth, backward draw of a very sharp knife followed by a roll of the wrist to prevent slices from sticking together. Tender, fleshy vegetables (celery cabbage) or cylindrical or stalky vegetables (celery) are sliced diagonally—or French cut—to avoid a stringy texture.

In mincing, a previously sliced ingredient is cut into very fine pieces with a chopping motion. This is tedious but the Chinese believe it to be so superior that they prefer it to grinding. If ground meat is to be used, it should be ground only once at the coarsest setting.

Dicing produces the same effect as coarse mincing by cutting first in one direction and crosshatching in the other. Shredding cuts thinly sliced food into fine slivers. To shred meat, it should be straight sliced first then cut lengthwise into ⅛- to ¼-inch shreds. To shred a fibrous vegetable (Chinese celery cabbage or celery), the stalk should be straight sliced (with the fibers) into 1- to 1½-inch pieces, about ⅛ inch wide. To shred a cylindrical vegetable (cucumber) it should be diagonally sliced, then shredded into ¼-inch slivers. To shred a firm vegetable, only the back end of the knife should be lifted; the tip remains on the board.

Stripping cuts a cylindrical vegetable (asparagus, carrot) diagonally as the left hand, after each slice, rolls the vegetable toward the cutter in such a way that the knife slices through part of the surface exposed by the previous cut. Stripping produces variously faceted shapes, which may not be as attractive as diagonal slicing.

As for fowl, the Chinese usually cut it into 2-inch pieces, without boning, which facilitates its handling by chopsticks. An advantage of the 2-inch size (at least) is that it makes for an easy cut and the juices and flavor are retained much better. Cuts can be made with a cleaver or poultry shears. Slicers, grinders, and blenders are frequently worth the time and effort saved by their use. However, Chinese chefs insist that there is a difference in the texture of foods prepared with such mechanical devices and do not favor these new conveniences for preparing meats.

Preparing Vegetables

After vegetables are cut, they are washed and drained and set aside for cooking. Frozen vegetables should be thawed completely before using, the pieces separated, and all excess moisture drained off. The Chinese housewife does not wash vegetables until the time of cooking because it is believed that once washed and put into the refrigerator, they may soften. Vegetables should not be left at room temperature for any length of time but should be kept in the refrigerator, preferably in the crisper compartment where light, water, air, and heat cannot reach them and affect their nutritional value. If it is necessary to wash vegetables long before using them, they should be placed in a plastic bag with holes. Vegetables with loose leaves that are washed too soon in advance tend to wilt and rot. Vegetables, especially nonleafy ones, are frequently parboiled beforehand to save time and to avoid overcooking the other ingredients in the recipe. Green vegetables are boiled in water only until they turn bright green, at which time they are removed and plunged briefly into cold water to retain their color, then set aside, ready to be cooked with the other ingredients. Salads consist of fresh, crisp, brightly colored and well-chilled vegetables tossed in a light oil (especially sesame oil in Mandarin foods because of its delicate flavor and fragrance); but any pure vegetable oil, including peanut oil, will do. Often, cold cooked meats or seafoods are added to make a more complete, filling dish. Ingredients should be washed well, dried, tossed lightly in the sauce, and then chilled in the refrigerator. Care must be taken not to leave the ingredients in the sauce too long or it may change their texture. General cooking-time rules are: lettuce, watercress, and bean sprouts require only 2 to 3 minutes; asparagus, bamboo shoots, celery, onions, snow peas, and string beans are stir-fried for about 3 to 5 minutes; Chinese cabbage and other leafy vegetables are stir-fried for 5 to 7 minutes; cucumbers, okra, tomatoes, yellow squash, and zucchini are stir-fried for about 5 minutes; eggplant and turnips, after being properly cut, the former into slices or cubes, the latter into slivers, are stir-fried for approximately 5 minutes; broccoli, brussels sprouts, cabbage, carrots, cauliflower, and corn are stir-fried for about 5 minutes.

When cooking green vegetables, whether stir-fried or boiled, never lift the lid more than once, to prevent deterioration of the green color. The lid is not required when reheating, and should never be used after cooking is complete to prevent the loss of natural colors and crispness.

Dried Ingredients

Dried ingredients (mushrooms, shrimp) should be soaked in hot water until soft. Certain varieties will require cleaning and resoaking in hot water until very soft. They can then be removed, drained, and cut as desired. The liquid often is used for making soup, or as a substitute for water or soup stock. The use of this water enhances rather than dilutes the flavor. Dry ingredients may be soaked in cold or lukewarm water until sufficiently expanded for thorough washing, while any unwanted parts (the tough stems of mushrooms) can be cut away. Occasionally squeezing and drying the ingredients following their removal from the water is necessary when only the flavor itself is desired in the final cooked dish.

Cornstarch

Meat is coated with cornstarch to give the surface a smooth texture and to prevent the loss of juices. The pan and oil must be sizzling hot (at which point the ingredients are added and must be turned constantly with a suitable instrument, with care not to break up the contents and cause a mushy consistency) to sear the meat and seal in its juices. Cornstarch is used also to thicken sauces: a mixture is prepared with stock in advance (½ cup of soup stock to 1 tablespoon of cornstarch) and mixed thoroughly just before introducing it into the cooking sauce so as to avoid lumpiness and to judge the amount needed. Boiling water should be available for diluting an over-thick sauce. A high heat should be maintained when adding the cornstarch mixture, which is introduced slowly but continuously for about 30 seconds or until all the cornstarch is thoroughly incorporated. Cornstarch not only thickens sauce and ensures that all the ingredients are evenly coated but also gives the entire dish a bright, piping hot, glistening appearance.

Fats and Oils

The Chinese choose lard over butter in cooking since lard provides a rich flavor and a clear color. Also, butter is scarce because of the paucity of China's dairy products. However, in the United States, animal fat is not considered as healthful as vegetable oils; among vegetable oils most commonly employed for cooking are peanut oil, soybean oil, and sesame oil.

Peanut oil is a favorite of the Chinese. Sesame oil is used as a flavoring oil. Crisco and such fats are not suitable in Chinese cooking as they tend to gel when cold, thus spoiling the food's appearance and consistency. Soybean oil is widely used in China with results almost equal to those obtained with the more expensive peanut oil. Occasionally, sesame oil is used, which imparts an extremely distinctive flavor to any dish.

When making Chinese pastries and dem sem, suet from pork is employed. This can be obtained from pork drippings or purchased melted down, strained, cooled, and resolidified.

Peanut oil complements best the flavor of the foods cooked in it. When a high-heat recipe is to be followed, as in stir-fry or tossed cooking, peanut oil is especially useful since it can withstand a high temperature without smoking and is not likely to burn. When, in fact, it does smoke, it imparts a distinctive and desirable aroma and flavor. All these vegetable oils absorb little food odor and can be used over again for deep-fry cooking, whereas fats and oil that have a low-smoke temperature impart unpleasant flavors and odors retained from previous use.

Some Tai See Foos purify peanut oil before use. This entails pouring 5 cups of peanut oil into a pan, adding about 5 slices of ginger and 1 leek cut into several sections, and heating the oil until both the ginger and leek turn brown. These are then removed, and the oil is considered improved and ready for use. This practice also gives the oil an excellent aroma and imparts a unique flavor to the dishes in which it is used. One should be aware though that when cold the oil may turn cloudy without, however, any change in its properties or flavor.

Garlic

It is important to know just how long and at what heat garlic can be cooked without burning it, and also when to add ingredients. Generally, garlic is cooked until it stops sizzling in the oil. Ingredients are then added at once. This lowers the temperature, and the garlic does not burn, provided that all the ingredients are stirred at once, and constantly thereafter. To leave garlic in the pan (if it has been used in a large piece) or not is the cook's prerogative. It is usually preferable to use the minced form—which leaves the cook no choice.

Seasoning

Seasoning and condiments are used extensively in Chinese cooking to bring out the flavor inherent in food, as well as to induce the important chemical reaction between food and seasoning that occurs at high temperatures. Seasonings and soy sauce (light or heavy, which are not interchangeable) should be added after the meat or fish has been partially cooked, and applied gradually throughout the remaining cooking process. If added too early, they may cause a toughening of the meat. Salt, however, is nearly always added in full to the oil or water at the very outset, which tends to preserve the brightness of green vegetables. Marinating sauces and seasonings, popular with meats and vegetables, are often added hours or days before cooking for proper penetration or curing.

Most Chinese chefs add sugar to many of their dishes, and some add it to all dishes. These master chefs know that, like salt, sugar should be used to enhance food flavor. Almost any dish, Chinese or American, is improved by the addition of a half teaspoonful of granulated sugar.

Cooking Time

A cooking time is given for each recipe, but it is the degree of heat that is the controlling factor, and attention must be given to the appearance of the food. Timing and temperature can be approximate only because the type and quality of utensil and heating unit affect the required cooking time drastically.

Generally the cooking sequence is as follows. When meat and vegetables are to be combined in a single dish, often they are first cooked separately, since they usually require different cooking conditions, and are later combined in the wok. Vegetables should be cooked first because a waiting period generally will not impair their quality, though some chefs do not see any difference and cook the meat first. The pan should be oiled, preferably with peanut oil, and brought to intense heat, the vegetable sautéed (perhaps parboiled first) for a minute until it turns bright green. Short exposure to intense heat is the key to stir-frying vegetables for color appeal and crispness. Then the vegetable usually is removed from the pan and set aside while the pan, with peanut oil added, reheats to the same degree for the stir-frying of the meat. The meat is sautéed until it is about three-quarters done; if beef, the center should still be slightly red, and if pork, because a concern for health is more important than additional succulence, *it must always be completely cooked* (even in China) until all traces of pink disappear, and then it should be overcooked slightly as additional ingredients are added. Stir-frying beef may take as little as thirty seconds before seasonings are added—the final addition usually is a sugar, stock, and cornstarch solution. Additional oil may be poured, but around the side of the pan so that it will be hot by the time it reaches the food. As for stock, meat and vegetables release their own juices so that its addition becomes a matter of personal preference. This practice of stretching a meal, although common in American kitchens, is frowned upon by the Chinese chef, who insists that every dish reaching the table be at its peak of taste perfection. However, if the preference is for stock, or water, unless otherwise specified, it should be added hot.

When the seasonings are added, the meat slices should be half-done. And when they are mixed with the meat, they, too, should be piping hot through having been added at the side of the pan. Pepper and certain other seasonings are added just before the dish is ready to be served, after the sugar has been added, in very small quantities. However, these are general rules, and are subject to change, depending on the recipe.

We all make mistakes, but it is the mark of a *Tai See Foo* to remedy them in time. If too much vinegar has been added, a pinch of salt will improve the taste. Conversely, if the dish is too salty, a little vinegar or sugar may help. When too cloying a taste is apparent, salt is the remedy; if too bland, a garnish may be added.

If, in the course of cooking, as in stir-fry (or chao), any ingredient shows signs of sticking or burning, a small amount of water should be added, and the stirring increased. The heat should not be lowered. There is nothing more distasteful to the Chinese gourmet than an overcooked vegetable, which is considered done when it is crisp and the flavor is at its height. But the taste should not be raw. Correct timing will come only through experience and training. Much depends on the nature and size of the vegetable, the heat, and the cooking utensil. Young, tender vegetables require less time. Color is an important guide to peak flavor. Remember that vegetables at their brightest color are at their pinnacle of taste and eye appeal.

Initially, it is wise not to attempt more than one stir-fry dish per meal and to depend instead upon steamed and boiled or other types of dishes that can be brought to the serving point and held at the proper temperature in a low oven (200°) or, if steamed, left in the vessel.

Generally, prepared dishes can await the completion of others if set in an oven at the lowest reading so as not to dehydrate or overcook them.

Organization is vital to success. In Chinese kitchens all dry ingredients and sometimes liquids, especially oil, are left in open containers near the range to be available for instant mixing. Other liquids are kept in containers with perforated tops to facilitate sprinkling or pouring. Ingredients are aligned in the order of use, all readily and instantly accessible. It is important that before cooking, everything be washed, where required, and arranged. Obviously, doing so in the midst of preparing a stir-fry dish will inevitably ruin the meal. But where possible it is wise to clean up along the way. Utensils and hands should be washed between handling different ingredients to avoid transmitting an alien flavor to any dishes prepared thereafter.

Whenever possible, groups of ingredients should be mixed beforehand, as indicated in the recipes; thus ingredients A, B, C are mixed and set aside, the D, E, F, G mixture prepared and set aside, and so on. Also, stock should be measured and set aside. This will save time and avoid confusion later. A considerable number of seasonings are frequently incorporated into the final cornstarch-and-water mixture. This is particularly true of the heavier soy sauce—a coloring and seasoning agent. Small mixing bowls or soup bowls that can be stacked are especially useful for holding cut ingredients such as meat or vegetables, as well as sauce mixtures. These bowls can then be stacked in the order of ingredients to be added to the stir-fry pan.

Proper planning should allow for all the elements of a meal to be served together and on time. For four persons having four entrees, 2 to 3 hours of preparation and cooking are usual.

COOKING TECHNIQUES

THE CHINESE EMPLOY WELL OVER A DOZEN COOKING METHODS, SOME UNIQUELY Chinese, which will be described in detail.

Each technique is chosen carefully. The nature of the ingredients, the degree of heat, and timing are considered; certain techniques seal in juices, others importantly affect flavor, and so on.

Stir-Frying (chao cooking)

Ingredients are fried in a small amount of oil over very high heat with constant stirring until cooking is complete, usually within a few minutes. The only oil (peanut oil) needed is that required to cover completely the bottom of the frying pan. Stir-frying resembles sautéeing and is one of the most common methods of Chinese cooking. Chao cooking is best done in a wok.

All ingredients should be on hand before stir-frying is begun. Meat and vegetables should be thinly sliced or cut into small cubes. Before the oil is introduced the pan should be heated sufficiently so that the oil is free-flowing, and then the ingredients added, and stirred vigorously and continuously during the entire cooking period. The highest heat obtainable must be used, while constantly stirring, since chao dishes can be ruined in a matter of seconds. Burned spots in the pan should be wiped with a paper towel and the pan reoiled for further use. This rapid form of cooking leaves comparatively little sauce.

Since stir-frying requires only a few minutes, such dishes are usually the last to be prepared; obviously, they are at their best when served immediately from the pan. Recommended cooking times are only approximate. Stir-frying preserves color, texture, and taste as well as nutritional values. (Another method, pon, is identical to chao cooking except that the basic sauce is used instead of oil.)

Steaming or Wet Steaming (ching)

Here the food is prepared in a chamber of steam comprised of a large pot filled one-third with water and separated into two compartments either by a perforated metal sheet or a rack. Ingredients are placed above the water level so that they will not be touched, but steamed, by the water, which of course is boiling vigorously before the ingredients are inserted. This method is not to be confused with the Western-style double boiler. Steaming is extremely popular because it is simple and does not require constant attention. The steaming utensil should have a tight-fitting lid but one which permits a slow escape of steam to prevent too much pressure building up inside. After a high heat has brought the water to a boil, and the ingredients inserted, the heat is lowered as the steaming process begins (to avoid vibrations and a burned pot). If the food has been placed initially on a serving platter, there will be no need to transfer it to another platter for serving at the table. Once cooked, food should not be left in the steamer unless the heat has been turned off before cooking is complete, after which the cooking process continues for a few minutes. Thus overcooking is avoided.

Steaming preserves flavors and food nutrients through the use of steam temperature rather than higher temperatures that destroy or leach these values in discarded boiling water. Several tiers can be used in the steamer to cook different foods simultaneously. Cooking time usually varies between 15 to 30 minutes for meat patties but can range from 20 minutes to 5 hours (which may require more water), depending upon the type of food to be steamed. However, meats cooked in this fashion must be of top quality. While steaming is often the best method for reheating leftover steamed meats, steamed fish and seafoods often become tough and lose flavor upon reheating.

Steaming is especially useful for persons recovering from gastrointestinal ailments, as well as for infants, because such dishes are easily digestible and are rich in natural flavor. Steamed Pork with Water Chestnuts; Steamed Pork Patties; Steamed Eggs with Minced Meat; Minced Pork (a smooth dish like a custard is obtained, but with meat interspersed); Dem Sem (wrapped meat balls), all require the steaming method. Sometimes a bowl with the ingredients is immersed partially in the boiling water, and a lid is placed over the entire steaming utensil but none over the bowl, so that the cooking action is performed both by the boiling water on the outside of the bowl and the steam directly on the food.

Red Stewing or Red Cooking (hung-shu)

Red stewing is uniquely Chinese, similar to ordinary stewing, but here the food is cooked in large quantities of soy sauce and water rather than in water alone. It is the soy sauce that makes the dish rich, tasty, and reddish brown. It is usually made of pork, beef, ham, chicken, duck, or carp. When these are prepared without soy sauce, but by the same technique, the color will always be light.

The technique is essentially that employed for making American beef stew. It is often necessary to brown the meat first. The laden pot is brought to a boil over high heat, which is progressively reduced until quite low. Red stewing is used primarily for cooking meats, and if vegetables are to be included, they should be fresh and added just before the dish is served, and only in relation to the quantity of stew being served; reheating leftover vegetables overcooks them. Various condiments are added to red-stewed dishes: sherry, ginger, scallions, and so on.

An exact cooking time is not critical. Meat may stew one to six hours, depending on the cut of meat, and may even be cooked a day ahead and rewarmed. In fact, with some dishes the flavor may be enhanced if the stew is refrigerated. It may be kept so for a week and sometimes reheated a number of times without harm. When served cold, vegetables should *not* be added. *Hung-shu* bean cake, squab, and chicken are commonly served cold. Cooked stew can also be poured into a mold and chilled, so that the sauce will become a rich aspic.

Boiling (chu)

In parboiling, ingredients are cut and washed first, then put in a large pot in which they can float freely, over high heat. Vegetables to be eaten crisp, like broccoli, are removed from the water just before they come to a full boil; those that cannot be eaten raw or take a long time to cook should remain in the pot for whatever time is required after boiling starts. Slow and prolonged boiling destroys flavor to some degree and certainly much nutritional value is lost in the boiling water that is discarded. Parboiled ingredients are poured with the water into a colander, rinsed or soaked in cold water until thoroughly cooled, and used as the recipe directs, or in salads. Parboiled vegetables are often used in banquet dishes where time may be limited. For full boiling, as in preparing soups, the Chinese employ a slow simmering process. As soon as the water boils, the heat is turned low and the soup allowed to simmer for whatever period of time is necessary. However, preparing soups by rapid boiling in which intense heat is used will result in the same preservation of color, texture, shape, and nutrition as in tossed cooking.

Deep Frying (tsa)

Ingredients are introduced into 2 inches (or more for conventional-type fryers) of very hot oil, generally 350° to 375° F. (The oil may be saved for future use except when fish has been fried in it.) To avoid spattering, foods should be dried first. Only foods that require a few minutes' cooking time, like shrimp, can be cooked in this fashion. Many meat or poultry dishes cannot be prepared this way because either they will be raw on the inside or burned on the outside, or they will break into little pieces. (Squab, duck, and pheasant often are precooked by steaming before they can be deep fried.)

Deep frying is very similar to what is done in making French-fried potatoes. Peanut oil is heated to 375°. A deep electric frying pan best maintains the oil at the proper temperature but an oil thermometer can be used. Ingredients usually are marinated in a sauce and then coated with cornstarch, flour, or breading before being slipped into the deep oil gently and deep fried until they become tender and deep golden brown. The marinade usually consists of soy sauce, sherry, and other seasonings, in which the ingredients are soaked for about half an hour. Adding water-chestnut flour to batter assures a crispy, crunchy texture to the outside portion of fried foods.

Meat should be cut into medium-sized pieces. If fish is to be served whole, deep gashes should be cut on either side of the fish so that the salt that is rubbed on can penetrate the skin. This type of frying must be done quickly. Coating will preserve the flavor and moisture.

Though the food is ready when it turns a golden brown (depending upon its density and size), some cooks use as an indicator the time at which the batter-coated food floats to the surface of the oil.

Shallow Frying (chien)

Shallow frying requires medium heat and a longer cooking time than deep frying. After heating sufficient oil to cover the entire bottom of the pan, ingredients are spread evenly in the pan and allowed to fry slowly for a few minutes, turned over once or twice, browning both sides. This technique seals in juices in meats and is particularly useful for the final cooking of prefried or preboiled foods.

Barbecuing (shu)

Barbecuing is done over charcoal on a spit or grill, or on a rotisserie.

Roasting (kow)

The Chinese do their roasting in ovens over a charcoal fire, with frequent basting. In this country, the roasting of many Chinese foods (a whole side of pig, etc.) is usually left to the large shopkeepers who specialize in it. However, Chinese roast dishes may be prepared in Western stoves according to directions indicated, with excellent results.

Cold Mixing (lun-ban)

Scalded or parboiled ingredients are mixed in salads and chilled before serving. Once used for hygienic reasons, parboiling is now used to tenderize vegetables.

Poaching (jum)

This method is similar to that of American-style poached eggs, that is, cooked in liquid just below the boiling point. A whole chicken can be prepared in this manner. Poaching is especially good for cooking delicate fish or boned fowl in a clear soup, slowly simmering until the meat is tender.

GUIDE TO INGREDIENTS

THE OBJECT OF THIS SECTION IS TO PROVIDE ALL THE VITAL INFORMATION NECESSARY TO PLAN A MEAL —from making up a menu to the point of purchase, to assure the reader of getting what he is paying for, without delay or embarrassment, as competently and economically as though he were a native Chinese.

The ingredients described below are the stock-in-trade of the Chinese grocery and are used throughout the recipes in this book. Many are uniquely Chinese even though most of the vegetables are grown in the United States. (However, most of the ingredients are purchasable only at Chinese shops.) Certain others are Western equivalents of Oriental varieties and may be substituted for them, but differences in their preparation are notable. Chinese transliterations of both Cantonese (the dialect for cooking terminology) and Mandarin (the official dialect), in the order here given, accompany the English name for each ingredient; it may be necessary to use one or the other when ordering. (The spelling—and pronunciation—of the Chinese ingredients named in the recipe titles may vary slightly, depending on the region the dish comes from, or the most commonly used form in Chinese-American restaurants. However, any variations should be easily reconciled with our official Cantonese/Mandarin spelling and pronunciation.) These Chinese terms (Fu yu, bok tsol, etc.), many of which have become incorporated into the English cooking language, appear in the general index and are cross-referenced with their English equivalents.

All ingredients have been graded by an index of importance, ranging from 4 down to 1. A 4 rating indicates either that the ingredient is most important or essential to a specific dish or that its widespread use makes it an absolute necessity in the Chinese cupboard. Rarely can a substitute of similar quality or flavor be found for a 4 ingredient.

Ingredients rated 3 are used in many Chinese dishes and add to the authenticity of such dishes. These ingredients are found in nearly any adequately stocked Chinese cupboard.

Ingredients rated 2 are used relatively infrequently, are required by fewer dishes, and are not essential. Substitutes can be made for these.

Ingredients rated 1 are difficult to obtain, those used rarely or limited to a few dishes, or are acceptable to only the most sophisticated palates. These would be the last to be purchased for the Chinese kitchen.

Costs are included, but only as generalized comparisons with familiar Western foodstuffs and standards. Certain items may seem expensive by the volume purchased but these are not actually costly because the recipes require only very small quantities. By American standards, therefore, the following cost generalizations may be made:

> Inexpensive: rice, potatoes, bread, chicken
> Moderately expensive: fresh fruits, flank steak, pork tenderloin
> Expensive: lobster, shrimp, prime beef
> Very expensive: caviar; sturgeon

ABALONE (bao yu/bao yu)
TYPE OF FOOD: mollusk
LENGTH: to 4 inches
SHAPE: oval
COLOR: cream
SURFACE: glossy, smooth; ridged or ribbed
CONSISTENCY: firm, moist, chewy
AROMA: slightly fishy; sweet; appetizing
TASTE: bland, delicate, meaty
USES: delicacy; main ingredient; often used on holiday occasions; usually included as a main dish at banquets
AVAILABLE FORMS: canned—shelled, water-packed, already cured and prepared; easy to use and entirely satisfactory as a canned food since it is more tender and tastier than the fresh variety; product of Mexico and Japan; fresh—sold in the shell, rarely obtainable except in California; dried—sold as unshelled, dried meat which requires cooking but, once cooked, should not be reheated; the best variety comes from Japan
STORAGE: canned—will keep indefinitely; opened, in refrigerator—will keep indefinitely but water should be changed every two days; fresh—should be used immediately, like any other mollusk; dried—will keep indefinitely
WHEN AVAILABLE: canned—always; fresh—rarely; dried—always
WHERE PURCHASED: Chinese and Japanese groceries (canned—in supermarkets)
APPROXIMATE COST: moderately expensive
SUBSTITUTES: none
IMPORTANCE: 3

AGAR AGAR (dung yong tsoi/dung yang tsai)
TYPE OF FOOD: vegetable (gum from seaweed)
LENGTH: about 1 foot
SHAPE: flat, stringlike
COLOR: transparent
SURFACE: dry
CONSISTENCY: hard until soaked
AROMA: none
TASTE: none
USES: salad ingredient, mixed with vegetables or meat
AVAILABLE FORMS: dried—in 4-oz. package

STORAGE: in pantry, will keep indefinitely
WHEN AVAILABLE: always
WHERE PURCHASED: Chinese grocery
APPROXIMATE COST: moderately expensive
SUBSTITUTES: none
IMPORTANCE: 1

ANISE, STAR (ba gok/ba chio)
TYPE OF FOOD: spice
LENGTH: to ½ inch
SHAPE: star-shaped seed
COLOR: brown
SURFACE: dull, smooth
CONSISTENCY: dry, brittle, fragile
AROMA: pungent; appetizing
TASTE: licorice
USES: condiment; flavoring agent; seasoning
AVAILABLE FORMS: dried—by the ounce in packages containing many cloves with seed enclosed; ground—as one of the five ingredients in Chinese Five (Fragrance) Spices Powder, which see
STORAGE: dry—in pantry in tightly covered jar will keep indefinitely
WHEN AVAILABLE: always
WHERE PURCHASED: Chinese grocery, also spice shops
APPROXIMATE COST: inexpensive
SUBSTITUTES: none
IMPORTANCE: 3

BACON, CHINESE (yin yoke/hsien ro)
TYPE OF FOOD: smoked meat
LENGTH: may be cut from cured side pork to desired length
SHAPE: may be cut to desired shape
COLOR: reddish brown meat between layers of yellowish fat
SURFACE: firm, smooth
CONSISTENCY: tender
AROMA: meaty, smoky
TASTE: meaty, smoky
USES: garnish; main ingredient
AVAILABLE FORMS: a whole pork leg or chunks sold by the pound
STORAGE: usually hanging in kitchen ready for slicing, will keep indefinitely

WHEN AVAILABLE: chiefly in winter
WHERE PURCHASED: Chinese grocery
APPROXIMATE COST: moderately expensive
SUBSTITUTES: cured sausage, lean bacon
IMPORTANCE: 3

BAMBOO SHOOTS (spring: jook sun/chu sun; winter: dung sun)
TYPE OF FOOD: vegetable
LENGTH: young shoots are about 4 inches long
SHAPE: chunky, tapered
COLOR: cream
SURFACE: glossy; ridged or ribbed
CONSISTENCY: crunchy, firm, fleshy, moist, stiff
AROMA: none
TASTE: delicate, bland
USES: main ingredient; garnish
AVAILABLE FORMS: salted (brine)—in cans, peeled, cleaned, boiled and shredded into chunks that fill about one-third to one-half a can; unsalted—packaged in cans; to be used in preference to salted variety; fresh—shredded into chunks; stored in pails of water in grocery; pickled—salty and sour in brine and sliced into thin strips, available loose or in cans; not popular in the United States; dried—precooked and ready to eat from can
STORAGE: canned varieties should be placed in tightly covered pint jars, completely covered with liquid from the can and stored in the refrigerator. This liquid should be drained off after two days and replaced by plain water. If water is changed every two days, the bamboo shoots will keep for several weeks. They may also be frozen.
WHEN AVAILABLE: always
WHERE PURCHASED: Chinese and Japanese groceries
APPROXIMATE COST: inexpensive
SUBSTITUTES: none
IMPORTANCE: 4

BEANS, BLACK: (wu dow/wu do)
TYPE OF FOOD: vegetable
LENGTH: to ¼ inch
SHAPE: bean seed

COLOR: black
SURFACE: dull
CONSISTENCY: dry, hard
AROMA: none
TASTE: beany, distinctive
USES: mainly in soups and gravies
AVAILABLE FORMS: dried, loose
STORAGE: will keep indefinitely in covered jar
WHEN AVAILABLE: always
WHERE PURCHASED: Chinese grocery
APPROXIMATE COST: inexpensive
SUBSTITUTES: none
IMPORTANCE: 2

BEANS, BLACK SALTED FERMENTED (dow si/do shih)
TYPE OF FOOD: vegetable or spice
LENGTH: to ¼ inch
SHAPE: bean seed
COLOR: black
SURFACE: dull, wrinkled
CONSISTENCY: moist, soft, tender
AROMA: fragrant, appetizing
TASTE: beany, salty, tangy
USES: condiment; flavoring agent; main ingredient; cuts odors, darkens sauces
AVAILABLE FORMS: plastic bags (preferable) or ½ to 1 pound cans; also in bottles
STORAGE: will keep in covered jar on pantry shelf indefinitely (saturate with peanut oil to prevent beans from drying out); will also keep frozen indefinitely
WHEN AVAILABLE: always
WHERE PURCHASED: Chinese grocery
APPROXIMATE COST: inexpensive
SUBSTITUTES: brown bean sauce
IMPORTANCE: 4

BEAN CAKE, FERMENTED (fu yu/fu yu)
TYPE OF FOOD: vegetable or spice
LENGTH: ½ to 1 inch
SHAPE: rectangle or cube
COLOR: cream, ivory, tan
SURFACE: glossy, shiny, smooth
CONSISTENCY: fragile, gelatinous, moist, soft, tender; paste or sauce when crushed
AROMA: strong, cheesy, pungent

TASTE: cheesy

USES: staple; condiment; flavoring agent

AVAILABLE FORMS: bottled (in small cubes), fermented, wine-drenched

STORAGE: unopened—will keep in the pantry indefinitely; opened—will keep in the refrigerator indefinitely

WHEN AVAILABLE: always

WHERE PURCHASED: Chinese grocery

APPROXIMATE COST: inexpensive

SUBSTITUTES: none

IMPORTANCE: 3

BEAN CURD (dow fu)

TYPE OF FOOD: bean cake or custard

LENGTH: ½ to 3 inches, as desired

SHAPE: flat, square about 3 inches by ½ inch thick

COLOR: cream, white

SURFACE: glossy, smooth

CONSISTENCY: creamy, firm, gelatinous, moist, soft, tender

AROMA: none

TASTE: bland, delicate, subtle

USES: main ingredient; may be used whole, cubed, sliced, shredded

AVAILABLE FORMS: usually as described above and dispensed from tins or containers filled with water; also deep-fried bean curd cakes; canned, which is similar in general characteristics to fresh, but somewhat firmer, very spongy, and with a more definite bean flavor; and pressed (dow fu kon), which is firmer, with the consistency of a stiff cheese (to prepare at home, wrap regular bean curd cakes in cheesecloth; place between 2 heavy boards or plates; place weights on top and add weight about every 10 minutes; allow to stand 5 or more hours until cakes are flat and firm); also available: bean curd skin

STORAGE: fresh—covered with water (which should be changed every other day) in refrigerator, it will keep for about one week; covered with brine (which should be changed every few days), it may be refrigerated for two weeks. Deep-fried bean curd cakes can be refrigerated but should not be kept for more than 3 or 4 days. It is preferable to use the fresh variety. Pressed variety can be kept about a few weeks, longer if frozen

WHEN AVAILABLE: always

WHERE PURCHASED: Chinese and Japanese groceries

APPROXIMATE COST: inexpensive

SUBSTITUTES: none

IMPORTANCE: 4

BEAN CURD, DRIED (tiem jook or fu jook pei/ t'ien ch'u or fu pi chi)

TYPE OF FOOD: soybean milk residue

LENGTH: 2 to 4 inches or ½ to 8 inches

SHAPE: thin rectangular sheets or curled, round sticks

COLOR: cream to tan

SURFACE: glossy, shiny, smooth; textured

CONSISTENCY: brittle, dry, firm; tender when cooked

AROMA: none

TASTE: beany, bland

USES: main ingredient

AVAILABLE FORMS: packaged sheets or dried sticks (fu jook pei)

STORAGE: in the pantry will keep for an indefinite period if wrapped well or kept in jar; both varieties may be stored in the freezer after being cooked

WHEN AVAILABLE: always

WHERE PURCHASED: Chinese grocery

APPROXIMATE COST: inexpensive

SUBSTITUTES: none

IMPORTANCE: 2

BEAN CURD CHEESE, RED (nam yu/nan yu)

TYPE OF FOOD: bean cheese

LENGTH: ½ to 2 inches

SHAPE: flat, square

COLOR: red

SURFACE: glossy, shiny, smooth

CONSISTENCY: creamy, fragile, gelatinous, moist, soft, tender

AROMA: none

TASTE: strong, unusual

USES: main ingredient

AVAILABLE FORMS: preserved, fermented in small square or oblong cans

STORAGE: will keep almost indefinitely in covered jar in refrigerator
WHEN AVAILABLE: always
WHERE PURCHASED: Chinese grocery
APPROXIMATE COST: inexpensive
SUBSTITUTES: none
IMPORTANCE: 2

BEAN FILLING, SWEET (dow sa/do sa)
TYPE OF FOOD: vegetable (derivative of kidney or mung bean)
COLOR: red (kidney beans), green (mung beans)
CONSISTENCY: dry, thick paste
AROMA: slight
TASTE: sweet
USES: flavoring agent, main ingredient, stuffing for pastry
AVAILABLE FORM: canned
STORAGE: will keep several months refrigerated
WHEN AVAILABLE: most commonly at Chinese New Year
WHERE PURCHASED: Chinese bakery or grocery
APPROXIMATE COST: inexpensive
SUBSTITUTES: dates or sweet potatoes
IMPORTANCE: 2

BEAN SAUCE, BROWN OR YELLOW (mien see jiong /do bahn jiang
TYPE OF FOOD: spice
COLOR: brown, yellow
CONSISTENCY: moist, thick paste
AROMA: sweet, appetizing
TASTE: beany, meaty, salty, rich
USES: condiment; flavoring agent for congee, barbecued dishes, festival dishes; breaded, slow-simmered, steamed, and stir-fried dishes
AVAILABLE FORMS: in 1-lb. can; occasionally in jar; may be bought as a bean sauce containing halves of soybeans (yellow)—as a prepared ready-to-use sauce or as a smoother bean paste
STORAGE: after can has been opened, contents should be transferred to a covered jar which may be kept either in the refrigerator or in the pantry. Sauce will keep indefinitely in the refrigerator but it changes color within 6 months if kept in the pantry
WHEN AVAILABLE: always
WHERE PURCHASED: Chinese grocery

APPROXIMATE COST: inexpensive
SUBSTITUTES: none
IMPORTANCE: 3

BEAN SPROUTS (small) (gna tsoi/ lo do ya)
TYPE OF FOOD: vegetable, mung bean sprouts
LENGTH: 1 to 2 inches by 1/16 inch
SHAPE: shoot or sprout
COLOR: green, yellow
SURFACE: glossy, has skin or hull like smooth shell
CONSISTENCY: crunchy, tender
AROMA: slight, appetizing
TASTE: beany, bland
USES: main ingredient
AVAILABLE FORMS: fresh—loose by the pound; canned—already cooked; dried
STORAGE: best if cooked on day of purchase; if stored (up to 4 days), sprouts should be washed thoroughly and covered with cold water, which should be changed daily, and refrigerated. If the canned variety is used, the can should be opened several hours before use, and the liquid discarded, sprouts rinsed and soaked in cold water to restore texture and sweet taste
WHEN AVAILABLE: always
WHERE PURCHASED: Chinese grocery; in supermarket for canned variety
APPROXIMATE COST: inexpensive
SUBSTITUTES: shredded lettuce heart (in fried rice, as only a small amount is needed)
IMPORTANCE: 4

BEAN SPROUTS (large) (wong dow gna/huang do ya)
TYPE OF FOOD: vegetable similar to small bean sprouts but grown from a larger soybean
LENGTH: 1 to 2 inches by 1/4 inch by 1/8 inch
SHAPE: shoot or sprout
COLOR: green; yellow
SURFACE: glossy, has skin or hull like smooth shell
CONSISTENCY: crunchy, tougher than small bean sprouts
AROMA: slight
TASTE: beany, bland
USES: main ingredient

AVAILABLE FORMS: fresh by the pound; can be grown from purchased seeds

STORAGE: treat same as small bean sprouts

WHEN AVAILABLE: always

WHERE PURCHASED: Chinese grocery

APPROXIMATE COST: inexpensive

SUBSTITUTES: none

IMPORTANCE: 2

BEANS, LONG GREEN (dow gok/do jiao)

TYPE OF FOOD: vegetable

LENGTH: 16 to 32 inches

SHAPE: like string bean but longer

COLOR: green

SURFACE: smooth, dull

CONSISTENCY: crispy when not overcooked

AROMA: none

TASTE: like string bean

USES: as vegetable or with meat dishes

AVAILABLE FORMS: fresh by the pound (loose)

STORAGE: treat like any green bean or fresh vegetable

WHEN AVAILABLE: always, except during winter

WHERE PURCHASED: Chinese grocery

APPROXIMATE COST: inexpensive

SUBSTITUTES: American green beans (not completely satisfactory)

IMPORTANCE: 2

BÊCHE-DE-MER (hai sum/hai sun)

TYPE OF FOOD: sea slug

LENGTH: to 8 inches by 4 inches

SHAPE: cucumber form; round, shrunken, wrinkled

COLOR: gray

SURFACE: dull, ridged or ribbed, textured

CONSISTENCY: dry, fleshy, gelatinous, moist, tender

AROMA: none

TASTE: meaty, little of its own; takes on flavor of other ingredients

USES: main ingredient

AVAILABLE FORMS: dried only, often sold wrapped in cellophane

STORAGE: will keep indefinitely in dried state

WHEN AVAILABLE: always

WHERE PURCHASED: Chinese grocery

APPROXIMATE COST: moderate

SUBSTITUTES: none

IMPORTANCE: 2

BIRD'S NEST (yin waw/yen wuo)

TYPE OF FOOD: protein (from cliff dwelling swallow nests)

SHAPE: curled, round, very thin strips; vari-shaped, wrinkled

COLOR: cream-tan-yellow

SURFACE: glossy, textured

CONSISTENCY: brittle, dry, firm, hard

AROMA: none

TASTE: bland, delicate, takes on flavor of other ingredients

USES: main ingredient; stuffing; tonic (it is believed that those who drink half a cup of bird's-nest soup attain good health and long life. A "must" for formal Chinese dinners)

AVAILABLE FORMS: prepared, dried bird's nest, often packaged in a cellophane-topped box; sold as clean, whole nests (expensive), or in clean, curved chips (bits of nesting, called loong ngaah or dragon's teeth). Sold in 6-ounce packages. 1½ ounces serve 6 to 8 persons

STORAGE: dry in package in pantry, will keep for years. Must be soaked and cleaned before use. Extremely troublesome to prepare. Procedure: (1) soak bird's nest in 10 cups of water overnight (8 hours); (2) discard water; put one or two drops of peanut oil in bird's nest, rub it with hands; fill with water again. Feathers will float to top with oil; (3) remove feathers and water; (4) and repeat procedure until nest is clean

WHEN AVAILABLE: always

WHERE PURCHASED: Chinese grocery

APPROXIMATE COST: expensive (there is a great scarcity of nests of required quality and considerable labor in preparation—removing feathers, etc.)

SUBSTITUTES: none

IMPORTANCE: 4 (for banquet only)

BROCCOLI, CHINESE (gai lan tsoi/chia lan tsai)

TYPE OF FOOD: vegetable

LENGTH: 12 to 14 inches long
SHAPE: similar to American broccoli but longer
COLOR: green stalks, leaves, flowers
SURFACE: dull, smooth
CONSISTENCY: crunchy firm, moist, stiff, tender
AROMA: pungent
TASTE: similar to American broccoli but more delicate flavor
USES: main ingredient; combined with meats
AVAILABLE FORMS: fresh only
STORAGE: in refrigerator, wrapped in plastic bag or paper, will keep for one week; may also be frozen after parboiling
WHEN AVAILABLE: summer
WHERE PURCHASED: Chinese grocery
APPROXIMATE COST: inexpensive
SUBSTITUTES: American broccoli
IMPORTANCE: 3

CABBAGE, WHITE CHINESE (bok tsoi*/bai tsai)
TYPE OF FOOD: vegetable
LENGTH: 16 inches (by 8 inches across)
SHAPE: leafy, long stalk
COLOR: white; green
SURFACE: dull, smooth
CONSISTENCY: crunchy, firm, moist, stiff (when raw); tender, crisp (when cooked)
AROMA: none
TASTE: subtle, bland
USES: main ingredient
AVAILABLE FORMS: fresh—by the pound; dried —in half-pound packages; for preserved, see celery cabbage
STORAGE: in refrigerator, wrapped in plastic bag or paper, will keep for one week; dried—indefinitely
WHEN AVAILABLE: always (winter crop is best)
WHERE PURCHASED: Chinese grocery; occasionally in supermarkets
APPROXIMATE COST: inexpensive
SUBSTITUTES: lettuce
IMPORTANCE: 4

CAUL FAT (mong yow/wang yo)
TYPE OF FOOD: thin covering of the lower part of the pig's intestines
SURFACE: thin and lacy

CONSISTENCY: doughy (when raw); crisp (when fried)
AROMA: none
TASTE: bland
USES: wrapping for foods to be fried or steamed
AVAILABLE FORMS: fresh by the pound
STORAGE: wrapped in food covering (Saran or aluminum foil) in the refrigerator, will keep for 3 to 4 days
WHEN AVAILABLE: always
WHERE PURCHASED: Chinese grocery or butcher shop
APPROXIMATE COST: moderately expensive
SUBSTITUTES: egg roll skin
IMPORTANCE: 2

CELERY CABBAGE, CHINESE (sheo tsoi/tientsin bai tsai)
TYPE OF FOOD: vegetable
LENGTH: to 16 inches
SHAPE: celery-like, leafy stalk (broader than American celery)
COLOR: green; yellow with white stalks
SURFACE: dull, smooth
CONSISTENCY: crunchy, firm, moist, tender
AROMA: none
TASTE: bland, delicate
USES: main ingredient
AVAILABLE FORMS: fresh by the pound
STORAGE: should be refrigerated in a plastic bag in the crisper; keeps for approximately one week but should be used before it wilts and becomes brown
WHEN AVAILABLE: always
WHERE PURCHASED: Chinese grocery and many American supermarkets
APPROXIMATE COST: inexpensive
SUBSTITUTES: bok tsoi
IMPORTANCE: 4

CHESTNUTS (loot tszee/li tze)
TYPE OF FOOD: nut
USES: in pastries and in red cooking with chicken or pork
AVAILABLE FORMS: shelled and dried halves by the pound, or fresh
STORAGE: will keep indefinitely in covered jar
WHEN AVAILABLE: always

* Tsoi Sum is a Chinese white cabbage similar to bok tsoi but is much tenderer, though slightly more expensive.

WHERE PURCHASED: most grocery stores
APPROXIMATE COST: inexpensive
SUBSTITUTES: none
IMPORTANCE: 2

CHESTNUTS, WATER (ma tie/ma ti)
TYPE OF FOOD: fruit, root
SHAPE: bulbous, round, tapered
COLOR: brown-purple skin, yellowish-white interior
SURFACE: dull
CONSISTENCY: chewy, crispy, crunchy, firm, fleshy, moist, meaty
AROMA: slight, fruity, appetizing
TASTE: bland, delicate, subtle, meaty
USES: garnish; main ingredient; stuffing
AVAILABLE FORMS: fresh—locally grown (sweet, tasty), by weight; canned—imported (somewhat less tasty); dried and ground into powder or flour (provides particularly desirable crispness for batter coating), imported; sugared—sold as sweetmeat at Chinese New Year
STORAGE: fresh—will keep 1 week in pantry, 2 weeks in refrigerator; canned—should be washed under cold water after opening can; will keep 4 weeks in refrigerator in closed jar covered with water (change water every other day or so or chestnuts lose texture as they age and crumble; dried powder—will keep indefinitely in the pantry; sugared—will keep indefinitely in a jar in the pantry
WHEN AVAILABLE: always
WHERE PURCHASED: Chinese grocery
APPROXIMATE COST: fresh and canned—inexpensive; water chestnut flour—expensive
SUBSTITUTES: none
IMPORTANCE: 4

CHIVES, CHINESE (gow tsoi/chiu tsai)
TYPE OF FOOD: vegetable
LENGTH: same as American chive
SHAPE: same as American chive
COLOR: same as American chive
SURFACE: same as American chive
CONSISTENCY: same as American chive
AROMA: strong, oniony
TASTE: onion-like

USES: flavoring agent, garnish
AVAILABLE FORMS: fresh by the bunch
STORAGE: to be kept as dry as possible in plastic bag in refrigerator crisper; should be used quickly—the longer they are kept the stronger the odor
WHEN AVAILABLE: always
WHERE PURCHASED: Chinese grocery
APPROXIMATE COST: inexpensive
SUBSTITUTES: American chives
IMPORTANCE: 2

CLOUD EARS (win yee/rin erh)
TYPE OF FOOD: fungus (also called wood ears [mook yee] or silver ears which is an albino form and is larger and tougher and less expensive and requires longer soaking and cooking; dried fungus; tree fungus; brown fungus)
LENGTH: to 1½ inch
SHAPE: curled, irregular, leafy, shrunken
COLOR: black-gray
SURFACE: dull, smooth, shriveled
CONSISTENCY: stiff, brittle, dry (before soaking); chewy, fleshy, gelatinous, rubbery, slippery, tender (after soaking)
AROMA: none
TASTE: subtle, little of its own, takes on flavor of other ingredients
USES: main ingredient
AVAILABLE FORMS: dried by the ounce
STORAGE: dried—will keep on pantry shelf indefinitely; soaked—will keep up to 6 days in covered container
WHEN AVAILABLE: always
WHERE PURCHASED: Chinese grocery
APPROXIMATE COST: inexpensive
SUBSTITUTES: none
IMPORTANCE: 3

COCONUT STRIPS, CHINESE (tong long/ping tang yea tze)
TYPE OF FOOD: fruit
LENGTH: to 2 inches
SHAPE: ½-inch-wide strip
COLOR: white
SURFACE: dull, pebbly, textured
CONSISTENCY: crunchy, dry, firm, fleshy, chewy

AROMA: none

TASTE: delicate, sweet

USES: confection, sweetmeat

AVAILABLE FORMS: as a crystallized sweetmeat, sold by the ounce, usually in cellophane bags

STORAGE: will keep in the pantry indefinitely in cellophane bag or covered jar

WHEN AVAILABLE: during and after Chinese New Year

WHERE PURCHASED: Chinese grocery

APPROXIMATE COST: inexpensive

SUBSTITUTES: crystallized fruits, peels, or melons

IMPORTANCE: 1

COOKIES, ALMOND (hong yong bang/hsin ren bing)

TYPE OF FOOD: dessert cooky

SHAPE: round

COLOR: light brown

SURFACE: textured

CONSISTENCY: crisp, dry

AROMA: almond

TASTE: almond

USES: dessert

AVAILABLE FORMS: loose or in packages or tins

STORAGE: will keep in freezer for several months or in pantry like any other cooky

WHEN AVAILABLE: always

WHERE PURCHASED: Chinese grocery or bakery

APPROXIMATE COST: inexpensive

SUBSTITUTES: any cookies

IMPORTANCE: 4 (for children)

CUTTLEFISH, DRIED (yow yu/yo yu)

TYPE OF FOOD: fish

LENGTH: 6 to 8 inches

SHAPE: fishlike (as packaged), fresh dried small squid

COLOR: powdery, gray

SURFACE: dried, textured

CONSISTENCY: dry (must be soaked before use)

AROMA: fishy

TASTE: fishy, salty

USES: soup ingredient, or stir fried

AVAILABLE FORMS: dried whole

STORAGE: will keep indefinitely in plastic bag

WHEN AVAILABLE: always

WHERE PURCHASED: Chinese grocery

APPROXIMATE COST: inexpensive

SUBSTITUTES: none

IMPORTANCE: 1

DATES, RED, DRIED (hung jo/hung tzao)

TYPE OF FOOD: fruit

LENGTH: 1 inch

SHAPE: oval to round

COLOR: red

SURFACE: glossy

CONSISTENCY: dry, firm, hard, moist interior; or, if so processed, a soft paste

AROMA: slight, sweet

TASTE: bland, delicate, sweet

USES: flavoring agent, garnish, stuffing for pastry

AVAILABLE FORMS: dried, in cellophane packages by the ounce. Although the red dates are the most commonly used (and are also known as dried jujubes), there are also white honey dates (jut jo) and black dates (huk jo). All three have a sweet flavor

STORAGE: will keep indefinitely in tightly covered container in pantry

WHEN AVAILABLE: always

WHERE PURCHASED: Chinese grocery

APPROXIMATE COST: moderately expensive

SUBSTITUTES: none

IMPORTANCE: 2

DUCK LIVER (GIZZARD), CURED (op gon/ya gan)

TYPE OF FOOD: meat

LENGTH: 1½ to 2 inches

SHAPE: flat figure 8

COLOR: brown-black

SURFACE: dry, textured

CONSISTENCY: hard

AROMA: meaty

TASTE: strong, meaty

USES: as a flavoring agent when finely chopped (after soaking for 2 hours)

AVAILABLE FORMS: loose by the ounce; sold wrapped in cured ducks' feet

STORAGE: will keep for several months in dry, cool pantry

WHEN AVAILABLE: always

WHERE PURCHASED: Chinese grocery

APPROXIMATE COST: moderately expensive

SUBSTITUTES: none

IMPORTANCE: 1

EGG, 100-YEAR-OLD (pei don/pi dan)

TYPE OF FOOD: duck egg artificially aged (by the application of a black coating of lime, salt, ashes, and tea; it is then cured for 100 days)

LENGTH: to 4 inches

SHAPE: ovoid

COLOR: black

SURFACE: salty and hard

CONSISTENCY: interior is dry, firm, gelatinous; yolk is cheeselike

AROMA: cheesy, sulfurous

TASTE: pungent, cheesy

USES: appetizer

AVAILABLE FORMS: sold individually (imported from Taiwan)

STORAGE: when refrigerated, will last for several months

WHERE PURCHASED: Chinese grocery

APPROXIMATE COST: inexpensive

SUBSTITUTES: none

IMPORTANCE: 2

EGG, SALTED, OR PRESERVED DUCK EGG (hahm don/hsien dan)

TYPE OF FOOD: egg

LENGTH: to 4 inches

SHAPE: ovoid

COLOR: white

SURFACE: dull, smooth

CONSISTENCY: loose when raw; solid when cooked

AROMA: none

TASTE: delicate, salty

USES: main ingredient; mixed raw into meats and cooked with them

AVAILABLE FORMS: cured in brine, sold individually

STORAGE: will keep about a month in refrigerator

WHEN AVAILABLE: always

WHERE PURCHASED: Chinese grocery

APPROXIMATE COST: inexpensive

SUBSTITUTES: hen's egg

IMPORTANCE: 3

EGG ROLL SKINS OR WRAPPERS (chwin guen pei/ chwin jwen pi)

TYPE OF FOOD: pastry

LENGTH: 6 inches

SHAPE: ⅛-inch-thick square

COLOR: fresh dough

SURFACE: doughy when raw; fragile when cooked

CONSISTENCY: crisp

AROMA: none

TASTE: delicate

USES: to be filled with meat or fish and vegetable mixture and deep fried

AVAILABLE FORMS: fresh by the pound

STORAGE: if refrigerated, may be kept for 3 or 4 days. If frozen, may be kept for several months, if well wrapped to preserve moisture, but becomes brittle in time

WHEN AVAILABLE: always

WHERE PURCHASED: Chinese grocery

APPROXMATE COST: inexpensive

SUBSTITUTES: none

IMPORTANCE: 4

EGGPLANT, CHINESE (ngai gwa/chieh tze)

TYPE OF FOOD: vegetable

LENGTH: 6 to 8 inches

SHAPE: cucumber-like

COLOR: white on outside and inside

SURFACE: smooth, shiny

CONSISTENCY: tender

AROMA: none

TASTE: delicate

USES: main ingredient; in stir-fried dishes

AVAILABLE FORMS: fresh by the pound

STORAGE: may be kept for a week in refrigerator crisper

WHEN AVAILABLE: always

WHERE PURCHASED: Chinese grocery

APPROXIMATE COST: inexpensive

SUBSTITUTES: American eggplant

IMPORTANCE: 2

FISH, SALTED, CURED (gon hahm yu/hsien yu)

TYPE OF FOOD: fish

LENGTH: depends on variety of fish; all types are cured and dried

CONSISTENCY: dry

AROMA: strong, fishy, pungent, disagreeable (probably the last ingredient for which an Occidental would acquire a taste)

TASTE: very fishy

USES: main ingredient; blended with meats as flavoring agent

AVAILABLE FORMS: dried and unwrapped by the pound

STORAGE: well wrapped in the pantry, it will keep indefinitely

WHEN AVAILABLE: always

WHERE PURCHASED: Chinese grocery

APPROXIMATE COST: inexpensive

SUBSTITUTES: none

IMPORTANCE: 1

FIVE SPICES POWDER (ng hiong fun/wu hsiang fun)

TYPE OF FOOD: spice (star anise or bot gok; Chinese cinnamon; fennel or aniseed; Szechuan pepper or Chinese pepper, and clove)

COLOR: brown-red

CONSISTENCY: powdery

AROMA: strong, sweet, appetizing, fragrant

TASTE: spicy, tangy

USES: flavoring agent, blending agent in sauce, cuts odors (as in fish)

AVAILABLE FORMS: in powdered dry form in cans; or in whole form when each item may be purchased separately

STORAGE: may be stored indefinitely in pantry

WHEN AVAILABLE: always

WHERE PURCHASED: Chinese grocery; occasionally in American specialty food stores

APPROXIMATE COST: inexpensive

SUBSTITUTES: mixture of 1 teaspoon each of powdered cinnamon, cloves, aniseed, and thyme

IMPORTANCE: 4

GINGER (FRESH) (giong/jiang)

TYPE OF FOOD: root

LENGTH: to 4 inches

SHAPE: irregular bulb, gnarled, knobby root, varishaped

COLOR: brown-gray (yellow-ivory inside)

SURFACE: dull, indented or pocked; has skin or hull which is textured

CONSISTENCY: crunchy, firm, fleshy, tender (if young), tough (if old)

AROMA: sweet, pungent

TASTE: sharp, spicy, tangy

USES: in sauce, as condiment, seasoning, flavoring agent, cuts odors, medicine

AVAILABLE FORMS: regular fresh (new)—roots sold loose by the pound; powder—in tins; liquid essence—in bottle; pickled red (bottled)—to be eaten plain as condiment; pickled in cans to go with other vegetables; crystallized—in packages (sugared, candied), used as dessert or to flavor dessert; preserved in syrup—in jar. Also, sub gum ginger available in jars. Can be used as dessert or garnish

STORAGE: fresh—may be kept wrapped in foil or plastic bag in vegetable compartment of refrigerator for about 2 months (do not let get wet or dried out); or indefinitely if peeled and cleaned, sliced or left in knobs in cheap sherry (covered tightly in jar); chopped and cooked in peanut oil and refrigerated it will keep for several months; dry powder—keeps indefinitely on shelf; crystallized—keeps indefinitely

WHEN AVAILABLE: fresh—always; fresh new roots, though, are best but are obtainable only in spring

WHERE PURCHASED: Chinese, Spanish, Japanese, and Greek groceries

APPROXIMATE COST: inexpensive

SUBSTITUTES: for fresh ginger: dried ginger powder ($\frac{1}{8}$ teaspoon is equivalent to 1 tablespoon fresh ginger)

IMPORTANCE: 4

ADDITIONAL INFORMATION: minced ginger may be mixed with scallion or crushed garlic and blended with soy sauce for use as a dipping sauce (especially with dem sem); or mixed with vinegar and soy sauce; for a hot drink recommended for upset stomachs, boil $\frac{1}{4}$ cup sliced ginger 10 minutes with 4 or more tablespoons brown sugar, 2 cups water, and additional sugar to taste. When shredded or finely chopped it may be frozen and kept indefinitely

GINKGO NUT (bok go/bai go)

TYPE OF FOOD: nut

LENGTH: to $\frac{1}{2}$ inch

SHAPE: oval or round

COLOR: tan

SURFACE: has skin or hull; after this is removed, the nut is smooth

CONSISTENCY: soft, tender, moist, firm, fleshy

AROMA: none

TASTE: bland, little of its own

USES: main ingredient, stuffing

AVAILABLE FORMS: canned—in liquid, shelled; also dried, loose

STORAGE: canned—will keep indefinitely if unopened; dried—will keep in the pantry indefinitely

WHEN AVAILABLE: always

WHERE PURCHASED: Chinese grocery

APPROXIMATE COST: moderately expensive

SUBSTITUTES: none

IMPORTANCE: 2

GOLDEN NEEDLES: (See Lily Flowers)

HOISIN SAUCE (RED SEASONING SAUCE) (hoy sin jiong/hai hsien jiang)

TYPE OF FOOD: condiment sauce, a combination of soybean flour, red beans, ginger, garlic, spices, salt, chili, and sugar

COLOR: brown-red

CONSISTENCY: thick fluid or thin paste

AROMA: pungent, sweet, garlic-like

TASTE: beany, spicy, sweet, tangy

USES: blends into other sauces or gravies; condiment; flavoring agent; cuts odors; marinating sauce; dip for meats

AVAILABLE FORMS: cans—usually 8-ounce size

STORAGE: will keep indefinitely in tightly covered jar kept in refrigerator

WHEN AVAILABLE: always

WHERE PURCHASED: Chinese grocery

APPROXIMATE COST: inexpensive

SUBSTITUTES: duck sauce

IMPORTANCE: 4

HOT SAUCE: (lot yow/la yu)

TYPE OF FOOD: condiment (made from chili peppers)

COLOR: red

CONSISTENCY: thick

TASTE: hot, spicy

USES: seasoning agent

AVAILABLE FORMS: in bottles (about 5 oz.)

STORAGE: will keep indefinitely in refrigerator

WHEN AVAILABLE: always

WHERE PURCHASED: Chinese grocery

APPROXIMATE COST: inexpensive

SUBSTITUTES: none

IMPORTANCE: 1

JELLYFISH (hoy jit pei/hai jih pi)

TYPE OF FOOD: seafood

LENGTH: 25 inches

SHAPE: generally squared (25 inches by 25 inches) by 1/8-inch thick (tentacles have been removed)

COLOR: brown; opaque; white-yellow

SURFACE: dull, shriveled, textured

CONSISTENCY: chewy, crunchy, firm, gelatinous, moist

AROMA: slight

TASTE: bland, delicate

USES: main ingredient

AVAILABLE FORMS: dry, by the individual fish; also available shredded and packaged in 1/2- to 1-pound bags.

STORAGE: will keep indefinitely in the pantry

WHEN AVAILABLE: always

WHERE PURCHASED: Chinese grocery

APPROXIMATE COST: inexpensive to moderately expensive

SUBSTITUTES: none

IMPORTANCE: 2

KOHLRABI (dye to tsoi/da tou tsai)

TYPE OF FOOD: root vegetable

LENGTH: 3 inches

SHAPE: round

COLOR: light green

CONSISTENCY: crisp, chewy

AROMA: pungent

TASTE: turnip-like

USES: salad, vegetable

AVAILABLE FORMS: fresh; also preserved (Szechuan style) in cans or jars

STORAGE: preserved—stored in jar in refrigerator, will keep for several months; fresh—

stored in refrigerator, will keep for about 1 week

WHEN AVAILABLE: always

WHERE PURCHASED: preserved — Chinese grocery; fresh—most markets

APPROXIMATE COST: inexpensive

SUBSTITUTES: turnip

IMPORTANCE: 2

KUMQUAT (gum quot/jin jiu)

TYPE OF FOOD: fruit

LENGTH: to 1 inch

SHAPE: oval (elongated)

COLOR: orange

SURFACE: shiny, smooth

CONSISTENCY: firm, fleshy, juicy, soft (on inside), seedy

AROMA: pungent, sweet, gingery

TASTE: spicy, syrupy (preserved), sweet on outside, tart inner meat

USES: garnish, stuffing, main ingredient, dessert

AVAILABLE FORMS: fresh—by the pint or quart in fruit baskets; preserved—in syrup packed in six-ounce jars or in gallon jars; preserved and sugared (crystallized)—loose by the pound or in smaller quantities in cellophane bags

STORAGE: fresh—will keep in refrigerator for about 2 weeks; preserved in syrup—will keep indefinitely in pantry or refrigerator; preserved and sugared—will keep for many months in tightly covered jar; tends to dry out after a month or two when kept in cellophane package

WHEN AVAILABLE: fresh—in winter; preserved in syrup—always; sugared—at time of Chinese New Year and for only two to three weeks thereafter

WHERE PURCHASED: fresh and preserved in syrup—in American and Chinese groceries; sugared—Chinese grocery

APPROXIMATE COST: moderately expensive

SUBSTITUTES: other syrup-packed or sugared fruits (orange peel)

IMPORTANCE: 4

LEMON SAUCE (ning mung jiong/ning mung jiang)

TYPE OF FOOD: sauce or jam

COLOR: yellow-gold-brown

CONSISTENCY: free-flowing, thin

AROMA: pungent, sweet, garlic flavor

TASTE: spicy, sweet, tangy

USES: condiment, flavoring agent, seasoning, spice

AVAILABLE FORMS: in cans or jars

STORAGE: will keep in covered jar in refrigerator indefinitely

WHEN AVAILABLE: always

WHERE PURCHASED: Chinese grocery

APPROXIMATE COST: inexpensive

SUBSTITUTES: none

IMPORTANCE: 1

LILY FLOWERS (gum tsum/jing tsen)

TYPE OF FOOD: flower (also known as golden needles, lily buds, dried tiger lilies, tiger lily petals)

LENGTH: to 2 inches

SHAPE: leafy, wrinkled

COLOR: gold-brown

SURFACE: dull, smooth, shriveled

CONSISTENCY: dry, tender to tough

AROMA: slightly pungent, sweet

TASTE: sweet, unusual, distinctive

USES: garnish, main ingredient to be mixed with other ingredients

AVAILABLE FORMS: dried, in cellophane packages by the ounce

STORAGE: will keep indefinitely in the pantry

WHEN AVAILABLE: always

WHERE PURCHASED: Chinese grocery

APPROXIMATE COST: inexpensive

SUBSTITUTES: other dried vegetables

IMPORTANCE: 2

LITCHIS (la-ee tzee/li tze)

TYPE OF FOOD: fruit

LENGTH: to 1 inch

SHAPE: round

COLOR: red-purple skin or hull; interior meat is opaque or white when canned or fresh; brown when dried

SURFACE: skin or hull is pebbly, textured; interior is smooth

CONSISTENCY: firm, fleshy, soft, tender; dried—chewy, pitted

AROMA: slight, sweet (fresh and canned)

TASTE: bland, delicate, sweet, tangy; dried—strong and sweet

USES: flavoring agent, dessert, garnish, for sweet and sour dishes

AVAILABLE FORMS: fresh—in cellophane bags by the pound; canned—in various sized cans, syrup-packed; dried—in boxes or cellophane bags

STORAGE: fresh—will keep in refrigerator for about 1 week; canned—will keep indefinitely in pantry; dried—will keep indefinitely

WHEN AVAILABLE: fresh—for about 1 month only in summer; canned—always; dried—always

WHERE PURCHASED: Chinese grocery

APPROXIMATE COST: fresh—expensive; canned—moderately expensive; dried—expensive

SUBSTITUTES: loquats (canned), longans (canned)

IMPORTANCE: 4

LONGANS (loong gnahn/lung yen)

TYPE OF FOOD: fruit

LENGTH: ½ to 1 inch

SHAPE: round

COLOR: yellow-tan

SURFACE: has smooth shell, interior is smooth

CONSISTENCY: fleshy, soft, tender; has pit

AROMA: slight, sweet

TASTE: delicate, fragrant, refreshing, distinctive

USES: desserts, garnish, sweet and sour dishes; dried longans are used in slow-cooked soups

AVAILABLE FORMS: dried—shelled, pitted, and packed solidly in the form of a bar; canned—packed in syrup

STORAGE: dried—will keep indefinitely in pantry; canned—will keep indefinitely in pantry

WHEN AVAILABLE: always

WHERE PURCHASED: Chinese grocery

APPROXIMATE COST: moderately expensive

SUBSTITUTES: raisins (dried), litchis

IMPORTANCE: 3

LOQUATS (pei pa/p'i pa)

TYPE OF FOOD: fruit

LENGTH: to 2 inches

SHAPE: round

COLOR: orange

SURFACE: glossy, smooth

CONSISTENCY: fleshy, tender, has pit

AROMA: slight, sweet

TASTE: delicate, bland

USES: dessert

AVAILABLE FORMS: canned—packed in syrup, from about 8- to 20-ounce cans; fresh—rarely found in this country; preserved—dried and packaged in boxes

STORAGE: canned—when opened, will keep in covered container in refrigerator for several days

WHEN AVAILABLE: always

WHERE PURCHASED: Chinese grocery

APPROXIMATE COST: moderately expensive

SUBSTITUTES: litchis or longans

IMPORTANCE: 3

LOTUS ROOT (leen gnow/lien ngo)

TYPE OF FOOD: vegetable root

LENGTH: to 8 inches

SHAPE: 4-inch by 8-inch bulb in cylindrical clusters

COLOR: brown-red-tan

SURFACE: has skin or hull, smooth

CONSISTENCY: firm, chewy, crisp, crunchy

AROMA: sweet

TASTE: sweet, bland, delicate

USES: soup ingredient, vegetarian dishes, sweetmeat (when crystallized)

AVAILABLE FORMS: fresh—by the whole bulb or segment sold by the pound; dried slices—by the ounce in boxes or cellophane bags; canned—packed in water and cut in thin crosswise slices; dried, powdered stem—in packages or boxes; sugared—in cellophane packages or loose by the pound

STORAGE: fresh—will keep 2 to 3 weeks in refrigerator crisper; dried—will keep indefinitely in pantry; canned—will keep 1 week in water in covered jar after being opened; dried powdered stem—will keep indefinitely in pantry; sugared—will keep indefinitely in covered jar in pantry

WHEN AVAILABLE: fresh—July to February; dried or canned—always
WHERE PURCHASED: Chinese grocery
APPROXIMATE COST: moderately expensive
SUBSTITUTES: none
IMPORTANCE: 3

LOTUS SEEDS (leen tszee/lien tze)
TYPE OF FOOD: vegetable seed
LENGTH: to ½ inch
SHAPE: ¼ inch by ½ inch seed form
COLOR: brown
SURFACE: has skin or hull
CONSISTENCY: hard
AROMA: none
TASTE: delicate
USES: candy, soup flavoring agent
AVAILABLE FORMS: canned or dried
STORAGE: will keep indefinitely
WHEN AVAILABLE: always
WHERE PURCHASED: Chinese grocery
APPROXIMATE COST: moderately expensive to expensive
SUBSTITUTES: none
IMPORTANCE: 1

MELON, BITTER (fu gwa/k'u gwa)
TYPE OF FOOD: vegetable (balsam pear)
LENGTH: to 8 inches
SHAPE: cucumber form and size
COLOR: green
SURFACE: glossy, ridged or ribbed, textured
CONSISTENCY: fleshy, soft, seeded
AROMA: slightly pungent
TASTE: extremely bitter
USES: main ingredient as vegetable dish, or added to meat dishes
AVAILABLE FORMS: fresh by the pound
STORAGE: will keep in vegetable crisper for a week
WHEN AVAILABLE: always
WHERE PURCHASED: Chinese grocery
APPROXIMATE COST: inexpensive
SUBSTITUTES: none
IMPORTANCE: 3

MELON, HAIRY (jit gwa or mo gwa/cheh gwa)
TYPE OF FOOD: vegetable
LENGTH: to 8 inches

SHAPE: 4-inch by 8-inch squash-shaped melon
COLOR: green; yellow
SURFACE: dull, hairy, has skin or hull
CONSISTENCY: fleshy, moist, soft
AROMA: none
TASTE: bland, delicate, takes on flavor of other ingredients
USES: main ingredient
AVAILABLE FORMS: fresh only
STORAGE: will keep 2 weeks in plastic bag in refrigerator crisper
WHEN AVAILABLE: summer
WHERE PURCHASED: Chinese grocery
APPROXIMATE COST: moderately expensive
SUBSTITUTES: cucumber
IMPORTANCE: 2

MELON SEEDS (gwa tzee/gwa tze)
TYPE OF FOOD: dried watermelon seeds
LENGTH: to ¼ inch
SHAPE: oval with pointed end
COLOR: red or black hull, white interior meat
SURFACE: smooth
CONSISTENCY: interior meat is chewy, crunchy
AROMA: none
TASTE: nutlike, delicate, sweet
USES: when shelled only: snack food, dessert
AVAILABLE FORMS: by the ounce in sealed plastic bags
STORAGE: will keep in pantry indefinitely
WHEN AVAILABLE: always
WHERE PURCHASED: Chinese grocery
APPROXIMATE COST: inexpensive
SUBSTITUTES: American pumpkin seeds
IMPORTANCE: 3

MELON, SILK (See Okra, Chinese)

MELON, TEA (tsa gwa/tsa gwa)
TYPE OF FOOD: fruit
LENGTH: to 2 inches
SHAPE: cucumber-like
COLOR: orange-brown
SURFACE: glossy, textured, shriveled
AROMA: sweet

TASTE: sweet, bland, delicate

USES: flavoring agent; main ingredient; appetizer; snack

AVAILABLE FORMS: canned—preserved in honey with or without ginger

STORAGE: will keep indefinitely after opening if placed in covered jar with (honey) syrup

WHEN AVAILABLE: always

WHERE PURCHASED: Chinese grocery

APPROXIMATE COST: moderately expensive

SUBSTITUTES: none

IMPORTANCE: 2

MELON, WINTER (dung gwa/dung gwa)

TYPE OF FOOD: vegetable

LENGTH: to 21 inches

SHAPE: oval or round

COLOR: green skin; white, seedy inner meat

SURFACE: skin—silvery, frosted; meat—white; cooked—translucent

AROMA: none

TASTE: bland, delicate, subtle

USES: soup ingredient; candied; not to be eaten raw

AVAILABLE FORMS: fresh by the pound and by the whole melon; sugared, as a sweetmeat in small cellophane bags at Chinese New Year

STORAGE: sections will keep in plastic bags in refrigerator for 6 days. A whole melon will keep in a cool, dark place for months

WHERE PURCHASED: Chinese grocery

APPROXIMATE COST: moderately expensive

SUBSTITUTES: none

IMPORTANCE: 4

ADDITIONAL INFORMATION: A half melon, with its pulp removed, may be steamed after being filled with soup, meat, and other ingredients, and placed on the table as a serving bowl

MOLASSES, CHINESE BEAD (ju yow/tsu yo)

TYPE OF FOOD: coloring agent

COLOR: black

CONSISTENCY: thick sauce

AROMA: pungent

TASTE: syrupy, bitter sweet

USES: coloring agent

AVAILABLE FORMS: canned or bottled

STORAGE: will keep indefinitely in pantry

WHEN AVAILABLE: always

WHERE PURCHASED: Chinese grocery

APPROXIMATE COST: inexpensive

SUBSTITUTES: caramelized sugar

IMPORTANCE: 2

MUSHROOMS (WINTER), DRIED CHINESE (dung gu/dung gu)

TYPE OF FOOD: fungus (thinner than flower mushrooms)

LENGTH: to 2 inches

SHAPE: round head with stem in center of underside

COLOR: black to cream

SURFACE: dull, ridged or ribbed, textured, shriveled

CONSISTENCY: before soaking (inedible)—brittle, dry, hard; after soaking—chewy, firm gelatinous, meaty, moist, tender

AROMA: slight, sweet

TASTE: meaty, delicate

USES: flavoring agent, main ingredient, can be added to almost any entree

AVAILABLE FORMS: in cellophane bags or boxes by weight

STORAGE: will keep indefinitely in closed jar in cool place

WHEN AVAILABLE: always

WHERE PURCHASED: Chinese grocery

APPROXIMATE COST: moderately expensive

SUBSTITUTES: flower mushroom

IMPORTANCE: 4

MUSHROOMS (FLOWER), DRIED CHINESE (fa gu/hwa gu)

TYPE OF FOOD: fungus

LENGTH, SHAPE, COLOR, AND SURFACE: similar to Chinese Dried Mushrooms (Winter) except that color is lighter; surface has striated indentations; body is thicker and shaped more like a flower.

CONSISTENCY, AROMA, TASTE, USES: same as Chinese Dried Mushrooms (Winter)

AVAILABLE FORMS: dried

STORAGE: will keep indefinitely in closed jar in cool place

WHEN AVAILABLE: always
WHERE PURCHASED: Chinese grocery
APPROXIMATE COST: moderately expensive to expensive
SUBSTITUTES: Chinese Dried Mushrooms (Winter)
IMPORTANCE: 2

MUSHROOMS, GRASS, DRIED (tso gu/tsao gu)
TYPE OF FOOD: fungus; although very similar to Chinese Dried Mushrooms (Winter), it is more fragrant and has a stronger flavor.
ALL OTHER CATEGORIES: *See* Chinese Dried Mushrooms (Winter)

MUSTARD, DRY (gai lat/gai mo)
TYPE OF FOOD: condiment, spice
CONSISTENCY: paste of powder and water
TASTE: sharp, pungent
USES: seasoning
AVAILABLE FORMS: dry in tins by the ounce
STORAGE: will keep in pantry indefinitely
WHEN AVAILABLE: always
WHERE PURCHASED: Chinese grocery
APPROXIMATE COST: inexpensive
SUBSTITUTES: Colman's English Mustard
IMPORTANCE: 4

MUSTARD GREENS (gai tsoi/gai tsai)
TYPE OF FOOD: vegetable
LENGTH: to about 12 inches
SHAPE: leafy stalk
COLOR: white stalk ending in green leaves
SURFACE: smooth stalk, textured leaf
CONSISTENCY: firm, crunchy
AROMA: none
TASTE: tangy, bitter, slightly sour
USES: soup, stir-fry dishes
AVAILABLE FORMS: fresh—by the pound; salted in brine—loose by the pound; pickled in quart jars (hsien tsai/ham tsoi)
STORAGE: fresh—will keep in the refrigerator for about one week; salted—in jar in refrigerator, will keep for about one week; pickled—will keep indefinitely unopened; will keep indefinitely opened in refrigerator

WHEN AVAILABLE: always
WHERE PURCHASED: Chinese grocery
APPROXIMATE COST: inexpensive
SUBSTITUTES: none
IMPORTANCE: 4

NOODLES, CELLOPHANE (fun see/fun si)
TYPE OF FOOD: noodle (of mung bean flour); also known as bean threads, Chinese vermicelli, shining noodles, transparent noodles
LENGTH: to 32 inches (cooked)
SHAPE: uncooked—8-inch rectangular mats of closely wound together noodles; cooked—thin, threadlike noodles
COLOR: translucent
SURFACE: smooth, glossy, shiny
CONSISTENCY: dry (uncooked); gelatinous, moist, slippery, soft (cooked)
AROMA: none
TASTE: bland, delicate, takes on flavor of other ingredients
USES: garnish, main ingredient
AVAILABLE FORMS: in cellophane packages of from 1 to 8 ounces
STORAGE: uncooked—will keep in the pantry indefinitely
WHEN AVAILABLE: always
WHERE PURCHASED: Chinese grocery
APPROXIMATE COST: inexpensive
SUBSTITUTES: egg noodles
IMPORTANCE: 3

NOODLES, FRESH (lo mein/lo mein)
TYPE OF FOOD: noodle (made with eggs)
LENGTH: to 24 inches (cooked)
SHAPE: uncooked—4 inch by 8 inch package of closely wound together noodles; cooked—shoelace-like
COLOR: whitish, doughy
SURFACE: dull
CONSISTENCY: doughy, firm
AROMA: none
TASTE: bland, takes on flavor of other ingredients
USES: as a side dish or main ingredient
AVAILABLE FORMS: in paper-wrapped (refrigerated) package by the pound

STORAGE: must be refrigerated; will keep several days or indefinitely if frozen
WHEN AVAILABLE: always
WHERE PURCHASED: Chinese grocery
APPROXIMATE COST: inexpensive
SUBSTITUTES: none
IMPORTANCE: 4

NOODLES, YEE FU (yee fu mein/ee fu mein)
TYPE OF FOOD: packaged fried dried egg noodles with seasoning
LENGTH: 3- by 5-inch package
SHAPE: loose, matted when opened
COLOR: yellow
SURFACE: glossy
CONSISTENCY: dehydrated; like regular noodles when cooked
AROMA: like regular noodles when cooked
TASTE: chicken flavored
USES: light lunch; main ingredient
AVAILABLE FORMS: dried
STORAGE: will keep in pantry indefinitely
WHEN AVAILABLE: always
WHERE PURCHASED: Chinese grocery
APPROXIMATE COST: inexpensive
SUBSTITUTES: none
IMPORTANCE: 2

OKRA, CHINESE (si gwa/se gwa)
TYPE OF FOOD: vegetable, also known as silk squash or silk melon
LENGTH: to 4 inches
SHAPE: similar to American okra
COLOR: green
SURFACE: textured, ribbed, fuzzy
CONSISTENCY: firm, fleshy, moist, tender
AROMA: none
TASTE: sweet, delicate
USES: main ingredient; also goes with many vegetable or meat ingredients
AVAILABLE FORMS: fresh by the pound
STORAGE: will keep for about 1 week in plastic bag in refrigerator crisper
WHEN AVAILABLE: summer only
WHERE PURCHASED: Chinese grocery

APPROXIMATE COST: inexpensive
SUBSTITUTES: American okra, zucchini
IMPORTANCE: 2

OLIVE, CURED (ham lam/hsien lan)
TYPE OF FOOD: fruit
LENGTH: to 1 inch
SHAPE: oval
COLOR: black; brown
SURFACE: wrinkled, dull, shriveled
CONSISTENCY: dry, fleshy, soft, has pit
AROMA: pungent
TASTE: salty, sweet, anise-like
USES: flavoring agent
AVAILABLE FORMS: dried, loose by the pound or in packages
STORAGE: will keep indefinitely in covered jar in the pantry
WHEN AVAILABLE: always
WHERE PURCHASED: Chinese grocery
APPROXIMATE COST: moderately expensive
SUBSTITUTES: none
IMPORTANCE: 1

ONE HUNDRED UNITIES (bok hop/bai ho)
TYPE OF FOOD: condiment, spice
APPEARANCE: dried, small iridescent white petals from a lily plant
AROMA: none
TASTE: none
USES: seasoning with other ingredients
AVAILABLE FORMS: dried, by the ounce
STORAGE: will keep indefinitely in covered jar in pantry
WHEN AVAILABLE: always
WHERE PURCHASED: Chinese grocery
APPROXIMATE COST: very expensive
SUBSTITUTES: none
IMPORTANCE: 1

OYSTER SAUCE (ho yow/hao yo)
TYPE OF FOOD: condiment
COLOR: brown
CONSISTENCY: free-flowing fluid but slightly thick
AROMA: meaty
TASTE: delicate, meaty
USES: flavoring agent, flavor heightener, staple;

enhances appearance of dishes; blends well into sauces

AVAILABLE FORMS: bottles (6 ounces or more) and cans (larger amounts). The imported variety is far superior; domestic variety is less flavorful.

STORAGE: will keep in bottle in the refrigerator indefinitely

WHEN AVAILABLE: always

WHERE PURCHASED: Chinese grocery

APPROXIMATE COST: moderately expensive

SUBSTITUTES: none

IMPORTANCE: 4

OYSTERS, CHINESE, DRIED (ho see/hao shih)

TYPE OF FOOD: shellfish

LENGTH: to 2 inches

SHAPE: flat, roundish

COLOR: gray-brown

SURFACE: dull, shriveled, ridged

CONSISTENCY: dry, hard (uncooked); chewy (cooked)

AROMA: slightly fishy when cooked

TASTE: delicate, fishy

USES: flavoring agent

AVAILABLE FORMS: in ½-lb. or 1-lb. cellophane bags or loose by the pound

STORAGE: will keep indefinitely in tightly covered jar in pantry

WHEN AVAILABLE: always

WHERE PURCHASED: Chinese grocery

APPROXIMATE COST: inexpensive

SUBSTITUTES: dried scallops or snails

IMPORTANCE: 2

ADDITIONAL INFORMATION: Dried Chinese Oysters must be soaked for at least 8 hours in warm water to remove sand. Some cooks recommend soaking them as long as 36 hours.

PARSLEY, CHINESE (yuin si tsoi/hsiang tsai)

TYPE OF FOOD: herb (coriander)

LENGTH: to 16 inches

SHAPE: thin stem ending in flat, serrated leaf

COLOR: green

SURFACE: leaf-textured

CONSISTENCY: crunchy, moist, tender

AROMA: pungent (stronger than American parsley)

TASTE: strong, tangy

USES: flavoring agent, garnish, cuts odors

AVAILABLE FORMS: fresh by the bunch

STORAGE: treat same as American parsley

WHEN AVAILABLE: always

WHERE PURCHASED: Chinese and Spanish (as coriander) groceries

APPROXIMATE COST: inexpensive

SUBSTITUTES: American parsley (as a garnish); none for flavoring

IMPORTANCE: 2

PEPPER, ANISE* (SZECHUAN) (fa jiu/hwa jiao)

TYPE OF FOOD: spice

LENGTH: 3/16 inch

SHAPE: round kernel

COLOR: light brown

SURFACE: rough, dried

CONSISTENCY: brittle

AROMA: stronger than black pepper

TASTE: stronger, more pungent than black pepper

USES: flavoring; dipping (in powdered form)

AVAILABLE FORMS: only in dried whole kernels, packaged; easily ground to a powder for immediate use

STORAGE: will keep indefinitely when tightly bottled

WHEN AVAILABLE: always

WHERE PURCHASED: Chinese grocery

APPROXIMATE COST: moderately expensive

SUBSTITUTES: none

IMPORTANCE: 2

PLUM SAUCE (DUCK SAUCE) (shwin mei jiong/ swan mei jiang)

TYPE OF FOOD: condiment

COLOR: brown; green; orange; red

CONSISTENCY: thick fluid or thin free-flowing sauce

AROMA: pungent, sweet

TASTE: tangy, tart, sweet and sour

USES: blending sauce, condiment, darkens sauce, flavoring agent, cuts strong odors in foods (such as fish)

---

* Not to be confused with Anise Pepper Salt, included in the recipes.

AVAILABLE FORMS: in jars or tins

STORAGE: in covered jar or bottle in refrigerator will keep indefinitely

WHEN AVAILABLE: always

WHERE PURCHASED: Chinese grocery for imported brands; most supermarkets for domestic brands

APPROXIMATE COST: inexpensive

SUBSTITUTES: none

IMPORTANCE: 4

RED-IN-SNOW (shiet lieh hung/shieh li hung)

TYPE OF FOOD: vegetable

LENGTH: to 12 inches

SHAPE: leafy stalk

COLOR: green

SURFACE: dull, smooth

CONSISTENCY: crunchy, firm, moist

AROMA: none

TASTE: similar to broccoli

USES: main ingredient; mixed with meats or in soups

AVAILABLE FORMS: fresh, by the pound; salted, in cans; also salted, in cans in combination with bamboo shoots

STORAGE: fresh—will keep in refrigerator for one week; salted—will keep in brine indefinitely

WHEN AVAILABLE: fresh—in late fall; canned—always

WHERE PURCHASED: Chinese grocery

APPROXIMATE COST: inexpensive

SUBSTITUTES: Chinese mustard greens

IMPORTANCE: 2

RICE, GLUTINOUS (noh my/noh mi)

TYPE OF FOOD: grain

LENGTH: shorter than long-grain rice

SHAPE: smaller and less elongated than long-grain rice

COLOR: white-cream

SURFACE: dull

CONSISTENCY: cooked—moist, pasty, slippery, tender, thick

AROMA: none

TASTE: sweet, little of its own, takes on flavor of other ingredients

USES: main ingredient; thickening agent; stuffing; dessert

AVAILABLE FORMS: dry in packages by the pound; rice powder finely ground for use in Chinese pastries

STORAGE: will keep indefinitely in covered jar in pantry

WHEN AVAILABLE: always

WHERE PURCHASED: Chinese grocery

APPROXIMATE COST: inexpensive

SUBSTITUTES: none

IMPORTANCE: 3

RICE STICKS (my fun/mi fun)

TYPE OF FOOD: grain

LENGTH: 8 inches

SHAPE: thin stick similar to spaghetti

COLOR: opaque, white

SURFACE: smooth, shiny when cooked

CONSISTENCY: brittle, dry, hard; cooked—moist, tender

AROMA: none

TASTE: little of its own, takes on flavor of other ingredients

USES: main ingredient

AVAILABLE FORMS: dry in paper packages by the half pound or pound or cut in short standard lengths and formed into small rolls

STORAGE: will keep indefinitely in can or jar in pantry

WHEN AVAILABLE: always

WHERE PURCHASED: Chinese grocery

APPROXIMATE COST: inexpensive

SUBSTITUTES: fresh noodles

IMPORTANCE: 2

SAUSAGE, PORK (lop chiong/la tsang)

TYPE OF FOOD: meat (pork alone or pork combined with pork liver)

LENGTH: 6 inches

SHAPE: frankfurter

COLOR: red with white (fat) marbling

SURFACE: glossy, shiny, slightly shriveled

CONSISTENCY: fatty, firm, meaty

AROMA: appetizing, meaty

TASTE: meaty, salty, spicy, strong

USES: flavoring agent; main ingredient; staple; stuffing

AVAILABLE FORMS: by individual sausage (or bunch) by weight

STORAGE: will keep indefinitely in the freezer
WHEN AVAILABLE: always
WHERE PURCHASED: Chinese grocery
APPROXIMATE COST: moderately expensive
SUBSTITUTES: none
IMPORTANCE: 3

SCALLOPS, DRIED (gong yu chu/gan bei)
TYPE OF FOOD: shellfish
LENGTH: to 2 inches (halved or quartered)
SHAPE: similar to American variety but shrunken
COLOR: amber
SURFACE: dull, textured, shriveled
CONSISTENCY: tough, chewy, fleshy
AROMA: fishy
TASTE: strong, fishy, sweet
USES: flavoring agent
AVAILABLE FORMS: dried segments loose by the pound
STORAGE: will keep indefinitely in covered jar in pantry
WHEN AVAILABLE: always
WHERE PURCHASED: Chinese grocery
APPROXIMATE COST: inexpensive
SUBSTITUTES: none
IMPORTANCE: 2

SEA CUCUMBER, DRIED (See Bêche-de-Mer)

SEAWEED (jee tsoi/tze tsai)
TYPE OF FOOD: seafood vegetable
LENGTH: 8 inches
SHAPE: square, flat sheet
COLOR: purple
SURFACE: matted, textured, shriveled; smooth when cooked
CONSISTENCY: brittle, stiff, dry; gelatinous, soft, tender, and limp when cooked
AROMA: strong, iodine-like
TASTE: iodine-like
USES: main ingredient, soups
AVAILABLE FORMS: in cellophane packets by the ounce; Japanese variety more common; also dried, almost black, variety known as "hair seaweed" (faat tsoi/faat tsai)

STORAGE: wrapped and stored in the pantry, it will keep indefinitely
WHEN AVAILABLE: always
WHERE PURCHASED: Chinese and Japanese groceries
APPROXIMATE COST: expensive
SUBSTITUTES: none
IMPORTANCE: 2

SESAME OIL (jee ma yow/tze ma yu)
TYPE OF FOOD: flavoring extract
COLOR: amber
CONSISTENCY: thin-flowing
AROMA: pungent, appetizing
TASTE: strong
USES: seasoning; flavoring agent; cuts odors; blends into sauces or salad dressings
AVAILABLE FORMS: bottled (6 ounces or more)
STORAGE: will keep in the pantry for a year or more
WHEN AVAILABLE: always
WHERE PURCHASED: Oriental or Middle East groceries or health food stores
APPROXIMATE COST: inexpensive
SUBSTITUTES: none
IMPORTANCE: 4

SHARK FIN (yu chi/yu tze)
TYPE OF FOOD: seafood (dried cartilage from the fin of a shark)
LENGTH: best quality, 5 inches; average quality, 2 to 3 inches; scraps, 1 inch
SHAPE: about as thick as thin spaghetti
COLOR: opaque
SURFACE: rough skin
CONSISTENCY: soft, fragile, crunchy
AROMA: none
TASTE: bland
USES: soup; red-cooked meats and poultry; a "must" in some form for formal Chinese dinners and especially weddings; believed to confer strength and virility
AVAILABLE FORMS: dried or in cans (partially prepared by having the skin and sand removed)
STORAGE: dried fins will keep for years in the

pantry; soaked fins can be kept in the refrigerator for several days before use

WHEN AVAILABLE: always

WHERE PURCHASED: Chinese grocery

APPROXIMATE COST: very expensive; the higher the quality, the more expensive ($5 to $50 per pound)

SUBSTITUTES: none

IMPORTANCE: 3

SHRIMP, DRIED (ha my/sha mi)

TYPE OF FOOD: shellfish

LENGTH: ½ inch to 2 inches

SHAPE: like common variety of shrimp, but very small

COLOR: amber

SURFACE: dull, shriveled

CONSISTENCY: dry

AROMA: strong, fishy

TASTE: very fishy, meaty

USES: flavoring agent, main ingredient, stuffing

AVAILABLE FORMS: dry by the ounce in cellophane bags

STORAGE: will keep indefinitely in covered jars; if too dry, it can be soaked in a little sherry or water

WHEN AVAILABLE: always

WHERE PURCHASED: Chinese and Japanese groceries

APPROXIMATE COST: inexpensive

SUBSTITUTES: none

IMPORTANCE: 3

SHRIMP CHIPS (OR SLICES) (ha bang/hsia bing)

TYPE OF FOOD: shellfish with flour dough

LENGTH: to 2 inches

SHAPE: curled, irregular, varishaped like potato chip

COLOR: red, yellow, or white

SURFACE: dull, pebbly, textured

CONSISTENCY: dry until deep-fried; then crisp, brittle, stiff

AROMA: slight, fishy

TASTE: delicate, sweet

USES: garnish, appetizer

AVAILABLE FORMS: in small cellophane bags by the ounce

STORAGE: will keep indefinitely in the pantry; deep-fried, will keep in tightly covered tin can or jar for a few days

WHEN AVAILABLE: always

WHERE PURCHASED: Chinese grocery

APPROXIMATE COST: inexpensive

SUBSTITUTES: potato chips

IMPORTANCE: 1

SHRIMP PASTE (hahm ha/shien sha)

TYPE OF FOOD: shellfish

COLOR: purple-white

CONSISTENCY: thick paste

AROMA: fishy, pungent

TASTE: strong, fishy, salty

USES: flavoring agent

AVAILABLE FORMS: in jars (up to 8 ounces)

STORAGE: will keep in the refrigerator indefinitely

WHEN AVAILABLE: always

WHERE PURCHASED: Chinese grocery

APPROXIMATE COST: inexpensive

SUBSTITUTES: none

IMPORTANCE: 2

SNOW PEAS (shieh dow/shieh do)

TYPE OF FOOD: vegetable

LENGTH: to 2 inches

SHAPE: flat pea pod

COLOR: green

SURFACE: glossy, smooth

CONSISTENCY: cooked—crispy, crunchy, firm, fleshy, moist, tender

AROMA: slight, tempting

TASTE: bland, delicate, pealike, distinctive

USES: flavoring agent; main ingredient

AVAILABLE FORMS: fresh by the ounce; frozen (imported from Japan, smaller, and not nearly as crisp or green) in packages

STORAGE: fresh—will keep in the crisper up to several weeks

WHEN AVAILABLE: always

WHERE PURCHASED: Chinese grocery or supermarket (for frozen variety)

APPROXIMATE COST: expensive (especially October to April)
SUBSTITUTES: none
IMPORTANCE: 4

SOY SAUCE (dark—lo tsow/lao tsou; heavy—jiong yow/jiang yu; light—sang tsow/sheng tsou; table soy sauce—sin tsow/shien tsou)
TYPE OF FOOD: fermented soy bean extract combined with salt. Dark soy sauce has caramel added for coloring. Heavy soy sauce, which has a slightly sweet smell, is also known as black soy. Light soy sauce is the most delicately flavored and is light brown in color. Japanese soy sauce, somewhere between the Chinese light and heavy, is preferable to domestic brands but inferior to Chinese brands. There are no standards for the color, saltiness, or taste of soy sauce but an inferior sauce can spoil a dish
COLOR: dark brown
CONSISTENCY: thin liquid
AROMA: fragrant, appetizing, meaty
TASTE: delicate, meaty, salty
USES: flavoring agent; flavor heightener; in stuffing; darkens other sauces; cuts odors
AVAILABLE FORMS: in pint or quart bottles; larger size, imported, comes in square or rectangular cans
STORAGE: will keep indefinitely tightly stoppered in pantry. Discard sediment at bottom of bottle because it is too salty for most recipes. If in opened can, it should be transferred to glass container. Soy sauce never sours or molds
WHEN AVAILABLE: always
WHERE PURCHASED: Chinese and Japanese groceries; also supermarkets
APPROXIMATE COST: inexpensive
SUBSTITUTES: none
IMPORTANCE: 4

SQUASH, SILK (See Okra, Chinese)

SQUID, DRIED (yow yu/yo yu)
TYPE OF FOOD: seafood
SHAPE: shrunken, dehydrated version of fresh variety (which is like small octopus)
COLOR: brown and whitish

SURFACE: smooth
CONSISTENCY: tough
AROMA: slight, fishy
TASTE: fishy
USES: main ingredient
AVAILABLE FORMS: by the piece by weight
STORAGE: will keep indefinitely when kept wrapped in pantry
WHEN AVAILABLE: always
WHERE PURCHASED: Chinese grocery
APPROXIMATE COST: inexpensive
SUBSTITUTES: none
IMPORTANCE: 1

SUGAR, ROCK (bing tong/bing tang)
TYPE OF FOOD: similar to rock candy, crystallized sugar
LENGTH: to 2 inches
SHAPE: irregular, knobby, varishaped
COLOR: amber, clear
SURFACE: glossy, shiny, smooth
CONSISTENCY: brittle, dry, hard
AROMA: none
TASTE: bland, syrupy, sweet
USES: flavoring agent; glaze; staple; in teas; blends into sauces
AVAILABLE FORMS: by the pound in packages
STORAGE: will keep indefinitely in covered jar in the pantry
WHEN AVAILABLE: always
WHERE PURCHASED: Chinese grocery
APPROXIMATE COST: inexpensive
SUBSTITUTES: granulated sugar
IMPORTANCE: 2

TANGERINE PEEL, DRIED (tsen pei/tsen pi)
TYPE OF FOOD: fruit rind
LENGTH: to 2 inches in diameter
SHAPE: curled, flat, wrinkled
COLOR: orange-amber
SURFACE: dull, indented or pocked, pebbly, textured, shriveled
CONSISTENCY: dry, stiff, hard until cooked; then, chewy, firm, fleshy, meaty, moist, tender
AROMA: slightly sweet, appetizing, fragrant
TASTE: sweet, spicy, tangy, tart

USES: condiment, flavoring agent; flavor heightener; garnish; stuffing; spice; cuts odors

AVAILABLE FORMS: by the ounce in cellophane bag

STORAGE: will keep indefinitely in the pantry

WHEN AVAILABLE: always

WHERE PURCHASED: Chinese grocery

APPROXIMATE COST: inexpensive

SUBSTITUTES: none

IMPORTANCE: 3

TARO ROOT (yu tau/yu t'ou)

TYPE OF FOOD: root vegetable

SHAPE: potato-like

COLOR: brown-tan

SURFACE: dull

CONSISTENCY: firm

AROMA: none

TASTE: potato-like

USES: auxiliary ingredient with duck, Chinese sausages, etc.

AVAILABLE FORMS: fresh by the pound

STORAGE: will keep several weeks in refrigerator crisper

WHEN AVAILABLE: autumn

WHERE PURCHASED: Chinese grocery

APPROXIMATE COST: inexpensive

SUBSTITUTES: none

IMPORTANCE: 2

TRIPE, FISH (yu toe/yu du)

TYPE OF FOOD: fish stomach

SHAPE: curled, long, sheet

COLOR: amber-yellow

SURFACE: dull, textured

CONSISTENCY: raw—dry, hard, stiff; cooked—chewy, moist

AROMA: none

TASTE: bland, delicate, unique

USES: main ingredient

AVAILABLE FORMS: dried loose by the pound

STORAGE: will keep in pantry for months

WHEN AVAILABLE: always

WHERE PURCHASED: Chinese grocery

APPROXIMATE COST: moderate

SUBSTITUTES: none

IMPORTANCE: 2

TURNIP, CHINESE (lo ba/lo bo)

TYPE OF FOOD: root vegetable

LENGTH: 8 to 12 inches

SHAPE: like a white radish

COLOR: white

SURFACE: carrot-like, unribbed

CONSISTENCY: crispy and crunchy when raw; firm when cooked

AROMA: none

TASTE: stronger than American variety

USES: main ingredient; soups; red-cooked or stir-fried

AVAILABLE FORMS: fresh by the pound

STORAGE: will keep 2 weeks in the refrigerator

WHEN AVAILABLE: always

WHERE PURCHASED: Chinese grocery

APPROXIMATE COST: inexpensive

SUBSTITUTES: American turnip

IMPORTANCE: 2

TURNIPS, SALTED (dy to tsoi/ta to tsai)

TYPE OF FOOD: cured root vegetable

LENGTH: 2 inches

SHAPE: sheeted or round

COLOR: brown

SURFACE: dull, shriveled

CONSISTENCY: firm, tough, chewy, crunchy

AROMA: strong

TASTE: salty, spicy

USES: flavoring agent; main ingredient

AVAILABLE FORMS: in packets

STORAGE: will keep indefinitely in the pantry in a closed container

WHEN AVAILABLE: always

WHERE PURCHASED: Chinese grocery

APPROXIMATE COST: inexpensive

SUBSTITUTES: none

IMPORTANCE: 2

VEGETABLE STEAK (mein gon/mein jing)

TYPE OF FOOD: meat substitute made from wheat gluten

SHAPE: 3-inch square or round patty ½ inch thick

COLOR: brown

SURFACE: smooth

CONSISTENCY: chewy, firm

AROMA: none

TASTE: meaty, beefy

USES: main ingredient

AVAILABLE FORMS: cans

STORAGE: opened will keep in refrigerator for a couple of weeks.

WHEN AVAILABLE: always

WHERE PURCHASED: Chinese grocery and health food shops

APPROXIMATE COST: inexpensive

SUBSTITUTES: meats

IMPORTANCE: 2

VINEGAR, RICE (ba tso/bai tsu)

TYPE OF FOOD: condiment—three varieties: light amber, used especially in sweet and sour dishes; a dark black native type (huck tso/hu ts'u) for red-cooking and added in small amounts to darken the color of sweet and sour sauces or used as a dip; and a red type used mainly as a dip

AROMA: strong, appetizing, pickled, fragrant, sweet

TASTE: sour, spicy, tangy, tart

USES: condiment; flavoring agent; blends into sauce

AVAILABLE FORMS: bottled

STORAGE: will keep indefinitely in the pantry

WHEN AVAILABLE: always

WHERE PURCHASED: Chinese grocery

APPROXIMATE COST: inexpensive

SUBSTITUTES: none

IMPORTANCE: 3

WATERCRESS (sih yong tsoi/hsi yang tsai)

TYPE OF FOOD: vegetable similar to American variety, with oval leaves and slightly acid flavor

USES: as soup green; garnish

AVAILABLE FORMS: fresh in small bunches

STORAGE: will keep in refrigerator for 1 week

WHEN AVAILABLE: always

WHERE PURCHASED: Chinese grocery

APPROXIMATE COST: inexpensive

SUBSTITUTE: American watercress

IMPORTANCE: 3

WOOD EARS (See Cloud Ears)

INGREDIENTS

Canned Abalone

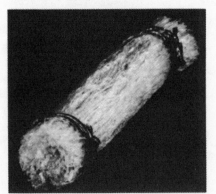

Agar Agar

Dried Star Anise

Chinese Bacon

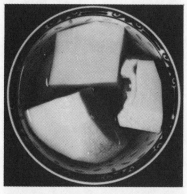

Canned Unsalted Bamboo Shoots

Fermented Black Beans

Sweet Bean Filling

Fresh Bean Curd

Bean Curd Sheets

Pressed Bean Curd

Bean Curd Sticks

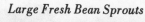

Large Fresh Bean Sprouts

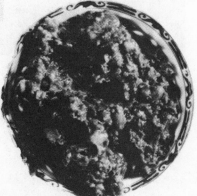

Brown Bean Sauce

Fresh Long Green Beans

Dried Bêche-De-Mer

Packaged Bird's Nest

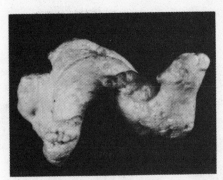

Caul Fat

Fresh Chinese Broccoli

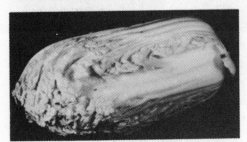

Celery Cabbage

White Chinese Cabbage

Canned Water Chestnuts

right: Fresh Water Chestnuts
left: Fresh Taro Roots

Cloud Ears (Wood Ears)

Dried Red Dates

Cured Duck Livers

left: Salted Duck Egg
right: 100-Year-Old Egg

Fresh Egg Roll Skins (Wrappers)

Mature Ginger

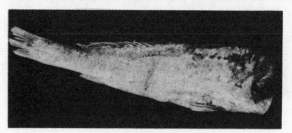
Dried Salted Fish

Packaged Crystallized Ginger and Loose
Crystallized Winter Melon

Preserved Ginger (Mixed) Pickles

Fresh Kohlrabi

Hoisin Sauce

Dried Packaged Jellyfish

Canned Litchis

Canned Shelled
Gingko Nuts

Dried Lily Flowers

Dried Litchis

Canned Longans

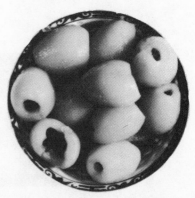

Canned Loquats

top: *Fresh Lotus Root*
bottom: *Fresh Young Ginger*

Dried Lotus Seeds

Fresh Bitter Melon

Hairy Melon

Canned Tea Melon

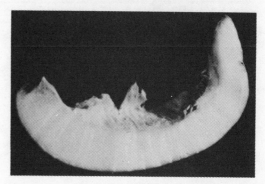

Fresh Winter Melon Slice

Dried Winter Mushrooms

*Fresh
Mustard Greens*

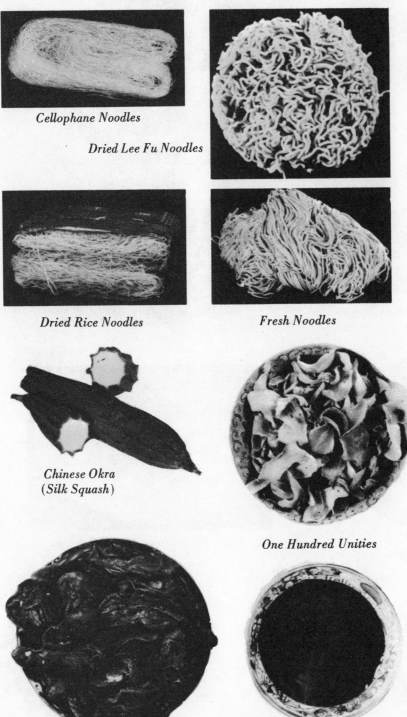

Cellophane Noodles

Dried Lee Fu Noodles

Dried Rice Noodles

Fresh Noodles

*Fresh Chinese Parsley
(Coriander)*

*Chinese Okra
(Silk Squash)*

One Hundred Unities

Dried Chinese Oysters

Oyster Sauce

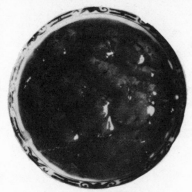

Plum Sauce (Duck Sauce)

Rock Sugar

Dried Pork Sausage

Sesame Oil

Purple Seaweed Sheets

Dried Scallops

Hair Seaweed

Packaged Shark's Fin

Sugared Winter Melon

Light Soy Sauce   Rice Vinegar
(Black)

Dried Shrimp

Shrimp Paste

Fresh Snow Peas

Dried Squid

Dried Tangerine Peel

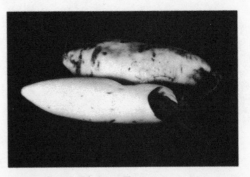

top: Fresh Chinese Turnip
bottom: Fresh Chinese White Eggplant

Canned Vegetable Steak

Watermelon Seeds

PREPARED DISHES

Egg Rolls and Fried Won Tons

Fun Goh (Meat Dumpling

Shrimp Dumplings and Mushroom Shu Mai
(Dumpling)

Szechuan Steamed Fish

Stir-Fried Shrimp with Green Peas

Lobster Cantonese

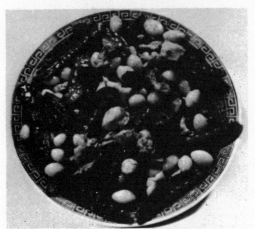

Stir-Fried Chicken Cubes with Gingko Nuts

Soy Sauce Chicken

Fire Pot (Chafing Dish): top row, left to right: Raw Spinach, Sliced Raw Chicken, Cut Chinese Celery Cabbage; bottom row: Cellophane Noodles, Sliced Raw Steak

Braised Bean Curd with Pork and Mushrooms

Litchi Snowball Pork

Beef Lo Mein

Braised Bamboo Shoots

*top: Flower Rolls; center: Chinese Bread;
bottom: Pork Stuffed Steamed Bread*

Agar Agar Salad with Sauce

Candied Fruit Coconut Rice Pudding

SHOPPING LIST
FOR CHINESE CUPBOARD

(American foodstuffs such as abalone, almonds, beef tenderloin, etc. are common to both Chinese and American cuisine. Such foods, a few of which are listed below because they are essential for Chinese cooking, may be purchased at any market by their English names.)

ENGLISH	CANTONESE		ENGLISH	CANTONESE	
Abalone, canned	bao yu	鮑魚	pressed	dow fu kon	豆腐乾
dried	bao yu		sticks	fu jook pei	腐竹皮
Agar Agar, dried	dung yong tsoi	東洋菜	**Bean Curd Cheese,** red	nam yu	南乳
Anise, Star, (Szechuan)			**Bean Filling,** sweet	dow sa	豆沙
dried	ba gok	八角	**Bean Sauce** (soy), brown	mien see jiong	麵豉醬
ground	ba gok		yellow	mien see jiong	
Bacon, Chinese	yin yoke	煙肉	**Bean Sprouts** (mung),		
Bamboo Shoots, dried	jook sun	竹筍	canned, small	gna tsoi	芽菜
fresh	jook sun		fresh, small	gna tsoi	
pickled	shwin sun ee	酸筍衣	**Bean Sprouts** (soy), large	wong dow gna	黃豆芽
salted	jook sun	竹筍	**Beans, Long Green,** fresh	dow gok	豆角
unsalted	jook sun,		**Bêche-de-Mer,** dried	hai sum	海參
	dung sun	冬筍	**Bird's Nest,** whole or parts	yin waw	燕窩
Bean, Black, dried	wu dow	烏豆	**Broccoli,** Chinese, fresh	gai lan tsoi	芥蘭菜
salted,			**Cabbage, White, Chinese,**		
fermented	dow si	豆豉	dried	bok tsoi	白菜
Bean Cake, fermented	fu yu	腐乳	fresh	bok tsoi	
Bean Curd, dried or sheets	tiem jook	甜竹	**Caul Fat**	mong yow	網油
canned,			**Celery Cabbage, Chinese,**		
water packed	dow fu	豆腐	fresh	sheo tsoi	紹菜
fresh	dow fu				

ENGLISH	CANTONESE		ENGLISH	CANTONESE	
preserved	dung tsoi	冬 菜	Litchis, canned	la-ee tzee	荔 枝
Chestnuts, dried	loot tzee	栗 子	dried	la-ee tzee gon	荔枝乾
shelled	loot tzee		fresh	la-ee tzee	
Chestnuts, Water, canned	ma tie	馬 蹄	Longans, canned	loong gnahn	龍 眼
fresh	ma tie		dried	loong gnahn	
powder	ma tie fun	馬蹄粉	Loquats, canned	pei pa	枇 杷
Chives, Chinese, fresh	gow tsoi	韮 菜	fresh	pei pa	
Cloud Ears	win yee	雲 耳	Lotus Root, canned	leen gnow	蓮 藕
Coconut, crystallized			fresh	leen gnow	
sweetmeat, strips	tong long	糖 郎	pqwdered stem	leen gnow fun	蓮 藕粉
Cookies, Almond	hong yang bang	杏仁餅	slices, dried	gon leen gnow	乾蓮藕
Cuttlefish, dried (whole)	yow yu	油 魚	Lotus Seeds, canned	leen tszee	蓮 子
Dates, red, dried	hung jo	紅 棗	dried	leen tszee	
Duck Liver (Gizzard),			fresh	leen tszee	
cured	op gon	鴨 肝	jam	leen tszee	
Duck Sauce	See Plum Sauce		Melon, Bitter, fresh	fu gwa	苦 瓜
Egg, 100-Year-Old	pei don	皮 蛋	Melon, Hairy, fresh	jit gwa	節 瓜
Duck, salted	hahm don	鹹 蛋	Melon Seeds	gwa tzee	瓜 子
preserved	hahm don		Melon Tea, canned	tsa gwa	茶 瓜
Egg Roll Skins			Melon, Winter, fresh	dung gwa	冬 瓜
(Wrappers), fresh	chwin guen pei	春卷皮	Molasses, Chinese Bead	ju yow	珠 油
Eggplant, Chinese, fresh	ngai gwa	矮 瓜	Mushrooms, Flower, dried	fa gu	花 菇
Fish, salted, cured, dried	gon hahm yu	乾鹹魚	Grass, dried	tso gu	草 菇
Five Spices Powder	ng hiong fun	五香粉	Winter, dried	dung gu	冬 菇
Ginger, crystallized	tong giong	糖 薑	Mustard, Dry	gai lat	芥 末
fresh	giong	薑	Mustard Greens, fresh	gai tsoi	芥 菜
pickled, canned	shwin giong	酸 薑	Noodles, Cellophane	fun see	粉 絲
pickled, red	shwin giong	紅酸薑	Fresh	lo mein	撈 麪
powder	giong moo	薑 末	Yee Fu	Yee Fu	伊府麪
preserved, sugared	tong giong	糖 薑	Okra or Silk Squash,		
Ginkgo Nuts, dried	bok go	白 果	Chinese	si gwa	絲 瓜
shelled	bok go		Olives, cured, dried	ham lam	鹹 欖
Golden Needles	See Lily Flowers		One Hundred Unities, dry	bok hop	百 合
Hoisin Sauce	hoy sin jiong	海鮮醬	Oyster Sauce	ho yow	蠔 油
Hot Sauce	lat yow	辣 油	Oysters, Chinese, dried	ho see	蠔 豉
Jellyfish, dried	hoy jit pei	海蜇皮	Parsley, Chinese, fresh	yuin si tsoi	芫茜菜
Kohlrabi, fresh	dye to tsoi	大頭菜	Pepper, Anise, Szechuan	fa jiu	花 椒
preserved	cha tsoi	榨 菜	Plum Sauce	shwin mei jiong	酸梅醬
Kumquats, crystallized	gum quot	金 橘	Red-in-Snow	shiet lieh hung	雪裏紅
fresh	gum quot		Rice, Glutinous, dried	noh my	糯 米
preserved	gum quot		powder	noh my fun	糯米粉
Lemon Sauce	ning mung jiong	檸檬醬	Rice Sticks, dried	my fun	米 粉
Lily Flowers or Golden			Sausage, Pork, dried	lop chiong	臘 腸
Needles, dried	gum tsum	金 針	Scallops, dried	gong yu chu	光魚柱

ENGLISH	CANTONESE		ENGLISH	CANTONESE	
Seaweed, Hair	faat tsoi	髮 菜	Squid, dried	yow yu	油 魚
Purple	jee tsoi	紫 菜	fresh	mook yu	墨 魚
Sesame Oil	jee ma yow	芝蔴 油	Sugar, Rock	bing tong	冰 糖
Shark Fin	yu chi	魚 翅	Tangerine Peel, dried	tsen pei	陳 皮
Shrimp, dried	ha my	蝦 米	Taro Root, fresh	yu tau	芋 頭
Shrimp Chips	ha bang	蝦 餅	Tripe, Fish, fresh	yu toe	魚 肚
Shrimp Paste	hahm ha	鹹 蝦	Turnip, Chinese, fresh	lo ba	蘿 葡
Snow Peas, fresh	shieh dow	雪 豆	salted	dy to tsoi	大頭 菜
Soy Sauce, dark	lo tsow	老 抽	Vegetable Steak	mein gon	麫 根
heavy	jiong yow	醬 油	Vinegar, Rice	ba tso	白 醋
light	sang tsow	生 抽	Watercress, fresh	sih yong tsoi	西洋 菜
Squash, Silk	See Okra		Wood Ears	mook yee	木 耳

RECIPES

APPETIZERS (DEM SEM)

SHU MAI
Shu Mai: Canton

A. ½ lb. ground pork
B. ½ cup minced raw shrimp
C. ¾ cup Chinese celery cabbage stalk
D. 3 water chestnuts
E. 3 scallions, sliced
F. 1 teaspoon light soy sauce
G. 1 teaspoon salt
H. 1 lb. won ton skins (from Chinese grocery)
I. 1 egg white

PREPARATION:

I. Boil water in steamer.
II. Chop C fine.
III. Chop D fine.
IV. Mix A, B, C, D, E, F, G well.
V. Beat I until stiff.

COOKING:

1. Place 2 tablespoons of mixture A–G in center of won ton skin.
2. Raise the sides of the skin until they meet at the top.
3. Seal by brushing with I and pressing together.
4. Place dem sem on small square of aluminum foil and put in steamer.
5. Steam 35 minutes.
6. Serve with duck sauce or soy sauce and vinegar.

WRAPPING SKIN FOR EGG ROLLS AND WON TONS
Chwin Guen Won Ton Pei: General

A. 2 cups flour
B. ½ teaspoon salt
C. 1 egg
D. ½ cup water

PREPARATION:

I. Sift A, B together.
II. Beat C, add D, and mix well. Blend thoroughly with A, B; knead until dough is smooth.
III. Roll dough on floured board until paper-thin. Be sure board is well dusted with flour.
IV. For egg rolls, make about 18 6-inch-square wrappings. If won ton wrappings are desired, cut each 6-inch square into four pieces. (If wrappings are not to be used immediately, they may be stacked together, but each piece should be well floured. Wrap stack in aluminum foil, and place in refrigerator. This will keep about a week. If skins become too hard and dry, place a wet dishcloth around them to remoisten.)

WRAPPING SKIN FOR EGG ROLLS AND WON TONS   *Approved Diabetic Recipe*
Chwin Guen Pei: General

A. 1 cup flour
B. ¼ teaspoon salt

C. 1 small egg
D. ¼ cup water

PREPARATION:

I. Sift A and B together.
II. Beat C and add D, mix thoroughly.
III. Mix A, B and C, D. Knead until dough is smooth.
IV. Roll dough on floured board until paper-thin. Be sure board is well dusted with flour.
V. For egg rolls, make about 9 6-inch-square wrappings. For won ton wrapping, cut each square into four pieces. Unused wrappings may be stacked together but each piece should be well floured and all wrapped with aluminum foil. They may be kept in refrigerator for a week; if hardening and dryness occurs, wrap in wet cloth.

WON TONS I
Won Ton: General

A. 1 egg
B. ½ lb. ground pork
C. 1 tablespoon chopped scallion
D. 8 water chestnuts, chopped

E. 1 teaspoon salt
F. ⅛ teaspoon pepper
G. 12 won ton skins (see Wrapping Skin for Egg Rolls and Won Tons)

PREPARATION:

I. Beat A.
II. Mix A, B, C, D, E, F well.
III. Cut each G into quarters.

COOKING:

1. Fill each G with ½ to 1 teaspoon A–F mixture. Shape each into a cap to make won tons by drawing the four corners together and seal by pressing gently at juncture.

2. Boil 2 qts. water, add won tons, bring to boil, and cook 5 minutes. Drain won tons in colander, run cold water over won tons to cool. Cooked won tons can be frozen or left in refrigerator for a few days.

WON TONS II
Shiao Tjang Chuen: Fukien

A. ¼ lb. ground pork
B. 2 oz. shrimp
C. 6 dried shrimp
D. 1 stalk celery, chopped
E. 2 teaspoons cornstarch
F. 1 teaspoon salt

G. 40 won ton skins (see Wrapping Skin for Egg Rolls and Won Tons)
H. 3 cups soup stock
I. 6 8-inch square sheets purple seaweed, shredded
J. few drops sesame oil
K. pepper to taste

PREPARATION:

I. Shell, devein, and wash B; mince.

II. Wash and clean C, soak in warm water 5 to 10 minutes; mince.

III. Mix A, B, C, D, E, F.

IV. Place about 1 teaspoon of A–F mixture in center of each G; moisten with water ½ inch from edges; fold like a nurse's cap.

COOKING:

1. Drop won tons into 2 qts. boiling water; cook until they float on surface (about 4 minutes). Drain.

2. Heat H (or 1 can chicken broth with enough water added to make 3 cups). Bring to a boil.

3. Add cooked won tons. When soup boils again, turn off heat and pour into tureen.

4. Sprinkle surface with I, J, K. Serve hot.

WON TONS *Approved Diabetic Recipe*
Won Ton: General

A. ¼ lb. ground pork
B. 1 teaspoon chopped scallion
C. 4 water chestnuts, chopped

D. ½ teaspoon salt
E. 6 egg roll skins, quartered (see Wrapping Skin for Egg Rolls and Won Tons)

PREPARATION:

I. Mix A, B, C, D thoroughly.

II. Fill each E with ½ to 1 teaspoon of A–D mixture. Moisten with water ½ inch from edges. Fold like a nurse's cap.

COOKING:

1. Boil 2 qts. water, add won tons, bring back to boil, and cook 5 minutes. Drain and run under cold water gently. Cooked won tons can be frozen or left in refrigerator for a few days.

FRIED WON TONS *Approved Diabetic Recipe*
Tza Won Ton: Canton

A. peanut oil for deep frying

B. 6 precooked won tons (see Index)

COOKING:

1. Heat A to 375°, deep-fry B a few at a time 2 to 3 minutes. Serve hot or cold.

WON TONS WITH CHICKEN SOUP
Won Ton Gee Tong: General

Dilute 1 can (13¾ ozs.) chicken broth with 1 can water; bring to boil. Add 24 cooked won tons and bring to boil again. Turn off heat. Serve with 1 tablespoon chopped scallion.

FRIED SWEET WON TONS
Tza Sue Won Ton: Shanghai

A. vegetable oil for deep frying
B. 4 teaspoons sesame seeds
C. ½ cup peanut butter
D. ½ cup packed brown sugar
E. 40 won ton skins (see Wrapping Skin for Egg Rolls and Won Tons)

PREPARATION:

I. In small frying pan, heat and brown B; shake so that they do not scorch. Remove from heat when golden.
II. Mix B, C, D thoroughly.
III. Lay out E. Moisten outside to ½ inch from edge; place about ½ to 1 teaspoon B–D filling in centers; fold over, press, and seal edges. Then fold like a nurse's cap.

COOKING:

1. Heat A to 375°; fry won tons 1 to 2 minutes until golden; drain on paper towel.

SHRIMP WON TONS   *Approved Ulcer Recipe*
Ha Won Ton: Canton

A. ¼ lb. frozen shrimp (peeled, skinned, deveined)
B. ¼ lb. double-ground pork
C. ½ cup chopped celery cabbage
D. 1 teaspoon light soy sauce
E. ½ teaspoon sesame oil
F. ½ teaspoon salt
G. 36 won ton skins (see Wrapping Skin for Egg Rolls and Won Tons)
H. 2 qts. chicken soup
I. 1 scallion

PREPARATION:

I. Chop A until very smooth (or double-grind).
II. Tie I into bundle.
III. Mix A, B, C, D, E, F.
IV. Wrap each G around ½ teaspoon A–F mixture. Form each G into a cup; seal by moistening with water.

COOKING:

1. Boil 2 to 3 qts. water, add stuffed G, bring to boil again; cook 5 minutes.
2. Drain in colander, rinse under cold water. Cooked G can be frozen for later use or refrigerated several days before using.
3. Bring H to boil in Dutch oven. Add G, I. As soon as H boils, it is ready to serve. Discard I before serving.

SWEET WON TONS WITH TANGERINES
Jing Jiu Sue Won Ton: Shanghai

A. ½ cup chunky style peanut butter
B. ½ cup packed brown sugar
C. 40 won ton skins (see Wrapping Skin for Egg Rolls and Won Tons)
D. 3 large tangerines or oranges
E. ¼ cup sugar
F. 2 to 4 teaspoons sherry

PREPARATION:

I. Mix A, B thoroughly.
II. Lay out C one at a time. Moisten outside to ½ inch from edge. Put ½ to 1 teaspoon filling A–B in center of each; fold over, press, and seal edges. Then fold like a nurse's cap.
III. Peel D; remove white rind and seeds; place tender meat in 4 to 6 serving bowls.

COOKING:

1. Boil 1 qt. water, add E and filled C. Allow C to boil 1 to 2 minutes; scoop out C.

2. Just before serving, add ½ to 1 teaspoon F to bowls; add hot C and serve.

EGG ROLLS (SPRING ROLLS)
Chwin Guen: General

A. 2 tablespoons peanut oil
B. ½ cup ground pork
C. ¼ cup minced raw shrimp
D. ½ cup shredded Chinese cabbage
E. 1 small onion, chopped
F. ½ cup chopped water chestnuts

G. ½ teaspoon salt
H. ¼ teaspoon pepper
I. ⅛ cup light soy sauce
J. 1-lb. pkg. egg roll skins, fresh
K. 1 egg white
L. 3 cups peanut oil

PREPARATION:

I. Beat K until stiff.

II. Mix D, E, F, G, H, I. Set aside.

COOKING:

1. Put A in very hot skillet and bring to high heat.
2. Add B. Stir-fry until done.
3. Add C. Stir-fry 3 minutes.
4. Add D–I mixture. Stir-fry 3 minutes.
5. Remove from heat. Cool and drain.
6. Place 2 to 3 tablespoons of cooked B–I mixture in center of each J in shape of an oblong mound.

7. Fold one long side of J skin over stuffing; then both short ends; fold over remaining long side.
8. Seal with K.
9. Heat L in deep-fat fryer to 375°. Fry egg rolls in deep-fat fryer to deep gold color and crisp texture.
10. Remove and drain on paper towels.
11. Serve with duck sauce and mustard, or soy sauce and vinegar.

EGG ROLLS *Approved Diabetic Recipe*
Chwin Guen: General

A. 1 tablespoon peanut oil
B. 1 teaspoon chopped scallion
C. ¼ lb. pork, shredded
D. ¼ lb. shrimp
E. ½ teaspoon light soy sauce
F. ½ cup shredded bamboo shoots
G. ½ cup shredded Chinese celery

H. ½ cup shredded Chinese cabbage
I. 4 water chestnuts, shredded
J. ½ teaspoon salt
K. 2 teaspoons cornstarch mixed with 1 tablespoon water
L. 18 egg roll skins (see Wrapping Skins for Egg Rolls and Won Tons)
M. oil for deep frying

PREPARATION:

I. Shell, devein D; mince.

COOKING:

1. Heat A, stir-fry B a few times. Add C, D, E, stir-fry 2 minutes.
2. Add F, G, H, I, mix well and stir-fry 3 more minutes.
3. Add J, mix thoroughly. Thicken with K.
4. Wait until meat mixture is completely cold before using as egg roll filling.
5. Put about 3 tablespoons of meat filling in center of each piece of L, and fold into a roll, seal the edge with water.
6. Deep fry at 375° in M until golden brown, about 4 to 5 minutes. Serve hot or cold.

CAUL FAT SHRIMP ROLLS
Mong Yow Ha Guen: Canton

A. 3 tablespoons peanut oil
B. ½ lb. small shrimp
C. ½ cup shredded Smithfield ham
D. 6 Chinese mushrooms
E. 2 stalks celery, shredded
F. 1½ cups shredded bamboo shoots
G. ½ cup shredded water chestnuts

H. 1 teaspoon salt
I. ½ teaspoon sugar
J. dash pepper
K. 1 lb. caul fat
L. ¼ cup cornstarch
M. 1 egg
N. 1 qt. peanut oil

PREPARATION:

I. Shell, devein, wash, and dice B.
II. Wash D, soak 15 minutes in warm water, drain, and shred.
III. Cut K into 7-inch squares.
IV. Beat M.

COOKING (filling):

1. Heat A in frying pan, add B, C, D, stir-fry 2 minutes. Remove B–D.
2. Place E, F, G in same pan, stir-fry 1 minute.
3. Return B–D mixture to pan, add H, I, J, and mix thoroughly. Drain and cool completely before using as filling.

COOKING (rolls):

1. Spread out one K square, dust surfaces with 1 teaspoon L. Fill center with ½ cup cooled B–J filling mixture, folding skin in the style of egg rolls.
2. Coat rolls with M, then dust each again with L.
3. Heat N to 375°. Deep fry shrimp rolls 2 to 3 minutes.
4. Reduce heat to 325°, and deep fry until golden brown. Yields 8 to 10 rolls.

EGG ROLLS
Chwin Guen: General

A. 3 tablespoons peanut or salad oil
B. 1 scallion, chopped
C. 2 slices ginger, chopped
D. ½ lb. shrimp
E. ½ lb. roast pork, shredded
F. 1 cup shredded bamboo shoots
G. 1 cup shredded celery
H. 1 cup shredded cabbage
I. ¼ cup chopped water chestnuts

J. 1 teaspoon light soy sauce
K. ½ teaspoon sugar
L. 1 teaspoon salt
M. 1 tablespoon cornstarch mixed with 2 tablespoons water
N. 18 egg roll skins (see Wrapping Skins for Egg Rolls and Won Tons)
O. salad or peanut oil for deep frying

PREPARATION:

I. Shell, devein, and wash D. Cut each into small pieces.
II. Mix B, C, D.
III. Mix E with F, G, H, I.

COOKING:

1. Heat A in large frying pan.
2. Add B–D; stir-fry 3 minutes.
3. Add E–I, mix well, and stir-fry 3 minutes.
4. Add J, K, L, cook 1 minute, and thicken with M mixture, stirring constantly until ingredients are thoroughly mixed.
5. Drain meat mixture in colander. Cool before using as filling.

6. Put about 3 tablespoons meat filling in center of each N. Starting with closest corner, fold skin over filling, short ends toward center; wet exposed edges with water; roll over until all edges of egg roll are sealed.

7. Deep fry egg rolls in O at 375° until golden brown, about 4 to 5 minutes. Serve hot or cold.

FUN GOH DOUGH (SKIN)
Fun Goh Pei: Canton

A. 1 cup wheat starch
B. ½ cup tapioca flour
C. 1 cup, 2 tablespoons boiling water
D. 1 teaspoon peanut oil

PREPARATION:

I. Sift A, B together in bowl.
II. Add C gradually. Stir with fork.
III. Grease hands with D.
IV. Knead dough until firm, about 4 minutes. Let stand 10 to 12 minutes.
V. Divide dough into 36 balls, 1 inch in diameter.
VI. Grease rolling pin and table, roll out balls as thin as possible to form patties 3 inches in diameter.

This is a basic recipe for a pastry that is to be filled with meats and then steamed.

FUN GOH
Fun Goh: Canton

A. 36 fun-goh skins (see Index)
B. 6 Chinese mushrooms
C. 1 cup chopped roast pork
D. ½ cup chopped Chinese celery cabbage (stem only) or ½ cup chopped bamboo shoots
E. 1 scallion
F. ½ teaspoon salt
G. ½ teaspoon sugar

PREPARATION:

I. Wash B, soak in warm water 15 minutes, drain, and chop.
II. Chop E very fine.
III. Mix B–G thoroughly.
IV. Prepare A.

COOKING:

1. Fill center of each A patty with 1 teaspoon B–G.
2. Fold over, shape in half-moon.
3. Arrange single layer on greased plate.
4. Steam 10 minutes.

WRAPPING FOR JAO TZE (CHINESE RAVIOLI)
Jao Tze Pei: Peking

A. 2 cups flour
B. ¼ teaspoon salt
C. ½ cup cold water

PREPARATION:

I. Sift A, B together.
II. Add C, mix well, and cover with cloth 25 minutes.
III. Knead thoroughly on floured board; shape A–C into several long strips. Cut each into several chestnut-size pieces, about 30 altogether. Shape each into a ball and roll into thin 3-inch-round patties.
IV. If jao tze is to be fried, use hot water.

JAO TZE (CHINESE RAVIOLI)
Jao Tze: Peking

A. 2 slices ginger, chopped
B. 2 scallions, chopped
C. 1 lb. ground pork (or beef)
D. 1 cup chopped Chinese celery cabbage
E. 1 tablespoon light soy sauce
F. ½ teaspoon salt
G. 1 teaspoon sherry
H. 1 teaspoon cornstarch
I. ¼ teaspoon sesame oil
J. 30 jao tze wrappings (see Wrapping for Jao Tze)

PREPARATION:

I. Mix A, B, C, D, E, F, G, H, I thoroughly.
II. Fill each J with A–I meat mixture. Fold over and shape in half moon. Press edge tight.

COOKING:

1. Put jao tze into 3 qts. boiling water. When it boils again, add 1 cup cold water. Repeat once. On final boil, remove jao tze and serve with vinegar and soy sauce.

JAO TZE
Jao Tze: Peking   *Approved Ulcer Recipe*

Substitute frozen chopped spinach for D; omit A and B.

FRIED JAO TZE
Go Te: Peking

A. 2 tablespoons peanut oil
B. ¼ lb. ground pork
C. ½ lb. shrimp
D. 2 cups chopped Chinese celery cabbage*
E. 3 slices ginger, chopped
F. 2 tablespoons chopped scallion
G. 1½ tablespoons light soy sauce
H. ½ teaspoon salt
I. 1 teaspoon sherry
J. 1 teaspoon cornstarch
K. ¼ teaspoon sesame oil
L. jao tze wrappings (see Wrapping for Jao Tze)
M. ⅓ cup soup stock

PREPARATION:

I. Shell, devein, and mince C.
II. Parboil D in boiling water for 1 minute and drain.
III. Mix B, C, D, E, F, G, H, I, J, K thoroughly.
IV. Fill center of each L with 1 teaspoon B–K mixture. Fold over and shape in half moon. Press edge tight.

COOKING:

1. Heat frying pan until very hot. Add A. Turn off heat.
2. Arrange jao tze in single layer in frying pan. Cover and brown over low heat 5 minutes. Sprinkle in half of M, cover and cook 5 minutes.
3. Sprinkle in the rest of M, cover and cook for another minute. It is not necessary to turn the jao tze.
4. Serve with vinegar and soy sauce or hot sauce.

* Frozen chopped spinach may be substituted for Chinese celery cabbage. Defrost and squeeze out water before mixing with other ingredients.

FRIED PUFFS
Yo Tiao: General

A. 2 qts. peanut oil

B. 1 envelope yeast

C. ½ cup lukewarm water

D. 1 teaspoon baking soda

E. 1 teaspoon salt

F. 1 teaspoon ammonium alum

G. 1 cup flour plus supply for pastry board

PREPARATION:

I. Dissolve B with C in bowl.

II. Add D, E, F, mix well.

III. Add G, stirring until well blended.

IV. Cover bowl with clean towel or lid; let stand at room temperature for 4 to 6 hours.

V. Sprinkle a little flour on pastry board; roll out one-half of dough into a strip 4 to 5 inches long and ¼ inch thick. (If dough is hard to handle, sprinkle a little more flour over it.) Cut into 10 to 12 strips. Repeat procedure with remaining half of dough.

VI. Place two strips together, one on top of the other and make lengthwise indentation down the middle with the back of a knife. Make 10 to 12 strips.

COOKING:

1. Heat A in deep-frying pan to 380° to 400°.

2. Holding a strip with two hands, stretch out as long as possible. Twist it around itself one or two times; drop into A.

3. Using chopsticks, tumble strip as it deep fries.

4. When strip is golden brown, remove from oil and drain on paper towel. Serve hot.

GOLDEN PUFF WITH SWEET BEAN PASTE
Gow Li Dow Sa: Peking

A. 2 cups peanut oil for deep frying

B. 2 egg whites

C. 1 tablespoon flour

D. 1 tablespoon cornstarch

E. ½ cup sweet bean paste (filling)

PREPARATION:

I. Beat B until fluffy.

II. Add C, D, continue to beat until B forms stiff peaks.

III. With teaspoon, scoop up E; use another spoon to form into about 10 little balls.

IV. Roll over B–D, so that each is well coated.

COOKING:

1. Heat A 325°, deep fry B–E for 1 to 2 minutes or until golden brown. Drain on paper towel.

STEAMED LITTLE BAO TZE WITH BEEF
Niu Ro Tong Bao: Shanghai

A. 2 cups flour

B. ¾ cup water

C. 1 cup ground beef chuck

D. 1 cup chopped water chestnuts

E. 2 tablespoons Chinese parsley

F. 1 teaspoon light soy sauce

G. ½ teaspoon sesame oil

H. ½ teaspoon sugar

I. ½ to 1 teaspoon salt (to taste)

PREPARATION:

I. Combine A, B, mix well. Knead into a soft dough. Cover, let stand at room temperature 30 to 60 minutes, while preparing filling, as follows:

II. Combine C, D, E, F, G, H, I; mix.

III. Knead dough, then divide into 24 parts. Roll as thin as possible. Place 1 to 2 teaspoons of filling in center of each piece; then wrap each.

COOKING: 1. Steam 15 to 20 minutes. Serve hot.

STEAMED LITTLE BAO TZE WITH TURKEY
Ho Gee Shiao Tong Bao: Shanghai

A. 2 tablespoons peanut oil
B. 6 Chinese mushrooms
C. 6 dried shrimp
D. 1 scallion, chopped
E. 1 cup chopped celery cabbage
F. 1 cup chopped cooked turkey

G. 1½ teaspoons salt
H. 2 teaspoons cornstarch mixed with ¼ cup B soak water
I. 2 cups flour
J. ¾ cup water

PREPARATION:

I. Combine I, J, mix well. Knead into a soft dough. Then cover and let stand at room temperature 30 to 60 minutes, while preparing filling, as follows:

II. Wash B, soak 15 minutes in warm water. Drain (save liquid) and chop B.

III. Wash C well, soak 15 minutes in cold water. Drain (discard water), and chop.

COOKING:

1. Heat A, add B, C, D, stir-fry 30 seconds.
2. Add E, F, stir-fry 2 minutes.
3. Add G, H, stir well until thick.

4. Knead dough once more, then divide into 24 parts. Roll as thin as possible. Place 1 to 2 teaspoons of filling in center of each piece; then wrap each. Steam 15 minutes. Serve hot.

STEAMED LITTLE BAO TZE WITH PORK
Tsu Ro Tong Bao: Shanghai

A. 2 cups flour
B. ¾ cup water
C. 1 cup ground pork
D. ½ cup chopped frozen shrimp
E. ½ cup chopped bamboo shoots
F. 1 tablespoon chopped scallion

G. 1 teaspoon chopped ginger
H. 1 teaspoon salt
I. ½ teaspoon sugar
J. ½ teaspoon sesame oil
K. 2 teaspoons light soy sauce

PREPARATION:

I. Combine A, B, mix well. Knead into a soft dough. Cover, let stand at room temperature 30 to 60 minutes, while preparing filling, as follows:

II. Combine C, D, E, F, G, H, I, J, K; mix thor-

oughly.

III. Knead dough, then divide into 24 parts. Roll as thin as possible. Place 1 to 2 teaspoons of filling in center of each piece; then wrap each.

COOKING:

1. Steam 20 to 25 minutes. Serve hot.

CHICKEN BAO I
Gee Bao: General

A. 2 tablespoons peanut oil
B. 2 cups chopped chicken meat
C. 2 teaspoons cornstarch
D. ¼ teaspoon sesame oil
E. ½ teaspoon sugar
F. 2 teaspoons oyster sauce

G. 1 teaspoon chopped scallion
H. ½ teaspoon chopped ginger
I. salt to taste
J. man to dough (see Index) without steaming

PREPARATION:

I. Mix B, C, D, E, F, G, H, I thoroughly.

COOKING:

1. Heat A and stir fry B–I 1 to 2 minutes. Cool completely.
2. Divide J into 20 parts; shape each into a ball, roll thin and shape into 3- to 4-inch round piece.
3. Fill center of each J dough with 1 tablespoon B–I. Fold dough around filling.
4. Steam in steamer 20 minutes.

CHICKEN BAO II
Gai Bao: Canton

A. 2 tablespoons peanut oil
B. 6 Chinese mushrooms
C. 1 scallion, chopped
D. 1 chicken breast
E. ¾ cup chopped bamboo shoots
F. 2 teaspoons light soy sauce
G. ½ teaspoon sugar
H. ¾ teaspoon salt
I. 2 teaspoons cornstarch mixed with 4 tablespoons water (from B)
J. ½ teaspoon sesame oil
K. man to bread (see Index)

PREPARATION:

I. Bone D, chop fine.
II. Rinse B and soak in warm water 15 minutes or until soft. Drain, save water. Chop fine.
III. Mix F, G, H.

COOKING:

1. Heat A to 350°, add B, C, stir-fry a few seconds.
2. Add D, stir-fry 1 minute.
3. Add E, continue stirring 1 to 2 minutes.
4. Add F–H mixture, mixing well, and thicken with I.
5. Add J.
6. Cool completely before using to fill K (will make 16 pieces).
7. Steam over boiling water for 20 minutes.

PORK CARROT BAO
Hung Lo Bo Ro Bao: Adapted

A. ½ lb. pork
B. 12 dry shrimp
C. 1 scallion, minced
D. 2 carrots
E. 2 teaspoons light soy sauce
F. 1 teaspoon sugar
G. 1 teaspoon salt
H. 2 teaspoons cornstarch
I. 2 tablespoons carrot water
J. man to dough (see Index)

PREPARATION:

I. Chop A with cleaver. Wash and mince B.
II. Shred and mince D. Cover with water, bring to boil, cook 5 minutes.
III. Mix all ingredients thoroughly.
IV. Stuff J.

COOKING:

1. Steam in steamer over hot water 25 minutes.

PORK CARROT BAO   *Approved Ulcer Recipe*
Hu Lo Bo Ro Bao: General

Omit B; steam dish 40 minutes instead of 25 minutes.

PEANUT BUTTER ROAST PORK BAO
Fa Sun Jiong Cha Shu Bao: Canton

A. 2 tablespoons peanut oil
B. 2 cups chopped roast pork (see Roast Pork)
C. 2 to 3 tablespoons peanut butter
D. 1 tablespoon light soy sauce
E. 2 teaspoons cornstarch

F. ⅔ cup chicken broth or water
G. snow-white steamed bread dough (see Index)
H. salt to taste

PREPARATION:

I. Mix C, D, H.

II. Mix E, F.

COOKING:

1. Heat A, add B, stir-fry ½ minute.
2. Add C mixture, stir well.
3. Thicken with E–F. Cool before using as filling.

4. Divide G into 18 pieces and use as wrappers for filling.
5. Steam over boiling water 15 minutes.

PORK MUSHROOM BAO
Dung Gu Ro Bao: General

A. 2 tablespoons peanut oil
B. 6 medium Chinese black mushrooms
C. 1 scallion, minced
D. 1 lb. pork, minced
E. 1 tablespoon cornstarch

F. 4 tablespoons mushroom water
G. 1 tablespoon light soy sauce
H. ½ teaspoon salt
I. ½ teaspoon sugar
J. snow-white steamed bread dough (p. 415)

PREPARATION:

I. Wash B, cover with hot water, soak 10 minutes; drain, saving water, and mince.

II. Mix E, F, G, H, I well.

COOKING:

1. Heat A in pot. Add B, C and stir-fry 30 seconds.
2. Add D. Stir-fry 5 minutes.

3. Add E–I, stir until well mixed. Wait until pork mixture is cold before it is used for stuffing.
4. Stuff and steam 15 minutes.

PORK MUSHROOM BAO *Approved Ulcer Recipe*
Dung Gu Ro Bao: General

Grind D fine; mince B very fine; omit C.

PEKING FLOWER ROLL
Hwa Jwen: Peking

A. 4 cups flour
B. ¼ cup sugar
C. 1 teaspoon salt
D. 1½ cups lukewarm water

E. 1 tablespoon sugar
F. 1 pkg. dry yeast
G. 1 teaspoon sesame oil

PREPARATION:

I. Sift A, B, C together in large bowl.
II. Mix D with E, stir in F slowly, mixing well.

III. Make hollow in center of flour mixture, add D–F and mix thoroughly.

IV. Knead on floured board until dough is smooth and elastic.

V. Place dough in well-greased bowl, cover and let rise at room temperature until it doubles in bulk (about 45 minutes).

VI. Remove from bowl and knead again for a few minutes; divide into two parts.

VII. Roll one part into a rectangle, about 14 by 7 inches; brush ½ of G over dough. Follow same procedure with remaining half of dough.

VIII. Form each half into a round roll, like a jellyroll; then cut each roll into 16 one-inch segments.

IX. With the loose ends against each other, press two segments together lightly to make a flat bun. Press chopstick through the buns to make them stick together; then remove.

X. Place each bun on a 2½- by 2½-inch square of waxed paper, let them rise at room temperature again until dough looks light and almost doubles in bulk (about 45 minutes).

COOKING:

1. Leave on paper and place buns in steamer; steam over boiling water 15 minutes. When buns are completely cooked, they will resemble butterflies. Makes 16 rolls.

LOTUS ROOT CHIPS
Ngo Bing: General

A. 2 fresh lotus root sections
B. 2 cups peanut oil

C. salt to taste

PREPARATION:

I. Peel A with potato peeler. Cut crosswise into thin slices (1/16 inch).

II. Have B heating in deep fryer.

COOKING:

1. Deep fry A in B at 370°F. until slices are deep golden brown.

2. Remove; drain well; sprinkle with C. Serve instead of potato chips.

LOTUS ROOT CAKES
Jien Ngo Bang: Canton

A. 1 tablespoon peanut oil
B. ½ lb. segment lotus root
C. ¼ lb. pork, chopped
D. 1 tablespoon chopped preserved kohlrabi

E. 2 teaspoons light soy sauce
F. 1 teaspoon sugar
G. ½ teaspoon salt
H. 1 tablespoon chopped scallion

PREPARATION:

I. Peel B; wash, slice thin, then chop.
II. Wash and clean D before chopping.

III. Mix B, C, D, E, F, G, H. Shape into 8 cakes, each 2½ inches in diameter.

COOKING:

1. Heat A in frying pan. Panfry B–H over medium heat until both sides are golden brown (2 to 3 minutes each side).

LOTUS ROOT CAKES *Approved Diabetic Recipe*
Lien Ngo Yoke Bang: Canton

A. 1 tablespoon peanut oil
B. ¼ lb. segment lotus root
C. ¼ lb. pork, chopped
D. 1 teaspoon chopped preserved kohlrabi

E. 1 teaspoon light soy sauce
F. ½ teaspoon salt
G. 1 teaspoon chopped scallion

PREPARATION:

I. Peel B; wash, slice thin, then chop.

II. Mix B, C, D, E, F, G. Shape into 8 cakes, each 2½ inches in diameter.

COOKING:

1. Heat A in frying pan. Panfry B–G over medium heat until both sides are golden brown (2 to 3 minutes each side).

LOTUS ROOT CAKES WITH BEEF *Approved Diabetic Recipe*
Ngo Yoke Ngo Bang: Canton

Substitute beef for C.

RINGING BELL
Shang Ling: Hangchow

A. 2 cups peanut oil
B. 2 tablespoons hoisin sauce
C. anise pepper salt to taste
D. ½ lb. ground pork
E. 1 egg

F. 2 teaspoons sherry
G. 1 teaspoon salt
H. 8 pieces fresh bean curd skin
I. 1 tablespoon scallion, chopped

PREPARATION:

I. Mix D, E, F, G well.

II. Place ⅛ of D–G mixture across each piece of H, about 2 inches below top, spread out 1½ inches wide.

III. Fold over, press down on D–G mixture, then roll.

IV. Cut each roll into 4 to 5 pieces about 1½ inches long.

COOKING:

1. Heat A to 350°. Deep fry rolls until golden brown, about 2 to 3 minutes.

2. Serve with B, C, mixed. Garnish with I. (Dish becomes so crispy that when chewed it is said to sound like the ringing of a bell.)

VEGETARIAN RINGING BELL
Tza Shang Ling: Shanghai

A. 1 tablespoon peanut oil
B. 3 Chinese mushrooms
C. 1 carrot
D. ½ cup shredded bamboo shoots
E. 1 tablespoon light soy sauce
F. 1 teaspoon sugar
G. 1 to 2 teaspoons sherry

H. 1 medium potato
I. ½ teaspoon salt
J. 8 pieces fresh bean curd skin
K. 3 tablespoons flour mixed well with 2 tablespoons water
L. 2 cups peanut oil
M. tomato sauce (to taste)

PREPARATION:

I. Peel H and cut into small pieces; using little water, cook until soft; mash, mix with I, making a thick paste.

II. Wash B and soak in warm water 15 minutes, drain, and shred very thin.

III. Peel C, slice and shred.

IV. Mix E, F, G.

V. Mix K with dash of salt.

COOKING:

1. Heat A, add B, C, D, stir-fry 1 to 2 minutes; add E–G, mix well.

2. Spread H–I paste on each J; put 2 pieces on top of each other.

3. Pláce ¼ B–G mixture across J, about 2 inches below top, spread out 1½ inches wide.

4. Fold top over and roll, cut each roll diagonally into 5 pieces.

5. Dip ends in K mixture.

6. Deep fry in L at 350° until golden brown (about 2 minutes).

7. Serve with M.

SHRIMP DUMPLINGS
Har Gow: Canton

A. 1 lb. fresh shrimp
B. 1 scallion, chopped
C. ¼ lb. ground pork
D. 2 teaspoons light soy sauce
E. 1½ teaspoons salt
F. ¼ teaspoon sesame oil
G. dash pepper
H. 36 fun-goh skins (p. 67)

PREPARATION:

I. Shell and devein A and cut into small pieces.

II. Mix A, B, C, D, E, F, G thoroughly.

III. Fill center of each H with 1 teaspoon A–G mixture.

IV. Gather edges of each H, squeeze tight, and press toward one side.

COOKING:

1. Arrange dumplings in single layer on greased plate.

2. Steam over boiling water 12 minutes.

3. Serve with hoisin sauce.

SHRIMP DUMPLINGS WITH WATER CHESTNUTS
Ma Tai Har Gow: Canton

A. ½ lb. frozen shrimp, chopped
B. ¼ cup chopped water chestnuts
C. 1 tablespoon chopped scallion
D. 2 teaspoons light soy sauce
E. 1½ teaspoons salt
F. ¼ teaspoon sesame oil
G. ½ teaspoon chopped ginger
H. 36 fun-goh skins (p. 67)

PREPARATION:

I. Mix A, B, C, D, E, F, G thoroughly.

II. Fill center of each H with 1 teaspoon A–G mixture.

III. Gather edges of each H, squeeze tight, and press toward one side.

COOKING:

1. Arrange dumplings in single layer on greased plate.

2. Steam over boiling water 12 minutes.

3. Serve with hoisin sauce.

SHRIMP WITH ANISE PEPPER SALT
Jiao Yen Sha: Tsenkiang

A. 2 cups peanut oil

B. 1 lb. large shrimp

C. 1 to 2 teaspoons anise pepper salt
(see Index)

D. 1 tablespoon light soy sauce mixed with

1 teaspoon Chinese hot sauce, for dipping

E. 1 egg white

F. 3 tablespoons rice flour

G. 1½ tablespoons glutinous rice flour

H. 1 teaspoon salt

PREPARATION:

I. Shell, devein, and wash B; dry between paper towels.

II. Beat E well, add to B.

III. Sift F, G, H and add to B, E. Be sure that B is well coated with F–H.

COOKING:

1. Heat A to 325°; deep fry B mixture until golden brown (about 2 minutes); drain on paper towel.

2. Sprinkle with C.

3. Serve with D.

SHRIMP TOAST
Sha Tze Mein Bao: Shanghai

A. peanut oil to fill deep-fat fryer

B. ½ lb. small shrimp

C. 12 water chestnuts, minced

D. 1 egg white

E. 1 tablespoon light soy sauce

F. ½ teaspoon salt

G. 1 teaspoon sherry

H. 1 tablespoon cornstarch

I. 6 slices white bread

PREPARATION:

I. Shell, devein, wash, and mince B.

II. Mix B, C, D, E, F, G.

III. Remove crust from I and cut into 1-inch

squares.

IV. Liberally spread each square of I with B–G mixture.

COOKING:

1. Heat A in deep fryer.

2. Deep fry B–I face down in A at 350° until

light brown.

3. Remove; drain well; serve with duck sauce.

GOLDEN SHRIMP TOAST
Kam Tsein Mein Bao Har: Canton

A. ½ lb. frozen small shrimp

B. 1 teaspoon lard or vegetable oil

C. ¼ cup flour

D. ¼ teaspoon baking powder

E. 1 egg

F. 1 teaspoon salt

G. 1 teaspoon fresh ginger, chopped

H. 6 slices light toast

I. Chinese parsley

J. peanut oil several inches deep in deep-fat fryer or saucepan.

PREPARATION:

I. Chop A.

COOKING:

1. Mix A, B, C, D, E, F, G.

2. Spread on H.

3. Press I on top.

4. Fry in J at 300° with shrimp side down 2

minutes. Turn over and fry the other side ½ minute.

5. Cut into bite-sized pieces.

6. Serve hot or cold.

SHRIMP TOAST WITH HAM
Ha Yoke Fo Twei To Si: Canton

A. 1 qt. peanut oil
B. ½ lb. frozen small shrimp
C. 2 tablespoons cornstarch
D. 1 teaspoon peanut oil
E. 1 teaspoon sherry

F. 1 teaspoon salt
G. 1 egg
H. 6 slices very light toast
I. 2 tablespoons chopped ham
J. Chinese parsley (optional)

PREPARATION:

I. Mince B.
II. Mix B, C, D, E, F, G, beat with fork until smooth.
III. Cut each H into 4 triangles.

IV. Spread I with B–G mixture; sprinkle I on top.
V. Garnish tops with J, press down slightly.

COOKING:

1. Heat A to 300°. Deep-fry each piece 2 minutes, shrimp side down.
2. Turn each over, fry 1½ minutes more. Remove, drain, and serve.

Note: This dish can be made ahead of time. It can be refrigerated or frozen if it is to be stored for a time, and reheated in the oven.

DRIED SHRIMPBURGERS
Kai Yang Niu Pa: Adapted

A. 10 dried shrimp
B. 1 large onion, chopped
C. 1½ lbs. ground chuck

D. 1 egg
E. 1½ tablespoons light soy sauce
F. 1 teaspoon salt

PREPARATION:

I. Soak A in warm water 10 minutes; shred A fine.

II. Mix A, B, C, D, E, F and make 8 to 10 patties.

COOKING:

1. Grease pan and cook A–F as hamburgers.

FLUFFY SHRIMP CAKES
Si Shi Sha Bing: Peking

A. 1 lb. large shrimp (or ½ lb. each of ground scallops and pork)
B. 2 to 3 oz. water chestnuts
C. 3 eggs
D. 2 teaspoons sherry
E. 1 teaspoon salt
F. 3 slices ginger

G. 2 scallions
H. 2 tablespoons cornstarch
I. 3 tablespoons vegetable oil
J. lettuce leaves
K. 3 teaspoons sugar
L. 3 tablespoons vinegar
M. 7 slices ginger, peeled and shredded

PREPARATION:

I. Shell, devein, and wash A, mince very fine.
II. Chop B well.

III. Mix A, B, C, D, E, F, G, H and form into golfball-size balls. Mix K, L, M.

COOKING:

1. Heat I in frying pan.
2. Flatten balls into cakes and fry in I until

golden brown.

3. Place on J and serve with K–M dip sauce.

STIR-FRIED SHRIMP CAKES
Tsao Har Kow: Canton

A. 3 tablespoons vegetable oil
B. 1 lb. large shrimp
C. 1 cup water chestnuts
D. 1 scallion
E. 2 slices ginger

F. 1 teaspoon salt
G. ¼ teaspoon pepper
H. 1 egg
I. 1 teaspoon cornstarch
J. 1 head Chinese cabbage (about 1 lb.)

PREPARATION:

I. Shell, devein, and wash B; chop very fine.
II. Mince C, D, E.
III. Wash J, cut into ½-inch-wide diagonal pieces; parboil 1 minute.

IV. Mix B, C, D, E, F, G H, I with fork.
V. Shape B mixture into cakes 1½ inches in diameter and ½ inch thick.

COOKING:

1. Heat A, fry B–I cakes until golden brown. Remove to dish. Pour any excess oil back into frying pan.

2. Stir-fry J a few times. Add additional salt to taste.

3. Replace B in frying pan, stir-fry gently 1 more minute. Serve with hot sauce.

CRAB MEAT SHU MAI
Hai Shu Mai: Canton

A. ¼ cup chopped bamboo shoots
B. 1 scallion, chopped
C. 1 small egg, beaten
D. ½ cup chopped fresh crab meat
E. ¼ cup ground pork
F. ½ cup shelled, minced shrimp
G. 1½ teaspoons salt

H. 1 tablespoon cornstarch
I. ½ teaspoon sugar
J. ½ teaspoon sesame oil
K. pepper to taste
L. 24 won ton skins (see Wrapping Skin for Egg Rolls and Won Tons)

PREPARATION:

I. Mix A, B, C, D, E, F, G, H, I, J, K thoroughly.
II. Trim corners of L, form each into a circle.

III. Fill each L with 1 tablespoon A–K mixture; gather each at top.

COOKING:

1. Steam in steamer 15 minutes over boiling water.

BEEF AND WATER CHESTNUT FUN GOH
Ngo Yoke Fun Goh: Canton

A. fun goh skins (see Index)
B. ¼ cup chopped water chestnuts
C. 1 teaspoon chopped preserved kohlrabi
D. 1 teaspoon light soy sauce

E. ½ teaspoon salt
F. ¼ teaspoon sugar
G. ½ lb. ground beef

PREPARATION:

I. Mix B, C, D, E, F, G thoroughly.

COOKING:

1. Fill each A skin with 1 teaspoon B–G mixture.
2. Fold over and shape like half moon.

3. Arrange in single layer on greased plate.
4. Steam over boiling water 20 minutes.

CURRIED CHICKEN ROLLS
Ga Li Gai Guen: Canton

A. 3 tablespoons peanut oil
B. 2 medium onions
C. 2 cloves garlic
D. 2 teaspoons curry powder
E. 2 chicken breasts
F. 2 teaspoons salt
G. ½ teaspoon sugar
H. 2 cups glutinous rice

PREPARATION:

I. Wash G, drain.
II. Bone E; shred.
III. Slice B, C thin.

COOKING:

1. Place H in pot, add 2½ cups water, and bring to boil. Lower heat, simmer 20 minutes.
2. Heat A, add B, C, stir-fry 1 minute.
3. Add D, mix well, and continue stirring 1 minute.
4. Add E, stir-fry 2 minutes.
5. Add F, mix thoroughly.
6. Add cooked H, mix well.
7. Form into 20 rolls, wrap each in foil. Bake 15 minutes in 375° oven.

STUFFED PORK PASTRY I
Har Shu Mai: Canton

A. ¼ lb. shrimp
B. ¼ lb. lean pork
C. 4 Chinese black mushrooms
D. 1 tablespoon chopped scallion
E. 1 teaspoon salt
F. ½ teaspoon sugar
G. 1 teaspoon sherry
H. 1 teaspoon cornstarch
I. ¼ teaspoon sesame oil
J. dash pepper
K. 6 egg roll skins, prepared or purchased (see Wrapping Skins for Egg Rolls or Won Tons)

PREPARATION:

I. Shell A, devein, wash, drain, and mince.
II. Slice and mince B.
III. Wash C, soak in hot water 15 minutes and cut into very small pieces.
IV. Mix all ingredients except K; divide into 24 portions.
V. Divide each K into 4 equal parts. Round off corners; fill each K with 1 portion of filling; gather skin at top.

COOKING:

1. Steam in steamer over boiling water 8 to 10 minutes.

STUFFED PORK PASTRY II
Shu Mai: Canton

A. ½ lb. ground pork
B. 2 scallions (white part only), chopped
C. 1 cup chopped Chinese celery cabbage (stem only)
D. 1 teaspoon salt
E. 1 teaspoon light soy sauce
F. 1 teaspoon cornstarch
G. 6 egg roll skins, prepared or purchased (see Wrapping Skins for Egg Rolls or Won Tons)

PREPARATION:

I. Mix A, B, C, D, E, F.
II. Quarter each G, round corners, add 1 portion of filling to each skin; gather skin at top.

COOKING:

1. Steam in steamer over boiling water 8 to 10 minutes.

PORK STUFFED STEAMED BREAD
Cha Shu Bao: Canton

A. 1 tablespoon fermented red bean curd cheese
B. ½ teaspoon sugar
C. 1 tablespoon cornstarch
D. 3 tablespoons water

E. 2 tablespoons peanut oil
F. 2 cups chopped barbecued pork (see Index)
G. salt to taste
H. man to dough (see Index)

PREPARATION:

I. Mix A, B.
II. Mix C, D.
III. Heat E, stir-fry F a few seconds. Add A–B. Mix well and thicken with C–D. Cool completely before use as filling.

IV. Divide H into 20 pieces, shape each into a ball. Roll thin to 3- to 4-inch round pieces.
V. Fill center of each piece with 1 tablespoon A–F mixture. Fold dough around filling.

COOKING:

1. Steam in steamer over boiling water 15 minutes.

PORK STUFFED STEAMED BREAD WITH OYSTER SAUCE
Ho Yu Cha Shu Bao: Canton

A. 2 cups roast pork, chopped (see Roast Pork)
B. 2 teaspoons cornstarch
C. ¼ teaspoon sesame oil
D. 1 teaspoon light soy sauce
E. ½ teaspoon sugar

F. 2 teaspoons oyster sauce
G. salt to taste
H. man to dough (see Index), without steaming
I. 2 tablespoons peanut oil

PREPARATION:

I. Mix A, B, C, D, E, F, G thoroughly. Stir-fry in I 1 minute.
II. Divide H into 20 pieces; shape each into a

ball. Roll thin to 3- to 4-inch round pieces.
III. Fill center of each piece with 1 tablespoon A–G mixture. Fold dough around filling.

COOKING:

1. Steam in steamer over boiling water 15 minutes.

RED BEAN CURD CHEESE ROAST PORK BAO
Nam Yu Cha Shu Bao: Canton

A. 1 tablespoon peanut oil
B. 2 cups chopped roast pork (see Index: Cha Shu I)
C. 1 scallion, chopped

D. 1-inch sq. red bean curd cheese
E. 2 tablespoons water
F. 2 teaspoons cornstarch
G. man to dough (see Index)

PREPARATION:

I. Prepare G.

II. Mix D, E, F into a smooth paste.

COOKING:

1. Heat A, stir-fry B, C 1 minute.
2. Add D–F mixture, stir until thick. Cool thoroughly before using as a filling for G.

3. Stuff and steam 20 minutes over boiling water (see Man to Dough).

CURRY CHICKEN TRIANGLES
Ga Li Gai Goh: General

A. 3 tablespoons peanut oil
B. 1 clove garlic, chopped
C. 1 large onion, chopped
D. 2 teaspoons curry powder
E. 2 pieces boned, minced chicken breast
F. ¾ teaspoon salt
G. 1 teaspoon sugar
H. 2 teaspoons cornstarch
I. 6-oz. pkg. piecrust mix
J. 1 egg yolk

PREPARATION:

I. Mix H with 2 tablespoons water.
II. Add F, G.
III. Mix J with 1 teaspoon water.

COOKING:

1. Put A in heated frying pan.
2. Add B, C; stir-fry 2 minutes.
3. Add D and stir a few seconds.
4. Add E and stir-fry 1 minute.
5. Add F–H mixture; stir until gravy thickens.
6. Pour out excess A.
7. Empty I into bowl and add 4 tablespoons ice-cold water. Mix well with fork. Divide into 12 portions.
8. Shape into 3 by 3 inch squares, fill each with 1 tablespoon B–H mixture and fold over in a triangle. Brush top with J.
9. Preheat oven to 425°.
10. Bake triangles on ungreased cookie sheet 35 to 40 minutes.
11. Triangle can be frozen. For reheating, defrost and bake in 425° oven 15 minutes.

CURRIED BEEF TRIANGLES
Ga Li Goh: Canton

A. 3 tablespoons peanut oil
B. 1 clove garlic, chopped
C. 1 large onion, chopped
D. 2 teaspoons curry powder
E. ½ lb. ground chuck
F. ¾ teaspoon salt
G. 1 teaspoon sugar
H. 2 teaspoons cornstarch
I. 6-oz. package piecrust mix
J. 1 egg yolk

PREPARATION:

I. Mix H with 2 tablespoons water.
II. Add F, G.
III. Mix J and 1 teaspoon water.
IV. Mix H with 1 tablespoon water.

COOKING:

1. Heat frying pan. Add A.
2. Add B, C; stir-fry 2 minutes.
3. Add D and stir a few seconds.
4. Add E and stir-fry 1 minute.
5. Add F, G, H; stir until gravy thickens.
6. Pour out excess oil. Cool.
7. Empty I into bowl and add 4 tablespoons ice-cold water. Mix well with fork. Divide into 12 portions.
8. Shape each into 3 by 3 inches square, fill each with 1 tablespoon B–H mixture and fold over in a triangle. Brush top with J.
9. Preheat oven to 425°.
10. Bake triangles on ungreased cooky sheet 35 to 40 minutes.
11. Triangles can be frozen. For reheating, defrost and bake in 425° oven 15 minutes.

LAMB (OR BEEF) BAO TZE
Yang Ro Bao Tze: General

A. 1 lb. lamb (with a little fat), minced

B. 1 scallion, chopped

C. 2 teaspoons chopped ginger

D. 2 tablespoons light soy sauce

E. ½ teaspoon salt

F. 1 to 2 teaspoons sesame oil

G. ¼ cup chicken broth

H. dough of Snow-White Steamed Bread (see Index)

PREPARATION:

I. Mix A well with B, C, D, E, F, G.

II. Divide H into 18 pieces; roll out each piece and put about 1 tablespoon of A–G on each as filling; shape into a ball. Place on waxed paper; cover with clean towel, let rise about ¾ to 1 hour.

COOKING:

1. Steam over boiling water 25 minutes.

TURNIP CAKE
Lo Bok Gow: Canton

A. 1½ lbs. Chinese or American white turnips

B. 2 cups chicken broth

C. ⅓ cup cornstarch

D. ½ cup E and F water

E. 10 dried shrimp

F. 8 Chinese black mushrooms

G. ½ cup finely chopped Virginia ham, or Chinese sausage

H. 1½ cups rice flour

I. 1 teaspoon salt

PREPARATION:

I. Peel, shred A.

II. Rinse E, F well. Cover with warm water and soak 15 to 20 minutes; drain, save the water and make enough for D for later use.

III. Chop E, F very fine.

IV. Mix C, D.

COOKING:

1. Add A to B, bring to boil, cook over low heat 10 minutes or until A is soft.

2. Add C–D slowly; mix well.

3. Add E, F, G, bring to boil.

4. Stir in H, I slowly, mix well.

5. Pour A–I into well-greased round cake pan. Steam over boiling water 1 hour.

6. Cool completely. Then cut into bite-size pieces (1½ inches square).

7. Serve cold, or fry in a little oil until both sides are golden brown.

MUSHROOM SHU MAI
Dung Gu Shu Mai: Canton

A. 18 Chinese black mushrooms

B. 1 scallion, minced

C. ¼ teaspoon salt

D. ¼ lb. ground pork

E. 1 teaspoon light soy sauce

F. ½ teaspoon cornstarch

G. 1 teaspoon sherry

PREPARATION:

I. Rinse A in cold water, then soak in warm water 15 minutes. Drain.

II. Mix B, C, D, E, F, G thoroughly. Divide into 18 portions.

III. Fill each A with equal portions of B–G.

IV. Arrange A on plate.

COOKING:

1. Steam over boiling water 10 minutes.

THREE-IN-ONE PATTIES
Sun Ee Bing: General

A. 1 lb. potatoes
B. 1 small tomato
C. 1 egg
D. ½ teaspoon sugar
E. 1 teaspoon salt
F. ¼ cup peanut oil
G. cornstarch for coating

PREPARATION:

I. Peel A, slice thin, wash, and place in cooking pot. Cover with water, cook until soft (about 15 minutes). Drain (saving water) and mash.

II. Place B in bowl, cover with reserved A water. Let stand several seconds, then peel. Cut B in half, discard seeds, mash.

III. Beat C.

IV. Mix D, E and add to C; beat well.

V. Add mashed A and mashed B to C–E, mix well.

VI. Form A–E mixture into patties 2½-inches in diameter. Coat each A–E with G.

COOKING:

1. Panfry A–E in F until both sides are golden brown.

THREE-IN-ONE PATTIES WITH SCALLIONS
Chung Hwa Sun Ee Bing: General

Add 2 tablespoons finely chopped scallion in Step VI.

FRIED BUTTERNUT SQUASH
Tza Bai Nahn Gwa: General

A. 1 qt. peanut oil
B. ½ to 1 lb. butternut squash
C. ½ cup flour
D. 5 tablespoons water
E. 1 tablespoon sugar
F. 2 tablespoons white sesame seeds
G. ¼ teaspoon salt

PREPARATION:

I. Discard B skin and seeds. Cut B into finger-size sticks.

II. Mix C, D into a paste.

III. Add E, F, G, stir well.

IV. Add B sticks, mix until each is well coated.

COOKING:

1. Heat A to 350°.

2. Deep fry B–G, ⅓ at a time, until golden brown (about 2 minutes). Sticks will float to top when they are done. Serve hot or cold.

SWEET-POTATO BALLS
Fahn Shu Dan: Canton

A. 1 lb. (about 3) sweet potatoes
B. 2 tablespoons sugar

C. ½ cup flour
D. 1 qt. peanut oil

PREPARATION:

I. Peel A, quarter each. Place in pan, cover with water, simmer until soft (about 30 minutes). Drain.
II. Mash A and mix with B.

III. Sift C gradually into A–B; mix thoroughly.
IV. Dust hands with C. Form A–C mixture into balls 1½ inches in diameter.

COOKING:

1. Deep fry balls in D at 350° until golden brown (2 to 3 minutes).

NEW YEAR'S DUMPLINGS I
Hwa Sun Jiang Tong Yuen: General

A. 2 cups glutinous rice flour
B. 1 cup water
C. ¼ cup peanut butter (chunk style)

D. ¼ cup brown sugar, packed
E. 1 teaspoon sesame seed
F. 6 teaspoons brown sugar for serving

PREPARATION:

I. Mix A, B into smooth dough; roll into about 30 1-inch balls.
II. Mix C, D, E well.

III. Flatten dough balls by hand into 2-inch discs. In center of each disc, place 1 teaspoon C–E mixture. Fold dough over, seal edges, and roll back into balls.

COOKING:

1. Boil 1½ qts. water in large saucepan. Add dumplings, stirring to prevent sticking. When dumplings float, simmer 7 more minutes.

2. For each serving, place 1 teaspoon F in a bowl, add hot water and 5 dumplings.

NEW YEAR'S DUMPLINGS I
Hung Tong Tong Yuen: General

Add garnish of tangerine slices to cooked dumplings and soup (dumpling soup may be used instead of hot water) in Step 2, and double F.

NEW YEAR'S DUMPLINGS II
Ro Tong Yuen: General

A. 2 cups glutinous rice flour
B. 1 cup water
C. 4 oz. ground pork
D. ¼ cup chopped celery cabbage
E. 1 slice ginger, minced
F. ¼ teaspoon cornstarch

G. 7 drops sesame oil
H. ½ teaspoon light soy sauce
I. ¼ teaspoon sherry
J. 2 tablespoons minced scallion
K. 1 qt. chicken broth

PREPARATION:

I. Mix A, B into smooth dough; roll into about 30 1-inch balls.

II. Mix C, D, E, F, G, H, I and half of J well.

III. Flatten dough balls by hand into 2-inch discs. In center of each disc, place 1 teaspoon C–J mixture. Fold dough over, seal edges, and roll back into balls. Cook 10 at a time.

COOKING:

1. Boil 1½ qts. water in large saucepan. Add 10 dumplings, stirring to prevent sticking. When dumplings float, simmer 10 more minutes.

2. Bring K to a boil, add rest of J. Remove from heat, transfer K to 6 small bowls, and add 5 dumplings per serving. Serve hot.

NEW YEAR'S DUMPLINGS II
Yang Ro Tong Yuen: General

Substitute ground chuck for C. In Step 1, simmer only 3 minutes.

NEW YEAR'S DUMPLINGS II
Sha Ro Tong Yuan: General

Substitute mixture of 2 oz. ground pork and 2 oz. ground shrimp for C.

NEW YEAR CAKE
Ham Goh: Canton

A. 2 tablespoons vegetable oil
B. 1 tablespoon chopped scallion
C. 10 Chinese mushrooms
D. ½ cup diced shrimp
E. ½ cup diced ham

F. 7 water chestnuts
G. ½ teaspoon sugar
H. ½ teaspoon salt
I. 2 cups glutinous rice flour
J. ⅔ cup hot water

PREPARATION:

I. Wash C, soak in warm water 15 minutes. Drain.

II. Dice C, F separately.

III. Mix I, J thoroughly, divide into 18 balls. By hand, flatten each ball as thin as possible.

COOKING:

1. Heat A, stir-fry B a few times.
2. Add C, stir-fry 1 minute.
3. Add D, stir-fry 1 minute.
4. Add E, F, and G, H, cook 1 to 2 minutes.

5. Fill each I–J patty with 1 tablespoon meat mixture. Fold over, shape each into half moon, press along edge.
6. Fry in deep fat at 230° until golden brown.

Since the Chinese are not in the habit of drinking water at the table (tea is traditionally served at the end of the meal), soup is usually served, as a beverage, throughout the meal.

Two soups are served at banquets, one in the middle, and one at the end of the feast, when a few heavy courses appear, accompanied by rice.

The Chinese often add soup to their rice, in the bowl. In Canton, soup is served before the main dishes; it is a large bowl, and a quantity for second and third helpings is placed in the center of the table.

Soups may be classified as light or heavy. Light soups, usually clear and with meat cooked only until done, and tender, are often served at dinner when there are a number of other dishes. Certain smooth, velvety soups (avoiding lumps at all costs), such as egg drop soup, are rich in flavor but are actually quite light. Sour pungent soup has an intriguing, unusual, and distinctive flavor but is not filling. However, for family lunches and light dinners, a "meal in a pot" soup is often concocted, which may include any number of ingredients.

Leftover rice may be cooked to make a thick congee, or liquid or semiliquid soup. Noodles may be combined with mushrooms, sliced abalone, chicken, ham, or celery for a satisfying noodle soup. In other instances, a clear chicken stock may be heated with leftover ingredients that have been cut into strips or shredded.

Stock rather than water should be used whenever possible, because of the flavor and nourishment it adds. In making stock, the Chinese use bones, such as from the neck and back, and meat scraps, as well as the liquid in which the vegetables have been cooked, the liquid from canned products, and water that has been used to soak dried foods. If chicken, duck, or pork bones are available, good stock can be made from them. Long cooking of these ingredients, however, is no substitute for the quantity of ingredients to be used. The American housewife may prefer to use a can of clear chicken broth rather than boil down several pounds of meat or bone to produce a quart of rich stock. The broth should be diluted with an equal part of water to prevent its masking the flavor of the other ingredients with its own strong broth taste.

The quantity of most soups may be increased when unexpected guests arrive by the addition of more water, stock, or canned chicken broth. Most soups can be prepared, at least in part, well in advance of serving. Thus, although won ton soup should be served as soon as the won tons are cooked, the soup itself could have been ready long before so that only the won tons need be added shortly before serving.

Cornstarch is added to a number of soups at the time of serving to thicken their consistency. This is especially true of egg drop soup. Before serving, cellophane noodles may be added but at a point when it is still possible to soak up a considerable amount of the soup. Dried foods, soaked until tender, may always be added to the soup to enrich its flavor.

CELESTIAL SOUP (SOUP FOR THE GODS)
Ching Tong: General

A. 6 cups water
B. 2 tablespoons light soy sauce
C. 1 scallion, sliced
D. 1 teaspoon peanut oil
E. 1 teaspoon salt
F. 3 drops sesame oil

PREPARATION:

I. Boil A.

II. Place B, C, D, E, F in large serving bowl.

COOKING:

1. Pour A over B–F mixture in bowl.

2. Serve. Clears the palate and refreshes taste.

GINGER BEEF TEA
Jiang Tze Niu Ro Tong: Adapted

A. ½ lb. boneless chuck

B. 1 tablespoon sherry

C. 6 slices ginger

D. dash black pepper (optional)

E. salt to taste

PREPARATION:

I. Cut A into 1½ inch cubes.

COOKING:

1. Place A, B in a heated, thick, 3-qt. saucepan. Brown A, stirring continuously to avoid scorching.

2. When A is browned, add C, D and 1 qt. water.

3. Simmer 1 to 1½ hours, adjust with E. Serve hot.

GINGER BEEF TEA WITH SPROUTS
Jiang Tze Niu Ro Huang Dow Ya Tong: Adapted

In Step 2, add ¼ lb. soy bean sprouts in addition to C, D and water.

GINGER BEEF TEA WITH CABBAGE
Jiang Tze Niu Ro Bai Tsai Tong: Adapted

In Step 3, simmer 50 minutes, add 1 cup celery cabbage, cut into 1-inch pieces, and cook 10 minutes more, salt to taste.

NUTRITIOUS, ECONOMICAL BEEF BROTH
Gin Gee Niu Ro Tong: General

A. 1 lb. lean chuck or shank of beef, minced

B. 3 slices ginger

C. 1 teaspoon salt

PREPARATION:

I. Place A in a bowl.

II. Add B, cover with 1 qt. cold water. Let stand 3 hours.

COOKING:

1. Place A–B mixture in pot, bring to boil and cook 5 minutes.

2. Add C.

3. Drain and serve hot as clear broth. A may be left in broth for further cooking with vegetables.

SIMPLE EGG DROP SOUP
Dan Hwa Tong: General

A. 13¾-oz. can chicken broth

B. 2 tablespoons cornstarch mixed with ¼ cup water

C. 1 egg

D. 1 tablespoon chopped scallion

PREPARATION:

I. Dilute A with 1 can water.

II. Beat C.

COOKING:

1. Bring diluted A to boil.
2. Thicken with B.

3. Turn off heat, slowly stir in C.
4. Garnish with D.

EGG DROP SOUP
Dan Hwa Tong: General

A. 4 cups soup stock

B. ½ teaspoon salt

C. ½ teaspoon sugar

D. 3 tablespoons cornstarch

E. ½ cup water

F. ½ egg

G. 1 teaspoon water

H. 2 scallions, sliced

PREPARATION:

I. Beat F but use only half for this recipe. Add G and mix.

II. Mix B, C. Set aside.

III. Mix D, E. Set aside.

COOKING:

1. Bring A to a rolling boil.
2. Add B–C mixture and stir well.
3. Add D–E mixture slowly to thicken the stock.

4. Remove pot from heat and immediately begin to pour in F–G mixture very slowly, stirring constantly. Serve with garnish of H.

EGG DROP SOUP   *Approved Ulcer Recipe*
Dan Hwa Tong: General

Halve H, tie in bundle, and add to soup in Step 1. Remove before serving.

BIRD'S NEST SOUP
Yen Wuo Tong: General

A. 2-oz. bird's nest

B. 1 qt. chicken soup

C. 3 slices ginger

D. dash black pepper

E. 1 teaspoon sherry

F. 1 boned chicken breast, chopped very fine

G. ¼ cup chopped lean Virginia ham

H. 2 teaspoons cornstarch

I. 1 egg white

J. several drops peanut oil

K. 5 drops sesame oil (optional)

PREPARATION:

I. Soak A in water overnight. Next day, sprinkle several drops J on A, wash with warm, clear water. Feathers should float to surface, making removal easier. Repeat oil-and-wash treatment until each A is clean.

II. Mix H with ¼ cup water.

COOKING:

1. Place A and 2 cups B in large bowl. Add C, D, E. Place in steamer, steam 1 hour.
2. Transfer A mixture to 3-qt. saucepan. Add F, G, rest of B, boil 2 minutes.
3. Add H mixture to soup, boil, then turn off heat.
4. Beat in I. Sprinkle with K. Serve hot.

BIRD'S NEST SOUP *Approved Ulcer Recipe*
Yen Wuo Tong: General

A. 2-oz. bird's nest
B. 1 qt. chicken soup
C. ⅛ teaspoon sherry
D. 1 boned chicken breast, chopped very fine
E. ¼ cup diced meat crumbs from Chinese grocery

F. 2 teaspoons cornstarch
G. 1 egg white
H. 5 drops sesame oil (optional)
I. several drops peanut oil

PREPARATION:

I. Soak A in water overnight. Next day, sprinkle several drops I on A, wash with warm, clear water. Feathers should float to surface, mak-ing removal easier. Repeat oil-and-wash treatment until A is clean.
II. Mix F with ¼ cup water.

COOKING:

1. Place A and 2 cups B in large bowl. Add C, D. Place in steamer, steam 1 hour.
2. Transfer A mixture to 3-qt. saucepan. Add D, E, rest of B, boil 2 minutes.
3. Add F mixture to soup, boil, then turn off heat.
4. Beat in G. Sprinkle with H. Serve hot.

BEAN CURD HOT AND SOUR SOUP
Dow Fu Swan La Tong: General

A. 1½ qts. pork stock (see Sliced Pork)
B. 3 Chinese mushrooms
C. ½ cup shredded pork
D. ½ cup shredded bamboo shoots
E. ½ cup shredded water chestnuts
F. 1½ tablespoons light soy sauce
G. 1 teaspoon salt

H. 3 cakes bean curd, sliced very thin
I. 3 tablespoons vinegar
J. ½ teaspoon pepper
K. 2 tablespoons cornstarch
L. ¼ cup water
M. 1 egg
N. 1 scallion, chopped

PREPARATION:

I. Wash B, soak 15 minutes in warm water. Drain, adding B water to A. Shred B.
II. Mix F, G.
III. Mix I, J, K, L. Beat M.

COOKING:

1. Bring mixture of A and B water to boil. Add B, C, D, E, cook 1 minute.
2. Add F–G mixture.
3. Add H, bring to boil again. Add I–L mixture, stir until thick.
4. Remove from heat, gradually stir in M.
5. Garnish with N and add sesame oil to taste; serve hot.

Note: Substitute 6 cups chicken broth or 6 chicken bouillon cubes in 1½ qts. water for A. This recipe is handy when soup stock is not available.

FROZEN BEAN CURD WITH SOYBEAN SPROUT SOUP
Dung Dow Fu Dow Ya Tong: Adapted

A. 13¾-oz. can chicken broth
B. 2 slices ginger
C. ½ lb. soy bean sprouts

D. 2 cakes frozen bean curd
E. 1 scallion, chopped

PREPARATION:

I. Wash C well; discard tail root.
II. Defrost D by covering with cold water, letting

stand 2 to 4 hours before cooking. Then cut each piece into 10 to 12 thin slices.

COOKING:

1. Empty A into cooking pot, add 1 can water.
2. Add B, C, bring to boil. Lower heat, cover, and cook 30 minutes.

3. Add D slices, cook 5 minutes. Serve hot; garnish with E.

BEAN CURD CHICKEN SOUP   *Approved Ulcer Recipe*
Dow Fu Gee Tong: General

A. 1 qt. chicken soup
B. 2 cakes bean curd, cut in 6 pieces
C. 4 dried black mushrooms

D. 1 chicken breast
E. 1 scallion, tied in bundle
F. salt to taste

PREPARATION:

I. Soak C in hot water 20 minutes; drain, saving water.

II. Bone D, double grind in meat grinder.

COOKING:

1. Bring A to boil in 3-qt. saucepan.
2. Add B, C, and C water.

3. Add D–F; simmer 5 minutes.
4. Remove C, E when soup is served.

MUSTARD GREEN AND BEAN CURD SOUP
Gai Tsai Dow Fu Tong: Shanghai

A. 3 to 4 cups soup stock
B. ¼ lb. mustard greens
C. ½ teaspoon chopped ginger
D. 2 teaspoons chopped scallion

E. 2 cakes bean curd
F. 1 tablespoon sherry
G. salt to taste

PREPARATION:

I. Wash and clean B, cut into ½-inch segments.

II. Slice each E into 8 to 10 thin pieces.

COOKING:

1. Bring A to boil, add B, C, D; when soup boils again, add E.

2. Let soup mixture boil ½ minute.
3. Turn off heat, add F, G; serve hot.

VELVET MUSHROOM SOUP
Fu Yong Sien Ku Tong: General

A. 8-oz. can chicken broth
B. ¼ cup diced Smithfield ham
C. ¼ cup green peas
D. ¼ cup diced bamboo shoots
E. ¼ lb. fresh mushrooms, sliced
F. 1 tablespoon cornstarch mixed with

    ¼ cup water
G. 1 tablespoon wine
H. salt, pepper to taste
I. 2 to 3 egg whites
J. ½ teaspoon salt
K. 2 teaspoons wine

PREPARATION:

I. Beat I slightly, add J, K and ½ cup A. Mix well.

II. Steam over boiling water until set (about 12 minutes).

COOKING:

1. Add enough water to rest of A to make 2½ cups liquid; bring to a boil.
2. Add B; cook 2 minutes.
3. Add C, D; cook 2 minutes.
4. Add E; cook 1 minute. Thicken with F.
5. Add G, H; pour over I–K mixture; serve hot.

MUSHROOM GO BA SOUP I
Tsao Gu Go Ba Tong: Shanghai

A.   3 tablespoons vegetable oil
B.   ¼ lb. pork, shredded
C.   1 teaspoon cornstarch
D.   2 teaspoons light soy sauce
E.   ½ lb. fresh mushrooms
F.   2 teaspoons cornstarch
G.   1 teaspoon light soy sauce
H.   1 tablespoon sherry

I.   ½ teaspoon sugar
J.   dash black pepper
K.   1 teaspoon sugar
L.   1 tablespoon cornstarch
M.   13¾-oz. can chicken soup
N.   fried rice patty (see Rice Patty or Rice Crust II)

PREPARATION:

I. Wash E, cut off ½ inch of stem, then cut into 3 to 4 pieces. Soak in cold water.

II. Mix E with F, G, H, I, J.

III. Mix B, C, D.

IV. Mix K, L, M. Make sure there are no lumps.

COOKING:

1. Heat A in frying pan. Stir-fry B–D mixture 1 to 2 minutes.
2. Add E–J mixture; stir-fry 1 minute, then cover and cook 2 minutes.
3. Add K–M mixture, cover, and bring to boil. Simmer 3 more minutes.
4. Heat oil in deep fryer to 375°. Fry patties until just golden. Do not wait until they are brown. Remove to cake pan and leave in 300° oven until ready to use.
5. When ready to serve, place N in a large bowl, pour soup over it, and serve. A crackling noise should be heard when soup comes in contact with the hot patties.

MUSHROOM GO BA SOUP II
Dung Gu Go Ba Tong: Peking

A.   12 Chinese mushrooms
B.   13¾-oz. can chicken soup
C.   1 tablespoon light soy sauce

D.   2 to 4 oz. fried rice patties (see Rice Patty or Rice Crust II)

PREPARATION:

I. Wash A in warm water and soak 15 minutes; drain; save water. Discard stems and cut each A into 2 or 3 pieces.

II. Cut D into 1-inch squares.

COOKING:

1. Place A, B, C with enough water added to mushroom water to make 1 cup in saucepan, bring to boil, and simmer 5 minutes.
2. When ready to serve, place hot and crispy D in soup bowl, pour A–C mixture over it and serve.

SUB GUM WON TON SOUP
Sub Gum Won Ton Tong: Canton

A. 1 small chicken breast
B. ¼ lb. ham
C. ½ cup sliced bamboo shoots
D. 3 black mushrooms

E. 5 cups chicken broth
F. 1 tablespoon chopped scallion
G. 12 snow peas
H. 24 won tons (see Index)

PREPARATION:

I. Wash D and soak in warm water 15 minutes. Drain and add mushroom water to E.

II. Cook A in E 10 minutes. Bone and shred.
III. Cut B, D, G in thin, narrow pieces.

COOKING:

1. Add A, B, C, D to E and cook 5 minutes.

2. Add F, G, H and bring to boil. Cook 1 minute. Serve hot.

WON TON SEA CUCUMBER SOUP
Won Ton Hai Sun: Szechuan

A. ¼ cup refined dried sea cucumbers
B. 1 cup sliced bamboo shoots
C. 8 Chinese mushrooms
D. 1 qt. chicken soup
E. 1 scallion, chopped

F. 3 slices ginger, chopped
G. 24 won tons (see Index)
H. dash salt, pepper
I. 2 slices ginger
J. 1 scallion

PREPARATION:

I. Soak A in water at room temperature for two days. Discard water, boil in fresh water with I, J for 35 minutes. Drain; wash and cut A

into 2- by ½- by ¼-inch pieces.

II. Soak C in warm water 20 minutes. Remove and discard stems; cut each in half.

COOKING:

1. Place A, B, C, D, E, F in large heavy pot. Bring to boil.

2. Add G, simmer for 3 minutes. Adjust with H. Serve hot.

RED-IN-SNOW FISH SOUP
Shieh Tsai Yu Tong: Ninpo

A. ¼ cup peanut oil
B. 1 scallion
C. 2 slices ginger
D. 1 porgy (about 1 lb.)

E. 1 tablespoon sherry
F. ¼ cup preserved red-in-snow
G. ½ cup sliced bamboo shoots
H. 1 teaspoon salt

PREPARATION:

I. Clean and wash D, dry between paper towels. Make 2 diagonal slashes on each side.

II. Tie B into a knot.

COOKING:

1. Heat A, add B, C, stir-fry 1 to 2 minutes.
2. Add D, brown on both sides; discard B, C; add E and cover for a few seconds.
3. Add 1 qt. cold water, bring to boil, cook 1 minute.

4. Spread F, G over fish, add salt, cover and simmer 15 minutes or until fish is done.
5. Turn heat high and cook 1 more minute. Remove oil that floats to top of soup.
6. Serve hot.

RED-IN-SNOW AND BEAN SOUP
Shieh Tsai Dow Ban Tong: Shanghai

A. 1½ qts. soup stock
B. ¼ lb. pork, shredded
C. 10-oz. pkg. frozen Fordhook lima beans

D. ½ cup preserved red-in-snow
E. salt to taste

PREPARATION:

I. Peel skin off C.

COOKING:

1. Bring A to boil, add B, C, D, cook 10 to 15 minutes.

2. Add E; serve hot.

PRESERVED KOHLRABI SOUP WITH PORK
Tza Tsoi Ro Si Tong: General

A. 2 tablespoons peanut oil
B. 3 slices ginger, chopped
C. 1 small scallion, chopped
D. ¼ lb. pork

E. ¼ cup preserved kohlrabi, cut as in Preparation I.
F. 2 oz. cellophane noodles
G. 2 teaspoons light soy sauce
H. 1 qt. water or pork stock

PREPARATION:

I. Slice D, E, then cut into pieces 1 inch to 1½ inches long.

II. Soak F in hot water 30 minutes.

COOKING:

1. Heat A, add B, C, stir-fry a few seconds.
2. Add D, continue stir-frying 1 to 2 minutes. Add E, F, G, mix well.

3. Add 1 qt. boiling H. Bring to boil. Cook over low heat 5 minutes. Salt to taste, serve hot.

PRESERVED KOHLRABI SOUP WITH SLICED CHICKEN
Tza Tsoi Gee Pien Tong: General

A. 1 chicken breast, sliced thin
B. 2 teaspoons light soy sauce
C. 1 teaspoon sherry
D. 1 teaspoon cornstarch

E. ½ cup diced bamboo shoots
F. ¼ cup thinly sliced preserved kohlrabi
G. 1 teaspoon salt
H. ½ teaspoon sugar

PREPARATION:

I. Bone A, place bone in saucepan. Add 1 qt. water, bring to boil, lower heat, and cook 10 minutes.

II. Marinate A with B, C, D.

COOKING:

1. Remove A bone from saucepan. Turn heat high, bring soup to boil.

2. Add A–D and E, F, stir well. When mixture boils again, add G, H. Lower heat, cook another 1 to 2 minutes. Serve hot.

TURNIP AND SPARERIB SOUP
Lo Bo Pai Gu Tong: General

A. 1 lb. spareribs
B. 1 medium turnip (about 1 lb.)

C. 1 tablespoon chopped scallion
D. 1 to 1½ teaspoons salt

PREPARATION:

I. Cut A into 1-inch pieces.

II. Peel B, cut into bite-size pieces.

COOKING:

1. Put A and 2 qts. water into a cooking pot, bring to boil. Lower heat, simmer 1 to 1½ hours.

2. Add B, cook another 30 to 45 minutes.
3. Add C, D.

TURNIP AND SPARERIB SOUP
Pai Gwut Lo Bo Tong: Canton

Add dried shrimp as follows: Wash 12 dried shrimp well, add to A along with B in Step 2, and cook as directed.

CELERY CABBAGE AND MEATBALL SOUP
Bai Tsai Chuan Yuan Tze Tong: Peking

A. 1 lb. celery cabbage
B. 1 qt. water (or 13¾-oz. can chicken broth plus 1 can water, without I)
C. ½ lb. pork, ground
D. 1 tablespoon chopped scallion (white part only)

E. 1 teaspoon chopped ginger
F. 2 teaspoons cornstarch
G. 2 teaspoons light soy sauce
H. 1 teaspoon sherry
I. 1 teaspoon salt
J. few drops sesame oil (optional)

PREPARATION:

I. Cut A into 2½-inch segments and wash.

II. Mix C, D, E, F, G, H well and make into balls 1 inch in diameter.

COOKING:

1. Place A in pot, add B, bring to boil, simmer 25 minutes.

2. Turn heat high, add C–H mixture and cook 5 to 8 minutes or until meatballs are done.
3. Add I, J and serve hot.

CELERY CABBAGE AND SHRIMP BALL SOUP
Bai Tsai Sha Yuan Tong: Peking

A. 1 lb. celery cabbage
B. 1 qt. water
C. 1 cup chopped frozen shrimp
D. 1 tablespoon chopped scallion
E. 1 teaspoon chopped ginger
F. ¼ teaspoon ground pepper

G. 2 teaspoons light soy sauce
H. 2 teaspoons sherry
I. 2 teaspoons cornstarch
J. 1 teaspoon salt
K. sesame oil to taste

PREPARATION:

I. Cut A into 2-inch segments and wash.

II. Cover C in cold water with ½ teaspoon salt until defrosted. Drain, dry between paper

towels. Chop.

III. Mix C with D, E, F, G, H, I well and make into balls 1 inch in diameter.

COOKING:

1. Place A in pot, add B, bring to boil; lower heat and simmer 20 to 25 minutes.

2. Turn up heat, add C–I mixture, and cook 1 minute or until shrimp are done.

3. Add J, K and serve hot.

CABBAGE SOUP WITH DRIED SHRIMP
Ha Mai Bok Tsoi Tong: Adapted

A. 2 tablespoons vegetable oil
B. 20 dried shrimp
C. 3 slices ginger
D. 1 tablespoon minced scallion

E. 6 cups pork stock or chicken stock
F. 2 oz. cellophane noodles
G. 4 cups (cut as below) celery cabbage (about 1 head)

PREPARATION:

I. Clean G, cut across leaf or stem into strips ½ inch wide.

II. Soak B 20 minutes in hot water. Drain, saving water.

III. Soak F 30 minutes in hot water.

COOKING:

1. Pour A into 3-qt. saucepan; heat. Add B, C, D; stir-fry 1 to 2 minutes.

2. Add E and B water; bring to boil.

3. Add F, simmer 5 to 10 minutes. Add G, cook another 5 minutes.

4. Add salt to taste. Serve hot.

CABBAGE SOUP WITH DRIED SCALLOPS
Gong Yu Chee Bok Tsoi Tong: Adapted

Substitute 6 pieces dried scallops for B. In Step II, increase hot-water soaking time to 45 minutes.

CURRIED BEEF SOUP
Ka Li Ngo Yoke Tong: Canton

A. 1 lb. stewing beef
B. 3 slices ginger
C. 1 tablespoon dry sherry

D. 1½ teaspoons salt
E. 1 to 2 teaspoons curry powder (to taste)
F. 2 medium potatoes

PREPARATION:

I. Cut A into bite-size pieces.

II. Peel F, cut each into 12 pieces. (Do not prepare until ready to cook.)

COOKING:

1. Place A in pot, cover with 2 qts. water. Bring to boil, cook 5 minutes. Skim off fatty froth.

2. Add B, C, reduce heat, and simmer until A is tender (about 2 hours).

3. Add D, E, F, cook 10 more minutes. Serve hot.

PORK TONGUE SOUP
Tsu Suh Tong: General

A. soup (see Braised Pork Tongue with Bamboo Shoots)
B. ½ cup shredded bamboo shoots
C. 6 slices ginger, shredded
D. 3 cakes bean curd
E. 2 teaspoons sherry
F. 1 teaspoon salt
G. 1 teaspoon chopped scallion

PREPARATION:

I. Cut D into halves, then cut into 8 to 10 slices.

COOKING:

1. Measure A into a pot, add enough water to make 2 to 3 cups, bring to a boil.
2. Add B, C, cook 1 to 2 minutes.
3. Add D, E, F, and cook 1 more minute; garnish with G and serve hot.

WINTER MELON SOUP
Dung Gwa Tsung: General

A. 1 winter melon, volleyball size
B. 2 qts. chicken soup
C. ¼ cup diced bamboo shoots
D. 5 dried mushrooms
E. 4 slices ginger
F. 2 tablespoons Virginia ham slivers
G. 1 chicken breast
H. 6 medium shrimp
I. 2 teaspoons cornstarch
J. salt to taste

PREPARATION:

I. Cut off 1½ inches from A top. (This will be used as a lid.) Remove melon seeds and clean inside of melon. Place in big bowl in upright position for easy removal.
II. Soak D in hot water 15 minutes. Cut into small slices.
III. Bone and dice G.
IV. Shell H, devein and dice.
V. Mix I with G, H.

COOKING:

1. Place A and bowl in steamer. Pour boiling B into center of A.
2. Add C, D, E, F. Steam 2 to 4 hours until melon meat is soft.
3. Add G–J to melon and steam an additional 15 minutes. Remove bowl with A, remove cover, and serve.

BITTER MELON AND PORK SOUP
Fu Gwa Ju Yoke Tong: Canton

A. 4 cups soup stock
B. ½ lb. sliced fresh pork
C. 3 slices ginger, minced
D. 1 bitter melon
E. 1 teaspoon light soy sauce
F. 3 drops sesame oil (optional)
G. ½ teaspoon salt
H. 2 eggs

PREPARATION:

I. Cut D in half lengthwise, remove and discard seeds, slice into thin pieces.

COOKING:

1. Bring A to rapid boil in large saucepan.
2. Add B, C; cook 5 minutes.
3. Parboil D 5 minutes in 1 qt. boiling water (in separate pot). Drain.
4. Add D to A–C and cook 5 minutes.

II. Mix E, F, G; set aside in small bowl.

5. Add E–G mixture; stir well, turn off heat.
6. Drop H one by one into soup; let stand 3 minutes.
7. Serve in large soup tureen.

WINTER MELON SOUP WITH CHICKEN
Dung Gwa Gee Tong: General

A. 6 cups soup stock
B. 1-lb. slice of winter melon
C. 4 dried black mushrooms
D. 1 slice ginger, minced
E. 2 chicken breasts
F. ⅛ teaspoon garlic powder

G. 1 teaspoon sherry
H. 1 teaspoon sugar
I. ½ teaspoon light soy sauce
J. ½ teaspoon salt
K. 1½ teaspoons light soy sauce
L. 2 teaspoons peanut oil

PREPARATION:

I. Soak C in warm water 15 minutes. Discard water. Slice C.
II. Cut B into ¼-inch slices. Skin may be left intact or cut off. Set aside.

COOKING:

1. Heat A to boiling.
2. Add B, C, D and simmer for 25 minutes.
3. Add E–I mixture. Stir well.
4. Add J–L mixture.

III. Bone E. Cut into bite-sized pieces.
IV. Mix E, F, G, H, I thoroughly and set aside to stand 15 minutes.
V. Mix J, K, L. Set aside.

5. Cook until chicken is tender and done.
   Note: Even though B skin may be left intact, it is *not* eaten.

HAIRY MELON SOUP
Mo Gwa Tong: Canton

A. 1 hairy melon (½ to 1 lb.)
B. 2 slices ginger
C. 1 tablespoon peanut oil
D. 3½ cups water

E. 6 dried scallops
F. ¼ lb. pork, sliced
G. 1 teaspoon salt
H. ½ teaspoon sugar

PREPARATION:

I. Peel A, wash and cut into bite-size pieces.
II. Rinse E, place in a small bowl; add 1 tablespoon of water and steam over boiling water 30 minutes.

COOKING:

1. Heat a 2-qt. saucepan. Add A, stir a few seconds.
2. Add B, C and stir ½ minute.

3. Add D, E, F, bring to boil. Lower heat and simmer 25 minutes.
4. Add G, H; serve hot.

CURRY SOUP WITH NOODLES
Ga Li Tong Mien: Canton

A. 5 cups soup stock
B. ½ lb. fresh noodles
C. ¼ to ½ teaspoon curry powder
D. ½ teaspoon salt
E. 3 tablespoons peanut oil

F. ½ cup finely chopped onions
G. ½ lb. beef tenderloin, sliced, or ground beef
H. ½ teaspoon sugar
I. ½ teaspoon salt
J. ¼ cup soup stock

PREPARATION:

I.   Parboil B. Set aside.
II. Mix C, D. Set aside.

III. Mix H, I. Set aside.

COOKING:

1. Heat A to boiling.
2. Add B, C, D and bring to boiling point again.
3. Place in large serving bowl. Set aside.
4. Put E in very hot skillet and bring to high heat.

5. Add F; stir-fry until brown.
6. Add G; stir-fry until just done.
7. Add H–I with J. Stir 15 seconds.
8. Spread E–J mixture over A–D mixture.

CHICKEN SOUP WITH PARTS
Gee Tong: Adapted

A. neck, back, gizzard, and breastbone of 2- to 3-lb. fryer
B. 3 slices ginger
C. 1½ to 2 qts. water

D. 1 teaspoon salt
E. 1 tablespoon chopped scallion or Chinese parsley

PREPARATION:

I. Wash and clean A.

COOKING:

1. Place A, B, C in a pot; bring to a boil, lower heat and cook for 1 to 2 hours or until about 3 cups of liquid are left.
2. Remove A, B and skim off fat.
3. Add D, garnish with E and serve hot.

Note: This soup is part of One Chicken: Three Flavors, which see. If desired, 2 to 4 oz. of a fresh vegetable may be added to soup and cooked until tender.

NOODLES IN CHICKEN SOUP
Gee Tong Mein: General

A. 1 tablespoon peanut oil
B. ¼ lb. boned breast meat of chicken
C. 2 teaspoons light soy sauce
D. ¾ teaspoon salt
E. ¼ teaspoon sugar

F. ½ cup bamboo shoots, diced
G. 3 to 4 Chinese mushrooms
H. 1½ qts. chicken broth
I. 1 lb. fresh noodles
J. 2 scallions, sliced

PREPARATION:

I.   Parboil I 4 minutes. Set aside in bowl.
II. Soak G 15 minutes. Slice into thin slivers. Discard water.

III. Dice B into ½-inch-square pieces.
IV. Dice F into ½-inch-square pieces.
V.   Mix C, D, E. Add C–E to B and stir well.

COOKING:

1. Put A in very hot skillet and bring to high heat.
2. Add B–E mixture and stir-fry 15 seconds.
3. Add F, G. Stir-fry 45 seconds.

4. Add H; bring to boil; simmer 10 minutes.
5. Reheat I under running hot tap water.
6. Place I in deep bowl. Pour soup mixture over I. Serve with garnish of J.

WON TONS WITH CHICKEN SOUP   *Approved Diabetic Recipe*
Won Ton Gee Tong: General

A.   2 to 3 cups chicken stock
B.   ½ cup shredded Chinese celery cabbage or any green-leaf vegetable

C.   24 won tons (see Index)
D.   salt to taste

PREPARATION:

I. Bring A to boil, add B, cook 1 to 2 minutes; add C, bring to boil.

II. Add D. Serve hot.

CHICKEN SOUP WITH CELERY CABBAGE
Gee Ro Bai Tsai Tong: General

A.   3-lb. roasting chicken
B.   4 dried mushrooms
C.   2 scallions
D.   3 slices ginger
E.   2 tablespoons sherry

F.   1- to 2-lb. celery cabbage
G.   salt to taste
H.   2 tablespoons light soy sauce
I.   ⅛ teaspoon sesame oil

PREPARATION:

I. Soak B in hot water 20 minutes. Drain, reserving water.
II. Clean F well. Split tender center piece in half. Then cut each into 2 to 3 parts.

III. Fold C 3 times. Take green end, tie into bundle with thread.

COOKING:

1. Place cleaned whole A in Dutch oven. Add B water, 1 additional qt. water, bring to boil. Add B, C, D, E. Simmer covered 35 to 40 minutes.
2. Add F, boil 5 minutes. Remove and discard C. Add G.

3. If desired, dipping sauce can be prepared by combining H, I, and 1 tablespoon minced scallion.
4. Serve whole and carve at table.

CHICKEN SOUP WITH CELERY CABBAGE AND CELLOPHANE NOODLES
Tien Tsin Bai Tsai Gee Tong: General

Soak 1 oz. cellophane noodles in hot water 30 minutes. Cut into short pieces. In Step 2, add cellophane noodles when F is added.

CHICKEN SOUP WITH BAMBOO SHOOTS
Dung Sun Gee Tong: General

Substitute 1 large piece bamboo shoot for F. In Step II, cut bamboo shoot in bite-size pieces. In Step 1, add bamboo shoot when B–E are added. Boil 35 to 40 minutes.

CHICKEN SOUP WITH ASPARAGUS SHOOTS
Lu Sun Gee Tong: General

Substitute 12 oz. asparagus shoots for F. In Step II, break off tender asparagus shoots, wash. Cook asparagus shoots same as cabbage.

STUFFED CHICKEN WING SOUP
Lung Chwan Feng Yi Tong: Shanghai

A. 1 lb. chicken wings
B. 1 oz. Virginia ham
C. ⅓ chunk of canned bamboo shoot
D. 1 tablespoon sherry

E. ½ teaspoon salt
F. 6 to 8 Chinese mushrooms
G. 13¾-oz. can chicken broth

PREPARATION:

I. Wash and disjoint A. Cook in boiling water 10 minutes, remove from liquid, and take out bones. Save water to mix with G.
II. Cut B, C into strips 3 inches long.
III. Stuff A with B, C. Place in soup bowl.

IV. Mix D, E and pour over A mixture.
V. Wash and soak F in warm water 15 minutes (save water), remove F and discard stems, cut each into 2 or 3 pieces and mix with A mixture.

COOKING:

1. Steam A–F mixture in steamer 30–45 minutes.
2. Dilute G with 1 can water plus mushroom water. Bring to boil and pour onto A, mix well, and serve hot.

CHICKEN GIBLETS WITH CUCUMBER SOUP
Hwang Gwa Gee Tza Tong: Shanghai

A. giblets and neck from 1 chicken
B. 13¾-oz. can chicken broth
C. 2 slices ginger
D. 1 cucumber

E. 1 tablespoon sherry
F. 1 tablespoon chopped scallion
G. few drops sesame oil

PREPARATION:

I. Clean and wash A.
II. Dilute B with 1½ cans water, add neck and C; bring to boil, cook over low heat 15 minutes.

III. Cut giblets into thin slices.
IV. Peel D, cut in half lengthwise. Discard seeds (if D is tender keep seeds and all), cut into ½-inch slices diagonally.

COOKING:

1. Add III to II and cook 15 to 20 minutes.
2. Add D, cook 3 more minutes.

3. Add E, F, G; stir well and serve hot.

CHICKEN WITH CUCUMBER SOUP
Huang Gwa Gee Pien Tong: General

A. 13¾-oz. can chicken broth
B. 2 slices ginger (optional)

C. 1 chicken breast
D. 1 teaspoon cornstarch

E. ½ teaspoon salt
F. 1 cucumber

PREPARATION:

I. Bone C, slice thin.
II. Mix C with D, E.

COOKING:

1. Empty A into saucepan, add B, dilute with 1 can water. (If desired, enrich stock by adding breastbone.) Bring to boil.

III. Peel F, cut in half lengthwise. Discard seeds, then cut into ¼-inch slices.

2. Add C–E mixture, stir well, cook 2 minutes.
3. Add F, bring to boil again, cook 2 to 3 more minutes. Serve hot.

PORK CHOPS WITH CUCUMBER SOUP
Huang Gwa Ro Pien Tong: General

Substitute 2 or 3 center-cut pork chops, boned and sliced thin, for C.

CHICKEN CORN SOUP
Gai Yung Sok Mai Tong: Canton

A. 13¾-oz. can chicken broth
B. 8-oz. can corn
C. 1 teaspoon sherry
D. 1 teaspoon salt
E. 1 chicken breast
F. 1 tablespoon cornstarch mixed with ¼ cup water
G. 1 egg

PREPARATION:

I. Bone and mince E.
II. Mix E with 1 tablespoon F and 2 tablespoons cold water. Beat until foamy.
III. Beat G well.

COOKING:

1. Empty A into a pot, add 1 can water and B, C, D. Bring to boil, lower heat, and cook 3 minutes.
2. Add E–F mixture, keep stirring until mixture reaches a boil, then thicken with remainder of F.
3. Remove from heat. Add G slowly. Serve hot, with several drops of sesame oil if desired.

CHICKEN, MUSHROOM, AND BAMBOO SHOOT SOUP
Gee Pien Dung Gu Tong: General

A. 13¾-oz. can chicken broth
B. 1 small chicken breast
C. 1 teaspoon cornstarch
D. ¼ teaspoon salt
E. ¼ lb. fresh mushrooms
F. ¼ cup canned bamboo shoots, sliced as in preparation
G. 2 teaspoons sherry

PREPARATION:

I. Bone B, slice meat into pieces ⅛ to ¼ inch thick. Add C, D, mix well.
II. Wash E well, cut each in half.
III. Cut F into slices ⅛ to ¼ inch thick and 2 inches long.

COOKING:

1. Empty A into saucepan, add 1½ cans water, bring to boil.
2. Add B–D mixture, stir well, add E, F, G. Cook 3 to 5 minutes. Serve hot.

CHICKEN SOUP WITH ASPARAGUS SHOOTS AND BEAN CURD
Lu Shun Dow Fu Tong: General

A. 1 qt. clear chicken broth and 2 cups water
B. 4 black dried mushrooms
C. 10 dried shrimp
D. 1 chicken breast
E. 1 tablespoon sherry
F. 3 slices ginger
G. ½ lb. asparagus shoots
H. 2 cakes bean curd
I. salt to taste

PREPARATION:

I. Clean tips of G, discard hard stems. French-cut tips into thin pieces.
II. Soak B in hot water 20 minutes.
III. Soak C in cold water 20 minutes.
IV. Cut H into thin ½- by 1-inch pieces.
V. Bone D and slice meat into thin pieces.

COOKING:

1. Place A in 3-qt. saucepan. Add B, C, D, E, F and cook 10 minutes.
2. Add G, H and cook 5 minutes. Add I. Serve hot.

ASPARAGUS SHOOTS, BEAN CURD, SPARERIB SOUP
Pai Gu Lung Shu Tsai Tong: Shanghai

Omit D. Add 1 lb. spareribs cooked in 2 qts. water 1 hour. Chop in 1-inch pieces. Substitute sparerib broth for chicken broth.

DUCK GIBLETS SOUP
Op Sun Tong: Adapted

A. giblets and neck (or bone) from 1 Peking duck or any roast duck
B. 4 slices ginger
C. ¼ cup preserved celery cabbage
D. 2-oz. pkg. cellophane noodles
E. ½ teaspoon salt

PREPARATION:

I. Clean and wash A, cover neck or bone with 2 qts. water, bring to boil, add B. Cook over low heat 1 hour.
II. Slice giblets into small pieces.
III. Place C in a cup of water, stir, then scoop up C. (The sand will sink to bottom.)
IV. Cover D with hot water, let stand ½ hour.

COOKING:

1. Add II to I and cook ½ hour.
2. Add C, D and cook 15 minutes; remove neck and bone.
3. Add E and serve hot.

ROAST DUCK SOUP
Shu Op Tong: Canton

A. 1 lb. Chinese white or American turnips
B. 1 qt. water
C. ½ lb. roasted duck
D. ½ to 1 teaspoon salt
E. 1 scallion, chopped

PREPARATION:

I. Cut C into bite-size pieces.

II. Peel A, cut into bite-size pieces.

COOKING:

1. Place A in cooking pot, cover wth B, bring to boil. Reduce heat, cook until soft (about 15 minutes).

2. Add C pieces, cook another 3 to 5 minutes.
3. Add D and garnish with E.

STEAMED DUCK SOUP
Dun Op Tong: Canton

A. 2- to 3-lb. duckling
B. 2 qts. boiling water
C. 2 teaspoons salt
D. 6 Chinese mushrooms

E. 1 scallion
F. 3 slices ginger
G. ½ cup shredded bamboo shoots
H. ½ cup shredded Virginia ham

PREPARATION:

I. Wash A well, cook 5 minutes in 1 qt. B. Drain, discarding water. Rub A with C inside and out. Place in large bowl, breast side up.

II. Wash D, soak 15 minutes in warm water. Drain, saving D water and adding it to remaining 1 qt. B. Slice D thin.

III. Cut E, F into pieces 1 inch to 2 inches long. Stuff half into A cavity.

IV. Mix G, H with D, rest of E, F. Spread evenly over A.

V. Add combination of D water and 1 qt. B to A.

COOKING:

1. Place bowl of A mixture in steamer. Steam over boiling water 2 hours until meat is soft and tender. Serve hot.

DUCK BONE SOUP
Ya Gu Tong: General

A. bones from duck (see Peking Duck)
B. 2 qts. water

C. 1 lb. Chinese celery cabbage
D. 2 teaspoons salt

PREPARATION:

I. Disjoint A.

II. Cut C into 1½-inch pieces.

COOKING:

1. Place A in pot, cover with B. Bring to boil, lower heat, and simmer 1 hour.

2. Add C, cook 10 minutes over low heat.
3. Remove A from soup. Add D and serve hot.

DUCK BONE SOUP WITH CELLOPHANE NOODLES
Fun See Ya Gu Tong: General

Reduce C to ½ lb. and add 1-oz. pkg. cellophane noodles. Soak noodles 30 minutes in hot water. After Step 1, drain soup and discard bones. Bring soup to boil. In Step 2, add C and noodles, cook 10 minutes over low heat. Serve hot.

DUCK BONE SOUP WITH DOW FU
Dow Fu Ya Gu Tong: General

Omit C. Cut 2 cakes bean curd into small cubes. Simmer A, B 1 to 2 hours; drain, discard bones. Bring soup to boil, add bean curd, bring to boil again. Remove from heat, garnish with chopped scallions, and serve hot.

DUCK LIVER SOUP
Ya Gahn Tong: Hunan

A. 1 can chicken broth
B. ½ cup sliced bamboo shoots
C. ¼ cup preserved celery cabbage

D. ¼ lb. duck liver
E. 1 teaspoon light soy sauce
F. 2 teaspoons sherry

PREPARATION:

I. Cut D into thin slices, mix with E, F and marinate 5 minutes.

II. To 2 cups boiling water, add D slices, stir well. When water boils again, turn off heat and drain.

COOKING:

1. Empty A into saucepan, add 1 can water, bring to boil.

2. Add B, C, cook 1 to 2 minutes.
3. Add D slices, cook 1 minute longer.

NUTRITIOUS, ECONOMICAL MUSTARD GREEN AND BEAN CURD BEEF SOUP
Niu Ro Gai Tsai Dow Fu Tong: General

A. ½ lb. lean chuck or shank of beef, minced
B. 3 slices ginger
C. 1 teaspoon salt

D. 1 cup mustard greens
E. 2 cakes bean curd

PREPARATION:

I. Place A in bowl.
II. Add B, cover with 1½ qts. cold water. Let stand 3 hours.

III. Slice D diagonally in bite-size pieces.
IV. Cut each E in 8 pieces.

COOKING:

1. Place A, B in pot, bring to boil over high heat. Cook 5 minutes.
2. Add C, D, E, cook 2 to 3 more minutes. Serve hot.
    Vegetable substitutes are: 2 or 3 tomatoes; 2 to 3 sheets purple seaweed; 1 beaten egg and 1 chopped scallion; ¼ cup preserved turnip and 1 oz. cellophane noodles; 1 cucumber; ½ cup shredded cabbage, ½ carrot, and 1 stalk celery; ½ lb. spinach; and 1 small onion and 2 tomatoes.

BEEF TOMATO SOUP
Fan Cheh Niu Gu Tong: Shanghai

A. 2 to 3 lbs. beef neck bones
B. 1½ lbs. fresh or canned tomatoes
C. 4 stalks celery, with leaves
D. 1 medium onion, sliced

E. 5 slices ginger
F. ½ teaspoon sugar
G. salt to taste

PREPARATION:

I. Wash C, cut across grain, into ½-inch pieces (save leaves for soup).

II. If B are fresh, quarter them.

III. Peel skin off E.

COOKING:

1. Using 5-qt. Dutch oven at high heat, brown A. Add 2 qts. water, and E, cover and simmer 2 hours. Add boiling water occasionally to replace water that evaporates, to make 1 qt. of soup.

2. Add B, C, D, cook 5 to 10 minutes. If canned tomatoes are used, add liquid to soup. Adjust taste with F and G.

MEATBALL SOUP
Ro Yuen Tong: Peking

A. 2 qts. pork broth
B. 6 dried mushrooms
C. ¼ lb. ground pork
D. ¼ lb. ground shrimp
E. 1 egg

F. 7 water chestnuts
G. ½ lb. Chinese celery cabbage hearts
H. salt to taste
I. ½ teaspoon sherry

PREPARATION:

I. Soak B in hot water 20 minutes. Drain, saving water. Remove and discard stems; chop into very fine pieces.

II. Chop F very fine.

III. Mix C, D, E, and F. Make spoon-size balls.

IV. Chop G into 2-inch pieces.

COOKING:

1. In saucepan bring A and water from B to boil, add B and C–F mixture, cook 5 to 10 minutes.

2. Add G, H, I and simmer 5 minutes. Serve hot.

CELLOPHANE NOODLES AND MEATBALL SOUP
Shien Fun Ro Yuen Tong: General

A. 1 qt. water
B. ¼ lb. ground pork or chicken
C. 1 tablespoon light soy sauce
D. 1 tablespoon sherry

E. 2 teaspoons cornstarch
F. 1 teaspoon salt
G. 1 oz. dried cellophane noodles
H. 2 scallions, sliced

PREPARATION:

I. Soak G in hot water 30 minutes. Drain.

II. Mix B, C, D, E and form into 16 balls.

COOKING:

1. Heat A to boiling.
2. Add B–E and F, G. Cook 5 minutes.

3. Serve hot in soup tureen with garnish of H.

CELLOPHANE NOODLES AND MEATBALL SOUP *Approved Ulcer Recipe*
Shien Fun Ro Yuen Tong: General

Double B, omit D and H.

BEEF MEATBALL SOUP WITH CELLOPHANE NOODLES
Ngo Yoke Yuen Fun See Tong: Adapted

A. 1-oz. pkg. cellophane noodles
B. ½ lb. ground chuck
C. 1 tablespoon chopped scallion
D. 2 slices ginger, chopped
E. 1 tablespoon light soy sauce
F. 1 teaspoon sugar

G. 2 teaspoons sherry
H. ½ teaspoon salt
I. 1 egg
J. 1 tablespoon cornstarch
K. salt to taste

PREPARATION:

I. Beat I, mix well with J.
II. Soak A 30 minutes in hot water. Drain.

III. Mix thoroughly B, C, D, E, F, G, H, I, J. Make into meatballs 1 inch in diameter.

COOKING:

1. Put A into 1½ qts. boiling water. Bring to boil, reduce heat, and cook 10 minutes over low heat.
2. Add meatballs, bring to boil, cook 5 minutes.

3. Add K.
4. Garnish with Chinese parsley or additional scallion.

BEEF MEATBALL SOUP AND CELLOPHANE NOODLES WITH CHINESE CELERY CABBAGE
Ngo Yoke Yuen Shiu Tsoi Tong: Adapted

Add 1 cup shredded Chinese celery cabbage to soup along with meatballs in Step 2.

BEEF MEATBALL SOUP AND CELLOPHANE NOODLES WITH SPINACH
Ngo Yoke Yuen Bo Tsoi Tong: Adapted

Add ½ lb. fresh spinach (washed well and drained) during last minute of cooking in Step 2.

DRAGON WHISKERS MEATBALL SOUP
Lung Shu Yen Yuen: Fukien

A. 4 oz. ground pork
B. 4 oz. shrimp
C. 6 to 8 dried shrimp
D. 4-oz. can water chestnuts
E. 1 teaspoon salt

F. 4 pieces won ton skin (see Wrapping Skin for Egg Rolls and Won Tons)
G. 13¾-oz. can chicken broth with enough water to make 3 cups
H. ¼ cup chopped celery

PREPARATION:

I. Shell, devein, and wash B; drain off water; mince.
II. Clean and wash C, soak in cold water 5 to 10 minutes, mince.
III. Drain D and chop.
IV. Mix A, B, C, D, E and make about 20 walnut-size balls.

V. Shred F into ¼-inch strips.
VI. Wet F a little with water and stick a few strips onto each meatball, leaving ends loose.
VII. Arrange meatballs in a single layer on a greased plate.

COOKING:

1. Steam meatballs over boiling water 7 minutes.
2. Bring G to a boil, add meatballs; when soup boils again, pour into large tureen. Add H and serve hot.

CALF BRAIN SOUP
Shiao Niu Nao Tong: General

A. 13¾-oz. can chicken broth and ½ can water
B. 1 calf brain
C. 2 teaspoons dry sherry
D. 1 egg white
E. 1 teaspoon minced ginger
F. 1 teaspoon lard

PREPARATION:

I. Place B in cold water; remove blood vessels with a toothpick, rinse and drain. Mince B.

II. Mix B with C.

COOKING:

1. Bring A to boil in saucepan.
2. Add B mixture, stir well.
3. Stir in D gradually.
4. When mixture boils again, add E, F; serve hot.

LAMB CHOP CUCUMBER SOUP *Approved Ulcer Recipe*
Yang Pai Hwang Gwa Tong: General

A. ½ lb. lean lamb chops (trim fat)
B. 2 scallions
C. 2 cups pork or chicken stock
D. 1 cucumber

PREPARATION:

I. Peel D lengthwise. Cut into ½-in. slices, removing all seeds.

II. Tie B into bundle (do not cut).

COOKING:

1. Cook A, B, C in 3-qt. saucepan 30 to 40 minutes or until A is well done.
2. Add D, cook 5 minutes. (If no roughage is permitted, cook 15 minutes).

PORK SOUP
Ro Si Tong: Shanghai

A. 1 can chicken broth
B. 6 Chinese mushrooms
C. 12 golden needles
D. ¼ lb. lean pork, shredded
E. 2 teaspoons light soy sauce
F. ½ cup shredded bamboo shoots
G. 1 scallion
H. 1 teaspoon sherry

PREPARATION:

I. Mix D with E.
II. Wash B, C, soak 15 minutes in warm water. Drain, save water, and add to A.
III. Discard tip (hard part) of C. Cut each into 1-inch pieces.
IV. Shred B.
V. Cut G into 1-inch pieces.

COOKING:

1. Empty A into saucepan, dilute with 1½ cans water and water from B, C. Bring to boil.
2. Add B, C, D–E, G, stir well, cook 2 to 3 minutes. Stir in H; serve hot.

WATERCRESS PORK SOUP I
Si Yang Tsai Tsu Ro Tong: Shanghai

A.　4 cups soup stock
B.　¼ lb. pork loin, shredded
C.　3 slices ginger, minced
D.　1 bunch watercress

E.　1 teaspoon light soy sauce
F.　3 drops sesame oil (optional)
G.　½ teaspoon salt
H.　2 eggs

PREPARATION:

I.　Cut D into 2-in. segments.

II.　Mix E, F, G. Set aside.

COOKING:

1.　Bring A to rapid boil in large saucepot.
2.　Add B, C. Cook 5 minutes.
3.　Add D. Cook 3 minutes without cover.
4.　Add E–G mixture. Stir well. Turn off heat.

5.　Drop H one by one into soup. Let stand 3 minutes.
6.　Serve hot in large soup tureen.

MUSTARD GREENS AND PORK SOUP
Gai Tsoi Ju Yoke Tong: Canton

Substitute 1 lb. mustard greens sliced in 1½-inch segments for D and ¼ lb. sliced pork for B.

HAIRY MELON AND PORK SOUP
Mo Gwa Ju Yoke Tong: Canton

Substitute 1 hairy melon (peeled with potato peeler and diced into ¾-inch cubes) for D and ½ lb. sliced pork for B.

WATERCRESS PORK SOUP II
Si Yong Tsoi Ju Yoke Tong: Canton

A.　13¾-oz. can chicken broth
B.　½ lb. watercress
C.　¼ lb. pork

D.　1 teaspoon light soy sauce
E.　1 teaspoon cornstarch
F.　2 teaspoons sherry

PREPARATION:

I.　Slice C thinly.

II.　Mix together D, E, F; marinate C a few minutes in mixture.

COOKING:

1.　Empty A into saucepan. Add 1 can water.
2.　Add B, bring to boil, and cook over low heat 10 minutes.

3.　Stir in C–F, bring to boil again, cook 5 to 10 minutes, serve hot.

WATERCRESS LIVER SOUP
Si Yong Tsoi Ju Gon Tong: Canton

A.　13¾-oz. can chicken broth
B.　½ lb. watercress
C.　¼ lb. pork liver
D.　1 teaspoon light soy sauce

E.　1 teaspoon cornstarch
F.　2 teaspoons sherry
G.　2 slices ginger, shredded

PREPARATION:

I. Wash C; slice thin.

II. Mix together C, D, E, F, G; marinate a few minutes.

COOKING:

1. Empty A into saucepan. Add 1 can water.
2. Add B, bring to boil, and cook over low heat 10 minutes.

3. Stir in C–G mixture, bring to boil again, cook 2 to 3 minutes, and serve hot.

PORK NOODLE SOUP
Tsu Ro Tong Mein: General

A. 6 cups soup stock
B. ¼ lb. pork loin, shredded
C. ½ lb. fresh noodles
D. 2 teaspoons peanut oil

E. 2 teaspoons light soy sauce
F. few drops sesame oil (optional)
G. 1 teaspoon salt
H. 2 scallions, sliced

PREPARATION:

I. Precook C by dropping into boiling water and cooking for 2 minutes. Drain.

II. Mix D, E, F, G.

COOKING:

1. Bring A to rolling boil.
2. Add B. Cook 5 minutes.

3. Add C and D–G mixture. Mix well. Bring to boil and boil another 5 minutes.
4. Serve with garnish of H.

PORK NOODLE SOUP   Approved Ulcer Recipe
Tsu Ro Tong Mein: General

Substitute ¼ lb. ground pork for B, halve H and tie in bundle for easy removal before serving.

PORK AND TURNIP SOUP
Ro Pien Lo Bo Tong: Shanghai

A. 1 lb. white turnip
B. ¼ lb. pork tenderloin (or boneless lamb)
C. 1 scallion, chopped
D. 2 slices ginger, chopped

E. 2 teaspoons light soy sauce
F. ½ teaspoon sugar
G. 2 teaspoons wine vinegar
H. ¼ teaspoon sesame oil
I. salt, pepper to taste

PREPARATION:

I. Slice B thin, mix with C, D, E, F, G, let stand several minutes.

II. Peel A, cut into bite-size pieces.

COOKING:

1. Place A in cooking pot, add 1 qt. water. Bring to boil, lower heat, and cook 30 minutes, or until tender.

2. Add B–G mixture, bring to boil, cook 1 to 2 minutes.
3. Add H, I. Serve hot.

SPARERIBS CUCUMBER SOUP
Pai Gu Hwang Gwa Tong: Adapted

A. 1 lb. spareribs
B. 3 slices ginger
C. 10 dried shrimp
D. 3 black dried mushrooms
E. salt to taste
F. 1 cucumber
G. 1 scallion, minced

PREPARATION:
I. Cut A into 1½-inch pieces.
II. Soak C in cold water 20 minutes.
III. Peel F and slice.
IV. Soak D in hot water 20 minutes, then slice and remove stems.

COOKING:
1. Place 1½ qts. water in saucepan. Bring to boil.
2. Add A, B, C, D. Simmer 1 hour or until A is done.
3. Add E.
4. Add F, G, simmer 10 minutes. Serve.

HAM AND MELON PATTY SOUP
Fo Twei Dung Gwa Tong: Adapted

A. 13¾-oz. can chicken broth
B. ½ cup diced Smithfield ham
C. 1 lb. Chinese winter melon
D. 2 slices ginger
E. 1 tablespoon sherry
F. salt, pepper to taste

PREPARATION:
I. Discard C skin and seeds. Cut C into bite-size pieces.

COOKING:
1. Empty A into pot, add 1 can water.
2. Add B, C, D, bring to boil, simmer 30 to 45 minutes.
3. Add E, F. Serve hot.

TOMATO, MEAT AND SHRIMP SOUP
Fan Chieh Ro Pien Sha Tze Tong: Shanghai

A. 13¾-oz. can chicken broth
B. ¼ lb. pork
C. 1 teaspoon cornstarch
D. 1 tablespoon sherry
E. ¼ lb. shrimp
F. 2 teaspoons light soy sauce
G. ½ lb. tomatoes
H. few drops sesame oil (optional)
I. 1 to 2 tablespoons chopped scallion

PREPARATION:
I. Cut B into thin slices and mix with C, D.
II. Shell, devein, and wash E. Mince.
III. Pour boiling water over G, let stand for a few seconds. Remove G, peel off skin and cut G into thin slices.

COOKING:
1. Empty A into saucepan, add 1 can of water, bring to a boil.
2. Add B–D mixture, stir well, cook 3 to 5 minutes.
3. Add E, F, stir well and cook 1 minute.
4. Add G and H, turn off heat. Pour into serving bowl.
5. Garnish with I and serve hot.

FLOATING LOTUS SOUP
Leen Fa Tong: Canton

A. ¼ lb. pork, chopped
B. ¼ cup chopped bamboo shoots
C. 1 tablespoon chopped scallion
D. ¼ teaspoon ginger juice (see Index)
E. 1 teaspoon light soy sauce
F. ¼ teaspoon salt
G. 1 teaspoon sherry
H. ½ teaspoon sugar
I. 18 medium Chinese mushrooms
J. 13¾-oz. can chicken broth
K. ½ cup thinly sliced bamboo shoots
L. ½ cup any thinly sliced green leaf vegetable

PREPARATION:

I. Mix A, B, C, D, E, F, G, H and form into 18 balls.

II. Wash I, soak 15 minutes in warm water. Drain (save water).

III. Empty J and I water into 1-qt. jar. Add enough tap water to fill.

IV. Remove I stems. Stuff each I with 1 meatball, pressing each down slightly.

COOKING:

1. Steam A–I 10 minutes over boiling water. Remove from heat.

2. Empty J mixture into pot, bring to boil.

3. Add K, L, cook 1 minute.

4. Add A–I, cook 1 more minute.

PORK MEATBALL SOUP
Yoke Yuan Shiu Tsoi Tong: Canton

A. 1 qt. pork broth
B. 6 dried mushrooms
C. ½ lb. ground pork
D. 1 egg
E. 7 water chestnuts, chopped
F. 3 slices ginger
G. ¾ lb. Chinese celery cabbage (or cauliflower)
H. salt to taste
I. 1 tablespoon minced scallion
J. 2 teaspoons sherry

PREPARATION:

I. Mix C, D, E. Make teaspoon-size balls.

II. Soak B in hot water 20 minutes. Drain, saving water. Remove stems; shred.

III. Cut G into 2-inch pieces.

COOKING:

1. In saucepan bring A and water from B to boil. add C–E mixture, B, F, cook 10 to 15 minutes.

2. Add G, H, I, J, simmer 5 minutes. Serve hot.

SHRIMP MEATBALL SOUP
Har Yuan Tong: Canton

Substitute mixture of ¼ lb. ground pork and ¼ lb. ground fresh shrimp for C.

BEEF MEATBALL SOUP
Ngo Yoke Yuan Tong: Canton

Substitute ½ lb. ground chuck for C, beef broth for A. In Step 1, reduce boiling time to 5 to 10 minutes.

SCALLOP MEATBALL SOUP
Kong Yu Ju Tsoi Fa Tong: Canton

Substitute mixture of ¼ lb. ground fresh scallops and ¼ lb. ground pork for C. Double F.

SPARERIBS SOYBEAN SPROUT SOUP
Pai Gu Dow Ya Tong: General

A. 1½ lbs. spareribs
B. 1½ qts. water
C. ½ lb. bean sprouts (soy)
D. 2 slices ginger
E. salt to taste

F. 1 tablespoon sherry
G. 1 tablespoon chopped scallions
H. ¼ teaspoon sesame oil
I. 2 tablespoons light soy sauce

PREPARATION:

I. Cut A into 1½-inch pieces.

II. Clean C in water so that no shells adhere. Discard tail.

III. Mix H, I.

COOKING:

1. Place A, B in 3-qt. saucepan. Bring to boil.
2. Simmer 1 hour then add C, D, E, F. Continue simmering ½ hour.

3. Add G (optional).
4. Serve ribs with sauce of H, I.

BEEF SHANK SOYBEAN SPROUT SOUP
Wu Hwa Niu Ro Hwang Dow Ya Tong: General

Substitute 1½ lbs. shank for A and cook 1½ to 2 hours in Step 2, before adding C, D, E, F.

PIGS' KNUCKLES WITH DRIED SCALLOP SOUP
Gong Yu Chee Ju Gyok Tong: Canton

A. 2 pigs' knuckles
B. 4 to 6 dried scallops
C. 2 slices ginger

D. 2 tablespoons wine
E. 1½ teaspoons salt

PREPARATION:

I. Cover A with boiling water and boil 30 seconds. Discard water, rinse A under cold water until meat and pot are clean.

II. Wash B well.

COOKING:

1. Add 2 to 3 qts. cold water to A, bring to boil. Skim and discard fatty froth that accumulates on top.
2. Add B, C, D, cook 15 to 20 minutes.

3. Lower heat, simmer until A is tender (about 1 to 1½ hours).
4. Add E; serve hot.

PIGS' FEET BEANSPROUT SOUP
Tsu Jio Dow Ya Tong: Shanghai

A. 2 to 3 pigs' feet
B. 3 slices ginger
C. ½ lb. soybean sprouts

D. 1½ teaspoons salt
E. 1 tablespoon sherry

COOKING:

1. Wash and clean A thoroughly, cut into 1- to 2-inch pieces. Cover with 3 qts. water, bring to boil.

2. Add B, lower heat and simmer 2 hours.
3. Add C and cook for another half hour.
4. Add D, E, and serve hot.

PIGS' FEET WITH DRIED BEAN CURD SOUP
Ju Gyok Tiem Jook Tong: Adapted

A.   3 to 4 pigs' feet
B.   2 slices ginger
C.   1 scallion

D.   10 sheets dried bean curd
E.   salt to taste

PREPARATION:

I. Wash A well. Place in 4-qt. saucepan.

II. Soak D in hot water 30 minutes. Drain, cut crosswise into pieces 1 inch wide.

COOKING:

1. Cover A, B, C with 3 qts. water, bring to boil, simmer 2 hours. Remove all large pieces of bone.

2. Add D, cook another 20 to 30 minutes. Add E. Serve hot.

PIGS' FEET WITH PEANUT SOUP
Ju Gyok Fa Sun Tong: Adapted

A.   3 to 4 pigs' feet
B.   2 slices ginger
C.   1 scallion

D.   1 cup fresh peanuts
E.   3 qts. water
F.   salt to taste

PREPARATION:

I. Wash A well. Place in 4-qt. saucepan.

II. Soak E in hot water 15 minutes; remove skin.

COOKING:

1. Cover A, B, C, D with E, bring to boil, skim and discard fatty froth, simmer 2 hours.

2. Add F. Serve hot.

PORK TAIL PEANUT SOUP
Ju Mei Fa Sun Tong: Canton

A.   1 lb. pork tail
B.   1 cup skinless, raw peanuts
C.   1 scallion

D.   1 to 1½ teaspoons salt
E.   1 tablespoon sherry (optional)

PREPARATION:

I. Wash A well, cut into 1-inch pieces, and place in cooking pot.

II. Cover with water, bring to boil; let boil 1 to 2 minutes and then discard water and wash A and pot.

COOKING:

1. Combine A, B, C in pot, add 2 qts. water, bring to boil.

2. Reduce heat, simmer 1½ to 2 hours.
3. Add D, E and serve.

SEAWEED SOUP
Jee Tsoi Tong: Canton

A. 1½ cups soup stock
B. 3 thin sheets purple seaweed
C. 1 tablespoon sherry
D. 1 slice ginger, minced

E. 1 egg
F. 1 tablespoon water
G. 2 scallions, sliced

PREPARATION:

I. Cut B into ½-inch slivers with kitchen shears or scissors.

II. Mix C, D. Set aside.
III. Mix E, F. Beat lightly.

COOKING:

1. Heat A to boiling.
2. Add B. Stir 15 seconds.
3. Add C–D mixture. Stir well.

4. Bring to boil again. Remove from heat and slowly pour in E–F mixture, stirring constantly.
5. Serve in soup tureen with garnish of G.

SLICED FISH WITH VEGETABLE SOUP
Yu Pien Tong: Adapted

A. 13¾-oz. can chicken broth
B. 2 slices ginger
C. 4 Chinese mushrooms
D. ½ cup sliced bamboo shoots
E. Chinese cabbage heart (few stalks)
F. ½ lb. flounder fillet
G. 1 tablespoon chopped scallion

H. 1 teaspoon ginger juice (see Index)
I. ½ teaspoon salt
J. ½ teaspoon sugar
K. 2 teaspoons sherry
L. 1 tablespoon cornstarch
M. 1 tablespoon water
N. few drops sesame oil

PREPARATION:

I. Slice F into thin pieces, mix well with H, I, J, K, L, M, N.
II. Dilute A with 1 can water.

III. Wash C in warm water and soak 15 minutes; drain and cut each in half.
IV. Cut E into 1-inch-long pieces.

COOKING:

1. Bring A to boil, add B, C, D, cook 3 minutes.
2. Add E and cook 1 minute.

3. Add F mixture and G; boil ½ to 1 minute.
4. Serve hot.

WATERCRESS FISH FILLET SOUP
Si Yong Tsoi Yu Pien Tong: Canton

A. 13¾-oz. can chicken broth
B. ½ lb. watercress
C. ¼ lb. flounder fillet
D. 1 teaspoon light soy sauce

E. 1 teaspoon cornstarch
F. ¼ teaspoon sesame oil
G. ⅛ teaspoon pepper
H. 2 teaspoons sherry

PREPARATION:

I. Rinse C, slice ¼ inch thick.

II. Mix C, D, E, F, G; marinate a few minutes.

COOKING:

1. Empty A into saucepan. Add 1 can water.
2. Add B, bring to boil, cook over low heat 10 minutes.

3. Stir in C–G, bring to boil again, add H, cook 1 to 2 more minutes. Serve hot.

FISH BALLS AND HAM SOUP
Yu Yuen Fo Twei Tong: Canton

A. 13¾-oz. can chicken broth
B. 6 Chinese mushrooms, shredded
C. ½ cup shredded bamboo shoots
D. ½ cup shredded Chinese cabbage
E. 2 slices ginger

F. 18 to 20 fish balls
   (see Tangerine Fish Balls)
G. ½ cup shredded Virginia ham
H. 1 scallion
I. salt to taste

PREPARATION:

I. Wash B, soak 15 minutes in warm water. Drain, save water, and add it to A.

II. Cut E and H into 1-inch pieces.

COOKING:

1. Place A (with B water added) in cooking pot; add 1 cup water, bring to boil.
2. Add B, C, D, E, cook 2 to 3 minutes.

3. Add F, G, H, cook 1 more minute. Add I. Serve hot.

ABALONE SOUP WITH BLACK MUSHROOMS
Bao Yu Dung Gu Tong: General

A. ½ cup abalone liquid
B. 5 cups soup stock
C. 4 large dried black mushrooms
D. 1 cup thinly sliced pork loin

E. ½ can (8 oz.) abalone
F. 1 tablespoon light soy sauce
G. ½ teaspoon salt
H. 3 drops sesame oil (optional)

PREPARATION:

I. Soak C in hot water 15 minutes. Squeeze dry, and cut into strips.

II. Cut E into slices. Save liquid for A above (and for other recipes). Mix E, F, G.

COOKING:

1. Pour A into a pot and add B. Heat to boiling.
2. Add C, D. Cook over low heat 10 minutes.

3. Add E–G. Continue to cook 2 minutes only.
4. Add H. Serve.

PRESERVED MUSTARD GREENS OYSTER SOUP
Shien Tsai Sun How Tong: General

A. 1 tablespoon peanut oil
B. ½ cup shredded preserved mustard greens
   (use stem only)
C. 3 slices ginger
D. 3 cups chicken broth
E. 1 tablespoon dry sherry

F. ¼ cup thinly sliced pork
G. 1 teaspoon cornstarch
H. 1 teaspoon light soy sauce
I. ½ pint oysters
J. 1 teaspoon salt

PREPARATION:

I. Mix F, G, H.

II. Rub I with J lightly in a colander; then rinse under cold water a few seconds. Drain.

COOKING:

1. Heat A, add B, C, stir-fry ½ minute.
2. Add D; bring to a boil.
3. Add E–H, cook 1 minute.

4. Add I and cook 2 to 3 more minutes; serve hot.

SPECIAL SHARK FIN SOUP
Song Gwan Yu Chi Gung: General

A. 1½ qts. chicken broth
B. 1 oz. shark fins
C. 2 tablespoons Smithfield ham shredded
D. ⅛ teaspoon pepper
E. ½ teaspoon salt
F. 6 Chinese mushrooms
G. ⅓ cup shredded bamboo shoots

H. ½ chicken breast (½ cup shredded chicken white meat)
I. 1 teaspoon cornstarch
J. 1 teaspoon light soy sauce
K. 3 tablespoons water chestnut flour mixed with ¼ cup water
L. 1 egg, beaten
M. 3 slices ginger

PREPARATION:

I. Soak B in cold water overnight; wash and clean well. Put B, M into 3 cups boiling water; bring to boil; simmer covered 30 minutes. Remove from heat and cook with cover on until water is cooled. Drain; rinse in cold water.
II. Mix H, I, J.
III. Rinse F, soak in warm water for 15 minutes; shred.

COOKING:

1. Bring A to boil; add B, C, D, E; lower heat and cook 1 hour.
2. Add F, G; cook 10 more minutes.
3. Add H–J mixture, cook 1 minute. Thicken with K so shark fins will float.
4. Add L gradually, stirring at the same time. Serve hot.

LOBSTER AND SWEET CORN THICK SOUP
Lung Sha Yu Mi Gung: Fukien

A. 1 cup water
B. 4 slices ginger, chopped
C. 3 tablespoons peanut oil
D. ½ cup tender raw corn kernels
E. 8-oz. pkg. frozen lobster

F. 1 teaspoon salt
G. 2 teaspoons sherry
H. 1 tablespoon cornstarch
I. 1 egg white
J. 1 tablespoon chopped scallion

PREPARATION:

I. Defrost E, squeeze out water, break into small pieces.

II. Beat I slightly.
III. Mix H with ¼ cup water.

COOKING:

1. Mix A, B, bring to a boil.
2. Heat C, stir-fry D 1 minute. Add to A–B mixture, cook 10 minutes.
3. Add E, F, G, cook 2 to 3 more minutes.
4. Add H mixture to thicken.
5. Gradually stir in I. Garnish with J. Mix well, serve hot.

CRAB MEAT CORN SOUP
Hai Yung Shok Mai Gung: Canton

A. 13¾-oz. can chicken broth
B. 8-oz. can corn kernels
C. ¼ teaspoon ginger juice (see Index)
D. ½ to 1 cup crab meat

E. 2 teaspoons sherry
F. ¼ cup chopped celery
G. 1 tablespoon cornstarch
H. 1 egg white

PREPARATION:

I. Mix G with 2 tablespoons water.

II. Beat H well.

COOKING:

1. Empty A into pot, add 1 can water, and bring to boil.
2. Add B, C, cook 5 minutes.
3. Add D, E, F, cook 3 minutes.
4. Thicken with G mixture. Remove from heat.
5. Slowly stir in H and serve hot.

HOT AND SOUR SOUP I
Swan La Tong: Szechuan

A. 13¾-oz. can chicken broth
B. ¼ cup shredded preserved kohlrabi
C. ½ cup shredded roast or fresh pork
D. ½ cup shredded bamboo shoots
E. 2 dried Chinese mushrooms
F. 2 soybean cakes
G. 2 tablespoons cider vinegar
H. 1 teaspoon light soy sauce
I. 2 tablespoons cornstarch

PREPARATION:

I. Wash red powder off B before shredding.

II. Soak E in warm water 20 minutes, remove and discard stems, shred.

III. Slice F very thin.

IV. Mix G, H, I until there are no lumps.

COOKING:

1. Dilute A with 1 can water, boil, add B, and cook 5 minutes.
2. Add C, D, E and boil 1 minute.
3. Add F.
4. When soup boils again, thicken with G–I.

HOT AND SOUR SOUP II
Swan La Tong: Szechuan

A. 3 cups soup stock
B. ⅛ cup dried cloud ears
C. 3 sheets dried bean curd
D. 8 small dried black mushrooms
E. ¼ cup water chestnuts
F. 2 tablespoons cornstarch
G. ½ cup water
H. 1 tablespoon light soy sauce
I. 1 teaspoon Chinese hot sauce
J. 1½ tablespoons vinegar
K. 1 egg
L. 1 teaspoon water

PREPARATION:

I. Separately soak B, C, D in 1 cup hot water each.

II. When soft, cut each sheet of C into eight pieces.

III. When soft, slice D into several slivers.

IV. Slice E. Mix with B, C, D.

V. Mix F, G. Set aside. Stir well before using.

VI. Mix H, I, J. Set aside.

VII. Beat K lightly and then mix with L. Set aside.

COOKING:

1. Heat A over high heat.
2. Add B–E mixture and continue to heat until soup boils.
3. Add F–G slowly, stirring constantly as soup thickens.
4. Add H–J mixture. Stir well.
5. When soup is again boiling vigorously, turn off heat and pour in K–L mixture slowly so as to obtain egg drop consistency.
6. Serve.

HOT AND SOUR SOUP III
Swan La Tong: Adapted

A.   13¾-oz. can chicken broth
B.   ¼ cup chopped ham
C.   1 stalk celery, diced
D.   1 tomato
E.   juice of ½ lemon

F.   ½ teaspoon black pepper
G.   2 tablespoons cornstarch mixed with
     ⅔ cup water
H.   1 egg, beaten

PREPARATION:

I. Dilute A with 1 can of water.

II. Peel and dice D.

COOKING:

1. Bring A to boil; add B, C, D.
2. Bring to boil again; add E, F.

3. Pour in G, stir until soup thickens.
4. Remove from heat; stir in H.

5. Serve hot.

HOT AND SOUR SOUP IV
Swan La Tong: Peking

A.   13¾-oz. can chicken broth
B.   4 wood ears
C.   12 golden needles
D.   2 Chinese mushrooms
E.   ¼ cup shredded preserved kohlrabi
F.   ½ cup shredded pork
G.   2 cakes bean curd
H.   2 tablespoons vinegar

I.   1 tablespoon light soy sauce
J.   1 teaspoon sugar
K.   ½ to 1 teaspoon pepper
L.   2 tablespoons cornstarch mixed with
     ¼ cup water
M.   1 egg, beaten
N.   2 scallions
O.   sesame oil to taste

PREPARATION:

I. Cover B with hot water and soak 15 to 30 minutes or until soft.
II. Discard water, wash and shred B.
III. Soak C in cold water for 15 to 20 minutes until soft; discard the hard tips, cut each

into 2 or 3 segments.
IV. Wash D in warm water and soak 15 minutes; shred; save water and add it to A.
V. Chop white part of N.
VI. Slice and shred G. Mix H, I, J, K.

COOKING:

1. In saucepan, dilute A with 1 can water plus mushroom water; bring to boil.
2. Add B, C, D, E and cook for 8 minutes.
3. Add F, cook 1 minute.

4. Add G and H–K; cook ½ minute.
5. Thicken with L.
6. Remove from heat; slowly stir in M.
7. Add N–O; serve hot.

HOT AND SOUR SOUP   *Approved Diabetic Recipe*
Swan La Tong: Szechuan

A.   ¼ cup shredded pork
B.   ¼ cup shredded bamboo shoots
C.   2 water chestnuts, shredded
D.   1 to 2 Chinese mushrooms
E.   1 cake bean curd
F.   1 tablespoon vinegar

G.   ¼ teaspoon red pepper sauce
H.   1½ teaspoons light soy sauce
I.   1 teaspoon cornstarch mixed with
     1 tablespoon water
J.   1 egg, beaten

PREPARATION:

I. Wash and soak D in hot water 15 minutes. Drain, save water, shred.

II. Slice E into thin pieces.

COOKING:

1. Add water to D water to make 1½ cups, bring to boil. Add A, B, C, D, cook 2 minutes.
2. Add E, F, G, H; when mixture boils again

add I, continue stirring until thick.

3. Turn off heat, stir in J gradually.
4. Serve hot.

FAMILY STYLE HOT AND SOUR SOUP
Ga Shong Shuen La Tong: Adapted

A. 13¾-oz. can chicken broth
B. ¼ cup shredded preserved kohlrabi
C. ½ cup shredded pork (or veal or beef)
D. 3 Chinese mushrooms
E. ½ cup shredded bamboo shoots
F. 2 cakes bean curd

G. 2 tablespoons vinegar
H. 2 teaspoons light soy sauce
I. 2 tablespoons cornstarch
J. pepper to taste
K. 1 egg, beaten

PREPARATION:

I. Wash D in warm water and soak 15 minutes; drain, save water and add to A. Shred.

II. Slice F, then shred.
III. Mix G, H, I, J.

COOKING:

1. Dilute A with a can of water and mushroom water, bring to a boil, add B and cook 5 minutes.
2. Add C, D, E, cook 1 minute.

3. Add F. When soup boils again, thicken with G–J; turn off heat.
4. Slowly stir in K; serve hot.

SQUID IN HOT AND SOUR SOUP
Swan La Yo Yu Tong: Szechuan

A. 13¾-oz. can chicken broth
B. 1 dried squid
C. ¼ cup shredded preserved kohlrabi
D. ½ cup shredded roast pork
E. ½ cup shredded bamboo shoots
F. 2 cakes bean curd
G. 2 tablespoons cider vinegar

H. 1 teaspoon light soy sauce
I. 2 scallions
J. salt to taste
K. 2 tablespoons cornstarch mixed with ¼ cup cold water
L. ½ teaspoon baking soda

PREPARATION:

I. Soak B overnight, remove soft bones and membrane. Change water. Add L, cover, and boil 30 minutes. Then soak ½ hour, drain

and rinse. Shred B.

II. Mix C, D, E.
III. Slice F into thin pieces.

COOKING:

1. Mix A with 1 can water. Bring to boil. Add B and C–E, cook 1 minute.
2. Add F, G, H, I, boil again.

3. Adjust with J and then, stirring gradually, add K. When soup has thickened, it is ready to serve.

HOT AND SOUR FISH WITH SOUP
Swan La Yu Tong: Adapted

A. 4 tablespoons vegetable oil
B. 1 to 2 lbs. sea bass
C. 4 cups pork soup
D. 1 tablespoon minced scallion
E. 4 slices ginger, minced
F. 2 teaspoons sherry

G. 1 tablespoon light soy sauce
H. 2 tablespoons cider vinegar
I. ¼ teaspoon Chinese hot sauce
J. 1 tablespoon cornstarch
K. 1 teaspoon salt
L. handful Chinese parsley (optional)

PREPARATION:

I. Clean B, slash skin diagonally at 1-inch intervals, and rub with K inside and out.

II. Place aluminum foil on broiling pan. Place B on top.
III. Mix J with ¼ cup water in small bowl.

COOKING:

1. Pour A over B. Place in broiler, broil 10 minutes. When slightly browned, turn over and broil 10 more minutes.
2. Place C in a Dutch oven, bring to boil. Add D, E, F, G.

3. Add B, cover and simmer 30 minutes.
4. Add H, I, J (with water); bring to boil.
5. Top with L. Serve hot.

TRIPLE SOUP I
San Sien Tong: Canton

A. 13¾-oz. can chicken broth
B. ½ cup diced deveined shrimp
C. ½ cup shredded pork
D. ½ cup shredded bamboo shoots

E. 1 teaspoon sherry
F. 2 teaspoons light soy sauce
G. pepper to taste

COOKING:

1. Empty A into a pot, add 1 can water.
2. Add B, C, D, bring to boil, and cook 3 to 5 minutes.

3. Add E, F, G, and serve hot.

TRIPLE SOUP   *Approved Diabetic Recipe*
San Sien Tong: Canton

A. 1 qt. dietetic chicken broth
B. ¼ cup shredded pork
C. ¼ cup diced, deveined shrimp

D. 12 snow peas
E. 1 teaspoon light soy sauce
F. pepper to taste

PREPARATION:

I. Remove D tips. D may be used whole or cut into two from end to end.

COOKING:

1. Empty A into saucepan; bring to boil.
2. Add B, C, cook 3 to 5 minutes.

3. Add D, cook 1 minute uncovered.
4. Add E, F, serve hot.

TRIPLE SOUP II
San Sien Tong: Shanghai

A. 13¾-oz. can chicken broth
B. ½ cup shredded abalone
C. ½ cup shredded Smithfield ham

D. ½ cup shredded white meat chicken
E. salt to taste
F. few drops sesame oil

COOKING:

1. Empty A into a pot, add 1 can water, and bring to boil.
2. Add B, C, D, mix well, cover, and bring back to boil.

3. Cook 1 to 2 minutes. Remove fatty foam from top, and discard.
4. Add E, F, and serve hot.

TRIPLE SOUP   *Approved Diabetic Recipe*
San Sien Tong: Shanghai

A. 1½ cups water
B. ½ to 1 teaspoon salt
C. ½ cup shredded abalone

D. ¼ cup shredded Virginia ham
E. ¼ cup shredded white meat chicken
F. few drops sesame oil

PREPARATION:

I. Combine A, B in saucepan.

COOKING:

1. Bring A–B to boil.
2. Add C, D, E, mix well, cover and cook 2 to 3

minutes, remove foamy froth.
3. Add F and serve hot.

YANGCHOW TRIPLE SOUP
San Si Tong: Yang Chow

A. ½ lb. lean pork
B. 1 scallion
C. 2 slices ginger
D. 13¾-oz. can chicken broth diluted with pork broth from I below

E. 1 egg
F. 3 Chinese mushrooms
G. ¼ cup shredded cooked ham
H. ¼ cup shredded chicken meat
I. 1 tablespoon sherry

PREPARATION:

I. Shred A, and dip in boiling water; remove immediately.
II. Beat E well, pour into hot greased pan, and spread as evenly as possible by tipping pan. When set, remove and shred.
III. Soak F in warm water 15 minutes, drain, and

remove stems.
IV. Cut B into 2-inch pieces.
V. Place F in bottom of small bowl, arrange E, G, H, along edge of bowl and place A in center.
VI. Spread B, C, I and 2 tablespoons D on top.

COOKING:

1. Steam A mixture in steamer over boiling water 35 minutes, discard B, C.
2. Bring D to boil.

3. Just before serving invert small bowl containing A mixture into large soup bowl. Add boiling D.

VEGETARIAN TRIPLE SOUP
Sue San Sien Tong: Shanghai

A. ½ cup sliced bamboo shoots
B. 1 cup fresh mushrooms
C. ¼ cup chopped preserved red-in-snow

D. 2-3 cups water
E. 1 teaspoon salt

PREPARATION:

I. Wash B, cut each into 3 to 4 pieces.

COOKING:

1. Place A, B, C in a pot, cover with D, and bring to boil.
2. Cover, cook over low heat 10 minutes.
3. Add E and serve.

SEA OF TRANQUILLITY SOUP
Ping On Dun Rieh Tong: Adapted

A. 1 large Chinese mushroom
B. ¾ cup shredded baked Virginia ham
C. ½ cup shredded bamboo shoots
D. ¼ cup shredded abalone

E. ¾ cup shredded cooked chicken meat
F. 3 to 4 cups chicken broth
G. salt to taste
H. 1 tablespoon chopped scallion

PREPARATION AND COOKING:

I. Wash A and soak in warm water 15 minutes or until soft; save the water and mix with F.
II. Place A, topside down, in center of shallow bowl; arrange B in 3 strips like the spokes of a wheel.
III. In two sections place C and in the third place D. Mushroom forms a hub, B forms the 3 spokes and C and D the background.
IV. Spread E over the top.
V. Steam over boiling water 10 minutes.
VI. Place a large soup bowl over the bowl with A mixture; invert.
VII. Just before serving, pour boiling F over mixture, add G and garnish with H.

FRIED NOODLES WITH SHREDDED MEAT SOUP
Yoke Si Yee Fu Mein: Adapted

A. 3 tablespoons peanut oil
B. ¼ lb. beef (pork or chicken), shredded
C. 1 carrot
D. 1 stalk celery, shredded
E. 1 cup shredded cabbage
F. 1 teaspoon salt
G. 2 pkgs. noodles (Yee fu mein) with soup base (or water and canned chicken broth to make qt.)

H. pepper to taste
I. 2 teaspoons chopped scallion
J. 2 slices ginger, chopped
K. 1 teaspoon cornstarch
L. 2 teaspoons light soy sauce
M. ¼ teaspoon sugar
N. few drops sesame oil

PREPARATION:

I. Mix B with I, J, K, L, M, N.
II. Peel C, slice, then shred.
III. Bring 1½ cups water to boil; add G, stir until noodles are loosened; add soup base and cook 3 to 4 minutes.

COOKING:

1. Heat 2 tablespoons A, add B mixture, stir-fry 1 to 2 minutes; remove to dish.
2. Heat 1 tablespoon A, add C, D, E, stir-fry 2 minutes; add F, and 1 to 2 tablespoons water, if necessary.
3. Add B mixture, stir well, cook ½ minute longer.
4. Add G, mix well.
5. Add H and serve hot.

SWEET CONGEE I
Tien Shi Fan: Shanghai

A. 20 dried lotus seeds
B. ½ cup glutinous rice
C. ½ cup dried longans or raisins
D. 10 Chinese or American dates
E. 2 tablespoons brown sugar

PREPARATION:

I. Cover A with hot water and soak for 30 to 45 minutes.
II. Place A, B in 3-qt. saucepan.
III. Add 2 qts. water.
IV. Add C, D.

COOKING:

1. Simmer 1 hour. Add 1½ to 2 cups water if needed.
2. When consistency is mushy, it is done. Add E.

SWEET CONGEE II
Tien Tso: General

A. ½ cup glutinous rice
B. ½ cup raisins
C. ½ cup American dates
D. 2 tablespoons brown sugar
E. 6 Bing cherries

COOKING:

1. Put A, B, C in 3-qt. saucepan. Add 2 qts. water, simmer 1 hour.
2. Add 1½ to 2 cups water and D (optional). When congee is mushy and soft, serve in bowl, adding E on top for color.

CONGEE   Approved Ulcer Recipe
Jook: Canton

A. ½ cup rice
B. ¼ lb. pork liver
C. 1 teaspoon heavy soy sauce
D. ¼ lb. ground lean chuck
E. 1 tablespoon light soy sauce
F. salt to taste

PREPARATION:

I. Slice B, removing white membrane and tough bloodvessels. Chop very fine into a puree.

COOKING:

1. Cook A with 6 cups water; simmer 1 hour. Add more water when congee becomes thick.
2. Add B, cook 15 minutes.
3. Add C.
4. Mix D into boiling congee.
5. Add E, F, mix well. Serve warm.

TRADITIONAL CONGEE
Shi Fan: General

A. 20 cups water
B. 2 cups rice
C. kettle of boiling water (add as necessary for desired consistency)
D. 4 tablespoons light soy sauce
E. 3 slices ginger, minced
F. 2 teaspoons heavy soy sauce

G. 1 tablespoon peanut oil
H. 1 teaspoon salt
I. 4 dried Chinese black mushrooms
J. ½ cup ginkgo nuts (optional)
K. 9 tablespoons water
L. 3 tablespoons cornstarch
M. 6 scallions, chopped

PREPARATION:

I. Wash B.
II. Soak I in warm water 15 minutes. Add water to A.

III. Mix D, E, F, G, H. Set aside.
IV. Mix K, L. Set aside. Stir well before using.

COOKING:

1. Bring A to boil.
2. Add B. Simmer 90 minutes or more until a thin paste is formed. Stir every 10 minutes, avoiding the very bottom.
3. Add C to thin congee toward completion of Step 2.

4. Add D–H mixture. Add I, J. Continue to simmer 30 minutes.
5. If necessary, add K–L slowly to thicken.
6. Serve congee in individual bowls with liberal sprinkling of M over each. Serves 8 to 10.

CHICKEN CONGEE I
Gai Jook: Canton

A. 2-lb. chicken
B. ½ cup rice
C. 2 qts. water
D. 1 scallion, chopped
E. 2 slices ginger, chopped

F. 1 tablespoon light soy sauce
G. ¼ teaspoon sesame oil
H. ½ of 12-oz. can abalone, sliced thin
I. salt, pepper to taste

PREPARATION:

I. Wash A, B well.

COOKING:

1. Place A, B, C in large pot, bring to boil, cover, simmer 1½ hours.
2. Remove A; bone. Mix boned A with D, E, F.

3. Add mixture A–F and G, H to B–C.
4. Bring to boil, stirring constantly. Add I. Serve hot.

CHICKEN CONGEE II
Gai Jook: Canton

A. 1 to 2 lbs. chicken parts
B. 3 qts. water
C. ½ cup rice
D. 2 tablespoons glutinous rice
E. 2 tablespoons light soy sauce
F. 3 slices ginger, minced

G. 1 teaspoon heavy soy sauce
H. 1 tablespoon peanut oil
I. 1 teaspoon salt
J. 4 dried Chinese black mushrooms
K. ½ cup ginkgo nuts (optional)
L. 2 scallions, chopped

PREPARATION:

I. Chop A into 1-inch segments.

II. Combine C, D and wash.

III. Soak J in warm water 15 minutes. Reserve water as part of B.

IV. Mix E, F, G, H, I. Set aside.

COOKING:

1. Place A in very large, heavy cooking utensil, at least 8-qt. capacity (or scale down all proportions of recipe).

2. Add B, C, D. Bring to boil and simmer 60 minutes. Stir every 10 minutes but do not scrape the very bottom. Add boiling water as necessary for thinning.

3. Add E–I mixture. Add J, K. Continue to simmer 30 minutes.

4. Serve congee and chicken parts in individual bowls with liberal sprinkling of L over each.

CHICKEN CONGEE WITH FERMENTED BEAN CAKE
Fu Yu Gai Jook: Canton

Serve 4 to 5 cakes (about a teaspoon each, with bean juice from jar) well mashed, in side dish to be added to congee to taste.

CHICKEN CONGEE WITH EGG DROP
Dan Fa Gai Jook: Canton

Slowly add 2 lightly beaten eggs just before Step 4 to obtain egg drop effect.

CHICKEN CONGEE III
Gee Tso: Peking

A. 1 qt. chicken soup

B. ½ cup rice

C. 2 qts. water

D. 2 tablespoons light soy sauce

E. 3 slices ginger, shredded

F. 1 tablespoon sesame oil

G. 3 scallions

H. salt to taste

I. black pepper to taste

J. 8 fried puffs (see Index)

PREPARATION:

I. Wash B.

II. Combine D, E, F, G.

III. Cut J into ½-inch segments.

COOKING:

1. Place A, B, C in a large, heavy cooking utensil. Bring to boil. Lower heat and simmer 60 minutes. Stir every 10 minutes to avoid scorching bottom of congee.

2. Add additional water when congee becomes too thick. Cook 30 minutes more.

3. Add D–G mixture and adjust with H, I. Serve in individual bowls, sprinkle with J.

DUCK CONGEE
Ya Tso: Shanghai

A. 4 Chinese mushrooms
B. ¼ cup chopped Virginia ham
C. ½ cup raw, skinless peanuts
D. ½ cup glutinous rice

E. 13¾-oz. can chicken broth
F. 1 duck breast
G. 2 teaspoons sherry
H. ½ teaspoon salt

PREPARATION:

I. Bone F and cut into cubes, drop into boiling water, let stand 30 seconds, drain.
II. Mix F, G, H, steam over boiling water 1 hour. Save liquid.

III. Wash A, soak in warm water 15 minutes. Drain, saving water. Add water to E to make 2 qts. liquid. Quarter each A.
IV. Wash C, D; drain.

COOKING:

1. Combine A, B, C, D, E, add liquid from steamed F, and bring to boil. Reduce heat, simmer 1 hour.

2. Add F pieces, serve hot, and garnish with Chinese parsley.

BEEF CONGEE
Ngo Yoke Jook: Canton

A. ½ cup rice
B. ½ lb. beef, shredded
C. 1 tablespoon chopped scallion
D. 2 slices ginger, chopped
E. 1 tablespoon light soy sauce

F. ½ teaspoon sugar
G. 1½ teaspoons cornstarch
H. 1½ teaspoons salt
I. ¼ teaspoon sesame oil
J. pepper to taste

PREPARATION:

I. Wash A, drain.

II. Mix B with C, D, E, F, G. Marinate ½ hour.

COOKING:

1. Cover A with 2 qts. of water and bring to boil.
2. After A has cooked 1¼ hours, add B–G mixture. Turn heat high and stir constantly until

each piece of beef is separated. Lower heat and cook 10 minutes. Add H, I, J. Serve hot.

PORK CONGEE
Ju Yoke Jook: Canton

A. 2 tablespoons peanut oil
B. 1 lb. pork
C. ⅛ teaspoon garlic powder
D. 2 teaspoons light soy sauce
E. 2 teaspoons heavy soy sauce
F. 15 cups soup stock
G. 2 cups rice
H. kettle of boiling water (to be added if necessary)
I. 4 tablespoons light soy sauce

J. 3 slices ginger, minced
K. 2 teaspoons heavy soy sauce
L. 1 tablespoon peanut oil
M. 1 teaspoon salt
N. 4 dried Chinese black mushrooms
O. ½ cup ginkgo nuts (optional)
P. 9 tablespoons water
Q. 3 tablespoons cornstarch
R. 6 scallions, chopped

PREPARATION:

   I. Wash G.

   II. Soak N in warm water 15 minutes; reserve water to use as part of F.

   III. Slice N into slivers and grind or slice B into slivers.

   IV. Mix I, J, K, L, M and set aside.

   V. Mix P, Q; set aside; stir well before using.

COOKING:

1. Place A in very hot skillet and bring to high heat.
2. Add B; stir-fry 1 minute.
3. Add C, D, E; stir-fry 5 minutes; turn off heat and set skillet and contents aside.
4. Bring F and G to boil in heavy large cooking utensil and simmer 90 minutes or more until rice and liquid form a thin paste; stir every 10 minutes, avoid scraping the bottom.
5. Have H available to thin the congee toward completion of Step 4.
6. Add B–E to congee.
7. Add I–M, then N, O; continue to simmer 30 minutes.
8. Keep P–Q available to add in slowly to thicken mixture—but only if necessary.
9. Serve congee in individual bowls with liberal sprinkling of R over top of each. Serves 10.

FISH CONGEE
Yu San Jook: Canton

A. ½ cup rice

B. 13¾-oz. can chicken broth plus 1½ qts. water

C. ½ lb. flounder fillet

D. 1 scallion, chopped

E. 2 slices ginger, chopped

F. 1 egg white

G. 2 teaspoons cornstarch

H. ½ teaspoon salt

I. few drops sesame oil

J. salt, pepper to taste

K. Chinese parsley leaves

PREPARATION:

   I. Wash A, drain.

   II. Slice C into ½-inch by 2-inch pieces.

   III. Mix C, D, E, F, G; let stand.

COOKING:

1. Mix A, B in 3-qt. pot, bring to boil. Lower heat, cover, simmer 1½ hours.
2. Five minutes before serving, bring A, B to boil. Add C–G. Turn heat high, stir gently and constantly 5 minutes.
3. Add H, I, J; garnish with K. Serve hot.

EGGS

Eggs are seldom served alone (soft-boiled or fried), as in the West. Because when they are raw they mix easily with other ingredients and yet solidify upon cooking, they are often used by the Chinese to give body to certain soft foods and to bind other ingredients—as with foo yong, or omelet dishes.

Omelets require only small amounts of expensive foods such as meat, fish, shellfish, or poultry, and yet create a dish high in protein content. Sometimes omelets are shredded into strips to be used as a garnish for main dishes and soups, largely because of their color rather than for their nutritional or taste value.

Many Chinese egg dishes are steamed, mixed with a variety of seasonings and flavorings, including many additional substantial ingredients. Often such dishes are very salty or highly seasoned, and these relatively solid but easily mixable concoctions are served over a bowl of rice.

SIMPLE SHRIMP OMELET
Sha Mi Tsao Don: Adapted

A. ¼ cup vegetable oil
B. 5 eggs
C. 1 oz. dried shrimp (about 30)
    or 3 dried scallops

D. 1 teaspoon salt
E. 2 scallions, minced

PREPARATION:

I. Soak C in hot water 20 minutes. Drain, save water; chop.

II. Break B. Add C, D, E, and whip. Add 2 tablespoons water from Step I.

COOKING:

1. Heat A in hot skillet.

2. Add B–E mixture to A. Stir-fry 3 to 7 minutes (according to preference).

SIMPLE MUSHROOM OMELET
Dung Gu Tsao Don: Adapted

Substitute 3 to 5 dried mushrooms for C.

FANCY OMELET
Gee Don Bing: General

A. ¼ cup vegetable oil
B. 4 oz. pork (or leftover chicken or white turkey meat), shredded
C. 2 teaspoons light soy sauce
D. 2 slices ginger, shredded

E. 6 dried Chinese mushrooms
F. 10-oz. pkg. frozen peas
G. 6 eggs
H. 1 teaspoon salt

PREPARATION:

I. Defrost F.
II. Soak E in hot water 20 minutes, drain, save water. Slice each E into 3 pieces.

III. Break G into bowl, beat, and add H.
IV. Marinate B with C, D.

COOKING:

1. Using high heat, add 2 tablespoons A to hot skillet. Add B–D mixture, stir-fry 1 minute. If water is needed, add some from soaking mushrooms. Add E, F, continue stir-frying 1 to 2 minutes. Remove to bowl.

2. Add remaining A to cleaned skillet. Use high heat. Add G–H mixture to pan without stirring. Allow skin to form. Lower heat when skin thickens.

3. Add A–F mixture to half of pan. Fold over G–H skin so that it forms a pouch. Serve hot.

FANCY OMELET
Yang Tsung Ro Si Don Jiao: General

Substitute 1 medium onion for F. Omit E. In Step 1, wash and skin onion, slice into rings, and cook onion and B together 3 to 5 minutes. Add small amount of water when needed. Remove to bowl.

FANCY OMELET
Ching Do Sha Ding Don Jiao: General

Substitute fresh shrimp for B. In Step IV, shell, devein, and dice shrimp. Marinate with C, D and 1 teaspoon sherry.

CRAB OMELET
Pong Shia Tsao Don: General

A. ¼ cup peanut oil
B. 7-oz. can crab meat (or lobster)
C. 6 eggs

D. 2 slices ginger
E. 1 scallion
F. 1 teaspoon salt
G. few drops hot sauce

PREPARATION:

I. Chop D, E very fine.

II. Beat C, mix with B, D–F.

COOKING:

1. Heat A in frying pan. Add B–F mixture, pan-fry both sides until golden brown (about 2 minutes). Serve hot or cold and add G.

EGG POUCH PORK OMELET WITH OYSTER SAUCE
Ho Yow Don Bao Ju Yoke: Canton

A. 1 tablespoon peanut oil
B. 4 eggs, beaten
C. ¼ lb. pork loin, minced
D. 4 scallions, sliced
E. 2 teaspoons light soy sauce
F. ½ teaspoon salt

G. ½ teaspoon sugar
H. 1 slice ginger, minced
I. ½ teaspoon cornstarch
J. 3 tablespoons oyster sauce
K. ½ cup water
L. 1½ teaspoons cornstarch

PREPARATION:

I. Boil water in steamer.
II. Mix C, D, E, F, G, H, I.

III. Mix J, K, L.

COOKING:

1. Heat A in center of frying pan.
2. Pour a small amount of B into center of pan; let fry to form thin small omelet.
3. Drop 1 teaspoon of C–I mixture to cover one half of omelet and fold other half over. Press edges together.
4. Repeat Steps 2–3 until ingredients are used up.
5. Place all omelets on serving dish in steamer and steam 15 minutes.
6. Heat J–L mixture to form smooth thickened sauce. Pour over omelets. Serve.

PLAIN EGG FU YONG
Ru Ee Fu Yong Don: Canton

A. 4 tablespoons peanut oil
B. 2 scallions, minced
C. 6 Chinese black mushrooms
D. 2 cups bean sprouts
E. ¼ cup shredded canned water chestnuts

F. 6 eggs
G. ½ teaspoon salt
H. ¼ teaspoon pepper
I. 2 teaspoons light soy sauce

PREPARATION:

I. Wash and soak C 15 minutes in warm water, drain, and slice into long, thin strips.

II. Wash D thoroughly. Drain.
III. Beat F, mix with G, H, I thoroughly.

COOKING:

1. Heat 1 tablespoon A, stir-fry B, C about a minute.
2. Add D, E, stir constantly 1 to 2 minutes.
3. Add cooked B–E mixture to F–I mixture, emptying frying pan contents.
4. Heat remaining A in frying pan. Cook egg-vegetable mixture over medium heat until one side is brown. Turn over, press, and fry until second side is brown. Serve hot.

Note: To serve as pancake (Fu Yong Don Bang) with oyster sauce, combine ¼ cup oyster sauce, ½ cup water, and 1 teaspoon cornstarch in a saucepan. Cook until thickened. Pour sauce over egg fu yong pancake and serve hot.

CHICKEN FU YONG
Fu Yong Gai: Canton

A. 4 tablespoons peanut oil
B. 4 oz. white meat of chicken, chopped
C. 4 egg whites
D. ½ teaspoon salt
E. 1 tablespoon sherry

PREPARATION:

I. Beat C until foamy.

II. Mix in D, E. Add B.

COOKING:

1. Heat A over low heat and add B–E mixture evenly in pan.
2. When cooked, about 5 minutes, turn mixture over and cook a while longer until under-surface is also firm.
3. Serve hot.

CHICKEN FU YONG   *Approved Ulcer Recipe*
Fu Yong Gee: General

Chop B very fine, and omit E.

PORK EGG FU YONG
Chai Shu Fu Yong Don: Canton

A. 3 tablespoons peanut oil
B. 4 eggs
C. 1 cup shredded roast pork
D. 1 scallion, minced
E. 2 slices ginger, minced
F. 1 teaspoon light soy sauce
G. ½ teaspoon sugar
H. ¾ teaspoon salt
I. ⅛ teaspoon pepper

PREPARATION:

I. Beat B, mix thoroughly with C, D, E, F, G, H, I.

COOKING:

1. Heat A in frying pan.
2. Add B–I mixture, brown one side over medium heat until golden brown. Then turn over and brown second side.

PORK EGG FU YONG WITH LETTUCE
Chai Shu Fu Yong Don: Canton

A. ¼ cup peanut oil
B. ½ cup shredded roast pork (see Roast Pork)
C. 1 cup shredded lettuce (center part)
D. 6 eggs, beaten
E. 1 scallion, chopped
F. 1 teaspoon salt
G. 1 teaspoon sherry

PREPARATION:

I. Mix B, C, D, E, F, G.

COOKING:

1. Heat A.
2. Add B–G mixture, fry over medium heat until both sides are golden brown; or scramble until B–G mixture is done. Serve hot with hot sauce or soy sauce.

GOLDEN THREAD FU YONG
Jing Sih Fu Yong: Fukien

A. 5 tablespoons peanut oil
B. 4 dried scallops
C. 1 teaspoon sherry
D. ½ teaspoon salt

E. 4 eggs
F. 1 teaspoon salt
G. dash pepper

PREPARATION:

I. Wash B well, add 2 tablespoons water, steam over boiling water 35 minutes; cool, break up into threads, mix with C, D.

II. Beat E, add F, G, and 1 tablespoon A, mix well.

COOKING:

1. Heat 4 tablespoons A, add B–D mixture, stir-fry 1 to 2 minutes.

2. Add E–G mixture, scramble, and serve hot. Do not overcook. Egg should remain tender and soft.

CRAB FU YONG
Fu Yong Hai Yoke Dung Gu: Adapted

A. ½ cup peanut oil
B. ½ cup crab meat
C. 4 Chinese mushrooms
D. 1 cup shredded lettuce hearts
E. 2 scallions, chopped
F. 2 slices ginger, chopped

G. 1 stalk celery, chopped
H. ½ teaspoon salt
I. ¼ teaspoon garlic powder
J. dash pepper
K. 4 large eggs

PREPARATION:

I. Wash C, soak 15 minutes in warm water. Drain and chop. Stir-fry in 1 tablespoon A for 1 minute.

II. Beat K, mix thoroughly with B, C, D, E, F, G, H, I, J.

COOKING:

1. Heat A. Add B–K mixture, fry until both sides are golden brown. If desired, serve with catsup or a few drops sesame oil.

OMELET CRAB FU YONG
Fu Yong Hai Yoke Bang: Adapted

In Step 1, divide B–K mixture into 6 portions. Fry as individual omelets until both sides of each omelet are golden brown (about 30 seconds each side). If desired, serve with catsup or a few drops sesame oil.

CRAB MEAT EGG FU YONG
Hai Yoke Fu Yong Don: Canton

A. 3 tablespoons peanut oil
B. 1 cup crab meat or 8-oz. pkg. frozen crab-meat (or lobster meat)
C. 6 water chestnuts, shredded
D. ½ cup shredded bamboo shoots

E. 4 Chinese mushrooms
F. 2 slices ginger, chopped
G. 2 scallions, chopped
H. ¼ teaspoon salt
I. 4 eggs

PREPARATION:

I. Break B into small pieces.
II. Wash E, soak in warm water 15 minutes or until soft, drain and shred. Stir-fry in 1 ta-blespoon A for 1 minute.
III. Mix B, C, D, E, F, G, H.
IV. Beat I, add to B–H mixture.

COOKING:

1. Heat A in frying pan.

2. Lower heat, add B–I mixture, fry both sides until golden brown.

CRAB MEAT EGG FU YONG   *Approved Diabetic Recipe*
Fu Yong Hai Yoke Dung Gu: Canton

A. 2 tablespoons peanut oil
B. 4 oz. crab meat
C. 2 to 3 eggs
D. 2 water chestnuts, shredded
E. ¼ cup shredded bamboo shoots
F. 1 to 2 Chinese mushrooms (optional)
G. 1 teaspoon chopped scallion
H. ½ teaspoon salt

PREPARATION:

I. Wash and soak F in hot water 15 minutes, drain and shred.
II. Beat C.
III. Mix B, C, D, E, F, G, H thoroughly.

COOKING:

1. Heat A. Add B–H mixture and fry on both sides until golden brown.

CHICKEN, TURKEY, PORK, SHRIMP, BEEF, OR HAM EGG FU YONG   *Approved Diabetic Recipe*
Fu Yong Don: Canton

Substitute either leftover chicken, turkey, roast pork or shrimp, for B.

SCRAMBLED EGGS
Ding How Tsao Don: Adapted

A. 3 tablespoons oil
B. 5 to 6 eggs
C. ½ cup shredded meat
D. 1 cup shredded lettuce heart
E. 1 scallion, chopped
F. 1 teaspoon salt
G. dash pepper

PREPARATION:

I. Beat B, add C, D, E, F, G, and mix well.

COOKING:

1. Heat A, add B–G mixture.
2. Scramble until almost firm. Serve with soy sauce or hot sauce, if desired.

Note: Any leftover cooked meat may be used —roast pork, chicken, turkey, beef, veal, ham.

SCRAMBLED EGGS WITH SOY SAUCE AND TOMATOES
Fan Chieh Tsao Don: General

A. 4 tablespoons peanut oil
B. 1 clove garlic, minced
C. ½ teaspoon salt
D. 8 eggs

E. 1 tomato
F. 1 tablespoon light soy sauce
G. 1 tablespoon heavy soy sauce
H. 1 scallion, sliced

PREPARATION:

I. Beat D.
II. Cut E into 8 wedges.

III. Mix B, C.
IV. Mix F, G.

COOKING:

1. Put A in very hot skillet and bring to high heat.
2. Add B, C. Stir-fry rapidly 15 seconds to brown garlic slightly.

3. Add D. Scramble until almost firm.
4. Add E. Stir-fry 1 minute.
5. Add F, G. Mix well.
6. Serve with garnish of H.

SCRAMBLED EGGS WITH SCALLIONS
Tsung Hwa Don: General

A. 4 tablespoons peanut oil
B. 8 eggs
C. 4 scallions, sliced
D. 1 teaspoon light soy sauce

E. ¾ teaspoon salt
F. 1 teaspoon heavy soy sauce
G. 1 scallion, sliced

PREPARATION:

I. Beat B slightly. Add C.

II. Mix D, E, F. Set aside.

COOKING:

1. Put A in very hot skillet and bring to high heat.
2. Add B, C. Scramble well.

3. Add D–F mixture. Stir well 15 seconds.
4. Remove from skillet at once; serve with garnish of G.

SCRAMBLED EGGS WITH FERMENTED BEAN CAKE
Fu Yu Don: Canton

A. 3 tablespoons peanut oil
B. 6 eggs
C. 1 teaspoon crushed fermented bean cake (including a little juice)
D. 1½ teaspoons light soy sauce

E. 1 teaspoon heavy soy sauce
F. 2 scallions, sliced
G. 2 teaspoons sherry
H. 2 cups rice, cooked
I. 2 scallions, sliced

PREPARATION:

I. Beat B slightly.

II. Mix C, D, E, F, G. Set aside.

COOKING:

1. Heat A in skillet to 300° F.
2. Scramble B until almost firm.
3. Add C–G mixture; stir 15 seconds.

4. Remove from skillet at once and serve with H and garnish of I.

SCRAMBLED EGGS WITH DRIED SHRIMP
Sha Mi Tsao Don: General

A. ¼ cup peanut oil
B. 12 dried shrimp
C. 6 eggs

D. 2 teaspoons dry sherry
E. 1 teaspoon salt
F. ½ teaspoon sugar

PREPARATION:

I. Wash B well, soak 5 minutes in hot water. Drain, and chop very fine. Save water.

II. Beat C; add B and its water, and D, E, F, and mix well.

COOKING:

1. Heat A until very hot.

2. Add B–F mixture, scramble, and serve hot.

SIMPLE SCALLION EGG FRIED RICE
Chung Hwa Don Tsao Fan: General

A. 3 tablespoons peanut oil
B. ¼ cup chopped scallion
C. 3 to 4 eggs

D. 2 to 2½ cups cold cooked rice
E. 1 tablespoon light soy sauce
F. salt and pepper to taste

PREPARATION:

I. Beat C slightly.

COOKING:

1. Heat A, add B, stir-fry a few seconds.
2. Add C, stir like scrambled eggs. When egg is almost done, add D; stir well 1 to 2 minutes over medium heat.
3. Add E, mix well.
4. Add F and serve.

FRIED EGGS WITH CHINESE BROWN SAUCE
Hung Tsup Don: General

A. 2 tablespoons peanut oil
B. 1 clove garlic, minced
C. 2 teaspoons brown bean sauce
D. 1 teaspoon heavy soy sauce
E. 2 teaspoons sherry

F. 1 teaspoon light soy sauce
G. ⅔ cup soup stock
H. 2 teaspoons cornstarch
I. 6 eggs
J. 3 tablespoons peanut oil

PREPARATION:

I. Break I. Do not beat.
II. Mix C, D, E, F. Set aside.

III. Mix G, H. Set aside.

COOKING:

1. Put A in very hot skillet and bring to high heat.
2. Add B. Stir-fry rapidly 15 seconds to brown garlic slightly.
3. Add mixture of C–F and stir-fry 15 seconds.
4. Add G–H mixture. Stir well until sauce thickens. Set aside.
5. In clean skillet, fry I in J as desired. Remove to individual bowls.
6. Pour sauce from Step 4 over each egg.
7. Serve.

STIR-FRIED EGGS WITH CALF BRAIN
Niu Nao Tsao Gee Don: General

A. ¼ cup lard
B. 1 calf brain
C. 2 teaspoons whiskey

D. 3 large eggs
E. 1 teaspoon salt
F. ½ teaspoon sugar

PREPARATION:

I. Place B in cold water; remove blood vessels with a toothpick. Rinse several times, drain, then mince.

II. Add C and mix well.
III. Beat D well. Add B, C and E, F and mix well.

COOKING:

1. Heat A until very hot.
2. Add B–F mixture. When bottom is set, turn it over and let the other side set. Then scramble a few times until egg is firm. Serve hot.

STIR-FRIED EGGS WITH PORK, BLACK MUSHROOMS, AND CLOUD EARS
Mo Shu Ro: Peking

A. 2 tablespoons peanut oil
B. ½ lb. ground pork
C. ½ teaspoon salt
D. ½ teaspoon minced ginger
E. 6 dried black mushrooms
F. 2 tablespoons cloud ears

G. ½ cup sliced bamboo shoots
H. 2 teaspoons light soy sauce
I. 2 teaspoons heavy soy sauce
J. 3 tablespoons peanut oil
K. 8 eggs
L. 3 scallions, sliced

PREPARATION:

I. Soak E in warm water 15 minutes. Discard water. Slice E in thin slivers.
II. Soak F in warm water 15 minutes. Discard water. Shred.

III. Beat K lightly. Set aside.
IV. Mix C, D. Set aside.
V. Mix E, F, G. Set aside.
VI. Mix H, I. Set aside.

COOKING:

1. Put A in very hot skillet and bring to high heat.
2. Add B and C–D. Stir-fry until pork is well done.
3. Add E–G mixture. Stir-fry 1 minute.
4. Add H–I mixture. Stir-fry 1 minute.

5. Remove B–I mixture from pan. Set aside.
6. Put J in very hot skillet and bring to high heat.
7. Add K. Stir-fry until set firmly. Place K on platter; pour B–J mixture over it.
8. Serve with garnish of L.

STEAMED EGGS
Tzing Don: Canton

A. 10 dried shrimp
B. 6 Chinese mushrooms
C. 1 scallion
D. 2 slices ginger
E. 6 eggs

F. ¼ cup ground pork
G. 2 teaspoons sherry
H. 2 tablespoons peanut oil
I. 1½ teaspoons salt

PREPARATION:

I. Wash and clean A, B. Soak in warm water 30 minutes; drain, saving ½ cup of the water.

II. Chop A, B, C, D very fine.

III. Beat E; combine with A–D, F, G, H, I, ½ cup mushroom and shrimp water; mix well.

IV. Place A–I mixture in a bowl.

COOKING:

1. Steam over boiling water in steamer 20 to 25 minutes.

STEAMED EGG CUSTARD WITH SCALLIONS AND SOY SAUCE
Tsung Fa Tsen Don: Canton

A. 4 eggs

B. 1 pint soup stock

C. 2 scallions, sliced

D. 2 teaspoons light soy sauce

E. 2 scallions, sliced

F. ½ teaspoon salt

PREPARATION:

I. Boil water in steamer.

II. Beat A; add F.

III. Heat B.

COOKING:

1. Place A in shallow serving dish suitable for placement in steamer.

2. Stir hot B into A.

3. Sprinkle with C.

4. Steam 15 to 20 minutes.

5. Remove from steamer. Sprinkle with D and E. Serve.

STEAMED EGG CUSTARD   *Approved Ulcer Recipe*
Tsen Don Ta: General

Halve C, tie in bundle for easy removal before serving. Omit E.

PEKING CUSTARD   *Approved Ulcer Recipe*
Kao Don: Peking

A. 4 eggs

B. 4-oz. can mushrooms (drained)

C. ¼ cup chopped frozen shrimp

D. ¼ cup ground pork

E. 1 teaspoon salt

F. ⅛ teaspoon sherry

G. 1 cup chicken broth

H. 1 teaspoon sesame oil

PREPARATION:

I. Beat A.

II. Chop B into small pieces.

III. Combine A, B, C, D, E, F, G; mix well.

IV. Pour A–G mixture into well-greased baking dish.

COOKING:

1. Preheat oven to 375°.

2. Bake A–G mixture until golden brown (about 35 minutes).

3. Sprinkle with H and serve.

STEAMED EGG CUSTARD WITH MINCED CHICKEN
Gai Yung Don Tat: Canton

A. 3 eggs
B. ¼ cup minced chicken breast
C. 1 tablespoon melted lard
D. 1 teaspoon salt

E. ½ teaspoon sugar
F. 2 teaspoons sherry
G. ¾ cup water
H. 1 tablespoon chopped scallion

PREPARATION:
I. Beat A.
II. Combine A, B, C, D, E, F, G; mix thoroughly.

III. Sprinkle top with H.

COOKING:
1. Steam 15 minutes over boiling water.

STEAMED EGG CUSTARD WITH MINCED MEAT   *Approved Diabetic Recipe*
Tsing Don: Canton

A. 2 eggs
B. 2 to 3 tablespoons minced white meat chicken, shrimp, or pork
C. 1 teaspoon peanut oil

D. 1 teaspoon salt
E. ½ cup water
F. 1 teaspoon chopped scallion

PREPARATION:
I. Beat A.
II. Combine A, B, C, D, E. Mix thoroughly.

III. Sprinkle F on top.

COOKING:
1. Steam over boiling water 15 minutes. Serve hot.

GOLDEN EGG WITH MEAT CONCENTRATE
Gee Don Ro Sung: Adapted

A. 3 tablespoons peanut oil
B. 4 eggs
C. ½ cup (cut as below) fresh mushrooms
D. ½ cup shredded lettuce hearts

E. 1 teaspoon salt
F. ½ cup meat concentrate (see Home-Style Beef Concentrate)
G. 2 scallions, minced

PREPARATION:
I. Cut C into 2 or 3 pieces each.

II. Break B into bowl; add C, D, E; beat slightly.

COOKING:
1. Put A in nonstick skillet over high heat, spreading A. Add B–E mixture and scramble.

As soon as B–E is firm, remove to a plate.
2. Spread F, G over B–E mixture and serve.

SMOKED EGGS
Shuin Don: Peking

A. 10 hard-cooked eggs
B. ¼ cup light soy sauce
C. ½ teaspoon pepper
D. 1½ teaspoons sugar

E. ⅓ cup dark brown sugar
F. ⅓ cup red tea leaves
G. ⅓ cup rice
H. ¼ teaspoon sesame oil

PREPARATION:

  I. Shell A. Slash each in 4 places, touching yolk.

  II. Mix B, C, D thoroughly.

  III. Soak A in B–D mixture at least 2 hours, turning A over after 1 hour.

  IV. Mix E, F, G.

  V. Line a heavy iron pot with aluminum foil. Spread E–G mixture on foil. Top with a rack.

  VI. Arrange A on rack, cover tightly. (Reserve B–D sauce.)

COOKING:

1. Place prepared A on low heat. After several minutes, smoke will appear. Smoke A for 3 to 5 minutes, turn over, and smoke for 3 more minutes.

2. Remove A, place back in B–D sauce, discard E–G, add H, and let cool.

3. When completely cold, quarter each A, and serve.

GOLDEN COIN EGG
Jing Tsen Don Bing: Hunan

A. 2 tablespoons peanut oil
B. 6 hard-cooked eggs
C. 1 hot green chili pepper
D. 2 slices ginger
E. 1 tablespoon chopped scallion
F. 2 tablespoons light soy sauce
G. 1 tablespoon vinegar

H. 1 teaspoon sugar
I. 2 teaspoons sherry
J. ½ teaspoon sesame oil
K. 1 teaspoon cornstarch mixed with 1 tablespoon water
L. a few lettuce leaves
M. 1 to 2 tablespoons cornstarch

PREPARATION:

  I. Slice each B into 5 pieces; sprinkle both sides with M until well coated.

  II. Discard seeds and stem of C, then chop.

(Two tablespoons chopped sweet green pepper may be substituted for C.)

  III. Mix C, D, E, F, G, H, I, J, K.

COOKING:

1. Heat A, brown B on both sides.
2. Add C–K mixture, mix well.

3. Place on top of L and serve.

PRESERVED 100-YEAR-OLD EGGS
Pi Don: General

A. 4 preserved eggs
B. 2 tablespoons vinegar

C. 3 slices ginger, minced
D. 1 tablespoon light soy sauce

PREPARATION:

  I. Remove shells from A. Whites will appear gray but translucent.

  II. Cut each egg into 6 lengthwise pieces. Yolk will appear gray-green-black.

  III. Arrange sections of A on serving dish.

  IV. Mix B, C, D.

  V. Pour over A. Serve.

PRESERVED 100-YEAR-OLD EGGS   *Approved Ulcer Recipe*
Pi Don: General

A. 2 preserved eggs
B. 2 tablespoons light soy sauce
C. ½ teaspoon sugar (optional)

PREPARATION:

I. Crack, peel A, rinse in water; cut each into eighths.

II. Pour B over A; sprinkle with C.
Note: Serve with congee or noodles. Sugar is used in Shanghai préparation.

FRIED 100-YEAR-OLD EGGS
Tza Pi Don: General

A. 1 cup peanut oil
B. 3 100-year-old eggs
C. 1 salted egg
D. 3 tablespoons flour
E. ½ teaspoon sugar
F. 2 teaspoons wine vinegar
G. ½ teaspoon salt
H. 2 tomatoes

PREPARATION:

I. Scrape ashes from B with a knife, wash. Cover B with water, bring to a boil and cook 3 minutes (so that B is firmed). Drain, cover with cold water a few seconds. Shell; quarter each B.

II. Break up yolk of C with fork and beat C until fluffy.

III. Mix in D gradually; add E, F, G, mix well.

IV. Dip H in boiling water a few seconds; remove skin and cut H into slices.

COOKING:

1. Heat A to 375°.
2. Dip each B in C–G until well coated. Deep-fry until all sides are golden brown.

3. Place in the middle of dish, garnish with H. Serve hot or cold.

TEA EGGS
Tsa Yieh Don: Peking

A. 6 eggs
B. 2 tablespoons red tea leaves
C. 1½ tablespoons salt

COOKING:

I. Boil A 5 to 10 minutes. Discard boiling water, let A stand in cold water until cool. Then crack, but do not shell.

II. Fill saucepan with 3 cups water, add B, C, bring to boil. Add A, cook over low heat 1 hour.

III. Remove from heat. Leave A in B–C mixture; remove when ready to eat.

SWEET TEA EGGS
Bing Tang Tsa Yieh Don: Peking

Substitute 2 tea bags for B and 3 tablespoons rock sugar for C.

FISH

Much of the fish eaten in China is similar to Western types: carp, porgy, sea bass, catfish, cod, herring, trout, millet, smelt, sea perch, salmon, shad, tuna, snapper, sole, sturgeon, turbot. Shellfish, too, include familiar varieties: shrimp, prawn, crab, lobster, clams, oysters, and scallops.

Fish in China often are bought alive and kept in large vats of water until ready to be cooked. This retains their freshness; also it combats the lack of commercial refrigeration. Preserving, salting, or cooking techniques, too, are widely used at the time of the catch. Some Chinese are so fond of salted fish that they eat it at almost every meal; it is soaked, seasoned with fresh ginger, and steam cooked over rice.

ABALONE SLICES (COLD)
Bao Yu Pien: General

A. ¼ teaspoon peanut oil
B. ½ can (8 oz.) abalone

C. ¼ cup abalone liquid
D. ½ teaspoon light soy sauce

PREPARATION:

I. Cut B into slices.
II. Mix C, D.

III. Soak B in marinade of C, D 15 minutes.

COOKING:

1. Heat A in skillet until smoking hot and pour over B–D. (Oil may be cooked in advance and allowed to cool first.)

2. Allow to cool (refrigerate if desired). Arrange on platter and serve with toothpick to spear individual slices.

BRAISED SLICED ABALONE
Hung Sao Bao Pien: General

A. 2 tablespoons peanut oil
B. 1 scallion (white part only), chopped
C. 2 tablespoons light soy sauce
D. 2 teaspoons sherry
E. ½ cup chicken broth
F. ½ teaspoon ground pepper

G. 1 teaspoon sugar
H. 1-lb. can abalone
I. 2 teaspoons cornstarch mixed with 2 tablespoons water
J. few drops sesame oil (to taste)

PREPARATION:

I. Slice H into thin pieces.

II. Mix C, D, E, F, G.

COOKING:

1. Heat A, add B, stir-fry a few seconds.
2. Add C–G mixture, bring to a boil.
3. Add H and cook 3 minutes.

4. Thicken with I.
5. Add J and serve.

ABALONE WITH MUSHROOMS AND BAMBOO SHOOTS
Tsao Bao Yu: Canton

A. 4 tablespoons peanut oil
B. 8 Chinese dry mushrooms
C. 1 scallion
D. 4 slices ginger

E. 1-lb. can abalone
F. 2 stalks Chinese cabbage heart
G. ½ can (8 oz.) bamboo shoots
H. salt and pepper to taste

PREPARATION:

I. Slice E into small pieces.
II. Wash B and soak in hot water ¼ hour; cut each into 4 pieces.
III. Wash F and cut diagonally same size as E.

Put into boiling water 1 minute; drain and let cold water run through.
IV. Slice G into small pieces.
V. Cut C into 1-inch pieces.
VI. Slice D into strips.

COOKING:

1. Heat A.
2. Stir-fry B, C, D one minute.

3. Add E, F, G. Mix well.
4. Add H, cover and cook 2 minutes and serve.

ABALONE WITH MUSHROOMS AND BAMBOO SHOOTS   *Approved Diabetic Recipe*
Er Dung Bao Yu: Canton

A. 2 tablespoons peanut oil
B. 1 teaspoon chopped scallion
C. 1 to 2 slices fresh or pickled ginger
D. ½ can (8 oz.) abalone

E. 2 to 3 Chinese black mushrooms
F. 1 cup shredded Chinese cabbage
G. ¼ cup shredded bamboo shoot
H. salt, pepper to taste

PREPARATION:

I. Slice D into thin, bite-size pieces.

II. Wash E, then soak in warm water 15 minutes; drain; cut each into 3 to 4 pieces.

COOKING:

1. Heat A, add B, C, and stir-fry briefly; add D, E, and stir 1 minute.

2. Add F, G and stir-fry another 2 to 3 minutes.
3. Add H and mix well.

ABALONE WITH CHINESE CABBAGE HEARTS
Bao Yu Bai Tsai Shing: Shanghai

A. 2 tablespoons peanut oil
B. 1 or 2 cloves garlic
C. 2 teaspoons sherry
D. ½ cup liquid from H
E. 2 tablespoons oyster sauce
F. 1 teaspoon sugar

G. ½ teaspoon sesame oil
H. 1-lb. can abalone
I. 2 teaspoons cornstarch mixed with 2 tablespoons water
J. 1 lb. Chinese cabbage heart
K. ½ teaspoon salt

PREPARATION:

I. Cut H into ¼-inch by 2½-inch slices.
II. Pound B with side of cleaver, discard skin.
III. Mix C, D, E, F, G.
IV. Clean and wash J, cut into 4- or 5-inch-long

pieces, parboil 1½ minutes. Bring water to boil, add K and J, bring back to boil and cook for a few seconds. Drain J and arrange on plate.

COOKING:

1. Heat A, add B, stir-fry until light brown, add C–G mixture, bring to boil.

2. Add H, cook 2 to 3 minutes.
3. Thicken with I, place on top of J, and serve.

ABALONE IN OYSTER SAUCE I
Ho Yow Bao Yu: Canton

A. 1 tablespoon peanut oil
B. ½ can (8 oz.) abalone
C. ⅓ cup abalone liquid
D. 1½ tablespoons oyster sauce

E. 1 teaspoon water chestnut flour or 2 teaspoons cornstarch
F. ¼ cup warm water

PREPARATION:

I. Cut B into slices ⅛ to 1/16 inch thick and no more than 1½ inches long.

II. Mix C, D, E, F. Set aside. Stir well before using.

COOKING:

1. Put A in very hot skillet.
2. Add B and stir-fry 1 minute over high heat.

3. Add C–F mixture. Stir-fry until sauce thickens. Remove from heat and serve at once.

ABALONE IN OYSTER SAUCE II
Ho Yow Bao Yu: Canton

A. 2 tablespoons peanut oil
B. 1-lb. can abalone
C. 2 tablespoons oyster sauce
D. ¼ teaspoon sesame oil
E. ½ cup chicken stock

F. 1 teaspoon sherry
G. dash pepper
H. 2 teaspoons cornstarch mixed with 2 tablespoons water

PREPARATION:

I. Cut B into bite-size pieces. (Liquid can be saved to add to chicken broth to make soup.)

II. Mix C, D, E, F, G.

COOKING:

1. Heat A, stir-fry B several seconds.
2. Add C–G mixture, bring to boil. Reduce heat, and cook 2 to 3 minutes.

3. Thicken with H mixture.

ABALONE WITH OYSTER SAUCE *Approved Diabetic Recipe*
Ho Yow Bao Yu: Canton

A. 1 tablespoon peanut oil
B. ½ can (8 oz.) abalone
C. 1 teaspoon light soy sauce
D. 2 teaspoons oyster sauce
E. ¼ cup dietetic soup stock or water

F. dash pepper
G. few drops sesame oil
H. 1 teaspoon cornstarch mixed with 1 tablespoon water

PREPARATION:

I. Cut B into bite-size pieces.

II. Mix C, D, E, F, G.

COOKING:

1. Heat A, add B, and stir-fry 15 seconds.
2. Add C–G mixture; bring to boil. Lower heat

and cook 2 to 3 minutes.
3. Thicken with H mixture.

ABALONE WITH ASPARAGUS AND TURKEY
Lu Shun Bao Yu: Shanghai

A. ¼ cup vegetable oil
B. ½ can (8 oz.) abalone
C. ½ lb. asparagus
D. 1 cup shredded cooked turkey breast
E. 4 oz. canned or fresh button mushrooms

F. 3 slices ginger
G. ¾ cup chicken or meat stock
H. 1 tablespoon cornstarch
I. 1 tablespoon light soy sauce

PREPARATION:

I. Slice B into thin pieces. Save juice as substitute for water later.

II. French-cut tender C tips; discard tough stems.
III. If fresh E are used, slice each into thirds.

COOKING:

1. Place A in hot skillet. Add B, C, stir-fry 2 minutes.
2. Add D, E, F, stir-fry 2 more minutes. If liquid is needed, add ¼ cup B juice.

3. Mix G, H, I, then add to skillet. Salt to taste. Serve hot.

BAKED FISH
Gook Yu: Adapted

A. 3 tablespoons peanut oil
B. 1½ lbs. sea bass
C. salt to taste
D. lemon or tomato sauce
E. 2 scallions

F. 1 tablespoon preserved horse bean chili sauce
G. 3 tablespoons light soy sauce
H. 1 teaspoon sugar
I. 1 tablespoon cornstarch
J. 1 cup water

PREPARATION:

I. Wash B well, dry with paper towels.
II. Slit B diagonally at about 2-inch intervals.

III. Rub B thoroughly inside and out with C.

COOKING:

1. Preheat oven to 425°.
2. Pour A over B. Wrap prepared B in aluminum foil. Bake 25 minutes.

3. Open foil, bake each side 10 to 12 minutes more.
4. Serve with D or catsup.

OPTIONAL:

5. Cut E into pieces 1 to 2 inches long.
6. Combine E, F, G, H, I, J thoroughly in saucepan and cook until thickened.

pan and cook until thickened.
7. Pour over fish and serve.

BOILED FISH
Shwintow Dow Si Yu: Canton

A. 4 cups water
B. 1 teaspoon salt
C. 2 lbs. porgy
D. 1 tablespoon vegetable oil
E. 3 teaspoons salted black beans

F. 2 cloves garlic, chopped
G. 1 tablespoon minced scallion
H. 1½ tablespoons light soy sauce
I. 3 slices ginger, minced
J. 2 teaspoons cornstarch in ¼ cup water

PREPARATION:

I. Scale C; slit skin diagonally at 1-inch intervals.

II. Combine D, E, F, G, H, I, J in saucepan, mix well.

COOKING:

1. Heat A, B in frying pan, bring to boil. Add C, continue boiling 5 minutes, covered. Remove pan from heat and let stand 15 minutes. Drain water, place C in shallow bowl.

2. Heat D–J mixture, stirring constantly, until it boils and thickens.

3. Pour D–J over C. Serve hot.

BOILED FISH WITH SZECHUAN SAUCE
Sao Yu: Szechuan

A. 1- to 1½-lb. sea bass
B. 2 tablespoons peanut oil
C. ¼ cup shredded bamboo shoots
D. 4 Chinese mushrooms
E. 1 tablespoon chopped scallion
F. 1 teaspoon chopped ginger
G. 1 clove garlic, minced
H. 2 teaspoons light soy sauce

I. 2 teaspoons brown bean sauce
J. ½ teaspoon salt
K. 2 teaspoons sherry
L. 2 teaspoons vinegar
M. 1 teaspoon sugar
N. 2 teaspoons cornstarch mixed with ½ cup mushroom water

PREPARATION:

I. Wash A, make 3 or 4 diagonal slashes on each side.

II. Wash and soak D in warm water 15 minutes. Drain (save water for N) and shred.

III. Mix H, I, J, K, L, M, N.

COOKING:

1. Place A in frying pan, cover with boiling water and cook over low heat 3 minutes. Remove from heat but leave in water 12 to 15 minutes, remove to plate.

2. Heat B, add C, D, E, F, G, stir-fry 1 minute, add H–N mixture, stir until gravy is thickened; pour over fish and serve.

BOILED FISH WITH SAUCE   *Approved Diabetic Recipe*
Shu Yu: Canton

A. 1-lb. sea bass
B. 1 small clove garlic, chopped
C. 1 teaspoon chopped scallion
D. 2 teaspoons light soy sauce

E. ¼ teaspoon salt
F. 1 teaspoon cornstarch mixed with 2 tablespoons water
G. 1 teaspoon salted black beans

PREPARATION:

I. Wash and clean A. Slash diagonally twice on each side.

II. Combine B, C, D, E, F, G.

COOKING:

1. Cover A with boiling water and cook over low heat 3 minutes. Remove from heat and leave A in water 12 to 15 minutes.

2. Place A in dish.

3. Heat B–G until it boils and thickens.

4. Pour B–G over A and serve.

BOILED SEA BASS WITH SAUCE
Shu Yu: Canton

A. 1- to 2-lb. sea bass
B. 3 slices ginger, minced
C. 2 to 3 cloves garlic, chopped
D. 2 scallions, sliced
E. ¼ teaspoon salt

F. 6 tablespoons light soy sauce
G. 1 tablespoon sherry
H. 5 tablespoons peanut oil
I. 2 scallions, sliced

PREPARATION:

I. Bring 4 quarts of water to a rapid boil in a pot large enough to hold A flat, lengthwise.

II. Clean and wash A thoroughly.
III. Mix B, C, D, E, F, G. Set aside.

COOKING:

1. Immerse A in boiling water. Simmer gently 3 minutes.
2. Remove pot from heat and let set for 15 minutes.
3. Remove A from water and place on serving dish.

4. Cover evenly with B–G mixture.
5. Bring H to smoking hot and pour over A–G combination.
6. Serve with garnish of I.

CANTONESE FRIED FISH   *Approved Diabetic Recipe*
Jien Yu: Canton

A. 1 cup peanut oil
B. 1- to 1½-lb. sea bass
C. 2 teaspoons salt

D. dash pepper
E. 1 egg
F. 2 tablespoons cornstarch

PREPARATION:

I. Cut B into quarters or use whole.
II. Mix C, D. Rub B thoroughly inside and out with C mixture, let B stand 15 minutes.

III. Beat E with 1 tablespoon F. Dip prepared B in E mixture, then roll in remaining portion of F.

COOKING:

1. Heat A to 350° and fry B–F mixture until golden brown (about 5 to 7 minutes each side).

2. Serve with Chinese hot sauce (optional).

PEKING FRIED FISH
Gahn Jien Yu: Peking

A. ¼ cup peanut oil
B. 1½-lb. porgy
C. 2 teaspoons chopped scallion
D. 1 teaspoon sesame oil
E. 1 teaspoon chopped ginger
F. 1 tablespoon vinegar

G. 1 scallion tied into a knot
H. 4 slices ginger
I. 2 teaspoons salt
J. 1 to 2 tablespoons flour
K. 1 egg, beaten

PREPARATION:

I. Clean and wash B, dry between paper towels. Make 2 or 3 slashes on each side.
II. Place G, H in B cavity and rub outside with

I. Let stand 15 minutes.
III. Coat B with J and roll in K.
IV. Mix E, F.

COOKING:

1. Heat A and in it brown B on each side for ½ to 1 minute.
2. Over medium heat, brown each side 3 to 5 minutes longer; turn B over once or twice or until it is done.
3. Remove B to plate.
4. Pour off excess oil, in same pan stir-fry C, D a few times, pour over B.
5. Serve with E–F mixture or Chinese hot sauce.

CRISPY BASS
Chui Pi Yu: Szechuan

A. 2 cups peanut oil
B. 1½-lb. sea bass
C. 1 tablespoon chopped scallion
D. 1 teaspoon chopped ginger
E. 2 tablespoons catsup
F. 2 tablespoons sugar
G. 2 tablespoons vinegar

H. salt to taste
I. 2 teaspoons cornstarch mixed with 2 tablespoons water
J. 1 tablespoon cornstarch
K. 1¼ teaspoons salt
L. ¼ teaspoon pepper
M. 1 tablespoon white or yellow wine

PREPARATION:

I. Clean and wash B, dry between paper towels.
II. Mix K, L, M and rub all over B.
III. Rub B with I, then coat with J.

COOKING:

1. Heat A to 325°, deep-fry B until it is golden brown, about 5 minutes, turn over once or twice during frying; remove to a dish.
2. Heat 1 tablespoon A, add C, D, stir-fry ½ minute; add E, F, G, H, and cook 1 to 2 minutes; place in small dish and serve with B.

PORK-COOKED WHOLE FISH
Chuan Cheh Gwa: Fukien

A. 1 to 2 cups peanut oil
B. 1-lb. sea bass
C. 2 teaspoons cornstarch
D. ¼ lb. pork
E. 10 dried shrimp
F. 1 scallion
G. 3 slices ginger
H. 1½ tablespoons light soy sauce

I. 1½ tablespoons vinegar
J. 2 teaspoons sugar
K. 2 teaspoons white wine
L. ½ teaspoon salt
M. ½ cup water
N. 2 teaspoons cornstarch mixed with 2 tablespoons water
O. pepper to taste

PREPARATION:

I. Clean and wash B; dry between paper towels. Make two diagonal slashes on each side; coat with C.
II. Cut D into thin slices, then into shreds.
III. Wash and clean E, then soak in cold water 15 minutes; drain and chop.
IV. Cut F into 1-inch pieces.
V. Mix H, I, J, K, L, M.

COOKING:

1. Heat A to 350°; deep fry B–C until golden brown (about 4 to 5 minutes on each side); remove to a dish.
2. Remove 2 tablespoons A to a pan, heat; add D, E, F, G, stir-fry about two minutes.
3. Add H–M mixture; mix well and cook 1 more minute.
4. Thicken with N. Pour sauce over fish, add O and serve.

FAMILY STYLE FISH
Jia Shiang Yu: Adapted

A. 5 tablespoons peanut oil
B. 2- to 3-lb. sea bass
C. ¾ to 1 cup flour
D. 2 scallions
E. 3 slices ginger

F. 1 teaspoon sugar
G. 1 tablespoon sherry
H. ½ cup light soy sauce
I. ¼ cup water

PREPARATION:

I. Wash B well, wipe with paper towels.
II. Make 4 diagonal slashes in skin on each side.
III. Spread C on paper; roll B in it.

IV. Cut D into 2-inch pieces.
V. Mix D, E, F, G, H, I.

COOKING:

1. Heat A, brown B–C on both sides.
2. Pour half of A away. Add D–I mixture to B.

Cover and cook over low heat until fish is done (about 10 minutes).

SZECHUAN STEAMED FISH
Do Jiang Tsen Yu: Szechuan

A. 1½- to 2-lb. carp
B. ¼ cup peanut oil
C. 1 clove garlic, minced
D. 2 slices ginger, chopped
E. 1 tablespoon brown bean sauce
F. ½ cup water
G. 2 teaspoons sherry
H. 1 tablespoon light soy sauce

I. 1 teaspoon sugar
J. 1 teaspoon salt
K. 1 tablespoon chopped scallions
L. 1 tablespoon cornstarch mixed with ¼ cup water
M. anise pepper to taste
N. ½ teaspoon salt
O. ¼ to ½ teaspoon ginger juice (see Index)

PREPARATION:

I. Scale, clean, and wash A, dry with paper towel, rub with N, O.

II. Mix C, D, E.
III. Mix G, H, I, J, K.

COOKING:

1. Place A in dish, steam in a steamer over boiling water 15 minutes or until done. Pour all the juice from A into another dish (may be added to H to make ½ cup).
2. Heat B to smoking, pour over A, return B to

pot, heat; when it is hot, add C–E, stir-fry 1 minute, add F, bring to boil.
3. Add G–K mixture, cook for 1 minute.
4. Thicken with L. Pour over fish, add M to taste and serve hot.

STEAMED FISH I
Tsen Yu: General

A. 1 to 2 lbs. fresh fish (sea bass, halibut, snapper, pike, swordfish)
B. 1 teaspoon salt
C. 2 scallions, sliced
D. 1 clove garlic, minced
E. 3 slices ginger, minced

F. 1 tablespoon salted black beans
G. 1 tablespoon sherry
H. 2 tablespoons light soy sauce
I. 2 tablespoons peanut oil
J. 2 scallions, sliced

PREPARATION:

   I. Boil water in steamer.

   II. Clean A.

   III. Rub B over A. Set aside 15 minutes. Wash A well.

   IV. Mash F.

   V. Mix C, D, E, F.

   VI. Mix G, H.

COOKING:

1. Set A–B in serving dish suitable for steaming.
2. Cover with C–F mixture.
3. Sprinkle with G, H, mixture.
4. Place dish in steaming utensil. Steam 18 minutes.
5. Remove platter and fish; set aside.
6. Heat I smoking hot and pour at once over fish.
7. Garnish with J and serve.

STEAMED FISH II
Ching Tsen Yu: Szechuan

A. 1- to 1½-lb. bass or trout
B. 1½ teaspoons salt
C. 1 tablespoon white wine
D. ¼ to ½ teaspoon pepper or to taste
E. 4 Chinese mushrooms
F. 1 scallion
G. 4 to 6 slices Virginia Ham
H. 4 slices ginger
I. few slices pork fat
J. ⅓ cup chicken broth

PREPARATION:

   I. Clean and wash A; make 2 or 3 slashes on each side.

   II. Mix B, C, D, rub over A; place A on a dish.

   III. Wash E and soak in warm water 15 minutes, drain, cut each into 4 or 5 pieces.

   IV. Cut F into 1½-inch pieces.

   V. Spread G on top of A.

   VI. Spread E on top of G.

   VII. Put F, H over E.

   VIII. Arrange I on top of all.

COOKING:

1. Steam in steamer over boiling water 15 minutes or until fish is done, discard pork fat and fish juice.
2. Boil J, add to steamed fish and serve.

CLEAR STEAMED TROUT
Ching Tsen Yu: General

A. 1 whole trout
B. 2 oz. Virginia ham, sliced
C. 4 Chinese mushrooms
D. ½ cup sliced bamboo shoots
E. 1 teaspoon salt
F. 4 slices ginger, slivered
G. 1 scallion, sliced
H. 1 tablespoon white wine
I. 1 tablespoon light soy sauce
J. 1 tablespoon peanut oil
K. salt to taste

PREPARATION:

   I. Rub A with E inside and out. Place on dish.

   II. Wash C and soak in hot water 15 minutes.

   Drain and cut each into 4 pieces.

   III. Mix H, I, J.

COOKING:

1. Arrange B, C, D, F, G over A.
2. Pour H, I, J over A.
3. Put dish on steaming rack in saucepan (be sure to prevent water from boiling over onto dish). Cover saucepan tightly and steam A 15 minutes.
4. Add K.
5. Serve hot.

STEAMED HOT AND SPICED FISH
Wong Yo Tsen Yu: Szechuan

A. 1½-lb. bass
B. 1½ teaspoons salt
C. 1 tablespoon sherry
D. 2 cloves garlic, chopped
E. 1 red-hot pepper

F. 3 tablespoons salted black beans
G. 1½ teaspoons sugar
H. 1 tablespoon light soy sauce
I. 1 piece caul fat 8 by 12 inches
J. 1 tablespoon cornstarch

PREPARATION:

I. Clean and wash A, dry between paper towels. Make 2 slashes diagonally on both sides. Rub inside and outside with B.
II. Sprinkle A with C and marinate 10 minutes.
III. Discard stem and seeds of E, chop.
IV. Soak F in a cup of water 1 minute so that any sand will settle on bottom; remove F, wash, drain, and mash.

V. Mix D, E, F, G, H well with 1 tablespoon water. Stuff A with 1 tablespoon of D–H mixture.
VI. Wash I in warm water, dry between paper towels, sprinkle lightly with J.
VII. Spread ½ of D–H mixture over I, J.
VIII. Place A on top of D–H mixture and place the other half of D–H mixture over A.
IX. Wrap I over fish and place in a dish.

COOKING:

1. Steam in a steamer 15 minutes or until fish is done.

FISH WITH SPICY BEAN SAUCE
La Dow Ban Jiang Yu: Szechuan

A. 1½-lb. sea bass or porgy
B. 1 teaspoon salt
C. ⅓ cup vegetable oil
D. ½ tablespoon spicy chili bean sauce

E. 2 tablespoons light soy sauce
F. 3 slices ginger, shredded
G. 1 scallion
H. 1 teaspoon cornstarch

PREPARATION:

I. Slit A skin diagonally, 1 to 1½ inches apart. Rub with B inside and out.
II. Place A on aluminum foil in pan for broiling. Pour C over A. Cover foil tightly over A.

III. Cut G into 1- to 2-inch pieces.
IV. Mix well D, E, F, G, H, and ¼ cup water. For a very spicy dish, add an extra teaspoon of D.

COOKING:

1. Broil A–C 25 minutes, turn over, broil 20 more minutes.
2. Place D–H mixture in pot, cook until thick-

ened. Pour over A.
3. Lower broiling pan, cover with aluminum foil, cook 15 to 20 more minutes. Serve hot.

SWEET AND SOUR FISH I
Tang Tsu Yu: Shanghai

A. 3 cups peanut oil
B. 1- to 1½-lb. porgy or bass
C. ½ cup shrimp, diced
D. ½ cup peas
E. 1 tablespoon light soy sauce
F. 1 tablespoon sherry
G. 3 tablespoons catsup
H. 1 tablespoon sugar

I. 1½ tablespoons vinegar
J. 2 tablespoons cornstarch
K. 1 tomato
L. 1 teaspoon cornstarch mixed with 2 tablespoons water
M. 1 teaspoon salt
N. dash pepper

PREPARATION:

I. Mix L, M, N thoroughly.

II. Slash both sides of B diagonally at 2-inch intervals, rub with L–N mixture. Roll in J so that B is coated with a thin layer.

III. Mix E, F, G, H, I and 1 tsp. J.

IV. Mix C with additional ½ teaspoon cornstarch and dash of salt.

V. Place K in boiling water for a few seconds, remove, peel, and cut into cubes.

COOKING:

1. Heat A to 325°; deep fry B until golden brown (about 5 minutes). Remove to dish.

2. Heat additional 1 tablespoon oil, stir-fry C 1 to 2 minutes, add D, stir for 1 minute.

3. Add E, K, J mixture, stir until thickened.

4. Pour over B and serve. Garnish with K.

SWEET AND SOUR FISH II
Tien Swan Yu: General

A. 1- to 2-lb. sea bass
B. 1 tablespoon light soy sauce
C. 1 tablespoon sherry
D. 1 tablespoon peanut oil
E. 3 tablespoons peanut oil
F. 1 small onion
G. 1 carrot
H. 1 sweet pickle
I. 1 scallion, sliced
J. 1 slice ginger, slivered
K. ¼ cup sugar
L. ¼ cup vinegar
M. 1 teaspoon cornstarch
N. 1 teaspoon salt
O. 2 tablespoons water

PREPARATION:

I. Make 3 slash cuts (slightly penetrating the meat) on both sides of A.

II. Mix B, C.

III. Marinate A in B, C mixture 10 minutes.

IV. Brush A with D.

V. Cut F, G, H into thin slices. Mix well.

VI. Combine F–H with I, J.

VII. Mix K, L, M, N, O. Preheat oven to 375°.

COOKING:

1. Bake A–D 25 minutes.

2. Put E into very hot skillet and bring to high heat.

3. Stir-fry F–J mixture 1-2 minutes.

4. Stir in K–O mixture until sauce thickens.

5. Pour over A and serve.

FIVE WILLOW SWEET AND SOUR SEA BASS
Wu Liu Yu: Hangchow

A. 1- to 2-pound sea bass (or pike, carp, haddock, halibut, mackerel, bluefish)
B. 1 teaspoon salt
C. 2 tablespoons peanut oil
D. sweet and sour sauce (see Index)

PREPARATION:

I. Eviscerate, clean, and wash A.   II. Rub with B.   III. Place on deep serving platter.

COOKING:

1. Place platter with A–B in steamer containing boiling water.

2. Steam 20 minutes (or until fish is done).

3. Remove platter and set aside.

4. Heat C to smoking; pour over A.

5. Pour D over A and serve at once.

WEST LAKE BOILED SWEET AND SOUR FISH
Si Wu Tsu Liu Yu: Shanghai

A. 1½-lb. bass or trout
B. 1½ teaspoons salt
C. 1 tablespoon sherry
D. 1 scallion cut into 2- to 3-inch pieces
E. 2 slices ginger
F. 3 tablespoons peanut oil
G. 1 or 2 cloves garlic, chopped
H. 1 cup fish soup
I. 3 tablespoons sugar

J. 2 tablespoons light soy sauce
K. 2 teaspoons sesame oil
L. 3 tablespoons wine vinegar
M. 1 tablespoon cornstarch mixed with ⅓ cup water
N. 2 scallions
O. ½ teaspoon pepper
P. 1 tablespoon shredded ginger

PREPARATION:

I. Clean and wash A, dry between paper towels. Split A open through stomach up to backbone, so that fish becomes one flat piece.

II. Add B, C, D, E to a pan of water (enough to cover fish), boil ½ minute.

III. Shred N diagonally into long strips.

IV. Mix I, J, K, L.

COOKING:

1. Add A to boiling B–E water mixture. Cover and cook 3 minutes; Remove pan from heat, but leave A in water 10 to 12 minutes more; place A on plate, being careful not to break A. Sprinkle O over A and arrange N, P over top of A.

2. Heat F, add G and stir-fry a few seconds.
3. Add H, bring to a boil.
4. Add I–L, stir well and thicken with M.
5. Pour over A and serve hot.

WEST LAKE STEAMED SWEET AND SOUR FISH
Si Wu Tsu Liu Yu: Shanghai

A. 1½-lb. bass or trout
B. 3 tablespoons peanut oil
C. 1 or 2 cloves garlic, chopped
D. 1 cup fish soup
E. 2 tablespoons light soy sauce
F. 3 tablespoons wine vinegar
G. 3 tablespoons sugar

H. 1 to 2 teaspoons sesame oil
I. 1 tablespoon cornstarch, mixed with ⅓ cup water
J. 2 scallions
K. 1 tablespoon shredded ginger
L. 1 teaspoon salt
M. 1 tablespoon sherry

PREPARATION:

I. Clean and wash A, dry between paper towels. Split through stomach up to backbone so that fish becomes one flat piece; rub both sides with L, M.

II. Shred J diagonally into long strips.

III. Mix E, F, G, H.

COOKING:

1. Place A back side up and steam in steamer over boiling water 15 minutes or until done.
2. Heat B, brown C, add D (chicken broth may be substituted), bring to boil, add E–H.
3. Thicken with I.
4. When A is done pour soup out, and arrange J and K on top of A.
5. Pour B–I mixture over A and serve hot.

FRIED FISH WITH SWEET AND SOUR SAUCE
Tiem Sween Tza Yu: Canton

A. 1 scallion
B. 4 slices ginger
C. 1 teaspoon light soy sauce
D. 3 tablespoons vinegar
E. 3 tablespoons sugar
F. 1 tablespoon cornstarch

G. ½ cup water
H. 1 large tomato
I. salt to taste
J. 1- to 1½-lb. fried sea bass (see Cantonese Fried Fish)

PREPARATION:

I. Chop A, B.
II. Mix A, B, C, D, E, F, G in saucepan.

III. Cut H into small wedges.

COOKING:

1. Bring A–G mixture to boil, stirring until thickened.

2. Add H, I; mix well; bring to boil again.
3. Remove from heat, pour over J. Serve hot.

FRIED FISH WITH SWEET AND SOUR SAUCE AND PEPPER
Tiem Sween La Chiu Yu: Canton

Add 2 tablespoons oil, 1 green pepper, and 1 or 2 red-hot peppers. In Step I, discard seeds of green pepper and red-hot peppers, slice each into long, thin pieces. In Step 3, heat oil in saucepan, stir-fry pepper and red-hot peppers 30 seconds and add A–I mixture from Step 2. Continue stirring until boiling and thickened. Pour over J, serve hot.

RED-COOKED MANDARIN FISH
Hung Sao Yu: Peking

A. 6 tablespoons peanut oil
B. 2-lb. sea bass
C. ¼ cup sliced bamboo shoots
D. 8 Chinese mushrooms
E. 1 scallion
F. 2 slices ginger, chopped

G. 1 clove garlic, chopped
H. ¼ cup light soy sauce
I. 1 tablespoon sherry
J. 1 teaspoon sugar
K. 2 teaspoons cornstarch
L. ½ cup chicken broth

PREPARATION:

I. Wash B well, dry with paper towels, and diagonally slash on each side about 2 inches apart.

II. Wash D, soak in warm water 15 minutes, drain. Cut each into 4- to 5-inch pieces.
III. Cut E into pieces 1½ inches long.
IV. Mix H, I, J, K, L.

COOKING:

1. Heat A. Brown B on both sides. Discard A, reserving 1 to 2 tablespoons.
2. Add C, D, E, F, G, H–L mixture to B. Bring

to boil, cover, and cook over low heat about 30 minutes. During this time, baste B two or three times with sauce. Serve hot.

FISH WITH BROWN BEAN PASTE I
Dow Ban Jiong Yu: General

A. 2-lb. sea bass or porgy
B. ½ teaspoon salt
C. 3 tablespoons brown bean paste
D. 1 tablespoon brown sugar
E. 3 slices ginger

F. 2 scallions, minced
G. 1 teaspoon cornstarch
H. 1 tablespoon light soy sauce
I. 4 tablespoons vegetable oil

PREPARATION:

I. Remove head from A, split A in half. Sprinkle with B. Place in shallow bowl for steaming.

II. Mix C, D, E, F, G, H, and spread over A.

COOKING:

1. Place A–H in steamer, steam 20 minutes. Remove.
2. In frying pan, heat I. When hot, add A–H.

Stir-fry 8 minutes; lower heat. If sauce becomes too thick, adjust with more fish juice. Serve hot.

FISH WITH BROWN BEAN PASTE II
Dow Ban Jiong Yu Pien: General

A. 4 tablespoons vegetable oil
B. 1 lb. haddock, fillet sole, or flounder
C. 1½ tablespoons cornstarch
D. 3 tablespoons brown bean paste
E. 1 tablespoon brown sugar

F. 3 slices ginger
G. 2 scallions, minced
H. 1 tablespoon light soy sauce
I. ¼ teaspoon salt
J. 1 clove garlic, chopped (optional)

PREPARATION:

I. Cut B into slices ¼ inch thick. Rub C over.

II. Mix D, E, F, G, H, I, J with ¼ cup water.

COOKING:

1. Place A in hot skillet. When heated, add B–C and stir-fry 1 to 2 minutes.

2. Add D–J, lower heat, simmer 2 minutes, and serve hot.

FISH KOW
Yu Kow: Canton

A. 1 lb. boned fish (sea bass, snapper, pike)
B. 3 tablespoons flour
C. 1 teaspoon sherry
D. 1 egg white
E. peanut oil for deep frying
F. 2 tablespoons peanut oil
G. 1 clove garlic
H. ½ teaspoon salt

I. ½ slice ginger, minced
J. ¼ pound Chinese cabbage, sliced
K. ¼ cup sliced bamboo shoots
L. 10 water chestnuts, sliced
M. ½ cup water
N. 1 teaspoon cornstarch
O. 3 tablespoons water
P. ¼ teaspoon sugar
Q. 1 slice ginger, minced

PREPARATION:

I. Cut A into 1-inch squares.
II. Mix batter of B, C, D; set aside.
III. Mix G, H, I; set aside.

IV. Mix J, K, L; set aside.
V. Mix N, O, P, Q; set aside; stir well before using.

COOKING:

1. Dip A into B–D mixture.
2. Deep fry in E at 400° 5 minutes; set aside.
3. Put F into very hot skillet and bring to smoking.
4. Add G–I and stir-fry rapidly 15 seconds to brown G slightly.

5. Add J–L and stir-fry 1 minute.
6. Add M, cover, cook 2 minutes.
7. Add A–D mixture and mix all thoroughly.
8. Add N–Q mixture slowly; stir-fry until sauce thickens and coats all ingredients well; serve.

SCALLION FISH
Tsung Shang Yu: Shanghai

A. 1½-lb. sea bass, porgy, or red snapper
B. 1 teaspoon salt
C. 4 scallions
D. 5 slices ginger, minced
E. 1 clove garlic, minced

F. 3 tablespoons vegetable oil
G. 1 teaspoon sugar
H. 2 tablespoons light soy sauce
I. 1 tablespoon cornstarch
J. ⅓ cup water

PREPARATION:

I. Clean and scale A. Slash skin diagonally at 1- to 1½-inch intervals. Rub on B inside and out.
II. Slit C. Place aluminum foil in flat pan and spread C on it. Place A on top.
III. Mix D, E, F, G, H.
IV. Preheat broiler.
V. Mix I, J and stir into D–H.

COOKING:

1. Broil A–C in pan 20 minutes, then turn over for another 20 minutes.
2. Pour D–J in pot. Stir and heat. Pour over A–C.
3. Lower broiling pan. Cover A–C with additional foil and cook 10 minutes.

STUFFED SCALLION FISH
Go Sao Yu: Shanghai

A. ¼ cup vegetable oil
B. 1½-lb. sea bass, porgy, or red snapper
C. 2 tablespoons light soy sauce
D. 1 tablespoon cornstarch
E. 1 teaspoon sugar

F. ⅓ cup water
G. 4 scallions
H. 1 tsp. salt
I. 3 slices ginger
J. 6 oz. ground pork

PREPARATION:

I. Clean and scale B. Slash skin diagonally at 1- to 1½-inch intervals. Rub H on both sides of B.
II. Chop one G with I and mix with J and a dash of additional salt. Stuff B cavity with mixture.
III. Mix C, D, E, F.

COOKING:

1. Heat A in frying pan and fry stuffed B until fully brown on both sides.
2. Remove ½ of A, lower heat, add C–F mixture and remaining G. Cover and simmer 15 minutes. Add a small amount of water if sauce becomes too thick.

Note: Only very fresh fish should be stuffed.

BASS, TURNIPS, AND SPARERIBS
Pai Gu Mun Yu: Peking

A. 1 lb. spareribs
B. 1½-lb. sea bass or porgy
C. 1 teaspoon salt
D. 2 turnips
E. dash black pepper
F. 1 teaspoon sherry

G. Chinese parsley (optional)
H. 4 slices ginger, minced
I. 2 scallions, minced
J. 1 tablespoon light soy sauce
K. 2 teaspoons cider vinegar
L. 1 teaspoon sesame oil

PREPARATION:

I. Clean and scale B. Slit skin diagonally every ¾ inch. Rub with C.

II. Cut A into pieces 2 inches long.
III. Peel and shred D.

COOKING:

1. Wash A and simmer 1 hour in 1 qt. water.
2. Add B–C, D, E, salt to taste, and boil 20 minutes. Add F. Serve in long dish; add G.

3. Prepare sauce by mixing H, I, J, K, L.
4. Fish is dipped in H–L sauce for eating.

PICKEREL BROILED IN FOIL
Kao Yu: General

A. 2-lb. pickerel or pike
B. 1 teaspoon salt
C. 3 tablespoons salted black beans
D. 3 slices ginger, shredded

E. 2 teaspoons light soy sauce
F. 1 tablespoon sherry
G. 6 slices bacon

PREPARATION:

I. Soak C in ¼ cup warm water 20 minutes or until soft. Mash C.

II. Scale and clean fish. Rinse in cold water and dry with paper towel. Slash skin diagonally, 1 inch apart, across its width on both sides. Rub B over A and inside cavity.

III. Place A on a piece of aluminum foil and spread C, D, E, F over A. Let stand 20 minutes.

IV. Cut strips of G in half and spread over A. Wrap foil tightly over A.

COOKING:

1. Preheat broiler for 10 minutes. Place foil-covered A about 3 inches below heat. Broil about 30 minutes or until meat separates from bone easily. Open foil and Brown A 5 to 10 minutes. Avoid scorching. Serve hot.

BUTTERFISH IN BEER SAUCE
Go Sao Gih Yu: General

A. ¼ cup peanut oil
B. 1½ lbs. butterfish (about 5)
C. ¾ teaspoon salt
D. 3 scallions, shredded
E. 4 slices ginger, shredded
F. 1 teaspoon sugar

G. 1 tablespoon brown bean sauce
H. 1 tablespoon cider vinegar
I. 1 teaspoon light soy sauce
J. 1 tablespoon sherry
K. ¾ cup beer
L. 2 teaspoons cornstarch

PREPARATION:

1. Scale and clean B. Rinse in cold water, then dry with paper towels. Slash skin diagonally 1 inch apart across the width of the fish on both sides. Rub C over B and inside cavity.

II. Mix D, E, F, G, H, I, J.

COOKING:

1. Heat frying pan. When hot, add A.
2. Brown B in A 3 to 4 minutes on each side.
3. Pour off excess A and add D–J.
4. Add ½ cup K, cover and simmer 15 minutes.
5. Mix L with rest of K so that no lumps remain. Add to frying pan to thicken sauce. Mix well and serve hot.

RED-COOKED BLACKFISH
Hung Sao Wu Yu: Shanghai

A. 4 tablespoons peanut oil
B. 1 scallion
C. 2 slices ginger
D. 1 blackfish (about 2 lbs.)
E. 1 tablespoon sherry
F. 3 tablespoons light soy sauce
G. 1 teaspoon rock sugar
H. ½ cup chicken broth
I. ½ teaspoon lard
J. ½ to 1 teaspoon sesame oil

PREPARATION:

I. Clean and wash D, cut into 6 to 8 pieces.
II. Cut B into 1-inch pieces.
III. Mix E, F, G, H.

COOKING:

1. Heat A, brown B, C; discard B and C.
2. Add D pieces, brown on all sides.
3. Add E–H mixture, bring to boil, cook over low heat 25 minutes.
4. Add I, cook on high heat until sauce is almost dry. Add J and serve.

RED-COOKED FISH WITH BEAN CURD
Hung Sao Dow Fu Yu: Szechuan

A. ¼ cup peanut oil
B. 1- to 1½-lb. porgy
C. 1 tablespoon brown bean sauce
D. 2 tablespoons light soy sauce
E. 1 tablespoon sherry
F. 2 slices ginger, chopped
G. ½ teaspoon salt
H. ½ teaspoon minced garlic
I. 3 cakes bean curd
J. 1 tablespoon cornstarch mixed with ¼ cup water
K. 1 tablespoon chopped scallion

PREPARATION:

I. Wash and clean B, dry with paper towel, slash both sides diagonally at 2-inch intervals.
II. Cut each I into 6 or 7 slices.
III. Mix C, D, E, F, G, H.

COOKING:

1. Heat A and brown B.
2. Pour off excess A, add C–H mixture and I, bring to boil, lower heat and cover, cook 5 to 7 minutes, spooning sauce over B and I once or twice.
3. Thicken sauce with J. Garnish with K.
4. Add Chinese hot sauce, to taste.

RED-COOKED CARP WITH BEAN CURD SKIN
Fu Pi Hung Sao Yu: Shanghai

A. bean curd skin to cover H.
B. 2 scallions, minced
C. 7 slices ginger, minced
D. 1 tablespoon sherry
E. 2 tablespoons light soy sauce
F. 1 clove garlic, chopped
G. 2 teaspoons brown sugar
H. 3-lb. carp, cleaned and scaled
I. 1 teaspoon salt
J. 2 teaspoons cornstarch
K. ½ cup broth
L. 3 tablespoons peanut oil

PREPARATION:

I. Soak A in hot water 20 minutes.
II. Mix B, C, D, E, F, G.
III. Slit skin of H diagonally every 1 inch and rub I over it. Take a piece of heavy-duty aluminum foil longer than H and place it in large cooky pan. Place H in foil.
IV. Drape A over H. Pour B–G, K, over H. Sprinkle with L. Fold foil over to seal A in steam.

COOKING:

1. Preheat oven to 350°.
2. Place foil-wrapped A–I in oven. Cook 1 hour.
3. Add ¼ cup water to J. Mix until smooth. Add to A–I as needed to thicken gravy. Check fish; if it comes off bone easily dish is ready to serve.

RED-COOKED CARP WITH BEAN CURD SKIN *Approved Ulcer Recipe*
Hung Sao Li Yu Dow Fu Pi: General

A. ¼ cup peanut oil
B. 2- to 3-lb. carp, cleaned and scaled
C. 1 tablespoon heavy soy sauce
D. ⅓ cup light soy sauce
E. 1 tablespoon cornstarch
F. 1 tablespoon brown sugar
G. 1 cup pork soup
H. ¼ lb. dried bean curd skin (about 20 pieces 1½ by 5 inches)
I. 1 teaspoon salt

PREPARATION:

I. Soak H 30 minutes in hot water. Drain, cut into 2-inch squares.
II. Cut B into strips 1½ inches thick. Rub with I. Mix C, D, E, F, G.

COOKING:

1. Heat Dutch oven, add A; when hot add B. Stir-fry 5 minutes.
2. Add C–G mixture; add H. Simmer, covered, 30 minutes. When meat comes off bones (it should be soft enough to cut with chopsticks; if it is not, cook 15 minutes longer, adding water if necessary), B is ready to serve.

CARP WITH BEAN CURD CAKE
Do Fu Mun Li Yu: Shanghai

A. 6 oz. frozen broccoli tips
B. 6 black dried Chinese mushrooms
C. 2- to 3-lb. carp, whole, cleaned, scaled
D. 2 tablespoons sherry
E. 4 slices ginger
F. 4 scallions
G. ⅓ cup peanut or salad oil
H. 2 tablespoons light soy sauce
I. 1 teaspoon salt
J. 3 tablespoons salad oil
K. 4 cakes bean curd
L. ½ cup shredded fresh pork
M. 2 teaspoons cornstarch mixed with 2 tablespoons water

PREPARATION:

I. Cut A into pieces 2 inches long.

II. Soak B in hot water ½ hour; discard stems; slice each B into 3 to 5 pieces.

III. Slit skin of C diagonally every ¾ inch and rub I over it. Take a piece of heavy-duty aluminum foil longer than C and place it in large cooky pan. Place C in foil.

IV. Mix D, E, F, G, H. Pour over C.

V. Add J to hot skillet. Add A, L. Stir-fry 3 minutes. Remove and place in dish.

VI. Dice K into squares and spread, with B, over C.

COOKING:

1. Preheat oven to 350°.

2. Place foil-wrapped fish in oven. Cook 50 minutes. Remove from oven; open foil. Put A, L over B–K. Seal foil, leave in oven 10 more minutes.

3. Add M to sauce in foil. Serve C with sauce poured over.

CARP WITH BEAN CURD CAKE   *Approved Ulcer Recipe*
Dow Fu Sao Li Yu: General

A. ¼ cup vegetable oil

B. 2- to 3-lb. carp, cleaned and scaled

C. 1 slice ginger

D. ⅓ cup light soy sauce

E. 1½ cups pork stock

F. 2 teaspoons heavy soy sauce

G. 4 cakes bean curd

H. ½ cup ground pork

I. 1 teaspoon cornstarch

J. 1 teaspoon salt

K. 1 cup flour

L. 1 scallion tied in bundle

PREPARATION:

I. Cut each G into 6 small pieces.

II. Mix H, I, and 1 tablespoon D.

III. Slit B skin diagonally, at about 1 inch intervals; sprinkle with J, roll in K until coated.

IV. Stuff B with H mixture.

COOKING:

1. Heat A in large frying pan. Add B, fry slightly on both sides 10 minutes.

2. Add C, remaining D, F and I. Simmer, covered, 25 minutes. Remove C; serve hot.

RED-IN-SNOW CARP
Shwe Tsai Li Yu: Shanghai

A. 2 tablespoons peanut oil

B. 1 scallion

C. 4 slices ginger, chopped

D. 1 carp (1 to 1½ lbs.), sea bass, or porgy

E. 1 tablespoon sherry

F. ½ cup sliced bamboo shoots

G. 1 cup chicken broth

H. ½ cup red-in-snow

I. salt to taste

PREPARATION:

I. Clean and wash D.

II. Cut B into 2-inch-long pieces.

COOKING:

1. Heat A, add B, C, stir-fry a few seconds.

2. Add D, E, F, G and bring to boil; cover and cook 5 minutes.

3. Add H, I, and cook 2 to 3 more minutes, or until fish is done.

BEAN SAUCE STEAMED CARP
Dow Ban Jiong Yu: Szechuan

A. 2-lb. carp or sea bass
B. ½ teaspoon salt
C. ¼ to ½ teaspoon ginger juice
D. ¼ cup peanut oil
E. 1 clove garlic, minced
F. 2 slices ginger, chopped
G. 1 tablespoon brown bean sauce
H. ½ cup water

I. 2 teaspoons sherry
J. 1 tablespoon light soy sauce
K. 1 teaspoon sugar
L. 1 teaspoon salt
M. 1 tablespoon chopped scallion
N. 1 tablespoon cornstarch mixed with ¼ cup water
O. anise pepper to taste

PREPARATION:

I. Clean and wash A, dry with paper towel, rub with B, C.

II. Mix E, F, G.

III. Mix I, J, K, L, M.

COOKING:

1. Place A–C in dish, steam in steamer over boiling water 5 to 8 minutes or until done. Pour juice into another dish (may be added to H to make ½ cup).
2. Heat D to smoking, pour over A–C, return D to pot, heat; when hot, add E–G, stir-fry ½ minute, add H, bring to boil.
3. Add I–M, cook 1 minute.
4. Thicken with N. Pour over fish; add O to taste and serve hot.

SHANGHAI SMOKED FISH
Shwin Yu: Shanghai

A. 2 to 3 scallions, chopped
B. 5 slices ginger, chopped
C. ⅓ cup sherry
D. ½ teaspoon five spices powder
E. 1 tablespoon sugar

F. ¼ cup light soy sauce
G. ½ teaspoon salt
H. 1 pt. peanut oil
I. 1- to 2-lb. carp

PREPARATION:

I. Wash I thoroughly. Dry well with paper towels.
II. Cut I into ½-inch pieces (cross section). Leave in cool, drafty place for air-drying 30 minutes.

III. Mix A, B well with C, D, E, F, G.
IV. Marinate I in A–G mixture. Refrigerate at least ½ day.
V. Drain I thoroughly before frying, saving sauce mixture in small cooking pot.

COOKING:

1. Heat A–G in pot, bring to boil. Turn off heat and add few drops sesame oil.
2. Heat H in 2-qt. pot. Deep fry I at 350° until brown and crisp (about 3 minutes).
3. Dip each piece of fried I in cooked sauce for a few seconds. Remove from sauce, and place in container. Fish will be tastier if left in refrigerator overnight and eaten cold.

ONION-BAKED FISH
Yang Chung Kow Yu: Shanghai

A. 2 medium onions
B. ½ lb. flounder
C. 2 tablespoons light soy sauce

D. 1 teaspoon sugar
E. 1 teaspoon salt
F. 2 teaspoons sherry

G. ¼ teaspoon pepper
H. 2 tablespoons peanut oil

PREPARATION:

I. Peel A and cut into thin slices.

II. Line cooky sheet with aluminum foil, arrange half of A on top of foil.

III. Place B on top of half of A and spread the other half of A over B.

IV. Mix C, D, E, F, G, H thoroughly; pour over B.

COOKING:

1. Preheat oven to 350°.

2. Bake flounder 30 minutes.

FISH BALLS
Yu Yuen: General

A. 1 lb. fillet of flounder

B. 3 water chestnuts

C. 1 egg, beaten

D. 3 scallions, chopped

E. 1 slice ginger, minced

F. ½ teaspoon salt

G. 4½ teaspoons cornstarch

H. 1 teaspoon light soy sauce

PREPARATION:

I. Chop or grind A into fine pieces. Place in mixing bowl.

II. Chop B fine.

III. Mix, B, C, D, E, F, G, H and add to A.

Combine thoroughly.

IV. Form A–H mixture into balls, each containing a heaping tablespoon of ingredients.

V. Bring 2 qts. water to a rolling boil.

COOKING:

1. Drop A–H balls into boiling water one at a time.

2. When they float to surface, remove.

3. Cool. Serve with duck sauce or light soy sauce.

TANGERINE FISH BALLS
Chen Pei Yu Yuen: Canton

A. 2 pieces (about 1-inch diameter) dried tangerine peel

B. 1 lb. fillet of flounder

C. 1 ball salted turnip

D. 1 egg white

E. ¾ teaspoon salt

F. ½ teaspoon sugar

G. 1½ teaspoons sherry

H. 1 tablespoon cornstarch

PREPARATION:

I. Soak A in warm water until soft (30 minutes). Clean, rinse, and chop until quantity measures 1 tablespoon.

II. Add A, C to B; chop very fine.

III. Beat D.

IV. Combine A, B, C, D, E, F, G, H, beat with fork or chopstick until smooth.

V. Using a porcelain Chinese soup spoon, scoop and form balls.

COOKING:

1. Place A–H balls in 1 qt. boiling water. When water returns to boil and balls float, they are done (about 2 to 3 minutes).

2. Remove balls to dish. Serve plain, with vegetables (see Fish Balls with Vegetables), or in soup (see Fish Balls and Ham Soup).

BRAISED FISH BALLS WITH OYSTER SAUCE
Ho Yow Yu Yuen: Canton

A. 6 tablespoons peanut oil
B. 1 tablespoon chopped scallion
C. 2 slices ginger, chopped
D. 18 to 20 fish balls (see Tangerine Fish Balls)
E. 6 to 8 Chinese mushrooms
F. 1 cup bite-size pieces bamboo shoots

G. 1 cup frozen peas
H. 1 tablespoon oyster sauce
I. 2 teaspoons cornstarch
J. 2 teaspoons sherry
K. ½ cup water
L. salt to taste

PREPARATION:

I. Wash E, soak 15 minutes in warm water. Drain, crosscut each into quarters.

II. Defrost G.
III. Mix H, I, J, K.

COOKING:

1. Heat A, stir-fry B, C a few seconds.
2. Add D, E, F, stir-fry 2 minutes.
3. Add G, cook 1 minute.

4. Add H–K mixture, stir well until thickened. Add L; serve hot.

FISH BALLS WITH VEGETABLES
Yu Yuen: Canton

A. 6 tablespoons peanut oil
B. 1 tablespoon chopped scallion
C. 4 slices ginger, chopped
D. 18 to 20 fish balls (see Tangerine Fish Balls)
E. 6 to 8 Chinese mushrooms
F. 1 cup bite-size pieces bamboo shoots

G. 1 to 2 cups 1-inch-wide pieces Chinese celery cabbage, cut diagonally
H. ½ cup chicken broth
I. 2 teaspoons sherry
J. 2 teaspoons cornstarch
K. salt to taste

PREPARATION:

I. Wash E, soak 15 minutes in warm water; drain, cut each into 3 or 4 pieces.

II. Mix I, J with ¼ cup water.

COOKING:

1. Heat A, stir-fry B, C a few seconds.
2. Add D, E, F, G, stir-fry 2 minutes.

3. Add H, cook 2 to 3 minutes.
4. Thicken with I–J mixture; add K.

GOLDEN FISH ROLLS
Don Pi Yu Guan: Hupeh

A. ¼ cup peanut oil
B. 6 eggs
C. ½ teaspoon salt
D. 1 lb. fillet of flounder, minced (or crab meat, freshly cooked; or shrimp, shelled and deveined)
E. 4 scallions, minced

F. 3 slices ginger, minced
G. 2 teaspoons sherry
H. ½ teaspoon salt
I. dash black pepper
J. 1 teaspoon cornstarch
K. ¾ cup soup stock

PREPARATION:

I. Mix D, E with F, G, H, I, J.

II. Break B into bowl, add C, beat mixture lightly.

COOKING:

1. Put 2 tablespoons A in 8-inch skillet, heat and spread. Add a cooking ladleful of B–C mixture to form skin about 8 inches in diameter. Using low heat, make 6 such skins.
2. Divide D–J mixture into 6 equal portions. Place 1 portion in each egg skin, and roll 6 fish rolls.

3. Fry fish rolls over medium heat in remaining A, turning to ensure even cooking. Add K, cover and simmer 10 minutes. To serve, cut rolls crosswise, thereby forming round slices with golden edges.

GOLDEN FISH ROLLS WITH SPINACH
Don Pi Yu Guan Bo Tsai: Hupeh

In Step 3, after rolls are fried, remove. Place ¼ cup chicken soup in frying pan, add 1 pkg. frozen (thawed) spinach (10 oz.), cover, simmer 2 minutes. Place spinach in a large shallow bowl. Place golden rolls on top and serve. Color contrast will be excellent.

GOLDEN SHRIMP AND PORK ROLLS
Don Pi Sha Guan: Hupeh

Substitute ½ lb. shelled and deveined shrimp and ½ lb. chopped pork for D. In Step 3, after frying rolls, add ½ cup hot water. Cover, and simmer 40 minutes.

FRIED FISH CAKES I
Yu Bing: Shanghai

A. 4 tablespoons peanut oil
B. ½ lb. fillet of flounder, bass, or haddock, minced
C. 1 cup thinly sliced bamboo shoots
D. 6 Chinese dried mushrooms
E. ½ cup thinly sliced Smithfield ham
F. 1 scallion
G. 1 teaspoon sugar

H. 1 tablespoon light soy sauce
I. 1 teaspoon cornstarch
J. dash salt, pepper
K. 3 tablespoons mushroom water
L. 1 teaspoon cornstarch
M. 10 dried shrimp, chopped
N. 2 teaspoons sherry
O. salt to taste

PREPARATION:

I. Mix B with I, J.
II. Wash M. Marinate M in N.
III. Mix B mixture and M, N and shape into 12 cakes.

IV. Wash D and soak in water 15 minutes; drain, saving 3 tablespoons (K); cut each D in half.
V. Slice F into 1-inch pieces.
VI. Mix K, L.

COOKING:

1. Heat A in frying pan; brown B cakes lightly on both sides (from Preparation Step III); remove to dish.
2. Add C, D, E, F to same pan, stir-fry 1 minute.

3. Replace B cakes in pan, mix well with other ingredients. Add G, H; cover and cook over low heat 2 minutes.
4. Add O and thicken with K, L; serve.

FRIED FISH CAKES II
Jien Yu Bing: General

A. 3 tablespoons peanut oil
B. 1 lb. fillet of flounder
C. 8 water chestnuts
D. 1 egg, beaten
E. 3 scallions, chopped
F. 1 slice ginger, minced
G. ½ teaspoon salt
H. 4½ teaspoons cornstarch
I. 1 teaspoon light soy sauce
J. water chestnut flour, as needed

PREPARATION:

I. Chop or grind B into fine pieces. Place in mixing bowl.
II. Chop C fine.
III. Mix C, D, E, F, G, H, I, and add to B. Combine thoroughly.
IV. Form mixture into flat patties, each containing a heaping tablespoon of ingredients.
V. Dust patties with J.

COOKING:

1. Heat A.   2. Fry patties until golden brown.   3. Serve with duck sauce or light soy sauce.

CORNMEAL FISH CAKES
Jien Yu Chio: Tientsin

A. peanut oil 1½ inches deep in deep-fat fryer
B. ¾ cup cornmeal
C. ¾ cup flour
D. ¼ cup minced scallions
E. ¼ teaspoon baking soda
F. 1½ teaspoons baking powder
G. 1½ teaspoons salt
H. 1 lb. flounder fillet or peeled shrimp (or ½ lb. shelled, chopped clams)
I. 1 egg
J. 1½ cups buttermilk

PREPARATION:

I. Mix B, C, D, E, F, G in large bowl.
II. Grind H or chop very fine.
III. Combine H, I, J with B–G mixture in bowl; mix well.

COOKING:

1. Heat A to 325°.
2. Drop 1 teaspoon B–J batter at a time into A, turning until cakes are browned (2 to 3 minutes).
3. Drain cakes on absorbent paper. Serve with catsup (optional).

FLOUNDER FILLET WITH WOOD EARS AND PEAS
Mo Er Ching Do Yu Pien: Shanghai

A. ⅓ cup peanut oil
B. ½ lb. fillet of flounder
C. 12 pieces wood ears
D. 2 cups defrosted frozen peas
E. 1 scallion
F. 3 slices ginger, shredded
G. 1 tablespoon light soy sauce
H. ½ teaspoon sugar
I. ¼ cup chicken broth
J. 2 teaspoons sherry
K. 1 tablespoon cornstarch mixed with ¼ cup water

PREPARATION:

I. Slice B into ½-inch pieces and mix with half of K mixture.

II. Wash C thoroughly, soak in hot water for 30 minutes, drain and shred.

III. Cut E into 1-inch pieces.

IV. Mix G, H, I, J.

COOKING:

1. Heat A, add B, stir-fry 1 to 2 minutes, remove to dish.

2. Leave 3 tablespoons oil in pan, add C, D, E, F, stir-fry 2 minutes; add G–J mixture, mix well.

3. Return B to pan, add rest of K, stir until thickened, serve hot.

FLOUNDER FILLET WITH CHINESE BROCCOLI
Gai Lan Yu Pien: Canton

A. ½ cup peanut oil
B. 4 slices ginger
C. ½- to 1-lb. fillet of flounder
D. 4 teaspoons cornstarch
E. 1 teaspoon salt
F. 6 Chinese mushrooms
G. ½ lb. Chinese (or American) broccoli or cabbage
H. 2 teaspoons sherry
I. 2 tablespoons oyster sauce
J. 1 teaspoon sugar
K. salt, pepper to taste

PREPARATION:

I. Cut C into pieces 1 inch wide, scoring each piece twice before severing.

II. Wash F, soak 15 minutes in warm water. Drain (saving water to mix with D) and quarter each.

III. Mix D with ¼ cup F water.

IV. Mix C, half of D mixture, and E.

V. Cut G into 2- to 3-inch diagonal segments.

VI. Mix H, I, J; add remaining D mixture.

COOKING:

1. Heat A, add B, stir-fry several seconds.

2. Add C–E mixture, stir 1 to 2 more minutes, and remove to a dish, leaving only 3 tablespoons A in pan.

3. Add F, G to remaining A in pan, stir-fry 3 minutes.

4. Add ¼ cup water and H–J mixture, stir until thick.

5. Return C–E mixture to pan, add K, mix well, and serve hot.

BARBECUED FLOUNDER FILLET
Kow Yu Pien: Adapted

A. 1-lb. fillet of flounder
B. 3 tablespoons peanut oil
C. 3 tablespoons light soy sauce
D. ½ teaspoon salt
E. ¼ teaspoon five spices powder
F. 2 tablespoons sherry
G. 2 teaspoons chopped or ½ teaspoon powdered ginger

PREPARATION:

I. Wash A and dry with paper towel.

II. Marinate A in B, C, D, E, F, G sauce and place on barbecue rack.

III. Start charcoal fire and let burn until coals are red-hot.

COOKING:

1. Place rack several inches above charcoal, barbecue fillet 15 minutes; brush on more marinade and cook 5 to 10 minutes longer—or until fully cooked.

FILLET OF SOLE WITH BEAN SPROUTS
Yu Pien Tsao Dow Ya: Shanghai

A. 2 cups vegetable oil
B. 1 lb. fillet of sole
C. 2 scallions
D. 4 slices ginger, shredded
E. 2 cloves garlic
F. 2 teaspoons brown bean sauce
G. 2 teaspoons light soy sauce
H. 2 teaspoons sherry

I. 2 teaspoons vinegar
J. 1 teaspoon sugar
K. ½ teaspoon salt
L. 2 teaspoons cornstarch mixed with
    ½ cup water
M. Chinese hot sauce to taste (optional)
N. ½ teaspoon salt
O. 1 lb. bean sprouts

PREPARATION:

I. Wash B and dry with paper towel, cut into 1½-inch pieces, then coat each side with cornstarch.
II. Cut C into 1-inch pieces.

III. Pound E with side of cleaver, discard skin, then mince. Mix F, G, H, I, J, K, L, M.
IV. Bring 1½ qts. water to boil, add N and O, stir well, remove from water and drain.

COOKING:

1. Heat A to 375°, deep fry B until golden brown (about 1 to 2 minutes), remove B to dish.
2. Leave 2 tablespoons A in pan, heat, and add C, D, E, stir-fry a few seconds.

3. Add F–M mixture to C–E mixture, stir until sauce is thickened.
4. Put B on a dish, add O and pour thickened sauce over all.

STIR-FRIED HADDOCK FLAKES
Tsao Yu Pien: General

A. 6 tablespoons vegetable oil
B. 1 lb. fillet of haddock
C. 2 heaping tablespoons cloud ears
D. 6 dried mushrooms
E. 2 stems celery
F. 1 package (10 oz.) frozen peas

G. 5 slices ginger
H. 2 to 3 scallions, minced
I. dash black pepper (optional)
J. 1 teaspoon salt
K. 3 tablespoons sherry
L. 3 tablespoons cornstarch

PREPARATION:

I. Slice B into strips ⅝ inch by 2 inches by ⅝ inch. Marinate in J, K. Then mix, and coat with L.
II. Soak D in hot water 20 minutes. Cut off stems, cut into 3 pieces each. Reserve water.

III. Cut E into pieces ⅛ inch thick, across grain.
IV. Defrost F.
V. Soak C in hot water 20 minutes, drain, and wash.

COOKING:

1. Place 5 tablespoons A in large frying pan. Stir-fry B 3 minutes, remove from pan.

2. Place remaining A in pan. Add C, D, E; cook 5 minutes. Add F, G, H, cook 1 minute more.
3. Add B, I. Stir a few times. Serve hot.

STIR-FRIED FILLET OF SOLE, FLOUNDER, OR SEA BASS FLAKES
Tsao Yu Pien: General

Substitute fillet of sole, flounder, or sea bass for B. Cook 2 minutes in Step 1.

FRIED SMELTS
Jien Sa Tsan Yu: General

A. 1 cup vegetable oil
B. 15 smelts (1 lb.)
C. ¼ cup light soy sauce
D. ¼ teaspoon five spices powder

E. 1 tablespoon sherry
F. 4 slices ginger
G. 1 bunch Chinese parsley (optional)
H. ¼ teaspoon sesame oil (optional)

PREPARATION:

I. Clean and scale B, drip dry in colander, then dry with paper towels.
II. Make sauce by mixing together C, D, E, F.

III. Marinate B in C–F sauce 30 to 60 minutes. Drip dry in colander.

COOKING:

1. Heat A to 375°. Deep fry B–F. Sprinkle with G, H. Use toasted salt and anise pepper mixture as dip (see Szechuan Pepper Salt).

FRIED BLOWFISH TAILS
Jien Yu Wei: General

Substitute 15 blowfish tails for B. (Tails are skinned and no scaling is required.)

SMELTS FRIED IN EGG BATTER
Jien Sa Tsan Yu: General

A. 1 cup vegetable oil
B. 1 lb. smelts or blowfish tails
C. ¾ teaspoon salt
D. dash black pepper

E. 5 tablespoons flour
F. 1 egg, beaten
G. 2 tablespoons water
H. 2 scallions, chopped

PREPARATION:

I. Scale and clean B. Dry with paper towels. (If blowfish tails are used, tails are skinned and no scaling is required.) Flavor B with C, D.

II. Mix E, F, G, H to a smooth batter.
III. Mix E–H batter with B; let stand 10 minutes.

COOKING:

1. Place A in frying pan; heat to 375°.

2. Add batter-covered B to pan. Deep fry on each side 5 minutes.

FLOUNDER FILLET FRIED IN EGG BATTER
Jien Bien Yu Pien: General

Substitute 1 lb. flounder fillet for B, and dry and cut fillet into 1-inch strips before dipping in E–G.

EEL FRIED IN EGG BATTER
Soo Tsao Wong San: General

Substitute 1 lb. skinned eel for B and increase cooking time to 6 minutes each side. To skin eel; take a piece of wood at least ¾ inch thick and 24 inches long, and place the eel on it. Force an ice pick (or nail) behind the head and into the board. With a sharp knife, cut the skin ½ inch below the pick. With pliers, pull skin off. Clean and slice eel into 1-inch pieces.

STEAMED SHAD
Tsen Sih Yu: Shanghai

A. 3-lb. shad, cleaned
B. 1½ teaspoons salt
C. 2 scallions
D. ¼ cup shredded Virginia ham
E. 5 slices ginger, shredded

F. 1 tablespoon sherry
G. 2 teaspoons shredded ginger
H. 3 tablespoons cider vinegar
I. 1 to 2 tablespoons light soy sauce

PREPARATION:

I. Scale and clean A, rub with B.

II. Cut each C into 4 sections.

COOKING:

1. Place A–B in large bowl. Place bowl in steamer.
2. Place C inside fish cavity.
3. Spread D, E and F over A–B.

4. Steam for 1½ hours or until meat separates easily from bones.
5. Mix G, H, I and serve as sauce for dipping.

STEAMED SHAD   Approved Ulcer Recipe
Tsen Sih Yu: Shanghai

Omit C, E, H and use I alone for dipping; mince D very fine.

SHAD WITH MELON
Fu Gwa Si Yu: Canton

A. 2-lb. shad
B. 1 tablespoon salted black beans
C. 4 slices ginger
D. 1 scallion, minced
E. 2 tablespoons sherry
F. 1 teaspoon sugar

G. 3 tablespoons light soy sauce
H. 4 tablespoons salad oil
I. 1 bitter melon or cucumber
J. 1 tablespoon cornstarch mixed with ¼ cup water
K. 1 teaspoon salt

PREPARATION:

I. Scale, clean, wash, and dry A. Rub with K.
II. Soak B in hot water 10 minutes, drain, then mash.

III. Peel I, remove seeds, and slice.

COOKING:

1. Preheat oven to 350°.
2. Place a large piece of heavy-duty aluminum foil on a cooky pan. Place A on it.
3. Mix B, C, D, E, F, G, H; pour over A. Seal foil over tightly.
4. Bake 40 minutes.

5. Remove from oven, open foil and add I around A. Close foil and bake 20 minutes.
6. Pour A juice into small pot. Add J. Cook to thicken gravy.
7. Pour over A. Serve hot.

SHAD ROE CAKES
Jien Yu Tze: Shanghai

A. peanut oil for deep frying
B. ½ lb. shad roe
C. 1 egg, beaten
D. 1 scallion, minced

E. 2 tablespoons cornstarch
F. ¾ teaspoon salt
G. dash black pepper or paprika

PREPARATION:

1. Wash B and remove membrane.

11. Mix B, C, D, E, F, G until smooth.

COOKING:

1. Heat A in deep fryer.

2. Add 1 tablespoonful B–G mixture at a time and fry until golden brown. Serve hot.

RED SNAPPER FLAKES
Tsu Yu Pien: Peking

A. 2 cups chicken soup
B. 2-lb. red snapper or sea bass
C. 5 slices ginger, chopped
D. 3 scallions, chopped
E. 3 tablespoons peanut oil

F. 1½ teaspoons sherry
G. dash black pepper
H. 1 teaspoon light soy sauce
I. Chinese parsley (optional)

PREPARATION:

1. Scale and clean B. Fillet, cut into 1½-inch squares.

11. Mix ½ C–D with F.

COOKING:

1. Put A and 1 cup water in 3-qt. saucepan. (If homemade chicken soup is available, use full strength.) Bring to boil, add B and rest of C, D. Boil 5 minutes or until B changes color. Transfer B flakes to platter. Keep hot.

2. Heat E in small frying pan. Stir in F, G, H.
3. Pour mixture over fish.
4. Sprinkle I over it and serve. Substitutes for B are 1 to 1½ lbs. flounder, sole, or haddock fillets.

STUFFED RED SNAPPER
Yu Riong Ro Bing: Shanghai

A. 2-lb. red snapper
B. 1 teaspoon salt
C. 4 oz. ground pork
D. 2 slices ginger, minced
E. 2 scallions, minced
F. 2 teaspoons sherry
G. 2 teaspoons light soy sauce
H. 1 teaspoon cornstarch

I. 1 teaspoon brown sugar
J. 3 slices ginger
K. 2 scallions
L. 1 tablespoon cornstarch
M. 1½ cups water
N. 2 tablespoons light soy sauce
O. 5 stalks Chinese parsley (optional)

PREPARATION:

1. Clean A. Make diagonal slashes in skin, one inch apart. Rub B over skin.

11. Mix C, D, E, F, G, H and stuff A with mixture.
111. Mix I, J, K, L, M, N for sauce.

COOKING:

1. Fry A–H in skillet with ½ cup hot oil, until browned on both sides. Pour off excess oil.
2. Add I–N sauce to skillet; cover tightly. Simmer A 15 to 20 minutes on each side. Add small amount of water, if needed. Serve hot. O may be sprinkled on top, if desired.

FISH MAW IN CRAB SAUCE
Sha Hwang Yu Du: Shanghai

A. 4 tablespoons vegetable oil
B. 4 slices ginger, chopped
C. 2 scallions, chopped
D. 2 cups chicken soup
E. ½ teaspoon salt
F. 6 Chinese mushrooms
G. 4 oz. fish maw

H. 4 oz. crab meat
I. 1 teaspoon sugar
J. 1 tablespoon cornstarch
K. 3 tablespoons sherry
L. 1 tablespoon light soy sauce
M. ½ cup mushroom water

PREPARATION:

I. Wash G in cold water and soak overnight. Squeeze out water. Cook in boiling water with 4 slices B and 2 tablespoons K for 10 minutes. Drain; rinse with cold water; squeeze out water. Cut into bite-size pieces.

II. Soak F in warm water 20 minutes. Discard stems and cut each into three pieces.

III. Mix I, J, 1 tablespoon K, L, M until smooth.

COOKING:

1. Put 2 tablespoons A into deep frying pan (or wok). Add B, C. Stir-fry ½ minute; add D, E, F. Bring to boil.
2. Add G and simmer 15 minutes. Place in serving bowl.
3. Into same frying pan put rest of A and heat. Add H, stir-fry ½ minute.
4. Add I, J, K, L, M to make crab sauce.
5. Pour sauce into fish maw soup and serve.

SWEET AND SOUR SAUCE FISH STICKS
Tien Swan Yu Tiao: General

A. 2 tablespoons peanut oil
B. ½ cup subgum ginger and juice to cover (mixed sweet pickles may be substituted)
C. ¼ teaspoon garlic powder
D. 4 tablespoons vinegar

E. 4 tablespoons sugar
F. 2 tablespoons heavy soy sauce
G. 1 cup soup stock
H. 2 tablespoons cornstarch
I. 1 package frozen fish sticks

PREPARATION:

I. Heat A to smoking hot. Set aside to cool.

II. Mix C, D, E, F.

III. Mix G, H.

COOKING:

1. Bring A to high heat again.
2. Add B and juice. Stir-fry 30 seconds.
3. Add C–F mixture. Add I. Stir well and bring to boil. Cook 2 minutes.
4. Add G, H slowly. Stir-fry until sauce thickens. Serve.

BRAISED FROGS' LEGS WITH VEGETARIAN STEAK
Tien Gee Mun Kow Fu: Shanghai

A. ½ cup vegetable oil
B. 5 oz. vegetarian steak
C. 2 scallions
D. 1 lb. frogs' legs
E. 2 teaspoons cornstarch
F. 3 tablespoons sherry
G. ½ teaspoon salt

H. 1½ tablespoons light soy sauce
I. 5 slices ginger
J. 1 teaspoon sugar
K. 1 cup chicken soup
L. ½ tablespoon cornstarch mixed with 2 tablespoons water
M. 1 teaspoon sesame oil (optional)

PREPARATION:

I. Wash and clean D, then drain.

II. Mix E, F, G, H, and M; separate into 2 portions.

III. Mix ⅔ of E–H with D; add I, J; let stand.

IV. Cut B into ½-inch by 1½-inch pieces, mix with ⅓ E–H mixture.

V. Cut C into 1½-inch pieces.

COOKING:

1. Heat A in frying pan.

2. Add B mixture, C and stir-fry 1 to 2 minutes.

3. Add D–J mixture and stir-fry 2 minutes. Add small amount of soup if pan dries out.

4. Add ¼ to ½ cup K and simmer 2 minutes. Thicken with L and serve.

SPICY FROGS' LEGS
Tsao Tien Gee Twei: Szechuan

A. 3 tablespoons vegetable oil

B. 2 large sweet green peppers

C. 2 hot red peppers (optional)

D. 1 clove garlic

E. 1 lb. frogs' legs

F. 2 tablespoons hoisin sauce

G. 1 teaspoon light soy sauce

H. 1 tablespoon sherry

I. ½ teaspoon salt

J. 5 slices ginger

K. ⅓ cup soup stock

L. 2 teaspoons cornstarch mixed with 2 tablespoons water

PREPARATION:

I. Clean and wash E; drain.

II. Split B, C; discard stems and seeds.

III. Mash D, remove skin.

IV. Mix F, G, H, I, J, K.

COOKING:

1. Heat A in frying pan. When smoking, add B, C, D. Stir-fry a few seconds; add E, stir-fry 1 minute.

2. Add F–K, cover and simmer 4 minutes.

3. Thicken with L and serve.

STIR-FRIED FROGS' LEGS
Tsao Tien Gee Twei: Shanghai

A. ⅓ cup peanut oil

B. ½ teaspoon sesame oil

C. ¼ cup sherry

D. 1 teaspoon salt

E. 2 teaspoons vinegar

F. 2 teaspoons sugar

G. 1 tablespoon light soy sauce

H. 1 lb. frogs' legs

I. 2 tablespoons cornstarch

J. 6-oz. can fried vegetable steak

K. 1 scallion, minced

L. 6 slices ginger, minced

PREPARATION:

I. Cut J into ½ inch chunks.

II. Clean H and cut each into 2 to 3 small pieces.

III. Mix B, C, D, E, F, G.

IV. Marinate H in B–G mixture ½ hour.

V. Place I in paper bag, add H and shake.

COOKING:

1. Heat A in skillet until hot.

2. Brown B–I in A. Add J, K, L, and cook additional 3 minutes with small amount of water.

FROGS' LEGS WITH FROZEN PEAS
Tien Gee Tsao Ching Do: Shanghai

A. ¼ cup vegetable oil
B. 1 lb. tender frogs' legs
C. ½ teaspoon sugar
D. 1 teaspoon sesame oil (optional)
E. 2 teaspoons sherry
F. 1 teaspoon salt

G. ½ teaspoon ginger juice (see Index)
    or ¼ teaspoon ginger powder
H. 2 teaspoons cornstarch
I. 1 tablespoon light soy sauce
J. 10-oz. pkg. frozen peas
K. 2 scallions, shredded

PREPARATION:

I. Cover J with boiling water 1 minute or until peas are thoroughly thawed out; drain.

II. Wash and clean B, drain and dry.
III. Mix B with C, D, E, F, G, H, I.

COOKING:

1. Heat A, add B–I mixture and stir-fry 2 minutes.

2. Add J and ¼ cup water, if needed; simmer 1 to 2 minutes or until B and J are done.
3. Remove to serving dish and garnish with K.

OYSTER SAUCE FROGS' LEGS
How Yo Tien Gee: Adapted

A. 3 tablespoons vegetable oil
B. 3 cloves garlic
C. 10 oz. frogs' legs
D. 3 scallions
E. 3 slices ginger
F. ½ cup meat stock

G. 2 teaspoons cornstarch
H. ½ teaspoon sesame oil (optional)
I. 3 tablespoons sherry
J. 1 teaspoon sugar
K. ½ teaspoon salt
L. 3 teaspoons oyster sauce

PREPARATION:

I. Wash and clean C; dry with paper towels.
II. Tie D into 3 small bundles.
III. Mash B, remove skin.

IV. Mix I, J, K, L, then mix with C.
V. Mix G with 2 tablespoons water.

COOKING:

1. Heat A in frying pan, fry B until brown.
2. Add C mixture, D bundles, and E, stir-fry 2 minutes; add liquid if needed.

3. Add F and simmer on low heat 15 to 20 minutes; remove B, D, E.
4. Thicken sauce with G; adjust with H.

BRAISED SHRIMP
Tsao Da Sha: Shanghai

A. 4 tablespoons vegetable oil
B. 1 tablespoon chopped scallion
C. 2 slices ginger, chopped
D. ½ lb. large shrimp
E. 8 water chestnuts
F. 6 dried Chinese mushrooms
G. ½ cup Smithfield ham cut into small pieces
H. 1 cup peas

I. 2 teaspoons light soy sauce
J. 2 teaspoons sherry
K. ½ cup chicken broth
L. 1½ teaspoons salt
M. 2 teaspoons cornstarch mixed with 2 tablespoons water
N. ½ teaspoon sesame oil
O. 1 teaspoon cornstarch

PREPARATION:

I. Shell, devein D, split each in half. Soak 15 minutes in water to which 1 teaspoon L has been added. Rinse well, drain.
II. Mix D with O.
III. Wash F, soak 15 minutes in warm water. Drain; quarter each.
IV. Cut E into small pieces.

COOKING:

1. Heat A. Stir-fry B, C a few seconds. Add D, stir-fry 1 minute.
2. Add E, F, G, H, mix well.
3. Add I, J, K, and rest of L, stir-fry another 1 to 2 minutes.
4. Thicken with M. Just before serving, mix in N.

BRAISED JUMBO SHRIMP
Chieh Tze Da Sha: Adapted

A. ¼ cup lard
B. 10 to 12 jumbo shrimp
C. ¼ cup sherry
D. 2 tablespoons light soy sauce

E. ½ cup catsup
F. 2 scallions
G. 1 teaspoon sugar

PREPARATION:

I. Wash B with shells on; dry thoroughly. Slit each shell along back, devein. Cut each B into thirds.
II. Cut F into 2-inch lengths.
III. Mix C, D, E.

COOKING:

1. Heat A until very hot. Add B, stir-fry until shells turn golden red (about 3 to 4 minutes). Avoid burning.
2. Add half C–E mixture; cook until sauce is re-duced, stirring constantly.
3. Add remaining C–E mixture, F, G. Continue cooking and stirring. When sauce is reduced to half, B is done.

FRIED SHRIMP
Tza Sha: Shanghai

A. 1 lb. large shrimp
B. 2 eggs
C. 1 teaspoon salt
D. dash pepper

E. ½ cup flour
F. peanut oil for deep frying
G. cocktail sauce or Tabasco

PREPARATION:

I. Shell A, except end part. Devein.
II. Cut lengthwise until back is connected slightly.

III. Beat B lightly.
IV. Sprinkle A with C, D; dip first in B, then in E.

COOKING:

1. Put several inches of F in deep fryer or saucepan. Heat.

2. Fry prepared A in hot F until golden brown.
3. Eat with G.

STIR-FRIED SHRIMP I
Ching Tsao Sha Ren: General

A. 4 tablespoons peanut oil
B. 1 lb. large shrimp
C. 1½ teaspoons cornstarch
D. ¾ teaspoon salt

E. 1 tablespoon sherry
F. 2 slices ginger, minced
G. ½ teaspoon sugar
H. 2 scallions, sliced

PREPARATION:

I. Shell, devein, and wash B.

II. Mix C, D, E, F, G well and pour over B. Marinate 15 minutes.

COOKING:

1. Put A in very hot skillet and bring to high heat.

2. Add B with C–G marinade. Stir-fry 3 to 5 minutes, depending on size of shrimp.
3. Serve with garnish of H.

STIR-FRIED SHRIMP II
Ching Tsao Sha Ren: Peking

A. ⅓ cup peanut oil
B. 1 lb. large shrimp
C. 1 egg white
D. 2 teaspoons sherry
E. 1½ teaspoons salt

F. 1 tablespoon cornstarch
G. 1 teaspoon sherry
H. few drops sesame oil
I. 1 tablespoon chopped scallion

PREPARATION:

I. Wash B, dry between paper towels, then shell and devein. (The outstanding feature of Peking shrimp is for the shrimp to be washed first, then shelled and cooked so that

shrimp pieces will be a brighter pink.)
II. Beat C, add D, E, F, mix well.
III. Add B, mix well.

COOKING:

1. Heat A to smoking, add B–F mixture, stir-fry 1 minute.
2. Remove B–F mixture to a dish, drain all the oil away.
3. In same pan, heat 2 more teaspoons peanut oil, add B–F mixture and G, and stir-fry 2 more minutes.
4. Add H and garnish with I.

STIR-FRIED SHRIMP III
Ching Tsao Sha Ren: Shanghai

A. ¼ cup peanut oil
B. 2 scallions, chopped
C. 1 lb. small shrimp
D. ½ teaspoon sugar
E. 1 teaspoon sesame oil

F. 2 teaspoons sherry
G. 2 teaspoons salt
H. ½ teaspoon ginger juice (see Index)
I. 2 teaspoons cornstarch

PREPARATION:

I. Shell, devein, and wash C.
II. Dissolve ½ G in cold water (enough to cover C), add C and soak 30 minutes.
III. Drain C, rinse thoroughly, dry with paper towels. Mix with D, E, F, ½ G, H, I.

COOKING:

1. Heat A, add B, stir-fry a few seconds, add C–I mixture, stir-fry 1 to 2 minutes or until C turns pink.
2. Remove C–I mixture to dish and serve hot.

STIR-FRIED SHRIMP WITH FROZEN PEAS
Sha Ren Ching Do: Shanghai

Add 10-oz. package frozen peas. Cover peas with boiling water 1 minute or until thoroughly thawed; drain. After removing C–I mixture to dish in Step 2, pour excess A back into pan. Heat A, add peas, stir-fry 1 minute, return C, mix well, and add salt and pepper to taste.

STIR-FRIED SHRIMP IN SHELL
Yo Bao Sha: Shanghai

A. 3 tablespoons peanut oil
B. 1 lb. large shrimp
C. 2 tablespoons light soy sauce
D. 1 tablespoon sugar
E. 2 tablespoons sherry
F. 1 tablespoon vinegar

G. 1½ teaspoons minced ginger
H. ⅛ teaspoon garlic powder
I. ½ teaspoon heavy soy sauce
J. ¼ cup water
K. 2 scallions, sliced

PREPARATION:

I. Remove legs from B (use small curved scissors). Wash well.
II. Mix C, D, E, F, G, H, I, J.

COOKING:

1. Put A in very hot skillet and bring to high heat.
2. Add B, stir-fry ½ minute.
3. Add C–J mixture. Cover. Cook over moderately high heat 5 minutes.
4. Serve with garnish of K. May be served cold.

FRIED PRAWN IN SHELL
Yo Bao Sha: Shanghai

A. ¼ cup peanut oil
B. ½ lb. jumbo shrimp
C. 1 tablespoon chopped scallion
D. 2 slices ginger, chopped

E. 1 tablespoon sherry
F. 2 tablespoons light soy sauce
G. 1 teaspoon sugar
H. several sprigs of Chinese parsley, chopped

PREPARATION:

I. Wash B with shells on, dry with paper towel, halve each, devein.

II. Mix C, D, E, F, G.

COOKING:

1. Heat A until smoking. Add B, stir-fry until shell turns golden red (about 1 minute), remove from heat, pour off excess A.

2. Return B to heat, add C–G, stir 3 more minutes (until sauce is reduced to half). Sprinkle with H. Serve hot or cold as hors d'oeuvres.

STIR-FRIED SHRIMP WITH BEAN CURD I
Sha Ren Dow Fu: Peking

A. ¼ cup peanut oil
B. 1 tablespoon chopped scallion
C. ½ teaspoon chopped ginger
D. ½ lb. small shrimp
E. 1 teaspoon cornstarch
F. ½ teaspoon salt

G. 4 cakes bean curd
H. ½ cup chicken broth
I. 3 teaspoons cornstarch mixed with ¼ cup water
J. salt to taste

PREPARATION:

I. Shell, devein, and wash D. Dry with paper towel, mix with E, F.

II. Cut each G into 8 pieces.

COOKING:

1. Heat A, stir-fry B, C 15 seconds.
2. Add D–F mixture, stir about ½ minute or until D turns pink.
3. Add G, mix well.

4. Add H, bring to boil, cook for ½ to 1 minute.
5. Thicken with I.
6. Add J and serve hot.

STIR-FRIED SHRIMP WITH BEAN CURD II
Dow Fu Tsao Sha Ren: General

A. 4 tablespoons peanut oil
B. 1 scallion, chopped
C. 2 slices ginger, chopped
D. 1 lb. large shrimp
E. 1 egg white
F. 1 teaspoon salt

G. 3 teaspoons cornstarch
H. 2 cakes bean curd
I. ½ cup frozen peas, defrosted
J. 1 tablespoon sherry
K. 1 tablespoon light soy sauce

PREPARATION:

I. Shell, devein, and wash D. Split each into 2 pieces. Dry with paper towels.

II. Mix D with E, F, and 1 teaspoon G.

III. Cut each H into 16 pieces.

IV. Mix J, K and 2 teaspoons G with ½ cup broth or water.

COOKING:

1. Heat A. Add B, C, stir a few times. Add D–G and sauté over high heat 2 minutes. Add H, I.
2. Mix well, keep stirring a minute or so.

3. Add J–K mixture, and stir until sauce is thickened. Serve hot with rice.

STIR-FRIED SHRIMP WITH GREEN PEAS
Ching Do Sha Ren: General

A. 3 tablespoons peanut oil
B. 2 slices ginger, chopped
C. 1 scallion, chopped
D. 1 10-oz. box peeled, ready-to-cook small shrimp

E. ½ package frozen peas
F. 1 tablespoon sherry
G. 1 teaspoon salt
H. 1 egg white
I. 4 teaspoons cornstarch

PREPARATION:

I. Dissolve G in 1 qt. cold water.
II. Add D; soak 10 minutes.
III. Drain D, rinse thoroughly, and dry with paper towel. When dry, mix D with F, H and

½ I.

IV. Cover E with 2 cups boiling water for 1 minute. Drain. Mix remaining I with ¼ cup water.

COOKING:

1. Heat A. Add B, C, stir a few times. Add D mixture, sauté mixture quickly over high heat 1 or 2 minutes.

2. Add E, F, continue to stir 1 more minute.
3. Thicken with I mixture; serve hot.

SHRIMP STIR-FRIED WITH MUSHROOMS
Dung Gu Sha Ren: General

Substitute 4-oz. can button mushrooms for E. Drain, using mushroom water to mix with cornstarch, in Step V.

STIR-FRIED SHRIMP WITH VEGETABLES
Ching Do Dung Gu Sha Ren: Peking

A. 3 tablespoons peanut oil
B. 1 tablespoon chopped scallion (white part only)
C. ½ teaspoon chopped ginger
D. 1 clove garlic, chopped
E. 1 small egg white

F. 1 teaspoon sherry
G. 1 teaspoon salt
H. 1½ teaspoons cornstarch
I. ½ lb. medium shrimp
J. 10-oz. pkg. frozen peas, defrosted
K. 6 to 8 Chinese mushrooms

PREPARATION:

I. Shell, and cut open the backs of I, devein, and wash.
II. Beat E, mix well with F, G, H.

III. Add I and mix well.
IV. Wash K and soak in warm water 15 minutes, drain, dice.

COOKING:

1. Heat A, and B, C, D, stir-fry ½ minute; add E–I mixture, stir-fry 1 minute, remove to a dish, return oil to pan.

2. Heat pan, add J and K, stir-fry 1 minute.
3. Add B–I, stir-fry with J–K 2 more minutes and serve.

SHREDDED BEAN CURD WITH DRIED SHRIMP
Sha Mi Tzu Gahn Si: Shanghai

A. ¼ cup peanut oil
B. 8 to 10 dried shrimp
C. 2 teaspoons sherry
D. 2 teaspoons light soy sauce
E. 4 to 6 Chinese mushrooms

F. 3 slices ginger, shredded
G. 4 pieces pressed bean curd
H. 1 cup chicken broth
I. ½ to 1 teaspoon sesame oil (to taste)
J. 1 stalk celery heart, chopped

PREPARATION:

I. Rinse B, drain, soak in C 15 minutes or until soft.
II. Wash and soak E in warm water 15 minutes or until soft, remove stems, shred. Save water and add to chicken broth to make 1 cup.
III. Cut G into slices, then shred.

COOKING:

1. Heat 2 tablespoons A, add B–C mixture, stir-fry for ½ to 1 minute, add D, mix well, remove to dish.
2. Heat remaining A until smoking, add E, F, stir-fry ½ to 1 minute, add G, mix well.
3. Add H, bring to boil, simmer until reduced to half, add B mixture and continue cooking until sauce is absorbed, about 2 to 3 minutes.
4. Add I, mix well and garnish with J.

PRESSED BEAN CURD SHRIMP
Sha Tze Gahn Si: Shanghai

A. ¼ cup peanut oil
B. ½ cup shrimp as in Preparation I
C. 2 teaspoons sherry
D. 2 teaspoons light soy sauce
E. 4 to 6 Chinese mushrooms

F. 3 slices ginger, shredded
G. 4 pieces pressed bean curd
H. 1 cup chicken broth
I. ½ to 1 teaspoon sesame oil (to taste)
J. 1 stalk celery heart, chopped

PREPARATION:

I. Shell, devein, wash, and dice B.
II. Soak B in C 15 minutes.
III. Wash E and soak in warm water 15 minutes or until soft, remove stem, shred; add E water to chicken broth.

COOKING:

1. Heat 2 tablespoons A, add B–C mixture, stir-fry ½ to 1 minute, add D, mix well, remove to dish.
2. Heat 2 tablespoons A until smoking, add E, F, stir a few times, add G, mix well.
3. Add H, bring to boil, simmer until gravy is reduced by half, add B mixture and continue cooking until gravy is completely absorbed.
4. Add I, mix well and garnish with J.

GLAZED SHRIMP
Gahn Tsao Sha: Shanghai

A. 3 tablespoons vegetable oil
B. 1 lb. medium shrimp
C. 1 egg white
D. 1 tablespoon cornstarch
E. dash baking soda

F. 1 tablespoon sherry
G. 3 slices ginger, chopped
H. 2 tablespoons light soy sauce
I. 2 scallions, minced

PREPARATION:

I. Shell B, devein, and wash in 1 pt. water containing 1 teaspoon salt. Drain, then dry on paper towels.

COOKING:

1. Place A in hot skillet. When oil is hot, add B–H mixture and stir continuously 1 minute. Lower heat, simmer 5 more minutes.

II. Mix B, C, D, E, F, G, H. Marinate for 30 minutes.

2. Add I, cover and cook on low heat for additional 5 minutes.

BROILED BACON WITH SHRIMP
Yen Ro Sha: Adapted

A. 1 lb. frozen shrimp (about 24 shrimp), defrosted
B. 1 tablespoon sherry
C. 1 tablespoon light soy sauce
D. ½ teaspoon sugar

E. ½ to 1 teaspoon ginger juice (see Index)
F. salt and pepper to taste
G. 1 teaspoon cornstarch
H. 6 strips bacon

PREPARATION:

I. Mix A, B, C, D, E, F, G and marinate 25 to 30 minutes.
II. Cut each H into 4 pieces.

III. Wrap pieces of A–G with pieces of H; fasten with wooden toothpicks.
IV. Arrange in a single layer in a foil-lined pan.
V. Pour rest of marinade over A.

COOKING:

1. Preheat broiler 15 to 20 minutes.

2. Broil A 3 to 4 minutes on each side or until H is cooked.

CURRIED SHRIMP WITH BAMBOO SHOOTS
Yeh Jiong Ga Li Har: Canton

A. 2 tablespoons peanut oil
B. 1 medium-size onion
C. 1 to 2 cloves garlic
D. 1 to 2 teaspoons curry powder
E. 1½ teaspoons salt
F. 1 cup cubed bamboo shoots

G. 1 cup coconut flakes
H. 1½ cups hot water
I. 1 lb. large shrimp
J. 2 teaspoons cornstarch mixed with 2 tablespoons water

PREPARATION:

I. Peel skin of B and C; chop into fine pieces.
II. Mix D, E.
III. Mix G, H and let stand 1 hour. Stir well, then squeeze out juice through a colander. Reserve juice; discard coconut.
IV. Shell, devein, and wash I. Dry between paper towels.

COOKING:

1. Heat A, add B, C; stir-fry over medium heat until onion is transparent (about 2 minutes).
2. Add D, E mixture; mix well.
3. Add F and G juice. Bring to a boil, then lower heat and simmer 10 minutes.
4. Turn up heat, add I and cook 5 minutes.
5. Thicken with J; serve with rice.

DRIED SHRIMP WITH CABBAGE
Jing Go Bai Tsai: General

A. 2 tablespoons peanut oil
B. 1 scallion, chopped
C. 2 slices ginger, chopped
D. 12 dried shrimp

E. ½ cabbage, cut into bite-size pieces
   (about 4 or 5 cups)
F. 1 teaspoon sugar
G. 1 teaspoon salt
H. 3 tablespoons shrimp water

PREPARATION:

I. Wash D, soak in water for 10 minutes; drain, save water.

COOKING:

1. Heat A in frying pan.
2. Add B, C, stir a few times.
3. Add D, stir-fry 30 seconds.

4. Add E, stir a few times.
5. Add F, G, H. Cook 5 more minutes.

STIR-FRIED SHRIMP WITH CABBAGE HEARTS
Sha Tsao Bai Tsai Shing: Szechuan

A. 2 tablespoons peanut oil
B. 8 to 10 dried shrimp
C. 1 teaspoon sherry
D. 1 to 1½ lbs. Chinese cabbage hearts
E. 1 teaspoon salt

F. ½ teaspoon sugar
G. 2 teaspoons light soy sauce
H. 1 teaspoon sherry
I. 1 tablespoon finely chopped scallion
J. ½ to 1 teaspoon sesame oil (to taste)

PREPARATION:

I. Cut D into pieces 2 to 3 inches long, parboil 1 minute, drain.

II. Clean, wash, and soak B in hot water 15 minutes; drain and mince.
III. Mix E, F, G, H.

COOKING:

1. Heat A, add B, stir-fry a few seconds, add C, continue stirring 1 minute.

2. Add D, stir few times, add E–H mixture; stir until no liquid is left.
3. Add I, J, mix well and serve.

DRIED SHRIMP WITH RADISHES
Sha Mi Sao Lo Bo: Shanghai

A. 3 tablespoons vegetable oil
B. 15 dried shrimp
C. 2 scallions, minced
D. 2 bunches red whole radishes

(or 1 cup shredded turnips)
E. ¾ cup meat or chicken broth
F. ¼ teaspoon salt
G. 1 teaspoon cornstarch

PREPARATION:

I. Soak B in hot water 20 minutes. Drain, reserving water.

II. Remove and discard green from D; wash D well in cool water; shred.

COOKING:

1. Place A in hot skillet, using high heat. Add B, C, stir-fry 1 minute.
2. Add D, E, F and water from B; cover, simmer

15 minutes.
3. Mix G with a little water; stir this mixture into other ingredients. Serve.

DRIED SCALLOPS WITH TURNIPS
Gahn Bei Sao Lo Bo Si: Shanghai
Substitute 1 cup shredded turnips for D and 6 dried scallops for B.

STIR-FRIED SHRIMP WITH CHINESE VEGETABLES
Shia Tze Lo Han Chai: General

A. 3 tablespoons peanut oil
B. 4 slices ginger, shredded
C. 1 pkg. frozen shrimp (about 1 lb.)
D. 10-oz. can Chinese vegetables
E. 2 tablespoons light soy sauce

F. 2 tablespoons heavy soy sauce
G. 4 tablespoons sherry
H. 1 can beef broth
I. 1 tablespoon cornstarch mixed with 2 tablespoons water

PREPARATION:

I. Mix E, F, G, H, I in saucepan; set aside.

COOKING:

1. Heat A to smoking in deep pot; turn off heat, let stand 30 seconds.
2. Add B, turn up heat, stir-fry 1 minute.
3. Add C, stir for 5 to 7 minutes or until cooked.
4. Add D, mix in well, then pour into a bowl.
5. Heat E–I mixture until it thickens.
6. Pour E–I mixture over C mixture. Serve with rice.

Note: Lo Han Chai is a traditional Buddhist vegetarian dish. It adds an unusual flavor to any meat.

STIR-FRIED SHRIMP AND KIDNEY
Tsao Sha Yao: Shanghai

A. 2 kidneys
B. ¼ lb. snow pea pods or 1 cup water chestnuts
C. ⅓ cup peanut oil
D. ½ lb. large shrimp
E. 1 teaspoon sherry
F. ½ teaspoon salt
G. 1 teaspoon cornstarch

H. 2 slices ginger
I. 1 scallion
J. 2 teaspoons light soy sauce
K. ½ teaspoon sugar
L. dash pepper, salt
M. 1 teaspoon cornstarch mixed with 2 tablespoons water

PREPARATION:

I. Wash and remove any outer membrane from A; split lengthwise, remove all the white veins; make tiny crisscross slashes on top, then cut into ¼-inch slices.

II. Shell, devein, and wash D; dry between paper towels, mix with E, F, G.
III. Remove tips of B (or slice water chestnuts).
IV. Shred H and cut I into 1-inch segments.
V. Mix J, K, L, M.

COOKING:

1. Put A slices into 2 cups of boiling water; when water returns to boil, turn off heat, drain.
2. Add B to boiling water, stir, then drain immediately.
3. Heat ½ of C, add D–G mixture, stir-fry 2 minutes; add B, stir-fry ½ minute. Remove to dish.
4. Heat rest of C, add H, I, stir-fry a few seconds; add A and stir-fry 1 minute.
5. Add J–M mixture, mix well.
6. Add D–G mixture, stir well and serve.

STIR-FRIED SHRIMP WITH DRAGON WELL TEA LEAVES
Lung Jing Tsao Sha Ren: Hangchow

A. 1/3 cup peanut oil
B. 1 lb. medium shrimp
C. 1 tablespoon dragon well tea leaves
D. 1 tablespoon sherry
E. 1 scallion, chopped
F. 1 egg white
G. 1 tablespoon cornstarch
H. 1 teaspoon salt

PREPARATION:

I. Shell, devein, and wash B, dry between paper towels.
II. Mix B with F, G, H.
III. Pour 1/2 cup boiling water over C, stir as leaves start to open; drain.

COOKING:

1. Heat A, add B mixture, stir-fry 1 minute; pour off excess oil.
2. Add C, stir-fry 1 minute.
3. Add D, mix well.
4. Add E, stir well and serve.

SHRIMP WITH WATER CHESTNUTS
Har Gow: Canton

A. 1/2 lb. medium shrimp
B. 1/4 cup water chestnuts
C. 1 scallion
D. 1 teaspoon salt
E. 1/8 teaspoon pepper
F. 1/4 teaspoon sesame oil
G. 36 fun goh skins (see Fun Goh Dough)
H. 2 teaspoons light soy sauce

PREPARATION:

I. Shell, devein, wash, dry, and chop A.
II. Chop B, C.
III. Mix A, B, C, D, E, F, H thoroughly.
IV. Fill each piece of G with 1 teaspoon A–H mixture.
V. Gather dough edges, pinch lightly, and press toward one side.

COOKING:

1. Arrange single layer of dough on greased plate.
2. Steam over boiling water 10 to 12 minutes.
3. Serve with hoisin sauce.

SHRIMP WITH TOMATO SAUCE I
Keh Tsup Har: Canton

A. 3 tablespoons peanut oil
B. 1 lb. large shrimp
C. 6-oz. can tomato paste
D. 1 1/2 teaspoons chopped ginger
E. 2 to 3 tablespoons chopped scallions
F. 1/2 teaspoon salt
G. 3 tablespoons cider vinegar
H. 1 tablespoon sugar
I. 4 tablespoons water

PREPARATION:

I. Shell, wash, and devein B.
II. Mix C, D, E, F, G, H, I.

COOKING:

1. Heat A until hot. Add B and stir until they turn pink.
2. Add C–I mixture; bring to boil. Cover and cook over low heat 2 minutes.
3. Serve hot with rice.

SHRIMP WITH TOMATO SAUCE II
Keh Tsup Har: Canton

A. 2 tablespoons peanut oil
B. 1 lb. large shrimp
C. 1 teaspoon salt
D. ¼ teaspoon garlic powder
E. 1 slice ginger, minced
F. 1½ teaspoons light soy sauce
G. 2 large tomatoes, or 2 cups canned tomatoes

H. 1 teaspoon sugar
I. ½ cup soup stock
J. ¼ cup water
K. 2 teaspoons heavy soy sauce
L. 2 tablespoons cornstarch
M. 2 scallions, sliced

PREPARATION:

I. Shell, devein, and wash B and place in bowl.
II. Cut G into 8 segments; mix with H. Set aside.

III. Mix C, D, E, F well. Add to B. Marinate 15 minutes.
IV. Mix J, K, L. Set aside. Stir well before using.

COOKING:

1. Put A in very hot skillet and bring to high heat.
2. Add B and stir-fry 2½ minutes.
3. Add G–H. Stir-fry 2 minutes.
4. Add I. Cover. Bring to boil.

5. Simmer over low heat 2 minutes.
6. Slowly add as much of J–L mixture as is necessary to thicken sauce and evenly coat shrimp and other ingredients.
7. Serve with garnish of M.

SHRIMP WITH BITTER MELON AND SALTED BLACK BEANS
Fu Gwa Dow Si Har: Canton

A. 2 tablespoons peanut oil
B. 2 tablespoons salted black beans
C. 2 cloves garlic, minced
D. ½ lb. medium shrimp
E. 1 teaspoon cornstarch
F. 1 teaspoon light soy sauce
G. 2 teaspoons sherry
H. ¼ teaspoon sugar

I. ¼ teaspoon peanut oil
J. 1 bitter melon
K. 1 teaspoon light soy sauce
L. ½ teaspoon sugar
M. 2 scallions, sliced
N. 1 teaspoon cornstarch
O. 1 cup soup stock

PREPARATION:

I. Shell, devein, wash D. Dry between paper towels and cut into ¾-inch segments. Mix E, F, G, H, I, and use as marinade for D. Soak 15 minutes.
II. Wash J, cut in half lengthwise and discard seeds. Cut into 1/16-inch slices and parboil in ½ teaspoon soda and 2 cups boiling water for 1-2 minutes. Drain, rinse well; discard water
III. Wash B and mash, mix with C. Set aside.
IV. Mix N, O. Set aside. Stir well before using.
V. Mix K, L, M. Set aside.

COOKING:

1. Put A in very hot skillet and bring to high heat.
2. Add B–C mixture. Stir-fry rapidly 15 seconds to brown C.
3. Add D and E–I. Stir-fry D about 3 minutes (so as to be slightly undercooked).
4. Add J, stir-fry 2 minutes and add K–M mixture; stir-fry well.
5. Add N, O, slowly. Stir-fry until sauce thickens and coats all ingredients well.

STEAMED SHRIMP WITH PORK
Sha Tze Ro Chio: General

A. ½ lb. medium shrimp
B. ⅛ lb. ground pork
C. 4 water chestnuts, chopped fine
D. 1 slice ginger, minced

E. 1 teaspoon light soy sauce
F. 1 tablespoon gin
G. 1 teaspoon salt
H. 1 scallion, sliced

PREPARATION:

I. Shell, devein, and wash A. Slice lengthwise partway through the back.
II. Mix B, C. Set aside.
III. Mix D, E, F, G. Pour over A and marinate 15 minutes.

IV. Arrange A on serving platter suitable for steaming.
V. Distribute B, C evenly over A. Pour marinade from A over A, B, C.

COOKING:

1. Boil water in steamer.
2. Place serving platter in steamer containing rapidly boiling water.

3. Cover and steam 25 minutes. Remove.
4. Serve with garnish of H.

FRIED SHRIMP WITH HOISIN SAUCE
Gahn Jien Sha: Peking

A. 3 tablespoons peanut oil
B. 2 cloves garlic, chopped
C. 1 tablespoon chopped scallion
D. 1 lb. large shrimp

E. 2 tablespoons hoisin sauce
F. 2 teaspoons light soy sauce
G. 1 teaspoon sherry

PREPARATION:

I. Shell, devein, and wash D.

II. Mix E, F, G.

COOKING:

1. Heat A, add B, C and stir-fry a few times.
2. Add D, continue stirring 1 to 2 minutes.

3. Add E–G mixture, mix well, stir until sauce is almost dry (about 4 to 5 minutes).

SHRIMP LIMA BEAN IN HEAVY SAUCE
Tsan Do Sha Ren: Shanghai

A. 4 tablespoons vegetable oil
B. 2 scallions, minced
C. ½ lb. small shrimp
D. ½ lb. small lima beans
E. 1 lb. asparagus
F. 2 slices ginger

G. dash pepper
H. ¾ teaspoon salt
I. 1 tablespoon sherry
J. 2 cups chicken soup
K. 2 tablespoons cornstarch mixed with ⅓ cup water

PREPARATION:

Shell and devein C. Wash and add to I. Marinate. Cut off E shoots and wash, discard stems.

COOKING:

1. Heat A in skillet.
2. Add B. Cover skillet immediately to prevent oil from spattering.
3. Remove cover. Add C, stir 2 minutes.

4. Add D, E, F. Keep heat high, cook and stir ½ minute.
5. Add G, H, I, J. Cook 5 minutes, add K. When sauce is thick, dish is ready.

SHRIMP BEAN CURD
Sha Tze Go Te Dow Fu: Peking

A. 1 cup peanut oil for deep frying
B. 4 cakes bean curd
C. ¼ lb. small shrimp
D. 1 to 2 eggs
E. ¼ cup chicken broth
F. few drops sesame oil (optional)
G. Chinese parsley (optional)
H. ½ teaspoon ginger juice (see Index)

I. 1 tablespoon minced scallion
J. 1 tablespoon light soy sauce
K. 1 teaspoon sherry
L. ½ teaspoon sugar
M. ½ teaspoon salt
N. 1 teaspoon peanut oil
O. ⅓ cup flour

PREPARATION:

I. Cut B horizontally and then into halves that make each B into 4 pieces.
II. Mix H, I, J, K, L, M, N well, and pour over B, marinate 15 minutes.

III. Shell, devein, and wash C. Wash, drain, and mix with 1 teaspoon cornstarch and dash of salt.
IV. Beat D.
V. Coat B pieces with O and then D.

COOKING:

1. Heat A to 375°, deep fry B until golden brown. Drain on paper towel. Drain excess oil into a container.
2. In same pan arrange B in single layer, spread C on top.

3. If any D is left from dipping, mix with E and pour over B, C mixture; cover and cook over medium heat 3 minutes; remove lid and cook until liquid is absorbed.
4. Remove B and C to plate in a flat layer.
5. Add F and garnish with G.

SHRIMP BALLS I
Sha Yuen: General

A. 1 lb. large shrimp (or fillet of flounder, minced)
B. 3 water chestnuts
C. 1 egg
D. 3 scallions, sliced

E. 1 slice ginger, minced
F. 1 teaspoon salt
G. 4½ teaspoons cornstarch
H. 1 teaspoon light soy sauce

PREPARATION:

I. Shell, devein, and wash A. Drain. Then chop or grind into fine pieces. Place in mixing bowl.
II. Chop B fine.

III. Mix B, C, D, E, F, G, H and add to A. Combine thoroughly.
IV. Form mixture into balls (a heaping tablespoon each).
V. Bring 2 qts. water to a rolling boil.

COOKING:

1. Drop shrimp balls into boiling water one at a time.

2. When shrimp balls float to surface, remove.
3. Cool. Serve with duck sauce.

SHRIMP BALLS II
Tza Sha Yuen: Adapted

A. peanut oil for deep frying
B. 1 lb. medium shrimp
C. ½ lb. fresh fat pork, minced
D. 1 teaspoon salt
E. ⅛ teaspoon pepper
F. 1 teaspoon sherry
G. ½ teaspoon ginger, minced
H. 3 tablespoons cornstarch
I. bread crumbs (optional)
J. head of lettuce
K. anise pepper (or Anise Pepper Salt—see Index)

PREPARATION:

I. Wash, shell, devein, wash, and mince B.
II. Mix B, C, D, E, F, G, H. Form lightly into 1-inch balls.
III. Coat with I, if desired.

COOKING:

1. Heat A to 300°.
2. Drop into A only as many B–I balls as can be deep fried without crowding. Fry 5 minutes. Repeat until all balls are fried.
3. Raise heat to 375°. Fry balls again until golden brown.
4. Serve on bed of J with small dish of K.

SHRIMP BALLS IN OYSTER SAUCE
Ho Yow Har Kew: Canton

A. 2 cups peanut oil
B. 1 lb. large shrimp
C. 6 water chestnuts, chopped
D. ¼ cup bamboo shoots, chopped
E. 1 egg white
F. 2 teaspoons lard (optional)
G. 2 tablespoons cornstarch
H. 1 tablespoon sherry
I. 1 teaspoon salt
J. dash pepper
K. ¼ cup oyster sauce
L. 1 scallion, chopped, or Chinese parsley

PREPARATION:

I. Shell, devein, and wash B. Chop fine.
II. Mix B, C, D, E, F, G, H, I, J, let stand 30 minutes.

COOKING:

1. Heat A in 2-qt. saucepan to about 350°.
2. Scoop B–J with a large soup spoon, drop balls gently into A. Deep fry until golden brown.

When balls float, remove and drain.

3. Place B–J on plate. Pour hot K over them. Garnish with L.

GOLDEN COIN SHRIMP
Jing Tsien Sha Bing: Yangchow

A. 2 tablespoons peanut oil
B. ½ lb. green leaf vegetable
C. ½ cup chicken broth
D. 1½ teaspoons cornstarch mixed with 1 tablespoon water
E. pepper to taste
F. 1 lb. medium shrimp
G. 2 oz. pork fat
H. 1 egg white
I. 2 teaspoons sherry
J. 2 teaspoons cornstarch
K. 1 tablespoon chopped scallion
L. 1 teaspoon salt

PREPARATION:

I. Shell, devein, and wash F, dry between paper towels.

II. Mix F, G, and mince.

COOKING:

1. Heat A in frying pan over medium heat.
2. Place shrimp balls in pan and flatten each lightly with ladle.
3. Brown on both sides until they are done; remove to platter.

III. Mix F–G and H, I, J, K, L thoroughly; form into 20 to 24 balls.

4. Stir-fry B with a little salt and place around the shrimp balls.
5. In saucepan, heat C and thicken with D; pour over the dish; sprinkle with E and serve.

SHRIMP ROLL
Sha Guan: General

A. 1 lb. large shrimp
B. 1 scallion, minced
C. 1 teaspoon salt
D. 2 slices ginger, minced
E. 2 teaspoons cornstarch
F. 1 teaspoon sesame oil (optional)

G. dash black pepper
H. 1 teaspoon sherry
I. 3 eggs
J. vegetable oil for greasing pan
K. 2 cups clear chicken soup
L. ½ cup shredded cooked ham

PREPARATION:

I. Shell, devein and wash A. Then chop or grind.

II. Mix A with half of C and all of D, E, F, G, H.

III. Beat I well. Add remaining C.

IV. Heat J in skillet and add 1 tablespoon I.

Spread as thin as possible by tilting skillet. After formed, egg skins should be about 5 inches in diameter. Remove egg skins when done. Repeat until I is used up.

V. Place A–H mixture in each I. Roll into 1-inch by 4-inch rolls.

COOKING:

1. Place rolls in skillet. Add K. Cover and simmer for 20 minutes.

2. Put rolls in shallow bowl. Spread L over rolls and serve hot.

SHRIMP ROLL   *Approved Ulcer Recipe*
Sha Guan: Fukien

Omit B, D, G, and H. Be sure to chop A and L very fine.

SHRIMP ROLL WITH CELLOPHANE NOODLES   *Approved Ulcer Recipe*
Sha Guan Fun See: Fukien

Add 2 oz. cellophane noodles, soak in hot water 30 minutes (noodles absorb water, so be generous); chop 3 cups Chinese celery cabbage very fine. In Step 1, add noodles and celery cabbage to egg rolls. Add soup, simmer covered 20 minutes. Add more water if necessary to prevent noodles and shrimp rolls from scorching.

SWEET AND SOUR SHRIMP
Tien Swan Sha: Shanghai

A. 4 to 6 tablespoons salad oil
B. 1 lb. large shrimp
C. ½ cup tomato paste
D. 3 to 4 tablespoons cider vinegar
E. 2 to 3 tablespoons sugar

F. 1 tablespoon chopped fresh ginger
G. 2 tablespoons chopped scallion
H. 1½ teaspoons salt
I. 1 tablespoon cornstarch

PREPARATION:

I. Shell, devein, and wash B.

II. Prepare sauce by mixing C, D, E, F with ¼ cup water, G, H and I.

COOKING:

1. Heat A in frying pan, sauté B 10 minutes, stirring constantly.

2. Add C–I, simmer 5 more minutes.

GOLDEN SHRIMP PATTIES
Jien Har Bang: Canton

A. 1 lb. medium shrimp
B. ¼ lb. pork, half fat, half lean, ground
C. 1 egg white
D. 2 teaspoons cornstarch
E. 1 teaspoon salt

F. dash pepper
G. ½ teaspoon sugar
H. 1 tablespoon Chinese parsley, chopped
I. peanut oil for frying

PREPARATION:

I. Shell, devein, wash, and mince A.

II. Mix A, B, C, D, E, F, G, H thoroughly. Make 24 patties.

COOKING:

1. Fry patties in G, over medium heat, until both sides are golden brown (about 2 to 3 minutes each side).

SIZZLING SHRIMP AND MEAT GO BA (PATTY)
Wei Go Ba: Canton

A. 3 tablespoons peanut oil
B. 2 slices ginger, shredded
C. ½ chicken breast, boned
D. 1 teaspoon cornstarch
E. 2 teaspoons sherry
F. ¼ lb. frozen or canned lobster meat or 6 pieces of cooked lobster meat, shelled
G. 6 pieces roast duck (See Index)
H. 6 pieces roast pork (See Index)
I. 6 shrimp
J. 6 Chinese mushrooms

K. 1 cup shredded bamboo shoots
L. ½ cup thinly sliced water chestnuts
M. 1 can (13¾ oz.) chicken broth
N. 1 tablespoon light soy sauce
O. 2 teaspoons vinegar
P. 1½ teaspoons sugar
Q. 1 tablespoon cornstarch mixed with ⅓ cup mushroom water
R. salt and pepper to taste
S. rice patties (Go Ba, see Index)

PREPARATION:

I. Cut C, F, G and H into bite-size pieces.
II. Mix C, D, E.
III. Wash J, soak in warm water 15 minutes; drain, save ⅓ cup of the water; cut each J into 4 to 6 pieces.
IV. Mix N, O, P, Q, R.

COOKING:

1. Heat A, add B and C–E mixture, stir-fry 1 minute.
2. Add F, G, H, I, J; stir-fry 1 minute.
3. Add K, L; mix well.
4. Add M, bring to boil, lower heat, cover and simmer 2 to 3 minutes.
5. Thicken with N–R mixture. Keep over very low heat.
6. Heat prepared S in 300° oven until very hot; then arrange on serving dish.
7. Pour hot A–R mixture over S. Dish will sizzle as ingredients hit go ba. Serves 6 to 8.

PHOENIX TAIL SHRIMP I
Tza Fung Wei Sha: Peking

A. peanut oil for deep frying
B. ½ lb. jumbo shrimp (about 8)
C. ¼ teaspoon ginger juice (see Index)
D. 2 teaspoons chopped scallion
E. 1 teaspoon salt
F. 1 teaspoon sherry
G. 2 egg whites
H. 2 tablespoons cornstarch
I. ¼ cup flour
J. ½ cup bread crumbs

PREPARATION:

I. Shell B, leaving tail parts intact. Split backs lengthwise and devein. Wash and drain.
II. Mix B, C, D, E, F thoroughly.
III. Beat G, gradually mix in H, and beat until mixture is stiff.
IV. Coat B–F mixture with I; then cover with G–H mixture.
V. Roll each B (but not tail parts) in I.

COOKING:

1. Heat A to 325°.
2. Deep fry B 3 to 4 minutes.

PHOENIX TAIL SHRIMP II
Fung Wei Sha: Szechuan

A. 2 cups vegetable oil
B. ½ lb. jumbo shrimp (about 8)
C. 2 egg whites
D. 1 tablespoon cornstarch
E. 2 teaspoons flour
F. 1 teaspoon cornstarch
G. 1½ tablespoons vinegar
H. 1½ tablespoons sugar
I. 1 teaspoon light soy sauce
J. 1 tablespoon chopped scallion
K. ½ teaspoon chopped ginger
L. ½ teaspoon salt

PREPARATION:

I. Shell B, leaving tail parts intact. Split backs lengthwise and devein. Wash and drain.
II. Beat C until stiff. Gradually add D, E, beating until mixture is stiff.
III. Coat B with C–E mixture.
IV. Mix F with 1 tablespoon water.
V. Mix G, H, I, J, K, L with F mixture thoroughly.

COOKING:

1. Heat A to 325°.
2. Deep fry B–E 3 to 4 minutes. Drain on paper towel and place on dish.
3. Heat F–L mixture until it thickens, pour over fried shrimp. Serve hot.

SHRIMP LO MEIN
Har Lo Mein: Canton

A. 3 tablespoons peanut oil
B. ½ lb. small shrimp
C. 2 teaspoons light soy sauce
D. 1 teaspoon sherry
E. 1 teaspoon cornstarch
F. 2 slices ginger, shredded

G. 1 scallion
H. 1 lb. string beans
I. 4-oz. can sliced mushrooms
J. ½ lb. thin spaghetti
K. ½ teaspoon sugar
L. salt, pepper to taste

PREPARATION:

I. Shell and devein B, wash and drain.
II. Cut G in 1½-inch pieces.

III. Cut H into 1½-inch pieces and cook in boiling water 3 minutes; uncover, drain.
IV. Mix B, C, D, E, F, G.

COOKING:

1. Cook J as directed on package; use no salt.
2. Put A in hot skillet and bring to high heat. Add B–G mixture, stir-fry 2 minutes.
3. Add H, stir-fry 1 minute.

4. Add I, cook 1 minute.
5. Add J, K, and mix well, cook for a minute. Add L and serve hot.

SHRIMP LO MEIN   *Approved Ulcer Recipe*
Har Lo Mein: Canton

A. ½ lb. thin spaghetti
B. 3 tablespoons vegetable oil
C. 1 scallion
D. ½ lb. small shrimp
E. 2 teaspoons light soy sauce
F. 1 teaspoon cornstarch

G. 1 lb. very tender string beans
H. 1 cup soup stock
I. ½ teaspoon sugar
J. salt to taste
K. 1 cup canned mushrooms

PREPARATION:

I. Shell, devein D; wash and drain. Chop until very fine and smooth.
II. Tie C into bundle.

III. French-cut G, cook in H 5 to 10 minutes until very soft.
IV. Mix D, E, F.

COOKING:

1. Cook A as directed on package but use no salt.
2. Heat B in frying pan; add C; add D–F mixture (break into small pieces), stir-fry 2 minutes, discard C.

3. Add G–H mixture; stir-fry 2 to 4 more minutes.
4. Add I, J, K, cook 1 to 5 minutes.

STEAK LO MEIN   *Approved Ulcer Recipe*
Ngo Yoke Lo Mein: Canton

Substitute steak for D; slice across grain into ⅛-inch cuts, 1½ inches by ½ inch. Omit C.

LOBSTER CANTONESE
Tsao Lung Ha: Canton

A. 2 tablespoons peanut oil
B. 2 cloves garlic, minced
C. 1 slice ginger, minced
D. 2 tablespoons salted black beans, mashed
E. ½ teaspoon salt
F. ½ lb. ground pork
G. 1 teaspoon sugar
H. 1½ tablespoons light soy sauce
I. 2 tablespoons sherry

J. 2 cups soup stock
K. 2 tablespoons heavy soy sauce
L. 2 tablespoons cornstarch
M. 1- to 1½-lb. lobster
N. 2 eggs
O. 2 tablespoons soup stock
P. 2 tablespoons peanut oil
Q. 4 scallions, sliced

PREPARATION:

I. Chop M (crosswise) into bite-sized (1-inch) pieces. Remove and crack claws. Discard gills (white), head shell, legs.
II. Mix B, C, D, E. Set aside.
III. Mix G, H, I. Set aside.
IV. Mix K, L. Set aside.
V. Mix beaten N slightly. Add O. Set aside.

COOKING:

1. Put A in very hot skillet and bring to high heat.
2. Add B–E mixture. Stir-fry rapidly 15 seconds to brown B slightly.
3. Add F. Stir-fry 2 minutes, add M, mix well.
4. Add G–I mixture. Stir-fry 1 minute.
5. Add J. Cover. Bring to boil. Cook 5 to 7 minutes.
6. Add K–L mixture slowly. Stir-fry until sauce thickens and coats all ingredients well.
7. Cover and cook 2½ minutes or until lobster is tender. Make certain lobster is well coated with sauce.
8. Turn off heat and add ¾ of N–O mixture all at once. Do not stir, but let N–O set 30 seconds.
9. Remove entire contents of skillet at once to serving dish. Pour remainder of N–O mixture over dish.
10. Heat P to smoking. Pour over lobster and sauce.
11. Serve with garnish of Q.

SHRIMP WITH LOBSTER SAUCE
Ha Tzee Lung Ha Joing: Canton

Substitute 1 lb. large shelled, washed, drained shrimp for M. Split along back but do not cut through completely. Cook 3 to 5 minutes in Step 7.

LOBSTER IN BROWN BEAN SAUCE
Mien Sie Jiong Lung Ha: Canton

A. 3 tablespoons peanut oil
B. 3 teaspoons brown bean sauce
C. 3 cloves garlic, minced
D. 1- 1½-lb. lobster
E. 1 slice ginger, minced
F. 1 tablespoon sherry
G. 1 tablespoon light soy sauce
H. ½ teaspoon sugar
I. 1 cup chicken broth
J. 1 tablespoon cornstarch
K. ¼ cup water
L. 2 scallions, sliced

PREPARATION:

I. Chop D into 1-inch pieces. Leave in shell. Head portion may be removed and discarded. Crack claws. Set aside. Discard gills (white) and legs.
II. Mix B, C into paste.
III. Mix E, F, G, H.
IV. Mix J, K.

COOKING:

1. Put A in very hot skillet and bring to high heat.
2. Add B–C mixture and stir-fry over moderate heat 1 minute.
3. Add D. Stir-fry 15 seconds.
4. Add E–H mixture. Stir-fry 2 minutes.
5. Add I. Cover. Simmer 5 to 8 minutes or until tender.
6. Slowly add as much of J, K mixture as is necessary to thicken sauce and coat lobster evenly.
7. Serve with garnish of L.

LOBSTER WITH CELLOPHANE NOODLES
Lung Ha Fun See: Canton

A. 3 tablespoons peanut oil
B. 1 clove garlic, minced
C. 2 small lobsters
D. ½ lb. shredded pork
E. 2 slices ginger
F. 2 scallions
G. ½ teaspoon salt
H. dash black pepper
I. 1 cup soup stock
J. 2 teaspoons cornstarch in 2 tablespoons water
K. 1 egg
L. 1 teaspoon sherry
M. 1 tablespoon light soy sauce
N. 1 oz. cellophane noodles
O. oil for deep frying

PREPARATION:

I. Remove head shell from C; discard head shell but save green liver; discard gills, legs. Split C endwise but leave rest of shell on. Split claws and joints.
II. Mix D with L, M.
III. Beat K.
IV. Mix E, F, G, H, I.
V. Deep fry N in O (see Cellophane Noodles for method).

COOKING:

1. Put A in a large frying pan; heat until smoking; add B and brown.
2. Add C and liver and stir-fry 1 to 2 minutes.
3. Add D mixture and stir-fry a few seconds.
4. Add E, F, G, H, I and lower heat, simmer covered 10 minutes.
5. Thicken sauce with J.
6. Add K to boiling mixture and turn off heat immediately; stir vigorously so that K solidifies; top with fried N and serve.

SAVORY STEAMED LOBSTER WITH PORK
Tsing Lung Ha Yoke Bang: Canton

A. 1 egg
B. ½ teaspoon salt
C. ½ teaspoon sugar
D. 1 tablespoon light soy sauce
E. 1 teaspoon sherry
F. 1 tablespoon peanut oil
G. 1 slice ginger, minced

H. 1 dash garlic powder
I. 1 teaspoon light soy sauce
J. 6 water chestnuts, chopped
K. ¼ lb. ground pork
L. 1- to 1½-lb. lobster
M. 1 tablespoon peanut oil
N. 3 scallions, sliced

PREPARATION:

I. Boil water in steamer.
II. Clean L, freshly killed; cut or chop into easily handled pieces; reassemble and place on serving platter suitable for steaming. Discard gills, head shell, and legs.
III. Mix B, C, D, E, F, G, H, I, J and set aside.

COOKING:

1. Beat A lightly. Add B–J mixture. Add K. Stir thoroughly.
2. Spread B–K over L.
3. Place A–L on platter in steamer.
4. Cover and steam over steady moderate heat 35 minutes.
5. Remove platter. Set aside.
6. Bring M to smoking heat. Pour over steamed lobster.
7. Serve with garnish of N.

SAVORY STEAMED LOBSTER WITH PORK AND SALTED EGG
Ham Don Yoke Bang Tsing Lung Ha: Canton

Use white only of salted duck egg instead of whole of A in Step 1; slice yolk of duck egg; place slices on B–L to complete Step 1.

LOBSTER CASSEROLE   *Approved Ulcer Recipe*
Sa Go Lung Sha: Fukien

A. 3 tablespoons peanut oil
B. 2 scallions, in bundle
C. 1 clove garlic
D. 1 lb. lobster meat

E. ⅓ cup chicken broth
F. 3 teaspoons cornstarch
G. 2 eggs
H. 1 teaspoon salt

PREPARATION:

I. Beat G slightly; add H.

II. Mix F with ¼ cup water.

COOKING:

1. Heat A. Add B, C, stir-fry until B is slightly brown. Discard B, C.
2. Add D, E, stir well. Cook over low heat for a few minutes.
3. Add F mixture; bring to a boil.
4. Add G mixture, stir well.
5. Place in casserole, cover, bake 30 minutes at 325°.

STEAMED CRAB
Tsen Pong Sha: Shanghai

A. 2 to 4 blue crabs per person
B. 2 large slices fresh ginger root per crab
C. 1 tablespoon cider vinegar per crab
D. 1 tablespoon light soy sauce per crab

PREPARATION:

I. Wash A well.
II. Place A in large steamer.
III. Peel B and chop very fine.
IV. Mix B, C, D for use as a dipping sauce.

COOKING:

1. Boil water in steamer; steam A (with visible steam escaping from steamer) 20 to 25 minutes. Place crabs on large tray and cover to keep hot.

2. Each person should shell his own crab, remove and discard gills, veins, food pouch (triangular-shaped pouch that is attached to the mouth), and shells. The rest of the crab is edible. Dip in sauce and eat hot.

SERVING AND EATING:

1. Place 3 to 4 layers of newspaper or paper towels on table to protect the surface from spattered juice.

BRAISED SOFT-SHELLED CRABS
Yo Mun Shiao Sha: Shanghai

A. 4 tablespoons peanut oil
B. 8 soft-shelled crabs
C. 1 teaspoon wine vinegar
D. 2 tablespoons minced ginger
E. 1 tablespoon light soy sauce
F. 1 teaspoon heavy soy sauce
G. 2 teaspoons sugar
H. ¼ cup chicken broth

PREPARATION:

I. Wash B well, and cut each in half.
II. Mix C, D; stuff into cut side of crab and let stand 15 minutes. Drain.
III. Mix E, F, G, H.

COOKING:

1. Heat A, brown both sides of B.
2. Add E–H and bring to boil. Cover and cook over low heat 3 minutes; turn over and cook another 2 to 3 minutes. Serve hot.

STIR-FRIED CRAB I
Tsao Hai: Canton

A. 2 tablespoons peanut oil
B. 1 scallion, chopped
C. 2 slices ginger, chopped
D. 2 cloves garlic, chopped
E. 3 to 4 medium crabs
F. 2 tablespoons sherry
G. 1 tablespoon yellow bean sauce
H. 1 tablespoon light soy sauce
I. 1 teaspoon sugar
J. ¼ teaspoon salt
K. ⅓ cup water

PREPARATION:

I. Wash E well; remove claws (crack with back of cleaver), legs, shell. Cut each E into quarters.
II. Combine F, G, H, I, J; mix well.

COOKING:

1. Heat A, stir-fry B–D a few seconds.
2. Add E, stir-fry 1 minute.
3. Add F–J mixture, continue stirring 1 to 2 more minutes.
4. Add K, mix well, bring to boil. Lower heat, simmer 10 minutes.
5. Serve hot with rice.

STIR-FRIED CRAB II
Tsu Pong Sha: Hunan

A. ¼ cup peanut oil
B. 3 to 4 live crabs
C. 3 tablespoons light soy sauce
D. 2 tablespoons sherry
E. 1 tablespoon sugar
F. 1½ tablespoons vinegar
G. 1 tablespoon chopped scallion
H. 1 teaspoon chopped ginger
I. 1 teaspoon cornstarch mixed with ¼ cup water
J. 1 teaspoon sesame oil
K. 2 tablespoons cornstarch

PREPARATION:

I. Wash B well; using cleaver, cut in quarters; remove claws, discard shell and legs; crack claws with back of cleaver; quarter each B.
II. Coat B with K.
III. Mix C, D, E, F, G, H, I.

COOKING:

1. Heat A, brown B.
2. Add C–I mixture, stir well, cook over low heat 10 minutes.
3. Sprinkle J on top and serve.

KING CRAB MEAT EGG FU YONG
Fu Yong Dai Hai: Canton

A. 4 tablespoons peanut oil
B. ½ lb. frozen king crab meat
C. 1 cup frozen peas
D. 1 teaspoon sherry
E. 2 scallions, sliced
F. 2 slices ginger, minced
G. ½ cup sliced water chestnuts
H. 1 teaspoon salt
I. dash pepper
J. 6 eggs

PREPARATION:

I. Defrost B, C; mix.
II. Mix B, C, D, E, F, G, H, I.
III. Beat J and add to mixture.

COOKING:

1. Put A into hot skillet and heat.
2. Fry B–J mixture on both sides until golden brown.
3. Serve with Tabasco or soy sauce.

KING CRAB MEAT EGG FU YONG   *Approved Ulcer Recipe*
Da Shieh Fu Yung Don: General

Omit D, E, F and I; keep J separated from B and C. In Step 2, fry B, C, G, H mixture 10 minutes in A so that C is well done. Add J, fry until tender; serve with light soy sauce.

STIR-FRIED CRAB MEAT WITH EGGS
Hai Yoke Tsao Don: Canton

A. 2 tablespoons peanut oil
B. 1 small onion
C. 10 large water chestnuts
D. ½ teaspoon salt
E. 3 oz. fresh crab meat
F. ⅔ tablespoon light soy sauce

G. ½ teaspoon sherry
H. ½ teaspoon ginger, chopped
I. 5 eggs
J. 2 tablespoons peanut oil
K. 1 teaspoon heavy soy sauce
L. 1 scallion, sliced

PREPARATION:

I. Remove all cartilage from E.
II. Beat I lightly and sauté with J in skillet until it reaches scrambled egg consistency. Set aside.

III. Chop B into large shreds.
IV. Chop C fine.
V. Mix F, G, H. Set aside.

COOKING:

1. Put A in very hot skillet and bring to high heat.
2. Stir-fry B until tender; add C and D.
3. Add E and stir-fry 2 minutes carefully with spatula.

4. Add F–H mixture and continue to stir-fry 2 minutes.
5. Add I–J, stir-fry 15 seconds; then add K.
6. Stir-fry 15 seconds. Serve with garnish of L.

STIR-FRIED CRAB WITH LEMON
Ning Mong Pi Tsao Hai: Canton

A. 4 tablespoons peanut oil
B. 1 or 2 cloves garlic, chopped
C. 1 scallion, chopped
D. 1 tablespoon fermented salted black beans
E. ½ teaspoon chopped ginger
F. 1 teaspoon chopped lemon rind
G. 3 or 4 medium crabs

H. 1½ tablespoons wine
I. 2 teaspoons light soy sauce
J. 1 teaspoon sugar
K. ½ teaspoon salt
L. 1 cup water or chicken broth
M. 2 teaspoons cornstarch mixed with 2 tablespoons water

PREPARATION:

I. Wash G well, remove claws, discard feet and shell. Cut each into 2 to 3 pieces and crack claws.

II. Place B, C, D, E, F on plate.
III. Mix H, I, J, K, L.

COOKING:

1. Heat A, stir-fry B–F a few seconds.
2. Add G pieces, stir-fry 1 to 2 minutes.
3. Add H–L mixture, stir well. Cover and cook

10 minutes over medium heat.
4. Remove cover and stir a few more seconds.
5. Thicken with M and serve hot.

CRAB MEAT WITH SWEET CORN SAUCE
Hai Yoke Suk Mai Gung: Canton

A. 2 cups soup stock
B. 4 slices ginger, chopped
C. 3 tablespoons peanut oil
D. ½ cup fresh tender corn kernels
E. 6-oz. can crab meat

F. 1 teaspoon salt
G. 2 teaspoons sherry
H. 1 tablespoon cornstarch
I. 1 egg white
J. 1 tablespoon chopped scallion

PREPARATION:

I. Drain E and remove cartilage, break up into shreds.

II. Wash D to remove silk; drain.

III. Beat I slightly.

IV. Mix H with ¼ cup water.

COOKING:

1. Mix A, B, bring to a boil.

2. Heat C, stir-fry D 1 minute. Add to A, B mixture, cook 10 minutes.

3. Add E, F, G, cook 2 to 3 more minutes.

4. Add H mixture to thicken.

5. Gradually stir in I. Garnish with J. Mix well, serve hot.

GOLDEN CRAB PATTIES
Gum Chien Hai: Canton

A. 1 lb. fresh crab meat
B. 1 teaspoon chopped ginger
C. 1 tablespoon chopped scallion
D. ¼ lb. pork, half fat, half lean, ground
E. 1 egg white

F. 2 teaspoons cornstarch
G. 1 teaspoon salt
H. dash pepper
I. water chestnut flour, as needed
J. peanut oil for frying

PREPARATION:

I. Remove cartilage from A and mince.

II. Mix A, B, C, D, E, F, G, H thoroughly. Make 24 patties.

III. Dust with I.

COOKING:

1. Fry A–I patties in J, over medium heat, until both sides are golden brown (about 2 to 3 minutes each side).

CRAB MEAT WITH CARROTS
Sha Ro Hung Lo Bo: Peking

A. ½ lb. spareribs
B. 2 cups chicken soup
C. 4 large carrots
D. 2 tablespoons vegetable oil
E. ¼ lb. fresh crab meat
F. 1 tablespoon sherry

G. 2 slices ginger
H. 2 teaspoons cornstarch mixed with ¼ cup water
I. 2 scallions, minced
J. salt to taste

PREPARATION:

I. Peel C and shred into pieces ¼ by ¼ by 1½ inches.

II. Remove all cartilage from E.

III. Cut A into 1½-inch pieces.

COOKING:

1. Place A, B in Dutch oven and cook ½ hour. Replace any B lost in cooking with water.

2. Add C and simmer additional 5 minutes.

3. Place D in large skillet. When hot, add E, F, G; stir for 1 minute.

4. Add H to sauce. Keep stirring.

5. Add all to Dutch oven and garnish with I. Add J.

CRAB MEAT WITH CARROTS   *Approved Ulcer Recipe*
Hai Pa Hung Lo Ba: Canton

A. 2 cups chicken soup
B. ¼ lb. ground pork
C. 2 teaspoons cornstarch
D. 1 scallion
E. 4 carrots

F. 2 tablespoons vegetable oil
G. ¼ lb. fresh crab meat
   (picked clean of cartilage)
H. salt to taste

PREPARATION:

I. Peel E, slice diagonally into ⅛-inch pieces.
II. Tie D into bundle.

III. Mix B, half of C, ¼ teaspoon salt. Make into meatballs.
IV. Mix remaining C with ⅛ cup of cold water.

COOKING:

1. Bring A to boil in Dutch oven. Add B–C mixture, then D and E. Simmer, covered, 20 minutes. Remove D.

2. Heat F in skillet, add G; stir-fry 1 minute.
3. Add F, G to mixture in Dutch oven. Add H.

CRAB MEAT WITH CELERY CABBAGE
Sha Ro Bai Tsai: Peking

A. 3 tablespoons vegetable oil
B. 2 scallions
C. 3 slices ginger
D. 1 clove garlic
E. 6 oz. canned crab meat
F. 1 teaspoon sherry
G. ½ teaspoon sugar

H. 2 teaspoons cornstarch
I. 2 tablespoons water
J. 1 cup chicken broth
K. 1½ lbs. celery cabbage
L. ½ cup thinly sliced bamboo shoots
M. salt to taste

PREPARATION:

I. Chop B, C, D and mix.
II. Cut K diagonally into 1-inch segments.

III. Mix F, G, H, I.

COOKING:

1. Heat A in frying pan; add B–D and stir-fry ½ minute.
2. Add E and stir-fry 2 minutes.
3. Add F–I mixture, simmer 2 to 3 minutes.

4. Heat J to boiling in large (11-inch) frying pan.
5. Add K, L; bring to boil; simmer 5 minutes; add M. Place in bowl and top with B–I mixture.

CRAB MEAT WITH CELERY CABBAGE HEARTS
Sha Huang Bai Tsai: Peking

A. 4 medium crabs
B. 1 teaspoon ginger juice (see Index) or
   ½ teaspoon black pepper
C. 1 tablespoon sherry
D. ½ teaspoon salt
E. 1 lb. celery cabbage hearts

F. 2 tablespoons vegetable oil
G. ½ teaspoon salt
H. 2 cups chicken soup
I. 1 tablespoon cornstarch mixed in
   ¼ cup water

PREPARATION AND COOKING:

I. Steam A 20 minutes, cool and shell. Remove triangular sack connected to shell. Also remove black vein and spongy gills. Save crab yellow and meat for making crab sauce.

II. Add B, C, D to A.

III. Cut E into 2-inch pieces.

IV. Put F into frying pan and stir-fry E, G, 1 to 2 minutes.

V. Add H and boil 2 minutes. Remove E, leaving soup in pan. Arrange E neatly on platter.

VI. Add A mixture to soup. Boil 1 to 2 minutes. Then add I to thicken. Pour over E and serve.

CRAB MEAT CASSEROLE
Sa Go Shia Ro: Fukien

A. 3 tablespoons peanut oil
B. 3 slices ginger
C. 2 scallions
D. 1 clove garlic

E. 1 lb. fresh crab (or lobster) meat
F. ⅓ cup chicken broth
G. 1 tablespoon cornstarch mixed with ⅓ cup water

H. 2 eggs
I. 1 teaspoon salt
J. dash pepper

PREPARATION:

I. Chop B, C, D.

II. Remove all cartilage from E.

III. Beat H slightly; add I, J.

COOKING:

1. Heat A. Add B–D, stir-fry until D is slightly browned.

2. Add E, F, stir well. Cook over low heat a few minutes.

3. Add G; bring to boil.

4. Add H–J mixture, stir well.

5. Place in casserole, cover, bake in 325° oven 30 minutes.

CRAB MEAT CASSEROLE   Approved Ulcer Recipe
Sa Go Shia Ro: Fukien

Omit B, C, D, and J. Add 1 teaspoon heavy soy sauce.

CRAB MEAT LION'S HEAD
Sha Hwang Si Tze Tou: Shanghai

A. 3 teaspoons vegetable oil
B. 1 lb. ground pork
C. 6 oz. chopped cooked or canned crab meat picked clean of cartilage
D. 2 eggs
E. 2 teaspoons sherry
F. 1 teaspoon salt
G. 1 tablespoon cornstarch

H. dash black pepper
I. 2 scallions, minced
J. 4 slices ginger, minced
K. 1 tablespoon light soy sauce
L. 2 cups chicken soup
M. 1 lb. celery or Chinese cabbage
N. 1 tablespoon cornstarch mixed with 3 tablespoons water

PREPARATION:

I. Cut M into 2-inch segments.

II. Mix B, C, D, E, F, G, H, I, J, K and form 5 large meatballs.

COOKING:

1. Heat A in heavy frying pan, then fry B–K until brown on all sides (approximately 8 minutes).

2. Add L and cover. Simmer 15 minutes.

3. Add M, cover. When M is cooked but still crisp (approximately 5 minutes), add N to thicken sauce.

CRAB WITH SWEET AND SOUR SAUCE
Tien Swan Pong Sha: Shanghai

A. 1½ cups peanut oil
B. 3 to 4 medium crabs
C. 1 tablespoon minced scallion
D. 2 slices ginger, minced

E. 1 tablespoon sherry
F. ¼ teaspoon salt
G. 2 tablespoons cornstarch
H. 1 egg

PREPARATION:

I. Wash B well; remove claws (crack with back of cleaver), legs, shell. Cut each B into quarters.
II. Mix C, D, E.

III. Marinate B in C–E mixture 10 minutes.
IV. Combine F, G, H to make batter.
V. Coat B with F–H.

COOKING:

1. Heat A to 375°. Deep-fry B–H mixture until golden brown (about 5 minutes). Remove from oil.

SAUCE:

A. 2 tablespoons peanut oil
B. 1 tablespoon chopped scallion
C. 1 teaspoon chopped ginger
D. 1 clove garlic, chopped
E. 2 tablespoons light soy sauce

F. ¼ cup vinegar
G. ¼ cup sugar
H. 2 teaspoons cornstarch
I. ¼ cup water

PREPARATION:

I. Mix E, F, G, H, I thoroughly.

COOKING:

1. Heat A in hot frying pan. Stir-fry B, C, D 1 minute.

2. Add E–I mixture, continue stirring until mixture comes to boil.
3. Add pieces B–D, mix well and serve hot.

STIR-FRIED FRESH SQUID
Tsao Mo Yu: Fukien

A. 4 tablespoons peanut oil
B. 2 to 3 oz. pork, minced
C. 4 Chinese mushrooms
D. ½ cup sliced bamboo shoots
E. 1 tablespoon chopped scallion
F. 1 lb. squid
G. ½ cup soup stock or chicken broth

H. 2 teaspoons light soy sauce
I. ½ teaspoon salt
J. 2 teaspoons cornstarch mixed with 2 tablespoons water
K. 2 teaspoons vinegar
L. 1 teaspoon sesame oil or to taste
M. pepper to taste

PREPARATION:

I. Pull out center bones of F, cut off tentacles, remove and discard black skin. Split open, clean out all internal organs. Wash remaining F under cold water.
II. Make deep crisscross pattern on one surface of F. Then cut into 1½-inch-square pieces.

Place pieces in one qt. boiling water and stir 1 minute. Drain.
III. Soak C 15 minutes in water, then cut into thin slices.
IV. Mix G, H, I.

COOKING:

1. Heat A, add B, C, D, E, stir-fry 1 to 2 minutes or until meat turns white.
2. Add F, mix well; add G–I, stir well. Cover,

let boil 1 minute. (Do not overcook squid.)
3. Thicken with J.
4. Add K, L, M. Serve hot.

SQUID WITH GREEN PEPPERS
Ching Jao Yo Yu: Shanghai

A. 4 tablespoons vegetable oil
B. 1 medium onion, shredded
C. 1 large pork chop
D. 3 dried squid
E. 1 large green pepper
F. 2 pieces pressed bean curd
G. 1 tablespoon sherry

H. 2 teaspoons light soy sauce
I. 1½ teaspoons cornstarch
J. ½ teaspoon sugar
K. dash pepper
L. ½ teaspoon baking soda
M. salt to taste

PREPARATION:

I. Soak D overnight. Remove soft bones and membranes. Change water. Add L and boil 30 minutes, covered. Then soak ½ hour, drain and rinse. Cut into thin shreds.
II. Bone C and cut into ¼- to ½-inch-wide strips.

III. Remove seeds from E and shred into ¼-inch-wide strips.
IV. Cut F into ¼-inch-wide strips.
V. Mix G, H, I, J, K with D and soak 20 minutes.

COOKING:

1. Heat A in frying pan. Add B, C, stir-fry 1 to 2 minutes.
2. Add E and D mixture, stir-fry 1 to 2 minutes.

3. Add F and a small amount of water or meat stock. Cover for a total cooking time of 6 minutes. Adjust with M.

BRAISED SQUID WITH CHICKEN
Sao Yo Yu Gee: Shanghai

A. 2 tablespoons vegetable oil
B. 3 dried squid
C. 2 chicken legs
D. 3 scallions
E. 5 slices ginger
F. 2 tablespoons light soy sauce
G. 1 teaspoon sugar

H. 2 tablespoons sherry
I. 6 Chinese mushrooms
J. ½ cup diced bamboo shoots
K. salt to taste
L. 1 tablespoon cornstarch mixed with ¼ cup water
M. ½ teaspoon baking soda

PREPARATION:

I. Soak B overnight. Remove soft bones and membranes. Change water. Add M, cover, and boil 30 minutes. Leave soaking ½ hour; drain and rinse. Cut into thin strips.

II. Soak I in hot water 30 minutes, save water, remove stems, cut each I into three pieces.
III. Cut C into bite-size pieces.
IV. Mix B, C, D, E, F, G, H.

COOKING:

1. Heat A in large frying pan. Add B–H and stir-fry 1 minute.
2. Add I, J and water from I; cover and sim-

mer 5 minutes or until B and C are tender. Add some soup or water if needed.
3. Adjust with K, L.

SQUID IN OYSTER SAUCE
How Yo Yo Yu: Fukien

A. 4 tablespoons vegetable oil
B. 4 small dried squid
C. 2 tablespoons oyster sauce
D. ½ cup clear chicken soup
E. 1 teaspoon sherry
F. 2 slices ginger, minced
G. salt to taste
H. 1 scallion, minced
I. 1 teaspoon baking soda

PREPARATION:

I. Soak B, I in water overnight in refrigerator. After softening, cut into 2-inch squares.

COOKING:

1. Heat 3 tablespoons A in skillet. Add B, stir-fry 1 minute.

2. Add C, D, E, F. Simmer, covered, until B is soft. Add water if needed.

3. Add G; stir in H, just prior to serving.

SQUID IN WHITE SAUCE
Bai Tze Yo Yu: Shanghai

A. 2 tablespoons vegetable oil
B. 3 dried squid
C. ½ teaspoon baking soda
D. 1 cup meat stock or chicken soup
E. 6 Chinese mushrooms
F. 1 lb. Chinese cabbage hearts
G. 4 oz. cooked ham
H. 1 tablespoon cornstarch
I. 5 slices ginger, chopped
J. 1 teaspoon salt
K. 2 tablespoons sherry

PREPARATION:

I. Soak B overnight. Remove soft bones and membranes. Change water. Add C, cover and boil 30 minutes. Then soak ½ hour, drain and rinse. Score B in crisscross fashion, then cut into 1-inch squares.

II. Soak E in hot water 30 minutes. Discard stems, save water, cut E into strips.

III. Wash F and cut into 1½-inch pieces.

IV. Cut G into same size pieces as B.

V. Mix I, J, K with B.

COOKING:

1. Heat A in frying pan, add B mixture. Stir-fry 1 minute.

2. Add D, cover and simmer 2 minutes.

3. Add E, F, G, simmer 3 minutes.

4. Mix E water with H, and add to thicken sauce.

SWEET AND SOUR SQUID
Tien Swan Yo Yu: Shanghai

A. 2 tablespoons vegetable oil
B. 2 tablespoons wood ears
C. 1 cup shredded bamboo shoots
D. ½ teaspoon salt
E. 3 dried squid
F. ½ teaspoon baking soda
G. 2 tablespoons light soy sauce
H. 2 tablespoons cider vinegar
I. 2 tablespoons sugar
J. 1 tablespoon sherry
K. 1 tablespoon cornstarch
L. 1 teaspoon salt

PREPARATION:

I. Soak E overnight. Remove soft bone and membrane. Change water. Add F and boil 30 minutes, covered. Then soak ½ hour, drain and rinse. Score E in crisscross fashion then cut into 1-inch-square pieces.

II. Soak B in hot water 40 minutes. Rinse and wash away extraneous material.

III. Mix E with G.

IV. Mix H, I, J, K, L.

COOKING:

1. Put 1 tablespoon A into frying pan, add B, C, stir-fry 1 to 2 minutes, add D. Remove mixture from pan.

2. Put rest of A into frying pan. Stir-fry E–G ½ minute, add B–D, and H–L sauce; cover, add ½ cup water, simmer 3 minutes or until E is tender.

RED BEAN CHEESE SQUID
Nam Yu Mun Mook Yu: Canton

A. 3 tablespoons vegetable oil
B. ½ lb. squid
C. ½ lb. pork tenderloin, shredded
D. 2 tablespoons sherry
E. 2 scallions
F. 5 slices ginger
G. 1 tablespoon light soy sauce

H. 1 tablespoon mashed red bean cheese
I. 1 teaspoon sugar
J. 1 cup soup stock
K. 2 teaspoons cornstarch mixed with 2 tablespoons water
L. 1 egg white
M. ¼ teaspoon salt

PREPARATION:

I. Clean B; discard ink pouch, eyes, bones, and gristle.
II. Mix C with L, M and half of D.

III. Cut E into 1½-inch pieces.
IV. Mix rest of D with E, F, G, H, I.

COOKING:

1. Heat A in heavy saucepan; when smoking, add B, stir-fry 1 to 2 minutes.
2. Add C and stir-fry 2 to 3 minutes.
3. Add D–I mixture, stir-fry 1 minute; lower heat, cover and simmer until B is tender (about 30 to 40 minutes), adding J when necessary.
4. When B becomes tender, thicken sauce with K and serve.

STIR-FRIED DRIED SQUID
Tsao Yow Yu: Canton

A. 5 tablespoons peanut oil
B. 4-oz. can water chestnuts
C. ¼ cup cloud ears
D. dash salt
E. 2 to 3 dried squid (4 oz.)
F. 2 teaspoons baking soda

G. 1½ tablespoons white wine
H. 1½ tablespoons light soy sauce
I. 1 tablespoon cornstarch
J. 4 slices ginger
K. 1 teaspoon sugar

PREPARATION:

I. Mix F with 2 qts. warm water.
II. Place E in F water and soak overnight. Rinse in running cold water at least 1 minute. Cut off tentacles so that they are separated. Discard the head part and soft bones and membranes. Make deep crisscross pattern on one side of E. Then cut into 1-inch-square pieces, cut tentacles in 1-inch lengths, and mix with G, H, I, J. Let stand 15 minutes.
III. Cut each B into 6 or 7 thin slices.
IV. Soak C in cold water 15 to 30 minutes or until they expand. Rinse with clean water several times; drain.

COOKING:

1. Heat 1 tablespoon A, add B, C, stir-fry 1 minute; add D. Remove to dish.
2. Heat rest of A to smoking (for safety's sake, turn off heat before adding E–J and place cover over pot as soon as E–J is added to the oil; then turn up heat again). Stir-fry E–J 1 minute after removing cover.
3. Add cooked B, C and K. Stir well and serve.

SQUID WITH PICKLED MUSTARD GREENS I
Sien Tsai Tsao Yo Yu: Shanghai

A. 2 tablespoons vegetable oil
B. 3 dried squid
C. ½ teaspoon baking soda
D. 1½ tablespoons sherry
E. 1½ teaspoons cornstarch
F. 1½ teaspoons sugar

G. 1 large pork chop
H. 1 cup chopped bamboo shoots
I. 1 cup pickled mustard greens
J. ½ cup meat stock
K. 4 slices ginger
L. salt to taste

PREPARATION:

I. Soak B overnight. Remove soft bones and membranes. Change water, add C, and boil 30 minutes, covered. Then soak ½ hour, drain and rinse. Cut into ¼-inch shreds.
II. Shred K.

III. Bone G and cut into pieces ¼-inch wide. Discard bone.
IV. Mix D, E, F with ¼ cup water and mix with B.

COOKING:

1. Heat A in frying pan, add B, D–F mixture, stir-fry 1 to 2 minutes.

2. Add G, H, I, J, K, cover, allow to simmer 5 minutes. Stir-fry 1 to 2 minutes.
3. Adjust with L and serve.

SQUID WITH PICKLED MUSTARD GREENS II
Sien Tsai Tsao Yo Yu: Fukien

A. 5 tablespoons peanut oil
B. 4-oz. can water chestnuts
C. ¼ cup cloud ears
D. dash salt
E. 2 to 3 dried squid (4 oz.)
F. 2 teaspoons baking soda
G. 1½ tablespoons white wine

H. 1½ tablespoons light soy sauce
I. 1 tablespoon cornstarch
J. 4 slices ginger
K. 1 teaspoon sugar
L. 1 cup pickled mustard greens
M. salt to taste

PREPARATION:

I. Mix F with 2 qts. warm water.
II. Place E in F water and soak at least 10 hours. Rinse in cold running water 1 minute. Cut off tentacles so that they are separated. Discard the head. Make deep crisscross pattern on one side of E. Cut each into 1-inch-squares and mix with G, H, I, J. Let stand 15 minutes.
III. Cut each B into 6 or 7 thin slices.
IV. Soak C in cold water for 15 to 30 minutes or until they expand. Rinse with clean water several times; drain.

COOKING:

1. Heat 1 tablespoon A, add B, C; stir-fry 1 minute; add D. Remove to dish.
2. Heat rest of A to smoking (for safety's sake, turn off heat before adding E–J and place cover over pot as soon as E–J is added; then turn up heat again). After removing cover, stir-fry E–J mixture 1 minute.
3. Add cooked B, C and K. Stir well.
4. Add L, M and serve.

SIMPLE SCALLOP OMELET
Jing Sih Tsao Don: Fukien

A. ¼ cup vegetable oil
B. 5 eggs
C. 3 dried scallops

D. 1 teaspoon salt
E. 2 scallions, minced

PREPARATION:

I. Steam C with 2 tablespoons water over boiling water 20 minutes. Drain, save water. Mince.

II. Break B. Add C, D, E, and whip. Add water from Step I.

COOKING:

1. Heat A in hot skillet.

2. Add B–E mixture to A. Stir-fry 3 to 7 minutes (according to preference).

DRIED SCALLOPS WITH TURNIPS
Gahn Bei Sao Lo Bo Si: General

A. 3 tablespoons vegetable oil
B. 6 dried scallops
C. 2 scallions, minced
D. 1 cup shredded turnip

E. ¾ cup meat or chicken broth
F. ¼ teaspoon salt
G. 1 teaspoon cornstarch

PREPARATION:

I. Soak B in hot water 30 minutes. Drain, reserving water.

II. Cut B into shreds.

COOKING:

1. Place A in hot skillet, using high heat. Add B, C, stir-fry 1 minute.
2. Add D, E, F, and water from B; cover, simmer 15 minutes.

3. Mix G with a little water; stir this mixture into other ingredients. Serve.

STEAMED SCALLOPS WITH CHINESE CABBAGE
Gahn Bei Bai Tsai: Peking

A. 6 dried scallops
B. 1 Chinese cabbage or celery cabbage (1 to 2 lbs.)

C. 1 teaspoon salt

PREPARATION:

I. Wash A, soak in ½ cup hot water 30 to 45 minutes until soft. Drain, saving water.

II. Discard few outside tough leaves of B. Wash, clean whole B, then cut into 2-inch cross-section pieces (try not to separate leaves). Put into a bowl.

III. Sprinkle B over A. Add ½ cup A water or chicken broth and C.

COOKING:

1. Steam in steamer over boiling water 30 minutes. Serve hot.

STIR-FRIED SCALLOPS WITH CHINESE VEGETABLES
Tsao Gahn Bei Ding: General

A. 3 tablespoons peanut oil
B. 3 slices ginger, shredded
C. 1 scallion, chopped
D. 1 clove garlic, chopped
E. ½ lb. bay scallops
F. 6 Chinese mushrooms
G. ½ cup sliced water chestnuts
H. ½ cup diced bamboo shoots
I. 1 tablespoon light soy sauce
J. 2 teaspoons dry sherry
K. ½ teaspoon sugar
L. ½ teaspoon salt
M. 3 tablespoons mushroom water
N. ¼ lb. snow peas
O. ½ to 1 teaspoon sesame oil

PREPARATION:

I. Dice E, place in colander, and rinse under cold water. Drain.
II. Rinse F and soak in warm water 15 minutes or until soft. Drain, saving water. Dice F.
III. Remove tips of N.
IV. Mix I, J, K, L, M.

COOKING:

1. Heat A to smoking, add B, C, D and stir-fry a few seconds.
2. Add E, F, stir-fry 1 to 2 minutes.
3. Add G, H; mix well; add I–M mixture, stir well; cover and cook 2 minutes.
4. Add N and continue to stir-fry 1½ more minutes.
5. Add O to taste.

FRIED SCALLOPS
Tza Kong Yu-Chu: Canton

A. 2 cups peanut oil for deep frying
B. 1 lb. sea scallops
C. 2 teaspoons dry sherry
D. 2 teaspoons light soy sauce
E. ½ teaspoon chopped ginger
F. 2 eggs
G. 3 tablespoons water chestnut flour
H. ½ cup flour
I. 1 teaspoon salt
J. 3 tablespoons water
K. dash pepper
L. catsup or few slices of lemon

PREPARATION:

I. Place B in a colander and rinse under cold water a few seconds. Drain and dry between paper towels.
II. Mix B, C, D, E and marinate ½ hour.
III. Beat F; mix well with G, H, I, J, K into a smooth paste.
IV. Dip B–E into F–K batter.

COOKING:

1. Heat A to 350°; deep-fry B–K until golden brown (about 5 to 7 minutes), turning frequently. Drain on paper towels.
2. Serve with L.

SWEET AND SOUR SCALLOPS WITH PINEAPPLE
Tiem Shwin Kong Yu-Chu: Canton

A. 2 cups peanut oil
B. ½ lb. bay scallops
C. ½ teaspoon minced ginger
D. 1 tablespoon chopped scallion
E. 1 teaspoon light soy sauce
F. 1 teaspoon sherry
G. 1 egg white
H. 2 tablespoons water chestnut flour
I. 1 tablespoon light soy sauce
J. 1 tablespoon vinegar

K. 2 teaspoons sugar

L. 1 tablespoon cornstarch

M. ¾ cup pineapple juice

N. 1 green pepper

O. 1 cup pineapple chunks

P. salt to taste

PREPARATION:

I. Place B in a colander and rinse under cold water a few seconds; drain.

II. Mix B, C, D, E, F; marinate ½ hour.

III. Mix G, H well; stir into B–F mixture.

IV. Mix I, J, K, L, M together in a saucepan.

V. Wash N, discard stem and seeds, and cut into 1-inch cubes.

COOKING:

1. Heat A to 325°; deep fry B–H 2 to 3 minutes, drain on paper towel.

2. Heat I–M mixture, stir until it thickens.

3. Add N and cook 1 minute; add B–N and O; stir well; add P.

CORNMEAL CLAM CAKES
Jien Ga Li Chio: Tientsin

A. peanut oil 1½ inches deep in deep-fat fryer

B. ¾ cup cornmeal

C. ¾ cup flour

D. ¼ cup minced scallions

E. ¼ teaspoon baking soda

F. 1½ teaspoons baking powder

G. 1½ teaspoons salt

H. 1 qt. fresh clams

I. 1 egg

J. 1½ cups buttermilk

PREPARATION:

I. Mix B, C, D, E, F, G in large bowl.

II. Grind H or chop very fine.

III. Combine H, I, J with B–G mixture in bowl; mix well.

COOKING:

1. Heat A to 325°.

2. Drop 1 tablespoon batter at a time into oil, turning until formed cakes are browned

(cooking time: 2 to 3 minutes).

3. Drain cakes on absorbent paper. Serve with catsup, optional.

CLAMS WITH PICKLED VEGETABLE SOUP
Ga Li Swan Tsai Tong: Shanghai

A. 2 tablespoons vegetable oil

B. 1 large pork chop

C. 1 teaspoon light soy sauce

D. 1 teaspoon cornstarch

E. 3 slices ginger

F. ½ cup pickled mustard greens

G. 1 qt. chicken soup

H. 10½-oz. can clams

I. 1 tablespoon sherry

J. dash pepper

K. salt to taste

PREPARATION:

I. Bone and shred B, mix with C and D.

II. Shred E.

III. Rinse F and slice into bite-size pieces.

IV. Mix H, I, J.

COOKING:

1. Heat A in frying pan.

2. Add B–D, stir-fry 1 to 2 minutes.

3. Add E, F, stir-fry 1 to 2 minutes.

4. Add G, bring to boil.

5. Add H–J. Boil 5 to 10 minutes.

6. Adjust with K.

STUFFED CLAMS WITH BEEF
Ngo Yoke Yuang Hien: Adapted

A.   2 to 3 lbs. clams (about 10 to 12 large
     or 18 medium, with shell)
B.   ½ lb. ground beef
C.   1 teaspoon ginger, chopped
D.   1 tablespoon chopped scallion
E.   1 tablespoon sherry

F.   ½ teaspoon salt
G.   ½ teaspoon sugar
H.   1 teaspoon light soy sauce
I.   dash pepper
J.   ¼ cup chicken broth
K.   1 tablespoon peanut oil

PREPARATION:

I.   Scrub A, rinse well under cold water; then
     place in bowl and pour boiling water over
     them. Drain, remove meat from shells. Mince.

Save shells.

II. Mix A, B, C, D, E, F, G, H, I, stuff mixture
     into shells, place in baking dish.

COOKING:

1.   Preheat oven to 425°.
2.   Mix J, K, bring to boil, and pour over A–I.

3.   Bake 10 to 15 minutes.

RED-COOKED SNAILS
Hung Shiu Tien Lo: Canton

A.   3 tablespoons vegetable oil
B.   10-oz. can snail meat
C.   6 dried mushrooms
D.   ½ lb. pork, shredded
E.   2 tablespoons diced ham
F.   2 tablespoons sherry

G.   1 cup sliced bamboo shoots
H.   1 tablespoon light soy sauce
I.   4 slices ginger, minced
J.   1 tablespoon minced scallions
K.   ½ cup pork or chicken stock
L.   2 teaspoons corn flour

PREPARATION:

I.   Slice B into thin, bite-size pieces. Marinate
     in F.

II. Soak C in hot water 20 minutes. Drain, sav-
     ing water, and cut each C into thirds.
III. Mix L with ¼ cup C water.

COOKING:

1.   Place A in large frying pan. Stir-fry B 5 min-
     utes over high heat.
2.   Add C, D, E, G, H, I, J; continue stir-frying.

3.   Add K. Lower heat, simmer covered 25 min-
     utes.
4.   When B is tender, add F, thicken with L mix-
     ture. Serve hot.

OYSTER BALLS
Tza Sun Ho Kew: Canton

A.   2 to 3 cups vegetable oil
B.   3 scallions, minced
C.   ⅓ cup cornstarch
D.   1½ teaspoons salt

E.   1½ teaspoons baking powder
F.   1 cup flour
G.   1 qt. oysters or clams, drained
H.   1 egg

PREPARATION:

I. Mix B, C, D, E, F.

COOKING:

1. Pour A into 3-qt. saucepan. Heat to 325°.
2. Drop 1 teaspoon B–H at a time into A. Turn

II. Add G, H and 1 cup water to B–F to form thick but smooth paste.

until balls are brown (cooking time: 2 to 3 minutes).

3. Drain balls on absorbent paper. Serve hot.

FRIED FRESH OYSTERS
Tza Sun How: General

A. 2 cups peanut oil
B. ½ pint oysters (about 12)
C. 1 teaspoon salt
D. 1 teaspoon dry sherry
E. 1 teaspoon light soy sauce
F. ¼ teaspoon ground pepper

G. 1 scallion, chopped
H. ½ teaspoon chopped ginger
I. ½ cup flour
J. ½ teaspoon baking powder
K. 1 teaspoon salt
L. 1 egg
M. ¼ cup water

PREPARATION:

I. Rub B lightly with C; place in colander and rinse under cold water ½ minute.
II. Put B into 2 cups boiling water, stir 30 seconds, drain.
III. Mix D, E, F, add B and marinate 10 min-

utes, turning once.
IV. Sift I, J, K together.
V. Beat L.
VI. Mix G, H, I, J, K, L, M well.
VII. Mix B with egg batter.

COOKING:

1. Heat A to 350°, add B–M a tablespoonful at a time; deep fry until golden brown (about

2 to 3 minutes) on each side. Serve with lemon or Szechuan pepper salt.

BRAISED SHARK FINS
Mun Yu Tse: General

A. 3 lbs. stewing chicken
B. ¼ lb. refined dried shark fins
C. 4 oz. Virginia ham, sliced
D. 4 dried scallops (2 to 3 oz.)
E. 5 slices ginger

F. 2 teaspoons sherry
G. 2 teaspoons water chestnut flour mixed with ¼ cup water
H. salt to taste

PREPARATION:

I. Clean and wash A. Remove fat.
II. Place B in cold water and soak overnight. Wash clean. Place B in pot with 2 qts. water, cover, bring to boil, simmer 30 minutes. Re-

move from heat; allow to cool. Rinse and drain.
III. Clean and rinse D. Soak D in hot water 20 minutes. Drain and save water.

COOKING:

1. Place A in Dutch oven, spread with B, C, D, E, F. Add D water and 2 qts. water. Boil 15 minutes, then simmer 4 hours. Add water

when necessary. At the end of 4 hours, soup should measure not more than 2 to 3 cups.

2. Remove A, C and skim off fat.
3. Mix in G and H. Serve hot.

SHARK FINS WITH SHREDDED CHICKEN
Gai Si Yu Chi: Canton

A. 1½ qts. chicken broth
B. 2 oz. dried refined shark fins (about 2 cups after soaking and cleaning)
C. 1 tablespoon sherry
D. ½ teaspoon salt
E. ¼ teaspoon pepper
F. ½ teaspoon sugar
G. 1 chicken breast

H. 1 egg white
I. few drops sesame oil
J. ½ teaspoon salt
K. ¼ teaspoon salt
L. 1 tablespoon light soy sauce
M. 3 tablespoons water chestnut flour mixed with ¼ cup water
N. 3 slices ginger

PREPARATION:

I. Soak B in cold water overnight; wash and clean well. In 5 cups boiling water add B, N, bring to boil; simmer covered 30 minutes. Remove from heat and cool with cover on. Drain, rinse in cold water several times. Drain.

II. Bone G, cut into thin slices, then shred, mix with H, I, J, K.

COOKING:

1. Heat A, add B, C, D, E, F, bring to boil, lower heat and cook 1 to 1½ hours.
2. Turn up heat, add G–K mixture and L, keep stirring for 1 minute.
3. Thicken with M, so shark fins will float, and serve hot.

SHARK FIN CASSEROLE
Mun Yu Tse: Szechuan

A. ½ stewing chicken
B. ¼ duck
C. 6 oz. ham
D. 1 qt. chicken soup
E. 2 oz. dried, refined shark fins
F. 4 slices ginger

G. 2 scallions
H. 2 tablespoons sherry
I. salt to taste
J. 3 tablespoons water chestnut flour with ⅓ cup water

PREPARATION:

I. Follow shark fin preparation (see Shark Fins with Cornish Hen and Abalone) using H and 2 pieces F with soaking water.

II. Slice C into thin pieces.

COOKING:

1. In a Dutch oven or flameproof casserole place A, B, C, D and simmer 30 to 60 minutes.
2. Add prepared E, rest of F, G, and I. Cover and simmer over low heat for 2 to 4 hours.
3. Add J to casserole for thickening.

SHARK FINS WITH CORNISH HEN AND ABALONE
Bao Yu Ju Gee Mun Yu Tse: General

A. 1½-lb. cornish hen (or fryer)
B. ½-lb. can abalone
C. 2 scallions
D. 2 teaspoons sherry
E. 6 dried mushrooms

F. 7 slices ginger
G. 2 teaspoons water chestnut flour
H. 1 egg white
I. ¼ lb. refined, dried shark fins
J. 1 teaspoon salt

PREPARATION:

I. Place I in cold water and soak overnight. Wash clean. Place I in pot with 1 qt. water, cover; simmer for 30 minutes. Remove pot from heat, allow to cool. Rinse and drain.

II. Slice B into thin, flat slices. Save liquid.

III. Clean and wash A. Cut in half and place in large shallow bowl. Add I, J, 2 slices F and half of liquid from B. Steam over boiling water 15 to 20 minutes. Bone A and leave soup in bowl.

IV. Mince 3 slices F.

V. Soak E in hot water 20 minutes, drain, remove stems, and quarter.

COOKING:

1. Put boned A in bowl. Spread B, C, D, E, remaining F, and remaining half of boiling soup from B over A. Steam 20 minutes.

2. Mix G with H and 2 tablespoons B soup. Beat mixture into hot soup. Salt to taste. Serve hot.

FRIED EELS IN EGG BATTER
Jien Hwang San Quai: General

A. 1 cup vegetable oil
B. 1 lb. eel
C. ¾ teaspoon salt
D. dash black pepper

E. 5 tablespoons flour
F. 1 egg
G. 2 tablespoons water

PREPARATION:

I. Skin and rinse B. To skin, take a piece of wood at least ¾ inch thick and 24 inches long; place B on board; force an ice pick (or nail) behind head and into board. With a sharp knife, cut skin ½ inch below nail, and with pliers, pull skin off. Clean and slice B into 1-inch pieces. Dry with paper towels. Flavor B with C, D; let stand 10 minutes.

II. Mix a smooth batter of E, F, G.

III. Mix E–G with flavored B.

COOKING:

1. Place A in frying pan; heat to 375°.

2. Add batter-covered B; fry 6 minutes.

TARO EEL
Yu Tow Mun Wong Hien: Canton

A. 3 tablespoons vegetable oil
B. 2 cloves garlic
C. 2 lbs. eel
D. 6 small taro roots
E. 2 teaspoons salted black beans
F. 3 slices ginger

G. 1 tablespoon sherry
H. 1 oz. Virginia ham, minced
I. 2 cups pork or chicken soup
J. 2 scallions, minced
K. salt to taste

PREPARATION:

I. Skin C, cut into 1-inch sections.

II. Skin D, cut each in quarters.

III. Crush B, remove outside skin.

IV. Soak E in hot water until soft, then mash.

COOKING:

1. Heat A in large, heavy pot. Add B, then C, stir-fry 7 minutes.

2. Add D, E, F, G, H, I. Cook until C and D are tender. Add water as needed, simmer covered 25 minutes. Sauce will thicken as taro softens.

3. Add J, adjust with K.

FRIED BLOWFISH TAILS
Jien Yu Wei: General

A. 1 cup vegetable oil
B. 15 blowfish tails
C. ⅓ cup light soy sauce
D. ½ teaspoon five spices powder

E. 1 tablespoon sherry
F. 4 slices ginger
G. 1 bunch Chinese parsley (optional)
H. ¼ teaspoon sesame oil (optional)

PREPARATION:

I. Rinse B in cold water, then dry with paper towels.
II. Make sauce by mixing D, E, F.

III. Marinate B in C–F 30 to 60 minutes. Drip dry in colander.

COOKING:

1. Heat A to 375°. Deep fry B–F. Sprinkle with G, H. Use toasted salt and anise pepper mixture as dip (see Anise Pepper Salt).

SPICY TARO EEL
Yu Tow Sun Kwai: Yunnan

A. 3 tablespoons vegetable oil
B. 1 clove garlic
C. 2 lbs. eel (or carp, cleaned and scaled) or fresh tuna chunks
D. 6 small taro roots
E. 2 slices Virginia ham, minced
F. 3 slices ginger

G. 1 tablespoon sherry
H. 1 teaspoon salt
I. 2 cups pork or chicken soup
J. salt to taste
K. 10 drops Tabasco sauce (or 1 teaspoon red pepper powder)

PREPARATION:

I. Skin C, cut into 1-inch sections.   II. Skin D, quarter each.   III. Crush B, remove outside skin.

COOKING:

1. Heat A in large, heavy pot. Add B, then C. Stir-fry 7 minutes.
2. Add D, E, F, G, H. Cook, covered, until C is soft. Add I as needed (cooking time: approximately 25 minutes).
3. Add J to taste and K.

SESAME EELS
Tsao San Hu: Shanghai

A. ⅓ cup vegetable oil
B. 2 cloves garlic
C. 8 eels
D. 10 slices ginger, shredded
E. ⅓ cup light soy sauce

F. 2 teaspoons sugar
G. 3 teaspoons sherry
H. 1 tablespoon cornstarch mixed with ¼ cup water
I. 1 tablespoon sesame oil

PREPARATION:

I. Skin, clean C. Cut into 1-inch segments.   II. Mix D, E, F, G.   III. Mash B, remove skin.

COOKING:

1. Heat A in frying pan; brown B.
2. Add C and stir-fry. Maintain high heat, cover, cook 1 minute.
3. Add D–G mixture, stir-fry 1 to 2 minutes; lower heat and simmer, adding water if necessary. After 6 minutes add H, stir and simmer ½ minute.
4. Heat I in small pot until smoking; pour over eels and serve.

BRAISED SEA CUCUMBER I
Hung Shiu Hoi Sum: Adapted

A. 3 tablespoons peanut oil
B. 1 cup sliced pork
C. 1 teaspoon cornstarch
D. 2 teaspoons light soy sauce
E. 1 teaspoon peanut oil
F. 2 cloves garlic, chopped
G. 2 scallions (white part only), chopped
H. 3 slices ginger, shredded
I. ¾ lb. dried sea cucumbers
J. 2 tablespoons light soy sauce
K. 1 tablespoon sherry

L. 1½ teaspoons sugar
M. ½ teaspoon pepper
N. 6 Chinese mushrooms
O. 1 cup chicken broth
P. 1 cup diced bamboo shoots
Q. ½ cup frozen shrimp, diced
R. 1 tablespoon cornstarch mixed with ⅓ cup water
S. ¼ to ½ teaspoon sesame oil
T. ½ teaspoon salt

PREPARATION:

I. Soak I in water 48 hours. Drain. Cut into bite-size pieces to make 2 cups.
II. Cut B into 1- by ½-inch pieces. Cook in 2 cups of boiling water with ½ G, 2 slices H for 3 minutes, drain.
III. Mix B, C, D, E.

IV. Wash N and soak in warm water 15 minutes; drain, save water and add to chicken broth; quarter each N.
V. Soak Q in cold water with T for 10 minutes; drain and dry between paper towels.
VI. Mix J, K, L, M well.

COOKING:

1. Heat 1 tablespoon A, add B–E, stir-fry 2 minutes, remove to dish.
2. Heat 2 tablespoons A, add F, and remaining G and H, stir-fry a few seconds, add I, stir-fry 2 minutes.
3. Add J–M, stir-fry 2 minutes.

4. Return B–E and add N; mix well, add O, bring to boil, and cook over low heat 10 minutes.
5. Add P, Q and cook 2 minutes.
6. Thicken with R.
7. Add S and serve.

BRAISED SEA CUCUMBER II
Hung Pa Hai Sun: Szechuan

A. 3 tablespoons peanut oil
B. 2 scallions
C. 4 slices ginger
D. 1 tablespoon light soy sauce
E. 1 tablespoon oyster sauce
F. 2 tablespoons sherry

G. 1 cup chicken broth
H. ⅛ teaspoon pepper
I. 1 cup refined dried sea cucumber
J. 1 tablespoon cornstarch mixed with ¼ cup water

PREPARATION:

I. Soak I in water 2 nights prior to cooking. Discard water; boil 15 minutes in fresh water with ½ B, ½ C. Drain I, wash, and cut into bite-size pieces.

II. Cut remaining B, C into 1-inch pieces.
III. Mix D, E, F, G, H.

COOKING:

1. Heat A, add B, C, brown a little.
2. Add D–H.

3. Add I, bring to boil; lower heat, simmer 30 to 35 minutes. Thicken with J.

BRAISED SEA CUCUMBER RED-COOKED WITH HAM AND CHICKEN
Sam Sun Wei Hoi Sum: Canton

A. 4 tablespoons peanut oil
B. 2 scallions
C. 4 slices ginger
D. ½ cup small dried sea cucumber
E. ½ cup thinly sliced white meat chicken
F. ½ cup thinly sliced Smithfield ham

G. 1 cup thinly sliced bamboo shoots
H. 2 tablespoons sherry
I. 2 cups chicken broth
J. salt, pepper to taste
K. 1 tablespoon cornstarch mixed with a little water

PREPARATION:

I. Soak D in water 2 nights prior to cooking. Discard water; boil 15 minutes in fresh water with ½ B, ½ C. Drain D, wash, and cut into bite-size pieces.

II. Cut remaining B, C into 1-inch pieces.

COOKING:

1. Heat A. Brown remaining B, C.
2. Add D, E, F, G, stir-fry 1 minute.
3. Add H, I, stir well, bring to boil; reduce heat, simmer 45 minutes. Add J, thicken with K.

BRAISED SEA CUCUMBER WITH PORK
Hung Sao Hai Sun: General

A. 4 tablespoons peanut oil
B. 2 scallions
C. 4 slices ginger
D. ½ lb. pork
E. ½ cup small dried sea cucumber
F. 1 cup bite-size pieces bamboo shoots
G. 8 Chinese mushrooms

H. ¼ cup cloud ears
I. 2 tablespoons light soy sauce
J. ½ teaspoon salt
K. ½ teaspoon sugar
L. 2 cups chicken broth
M. 1 tablespoon cornstarch mixed with a little water

PREPARATION:

I. Soak E in water 2 nights prior to cooking. Discard water; boil 15 minutes in fresh water with ½ B, ½ C. Drain E, wash, and cut into bite-size pieces.

II. Cut D into thin 1- by ½-inch pieces.

III. Wash G, soak 15 minutes in warm water; drain, save water and add it to L. Cut each G in quarters.

IV. Soak H 15 to 30 minutes in hot water or until crisp and crunchy. Drain, wash well in cold water, drain again.

V. Cut remaining B into 1-inch pieces.

COOKING:

1. Heat A. Add remaining B, C; add D; stir-fry 2 minutes.
2. Add E, F, G, mix well; stir-fry 3 to 5 minutes.
3. Add H, I, J, K, L, mix well, bring to boil. Lower heat, simmer 45 to 60 minutes.
4. Thicken with M.

RED-COOKED SEA CUCUMBERS
Hung Sao Hai Sun: Peking

A. ½ cup bite-size dried sea cucumber
B. 6 chicken gizzards (or pork stomach)
C. 2 oz. Virginia ham, shredded
D. 2 chicken legs (or pork shoulder)
E. 2 teaspoons light soy sauce

F. 1 teaspoon oyster sauce
G. 2 scallions
H. 1 teaspoon sugar
I. 1½ teaspoons sherry
J. salt to taste

K. dash pepper

L. 1 cup chicken soup

M. 3 tablespoons cornstarch

N. 2 slices ginger

O. 1 scallion

PREPARATION:

I. Soak A in water 48 hours. Discard water, then boil A in 2 cups fresh water with N and O 15 minutes; wash, cut into bite-size pieces.

II. Cut each B into 2 pieces, slit each piece.

III. Bone D.

COOKING:

1. Place A, B, C, D, E, F, G, H, I, J, K, L in bowl. Steam 30 to 45 minutes, until A is soft.

2. Mix ⅓ cup water with M. Add to A–L for thickening. Serve.

SEA CUCUMBER IN MUSHROOM SAUCE
Hai Sun Sao: Shanghai

A. 4 tablespoons peanut oil

B. 2 teaspoons light soy sauce

C. 1 teaspoon salt

D. 1 cup dried sea cucumber

E. 2 cups clear chicken soup

F. ½ lb. Chinese white cabbage or celery cabbage

G. 8 dried black mushrooms

H. 1 tablespoon cornstarch

I. 2 scallions, minced

J. 2 slices ginger

K. 1 teaspoon sesame oil

L. 3 tablespoons water

PREPARATION:

I. Soak D in water 48 hours. Discard water, then boil D in 2 cups of fresh water with ½ I and J 15 minutes.

II. Cut each D into 2 to 4 pieces.

III. Cut F into ½- by 2-inch pieces.

IV. Soak G in hot water 20 minutes. Cut off stems, then cut each into 3 pieces.

COOKING:

1. Place A in skillet. Heat, then add B, C, D. Bring to boil.

2. Add E, then F, G. Keep stirring over high heat.

3. Mix H, remaining I, J, K, L. Add to sauce, keep stirring. When sauce thickens, it is ready to serve.

SEA CUCUMBER BEAN CURD IN HEAVY SAUCE
Hung Siu Dow Fu Hoi Sen: Canton

A. 2 cups chicken soup

B. 1 cup refined dried sea cucumber

C. 2 slices ginger, diced

D. 1 scallion

E. 4 cakes bean curd

F. 1 tablespoon cornstarch mixed with ¼ cup water

G. 1 tablespoon sherry

H. 1 scallion

I. salt to taste

J. 2 eggs

PREPARATION:

I. Prepare B as in Sea Cucumber with Shrimp Seeds.

II. Cut B, E into 1-inch squares.

III. Crack J into bowl and beat.

COOKING:

1. Place A in saucepan. Bring to boil. Add B, C, D, simmer 20 minutes. Add E. When liquid boils again, add F so that E just barely floats.

Add G, H, I. Turn off heat and beat in J. Serve.

SEA CUCUMBER WITH SHRIMP SEEDS
Sha Tze Hai Sun: Shanghai

A. ¼ cup peanut oil
B. 2 scallions
C. ¾ to 1 cup refined, dried sea cucumber
D. 15 dried shrimp
E. 2 tablespoons light soy sauce
F. 1 teaspoon sugar
G. ½ lb. bamboo shoots
H. 1 cup chicken broth

I. 1 tablespoon cornstarch mixed with ⅓ cup water
J. ¼ teaspoon sesame oil
K. ¼ teaspoon pepper
L. 1 scallion tied into a knot
M. 2 slices ginger
N. 3 tablespoons sherry

PREPARATION:

I. Soak C in water 48 hours. Drain. Boil 15 minutes in fresh water with L and M. Drain; wash and cut into bite-size pieces. Boil 3 cups water in saucepan, add C, L, M and 1 tablespoon N. Cook 5 minutes; drain and discard L, M.

II. Clean and wash D; soak in 2 tablespoons N.

III. Cut G into ½-inch slices.

IV. Cut B diagonally into pieces 1½-inches long.

COOKING:

1. Heat A, add B, stir-fry a few seconds; add C, D, E, F; stir-fry 1 minute.
2. Add G, mix well.
3. Add H, stir, bring to boil, then lower heat and simmer 15 minutes.
4. Thicken with I.
5. Add J, K, mix well and serve hot.

STIR-FRIED SEA CUCUMBER AND MUSHROOMS
Dung Gu Hai Sun: General

A. 3 tablespoons vegetable oil
B. 6 dried Chinese mushrooms
C. 1 bamboo shoot, shredded
D. 3 scallions
E. 2 slices ginger
F. 1 cup chicken soup

G. ½ cup refined dried sea cucumber
H. 4 oz. turkey white meat, shredded
I. 2 teaspoons cornstarch mixed with a little water
J. salt to taste

PREPARATION:

I. Soak G in water 48 hours prior to cooking. Discard water and boil G with 1 D and E 15 minutes. Slice G into 1½- by ½-inch pieces and wash.

II. Soak B in hot water 20 minutes. Drain, saving water. Slice B into quarters; discard stems.

III. Mix I with ¼ cup B water.

IV. Cut remaining D into 1½-inch pieces.

COOKING:

1. Place A in hot frying pan. When A is smoking, add B, C, and remaining D. Stir-fry 5 minutes. Add ½ F if needed.
2. Add G and rest of F; stir-fry 2 more minutes.
3. Add H. Cook 2 minutes.
4. Thicken with I. Add J. Serve hot.

SIMPLE FRIED CHICKEN
Ru Ee Tza Tze Gee: General

A. peanut oil for deep frying
B. 2 tablespoons light soy sauce
C. 1 teaspoon sugar
D. ½ teaspoon salt
E. 1 tablespoon cornstarch
F. 2-lb. fryer

PREPARATION:

I. Disjoint F and cut it into 10 pieces.
II. Mix B, C, D thoroughly.
III. Marinate F in B–D mixture 1 hour.
IV. Sprinkle E over F; mix well.

COOKING:

1. Heat A to 350°. Deep fry B–F until golden brown.

SHANGHAI FRIED CHICKEN
Yo Ling Gee: Shanghai

A. 2-lb. fryer
B. 3 slices ginger, chopped
C. 2 scallions, chopped
D. 3 tablespoons light soy sauce
E. 2 teaspoons anise pepper
F. 2 teaspoons whiskey
G. ⅛ teaspoon five spices powder
H. ½ teaspoon salt
I. 1 pint peanut oil

PREPARATION:

I. Wash A and clean.
II. Mix B, C, D, E, F, G, H.
III. Rub A inside and out with B–H mixture. Let stand 45 minutes.

COOKING:

1. Place A–H on plate, steam over boiling water 30 minutes; remove seasoning, and dry A with paper towel.
2. Fry A in I at 350° until golden brown (about 3 minutes each side).
3. Cut A into bite-size pieces and serve.

PEKING FRIED CHICKEN I
Tza Ba Quai: Peking

A. 1 qt. peanut oil for deep frying
B. 2-lb. fryer
C. 1 scallion, cut into 1-inch pieces
D. 1 teaspoon ginger juice (see Index)
E. 3 tablespoons light soy sauce
F. 1 teaspoon sugar
G. 1 tablespoon sherry

PREPARATION:

I. Clean and wash B, cut into 8 pieces.
II. Mix B, C, D, E, F, marinate for 3 to 4 hours.
III. Remove B from sauce and dry between paper towels.

COOKING:

1. Heat A to 350°, deep fry B until golden brown (about 6 minutes) and is done.
2. Serve with anise pepper salt (see Index).

PEKING FRIED CHICKEN II
Yo Tza Gee: Peking

A. 6 to 8 chicken drumsticks (about 2 lbs.)
B. 2 to 3 cups peanut oil for deep frying
C. 1½ teaspoons salt
D. 1 tablespoon sherry
E. 1 egg
F. ¼ cup cornstarch

PREPARATION:

I. Mix C, D and rub all over A, marinate 30 minutes.
II. Beat E.
III. Dip A in E and coat lightly with F.

COOKING:

1. Deep fry A in B (350°) until golden brown.
2. Serve with anise pepper salt (see Index).

CANTON FRIED CHICKEN
Tza Gai: Canton

A. 5 tablespoons peanut oil
B. 6 chicken legs
C. 1 clove garlic, chopped
D. 1 teaspoon salt
E. 1 tablespoon light soy sauce
F. 1 tablespoon peanut oil
G. ½ cup flour
H. 1 tablespoon cornstarch
I. ¼ cup sherry
J. ½ cup chicken broth
K. 8-oz. can whole mushrooms
L. 1 cup peas

PREPARATION:

I. Cut each B into 4 pieces.
II. Rub B with C, D.
III. Mix E, F. Pour over B–D and mix well. Let B–F mixture stand 10 minutes.
IV. Mix H, I, J.
V. Put G in a paper bag; add B–F mixture. Shake.

COOKING:

1. Heat A.
2. Fry B–G in A until light brown on all sides.
3. Add H–J mixture and cook about half an hour on low heat.
4. Add K, L. Cook for another 3 minutes (optional).
5. Serve hot on rice.

FRIED CHICKEN WITH WHITE SAUCE
Nai Yow Gai: Canton

A. 2- to 3-lb. chicken
B. 1 cup water
C. ½ cup half-and-half
D. 2 tablespoons cornstarch
E. 1 teaspoon salt
F. ¼ teaspoon garlic powder
G. 1 slice ginger, minced

PREPARATION:

I. Chop A intact, or boned, into bite-size pieces.
II. Mix B, C, D, E, F, G. Set aside.

COOKING:

1. Prepare batter-fried A (see Batter for Frying in Deep Fat) and place in serving dish.
2. Prepare white sauce by cooking B–G mixture at low heat, stirring continuously.
3. When sauce is smooth and hot, pour over A. Serve.

CRISPY FRIED CHICKEN
Chui Pi Gai: Canton

A. 4 to 5 chicken legs (about 2 lbs.)
B. 1 cup chicken broth
C. ½ teaspoon anise pepper
D. 1 clove star anise
E. 3 slices ginger
F. 1 tablespoon light soy sauce

G. 2 tablespoons wine
H. 1 egg white
I. 1 teaspoon flour
J. 2 teaspoons cornstarch
K. 2 cups peanut oil

PREPARATION:

I. Cut each A in half.

II. Mix B, C, D, E, F, G.

III. Mix H, I, J thoroughly.

COOKING:

1. Arrange A in single layer in frying pan.
2. Add B–G mixture, bring to boil; lower heat, simmer 5 to 10 minutes each side.
3. Remove A pieces, drain on paper towels. Save B–G mixture for other cooking uses.
4. Coat each A piece well in H–J mixture.
5. Deep fry A pieces in K at 350° until golden brown.
6. Serve with anise pepper salt (see Index) or catsup.

SALT ROAST CHICKEN
Yen Ju Gee: Peking

A. 5 to 6 lbs. coarse salt

B. 2-lb. fryer

C. 1 tablespoon salt

PREPARATION:

I. Wash and clean B, dry with paper towel.

II. Rub C all over B inside and out. Let stand 2 to 3 hours. Wrap aluminum foil over B.

COOKING:

1. Place A in deep frying pan. Heat until hot, stirring occasionally.
2. Make hole in A, insert B–C and cover with A.
3. Cover frying pan, lower heat and cook on top of stove 30 minutes.
4. Turn B–C and cook another 30 minutes.
5. Remove B–C from A, discard foil and cool B.
6. Cut into bite-size pieces and serve with ginger oil (see Index).

SALT-CURED CHICKEN I
Yen Fung Gee: Peking

A. 2-lb. fryer
B. 1½ tablespoons salt

C. 1 scallion
D. 3 slices ginger, shredded

PREPARATION:

I. Wash A well, dry with paper towels, rub with B inside and out. Place in bowl, refrigerate at least 1 day (3 days preferably).

II. Cut C in half, cut 2 or 3 times crosswise.

III. Drain excess water from A, split breast open, place on dish. Cover wth C, D.

COOKING:

1. Steam A–B in steamer 30 to 45 minutes. Remove from heat, let cool. Discard C, D.

2. When cold, cut into bite-size pieces. Serve.

SALT-CURED CHICKEN II
Yen Tsa Gee: Shanghai

A. 2- to 3-lb. fryer
B. 1 tablespoon salt
C. 1 teaspoon anise pepper
D. 6 cups chicken broth
E. ¼ cup sherry
F. 1 scallion
G. 3 slices ginger

PREPARATION:

I. Mix B, C.
II. Wash A, dry with paper towel, rub with B–C mixture inside and out. Place in bowl and refrigerate at least ½ day.
III. Mix D, E, bring to boil, cool.
IV. Slice F into thin strips.
V. Cut G crosswise into small pieces.
VI. Marinate A–C in D–E 3 hours, then turn and marinate 3 more hours.
VII. Remove A from sauce, place in bowl and garnish with F, G.

COOKING:

1. Steam A in steamer 30 to 45 minutes. Remove from heat, cool, and cut into bite-size pieces.

Serve. Sauce may be reused; just add chicken broth, if necessary, for marinating.

SALT-CURED CHICKEN *Approved Diabetic Recipe*
Yen Fung Gee: Peking

A. 2-lb. fryer
B. 1 to 1½ tablespoons salt

PREPARATION:

I. Wash A well and remove all fat. Dry with paper towel.
II. Rub A with B thoroughly, inside and out.
III. Place A in bowl and refrigerate at least 1 to 2 days.

COOKING:

1. Drain excess water from A. Split open breast side. Steam over boiling water for 30 to 45 minutes. Remove from heat.
2. Cool completely before cutting into bite-size pieces. Serve.

CHICKEN ROASTED IN SALT
Yem Gook Gai: Dungkiang

A. 7 lbs. coarse salt (kosher type)
B. ½ teaspoon five spices powder
C. 2- to 2½-lb. roasting chicken
D. 5 slices ginger, minced
E. ⅛ teaspoon black pepper
F. ⅓ cup sherry
G. ½ teaspoon sesame oil
H. 1 tablespoon light soy sauce
I. 1 teaspoon salt
J. sauce for dipping (1 scallion, minced, 1 tablespoon light soy sauce)

PREPARATION:

I. Wash C and dry with paper towels.
II. Mix D, E, F, G, H, I.
III. Marinate C in D–I mixture 30 minutes.
IV. Wrap C in paper towels and tie securely.

COOKING:

1. Place A, B in deep frying pan. Cook, with occasional turning, until hot.
2. Make a depression in A–B. Place C–I inside, cover with A–B and cook over medium heat 30 minutes.
3. Turn C over and continue to cook 40 minutes.
4. Remove C and paper towels; cut C into bite-size pieces, and serve with J.

CHICKEN IN RED BEER
Jiu Tzao Gee: Fukien

A. 1½ cups peanut oil
B. 1½- to 2-lb. roasting chicken
C. 1 tablespoon peanut oil
D. 1½ teaspoons garlic salt
E. 1 teaspoon sugar
F. 1½ cups beer
G. 1 to 2 drops red food coloring

H. 1 scallion
I. 1 slice of ginger (about size of a nickel and ½ inch thick)
J. 1 tablespoon cornstarch mixed with 2 tablespoons water
K. salt to taste

PREPARATION:

I. Cut B into bite-size pieces. Rub with D and let stand 15 minutes.

II. Tie H into a knot and pound with side of cleaver.

COOKING:

1. Heat A to 375°; deep fry B 1 to 2 minutes. Drain.
2. Heat C in another pot, add B, stir-fry a few seconds, then add E, F, G, H, I; bring to a boil.

3. Lower heat and simmer 15 minutes or until B is tender.
4. Remove H and I and thicken with J.
5. Add K and serve.

BRAISED CHICKEN
Hung Sao Gee: Shanghai

A. ½ cup soup stock
B. ⅛ cup sherry
C. ⅛ cup light soy sauce

D. 2-lb. fryer
E. ¼ cup bamboo shoots
F. 8 Chinese mushrooms

G. 1 scallion
H. 3 slices ginger

PREPARATION:

I. Cut D into bite-size pieces.
II. Slice E thin.
III. Wash F, soak in warm water 15 minutes. Drain, cut each in half.

IV. Cut G, H into 1- to 2-inch pieces.
V. Place D in frying pan. Spread E, F, G, H on top.
VI. Mix B, C.

COOKING:

1. In a saucepan, bring A to boil.
2. Add B–C mixture, bring to boil again, pour over D–H mixture.

3. Bring to boil, cover, and simmer until D is tender (about 15 to 20 minutes).

STEAMED WHOLE CHICKEN
Ching Tsen Chwan Gee: Szechuan

A. 3-lb. chicken
B. 2 tablespoons chopped scallion
C. 3 slices ginger, chopped

D. 1 tablespoon sherry
E. 1½ teaspoons salt

PREPARATION:

I. Rub A thoroughly inside and out with E.

II. Place prepared A in bowl. Sprinkle with B, C, D.

COOKING:

1. Cook A–D in a steamer over boiling water until tender (about 30 to 45 minutes).

STEAMED CHICKEN WITH GLUTINOUS RICE
Lo Mi Gai: Canton

A. 2 cups glutinous rice
B. ½ cup dried black mushrooms
C. 1 teaspoon rice wine or
   1 tablespoon gin
D. 1 teaspoon sugar
E. 2 scallions, sliced
F. ⅛ teaspoon garlic powder
G. 1 teaspoon light soy sauce

H. 1 tablespoon heavy soy sauce
I. 2 tablespoons peanut oil
J. ¼ cup bamboo shoots
K. 4- to 5-lb. chicken
L. ⅛ teaspoon garlic powder
M. 2 teaspoons light soy sauce
N. ½ teaspoon salt

PREPARATION:

I. Wash A and cook in 1½ cups boiling water 5 minutes. Drain.
II. Soak B in warm water 15 minutes. Drain. Chop fine.
III. Chop K into bite-size pieces; mix well with L, M, N. Set aside.

IV. Dice J.
V. Mix A, B, C, D, E, F, G, H, I, J in large wide-topped steaming dish.
VI. Have water boiling in steamer.

COOKING:

1. Place steaming dish with A–J mixture in large steaming vessel.
2. Steam 60 minutes, adding water to bottom of steaming vessel if needed.

3. Open steamer and place K–N on top of A–J mixture.
4. Cover and steam 30 minutes. Serve in steaming dish set on trivet or on another plate of the same size and shape.

BOILED CHICKEN WITH PORK AND GLUTINOUS RICE STUFFING
No Mai Ju Yoke Gai: Canton

A. 2 tablespoons peanut oil
B. ¼ lb. lean pork, diced
C. ¼ cup canned bamboo shoots, diced
D. 3 dried black mushrooms

E. 1 tablespoon gin
F. 2 tablespoons light soy sauce
G. 1 cup glutinous rice
H. 3-lb. chicken

PREPARATION:

I. Wash G and cook in rapidly boiling water 5 minutes. Drain. Rinse with cold water. Drain.

II. Soak D in warm water 15 minutes. Drain and slice into slivers.
III. Mix C, D, E, F. Set aside.

COOKING:

1. Put A in very hot skillet and bring to high heat.
2. Add B and stir-fry 1 to 2 minutes.
3. Add C–F mixture and stir-fry 1 minute.
4. Add G. Mix well.
5. Stuff H with this mixture. Fasten opening with skewers.

6. Wrap H in cheesecloth and immerse in water (just enough to cover) at the simmering point. Simmer 30 to 40 minutes or until tender.
7. Remove from water. Unwrap. Carve at table and serve with a spoonful of stuffing.

STEAMED CHICKEN
Tze Fung Gee: Shanghai

A. 2 chicken breasts (1½ lbs.)
B. 6 Chinese mushrooms
C. ¼ cup thinly sliced Virginia ham
D. 1 scallion

E. 3 slices ginger, shredded
F. 1 teaspoon salt
G. 2 teaspoons sherry

PREPARATION:

I. Bone A, cut into cubes, place in dish.
II. Wash B, soak in warm water 15 minutes; drain and save 1 cup of soak water; discard stems and cut each mushroom in half.
III. Spread B, C over A.

IV. Cut D into 1-inch pieces.
V. Spread D, E, F, G and B water over A mixture.
VI. Cover tightly with aluminum foil.

COOKING:

1. Steam A–G in steamer 1 to 1½ hours or until A is tender.

2. Remove foil and serve hot.

STEAMED CHICKEN WITH SOUP
Dun Gee: General

A. 2-lb. chicken
B. 6 dried black mushrooms
C. 1 cup cold water
D. ¼ teaspoon salt

E. 2 teaspoons light soy sauce
F. 3 slices ginger, slivered
G. 1 tablespoon sherry

PREPARATION:

I. Boil water in steamer.
II. Soak B in warm water 15 minutes. Drain; remove stems.

III. Place A, B, C, D, E, F in a deep serving bowl suitable for steaming.

COOKING:

1. Place bowl containing A–F in steaming utensil.
2. Steam over moderate heat 2 hours.
3. Add G.
4. Serve with concentrated soup. Very nourishing.

Note: Soup may be converted to sauce by adding approximately one tablespoon cornstarch mixed in ¼ cup water to each cup of soup, mixing well, and heating until sauce thickens.

STEAMED CHICKEN WITH SOUP   *Approved Ulcer Recipe*
Ching Tsen Gee: General

Reduce F to ½ slice; omit G; use B as flavoring. Remove B and F before serving; use white meat only.

SMOKED CHICKEN
Shwin Gee: Shanghai

A. 3- to 4-lb. roasting chicken
B. 3 scallions
C. ½ cup brown sugar
D. 2 slices ginger, chopped
E. 2 tablespoons salt
F. few drops sesame oil (optional)

PREPARATION:

I. Wash A thoroughly. Dry with paper towels.
II. Mix D with E.
III. Rub A thoroughly with D–E mixture inside and out. Refrigerate overnight.

COOKING:

1. Place B in A cavity; steam over boiling water 30 minutes.
2. Turn off heat, leave A in steamer another 15 minutes.
3. Line Dutch oven with aluminum foil; sprinkle C over foil. Place a rack over C.
4. Place A on top of rack. Cover and cook over medium heat 10 to 15 minutes.
5. Remove pot from heat, allowing it to cool before uncovering.
6. Cut A into bite-size pieces; serve. If desired, rub A with a little F before cutting.

LEMON BAKED CHICKEN
Ning Mung Gook Gai: Adapted

A. ⅓ cup peanut oil
B. 3-lb fryer
C. juice of 1 lemon
D. 3 tablespoons honey
E. 3 tablespoons peanut oil or butter
F. 1 teaspoon paprika
G. dash pepper
H. 1½ teaspoons salt
I. ¾ cup flour

PREPARATION:

I. Cut B into 8 to 10 pieces; mix with F, G, H thoroughly; let stand ½ hour.
II. Place I in a paper bag; shake B in the bag until the pieces are well coated.
III. Mix C, D, E.

COOKING:

1. Line cooky sheet with aluminum foil.
2. Spread A thoroughly over floured B pieces.
3. Place B on foil skin side down in a single layer.
4. Preheat oven to 400° and bake B 30 minutes.
5. Turn B over; pour C–E mixture over B and bake 20 to 30 minutes longer or until B is tender. During the last 10 minutes spoon C–E over pieces as they bake. Serve hot or cold.

LEMON CHICKEN
Ning Mung Gai: Canton

A. 2 chickens (2 to 3 lbs. each)
B. ½ lemon
C. 1 slice ginger
D. 1 teaspoon dried mandarin orange peel
E. 1 large clove garlic, minced
F. 1 teaspoon light soy sauce
G. 1 teaspoon salt
H. 1 tablespoon sugar
I. ¼ to ½ teaspoon ground cinnamon
J. 2 teaspoons cornstarch
K. 2 tablespoons water

PREPARATION:

I. Slice B thinly.

II. Mince D fine.

COOKING:

1. Place A in deep steaming bowl.

2. Spread B–I over surface of A.

3. Place bowl in steaming utensil, cover and steam 15 minutes.

4. Uncover, turn A–I over, cover again, and steam 15 to 20 minutes more.

III. Mix B, C, D, E, F, G, H, I thoroughly.

IV. Mix J, K. Set aside.

5. Remove A to serving dish. Reserve juices.

6. Bring juices to boil in small pot.

7. Add J–K, stirring until sauce thickens.

8. Pour sauce over A–I, serve.

MUSHROOM CREAMED CHICKEN
Ba Tsup Dung Gu Gai: Canton

A. 3½-lb. fowl

B. 4 slices ginger

C. 10 dried mushrooms

D. 6 carrots

E. ¼ cup flour

F. ½ cup evaporated milk

PREPARATION:

I. Clean A, remove fat.

II. Soak C in hot water 20 minutes until soft.

Drain and save water. Cut C into 2 to 3 pieces each.

III. Peel D and cut each into bite-size pieces.

COOKING:

1. Place A and B in Dutch oven. Add 4 cups water and boil 1 to 2 hours (or, depending on how tough chicken is, until tender).

2. When tender, add C, D, and continue cooking 20 minutes. Remove all but 2 cups liquid from pot.

3. Add E to mushroom water to form paste. Add flour paste to pot and bring to boil.

4. Add salt to taste, remove Dutch oven from heat immediately, add F, stirring continuously. Serve.

MUSHROOM CREAMED CHICKEN   *Approved Ulcer Recipe*
Nai Yo Dung Gu Gee: Shanghai

Chop A and serve only mixed in sauce with carrots over rice or steamed bread. Omit B.

CHICKEN CREAM OF RICE
Fun Tsen Wu Shiang Gee: Hupeh

A. 2½-lb. chicken

B. 1 teaspoon salt

C. 1 tablespoon sherry

D. ¼ teaspoon five spices powder (optional)

E. 2 tablespoons light soy sauce

F. 4 slices ginger, minced

G. ½ cup Cream of Rice

H. 1 scallion, minced

I. 2 tablespoons vegetable oil

J. ¼ teaspoon sesame oil (optional)

PREPARATION:

I. Cut A into bite-size pieces and add B, C, D, E, F.

II. Place G in paper bag and shake A–F in it.

III. Place A–F in large bowl and garnish with H. Pour I, J over and place in steamer.

COOKING:

1. Cover bowl with aluminum foil and steam 40 minutes. Serve.

SPARERIBS CREAM OF RICE
Fun Tsen Pai Gu: General

Substitute 3 lbs. spareribs for A and steam 1 hour.

CHICKEN CREAM OF RICE   *Approved Ulcer Recipe*
Fun Tsen Wu Shiang Gee: General

Omit C, D, F and tie H in bundle. Remove H before serving.

CHICKEN WITH BARBECUE SAUCE
Ke Tsup Gai: Canton

A. 2- to 3-lb. fryer
B. 3 cloves garlic, chopped
C. 3 slices ginger, chopped
D. 2 scallions, chopped
E. 4 tablespoons light soy sauce
F. 2 tablespoons catsup
G. 2 tablespoons bottled seafood sauce
H. 1 teaspoon sesame oil (optional)
I. ½ teaspoon salt
J. 3 tablespoons vegetable oil

PREPARATION:

I. Clean A thoroughly, cut into 8 to 10 pieces.
II. Mix B, C, D, E, F, G, H, I, J.
III. Marinate A in B–J 30 minutes.
IV. Place A and sauce in a baking dish. Cover with aluminum foil.

COOKING:

1. Bake A in 375° oven 30 minutes.
2. Turn A pieces over, remove foil, and bake another 20 minutes. Turn once during this baking period.

BARBECUED CHICKEN
Jiang Yo Sao Gee: Shanghai

A. 2 chickens (2 to 3 lbs. each)
B. ½ cup light soy sauce
C. 2 tablespoons sherry
D. ¼ teaspoon paprika
E. ¼ cup peanut oil
F. 1 teaspoon sugar

PREPARATION:

I. Wash A; dry with paper towels. Cut into 8 pieces.
II. Mix B, C, D, E, F; marinate A in mixture 1 hour.

COOKING:

1. Get coals red-hot on horizontal grill. Put on A. Cover A with aluminum foil to retain juices. If half hood is on grill, place one end of foil on top of hood (with weights) and allow foil to hang extended over edge of grill. When A browns, turn over. Cooking time: 25 to 40 minutes. Serves 6 to 8.

BARBECUED PORK
Jiang Yo Sao Ro: Shanghai

Substitute 4 lbs. pork chops for A. Eliminate E. Cook chops 40 to 60 minutes.

BARBECUED LAMB
Jiang Yo Sao Yang Pai: Shanghai

Substitute 4 lbs. lamb chops for A. Eliminate E. Sprinkle lamb with garlic salt.

BARBECUED DUCK
Jiang Yo Sao Yah: Shanghai

Substitute 3 to 4 lbs. duck for chicken. Eliminate E. Cook duck 40 to 60 minutes.

CHICKEN CURRY
Ga Li Gai: Canton

A. 2 tablespoons peanut oil
B. 1 medium onion, sliced
C. 2 teaspoons curry powder
D. 2- to 3-lb. frying chicken
E. 1 tablespoon light soy sauce
F. 3½ oz. pkg. coconut flakes.

PREPARATION:

I. Cut D into small pieces.
II. Combine C with a little water to form paste.
III. Soak F in 1 cup warm water; squeeze out juice to provide 1 cup coconut milk. (½ cup evaporated milk mixed with ½ cup water may be substituted.) Discard coconut.

COOKING:

1. Heat A; add B; stir until brown.
2. Add C paste; stir well.
3. Add D, E; stir well.
4. Add F juice, bring to boil and cook over low heat ½ hour, salt to taste.
5. Serve with rice.

CURRIED CHICKEN CANTONESE
Yea Tsup Ga Li Gai: Canton

A. 3 tablespoons peanut oil
B. 1 medium onion, chopped
C. 2 slices ginger, chopped
D. 2 teaspoons curry powder
E. 2 cups chicken broth
F. 1½ teaspoons salt
G. 2-lb. chicken
H. 1 cup milk
I. ½ cup coconut flakes
J. 1 tablespoon flour

PREPARATION:

I. Cut G into bite-size pieces.
II. Mix H, I in a pan, warm 30 minutes over low heat (do not boil), stirring occasionally.
III. Pour H–I from pan through a wire strainer, squeeze I, discard coconut residue, and mix liquid with J.

COOKING:

1. Heat A, brown B, C 1 minute.
2. Add D, stir 2 minutes more.
3. Add E, F, bring to boil. Lower heat, cook 5 minutes. Remove B, C.
4. Add G, cook 30 minutes.
5. Thicken with H–J mixture. Serve hot with rice.

SWEET AND SOUR CHICKEN
Tien Swan Gee Jiu: General

A. 2 eggs, beaten
B. ¾ teaspoon salt
C. ½ teaspoon garlic powder
D. ½ cup all-purpose flour
E. ¼ cup cornstarch
F. ½ cup milk
G. 1 tablespoon honey

H. 1 teaspoon lemon juice
I. 1 teaspoon rice wine or 2 tablespoons sherry
J. 1 teaspoon fresh ginger put through garlic press
K. 2½-lb. chicken
L. Sweet and sour sauce (see Index)

PREPARATION:

I. Bone K and cut into pieces 1 by 2 inches.
II. Mix G, H, I, J.
III. Marinate K in mixture 15 minutes.

IV. Mix A, B, C, D, E, F to make a smooth batter.
V. Dredge K in batter.

COOKING:

1. Fry A–K in peanut oil at 350° F. until light brown. Drain and remove to deep bowl.
2. Heat L and pour over A–K. Serve hot.

SWEET AND SOUR GINGER CHICKEN
Tien Swan Jiang Se Gee: Hunan

A. 1½-lb. frying chicken
B. 2 tablespoons ginger

C. 2 tablespoons distilled vinegar
D. 2 teaspoons sugar

E. 1 teaspoon salt
F. ½ teaspoon sesame oil

PREPARATION:

I. Shred B very fine.

II. Mix B, C, D, E, F well. Let stand ½ hour. Drain, save liquid.

COOKING:

1. Put 2 qts. of water in a pot and bring to a boil.
2. Add A, cover and simmer 15 minutes with occasional turning.

3. Turn off heat, leave A in pot another 20 minutes.
4. Cut A into bite-size pieces.
5. Add B–F mixture to A, mix well, and serve.

CHICKEN WITH HOISIN SAUCE
Hoi Shien Jiong Gai: Canton

Add 1 teaspoon salt in Step 1. Save stock for other dishes. Allow A to cool completely before cutting in Step 4 to avoid crumbling. Serve with hoisin sauce, mixed with chopped and pickled scallion.

SIMPLE SPICY CHICKEN
Ru Ee La Tze Gee: Adapted

A. 3 tablespoons vegetable oil
B. 1½- to 2-lb. frying chicken
C. 2 onions, sliced
D. 5 to 10 drops tabasco

E. ¼ cup light soy sauce
F. 1 teaspoon sugar
G. dash paprika (optional)
H. salt to taste

PREPARATION:

I. Cut B into 12 to 15 pieces.

II. Marinate B in D, E 20 minutes. Drain, saving liquid.

COOKING:

1. Heat A in large frying pan.
2. Using high heat, stir-fry B 5 minutes.
3. Add C, cook 3 minutes, then cover, lower heat to medium.

4. Add D, E marinating liquid and F, G. Continue cooking 3 to 5 minutes until done. Add H.

SPICY CHICKEN I
La Tze Gee: Shangtung

A. ¼ cup peanut oil
B. 2 chicken breasts
C. 1 tablespoon sherry
D. 1 tablespoon light soy sauce
E. 1 tablespoon cornstarch

F. 8-oz. can bamboo shoots, diced
G. 2 tablespoons hoisin sauce
H. ½ teaspoon crushed red-hot pepper
I. 1 tablespoon chopped scallion
J. 1 teaspoon chopped ginger

PREPARATION:

I. Bone B, cut into cubes.
II. Mix C, D, E.

III. Marinate B in C–E mixture. Let stand a few minutes.

COOKING:

1. Heat A.
2. Add B–E; stir 2 minutes; take out B.
3. Add F, G, H, I, J; stir 2 minutes.

4. Put B back into mixture and stir well.
5. Serve.

SPICY SMOKED CHICKEN II
Woo Siang Shwin Gee: Adapted

A. 3-lb. roasting chicken
B. 2 tablespoon sherry
C. 2 teaspoons salt
D. ¼ teaspoon cinnamon
E. 2 cloves star anise
F. ½ cup sugar

G. 1 tablespoon molasses
H. 2 scallions
I. 3 tablespoons light soy sauce
J. ¼ teaspoon sesame oil
K. 7 drops tabasco sauce

PREPARATION:

I. Clean A, dry thoroughly with paper towels.
II. Mix B, C; rub on A.

III. Stuff A cavity with H. Refrigerate overnight.
IV. Mix D, E, F, G.

COOKING:

1. Steam prepared A over boiling water 30 minutes. Remove from heat, let A stand in steamer 15 more minutes.
2. Line a Dutch oven with aluminum foil. Spread D–G uniformly over foil. Place a rack above D–G mixture.

3. Place prepared A on rack, cover, and cook over low heat 10 to 15 minutes. Remove from heat.
4. When Dutch oven is cool remove prepared A and cut into bite-size pieces.
5. Mix I, J, K, paint on A. Serve hot or cold.

SPICY WHITE-CUT CHICKEN
Bai Dzan Gee: Peking

A.   2 qts. water
B.   2½-lb. frying chicken (or Cornish hen)
C.   1 teaspoon salt

D.   2 to 3 oz. cooked ham
E.   2 to 3 tablespoons oyster sauce
F.   1 tablespoon hot mustard

PREPARATION:

I.   Wash B, dry with paper towel. Rub C on B inside and out.

II.   Slice D in thin, small pieces.
III.   Mix E, F.

COOKING:

1. Place A in Dutch oven, bring to boil, then add prepared B. Cover and lower to medium heat; boil for 10 to 15 minutes.

2. Remove from heat but leave cover on. After 5 minutes, remove B.

3. Cut B into bite-size pieces. Place D over it. Pour over E–F mixture.

HOT AND SPICY CHICKEN
Ma La Tze Gee: Hunan

A.   4 tablespoons peanut oil
B.   1 scallion
C.   2 to 3 red-hot peppers
D.   1 tablespoon shredded ginger
E.   1 tablespoon sherry
F.   2 tablespoons light soy sauce
G.   2-lb. fryer
H.   ½ cup chicken broth

I.   1 tablespoon light soy sauce
J.   2 tablespoons wine vinegar
K.   1 tablespoon sugar
L.   ½ teaspoon sesame oil
M.   ½ teaspoon salt
N.   1 to 2 teaspoons anise pepper
O.   1 tablespoon cornstarch

PREPARATION:

I.   Cut G into bite-size pieces, marinate 15 to 20 minutes in D, E, F.

II.   Cut B, C diagonally in 1-inch pieces.

III.   Grind N to powder.
IV.   Mix H, I, J, K, L, M, N.

COOKING:

1. Heat A. Add B, C, stir-fry several times.

2. Add D, E–G mixture to B, C mixture, and stir-fry 1 to 2 more minutes.

3. Add H–N, mix well, cook over low heat until G pieces are tender (about 10 to 12 minutes). Add O to thicken, stir well. Serve with rice.

CHICKEN WITH HOT PEPPER
La Gee Sih: Hunan

A.   3 tablespoons peanut oil
B.   4 hot peppers
C.   2 chicken breasts
D.   ½ teaspoon salt

E.   1 teaspoon cornstarch
F.   2 teaspoons sherry
G.   2 teaspoons light soy sauce
H.   10-oz. pkg. spinach

PREPARATION:

   I. Bone C, cut into cubes.

   II. Mix C, D, E, F, G.

III. Cut each B in half, chop.

IV. Wash and drain H.

COOKING:

1. Heat A. Stir-fry B ½ minute; remove.
2. Add C–G mixture, stir-fry until meat turns white (about 2 to 3 minutes). Remove to plate.

3. Put 1 tablespoon A into same frying pan; add H. Stir-fry 1 to 2 minutes. Add another dash of D. Mix well.
4. Serve C beside H or top H with C. Garnish with chopped fried B.

FIVE FLAVORS CHICKEN
Ng Heong Gai: Canton

A. 3 tablespoons peanut oil
B. 2-lb. fryer (or 2 squabs)
C. 1 teaspoon salt
D. 1 teaspoon anise pepper, ground (see Index)
E. 1 star anise, ground

F. 1 tablespoon chopped scallion
G. 3 slices ginger, chopped
H. 1 tablespoon light soy sauce
I. 1 tablespoon sherry
J. 2 teaspoons hoisin sauce

PREPARATION:

I. Cut B into bite-size pieces; rub with C.

II. Mix D, E, F, G, H, I, J.

COOKING:

1. Heat A, stir-fry and brown prepared B pieces about 5 minutes.

2. Add D–J mixture, mix well. Reduce heat, cover, and cook 10 to 15 more minutes (or until B is tender), stirring once or twice.

CHICKEN WITH BROWN BEAN SAUCE I
Jiang Gee: Shanghai

A. 2- to 2½-lb. fryer
B. 2 tablespoons brown bean sauce
C. 1 teaspoon sugar
D. 2 tablespoons sherry

E. ¼ cup light soy sauce
F. ½ teaspoon five spices powder
G. 1 scallion
H. 3 to 4 slices ginger

PREPARATION:

   I. Wash A well.

  II. Cut G, H in 1-inch to 2-inch pieces.

III. Mix B, C, D, E, F with 1 cup water.

IV. Rub A inside and out with B–F. Save excess mixture.

COOKING:

1. Place A in cooking pot, add any excess B–F mixture. Add G, H.
2. Bring to boil, lower heat, simmer 1 hour.

During this time, turn A over 3 or 4 times, basting with sauce.

3. Remove from heat, let cool. When cold, cut A into bite-size pieces and serve.

CHICKEN WITH BROWN BEAN SAUCE II
Jiang Bao Gee: Shanghai

A. 2 tablespoons peanut oil
B. 2- to 3-lb. frying chicken
C. 2 tablespoons brown bean sauce
D. 1 clove garlic, minced
E. 1 slice ginger, minced
F. 7 dried black mushrooms
G. ½ cup canned bamboo shoots
H. ¾ cup soup stock

I. ¼ cup sherry
J. ½ teaspoon salt
K. ½ teaspoon sugar
L. 2 teaspoons light soy sauce
M. 1 tablespoon cornstarch
N. 2 teaspoons heavy soy sauce
O. ¼ cup water

PREPARATION:

I. Boil B until tender (about 25 minutes). Remove bones and cut B into bite-sized cubes.
II. Soak F in warm water 15 minutes. Drain.
III. Mash C with back of spoon.

IV. Mix C, D, E. Set aside.
V. Mix H, I, J, K, L. Set aside.
VI. Mix M, N, O. Set aside.
VII. Slice F and G into ⅛-inch-thick pieces.

COOKING:

1. Heat skillet over high heat. Add A. Heat 30 seconds.
2. Add B and stir-fry 1 minute.
3. Add C–E mixture and stir-fry 1 minute.
4. Add F, G and stir-fry 30 seconds.

5. Add H–L mixture, cover, and cook 1 minute.
6. Add M–O mixture slowly while stirring constantly.
7. Serve as soon as sauce thickens and coats all ingredients well.

SOY SAUCE CHICKEN I
Si Yow Gai: Canton

A. 2 cups light soy sauce
B. ¼ cup brown sugar

C. ½ cup sherry
D. ½ cup water

E. 2- to 3-lb. fryer
F. 2 teaspoons sesame oil

PREPARATION:

I. Clean and wash E, dry between paper towels.

COOKING:

1. Place A, B, C, D in a 5-qt. saucepan, bring to boil.
2. Add E, return to boil, cover and simmer E 5 minutes per lb. turning over every 5 minutes.

3. Turn off heat and leave E in sauce 20 minutes longer.
4. Take cover off; remove E to a dish and brush with F.
5. Cool, then cut into bite-size pieces and serve.

SOY SAUCE CHICKEN II
Jiang Yo Gee: Shanghai

A. 1 slice ginger (½ in. thick) about size of a quarter
B. 1 scallion
C. 1 teaspoon anise pepper
D. 1 to 1½ star anise seeds

E. 2 cups light soy sauce
F. 2 cups chicken broth
G. ½ cup sherry
H. 1 tablespoon sugar
I. 2- to 3-lb. fryer

PREPARATION:

I. Clean and wash I, dry between paper towels.

II. Place A, B, C, D in a piece of cheesecloth, gather at the top, and tie with string.

III. Mix E, F, G, H.

COOKING:

1. Place A–H in 5-qt. saucepan; bring to boil, lower heat and simmer 15 minutes.

2. Turn heat to high, add I; when sauce boils, lower heat, cover pan tightly, and simmer 5 minutes for each pound of I, turning it over every 5 minutes.

3. Turn off heat and leave I in sauce 20 minutes. Do not remove cover during this period.

4. Remove I to dish; cool and cut into bite-size pieces. Pour some sauce over I to serve. Remaining sauce can be stored under refrigeration for reuse.

DRUNKEN CHICKEN I
Jwei Gee: Shanghai

A. 2-lb. fryer or Cornish hen (or 4 chicken breasts)

B. 1 scallion

C. 2 slices ginger

D. 2 teaspoons salt

E. ½ cup dry sherry or whiskey

PREPARATION:

I. Wash A well.

II. Stuff B, C in cavity.

COOKING:

1. Cover A with boiling water, bring to boil; lower heat, simmer, turning over once, 10 minutes. Remove from heat and leave A in water 5 more minutes.

2. Remove A from water. Cool.

3. Quarter A.

4. Rub prepared A with D; pour E on top. Place in covered container.

5. Refrigerate at least 1 to 2 days. Turn pieces over at least once a day.

6. Cut A into bite-size pieces. Serve.

DRUNKEN CHICKEN II
Jwei Gee: Shanghai

A. 2-lb. fryer

B. 1 tablespoon salt

C. ½ to 1 cup sherry or whiskey

PREPARATION:

I. Clean and wash A, dry with paper towel, split in halves.

II. Rub A all over with B. Let stand 2 hours; pour off excess liquid.

III. Add ¾ cup C to A, marinate 1 to 2 days in refrigerator. Turn A over a few times.

COOKING:

1. Steam prepared A in steamer over boiling water 25 minutes. Remove from steamer and cool.

2. Pour remainder of C over A. Marinate 3 to 4 hours or leave in refrigerator for few days (can be soaked up to 1 to 2 weeks, the longer, the stronger).

3. Cut into bite-size pieces or bone and cut into strips and serve.

STEAMED CHICKEN WITH WINE
Jiu Tsen Gee: Peking

A. 1½-lb. chicken
B. 1½ teaspoons salt
C. 2 scallions (white part only)

D. 4 slices ginger
E. ½ cup sherry

PREPARATION:

I. Clean and wash A, dry between paper towels, rub with B inside and outside.

II. Cut C into 1½-inch-long pieces.

III. Arrange A in a bowl breast side up, spread C, D, on top.

IV. Pour E over.

COOKING:

1. Steam A–D over boiling water for 35 to 45 minutes or until chicken is tender.

2. Remove C, D, place A in a dish breast side up.

3. Boil ½ cup of soup from A, pour over A and serve.

CHICKEN IN SHERRY
Tsow Mun Gai: Canton

A. 2 tablespoons peanut oil
B. 1½ cups sherry
C. 6 slices ginger, slivered
D. 2 cups water
E. 1 teaspoon heavy soy sauce
F. 2 teaspoons light soy sauce

G. 2 teaspoons salt
H. 3 cloves garlic, minced
I. 3-lb. chicken
J. 3 tablespoons cornstarch
K. 6 tablespoons water

PREPARATION:

I. Mix B, C, D, E, F, G, H. Set aside.

II. Mix J, K. Set aside.

COOKING:

1. Put A in very hot skillet and bring to high heat.

2. Add B–H. Mix well.

3. Add I (whole). Bring sauce to a boil.

4. Simmer 30 minutes.

5. Remove I, disjoint, cut into pieces, place in deep serving bowl.

6. Put remaining sauce over high heat. Add as much of J, K mixture as is necessary to thicken to taste.

7. Pour thickened sauce over I. Serve.

CHICKEN IN OYSTER SAUCE
Ho Yow Gai: Canton

A. 3 tablespoons peanut oil
B. 2-lb. frying chicken
C. 1 scallion

D. 4 slices fresh ginger
E. 4 tablespoons oyster sauce
F. salt to taste

PREPARATION:

I. Cut B into small pieces.

II. Cut C into 1-inch pieces.

COOKING:

1. Heat A. Add B, C, D. Sauté until golden brown.

2. Add E. Cook, covered, 25 minutes over low heat.

3. Add F.

4. Serve hot or cold.

BONG BONG CHICKEN
Bong Bong Gee: Szechuan

A. 2 tablespoons peanut oil
B. hot pepper powder, to taste
C. 1 scallion, chopped
D. 4 to 6 slices ginger, shredded
E. 1 tablespoon light soy sauce
F. 1 tablespoon sesame seed paste
G. 1 tablespoon vinegar

H. 1½ teaspoons sugar
I. ½ teaspoon salt
J. ¼ to ½ teaspoon sesame oil
K. 1½-lb. fryer (or 2 whole breasts)
L. 1 teaspoon salt
M. Chinese parsley (optional)

PREPARATION:

I. Rub K with L. Cut open. Steam in steamer over boiling water 15 minutes, or until tender. Remove K to dish and cool.

II. Bone K and tear into long thin pieces. (In Szechuan a rolling pin is used to beat the meat to loosen and separate it from the bone.) Arrange K on plate.

III. Mix C, D, E, F, G, H, I, J.

COOKING:

1. Heat A until very hot, remove from heat. Add B, stir well, and add C–J mixture; mix well. Sprinkle over K–L, garnish with M.

BONG BONG CHICKEN WITH CUCUMBER
Hwang Gwa Bong Bong Gee: Szechuan

Add two small, tender, sweet and sour cucumbers. Wash, cut lengthwise, then slice diagonally into thin pieces. Mix with 1 teaspoon salt and marinate 30 minutes. Squeeze out salt water from cucumber, add 1 tablespoon vinegar and 1 tablespoon sugar, mix well and serve under chicken.

CLUB CHICKEN
Bong Bong Gee: Szechuan

A. 2 tablespoons peanut oil
B. hot pepper powder, to taste
C. 1 scallion, chopped
D. 4 to 6 slices ginger, shredded
E. 1 tablespoon light soy sauce
F. 2 tablespoons peanut butter
G. 1 tablespoon vinegar
H. 1½ teaspoons sugar

I. ½ teaspoon salt
J. ¼ to ½ teaspoon sesame oil
K. 1 fryer (about 1½ lbs.) or two whole breasts
L. 1 teaspoon salt
M. Chinese parsley (optional)
N. ½ head lettuce, shredded

PREPARATION:

I. Rub K with L. Cut open. Steam in steamer over boiling water 15 minutes, or until tender. Remove K to dish and cool.

II. Bone K and tear into thin long pieces. Spread N on plate. Arrange K on N.

III. Mix C, D, E, F, G, H, I, J.

COOKING:

1. Heat A until very hot, remove from heat. Add B, stir well and add C–J mixture; mix well. Sprinkle over K–L, garnish with M.

PAPER-WRAPPED CHICKEN I
Tze Bao Gee: Shanghai

A. 2 cups vegetable oil
B. 3 lbs. breast meat of frying chickens
C. 1 tablespoon light soy sauce
D. 1 tablespoon gin

E. 1 teaspoon salt
F. ½ teaspoon ground white pepper
G. 1 to 3 teaspoons sesame oil (to taste)

PREPARATION:

I. Slice B into pieces 2 inches long by ¼ inch wide. Place in bowl.

II. Mix C, D, E, F, G and pour over B in bowl. Mix well and let stand 1 hour.
III. Wrap each piece of B in wax paper.

COOKING:

1. Heat A to 375°, and deep fry packages 1 minute on each side.

2. Serve hot in wrapping (to be unwrapped at the table).

PAPER-WRAPPED CHICKEN II
Tzee Bao Gai: Canton

A. breast meat of a 3-lb. frying chicken
B. 6 scallions
C. 2 cups peanut oil
D. ½ teaspoon minced ginger
E. 1 tablespoon light soy sauce

F. 1 teaspoon sugar
G. 1 teaspoon salt
H. ¼ teaspoon garlic powder
I. 1 tablespoon gin

PREPARATION:

I. Slice A into pieces 1 inch wide by 1 inch long. Place in bowl.

II. Mix D, E, F, G, H, I and pour over A in bowl. Mix well. Set aside for 30 minutes.
III. Cut B into thirds.

COOKING:

1. In pieces of aluminum foil wrap 2 to 3 pieces of prepared A with 2 to 3 sections of B.
2. Heat C to 350° and deep-fry A–B packages 1½ minutes.

3. Serve hot in foil wrapping—to be unwrapped at the table.

HOT SWEET SAUCE CHICKEN
Jiang Bao Ro Ding: Szechuan

A. 3 tablespoons peanut oil
B. 1 chicken breast (or ½ lb. veal or lean pork)
C. 1 cup diced bamboo shoots
D. 1 or 2 red-hot peppers or to taste (optional)
E. 2 tablespoons brown bean sauce
F. 1 teaspoon sugar
G. 2 teaspoons sherry

H. 1 teaspoon light soy sauce
I. 2 teaspoons chopped scallion
J. 1 teaspoon chopped ginger
K. 1 teaspoon cornstarch
L. 1 egg white
M. 2 teaspoons cornstarch
N. dash salt

PREPARATION:

I. Bone B and dice, mix with L, M, N.

II. Cut D in half, remove and discard seeds, dice.

III. Mix E, F, G, H, I, J, K thoroughly.

COOKING:

1. Heat A, add B mixture, C and D, stir-fry for 3 to 5 minutes.

2. Add E–K, stir until thoroughly mixed.

DICED CHICKEN WITH SWEET SAUCE I
Jiang Bao Gee Ding: Peking

A. ¼ cup peanut oil

B. 1 chicken breast

C. 2 teaspoons light soy sauce

D. 2 teaspoons cornstarch

E. 1 to 2 cloves garlic

F. 2 scallions (white part only), diced

G. 1 tablespoon brown bean sauce

H. 1 teaspoon sugar

I. 2 teaspoons sherry

J. ½ teaspoon sesame oil

K. ½ cup drained and diced water chestnuts

PREPARATION:

I. Bone B and dice, mix well with C, D.

II. Pound E with side of cleaver, discard skin. Mince.

III. Mix G, H, I, J, K.

COOKING:

1. Heat A, add B–D, and stir-fry 1 to 2 minutes. Remove B–D, leaving about 1 tablespoon A in pan.

2. Reheat A, add E, F, stir-fry 1 to 2 minutes.

Add G–K mixture, continue stirring for ¾ minute.

3. Return B–D mixture, mix well, add salt to taste.

DICED CHICKEN WITH SWEET SAUCE II
Jiang Bao Gee Ding: Shanghai

A. 4 tablespoons peanut oil

B. 1 scallion, chopped

C. 2 slices ginger, chopped

D. 2 chicken breasts

E. 3 tablespoons brown bean sauce

F. 6 Chinese mushrooms

G. 1 green pepper, cubed

H. 1 sweet red pepper, cubed

I. ½ cup cubed bamboo shoots

J. salt to taste

K. 1 teaspoon light soy sauce

L. 1 teaspoon cornstarch

M. 2 teaspoons sherry

N. 1 teaspoon sugar

PREPARATION:

I. Bone D and cut into cubes. Mix with K, L, M, N.

II. Wash F and soak in warm water 15 minutes. Drain, saving ¼ cup water. Cut each F into quarters.

COOKING:

1. Heat A. Add B, C; stir-fry a few seconds.

2. Add prepared D, stir-fry 2 minutes. Transfer contents of frying pan to plate.

3. Pour excess A back into frying pan. Add E, stir-fry several times.

4. Add F, G, H, I, stir-fry 1 to 2 minutes.

5. Replace D in pan, add water from F. Mix well with F–I mixture and J. Cook 1 more minute. Serve.

ONE CHICKEN: THREE FLAVORS
I Gee San Wei

It is possible to prepare one chicken in three different ways with three distinctive flavors, as follows. This is particularly desirable for small families that cannot finish a whole chicken in one meal:

1. CHICKEN WINGS AND LEGS WITH SOY SAUCE
Jiang Yo Gee: Adapted

A. 1 cup light soy sauce
B. 1 scallion
C. 1 slice ginger (½ inch thick) about size of a nickel
D. ¼ cup of wine

E. ¼ cup water
F. 2 tablespoons brown sugar
G. wings and legs from 2- to 3-lb. fryer
H. 1 to 2 teaspoons sesame oil
I. 1 scallion, chopped

PREPARATION:

I. Tie B in a bundle.

II. Peel C and pound lightly with side of cleaver.

COOKING:

1. Place A, B, C, D, E, F in a saucepan, bring to a boil.
2. Add G spread out in a single layer; when mixture boils again, lower heat, cover, and simmer 5 minutes.
3. Turn G pieces over, turn up heat until sauce boils again; then lower heat, cover and simmer 5 minutes. Turn G, bring to boil, lower heat, and simmer 15 minutes.

4. Remove saucepan from heat. Keep covered and let stand 10 minutes.
5. Remove G from pan, brush with H, and let cool completely.
6. With cleaver, cut G into bite-size pieces.
7. Place on platter and garnish with I. Pour 2 to 3 tablespoons of the sauce over G. Serve. (The remaining sauce can be used over again as a sauce for hard-cooked eggs, gizzards, or any red-cooked dish.)

2. CHICKEN CUBES STIR-FRIED WITH GINKGO NUTS
Bai Go Gee Chiu: Adapted

A. 3 tablespoons peanut oil
B. 1 tablespoon chopped scallion
C. 6 Chinese mushrooms
D. chicken breast from 2- to 3-lb. fryer
E. 1 teaspoon wine
F. 1 teaspoon cornstarch

G. 1 teaspoon peanut oil
H. 4 oz. snow peas
I. 6½-oz. can ginkgo nuts
J. 2 teaspoons light soy sauce
K. ½ teaspoon salt
L. 2 tablespoons mushroom water

PREPARATION:

I. Rinse C under cold running water, then soak in warm water 15 minutes or until soft. Cut each into 4 pieces. Save 2 tablespoons mushroom water for L.

II. Bone D and cut into cubes, mix with E, F, G. (Save bone for soup.)
III. Remove tips of H and wash.
IV. Drain I.

COOKING:

1. Heat A, add B, C, and stir-fry a few seconds.
2. Add D–G, stir-fry 1½ minutes.
3. Add H, I and mix well.

4. Add J, K, L, stir well, cover and cook 1 minute. Serve.

3. CHICKEN SOUP WITH PARTS
Gee Tong: Adapted

See Index.

CHICKEN WHITE CUT
Bai Tzahn Gee: General

A. water to cover B
B. 2- to 3-lb. chicken
C. 2 slices ginger, slivered
D. 1½ teaspoons salt
E. 1 tablespoon light soy sauce

F. 1 to 2 tablespoons sherry (optional)
G. 4 tablespoons peanut oil
H. 1 tablespoon light soy sauce
I. 3 scallions, chopped
J. 2 tablespoons oyster sauce (optional)

PREPARATION:

I. Mix C, D, E, F.

II. Mix H, I, J. Set aside for use as dip (Step 6, optional).

COOKING:

1. Boil A vigorously.
2. Place B in pot, cover and cook over moderate heat 25 to 30 minutes.
3. Remove B. Cool. Reserve the soup stock for use in another dish.
4. When cold, chop B into bite-size pieces and place in serving dish. Add C–F mixture and mix well.
5. Heat G in skillet until smoking hot.
6. Pour G over A. Serve at once, or after refrigeration, with or without mixture of H–J (served separately as a dip).

CHICKEN VELVET I
Fu Yung Gee Pien: General

A. 2 chicken breasts
B. 3 tablespoons peanut oil
C. 1 scallion, chopped
D. 4 slices ginger, chopped
E. 10 Chinese mushrooms

F. 4 stalks Chinese cabbage
G. ½ teaspoon salt
H. dash sugar
I. ½ cup cornstarch

PREPARATION:

I. Slice A into 2-inch by ¾-inch pieces; roll each piece in I.
II. Wash E and soak in hot water for 15 minutes. Drain (save water); cut each E into halves.
III. Cut F diagonally same size as chicken pieces.

COOKING:

1. Put prepared A in boiling water to cook; stir and cook 2 minutes; remove.
2. Heat B; add C, D. Stir for a few seconds; add E, F; stir well.
3. Add ¼ cup mushroom water, cover and cook five minutes.
4. Add A and G, H. Stir for another two minutes and serve.

CHICKEN VELVET II
Gai Yung: Canton

A. ½ cup ground breast meat of chicken
B. 1 teaspoon cornstarch
C. ¼ teaspoon salt
D. ¼ cup water
E. 4 egg whites

F. 2 tablespoons peanut oil
G. 1 cup chicken soup stock
H. 1 teaspoon sherry
I. ¼ teaspoon salt
J. 1 tablespoon cornstarch

PREPARATION:

I. Mix B, C. Set aside.

II. Mix G, H, I, J. Set aside.

COOKING:

1. Combine A thoroughly with B, C.
2. Very slowly add D, a few drops at a time (if added too fast, mixture will not hold together).
3. Beat E until stiff and slowly fold into A–D mixture.
4. Heat F to moderate heat. Pour A–E mixture into skillet. Remove from heat at once. Stir and mix well and rapidly.
5. Return to heat. Cook until just set (firm, but do *not* brown).
6. Remove to warm serving dish.
7. Heat G–J sauce. Mix until sauce thickens and boils.
8. Pour over chicken velvet and serve at once.

CHICKEN VELVET SHRIMP
Gee Yung Sha: Peking

A. 3 tablespoons vegetable oil
B. 10 oz. shelled shrimp
C. 3 slices ginger
D. 3 scallions
E. ½ teaspoon salt
F. 1 teaspoon sherry
G. 2 teaspoons light soy sauce

H. 3 oz. chicken breast meat
I. 6 egg whites
J. 2 tablespoons cornstarch
K. dash pepper
L. 1 tablespoon vegetable oil
M. 1 oz. cooked ham
N. 6 stalks asparagus

PREPARATION:

I. Devein and wash B. Split each into 2 pieces.
II. Chop C and D fine and mix with E, F, G.
III. Marinate B in C–G mixture 2 hours.
IV. Mince M.

V. Break off tough stems of N; French-cut tips very thin. Precook in boiling water 2 minutes.
VI. Mince H very fine, mix with I, J, K.

COOKING:

1. Heat A in frying pan. Stir-fry B–G mixture 1 minute, then add H–K mixture, stir-fry 2 more minutes. Remove and place in warm bowl.
2. In same frying pan, heat L, add M, N; stir-fry 1 minute, spread over B and serve.

CHICKEN VELVET SHRIMP
Gee Yung Sha: Peking

Omit L and substitute 2 oz. canned bamboo shoots for N and shred in Step V. In Step 2, spread minced M over B and serve.

CHICKEN VELVET SHRIMP
Dung Sun Gee Yung Sha: Peking

Substitute 5 Chinese mushrooms for N and soak in warm water (Step V) 20 minutes. Drain, discard stems, and shred.

CHICKEN VELVET AND PEAS
Gee Yung Ching Do: Peking

A. 6 tablespoons vegetable oil
B. 6 oz. fresh peas, shelled (or snow peas)
C. 3 tablespoons chicken soup
D. 2 chicken breasts
E. 3 slices ginger, chopped
F. 3 scallions, chopped

G. 1 teaspoon sherry
H. 2 teaspoons light soy sauce
I. 6 egg whites
J. 2 tablespoons cornstarch
K. dash pepper
L. 2 oz. cooked ham, minced

PREPARATION:

I. Bone D, mince very fine.
II. Mix E, F.

III. Mix E, F, G, H, I, J, K until any lumps disappear.

COOKING:

1. Heat A in frying pan, add B, stir-fry 2 minutes (1 for snow peas). Add C and stir-fry 1½ minutes.

2. Add D–K, stir-fry vigorously 2 minutes. Break up any large lumps.
3. Place mixture in bowl. Garnish with L and serve.

KUNG BAO CHICKEN DING
Kung Bao Gee Ding: Szechuan

A. ¼ cup peanut oil
B. 2 chicken breasts
C. 1 egg white
D. 2 teaspoons cornstarch
E. 1 to 2 scallions, chopped
F. 2 to 4 slices ginger, chopped
G. 2 to 3 red-hot peppers
   (dried hot or pepper flakes)

H. ¼ cup water chestnuts (optional)
I. 1 tablespoon soybean sauce (mien see)
J. 1 teaspoon sugar
K. 2 teaspoons light soy sauce
L. 2 teaspoons sherry
M. 2 teaspoons vinegar
N. ¼ teaspoon sesame oil
O. salt to taste

PREPARATION:

I. Bone B, discard skin, dice and mix with C, D.

II. Split G into halves, discard stem and seeds, cut each into ½-inch pieces.
III. Mix I, J, K, L, M, N.

COOKING:

1. Heat A, stir-fry B–D mixture for 1 to 2 minutes, remove to dish.
2. Leave excess oil in same pan, and heat. Add E, F, G, H (drained and diced); stir-fry 1 to 2 minutes.

3. Add B–D mixture, stir-fry 1 to 2 minutes.
4. Add I–N mixture, continue stirring until well mixed. Add O.

STEAMED CHICKEN BREASTS
Ching Tsen Gee Ro: Fukien

A. 2 chicken breasts
B. 1½ teaspoons salt
C. 2 teaspoons sherry
D. ½ teaspoon sugar
E. 2 teaspoons cornstarch

F. 8 Chinese mushrooms
G. 20 golden needles
H. 6 slices ginger, shredded
I. 1 tablespoon peanut oil

PREPARATION:

I. Bone A, cut into 1¼-inch cubes, and mix thoroughly with 1 teaspoon B, ¼ teaspoon each of C, D, E.

II. Wash F, G, soak 15 minutes in warm water; drain. Cut each F into 3 or 4 pieces, discard G tips (hard part), and cut each again into pieces 1-inch long.

III. Place A–E in dish, spread with F, G, top with H, and sprinkle with rest of B–E and I.

COOKING:

1. Steam A–I over boiling water until done (about 15 to 20 minutes).

STEAMED CHICKEN BREASTS WITH RICE FLOUR
Fun Tsen Gee: Hupeh

A. 2 chicken breasts (or 2 lbs. pork chops)
B. 2 teaspoons sherry
C. 2 teaspoons light soy sauce
D. ¾ teaspoon salt

E. ½ cup Cream of Rice
F. 2 scallions
G. 2 slices ginger

PREPARATION:

I. Cut A into 1½-inch squares.
II. Marinate with B, C, D.

III. Mix in E and place in shallow bowl.
IV. Slice F. Scatter F and G over A.

COOKING:

1. Place bowl of A–G in steamer and steam 30 minutes (45 for pork chops). Serve hot.

STEAMED SPARERIBS WITH RICE FLOUR
Fun Tsen Pai Gu: General

Substitute 2 lbs. spareribs for A. Cut into 1- by 2-inch pieces; steam 45 minutes.

STEAMED CHICKEN BREASTS WITH RICE FLOUR   *Approved Ulcer Recipe*
Fun Tsen Gee: Adapted

Omit B, F, G.

STEAMED CHICKEN BREASTS WITH RICE FLOUR AND MUSHROOMS
Fun Tsen Dung Gu Gee: Hupeh

A. 2 chicken breasts
B. 2 teaspoons sherry
C. 2 teaspoons light soy sauce
D. ¾ teaspoon salt

E. ½ cup rice flour
F. 6 dried mushrooms
G. 2 slices ginger

PREPARATION:

I. Bone A and cut into 1½-inch squares. Marinate with B, C, D.

II. Mix E with A–D. Place in shallow bowl.

III. Soak F in hot water until soft. Drain. Cut into small pieces.

IV. Spread F, G over A.

COOKING:

1. Steam A–G 30 minutes.

MINCED CHICKEN BREASTS ON LETTUCE
Gai Si Sang Tsoi: Canton

A. ¼ cup vegetable oil

B. 2 chicken (or turkey) breasts

C. 5 black dried mushrooms

D. 1 large bamboo shoot

E. ½ cup diced celery

F. 2 teaspoons cornstarch

G. 1 tablespoon sherry

H. ½ teaspoon salt

I. 2 teaspoons light soy sauce

J. romaine lettuce

K. hoisin sauce (optional)

PREPARATION:

I. Bone and dice B.

II. Soak C in hot water 20 minutes. Drain, saving water, remove stems, dice.

III. Dice D (about ½ cup).

IV. Mix B with F, G, H, I.

COOKING:

1. Place A in hot skillet. Stir-fry B 2 minutes.

2. Add C, D, E. Simmer 3 minutes.

3. Mix F–I with ¼ cup mushroom water; add to mixture in skillet.

4. Place J leaves on plates, top with A–I, and serve. K may be used as dip.

SNOW-WHITE MINCED MEAT
Bai Shueh Gee: Fukien

A. ½ chicken breast

B. dash salt

C. 1 teaspoon sherry

D. 1 teaspoon cornstarch

E. 10 medium-size frozen shrimp, minced

F. ⅓ cup minced flounder fillet

G. ⅓ cup ground pork (½ lean, ½ fat)

H. ¾ teaspoon salt

I. 2 teaspoons sherry

J. 1 tablespoon water

K. 2 tablespoons chopped ham

L. 3 egg whites

M. 1 to 2 tablespoons chopped scallion

N. 2 teaspoons peanut oil

PREPARATION:

I. Bone A, remove skin, mince and mix with B, C.

II. Arrange on a plate in a rectangle, about 4 inches by 7 inches, and sprinkle with D.

III. Mix E, F, G, H, I, J and 1 teaspoon cornstarch well and spread on top of A–C mixture.

IV. Beat L until peaks are formed.

COOKING:

1. Steam A–J over boiling water 15 minute.

2. Spread beaten L on top of A–J mixture and then sprinkle on K.

3. Return to steamer and steam 5 more minutes.

4. Cut into 6 to 8 pieces.

5. Heat N, add A–J; brown pieces on three sides, but not the egg-white side. Garnish with M. Serve hot.

DICED CHICKEN WITH CHILIES
La Tze Gee Ding: Szechuan

A. 3 tablespoons peanut oil
B. 1 chicken breast
C. 1 egg white
D. 2 teaspoons cornstarch
E. ½ teaspoon salt
F. 1 clove garlic, chopped
G. 1 green pepper
H. 2 red-hot peppers

I. 3 slices ginger, chopped
J. 1 scallion, chopped
K. ½ cup diced bamboo shoots
   (or water chestnuts)
L. 1 teaspoon salt
M. 2 tablespoons light soy sauce
N. 1 tablespoon vinegar
O. 2 teaspoons sugar

PREPARATION:

I. Bone B and dice, mix with C, D, E.
II. Wash and discard stem and seeds of G, H; dice.

III. Mix M, N, O.

COOKING:

1. Heat A, add B–E mixture, stir-fry 1 to 2 minutes, remove to dish.
2. Pour excess A back into frying pan and heat.

Add F, G, H, I, stir-fry 1 to 2 minutes, add J, K, L, stir until done (1 to 2 minutes).
3. Return B–E mixture to pan, add M–O, mix well and serve.

FLUFFY CHICKEN PANCAKE
Fu Yung Gee Pien: Peking

A. ¼ cup peanut oil
B. ½ chicken breast
C. 2 teaspoons sherry

D. salt and pepper to taste
E. few drops sesame oil
F. 3 egg whites

PREPARATION:

I. Bone and mince B.

II. Beat F with chopsticks until foamy; mix in B, C, and D thoroughly.

COOKING:

1. Put A into flat frying pan over medium heat.
2. When slightly hot, add B–F mixture. Tip frying pan so that it is evenly coated by mixture.

3. When firm, turn mixture over; cook until both sides are firm, but do not brown.
4. Add E and serve.

PEKING JELLED CHICKEN
Dung Gee: Peking

A. 2- to 3-lb. chicken
B. 1 lb. pigskin
C. 2 scallions
D. 3 to 4 slices ginger
E. ⅓ cup light soy sauce

F. 2 tablespoons sherry
G. 1½ teaspoons sugar
H. salt to taste
I. Chinese parsley

PREPARATION:

I. Clean and wash A; cut into bite-size pieces.

II. Clean and wash B.

III. Tie C into knot.

COOKING:

1. Place A, B in cooking pot, add 1½ cups water, bring to boil.
2. Add C, D, E, cook 1 minute, lower heat and simmer for 35 minutes.
3. Place A pieces in dish, dice B and discard C, D.
4. Place B back in pot with sauce, simmer for 1½ hours or until sauce is half gone. Drain and save sauce.

5. Mix A with sauce and F, G, bring to boil, lower heat and simmer 5 to 10 minutes or until A is tender. Add a little boiling water if necessary.
6. Add H.
7. Place A in bowl and let stand until jelled.
8. When serving, turn bowl upside down on a plate, garnish jelled chicken with I.

PEKING JELLED CHICKEN
Dung Gee: Peking

Bone A before cooking. In Step 5, chop A, then mix with sauce and F, G, bring to boil, and simmer 5 to 10 minutes. Place A in 1 or 2 long pans and let stand until jelled. Slice and serve or use as hors d'oeuvres.

COLD CHICKEN
Lun Ban Gee: General

A. 1½ teaspoons peanut oil
B. 1 cup thinly sliced cooked white meat of chicken
C. 1 tablespoon light soy sauce

D. 6 drops sesame oil
E. ½ teaspoon peanut oil
F. 2 scallions, sliced

PREPARATION:

I. Mix C, D, E.

II. Pour C–E mixture over B.

COOKING:

1. Heat A to smoking hot and pour over B–E. Mix gently but well.

2. Serve with garnish of F.

COLD SAVORY NOODLES WITH CHICKEN   Approved Ulcer Recipe
Lun Ban Gee Si Mein: General

A. ¼ lb. spaghetti
B. 1 cup grated carrots
C. 1 cup chicken broth

D. 1 cup white meat chicken, cooked and chopped
E. 2 tablespoons light soy sauce
F. salt to taste

COOKING:

1. Cook A in 2 qts. boiling water 5 to 8 minutes. Drain, cool with cold water.
2. Place B in C, add D; simmer until very soft. Cool.

3. Mix A with B–D, E, and F.
4. Serve cold.

FRIED SPICY CHICKEN NUGGETS
Tswei Pi Dza Gee: Shantung

A. 2 tablespoons vegetable oil
B. 1 clove garlic, chopped
C. 3 slices ginger, chopped
D. 2 scallions, chopped
E. 2 chicken legs (or 4 pork chops)
F. 1 tablespoon cornstarch
G. 1 egg white
H. 3 to 10 drops hot sauce or ¼ to 1 teaspoon red pepper (optional)

I. 1 teaspoon sherry
J. ½ teaspoon salt
K. ½ cup diced bamboo shoots
L. ¼ cup button mushrooms with liquid
M. 1 teaspoon light soy sauce
N. 1 teaspoon cider vinegar
O. 1 tablespoon catsup
P. 1 teaspoon sugar

PREPARATION:

I. Bone E and cut into 1-inch nuggets.
II. Mix E, F, G, H, I, J.

III. Mix B, C, D.
IV. Mix K, L, M, N, O, P.

COOKING:

1. Heat A in frying pan. When hot add B–D and stir-fry ½ minute.
2. Add E–J mixture, stir-fry 3 minutes 10 minutes for pork) over medium heat until nuggets are brown outside and tender in the center.
3. Add K–P, including liquid from L. Cover and simmer for 5 minutes, stirring occasionally.

FRIED SPICY CHICKEN NUGGETS WITH ASPARAGUS
Gee Jiu Lu Sun: Adapted

Substitute asparagus shoots for K. Break off tender shoots and dice. Discard stems.

FRIED SPICY SHRIMP NUGGETS
Tsao Sha Jiu: General

Substitute shrimp for E. Cut each shrimp into 2 pieces. In Step 2 stir-fry with E–J mixture for 1½ to 2 minutes only. In Step 3 simmer for 3 minutes only, stirring occasionally.

STUFFED CHICKEN WINGS
Yiong Gai Yik: Adapted

A. 10 chicken wings
B. 1 teaspoon salt
C. 3 Chinese mushrooms
D. ½ cup finely shredded bamboo shoots

E. ⅓ cup finely shredded Virginia ham
F. 2 tablespoons chopped scallion
G. 1 tablespoon cornstarch

PREPARATION:

I. Remove tips of A (which may be saved for other uses). Make 2- to 3-inch slits in skin of elbow portions. Sprinkle A with ½ teaspoon B.
II. Wash C, soak 15 minutes in warm water. Drain.

III. Shred C, D, E very fine.
IV. Chop F, mix with C–E and remaining ½ teaspoon B.
V. Stuff A slits with C–F mixture, using about 1 tablespoon per wing.
VI. Mix G with 1 tablespoon water.

COOKING:

1. Place A–F in shallow dish, steam over hot water 30 to 45 minutes.
2. Pour A drippings into pot; thicken with G mixture.
3. Pour over A, garnish with additional F. Serve hot.

BRAISED CHICKEN WINGS I
Kwei Fei Gee: Shanghai

A. 2 tablespoons peanut oil
B. 8 chicken wings (1 to 1½ lbs.)
C. 1 cup canned bamboo shoots
D. 6 Chinese mushrooms
E. 3 teaspoons light soy sauce
F. 2 slices ginger
G. 1 teaspoon salt
H. ½ cup chicken broth
I. 2 teaspoons sesame oil
J. 2 scallions
K. 2 teaspoons sherry
L. 1 teaspoon sugar
M. 1 teaspoon cornstarch mixed with 2 tablespoons water

PREPARATION:

I. Disjoint B.
II. Cut C into bite-size pieces.
III. Wash D and soak in warm water until soft (about 15 to 30 minutes). Drain and quarter each.
IV. Mix E, F, G, H.
V. Cut J into 1- to 2-inch pieces.

COOKING:

1. Heat A, brown B 5 minutes, remove B pieces to cooking pot. Add C and D–H, bring to boil, lower heat and simmer 25 minutes.
2. Heat I in frying pan and stir-fry J for a few seconds, then add to chicken mixture.
3. Add K, L and simmer another 10 to 15 minutes.
4. Remove B to dish. Thicken gravy with M mixture and pour over B. Serve hot.

BRAISED CHICKEN WINGS II
Kwei Fei Gee: Szechuan

A. 3 tablespoons lard (or vegetable oil)
B. 1 teaspoon rock sugar
C. 6 to 8 chicken wings (1 to 1½ lbs.)
D. 1 tablespoon chopped scallion
E. 1 teaspoon chopped ginger
F. 3 teaspoons light soy sauce
G. 2 teaspoons sherry
H. 1 teaspoon salt
I. ½ cup chicken broth
J. 1 cup sliced bamboo shoots
K. 8 Chinese mushrooms
L. ½ teaspoon sugar
M. 1 teaspoon cornstarch mixed with 2 tablespoons water

PREPARATION:

I. Disjoint C.
II. Wash K and soak in warm water until soft (15 to 30 minutes), drain, and quarter each.
III. Mix D, E, F, G, H, I.

COOKING:

1. Heat A and brown B. Add C pieces, stir-fry 1 minute.
2. Add D–I mixture, bring to boil; lower heat and simmer 25 minutes.
3. Add J, K, L and cook another 3 to 5 minutes (until wings are tender).
4. Thicken with M.

FRIED CHICKEN WINGS WITH HOISIN SAUCE
Hoisin Jiang Gee Tse Pong: Fukien

A.   3 tablespoons peanut oil
B.   1 scallion
C.   3 slices ginger
D.   1 clove garlic, chopped
E.   8 chicken wings

F.   1½ tablespoons hoisin sauce
G.   3 teaspoons soy sauce
H.   2 teaspoons sherry
I.   ½ teaspoon salt

PREPARATION:

I.   Disjoint E.
II. Cut B, C into 1-inch pieces.

III. Mix F, G, H, I.

COOKING:

1.   Heat A, add B, C, D and stir-fry ½ minute.
2.   Add E pieces and brown 3 minutes.

3.   Add F–I mixture, mix well, cover and cook over low heat 20 to 25 minutes or until E is tender. Stir occasionally.

SPICED CHICKEN WINGS   *Approved Diabetic Recipe*
Wu Shiang Gee Yeh: General

A.   1 tablespoon peanut oil
B.   1 teaspoon chopped scallion
C.   1 to 2 slices unsweetened pickled or fresh ginger
D.   1 lb. chicken wings

E.   1½ tablespoons light soy sauce
F.   ½ teaspoon anise pepper
G.   ½ star anise
H.   ½ teaspoon salt
I.   ½ cup water

PREPARATION:

I.   Wash D and cut each into 2 pieces.

COOKING:

1.   Heat A, add B, C and stir-fry a few seconds.
2.   Add D and brown 1 to 2 minutes.

3.   Add E, F, G, H, I. Mix well, bring to boil, lower heat and simmer 30 minutes.

CHICKEN WINGS WITH OYSTER SAUCE
Ho Yow Gai Yik: Canton

A.   2 tablespoons peanut oil
B.   3 slices ginger, minced
C.   ¼ teaspoon salt
D.   8 chicken wings (or 3 chicken breasts)
E.   2 scallions, sliced
F.   1 cup water

G.   3 teaspoons lemon juice
H.   1 teaspoon sugar
I.   1½ tablespoons cornstarch
J.   ½ cup water
K.   3½ tablespoons oyster sauce
L.   2 scallions, sliced

PREPARATION:

I.   Disjoint D or cut breasts into bite-size pieces.
II. Mix B, C. Set aside.

III. Mix G, H, I, J. Set aside. Stir well before using.

COOKING:

1. Put A in very hot skillet and bring to high heat.
2. Add B–C mixture. Stir-fry 15 seconds.
3. Add D and stir-fry 2 minutes.
4. Add E and F.
5. Cover and simmer 10 minutes.
6. Add G–J mixture, slowly. Stir-fry until sauce thickens and coats all ingredients well.
7. Add K. Stir-fry 15 seconds.
8. Serve with garnish of L.

STIR-FRIED CHICKEN LIVERS I
Tsao Gee Gahn: General

A. 3 tablespoons peanut oil
B. ½ lb. chicken livers, sliced
C. 1 tablespoon gin
D. 1 tablespoon light soy sauce
E. 1 tablespoon sherry
F. ¼ cup sliced bamboo shoots
G. ¼ cup sliced water chestnuts
H. 1 teaspoon salt
I. ¼ cup soup stock
J. 1 teaspoon cornstarch
K. ½ teaspoon sugar
L. 2 scallions, sliced

PREPARATION:

I. Mix B with C. Set aside for 10 minutes. II. Mix F, G, H, I, J. Set aside. III. Mix D, E. Set aside.

COOKING:

1. Put A in very hot skillet and bring to high heat.
2. When A begins to smoke add B–C. Stir-fry 30 seconds.
3. Add D–E. Stir-fry 30 seconds.
4. Add F–J. Stir-fry until sauce thickens and coats all ingredients well.
5. Add K and half of L. Cook 30 seconds more.
6. Serve with garnish of remaining L.

STIR-FRIED CHICKEN LIVERS II
Tsao Gee Gahn: General

A. 4 tablespoons peanut oil
B. 10 chicken (or duck) livers
C. 1 clove garlic, chopped
D. 1 scallion, chopped
E. 2 slices ginger, chopped
F. 6 dried Chinese mushrooms
G. ¼ cup shredded bamboo shoots
H. ½ teaspoon salt
I. 1 tablespoon light soy sauce
J. ¼ cup chicken broth
K. 2 teaspoons sherry
L. 2 teaspoons cornstarch mixed with ¼ cup water
M. dash pepper and salt

PREPARATION:

I. Cut each B into thin slices. Mix with ½ L and all of M.
II. Wash F, soak in warm water 15 minutes. Drain, saving 2 tablespoons F water. Mix this with remainder of L.
III. Slice F into strips ¼ inch wide.
IV. Mix H, I, J, K.

COOKING:

1. Heat A in frying pan. Add B, stir-fry 1 to 2 minutes. Remove to dish. Pour excess oil back into frying pan.
2. Stir-fry C, D, E 30 seconds.
3. Add F, G, and H–K mixture. Stir well, cook 2 minutes.
4. Return B to frying pan, mix well with F–K. Continue stir-frying 1 minute.
5. Add L, M to thicken. Serve hot.

STIR-FRIED CHICKEN LIVERS *Approved Diabetic Recipe*
Tsao Gee Gahn: General

A. 2 tablespoons peanut oil
B. 5 chicken livers
C. ½ teaspoon cornstarch
D. salt and pepper to taste
E. 1 small clove garlic, chopped
F. 1 teaspoon chopped scallion

G. 2 Chinese black mushrooms
H. ¼ cup shredded Chinese cabbage
I. ¼ teaspoon salt
J. 1 teaspoon light soy sauce
K. 1 teaspoon cornstarch mixed with 1 tablespoon mushroom water

PREPARATION:

I. Slice B into thin pieces and mix with C and D.
II. Wash and soak G 15 minutes in hot water.

Drain; save water, cut each G into 4 to 5 pieces.
III. Mix I, J with 1 tablespoon water.

COOKING:

1. Heat A; add B–D mixture, stir-fry 1 to 2 minutes. Remove to dish. Pour excess oil back into frying pan.
2. Stir-fry E, F a few seconds, add G, H, I, J, mix well and cook 2 minutes.

3. Return B to E–J mixture; continue to stir-fry for 1 minute.
4. Thicken with K and serve hot.

SWEET AND SOUR CHICKEN LIVERS
Tiem Shwin Gai Gon: Canton

A. 3 tablespoons peanut oil
B. 1 scallion, chopped
C. 2 slices ginger, chopped
D. 1 clove garlic, chopped
E. 8 chicken (or 8 duck) livers
F. 2 teaspoons light soy sauce
G. 1 teaspoon cornstarch

H. ½ teaspoon sugar
I. 1 teaspoon sherry
J. 1 cucumber
K. 3 tablespoons vinegar
L. 3 tablespoons sugar
M. ½ teaspoon salt
N. 2 teaspoons cornstarch

PREPARATION:

I. Cut E into thin slices. Mix with F, G, H, I.
II. Peel J, cut in half, discard seeds. Slice di-

agonally into ¼-inch pieces.
III. Combine K, L, M, N; mix well.

COOKING:

1. Heat A. Add B, C, D, stir-fry a few seconds.
2. Add E–I mixture, stir-fry 2 minutes. Remove E to dish, pouring excess oil back into pan.

3. Add J. Stir-fry 3 minutes.
4. Return E mixture to pan. Add K–N mixture. Stir until sauce thickens. Serve hot.

SWEET AND SOUR CHICKEN GIBLETS
Tiem Shwin Gai Jap: Canton

Substitute chicken gizzards and hearts for E. Slice gizzard very thin, and cook a few minutes longer.

CHICKEN LIVERS WITH OYSTER SAUCE
Ho Yu Fung Gon: Canton

A. 3 tablespoons peanut oil
B. 2 slices ginger
C. 1 scallion
D. 1 clove garlic
E. ½ lb. chicken livers
F. 1¼ tablespoons oyster sauce
G. 2 tablespoons water

H. 6 Chinese mushrooms
I. ¼ lb. snow peas
J. 1 cup sliced bamboo shoots
K. ½ to 1 teaspoon salt
L. ½ teaspoon sugar
M. 1 tablespoon water

PREPARATION:

I. Cut C into 1-inch-long pieces.
II. Pound D with side of cleaver, discard skin.

III. Wash H and soak in warm water for 15 minutes; drain, cut each into 4 or 5 pieces.
IV. Discard tips of I.

COOKING:

1. Heat 1 tablespoon A, stir-fry B, C, D ½ minute, add E, stir-fry 1 to 2 minutes longer.

2. Add F, mix well; add G, stir well; bring to boil, then lower heat and simmer until E is cooked (about 15 minutes).

3. Heat 2 tablespoons A in another pan, add H, stir-fry ½ minute.
4. Add I, J, stir-fry 1 minute, add K, L, mix well.
5. Add M and A–G, mix well, cover, and cook ½ minute.

CHICKEN LIVERS WITH QUAIL EGGS
Fung Gahn An Don: Adapted

A. 3 tablespoons peanut oil
B. 3 slices ginger, shredded
C. 1 clove garlic, minced
D. 12 chicken livers
E. ½ cup water chestnut flour
F. 4 water chestnuts, sliced thin
G. 9½-oz. can quail eggs

H. ½ tablespoon black beans
I. 2 tablespoons light soy sauce
J. 2 tablespoons heavy soy sauce
K. 1 cup chicken soup
L. 1 tablespoon cornstarch mixed with 2 tablespoons water

PREPARATION:

I. Rinse D under cold water; coat lightly with E.
II. Drain G and rinse in cool water. Set aside in a bowl.

III. Wash H, then mash into a paste.
IV. Mix I, J, K, L; add H.

COOKING:

1. Heat A to smoking, add B, C; stir-fry 1 minute.
2. Add D–E; stir-fry until livers are cooked (about 8 to 10 minutes).
3. Add F, stir-fry 1 minute.

4. Place G in a bowl. Pour B–F over.
5. Heat H–L mixture until thick, then pour over D.
6. Serve hot with rice.

FRIED CHICKEN GIZZARDS
Tza Gee Tzen: Shanghai

A. 1 lb. chicken gizzards
B. 1 cup peanut oil
C. 3 stalks Chinese parsley
D. 1 scallion
E. 1 clove garlic

F. ½ teaspoon anise pepper
G. 1 teaspoon salt
H. 1 tablespoon sherry
I. 1 teaspoon vinegar
J. ½ teaspoon sesame oil

PREPARATION:

I. Clean and wash A, remove all fat, quarter each A; cross slash each piece several times.
II. Cut C, D into 1-inch pieces.

III. Discard skin of E, then slice into thin pieces.
IV. Mix C, D, E, F, G, H, I, J.

COOKING:

1. Cook A in boiling water 1 to 2 minutes. Drain.
2. Heat B to 375°, deep-fry A 1 minute. Pour off B.

3. Add C–J mixture to A, bring to boil, mix well.

SPICED CHICKEN GIZZARDS I
Woo Siang Tsen Gahn: General

A. 2 tablespoons peanut oil
B. 1 scallion
C. 2 slices ginger
D. 1 to 1½ lbs. chicken gizzards and hearts
E. 3 tablespoons light soy sauce

F. 1 tablespoon sherry
G. 1 teaspoon sugar
H. ¼ teaspoon anise pepper
I. ½ star anise
J. ½ cup water (or chicken broth)

PREPARATION:

I. Clean D well, removing all fat.
II. Combine E, F, G, H, I.

III. Cut B into 1-inch pieces.

COOKING:

1. Heat A, stir-fry B, C several seconds.
2. Add D, stir-fry 1 minute.
3. Add E–I mixture, mix well.

4. Add J, bring to boil. Reduce heat, simmer 1 hour.

SPICED CHICKEN GIZZARDS *Approved Diabetic Recipe*
Wu Shiang Gee Tsen: General

A. 1 lb. chicken gizzards
B. 1½ tablespoons light soy sauce
C. 1 teaspoon chopped scallion

D. ½ teaspoon salt
E. ½ cup water

PREPARATION:

I. Wash A and remove all fat.

II. Combine all ingredients in saucepan.

COOKING:

1. Bring mixture to boil, lower heat, and simmer 1 hour.

SPICED CHICKEN GIZZARDS II
Bao Gee Chun: Peking

A. 1 to 1½ lbs. chicken gizzards
B. 2 tablespoons peanut oil
C. 1 scallion
D. 3 slices ginger
E. 1 teaspoon anise pepper
F. 1 tablespoon sherry
G. 1 teaspoon salt
H. ¼ cup chicken broth

PREPARATION:

I. Clean A and wash well, removing all fat; make several ½-inch crisscross slashes on each.
II. Cut C into 1- to 2-inch pieces.

COOKING:

1. Cover A with boiling water and cook 15 to 20 minutes. Drain.
2. Heat B, add C, D, E and stir-fry 30 seconds, add A, F, G, H, bring to boil; lower heat and cook 3 to 5 minutes or until very little sauce is left.
3. Discard C–E and serve.

STEAMED CHICKEN WITH HAM AND BAMBOO SHOOTS
Won Twei Tsen Gai: Canton

A. 3 slices ginger, shredded
B. ½ cup shredded bamboo shoots
C. 1 scallion
D. 1½- to 2-lb. frying chicken
E. ½ teaspoon salt
F. 1 teaspoon light soy sauce
G. 1 teaspoon sherry
H. 4 teaspoons cornstarch
I. 4 mushrooms
J. ½ cup shredded Virginia ham

PREPARATION:

I. Cut C into 1-inch pieces.
II. Cut D into bite-size pieces.
III. Mix A, C, E, F, G, and 2 teaspoons of H. Marinate D in this mixture.
IV. Wash I, soak 15 minutes in warm water. Drain and shred.
V. Mix B, I, J; spread over D in marinade.

COOKING:

1. Steam entire mixture over boiling water 30 minutes.
2. Transfer gravy into a pot, thicken with 2 teaspoons cornstarch mixed with a little water.
3. Pour gravy over D; serve with rice.

SCALLION STEAMED CHICKEN
Tsung Tsen Gee: Shanghai

A. 2- to 3-lb. chicken
B. 1 tablespoon salt
C. 1 bunch scallions
D. 5 slices ginger, minced
E. 2 tablespoons sherry

PREPARATION:

I. Rub B over A inside and out and place in bowl. Then place C, D inside A and let stand for 1 hour.

COOKING:

1. Place A–E in steamer. Steam over high heat 30 minutes.

SCALLION STEAMED CHICKEN   *Approved Ulcer Recipe*
Tsung Tsen Gee: Shanghai

Substitute 2 to 3 lbs. chicken breasts for A, C (do not cut, and remove before serving) ; omit D and E.

STEAMED CHICKEN WITH CHINESE SAUSAGE
Heong Chong Tsing Gai: Canton

A. 1- to 2-lb. fryer

B. 2 Chinese sausages

C. 6 Chinese mushrooms

D. 1 scallion, chopped

E. 2 slices ginger, chopped

F. 2 teaspoons light soy sauce

G. 2 teaspoons sherry

H. 1 teaspoon salt

I. ½ teaspoon sugar

J. ½ to 1 teaspoon sesame oil

K. 1 tablespoon cornstarch

PREPARATION:

I. Cut A into bite-size pieces.

II. Cut each B into 10 to 12 diagonal slices.

III. Wash C, soak 15 minutes in warm water. Drain, cut each into quarters.

IV. Combine all ingredients, place in dish.

COOKING:

1. Steam A–K 30 minutes over boiling water.

STEAMED CHICKEN WITH CHINESE PRESERVED SAUSAGE   *Approved Diabetic Recipe*
Tsing Heong Chong Gai: Canton

A. ½ chicken (about 1 lb.)

B. 1 Chinese preserved sausage

C. 2 Chinese mushrooms

D. 1 teaspoon chopped scallion

E. 1 teaspoon light soy sauce

F. ½ teaspoon salt

G. ¼ teaspoon sesame oil

H. 2 teaspoons cornstarch

PREPARATION:

I. Cut A into bite-size pieces.

II. Cut B diagonally into 12 pieces.

III. Wash C and soak in hot water 15 minutes. Drain, quarter.

IV. Combine all ingredients and mix well, place in a dish.

COOKING:

1. Steam A–H over boiling water 30 minutes.

CUBED SUB GUM CHICKEN
Gai Kow Sub Gum: Canton

A. 3 tablespoons peanut oil

B. 1 onion

C. 1 chicken breast

D. ½ teaspoon salt

E. 2 teaspoons sherry

F. ½ cup sliced bamboo shoots

G. ¼ cup sliced water chestnuts

H. ½ cup sliced celery

I. 1 cup sliced fresh mushrooms

J. 1 cup frozen peas

K. ½ cup chicken broth with ¼ cup water

L. 1 tablespoon cornstarch

M. salt, pepper to taste

N. 1 to 2 oz. toasted almonds

PREPARATION:

I. Bone C and cut into cubes. Marinate ½ hour with D, E.

II. Slice B into thin strips. Mix F, G, H, I, J.

COOKING:

1. Heat A in frying pan, stir-fry B 1 minute.
2. Add C–E mixture, stir-fry until it turns white (about 2 minutes).

3. Add F–J, stir-fry 3 minutes.
4. Add K, L, cook until thickened. Add M.
5. Garnish with N; serve hot.

CHICKEN WITH VEGETABLES
Fu Yung Gai Pien: Canton

A. 4 tablespoons peanut oil
B. 3 slices ginger
C. 2 scallions
D. ¼ cup sliced mushrooms
E. 1 pkg. frozen peas

F. 2 chicken breasts
G. 2 egg whites
H. 1 teaspoon salt
I. ½ tablespoon cornstarch

PREPARATION:

I. Bone and slice F into very thin strips.
II. Beat G, mix well with H, I.
III. Add F to G–I; mix well.

IV. Chop B. Cut C into 1-inch pieces.
V. Defrost E; drain D.

COOKING:

1. Heat 1 tablespoon A. Add B, C; stir-fry a few times.
2. Add D, E, continue stir-frying 1 minute. Remove to a plate.

3. Heat rest of A over high heat, stir-fry F–I mixture quickly 2 minutes.
4. Add B–E mixture, mix well. Serve hot.

CHICKEN WITH SNOW PEAS
Ho Lan Dow Tsao Gai Yoke: Adapted

A. 3 tablespoons peanut oil
B. 1 scallion
C. 2 slices ginger
D. 2 chicken legs
E. 1 teaspoon cornstarch
F. 1 tablespoon sherry

G. 10 Chinese mushrooms
H. ¼ lb. snow peas
I. 1 cup whole water chestnuts
J. 1 teaspoon salt
K. ¼ cup mushroom water

PREPARATION:

I. Cut D into ¼-inch pieces. Mix E, F and roll D in mixture.
II. Slice each I thin (about 5 slices each).

III. Wash G and soak in warm water. Drain, saving ¼ cup G water. Cut each G in half.
IV. Cut B, C into 1-inch pieces.

COOKING:

1. Heat A, add B, C, stir-fry a few seconds.
2. Add D–F mixture and G. Stir-fry 2 minutes, add 2 tablespoons water, simmer 10 minutes.

3. Add H, I, J. Mix well, add K, cover, and cook over medium heat 1 to 1½ minutes. Serve hot.

MINCED CHICKEN WITH CREAMED CORN
Gee Yung Yu Mi: Shanghai

A. 2 cups chicken broth
B. 8-oz. can creamed corn
C. 1 tablespoon cornstarch

D. 3 tablespoons water
E. 2 egg whites
F. 2 chicken breasts, minced

PREPARATION:

I. Beat E until foamy. Add F.

II. Mix C, D to form paste.

COOKING:

1. Bring A to boil.
2. Add B. Cook 5 minutes; add C–D mixture, stirring constantly.

3. Add E–F and stir a few seconds.
4. Serve hot.

CHICKEN WITH TOMATO AND POTATO
Fan Keh Shu Tzai Gai: Adapted

A. 3 tablespoons peanut oil
B. 1 medium onion
C. 2-lb. fryer
D. 3 to 4 tomatoes
E. 2 tablespoons light soy sauce

F. 2 to 3 medium potatoes
G. ¾ teaspoon salt
H. dash pepper
I. ¼ cup water

PREPARATION:

I. Cut C into bite-size pieces.
II. Pour boiling water over D, let stand several seconds. Peel D, slice each into 6 or 7 pieces.

III. Peel F, cut into bite-size pieces.
IV. Cut B in half, then slice.

COOKING:

1. Heat A; brown B slightly.
2. Add C, D, E, stir-fry 1 to 2 minutes. Lower heat, simmer 10 minutes.

3. Add F, G, H, I. Bring to boil, lower heat, and cook 15 more minutes or until F is done.

CHICKEN MUSHROOM RICE
Gai Fan: Canton

A. 2 cups chicken broth
B. 6 Chinese mushrooms
C. 1½ cups rice
D. 2-lb. chicken
E. 3 slices ginger, chopped

F. 1 teaspoon sherry
G. ½ teaspoon sesame oil
H. salt, pepper to taste
I. 1 tablespoon chopped scallion

PREPARATION:

I. Cut D into bite-size pieces, and mix with E, F, G, H.
II. Wash B, soak in warm water 15 minutes. Drain, saving water; cut each into 3 or 4 pieces. Add to D mixture.

III. Wash C several times with cold water; drain.
IV. Add B water and enough additional water to A to make 2¼ cups liquid.

COOKING:

1. In 3-qt. pot, bring A mixture to boil. Add C, let liquid boil down until very little remains.
2. Spread D–H mixture over A, cover tightly, reduce heat to very low, simmer 15 to 20 minutes.
3. Add I, mix well, and serve hot. Add light soy sauce if desired.

CHICKEN MUSHROOM RICE WITH OYSTER SAUCE
Ho Yo Gai Fan: Canton

Add 1 tablespoon oyster sauce to D–H mixture in Step I.

DICED CHICKEN WITH PEPPER
Kung Bao Gee Ding: Szechuan

A. 6 tablespoons peanut oil
B. 2 chicken breasts
C. 1 egg white
D. 2 teaspoons cornstarch
E. 1 teaspoon salt
F. 1 green pepper
G. 2 sweet red peppers
H. ½ cup diced bamboo shoots
I. ½ teaspoon sugar
J. 2 teaspoons white wine
K. 1 tablespoon light soy sauce

PREPARATION:

I. Bone, dice B, mix with C, D and ½ teaspoon E.
II. Wash F, G, discard seeds; dice same size as B.
III. Mix remaining E with I, J, K.

COOKING:

1. Heat A, add B–E mixture, stir-fry 1 to 2 minutes. Remove to dish, pour any excess oil back into pan.
2. Add F, G, H, stir-fry 30 seconds. Return B–E mixture to pan, stir several more seconds.
3. Add remaining E and I–K mixture, mix well.

CHICKEN CUBES WITH GREEN PEPPERS
Ching Jiu Gai Kew: Canton

A. 4 tablespoons peanut oil
B. 2 small chicken breasts
C. 2 teaspoons sherry
D. 1 teaspoon light soy sauce
E. 4 slices ginger, chopped
F. 2 green peppers
G. 2 tablespoons salted black beans
H. 2 teaspoons cornstarch
I. ½ teaspoon sugar
J. salt to taste

PREPARATION:

I. Bone B, cut into cubes.
II. Mix B, C, D, E.
III. Wash F, discarding seeds; cut into cubes.
IV. Mash G with fork; mix well with ½ cup water. Drain through strainer. Mix juice with H, then with mashed G.

COOKING:

1. Heat A, stir-fry B–E mixture 1 minute.
2. Add F, stir-fry 1 more minute.
3. Add G–H mixture, cook until thickened.
4. Add I, J.

DICED CHICKEN WITH PEPPER   *Approved Diabetic Recipe*
Ching Jao Gee Ding: General

A. 2 tablespoons peanut oil
B. 1 chicken breast
C. 1 egg white
D. ½ teaspoon cornstarch
E. 1 teaspoon salt

F. 1 small green pepper
G. 1 small sweet red pepper or
    1 to 2 red-hot peppers
H. ¼ cup diced bamboo shoots
I. 1 teaspoon light soy sauce

PREPARATION:

I. Bone and dice B, mix with C, D and ¼ teaspoon E.

II. Wash F, G; discard seeds and stems; dice.
III. Mix rest of E with I.

COOKING:

1. Heat A, add B–E mixture, stir-fry 1 to 2 minutes.
2. Remove to dish, pour excess oil back into pan.

3. Add F, G, H, stir-fry ½ minute, add B to F–H mixture. Continue stirring for ½ to 1 minute more. Add E and I mixture, mix well.

RED-COOKED CHICKEN WITH MUSHROOMS
Dung Gu Gee Chiu: General

A. 4 tablespoons peanut oil
B. 2 chicken breasts
C. 1 scallion
D. 4 slices ginger
E. 12 Chinese mushrooms
    (or 1 cup bite-size bamboo shoots)

F. 2 teaspoons light soy sauce
G. 1 tablespoon sherry
H. ½ cup chicken broth
I. 1 teaspoon sugar
J. 2 teaspoons cornstarch

PREPARATION:

I. Bone B, cut into 1-inch cubes.
II. Wash E, soak 15 minutes in warm water. Drain, cut each into 3 or 4 pieces.

III. Cut C into 1-inch pieces.
IV. Cut D into long, thin pieces.
V. Mix F, G, H, I.

COOKING:

1. Heat A. Add B, C, D; stir-fry a few seconds.
2. Add E, mix well.

3. Add F–I mixture, stir well, bring to boil. Lower heat, simmer 7 to 10 minutes.
4. Thicken with J mixed with a little water.

STEAMED CHICKEN WITH CAULIFLOWER
Hwa Tsai Tsen Gee: Shanghai

A. 1 to 1½ lbs. chicken meat
B. 1 tablespoon light soy sauce
C. 3 teaspoons sherry
D. 1 tablespoon chopped scallion
E. 1 teaspoon chopped ginger

F. 1 teaspoon salt
G. 1 teaspoon sugar
H. ¼ cup rice flour
I. 1 to 1½ cups cauliflower flowerets
J. ½ teaspoon salt

PREPARATION:

I. Cut A into bite-size pieces, mix with B, C, D, E, F, G and let stand 30 minutes to 1 hour.
II. Mix with H.

III. Mix I, J and arrange in dish.
IV. Arrange A–G mixture on top of I–J.

COOKING:

1. Steam A–J in steamer over boiling water for 25 minutes (or until A is tender).

CHICKEN AND MUSHROOM CASSEROLE
Dung Gu Mun Gee: Peking

A. 4 chicken legs
B. ¼ teaspoon pepper
C. 1 teaspoon salt
D. 4 tablespoons peanut oil
E. 1 large onion, sliced

F. ½ lb. fresh mushrooms
G. 1 tablespoon sherry
H. 2 tablespoons light soy sauce
I. ½ teaspoon sugar

PREPARATION:

I. Cut each A in 2 pieces, wash well, dry with paper towel.
II. Mix thoroughly with B, C, and ½ D.

III. Line baking pan with aluminum foil, arrange single layer of A.
IV. Cut each F in half.
V. Mix G, H, I.

COOKING:

1. Preheat oven at 375°. Bake A–D mixture 25 minutes each side.
2. Heat remainder of D in frying pan, stir-fry E 1 minute, add F, stir-fry 1 more minute. Add G–I.
3. Put A–D in casserole dish, add E–I over A and bake 10 more minutes.

GOLDEN NEEDLES CHICKEN
Jing Tsen Gee: General

A. 1 tablespoon peanut oil
B. ½ cup golden needles
C. ½ cup cloud ears
D. 7 Chinese mushrooms
E. 2 scallions
F. 4 thin slices ginger, shredded

G. 2 tablespoons light soy sauce
H. 1 tablespoon sherry
I. 2- to 3-lb. frying chicken
J. ½ cup peanut oil
K. 1 teaspoon salt
L. 2 teaspoons cornstarch

PREPARATION:

I. Soak B in hot water 30 minutes. Cut off tips and cut each into 2 pieces.
II. Soak C in warm water; when soft, wash in cold water.

III. Wash D and soak in 1¼ cups hot water 30 minutes (save water); cut each D into 4 pieces.
IV. Slice E into 1-inch strips.

COOKING:

1. Heat A, stir in B, C, D. Add E, F, G, H. Stir well a few seconds. Put in Dutch oven.
2. Brown I in J. Remove and put on top of B–H mixture. Add K and 1 cup mushroom water (save some for Step 4). Cover tightly and simmer 30 minutes.
3. Before serving, cut cooked I into small pieces. Arrange on plate, surrounded by rest of mixture.
4. Use a little mushroom water and L to make gravy in pot. Pour over I. Serve with rice.

CLOUD EAR CHICKEN   *Approved Ulcer Recipe*
Rwing Er Gee: General

Omit E, F, H; halve J; and use 2 lbs. chicken breasts for I; use D whole and remove before serving.

CHICKEN WITH SIMPLE SAVORY NOODLES
Gee Si La Hu Jiang Mein: Shanghai

A. 2 tablespoons peanut oil

B. 1 scallion, chopped

C. 1 cup shredded chicken (or pork or beef)

D. 1 tablespoon light soy sauce

E. ½ cup water

F. 14-oz. can braised mixed vegetables in chili sauce

G. ½ lb. noodles or spaghetti, cooked

COOKING:

1. Heat A, add B, stir-fry a few seconds.
2. Add C, stir-fry 2 minutes.
3. Add D, E, F, mix well.
4. Add G, stir until thoroughly mixed. Cover, cook 5 to 10 minutes over low heat, stirring occasionally.

CHICKEN CUBES WITH CHERRY, PINEAPPLE AND LITCHI
Bo Lo Lychee Gai Kew: Adapted

A. 2 cups peanut oil

B. 1 chicken breast

C. 2 tablespoons sugar

D. 3 tablespoons catsup

E. 3 tablespoons vinegar

F. 1 tablespoon cornstarch

G. 1 cup litchi juice

H. 1 cup litchi meat

I. ½ cup maraschino cherries

J. ½ cup pineapple chunks

K. 1 teaspoon sherry

L. 2 teaspoons light soy sauce

M. ½ teaspoon anise pepper

N. 1 tablespoon chopped scallion

O. 1 egg white

P. 2 tablespoons cornstarch

PREPARATION:

I. Bone B and cut into cubes, mix with K, L, M, N, marinate ½ hour.

II. Beat O, P thoroughly, pour over B mixture.

COOKING:

1. Heat A to 325°, deep-fry B 2 minutes, drain on paper towels.
2. Mix C, D, E, F, G in a saucepan, stir until thickened.
3. Add H, I, J and B mixture, mix well and serve.

CHICKEN IN PLUM SAUCE I
Sue Mei Jiang Gai: Shanghai

A. 3 tablespoons peanut oil

B. 1 tablespoon chopped scallion

C. 1 teaspoon chopped ginger

D. 2 chicken legs or 1 chicken breast

E. 1½ tablespoons plum sauce

F. 2 teaspoons soy sauce

G. 1 cup sliced carrot

H. 1 cup sliced celery

I. ½ to 1 teaspoon salt

PREPARATION:

I. Bone and cut into bite-size pieces.

COOKING:

1. Heat A, add B, C, stir-fry 1 to 2 minutes, add D pieces and brown on all sides.
2. Add E, F, mix well, simmer 15 minutes.
3. Add G, H, I, turn heat higher, stir well, then lower heat and simmer for another 5 to 10 minutes (until chicken pieces are tender).

CHICKEN IN PLUM SAUCE II
Mwei Jiong Gai: Canton

A. ¼ cup vegetable oil
B. 1 clove garlic
C. 2½- to 3-lb. frying chicken
D. ⅓ cup plum sauce
E. 5 celery stalks, diced
F. 4 slices ginger
G. 3 tablespoons sherry
H. 4 carrots

I. 2 teaspoons sugar
J. 1 teaspoon salt
K. ⅓ cup spoon-size Chinese pickles (or equivalent)
L. ¼ cup water
M. 2 teaspoons cornstarch mixed with ¼ cup water

PREPARATION:

I. Cut C into bite-size pieces.
II. Peel H, cut into cubes.
III. Crush B with flat side of cleaver; remove skin.

COOKING:

1. Place A, B in skillet. Using high heat, brown C. Stir 5 minutes, cover, reduce heat, and simmer 10 minutes.
2. Add D, E, F, G, H, I, J, K, L. Simmer, covered, 12 minutes.
3. Add M to thicken gravy.

PINEAPPLE CHICKEN
Bo Lo Gai: Canton

A. 4 tablespoons vegetable oil
B. 2 lbs. chicken (or duck)
C. 5 slices ginger
D. 1 cup pineapple chunks and 1 cup juice
E. 2 stalks celery
F. 2 carrots

G. 1 medium green pepper
H. 1 tablespoon sherry
I. salt to taste
J. 1 tablespoon cornstarch, mixed with ½ cup water
K. ½ tablespoon sugar

PREPARATION:

I. Cut B into bite-size pieces.
II. Slice E diagonally into ½-inch pieces.
III. Skin F, then slice into ½-inch pieces.
IV. Split G endwise. Remove core and seeds. Slice into pieces.
V. Mix J and K.

COOKING:

1. Heat A in skillet.
2. Add B, C and stir-fry 2 minutes.
3. Add D juice and ½ cup water, bring to boil and simmer 10 minutes.
4. Add E, F, cook 5 minutes.
5. Add G, H, I. Mix well 1 minute.
6. Thicken with J–K.

PINEAPPLE CHICKEN DELIGHT I
Bo Lo Gee: Shanghai

A. 4 tablespoons peanut oil
B. 2 chicken breasts (1 to 1½ lbs.)
C. 1 teaspoon chopped ginger
D. 1 small egg white
E. ½ teaspoon salt
F. 2 teaspoons cornstarch
G. 1 clove garlic, chopped
H. 1 green pepper
I. 2 carrots

J. 1 cup pineapple chunks
K. 2 teaspoons sherry
L. 2 teaspoons light soy sauce
M. 3 teaspoons vinegar
N. 1 teaspoon sugar
O. ½ cup pineapple juice
P. 1 tablespoon cornstarch
Q. 1 to 1½ teaspoons salt

PREPARATION:

I. Bone B and cut into 1-inch cubes. Mix with C, D, E, F and 1 teaspoon A.
II. Wash H, discard stem and seeds, cut into 1-inch cubes.
III. Peel I, cut into ¼-inch thick slices, parboil 3 minutes.
IV. Drain J and save ½ cup juice.
V. Mix K, L, M, N, O, P, Q.

COOKING:

1. Heat 3 tablespoons A, add B–F mixture, stir-fry 2 minutes, remove to a dish.
2. Heat 1 tablespoon A, stir-fry G for a few times, add H, I, stir-fry ½ minute.
3. Add B–F mixture and J, stir well for a minute.
4. Add K–Q mixture, continue stirring until it is thickened; serve with rice.

PINEAPPLE CHICKEN DELIGHT II
Bo Lo Gai: Canton

A. 3 tablespoons peanut oil
B. 1 chicken breast
C. ½ egg white
D. 1 teaspoon chopped ginger
E. 2 teaspoons cornstarch
F. ½ teaspoon salt
G. 1 teaspoon peanut oil
H. 1 or 2 cloves garlic
I. 6 Chinese mushrooms
J. 8 water chestnuts, sliced

K. ½ cup sliced bamboo shoots
L. 15 snow peas
M. 2 canned pineapple rings
N. ⅓ cup pineapple juice
O. 1 teaspoon sugar
P. 2 teaspoons sherry
Q. 2 teaspoons soy sauce
R. 1 tablespoon vinegar
S. 1 tablespoon cornstarch
T. 1 teaspoon salt

PREPARATION:

I. Bone B and cut into 1-inch cubes, mix with C, D, E, F, G.
II. Pound H with side of cleaver, discard skin, chop.
III. Drain M, save juice, cut each ring into 10 pieces.
IV. Soak I in warm water 15 minutes, drain, discard stems; quarter each.
V. Discard tips of L; wash.
VI. Combine N, O, P, Q, R, S, T.

COOKING:

1. Heat 2 tablespoons A, add B–G mixture, stir-fry 2 minutes, remove to a dish.
2. Heat rest of A, add H, stir-fry a few times; add I, J, K, L, stir-fry 1 to 2 minutes, add 1 or 2 tablespoons water if necessary.
3. Add A–L mixture and M, mix well.
4. Add N–T mixture, continue stirring until it is thickened. Serve with rice.

ROASTED CHICKEN WITH TANGERINE PEEL
Chen Pei Shiu Gai: Canton

A. 4-lb. frying chicken
B. 2 to 3 pieces dried tangerine (or fresh orange) peel
C. 1 tablespoon yellow bean sauce
D. 3 slices ginger
E. 1 clove garlic
F. 2 tablespoons light soy sauce
G. 1 teaspoon sugar
H. 2 tablespoons whiskey
I. 1 teaspoon salt
J. 3 tablespoons peanut oil

PREPARATION:

I. Wash A well.
II. Wash B, soak in warm water until soft (about 30 minutes). Rinse, chop fine.
III. Mash C into a paste.
IV. Chop D, E very fine.
V. Mix B, C, D, E, F, G, H, I, J with a fork.
VI. Rub A thoroughly with B–J mixture, inside and out.

COOKING:

1. Place A with B–J mixture in large pot; braise each side 1 minute, or until very little sauce remains.
2. Line roasting pan with aluminum foil. Place A on top, roast 5 minutes each side in 450° oven.
3. Reduce heat to 325°, roast each side 30 more minutes.

WATERMELON CHICKEN
Shi Gwa Tsen Gee: Shanghai

A. 6 large Chinese mushrooms
B. 2-lb. fryer
C. 1½ teaspoons salt
D. ¼ cup diced ham
E. 1 cup diced bamboo shoots
F. 1 egg
G. 1 tablespoon cornstarch
H. 1½ teaspoons sherry
I. 3 slices ginger
J. dash pepper
K. 1 medium watermelon
L. salt to taste

PREPARATION:

I. Soak A in hot water 20 minutes. Discard stems and dice.
II. Rub C on B. Place B in bowl, steam for 35 minutes. Remove and bone, cut into 1½-inch cubes; save soup.
III. Mix A with D, E, F, G, H, I, J until smooth; combine with B.
IV. Cut 8 inches off K. With large, sharp spoon hollow out K, leaving 2-inch-thick shell. Cut thin slice off bottom to make flat surface, place in bowl, open end up.

COOKING:

1. Place bowl on rack inside tall steamer.
2. Put A–J into K, cover with foil, steam until melon is soft.
3. Add L to taste and serve.

WATERMELON CHICKEN
Shi Gwa Tsen Gee: Shanghai

Substitute 1 cup French-cut asparagus for E and add in Step II after steaming B for 35 minutes; then continue steaming for 5 more minutes. Continue with preparation as above. Optional: Substitute ½ cup small, fresh shrimp for D.

ROCK SUGAR CHICKEN
Bing Tong Gee: Shanghai

A. 4 tablespoons peanut oil
B. 2 chicken legs
C. 2 chicken wings
D. 1½ tablespoons light soy sauce
E. 1 tablespoon sherry
F. 5 Chinese black mushrooms

G. ½ cup diced bamboo shoots
H. 2 teaspoons salt
I. 2 teaspoons rock sugar
J. 2 scallions
K. 2 teaspoons cornstarch mixed with ¼ cup water

PREPARATION:

I. Cut each B into 4 small pieces, and each C into 2.
II. Mix D, E. Add to B, C. Marinate 5 minutes.

III. Wash F, soak in warm water 15 minutes. Drain. Save mushroom water. Then cut each F into 4 pieces.
IV. Cut each J into inch-long pieces.

COOKING:

1. Heat A, add B–E mixture, brown each side 2 minutes.
2. Add F, G, stir-fry 1 minute.
3. Add ½ cup mushroom water from Step III, H, I; cover, and cook 20 minutes.
4. Add J, mix well, cook another 10 minutes.
5. Thicken with K, serve hot.

DICED WALNUT CHICKEN DING
Heh Tao Gee Ding: General

A. 4 tablespoons peanut oil
B. 2 chicken breasts
C. 1 egg white
D. 1 teaspoon cornstarch

E. 1 teaspoon sherry
F. ½ teaspoon salt
G. 1 cup walnuts

PREPARATION:

I. Bone B and dice.
II. Mix B, C, D.

III. Fry G in deep oil. When light brown, take out and drain on paper towel.

COOKING:

1. Heat A until hot.   2. Add B–D. Stir 2 to 3 minutes.   3. Add E, F, G. Mix well and serve hot.

STIR-FRIED CHICKEN WITH WALNUTS
Heh Tao Bao Gee Ding: Peking

A. 2 cups peanut oil for deep frying
B. 1 cup walnuts (or cashew nuts)
C. 2 chicken breasts
D. 1 egg white
E. ½ teaspoon salt

F. 2 teaspoons light soy sauce
G. 2 teaspoons sherry
H. ½ teaspoon sugar
I. ½ teaspoon sesame oil
J. 2 teaspoons cornstarch

PREPARATION:

I. Bone C and dice.

II. Beat D and mix with C, E, F, G, H, I, J; mix with C.

III. Pour boiling water over B, let stand for 1 to 2 minutes or until skin comes off easily. Peel off skin. Spread walnuts on paper towel and dry completely before frying.

COOKING:

1. Heat A to 325°. Deep fry B until golden brown, about ½ to 1 minute. (Do not overfry or burn). Remove and drain on paper towel.

2. Heat 3 tablespoons A, add C–J mixture, stir-fry 1 to 2 minutes.

3. Add B, mix well, and serve hot.

DICED CHICKEN WITH PEANUTS
Kung Bao Gee Ding: Szechuan

A. 4 tablespoons peanut oil
B. 1 chicken breast
C. 1 egg white
D. 2 teaspoons cornstarch
E. 1 tablespoon chopped scallion
F. ½ cup skinless, roasted peanuts (canned are suitable)
G. ½ cup diced bamboo shoots
H. 1 sweet red pepper
I. ½ teaspoon sugar
J. 2 teaspoons sherry
K. 1 tablespoon light soy sauce
L. ½ teaspoon salt

PREPARATION:

I. Bone, dice B. Mix with C, D.

II. Dice H.

III. Mix I, J, K.

COOKING:

1. Heat A. Add B–D mixture, stir-fry 1 to 2 minutes. Remove to dish, pour excess oil back to pan.

2. Add E, F, G, H, stir-fry 1 minute.

3. Return B–D mixture to pan, mix well.

4. Add I–K, stir-fry a few seconds. Add L. If canned F is used, salt to taste.

CHICKEN BREASTS WITH PEANUTS
Hwa Sun Gee Ding: Adapted

A. ¼ cup peanut oil
B. ½ cup blanched peanuts (or cashew nuts)
C. ½ to 1 teaspoon hot chili pepper flakes (to taste)
D. 2 chicken breasts
E. 1 scallion
F. 1 small clove garlic
G. ½ teaspoon salt
H. 4 teaspoons light soy sauce
I. 2 teaspoons cornstarch
J. few drops vinegar
K. 1 teaspoon sherry
L. 2 slices ginger, minced
M. ⅛ teaspoon sesame oil

PREPARATION:

I. Bone D, discard skin. Dice.

II. Split E lengthwise; cut into 1-inch sections.

III. Cut F into slivers.

IV. Mix D, E, F, G, 1 teaspoon H, and 1 teaspoons I.

V. In small bowl, mix remaining H, I with J, K, L, M. Stir until smooth.

COOKING:

1. Heat A, add B, stir-fry until golden brown.

2. Add C, then D–G mixture. Stir-fry 1 minute.

3. Add H–M mixture, stir-fry just until sauce thickens and coats D.

RED AND WHITE CHICKEN WITH ALMONDS
Hoisin Tou Yen Gai: Canton

A. 3 tablespoons vegetable oil
B. ½ cup blanched almonds (2 to 3 oz.)
C. 1 chicken breast
D. 1 egg white
E. 2 teaspoons cornstarch
F. ½ teaspoon salt

G. 2 tablespoons hoisin sauce
H. 2 teaspoons light soy sauce
I. 2 teaspoons sherry
J. 2 scallions
K. dash pepper

PREPARATION:

I. Bone C, discard skin, cut into ½-inch cubes.
II. Mix C with D, E, F.

III. Mix G with H, I, J, K to make sauce.

COOKING:

1. Heat A until smoking, lower heat, add B, stir-fry ½ minute until edges turn golden. Do not brown or overcook. Remove B from A and drain on paper towel.
2. While pan is still hot, add C–F, stir-fry over high heat, turn to medium heat; cook 2 minutes.
3. Add G–K sauce and cook for 2 to 3 minutes. Lower heat if sauce starts to dry up.
4. Transfer to serving dish, cover with B and serve.

CHICKEN BREAST WITH CASHEW NUTS I
Yah Goh Gee Ding: Shanghai

A. 3 tablespoons peanut oil
B. 2 scallions
C. 2 boned chicken breasts
D. 1 tablespoon hoisin sauce
E. 2 tablespoons light soy sauce
F. 2 teaspoons sherry

G. 2 teaspoons cornstarch
H. ⅛ teaspoon pepper
I. 1 cup cashew nuts (or blanched peanuts or walnuts)
J. salt to taste

PREPARATION:

I. Slice C into pieces ½ inch thick.
II. Mix C with D, E, F, G, H thoroughly.

III. Using only white part of B, cut into ¼-inch pieces.

COOKING:

1. Heat A, stir-fry B until slightly brown.
2. Add C–H mixture, stir-fry constantly over medium heat until C changes color (about 2 minutes).
3. Add I, mix well.
4. Add J. Serve hot.

CHICKEN BREAST WITH CASHEW NUTS II
Yao Goh Gee Ding: Peking

A. 3 tablespoons peanut oil
B. 2 chicken breasts
C. 1 egg white
D. ½ teaspoon salt
E. 2 teaspoons light soy sauce

F. 2 teaspoons sherry
G. ½ teaspoon sugar
H. ½ teaspoon sesame oil
I. 2 teaspoons cornstarch
J. 1 cup salted cashew nuts

PREPARATION:

I. Bone B and dice.

COOKING:

1. Heat A, add B–I, stir-fry 1 to 2 minutes.

II. Beat C and mix with B, D, E, F, G, H, I.

2. Add J, mix well, and serve hot.

LITCHI SNOWBALL CHICKEN
La-ee-tzee Gai Kew: Canton

A. 2 cups peanut oil
B. 1 chicken breast
C. 2 tablespoons sugar
D. 2 tablespoons catsup
E. 2 tablespoons vinegar
F. 2 teaspoons cornstarch
G. ¾ cup litchi juice

H. 20-oz. can whole litchis
I. 1 teaspoon sherry
J. 2 teaspoons light soy sauce
K. ½ teaspoon anise pepper
L. 1 tablespoon chopped scallion
M. 1 egg white
N. 2 tablespoons cornstarch

PREPARATION:

I. Bone B, cut into cubes.
II. Mix I, J, K, L. Marinate B in mixture 30 minutes.

III. Beat M and add N; coat B with this.
IV. Drain H, reserving juice for G.

COOKING:

1. Heat A to 325°. Deep fry B 2 minutes, stirring to prevent sticking together. Drain on paper towels.

2. Mix C, D, E, F, G in a saucepan, bring to boil, stir until sauce is thickened.
3. Add B and H, mix well, and serve.

STEWED CHICKEN WITH CHESTNUTS
Hung Sao Li-Tze Gee: Shanghai

A. 4 tablespoons peanut oil
B. 1 scallion
C. 3 slices ginger
D. 2-lb. fryer
E. 3 tablespoons light soy sauce

F. 1 teaspoon salt
G. 2 teaspoons sugar
H. 2 tablespoons sherry
I. ½ cup water
J. 1 lb. chestnuts

PREPARATION:

I. Wash D thoroughly. Cut into bite-size pieces (do not bone).
II. Make slits on J, cover with water and boil 3

minutes, shell and skin.
III. Cut B into 1½-inch pieces.
IV. Mix together E, F, G, H.

COOKING:

1. Heat A; stir-fry B, C a few times.
2. Add D, stir-fry 3 minutes. Add E–H mixture and mix well.

3. Add I. Bring to boil, simmer 15 minutes.
4. Add J, bring to boil again, simmer 15 minutes more. Serve hot.

STEWED DUCK WITH CHESTNUTS
Gan Li Yah: Shanghai

Substitute 3-lb. duckling for D. Increase C–J by ½ and increase Step 3 cooking time to 35 minutes. Skim off excess fat just prior to serving.

DUCK

Duck is a Chinese favorite and some of the duck recipes are famous throughout the world. For various Chinese festivals and holidays, numerous special duck dishes are prepared, all likely to be different depending on the season. Salted duck is usually eaten in winter, since it is less likely to spoil. Salted dried ducks are available during the Chinese New Year and are used as a flavoring agent, with relatively small pieces added to a pot of boiling rice or soup.

Duck gizzards are used much like chicken gizzards. They are salted, dried, cooked, sliced, and served with congee at breakfast. Duck feet are a great delicacy, also duck tongue, kidney, and liver. Dried duck feet are believed to be the best portion for flavoring; they are an important ingredient in many soup stocks.

The reddish-brown, glistening ducks hanging in Chinese food shops have been roasted whole and may be purchased whole and eaten with or without reheating.

Roast duck may be served with its own sauce, with litchis and other fruit, or with a sweet and sour sauce.

Peking duck has an aroma and flavor unsurpassed by any other method of preparation. It is a favorite in this country as well as abroad. Peking duck is usually eaten with doilies (a thin pancake), which can be made the day before and reheated in a double boiler at the time of serving. These doilies can be frozen thereafter, kept for several weeks, and steamed again without thawing when ready to be used.

CHARCOAL ROAST DUCK
Kao Ya: Shanghai

A. 1 can pickled red-in-snow
B. 4-lb. duck
C. dash black pepper
D. 2 teaspoons sugar

E. 2 tablespoons light soy sauce
F. ½ teaspoon cornstarch
G. hoisin sauce for dipping
H. 1 bunch scallions

PREPARATION:

I. Wash B well, remove fat from cavity, dry with paper towels.
II. Stuff B with A, and sew up openings.
III. Mix C, D, E, F and paint on B.

IV. Slice each H vertically 3 inches down from bulb end; make another 3-inch vertical cut perpendicular to the first cut. Soak H in ice-cold water 10 to 15 minutes. They should spread out like brushes.

COOKING:

1. Attach duck firmly on automatic spit and roast about 2 hours or until B becomes chop-stick tender; baste occasionally. Serve with G, H.

PEKING CRISPY DUCK
Go Sao Ya Tze: Peking

A. 3-lb. duck
B. 1½ tablespoons salt
C. 2 tablespoons sherry
D. 1 tablespoon chopped scallion
E. 1 teaspoon chopped ginger
F. ¼ cup flour

G. 2 small eggs
H. 2 teaspoons light soy sauce
I. 1 tablespoon cornstarch mixed with ¼ cup water
J. 2 cups peanut oil

PREPARATION:

I. Wash A thoroughly.

II. Mix B, C, D, E.

COOKING:

1. Place A in dish, steam over boiling water 1 to 2 hours or until tender.

2. Bone A or simply dry between paper towels. Coat lightly with F.

3. Rub A with G–I.

III. Rub A inside and out with B–E.

IV. Beat G, mix with H, I.

4. Deep fry A in J at 350° until golden brown (about 3 minutes each side).

5. Cut into strips, arrange on plate in a row or cut into bite-size pieces and serve.

PEKING ROAST DUCK
Jia Ting Peking Ya: Peking

A. 4- to 6-lb. duck

B. 2 tablespoons molasses

C. 1 to 2 bunches scallions (white part only)

D. hoisin sauce

PREPARATION:

I. Mix B with 1 tablespoon water.

II. Wash A well, remove fat from cavity, dip in boiling water 5 minutes.

III. Hang A in airy spot half a day. Rub with B mixture, hang again overnight.

IV. Slit the bulbs of C 2 inches down the stems, make a second 2-inch cut at right angles to the first cut, cover with ice-cold water until serving time.

COOKING:

1. Preheat oven to 350°. Line a baking sheet with aluminum foil, place a rack over foil.

2. Place A on rack, roast 1½ hours.

3. Raise oven temperature to 425°, roast A 15 to 20 more minutes.

4. To serve, slice off A skin, cut into pieces 1½ inches by 3 inches. Slice meat into bite-size pieces; arrange in center of platter, surrounded with skin. Serve with C, D, and sliced Chinese steamed bread or thinly sliced American bread.

ROASTED DUCK WITH ORANGE PEEL
Chan Pei Shiu Op: Canton

A. 3- to 4-lb. duck

B. 2 to 3 pieces dried orange peel

C. 1 tablespoon yellow bean sauce

D. 5 slices ginger

E. 1 clove garlic

F. 2 tablespoons light soy sauce

G. 1 teaspoon sugar

H. 2 tablespoons whiskey

I. 1 teaspoon salt

PREPARATION:

I. Wash A well, remove fat from cavity, dry with paper towels.

II. Wash B, soak in warm water until soft (about 30 minutes). Rinse, chop fine.

III. Mash C into a paste.

IV. Chop D, E very fine.

V. Mix B, C, D, E, F, G, H, I with a fork.

VI. Rub A thoroughly with B–I mixture, inside and out.

COOKING:

1. Place A in large pot; braise each side 2 minutes, or until very little sauce remains.

2. Line roasting pan with foil. Place A on top,

roast 20 minutes each side in 450° oven.

3. Reduce heat to 325°, roast each side 30 more minutes. Serve.

CRISPY DUCK I
Tswei Pi Ya: Shanghai

A. 3-lb. duck
B. 3 slices ginger
C. 1 scallion
D. 1 clove garlic, peeled
E. 2 teaspoons anise pepper

F. 4 tablespoons light soy sauce
G. 1 teaspoon salt
H. 1 tablespoon sherry
I. peanut oil for deep frying

PREPARATION:

I. Wash A well, remove fat from cavity, dry with paper towels.
II. Chop B, C, D very fine.
III. Break up E with back of cleaver or with mortar and pestle.
IV. Mix E, F, G, H with B–D.
V. Rub A inside and out with B–H mixture. Let stand 1 to 2 hours.

COOKING:

1. Place A–H in dish. Steam over boiling water 1½ to 2 hours or until tender. Cool.
2. Remove all ingredients from A; dry A with paper towel.
3. Deep fry A in I until golden brown (about 3 minutes each side).
4. Cut into bite-size pieces. Serve.

CRISPY DUCK II
Siang Sue Yah: Szechuan

A. 3- to 4-lb. duck
B. 2 teaspoons anise pepper
C. ¼ teaspoon nutmeg
D. ¼ teaspoon cinnamon
E. ½ teaspoon ground cloves
F. 2 tablespoons salt
G. 2 tablespoons sherry

H. 1 tablespoon chopped scallion
I. 4 slices ginger, chopped
J. 1 egg white
K. 2 teaspoons cornstarch
L. 1 teaspoon flour
M. 2 cups peanut oil

PREPARATION:

I. Wash A thoroughly, remove fat from cavity, dry with paper towels.
II. Mix B, C, D, E, F, G, H, I.
III. Rub A inside and out with B–I mixture; marinate 1 to 2 hours.
IV. Mix J, K, L thoroughly.

COOKING:

1. Place A in dish; steam over boiling water 1½ to 2 hours, or until done.
2. Be sure all of B–I mixture has been removed from A; dry A with paper towel.
3. Rub outside of A all over with J–L mixture.
4. Deep fry A in M at 350° until golden brown (about 3 minutes each side).
5. Cut A into bite-size pieces. Serve with anise pepper salt (see Index) or catsup.

BRAISED DUCK
Sao Yah: Peking

A. 4- to 5-lb. duck
B. ¼ cup light soy sauce
C. ¼ cup brown sugar

D. 1 teaspoon sesame oil
E. 3 slices ginger, chopped
F. 1 tablespoon salt

G. 2 tablespoons sherry
H. 3 scallions

PREPARATION:

I. Wash A, remove all fat from cavity, dry with paper towels.

II. Mix E with F, G. Rub A with some of E–G

mixture thoroughly inside and out.

III. Put H and remaining E–G mixture in cavity of A. Let stand 1½ hours.

COOKING:

1. In Dutch oven, place A in 2 qts. boiling water. Simmer each side about 25 minutes.
2. Remove A. Pour stock out and save 1 qt. Mix this stock with B, C, D in pot.

3. Bring sauce to boil; add A. Simmer 1 more hour. Continue turning and basting every 10 to 15 minutes until all the stock is worked off and A is browned evenly. Serve hot or cold.

PICKLED GINGER DUCK
Tse Jiang Ya Pien: Szechuan

A. 3 tablespoons peanut oil
B. 1 breast of roasted duck or
    2 roasted duck legs
C. 1 walnut-sized piece pickled ginger
D. 1 clove garlic, chopped
E. 2 teaspoons sherry
F. 2 teaspoons light soy sauce

G. 1 teaspoon brown bean sauce
H. 1 or 2 pickled peppers, diced
I. ¼ cup chicken broth
J. 1 scallion
K. 1 green pepper
L. 1 teaspoon sugar
M. Chinese hot sauce to taste

PREPARATION:

I. Bone B and cut into long strips.
II. Cut C into thin slices.
III. Mix D, E, F, G, H.

IV. Cut J into 1-inch-long strips.
V. Discard stem and seeds of K; wash and cut into long strips.

COOKING:

1. Heat A, stir-fry B 1 minute, add C, mix well.
2. Add D–H mixture, stir thoroughly; add I, lower heat and simmer 3 minutes or until

gravy has almost evaporated.
3. Turn heat high, add J, K, stir ½ minute, add L, M and serve.

PRESSED DUCK
Ban Yah: Nanking

A. 4- to 5-lb. duck
B. 1 teaspoon saltpeter (obtained in drugstore)

C. 6 tablespoons salt
D. 2 teaspoons anise pepper

PREPARATION:

I. Wash A thoroughly, remove fat from cavity, dry with paper towels.
II. Mix B, C, D well. Rub A with B–D mixture

inside and out thoroughly.
III. Place a rack in large pan. Place A on rack; refrigerate 3 days. Hang A in sun 1 day.

COOKING:

1. Cut A in halves or quarters. Wash away salt under cold water.
2. Place A pieces in deep plate; steam 1 hour.

Note: Hung or pressed duck can be refrigerated several weeks. Cook when needed. (When processed for commercial sale, it is flattened, or pressed.)

RED-COOKED DUCK I
Hung Sao Ya: Peking

A. 2 tablespoons peanut oil
B. 3 slices ginger
C. 1 or 2 cloves garlic
D. 3- to 4-lb. duck

E. ⅓ cup light soy sauce
F. 2 tablespoons sherry
G. 1 teaspoon sugar
H. 4 to 6 cloves

I. 1 star anise
J. 2 cups water
K. salt to taste

PREPARATION:

I. Clean and wash D, remove fat from cavity, dry between paper towels, chop, and cut into bite-size pieces.

II. Pound C lightly with side of cleaver, discard skin.

COOKING:

1. Heat A, stir-fry B, C a few times.
2. Add D, continue stirring for 3 to 5 minutes.

3. Add E, F, G, H, I, J, bring to boil, lower heat and simmer for 1½ hours or until D is tender.
4. Add K and serve.

RED-COOKED DUCK WITH POTATO
Yang Yu Hung Sao Ya: Peking

Add 3 to 4 potatoes (about 1 lb.) peeled and cut into 8 pieces each. In Step 3 add to D during last 15 minutes of cooking. Add water if necessary.

RED-COOKED DUCK II
Hung Siu Op: Adapted

A. 3- to 4-lb. duck
B. 8 Chinese black mushrooms
C. 3 slices ginger
D. 1 scallion
E. 5 tablespoons light soy sauce
F. 2 tablespoons sherry

G. 1 teaspoon sugar
H. 1 teaspoon salt
I. 1 teaspoon sesame oil
J. enough water added to mushroom water to make 1½ cups

PREPARATION:

I. Wash A well and remove fat from cavity. Place in Dutch oven.

II. Wash B, soak in warm water 15 minutes. Drain, save water. Cut each B in half.
III. Combine all ingredients.

COOKING:

1. Bring all ingredients mixture to boil, then reduce heat. Simmer 1 to 2 hours until A is tender, turning once or twice. Baste A several times. Serve hot with gravy.

RED-COOKED DUCK   *Approved Diabetic Recipe*
Hung Sao Yah: General

A. 3-lb. duck
B. 6 Chinese black mushrooms
C. 1 teaspoon chopped scallion
D. 3 tablespoons light soy sauce

E. 1 teaspoon salt
F. ¼ teaspoon sesame oil
G. water added to mushroom water to make 1½ cups

PREPARATION:

I. Wash A well and remove fat from cavity. Place in Dutch oven.

II. Wash B and soak in warm water 15 minutes.

Drain, save water. Cut each into 3 to 4 pieces.

III. Combine all ingredients.

COOKING:

1. Bring A with marinade to boil; reduce heat and simmer 1 to 2 hours until A is tender, turning once or twice. Baste A several times.

Add a little more boiling water if necessary. Serve hot with gravy.

SALT-CURED DUCK
Yen Swei Ya: Nanking

A. 3-lb. duck

B. 1 to 2 tablespoons salt

C. 1 tablespoon anise pepper

D. 3 slices ginger, shredded

E. 2 tablespoons dry sherry

PREPARATION:

I. Clean A well and remove fat from cavity.

II. Crush C with back of cleaver.

III. Heat frying pan, add B, C, stir-fry over

medium heat 3 to 5 minutes.

IV. Rub A with B, C inside and out.

V. Place A in bowl, refrigerate 1 to 2 days.

COOKING:

1. Wipe A free of excess moisture and B–C mixture. Split A open through breast.

2. Place A in bowl, sprinkle D, E over cavity, steam over boiling water in steamer 45 to 60

minutes. Turn off heat; leave A in steamer until cold. Remove. Remove D.

3. Cut A into bite-size pieces. Serve.

SALT-CURED DUCK *Approved Diabetic Recipe*
Fung Yah: Shanghai

Substitute a duckling (2 lb.) for A; omit D, E.

STEAMED WHOLE DUCK
Ching Tsen Chwan Yah: Szechuan

A. 2 teaspoons salt

B. 2 tablespoons sherry

C. ¼ teaspoon pepper

D. 3-lb. duck

E. 1 scallion, chopped

F. 4 slices ginger, chopped

G. 1 cup chicken broth

PREPARATION:

I. Mix A, B, C. Rub D inside and out with mixture.

II. Sprinkle E, F over D.

III. Let D stand 1 to 2 hours.

COOKING:

1. Place prepared D and G in bowl. Steam over boiling water 2½ hours. Serve hot.

CLEAR STEAMED WHOLE ROASTED DUCK
Ching Dun Chwan Sao Ya: Shanghai

A. 2- to 3-lb. roasted duck
B. ½ cup thinly sliced bamboo shoots
C. 1 scallion, halved
D. 3 slices ginger

E. 1 tablespoon sherry
F. enough chicken broth to cover duck
G. salt to taste
H. ½ cup thinly sliced baked Virginia ham

PREPARATION:

I. Split open A through the back; place in a bowl. Add B, C, D, E, F, G.

COOKING:

1. Steam A–G in steamer over boiling water 45 minutes or until duck meat is very tender.

2. Remove C, D; place A breast side up on platter; put H on top and serve.

SOY SAUCE DUCK
Jiang Yo Yah: Shanghai

A. 3-lb. duck
B. ½ teaspoon five spices powder
C. ½ teaspoon salt
D. 3 scallions

E. 4 slices ginger
F. ¼ cup light soy sauce
G. 2 tablespoons sherry

COOKING:

1. Place A in Dutch oven, adding enough water to half cover it. Cover pan and simmer 1 hour.
2. Drain, saving soup; let stand and remove grease from top; return A to Dutch oven. Rub B and C over A; place D, E in A cavity.
3. Add F, G, and 4 cups soup. Boil 30 minutes, or until duck is tender.

SOY SAUCE DUCK WITH GRAPES (ONE DUCK, TWO FLAVORS)
Yet Op Liang Mei (Pu To Op): Canton

A. 3-lb. duck, cooked (see Soy Sauce Duck)
B. 40 seedless grapes

C. ½ teaspoon sesame oil
D. 2 teaspoons light soy sauce

PREPARATION:

I. Split A lengthwise. Bone, shredding meat with grain. Skin B and cut each in half.

SERVING:

1. Place A on platter.

2. Mix B, C, D and neatly cover A. Serve cold.

SOY SAUCE DUCK WITH PINEAPPLE RINGS (ONE DUCK, TWO FLAVORS)
Yet Op Liang Mei (Bo Lo Op): Canton

A. 3-lb. duck, cooked (see Soy Sauce Duck)
B. 2 16-oz. cans pineapple rings
C. handful Chinese parsley, chopped

D. 4 tablespoons light soy sauce
E. ½ teaspoon sesame oil

PREPARATION:

I. Bone A and slice in thin broad slices.

II. Mix D, E to make dipping sauce.

SERVING:

1. Place A slices on platter, alternating with B. Sprinkle with C. Serve cold, with or without dipping sauce.

PINEAPPLE DUCK
Bo Lo Op: Canton

A. 4 tablespoons vegetable oil
B. 3- to 4-lb. duck
C. 2 cups pineapple chunks with juice
D. ½ tablespoon sugar
E. 2 stalks celery
F. 2 carrots

G. 1 medium green pepper
H. 1 tablespoon cornstarch mixed with ¼ cup water
I. 1 tablespoon sherry
J. 5 slices ginger, minced
K. 1 tablespoon soy sauce

PREPARATION:

I. Cut B into bite-size pieces, add I, J, K; mix thoroughly.
II. Slice E diagonally into ½-inch pieces.
III. Skin F, then slice into ½-inch pieces.
IV. Split G endwise. Remove core and seeds. Slice.

COOKING:

1. Heat A in skillet.
2. Add B and stir-fry 2 minutes.
3. Drain off most of oil and duck grease.
4. Add C juice and ½ cup water, bring to boil and simmer 30 minutes.
5. Add D, E, F, cook for 5 minutes.
6. Add G, C and salt to taste. Mix well for a minute.
7. Thicken with H.

SOY SAUCE AND CINNAMON DUCK
Jiang Yah: Shanghai

A. 1 stick cinnamon (½ to 1 inch long)
B. 1 star anise
C. 1 scallion
D. 1 slice ginger (nickel-sized) pounded with side of cleaver
E. 3-lb. duckling (or roasting chicken)

F. 2 tablespoons sherry
G. 5 tablespoons light soy sauce
H. 1 teaspoon rock sugar
I. ½ teaspoon salt
J. 1 to 1½ teaspoons sesame oil
K. 1 teaspoon salt

PREPARATION:

I. Wash E well, remove fat from cavity, and rub inside with K.
II. Place A, B, C, D in a piece of clean cheese- cloth, gather corners and tie with a piece of string.
III. Combine F, G, H, I.

COOKING:

1. Place A–D in large pot, add 2 cups of water, bring to boil, simmer ½ hour (to 45 minutes for chicken) or until there are about 1½ cups liquid left; remove and discard A–D bag.
2. Place E in liquid, add F–I mixture, bring to boil, reduce heat; simmer 1 to 2 hours until E is tender, turning once or twice.
3. Remove E to a dish and rub with J.
4. Cook remaining liquid until about ¼ cup is left; pour over duck and drain, repeating this procedure several times.
5. Cut into bite-size pieces and serve.

DUCK IN BEER SAUCE
Jiu Tzow Ya: Shanghai

A. ¼ cup peanut oil
B. 3- to 4-lb. duck
C. 1 tablespoon garlic salt
D. 3 tablespoons light soy sauce
E. 1 cup beer

F. 2 teaspoons cornstarch mixed with ¼ cup water
G. ⅛ cup sugar
H. 2 to 3 tablespoons chopped scallion

PREPARATION:

I. Remove fat from cavity and wash B thoroughly, dry and quarter. Rub each quarter with C.

II. Mix F with G.

COOKING:

1. Heat A in large pot. Brown B, then remove from pot.
2. In same pot, add D, E, and bring to boil.
3. Add B, cover. Turn B over once or twice during cooking, and simmer until done (about 1½ hours). Remove B, allow to cool. When cold, cut into bite-size pieces.
4. Thicken sauce in pot with F–G.
5. Pour this gravy over cold B pieces, and serve, garnished with H.

STIR-FRIED DUCK WITH SPRING GINGER
Tse Jiang Tsao Ya Pien: Szechuan

A. ½ cup peanut oil
B. ½ duck (or whole duck breast)
C. 1 clove garlic, chopped
D. ¼ lb. spring ginger
E. 3 teaspoons light soy sauce
F. 2 teaspoons sherry
G. ½ teaspoon sugar
H. ¼ to ½ teaspoon sesame oil or to taste

I. 2 teaspoons cornstarch mixed with ¼ cup chicken broth
J. ½ teaspoon salt
K. 1 egg white
L. 2 teaspoons cornstarch
M. 1 teaspoon sugar
N. 1 teaspoon salt

PREPARATION:

I. Bone B, slice meat into very thin pieces, mix with J, K, L.

II. Peel skin of D and slice D into thin pieces; mix thoroughly with M, N; squeeze out water before using.

III. Mix E, F, G, H, I.

COOKING:

1. Heat A, add B mixture, stir-fry 1 minute; remove to dish.
2. Heat 1 tablespoon A in same pan, add C, stir-fry a few times, add D, continue stirring 1 minute.
3. Add B, stir well.
4. Add E–I, continue stirring until gravy is thickened.

DUCK WITH FERMENTED BEAN CAKE
Fu Yu Yah: Adapted

A. ⅓ cup peanut oil
B. 4 cubes fermented bean cake
C. 1 cup mushroom water
D. 4-lb. duckling

E. 12 Chinese mushrooms
F. 1 cup bite-sized pieces bamboo shoots
G. ¼ cup light soy sauce
H. 2 tablespoons sherry

PREPARATION:

I. Rinse D in cold water, remove fat from cavity, pat D dry with paper towels. Cut into quarters; spread quarters out to air until excess moisture evaporates.

II. Wash E, soak 15 minutes in warm water. Drain, saving liquid, and add enough water to make 1 cup (C). Trim off stems of E, cut each in half.

III. Mix B with 2 tablespoons C; make a smooth paste.

IV. Cut F into bite-size pieces.

COOKING:

1. Heat A in a Dutch oven. Add B, C paste, stir-fry a few seconds.

2. Add D, brown on all sides.

3. Add E, F, G, H and reserved C liquid.

4. Bring to boil; reduce heat, simmer covered 1½ hours, or until D is chopstick tender.

STEAMED DUCK WITH CHINESE CABBAGE
Sheo Tsoi Pa Op: Canton

A. 3- to 4-lb. duck
B. 2 qts. oil for deep frying
C. ½ cup light soy sauce
D. 2 tablespoons sherry
E. 1 teaspoon salt

F. 1 teaspoon sugar
G. 2 scallions
H. 4 slices ginger
I. 1 to 2 lbs. Chinese white cabbage
J. 1 tablespoon cornstarch in ¼ cup water

PREPARATION:

I. Wash A well, dry with paper towels, remove fat from cavity, and rub all over with ½ of C.

II. Wash I well; cut diagonally into 2-inch pieces. Cut G, H into 1-inch pieces.

III. Mix remainder of C with D, E, F, G, H.

COOKING:

1. Deep fry A in B until golden brown. Remove to dish.

2. Add C–H mixture to A, steam over boiling water until A is tender (about 1 to 1½ hours).

3. Pour A gravy into a pot, add I, cook until soft (about 3 to 5 minutes).

4. Thicken with J.

5. Place A on a platter, arrange I alongside it, and serve with rice.

PRESERVED CELERY CABBAGE DUCK
Dung Tsoi Yah: Fukien

A. ½ duck (about 2 lbs.)
B. 1 cup water
C. 1 slice ginger (about ½ inch wide)
D. 1 tablespoon sherry

E. ½ cup preserved Chinese celery cabbage
F. 2 tablespoons light soy sauce
G. 1 teaspoon sugar
H. 1 cup bamboo shoots

PREPARATION:

I. Wash A and cut into bite-size pieces.

II. Rinse E once in cold water.

III. Pound C with back of cleaver.

COOKING:

1. Place A in saucepan; add B, bring to boil.

2. Add C, D, lower heat, cook 30 minutes.

3. Add E, F, G, H; bring to a boil; lower heat, simmer 30 minutes or until A is tender. If necessary, add more water.

DUCK WITH PICKLED CUCUMBER
Cha Gwa Dun Op Tong: Canton

A. 3-lb. duck
B. 4 slices ginger
C. 6-oz. can tea melon

D. 2 tablespoons sherry
E. salt to taste

PREPARATION:

I. Wash A and quarter.

COOKING:

1. Place A in boiling water, cook 3 to 5 minutes.
2. Remove A to a bowl, adding just enough boiling water to cover.
3. Add B.

4. Steam A, B in steamer 1 hour.
5. Add C, steam another 30 minutes, or until A is tender.
6. Add D, E, and serve.

DUCK WITH HAIR SEAWEED
Faat Tsoi Pa Op: Canton

A. 3- to 4-lb. duck
B. 2 qts. oil for deep frying
C. ¼ cup light soy sauce
D. 2 scallions
E. 4 slices ginger
F. 1 teaspoon salt

G. ½ cup boiling water
H. 1 oz. hair seaweed
I. 2 tablespoons sherry
J. 1 teaspoon sugar
K. 1 cup chicken broth
L. 1 teaspoon cornstarch

PREPARATION:

I. Wash A well, cut open breast side. With back of cleaver, press until A is flattened. Dry with paper towels, and rub all over with ½ of C.

II. Soak H 1 hour in hot water. Wash until water runs clear; drain. Heat 2 tablespoons oil, stir-fry H 1 minute.
III. Cut D into 2-inch pieces.
IV. Mix I, J, K. Set aside.

COOKING:

1. Fry A in B 350° until golden brown (about 2 minutes). Remove to saucepan.
2. Add remainder of C and D, E, F, G, bring to boil, reduce heat and simmer 1 hour.

3. Place H under A; add I–K. Cook over low heat 1 more hour.
4. Remove A to platter, arrange H around it. Thicken gravy with L; pour over A.

SILVER SPROUTS WITH SHREDDED ROAST DUCK
Ngun Nga Op Si: Canton

A. 2 tablespoons peanut oil
B. 1-lb. Cantonese roast duck
C. 1 lb. bean sprouts
D. 2 teaspoons sherry
E. 2 teaspoons light soy sauce
F. ½ teaspoon sugar

G. 1 teaspoon salt
H. 1 teaspoon sesame oil
I. ¼ teaspoon pepper
J. 1 teaspoon cornstarch mixed with 2 tablespoons water

PREPARATION:

I. Bone B and shred as thin as C.

II. Remove tail part of C, wash and drain; drop into boiling water, stir for a second; drain and rinse under cold water.

III. Mix D, E, F, G, H, I.

COOKING:

1. Heat A, add B, stir-fry 1 to 2 minutes.
2. Add C and D–I, mix well.
3. Thicken with J.

TARO ROOT DUCK
Yu Tao Op: Canton

A. 3-lb. duck

B. 12 small taro roots

C. 1 tablespoon salt

D. 6 Chinese mushrooms

E. few slices Virginia ham

F. 3 slices ginger

G. 1 scallion

H. ⅛ cup sherry

PREPARATION:

I. Peel, wash B.

II. Wash A well, remove fat from cavity, rub inside and out with C.

III. Wash D and soak in warm water 15 minutes; drain. Cut each in half.

IV. Cut G in 1-inch to 2-inch pieces.

V. Stuff A with ⅓ of B. Do not overstuff, as B will expand. Close cavity with poultry pins.

VI. Place A in Dutch oven, breast side up. Arrange D, E, F, G over A and rest of B around A.

COOKING:

1. Pour boiling water on A, barely covering it. Bring to boil, cover and simmer 2 to 3 hours or until tender. Just before serving, add H.

ALMOND DUCK
Shing Jen Ya: Szechuan

A. 4-lb duck

B. 1 teaspoon salt

C. 5 slices ginger, chopped

D. 3 scallions, chopped

E. 2 tablespoons sherry

F. 2 tablespoons light soy sauce

G. dash anise pepper

H. dash black pepper

I. 4 oz. green peas

J. 2 oz. ham, chopped

K. 4 oz. almonds

L. 4 oz. water chestnuts, sliced

M. 4 eggs

N. 2 tablespoons cornstarch

PREPARATION AND COOKING:

I. Clean and wash A, remove fat from cavity.

II. Mix B, C, D, E, F, G, H in shallow bowl. Rub mixture on A, let stand 2 hours.

III. Place bowl in steamer and steam A for 30 minutes or until just done.

IV. Allow A to cool. Bone A. Separate skin from meat.

V. Cook I in boiling water 3 minutes.

VI. Mix J, K, L, M, N. Make sandwich of J–N mixture between meat (bottom layer) and skin (top layer).

VII. Place duck sandwiches in pan and cook in preheated 350° oven 30 minutes.

STEWED DUCK WITH CHESTNUTS
Li Tze Dun Ya: Shanghai

A. 4 tablespoons peanut oil
B. 1 scallion
C. 5 slices ginger
D. 3-lb. duck
E. 4 tablespoons light soy sauce

F. 1½ teaspoons salt
G. 3 teaspoons sugar
H. 3 tablespoons sherry
I. ¾ cup water
J. 1 lb. chestnuts

PREPARATION:

I. Wash D thoroughly. Cut into bite-size pieces, with bone in.
II. Make slits in J, cover with water and boil 3 minutes, shell and skin.
III. Cut B into 1½-inch pieces.
IV. Mix E, F, G, H.

COOKING:

1. Heat A; stir-fry B, C a few seconds.
2. Add D, stir-fry 4 minutes.
3. Drain off most of A and duck grease.
4. Add E–H mixture and mix.
5. Add I. Bring to boil, simmer 35 minutes.
6. Add J, bring to boil again, simmer 15 minutes more. Serve hot.

LITCHI DUCK
La-ee-tzee Op: Canton

A. 2 tablespoons sugar
B. 2 tablespoons catsup
C. 2 tablespoons vinegar
D. ½ cup litchi juice
E. 2 teaspoons cornstarch

F. 2 teaspoons light soy sauce
G. ½ Cantonese roasted duck
H. 20-oz. can whole litchis
I. 1 to 2 stalks Chinese parsley

PREPARATION:

I. Bone G and cut into cubes.
II. Break up I.

COOKING:

1. Combine A, B, C, D, E, F in saucepan, stir until thickened.
2. Add G, H, mix well.
3. Place on a platter, garnish with I and serve.

DUCK WITH PEANUT BUTTER AND PINEAPPLE
Bo Lo Bon Shu Op: Canton

A. 1 lb. Cantonese roast duck
B. 1 cup pineapple pieces (1½ inches)
C. ¼ cup peanut butter

D. 1 tablespoon vinegar
E. 1 tablespoon sugar
F. 2 tablespoons pineapple juice

PREPARATION:

I. Bone A and slice into 1½-inch pieces.
II. Mix C, D, E, F well.
III. Mix A, B.
IV. Pour C–F over mixture, mix well and serve.

BARBECUED DUCK
Jiang Yo Sao Yah: Shanghai

A. 2 ducks, 2 to 3 lbs. each
B. ½ cup light soy sauce
C. 2 tablespoons sherry
D. ¼ teaspoon paprika
E. ¼ cup peanut oil

PREPARATION:

I. Rinse A, remove fat from cavity, and dry with paper towel.

II. Mix B, C, D, E; marinate A in mixture for 2 hours, turning a few times.

COOKING:

1. Place A on horizontal grill over red-hot coals. Cover A with 18-inch-wide aluminum foil to retain juices. If half hood is on grill, place one end of foil on top of hood (with weights) and allow foil to hang extended over edge of grill. When A browns, turn over. Cooking time: 30 to 45 minutes.

TANGERINE PEEL DUCK
Chen Pi Ya: Szechuan

A. 2 cups peanut oil
B. 3-lb. duck
C. 2 to 3 small pieces tangerine peel
D. ½ star anise
E. ½ teaspoon anise peppercorns
F. 1 scallion
G. 2 slices ginger
H. ⅓ cup light soy sauce
I. 2 tablespoons sherry
J. 1½ teaspoons brown sugar
K. ½ teaspoon sesame oil
L. 2 teaspoons cornstarch mixed with ¼ cup water
M. 1 teaspoon salt
N. 1 to 2 tablespoons honey

PREPARATION:

I. Remove fat from cavity of B. Rub cavity of B with M, and outside with N; let stand 1 to 2 hours; hang up and let drip dry, finish drying with paper towel.

II. Place C, D, E, F, G on a piece of cheesecloth, gather at the top, and tie with a piece of string.

III. Mix H, I, J, K.

COOKING:

1. Heat A to 350°, deep fry B until golden brown (about 2 to 3 minutes); drain on paper towel.
2. Put 1½ cups water in Dutch oven; bring to boil with C–G and H–K and cook 1 minute.
3. Add B, simmer 1 to 2 hours or until B is tender (adding boiling water if necessary). Turn B over a few times during simmering; when done, remove to platter.
4. Thicken gravy with L and pour over A; serve hot.

TANGERINE PEEL DUCK WITH GREENS
Fei Tswei Chen Pi Ya: Szechuan

Add ½ to 1 lb. any stir-fried green-leafed vegetable. Spread under duck before serving.

EIGHT PRECIOUS DUCK I
Ba Bao Op: Canton

A. 6 tablespoons peanut oil
B. 4 black mushrooms
C. 2 tablespoons chopped Smithfield ham
D. 1 Chinese sausage, diced
E. 6 dried shrimp
F. ¼ cup raw peanuts
G. ½ cup diced bamboo shoots
H. ½ cup glutinous rice
I. 2 slices ginger, chopped

J. 2 teaspoons light soy sauce
K. 1 teaspoon sherry
L. ½ teaspoon salt
M. 1 scallion, chopped
N. 4- to 5-lb. duck
O. 2 tablespoons light soy sauce
P. 1 tablespoon sherry
Q. 1 teaspoon sugar
R. 1 cup broth

PREPARATION:

I. Wash H, drain, cover with ⅔ cup water, bring to boil, simmer 5 minutes.

II. Wash B, soak in warm water 15 minutes, drain, dice.

III. Wash E, soak in water 10 minutes, dice.

IV. Soak F in hot water 1 hour, discard skins.

V. Chop G.

COOKING:

1. Heat 2 tablespoons A in frying pan.
2. Add B, C, D, E, F, G; stir-fry 1 minute.
3. Add H, I, J, K, L, mix well.
4. Stuff N with B–L.
5. In large pot, measure remaining 4 tablespoons A, and stir-fry M. Add N and brown a little.
6. Add O, P, Q, R, bring to boil, lower heat, and simmer 2 hours.
7. Put duck in large shallow bowl, steam in steamer ½ hour. Serve hot.

EIGHT PRECIOUS DUCK II
Tsen Ba Bao Yah: Shanghai

A. 10 dried shrimp
B. 5 dried mushrooms
C. ¼ cup fresh peanuts
D. ¼ cup barley
E. ½ cup ground pork tenderloin
F. ¼ cup ground fresh scallops
G. 1 teaspoon cornstarch

H. 2 tablespoons vegetable oil
I. ½ cup glutinous rice
J. 2 tablespoons light soy sauce
K. 2 tablespoons sherry
L. 1 teaspoon salt
M. 4-lb. duck

PREPARATION:

I. Soak A, B each in a cup of hot water for 20 minutes. Drain and save water. Cut A, B into small pieces.

II. Soak C in hot water, peel skins.

III. Boil D in water in small pot until soft and done. Drain excess water.

IV. Mix E with F. Add G and mix. Place H in hot skillet. Stir-fry E, F, G.

V. Place A, B, C, D, E, F, G, H, I, J, K, L in large bowl and mix well. Add ¼ cup extra water. Stuff into M and sew up duck.

COOKING:

1. Place M in steamer and steam for 1 to 2 hours until tender.

STIR-FRIED DUCK LIVERS
Tsao Yah Gahn: General

A. 4 tablespoons peanut oil
B. 10 duck livers
C. 1 clove garlic, chopped
D. 1 scallion, chopped
E. 3 slices ginger, chopped
F. 6 dried Chinese mushrooms
G. ½ cup shredded bamboo shoots

H. ½ teaspoon salt
I. 1 tablespoon light soy sauce
J. ½ cup chicken broth
K. 2 teaspoons cornstarch mixed with
   ⅔ cup water
L. 2 teaspoons sherry
M. dash pepper, salt

PREPARATION:

I. Cut each B into thin slices. Mix with ½ L and all of M.

II. Wash F, soak in warm water 15 minutes. Drain, saving 2 tablespoons F water. Mix F water with remainder of L.

III. Slice F into strips ¼ inch wide.

IV. Mix F, G, H, I, J.

COOKING:

1. Heat A in frying pan. Add B, stir-fry 2 to 3 minutes. Remove to dish. Pour excess oil back into frying pan.

2. Stir-fry C, D, E 30 seconds.

3. Add F–J mixture. Stir well, cook 2 minutes.

4. Place B back in frying pan, mix well with vegetable mixture. Continue stir-frying 1 minute.

5. Add K to thicken gravy. Serve hot.

CRISPY CORNISH HEN
Tswei Pi Gee: Shanghai

A. peanut oil for deep frying
B. 2-lb. Cornish hen
C. 2 scallions
D. 4 slices ginger
E. 1½ teaspoons salt
F. 1 teaspoon sherry

G. 1 teaspoon malt sugar
H. 2 tablespoons cornstarch
I. 2 tablespoons water
J. 1 pt. water
K. 6 pineapple rings
L. ¼ cup maraschino cherries

PREPARATION:

I. Stuff B with C, D. Place in 3-qt. saucepan. Add E, J. Cover and boil 20 minutes or until B is just about done. Drain, save soup.

II. Mix F, G, H, I. Paint mixture on B.

COOKING:

1. Heat A in deep fryer to 350°.
2. Deep fry B until golden brown.
3. Place B on large platter. Remove C, D. Decorate with K, L.

STEAMED MUSHROOM CORNISH HEN
Tsao Gu Tsen Gee: Peking

A. 2-lb. Cornish hen (or 2½-lb. fryer)
B. 3 oz. fresh mushrooms
C. 2 scallions, chopped
D. 3 slices ginger, chopped
E. 1 teaspoon sherry

F. 1 teaspoon sugar
G. 2 tablespoons light soy sauce
H. 1 tablespoon cornstarch
I. ½ teaspoon salt

PREPARATION:

I. Cut A into bite-size pieces and place neatly in shallow bowl for steaming.
II. Cut B into 3 pieces each.

III. Mix B, C, D, E, F, G, H, I and spread over A. Make sure it is spread evenly.

COOKING:

1. Place bowl in steamer and steam 30 to 40 minutes.

FIVE SPICES PIGEON
Wu Shiang Koh Tze: Hunan

A. 2 cups vegetable oil
B. 2 pigeons, about 1 to 1½ lbs. each
C. 1 teaspoon five spices powder

D. 2½ tablespoons light soy sauce
E. ¾ teaspoon salt

PREPARATION:

I. Clean B well, dry with paper towels.

II. Mix C, D, E and paint B with mixture, inside and out. Let stand 2 to 4 hours.

COOKING:

1. Heat A to 350° in 3-qt. saucepan, and deep fry B 15 to 20 minutes. Use toasted salt and anise pepper mixture as dip (see Index).

FIVE SPICES CORNISH HEN
Wu Shiang Ju Gee: Hunan

Substitute 2-lb. Cornish hen (or fryer) for B. Frying time: 25 to 30 minutes.

SQUAB PEKINESE
Shang Sue Bai Ko: Peking

A. 1 qt. vegetable oil for deep frying
B. 2 squab
C. 1 tablespoon light soy sauce
D. 1 clove garlic, chopped
E. 4-oz. can button mushrooms
F. ¾ cup chopped chestnut meat
G. ¼ cup raisins
H. ½ cup chopped ginkgo nuts

I. 1 medium kohlrabi
J. ¼ teaspoon powdered ginger
K. 1 tablespoon heavy soy sauce
L. 1 teaspoon sugar
M. ¼ cup sherry
N. 1 teaspoon salt
O. ½ cup soup stock combined with E water

PREPARATION:

I. Dress and clean B; rub with C and D.

II. Drain E and save water for O.

III. Peel I and shred into small thin pieces.

IV. Mix E, F, G, H, I.

V. Mix J, K, L, M, N, O.

COOKING:

1. Heat A to 325° in deep skillet; deep fry B until golden brown. Rinse under cold water.

2. Place B in casserole; spread E–I mixture over B, then pour J–O mixture over all.

3. Bake in 375° oven 30 minutes or until tender.

SPICED SQUAB
Ru Koh: Peking

A. 3 squab
B. 1 cup chicken soup
C. dash anise pepper (see Index)
D. 1 star anise
E. ¼ teaspoon cinnamon

F. 1 tablespoon sherry
G. 2 tablespoons light soy sauce
H. 1 teaspoon sugar
I. 1 teaspoon sesame oil (optional)

PREPARATION:

I. Clean and wash A; drain.

II. Place B in 3-qt. saucepan. Mix in C, D, E, F, G, H.

COOKING:

1. Place A in saucepan with B–H mixture; bring to boil; cover and simmer until soup has nearly evaporated (about 20 to 25 minutes). Add more liquid if necessary.

2. Smear I over A and serve.

SQUAB IN HOT OIL
Yow Tza Bok Gop: Canton

A. 1 qt. peanut or salad oil
B. 5 squab
C. 2 stalks celery, minced
D. 1 scallion, minced
E. 5 slices ginger, minced

F. ¼ teaspoon black pepper
G. 2 tablespoons sherry
H. 5 tablespoons light soy sauec
I. 1 lemon

PREPARATION:

I. Mix C, D, E with F, G, H.
II. Dress and clean B and marinate B in C–H mixture 30 minutes. Make sure sauce reaches into cavities of B. Dry with paper towels.

COOKING:

1. Bring A to 350° in deep skillet and deep fry prepared B until golden brown.

2. Squeeze on I juice just before eating.

SESAME SQUAB
Yo Ling Ru Go: Hunan

A. 3 young squab
B. 1 tablespoon light soy sauce
C. 1 tablespoon sherry
D. ½ teaspoon sugar
E. ½ teaspoon anise pepper

F. 1 teaspoon salt
G. 1 scallion
H. 4 slices ginger, shredded
I. 1 tablespoon sesame oil

PREPARATION:

I. Slit backs of A, remove and discard intestines, and clean giblets. Clean A, dry with paper towels, and place in dish.
II. Mix B, C, D, ½ E, and F.

III. Add A, mix, and let stand 30 minutes.
IV. Cut G into 2-inch pieces. Place on top of A.
V. Place H on top of A.

COOKING:

1. Steam A–H mixture 20 minutes in steamer.
2. Cut each A into quarters, arrange on dish, and top with 2 tablespoons drippings.

3. Heat I. Stir-fry remaining E a few times, strain to remove E. Pour over A.

SESAME CORNISH HEN
Yo Ling Juh Gee: Szechuan

Substitute 1 Cornish hen for A. In Step 1, steam for 25 minutes.

FRIED SQUAB
Tza Ba Gup: Canton

Following Step 1, remove A from drippings, dry with paper towels, and cut each into quarters. Mix 1 egg white with 1 tablespoon cornstarch. Coat A pieces with this mixture, and deep fry at 350° 1 to 2 minutes.

STIR-FRIED SQUAB WITH OYSTER SAUCE
Ho Yow Ba Gup: Canton

A. 4 tablespoons peanut oil
B. 1 clove garlic
C. 4 slices ginger, shredded
D. 3 squab
E. 1 tablespoon oyster sauce
F. 2 teaspoons light soy sauce

G. 1 teaspoon sherry
H. 1 teaspoon sugar
I. 1 scallion
J. 2 teaspoons cornstarch
K. ¾ cup water

PREPARATION:

I. Slit backs of D, remove and discard intestines, and clean giblets. Cut D into bite-size pieces.
II. Pound B with side of cleaver, discard skin, and chop B.

III. Cut I into 1½-inch pieces.
IV. Mix E, F, G, H thoroughly.
V. Mix J with ¼ cup K.

COOKING:

1. Heat A, add B, C, stir-fry several times.
2. Add D, stir-fry several minutes.
3. Add E–H mixture, stir-fry thoroughly 2 minutes.

4. Add rest of K. Cook 15 minutes over low heat.
5. Add I; thicken with J–K mixture.

ROAST TURKEY
Kao Fo Gai: Canton

A. 3 cups water
B. 10- to 12-lb. turkey
C. 1 teaspoon salt
D. 3 tablespoons cornstarch

E. 6 tablespoons water
F. stuffing (see Stuffing for Turkey, Chicken, Duck)

PREPARATION:

I. Wash and clean B.
II. Stuff with F.

III. Sew or skewer B closed.
IV. Mix D, E.

COOKING:

1. Pour A into roasting pan. (Utilize mushroom soak water from F preparation.)
2. Place B on its back in roasting pan.
3. Cover tightly and roast at 450° for 2½ hours or more.

4. Uncover and bake 15 minutes more.
5. Remove B and serve on large platter.
6. Bring pan gravy to boil. Add C. Stir well. Slowly add sufficient D–E mixture to thicken gravy evenly.

PORK

Countless ways have been found to prepare pork, and the pig is small enough to enable its unused portions to be preserved quickly after slaughter, either by salting or smoking.

For stir-fried dishes, the following cuts are used: pork tenderloin, pork shoulder, fresh butt, boned shoulder, and chops. Ground pork is used in Lobster Cantonese, Shrimp with Lobster Sauce, and Steamed Pork with Water Chestnuts. Belly pork or uncured bacon, which is rarely used by the American housewife, has alternating layers of lean meat and fat, with the skin on one side. This cut closely resembles our salt pork.

Pork may be considered cooked when it has turned white. When used in soup, thin slices are usually done after 3 minutes of boiling. When recooking pork, since additional cooking will only cause it to lose flavor, it should be added to a dish at the last possible moment.

SLICED PORK
Bai Chieh Ro: General

A. 1½ lbs. fresh ham
B. 1 clove garlic, minced
C. 2 tablespoons light soy sauce
D. 1 tablespoon vinegar
E. 1 teaspoon sesame oil
F. 1½ teaspoons sugar

G. 2 tablespoons chopped scallion
H. 2 teaspoons chopped ginger
I. 1 to 2 teaspoons crushed red pepper (to taste)
J. salt to taste

PREPARATION AND COOKING:

1. Place A in 2 qts. cold water, bring to boil, lower heat, and cook 30 minutes. Turn off heat, leaving A in water until water is nearly cold.
2. Remove A from water. Save stock for use with other recipes. Slice A very thin, arrange on dish.
3. Mix B, C, D, E, F, G, H, I, J thoroughly. Dip A slices in B–J mixture, or pour mixture over A, mix well, and serve.

SLICED PORK WITH VEGETABLES
Er Dung Ro Pien: Peking

A. 3 tablespoons peanut oil
B. ½ lb. pork tenderloin
C. 1 small egg white
D. 1 teaspoon cornstarch
E. few drops sesame oil
F. ½ teaspoon chopped ginger
G. 1 tablespoon chopped scallion (white part only)

H. 1 cup sliced bamboo shoots
I. ½ cup button mushrooms
J. 1 tablespoon light soy sauce
K. 2 teaspoons sherry
L. ½ cup chicken broth
M. ½ teaspoon salt
N. 2 teaspoons cornstarch mixed with I liquid

PREPARATION:

I. Slice B into 1- by 2-inch thin pieces, mix well with C, D, E.

II. Drain I and save liquid for N.

III. Mix J, K, L, M.

COOKING:

1. Heat A, add B–E mixture, stir-fry 1 to 2 minutes, remove to dish; leave oil in pan.
2. Heat oil in pan, stir-fry F, G a few times; add H, I, continue frying 1 minute.

3. Add J–M mixture, bring to boil, thicken with N.
4. Add B mixture, cook 1 minute and serve.

JADE GREEN MEAT DING
Fei Chwee Yoke Ding: Canton

A. 3 tablespoons peanut oil
B. ½ lb. pork tenderloin, diced
C. 1 teaspoon light soy sauce
D. 1 teaspoon cornstarch
E. 1 teaspoon peanut oil

F. 1 cup diced bamboo shoots
G. ¼ lb. snow peas
H. 1 teaspoon salt
I. 1 tablespoon water
J. ½ teaspoon sugar

PREPARATION:

I. Mix B, C, D, E.

II. Discard tips of G. Wash G, drain.

COOKING:

1. Heat A, stir-fry B–E mixture 2 minutes.
2. Add F, continue stir-frying 30 seconds.

3. Add G, H, I, J, stir-fry 1 to 2 more minutes.

JADE GREEN MEAT DING *Approved Diabetic Recipe*
Fei Tsuei Ro Ding: Canton

A. 1 tablespoon peanut oil
B. ¼ lb. pork tenderloin, diced
C. ½ teaspoon light soy sauce
D. ½ teaspoon cornstarch
E. ½ teaspoon peanut oil

F. ¼ cup diced bamboo shoots
G. ¼ lb. snow peas
H. 1 teaspoon salt
I. 1 tablespoon water

PREPARATION:

I. Dice B and mix with C, D, E.

II. Discard tips of G, wash and drain.

COOKING:

1. Heat A, stir-fry B–E mixture 2 minutes.
2. Add F, continue to stir-fry ½ minute.

3. Add G–I, stir-fry 1 to 2 more minutes.

JADE GREEN MEAT DING *Approved Diabetic Recipe*
Fei Tsuei Ro Ding: Canton

Substitute chicken, beef, lamb, veal, or shrimp for B.

PAPER-WRAPPED PORK
Tzee Bao Yoke Ding: Canton

A. 1 lb. fresh pork
B. 4 slices ginger, minced
C. ¼ cup light soy sauce
D. 2 teaspoons heavy soy sauce
E. 2 teaspoons duck sauce
F. 1 teaspoon salt
G. 1 teaspoon sugar
H. ¼ teaspoon garlic powder
I. 1 tablespoon gin
J. 6 scallions
K. 2 cups peanut oil

PREPARATION:

I. Slice A into ¾-inch cubes; place in bowl.
II. Mix B, C, D, E, F, G, H, I and pour over A in bowl; mix well; set aside 30 minutes.
III. Cut J into 1 inch pieces.

COOKING:

1. Wrap 2 to 3 pieces A–I in aluminum foil with 2 or 3 pieces of J.
2. Heat K to 350° and deep fry packages 10 minutes.
3. Serve hot in foil wrapping (to be unwrapped at table).

STEAMED PORK
Tsen Tsu Ro: Szechuan

A. 1 lb. pork
B. 1½ tablespoons light soy sauce
C. 1 tablespoon brown bean sauce
D. 1 teaspoon sugar
E. 2 teaspoons sherry
F. 1 teaspoon chopped ginger
G. 1 tablespoon chopped scallion
H. 2 tablespoons water
I. ½ teaspoon anise pepper
J. ⅓ cup rice flour

PREPARATION:

I. Cut A into slices 1½ by ⅛ inches.
II. Mix with B, C, D, E, F, G, H, I and marinate ½ hour.
III. Mix with J.

COOKING:

1. Steam all ingredients in steamer over boiling water 30 to 45 minutes.

STEAMED PORK   *Approved Diabetic Recipe*
Tsen Tsu Ro: Peking

A. ½ lb. pork
B. 1 teaspoon chopped scallion
C. 1 slice fresh ginger (or sour pickle ginger, chopped)
D. ½ teaspoon light soy sauce
E. ½ teaspoon salt
F. 1 teaspoon fermented bean cake
G. 3 tablespoons rice flour

PREPARATION:

I. Slice A into thin pieces.
II. Mix A, B, C, D, E, F and marinate 45 to 60 minutes.
III. Add G to A mixture and mix well.

COOKING:

1. Steam A–G over boiling water 30 to 45 minutes.

STEAMED PORK WITH SALT EGG
Ham Don Tseng Ju Yoke: Canton

A. ½ lb. ground pork
B. ½ teaspoon chopped ginger
C. 1 teaspoon sherry
D. 2 teaspoons light soy sauce

E. ½ teaspoon sugar
F. 1 teaspoon cornstarch
G. ½ teaspoon salt
H. 1 salt egg

PREPARATION:

I. Combine A, B, C, D, E, F, G, mix thoroughly, and form into a ball.
II. Beat H as thoroughly as possible. (Its yolk is hard, and not easy to mix.)

III. Roll meatball in H, place on a greased 8-inch pie tin. Press ball flat, pour excess H over it.

COOKING:

1. Steam all ingredients 30 minutes over boiling water.

STEAMED PORK WITH SALTED BLACK BEANS
Dow Si Tsing Ju Yoke: Canton

A. ½ lb. ground pork
B. 1 tablespoon salted black beans
C. 1 scallion, minced
D. 1 tablespoon light soy sauce

E. 1 teaspoon sherry
F. 1½ teaspoons sugar
G. 1 scallion, sliced

PREPARATION:

I. Mix A, B, C, D, E, F.

II. Place mixture on serving platter suitable for steaming and shape into a thin meatcake.

COOKING:

1. Boil water in steamer.
2. Place meatcake platter in steaming utensil containing rapidly boiling water.

3. Steam 30 minutes. Remove. Serve on trivet or platter of same size.
4. Serve with garnish of G.

STEAMED PORK WITH SALTY FISH
Ham Yu Tsen Yoke Bang: Canton

A. ½ lb. ground pork
B. 2 teaspoons light soy sauce
C. ½ teaspoon sugar
D. ½ teaspoon salt
E. 1 teaspoon cornstarch

F. 1 egg
G. dash pepper
H. ½ teaspoon sesame oil
I. 1 salty fish (Chinese style)
J. ½ teaspoon peanut oil

PREPARATION:

I. Mix A, B, C, D, E, F, G, H, place in a dish.
II. Wash and clean I; place on top of A mixture.
III. Pour J over I.

COOKING:

1. Steam in a steamer over boiling water 30 minutes; serve with rice.

STEAMED PORK WITH SHRIMP PASTE
Hom Har Tsing Ju Yoke: General

A. ¼ lb. pork
B. 3 slices ginger, shredded
C. 2 to 3 teaspoons shrimp paste

D. ½ teaspoon sugar
E. 1 teaspoon peanut oil
F. 1 teaspoon cornstarch

PREPARATION:

I. Cut A into thin slices.

II. Mix all ingredients well and spread out evenly on a dish.

COOKING:

1. Steam all ingredients over boiling water 20 minutes and serve with rice.

STEAMED PORK WITH FERMENTED BEAN CAKE
Fu Yu Tsing Ju Yoke: Canton

A. ½ lb. pork loin, sliced
B. 1 cube fermented bean cake
C. ¾ teaspoon light soy sauce

D. ¾ teaspoon water chestnut flour
E. 1½ tablespoons cold water

PREPARATION:

I. Mix B, C, D, E into smooth paste.
II. Combine all ingredients thoroughly and place evenly in a shallow platter suitable for steaming.

COOKING:

1. Bring water in steaming vessel to vigorous boil.
2. Place platter on steaming rack after water is boiling.
3. Cover and steam 30 to 40 minutes. Remove and serve in same platter (using trivet or a second platter of same size).

PORK WITH ALMOND BEER SAUCE
Tao Jen Jiang Tze Ro: Peking

A. 3 tablespoons vegetable oil
B. ½ cup blanched almonds
C. 2 lbs. pork butt
D. 3 scallions
E. 1 tablespoon sugar

F. 2 tablespoons light soy sauce
G. 5 slices ginger
H. 1 can beer
I. 1 tablespoon cornstarch
J. ⅛ teaspoon red food coloring

PREPARATION:

I. Bone and cut C into 1½-inch cubes.
II. Cut D into 2-inch pieces.

COOKING:

1. Heat A in heavy 3-qt. saucepan.
2. Add B and brown ½ minute. Remove B.
3. Add C and stir-fry until pork pieces glisten.
4. Add D, E, F, G and stir-fry 1 to 2 minutes.
5. Add H, cover and simmer 45 to 60 minutes.
6. Add B, cook 3 minutes.
7. Mix I, J with 2 tablespoons water, add to pot to thicken gravy.

PORK WITH BRAISED BEAN AND VEGETABLES
Shueh Tsai Mao Dow Ro Si: Adapted

A. 3 tablespoons peanut oil
B. ½ lb. pork (or beef), shredded
C. 1 tablespoon light soy sauce
D. 2 teaspoons cornstarch
E. ½ teaspoon sugar

F. 1 tablespoon chopped scallion
G. 1 cup shredded bamboo shoots
H. 10-oz. can braised bean and vegetables from Chinese grocery

PREPARATION:
I. Mix B with C, D, E, F.

COOKING:
1. Heat A. Stir-fry B–F mixture 1½ minutes.
2. Add G, stir-fry 1 more minute.
3. Add H, mix well, continue stirring 1 minute.

DOUBLE-COOKED PORK WITH HOISIN SAUCE
Hwei Gwo Ro: Szechuan

A. 3 tablespoons peanut oil
B. 1 tablespoon chopped scallion
C. 2 tablespoons hoisin sauce
D. ½ lb. pork

E. 2 small green peppers
F. 1 to 2 small sweet red peppers
G. salt to taste
H. 1 tablespoon water

PREPARATION:
I. Cover D with water, bring to boil, lower heat, cook 30 minutes. Broth may be saved for soup.
II. Discard E seeds, cut each E into eighths, each eighth into quarters.
III. Discard F seeds, cut each same as E.
IV. Cut cooked D in slices 1½ by ¾ inches.

COOKING:
1. Heat A, add B, stir-fry a few seconds.
2. Add C, mix well.
3. Add D slices, stir a few times.
4. Add E, F, G, H. Continue stir-frying 1 minute.

DOUBLE-COOKED PORK WITH BROWN BEAN SAUCE
Hwei Gwo Ro: Szechuan

Substitute bean sauce for C. The bean sauce is made as follows:

A. 4 tablespoons peanut oil
B. 2 small green peppers
C. 2 small red peppers or hot red peppers
D. ½ lb. Double-Cooked Pork with

Hoisin Sauce
E. 2 tablespoons brown bean sauce
F. 1 teaspoon sugar
G. 1 tablespoon water

PREPARATION:
I. Discard seeds of B, C and cut peppers into eighths and then quarters. Mix E, F, G.

COOKING:
1. Heat 2 tablespoons A in frying pan. Stir-fry B, C until almost done (about 40 to 50 seconds). Remove B, C to plate.
2. Heat remaining A. Add cooked D, stir-fry a few seconds.
3. Add E–G, mix well, stir-fry 1 minute.
4. Add B, C, stir-fry a few seconds.

RED-COOKED PORK WITH BAMBOO SHOOTS (FAMILY STYLE)
Jia Shiang Hung Sao Ro: General

A. 1 lb. pork butt
B. 1½ cups water
C. 4 slices ginger
D. 1 scallion
E. 1 tablespoon sherry

F. 1½ cups bite-size pieces bamboo shoots
G. ⅓ cup light soy sauce
H. 1 teaspoon sugar
I. salt to taste

PREPARATION:

I. Cut A into 1-inch cubes.

II. Cut D into 1-inch pieces.

COOKING:

1. Cover A with B in saucepan, bring to boil. Remove foamy froth.
2. Add C, D, E, cook 20 minutes.

3. Add F, G, H, bring to boil; lower heat, simmer until A is soft (about 30 minutes). Add I.

FAMILY-STYLE RED-COOKED PORK
Hung Shu Ju Yoke: General

Substitute 1½ cups tender asparagus shoots for F, ¼ teaspoon powdered ginger for C. In Step II, break off tough stems, French-cut into ½-inch pieces. In Step 3, add B after 25 minutes of simmering.

RED-COOKED PORK WITH BAMBOO SHOOTS AND MUSHROOMS
Jia Siang Hung Sao Ro: General

Add 8 Chinese mushrooms (wash, soak mushrooms in water; drain, and cut each in half) in Step 3.

RED-COOKED PORK WITH CARROTS
Tsu Ro Hung Sao Hung Lo Bo: General

Substitute 1 bunch fresh carrots or turnips for F. Peel and cut into bite-size pieces.

RED-COOKED PORK WITH CHESTNUTS
Tsu Ro Mun Li Tze: Shanghai

A. 2 tablespoons peanut oil
B. 1 boned pork shoulder (about 2 lbs.)
C. 2 scallions
D. ⅓ cup light soy sauce

E. 2 teaspoons sugar
F. 1 cup water
G. 1 lb. fresh chestnuts

PREPARATION:

I. Cut B into 1½-inch cubes.
II. Cover G with boiling water and simmer 20

minutes; drain, shell and skin.

III. Cut C into 1-inch pieces.

COOKING:

1. Heat A in pot.
2. Add B, C, and brown slightly.
3. Add D, E, F, simmer 1½ hours.

4. Add G, cook until done (about 15 to 20 more minutes).

RED-COOKED PORK WITH CELERY CABBAGE
Hung Sao Ro: Shanghai

A. 1 cup water
B. 3 lbs. pork (fresh ham piece or shoulder)
C. 1 tablespoon sherry
D. 2 scallions

E. 2 slices ginger
F. 8 tablespoons heavy soy sauce
G. 1 tablespoon sugar
H. 1 lb. celery cabbage

PREPARATION:

I. Cut H to fit into Dutch oven.

COOKING:

1. Place A in Dutch oven, bring to boil.
2. Add B, C, D, E, F, G. Simmer with lid on 2 to 3 hours or until skin breaks when poked with fork. Add water when needed.
3. Add H. Remove cover, simmer until only ½ cup liquid remains.
4. Slice B and serve with H.

STEAMED MINCED PORK WITH WATER CHESTNUTS (OR WATER CHESTNUT MEATCAKE)
Ma Ti Tsen Tsu Ro: General

A. ½ lb. ground pork
B. 9 canned water chestnuts, chopped fine
C. 1 teaspoon cornstarch
D. 2 tablespoons water

E. 1 tablespoon light soy sauce
F. ½ teaspoon sugar
G. ½ teaspoon salt

PREPARATION:

I. Mix A, B, C, D, E, F, G, well.

COOKING:

1. Flatten A–G in a flat serving dish suitable for steaming.
2. Place dish in steaming utensil and steam 25 minutes.
3. Remove from steaming utensil and serve.

STEAMED MINCED PORK WITH WATER CHESTNUTS AND SALTED DUCK EGG
Shien Dan Tsen Ro Bing: General

Spread contents of 1 uncooked salted duck egg over mixture A–G to complete Step 2.

STEAMED MINCED PORK WITH WATER CHESTNUTS AND CHINESE PORK SAUSAGE
Lap Tsong Tsing Ju Yoke: Canton

Add one finely chopped Chinese pork sausage to mixture A–G to complete Step I.

STEAMED MINCED PORK WITH SWEET PRESERVED CHINESE CUCUMBER
Jiang Gwa Tsen Tsu Ro: General

Substitute 3 tablespoons chopped preserved sweet Chinese cucumbers for B.

LUNAR LANDING
Lau Yin Dun Rieh: Adapted

A. 2 cups peanut oil for deep frying
B. ¼ lb. pork
C. ½ teaspoon cornstarch
D. ½ teaspoon light soy sauce
E. ½ chicken breast cubed (about ½ cup)
F. ½ egg white
G. 1 teaspoon cornstarch
H. 1 teaspoon sherry
I. dash salt
J. 5 Chinese mushrooms
K. 1 carrot
L. ½ cup sliced water chestnuts
M. 1 scallion
N. 3 slices ginger, shredded

O. 8½-oz. can sliced pineapple
P. 4 oz. lobster or king crabmeat
   (frozen or canned)
Q. 3 tablespoons vinegar
R. 1½ tablespoons sugar
S. 1 tablespoon sherry
T. ½ tablespoon heavy soy sauce
U. ½ tablespoon light soy sauce
V. 1 tablespoon cornstarch
W. ½ cup pineapple juice
X. ½ cup sliced blanched almonds
Y. salt to taste
Z. 1 oz. cellophane noodles

PREPARATION:

I. Loosen Z and form into a round shape; deep fry in A at 375°. When noodles expand, remove them to a platter. (It should take only a second for them to expand.)
II. Cut B into ¾-inch cubes, mix with C, D.
III. Cut E into ¾-inch cubes, mix with F, G, H, I.

IV. Soak J in warm water 15 minutes, drain, and cut each into 4 to 5 pieces.
V. Peel K, cut into ⅛-inch diagonal slices.
VI. Cut M into ½-inch pieces.
VII. Slice each O into 6 pieces.
VIII. Mix Q, R, S, T, U, V, W.
IX. Heat 1 tablespoon A, add X, stir until X turns golden brown.

COOKING:

1. Heat 3 tablespoons A, add B–D, stir-fry 2 minutes.
2. Add E–I, stir-fry ½ minute.
3. Add J, K and 2 tablespoons water, stir well and cook 2 minutes.
4. Add L, M, N, O, P, stir and mix well.

5. Add Q–W, stir well and cook 1 to 2 additional minutes. Turn off heat.
6. Add X, Y; mix well.
7. Just before serving, pour B–Y over Z. Serve immediately, for six.

STIR-FRIED MINCED PORK WITH WATER CHESTNUTS AND LETTUCE LEAVES
Sang Tsoi Bao Yoke Bang: Canton

A. 2 tablespoons peanut oil
B. 1 lb. ground pork
C. 2 tablespoons peanut oil
D. ¼ teaspoon salt
E. ½ clove garlic, minced
F. 1 slice ginger, minced
G. ¼ lb. fresh water chestnuts
   (or 1 cup canned)
H. 1 tablespoon light soy sauce

I. 1 teaspoon heavy soy sauce
J. ½ teaspoon sugar
K. 1 tablespoon gin
L. 2 teaspoons cornstarch
M. ¾ cup water
N. ½ cup soup stock
O. 1 scallion, sliced
P. ½ head lettuce

PREPARATION:

I. Chop G fine.

II. Prepare P either as shreds or as individual whole leaves.

III. Mix D, E, F. Set aside.

IV. Mix H, I, J, K, L, M. Set aside. Stir well before using.

COOKING:

1. Put A in very hot skillet and bring to high heat.

2. Add B and brown thoroughly. Discard excess fat.

3. Add C. Cook 2 minutes.

4. Add D–F and stir-fry 1 minute.

5. Add G; stir well.

6. Add H–M and stir-fry 3 minutes.

7. Add N. Cover and cook 5 minutes. Sauce should be thick and all ingredients well coated.

8. Serve in bowl with garnish of O either on a bed of P shreds or along with a separate bowl of P leaves, which are used to wrap a small portion of cooked B in a roll—like a pancake with a filling.

RED BEAN CURD CHEESE PORK
Nam Yu Tsu Ro: Shanghai

A. 1 lb. pork butt
B. 1 scallion tied into a knot
C. 2 slices ginger
D. 1 tablespoon sherry

E. 1 teaspoon sugar
F. 2 tablespoons mashed red bean curd cheese
G. salt to taste
H. 1½ cups water

COOKING:

1. Mix all ingredients in pot, bring to boil and simmer 45 minutes.

2. Place mixture in dish and steam in steamer over boiling water 30 minutes or until meat is very soft and tender.

3. Before serving, pour all gravy into pot, discard B, C, boil down gravy until very thick, pour over A and serve.

STIR-FRIED ROAST PORK WITH VEGETABLES
Cha Shu Bok Tsoi: Canton

A. 3 tablespoons peanut oil
B. 2 teaspoons chopped scallion
C. 1 clove garlic, chopped
D. ½ lb. roast pork (see Index)

E. 8 Chinese mushrooms
F. 4 cups 1-inch pieces celery cabbage
G. 1 teaspoon salt
H. ½ teaspoon sugar

PREPARATION:

I. Cut D into thin, bite-size pieces.

II. Wash E, soak 15 minutes in warm water; drain, cut each into 3 to 4 pieces.

COOKING:

1. Heat A. Add B, C, stir-fry a few seconds.

2. Add D, E, stir-fry 1 minute.

3. Add F, mix well, and stir until F becomes tender (about 3 to 5 minutes).

4. Add G, H, mix well; serve.

FIRE POT (OR CHAFING DISH)
Ho Go: General

A. 2 qts. meat stock, canned
chicken broth, or stock

B. 1 scallion, sliced

C. 1 slice ginger, slivered

D. ½ lb. pork loin

E. ¾ lb. boned chicken

F. 1 lb. fresh shrimp

G. 2 cups spinach

H. 2 cups lettuce

I. 2 cups Chinese cabbage

J. 1 cup watercress, tough stems cut off

K. 12 raw eggs in shell

PREPARATION:

I. Slice D, E as thinly as possible and place
each on separate plate.

II. Shell F and cut in half lengthwise.

III. Wash and drain G, H, I, J. Cut into bite-
sized pieces and place each ingredient in
separate bowl.

IV. Place K unbroken on table.

V. Mix B, C and set aside.

COOKING:

1. Heat A just to boiling in regular pot.

2. Transfer A to lit chafing dish or fire pot.

3. Add B–C.

4. Cook D, E, F, G, H, I, J, K in soup as follows:
Each person cooks his own portions of meats
and vegetables on a skewer in the soup in fire
pot or chafing dish. K boils in soup.

5. Arrange soy, oyster, duck (plain), etc.,
sauces in small bowls around the table for
use as "dips" as desired. Serves 8 to 10.

ROAST PORK I
Cha Shu: Canton

A. 2 lbs. skinless fresh ham or
boneless butt of pork

B. 1 tablespoon light soy sauce

C. 3 tablespoons sugar

D. ½ tablespoon hoisin sauce

E. ½ tablespoon soy bean sauce

F. ½ teaspoon salt

G. few drops red food coloring

PREPARATION:

I. Cut A into pieces 1 inch to 1½ inches wide
and 6 to 7 inches long.

II. Mix B, C, D, E, F, G.

III. Soak A in B–G several hours or overnight,
refrigerated.

COOKING:

1. Preheat oven to 375°.

2. Line roasting pan with aluminum foil. Add 1
to 2 inches of boiling water to pan.

3. Arrange single layer of A on cake rack and
place in pan. (If necessary during cooking,
add more water. This prevents the meat from
drying out.)

4. Roast 1¼ hours, turning meat over after 45
minutes.

5. Slice, serve hot or cold, or stir-fry with a
vegetable.

ROAST PORK II
Shiu Yoke: Canton

A. 1 to 2 lbs. fresh ham, without skin

B. 2 scallions

C. 2 to 3 cloves garlic

D. 3 slices ginger

E. 1 tablespoon sugar

F. 2 tablespoons sherry

G. ¼ cup light soy sauce

H. ½ teaspoon five spices powder

PREPARATION:

I. Cut A into pieces 1 inch thick by several inches long.

II. Cut B in 1- to 2-inch pieces.

III. Crush C with back of cleaver, discard skin; chop C fine.

IV. Slice D into long, thin pieces.

V. Mix B, C, D, E, F, G, H.

VI. Marinate A in B–H several hours.

COOKING:

1. Preheat oven to 375°.

2. Line pan with aluminum foil. Add 1 to 2 inches of hot water. Arrange single layer of A on cake rack and place in pan after water comes to a boil.

3. Roast 1 hour, 15 minutes, turning meat over after 45 minutes.

4. Slice, serve hot or cold or stir-fry with a vegetable.

SZECHUAN PORK WITH ASPARAGUS
Lu Sun Tsu Ro: Szechuan

A. 3 tablespoons peanut oil
B. ½ lb. pork
C. 2 teaspoons light soy sauce
D. 1 teaspoon cornstarch
E. 1 bunch asparagus (½ lb.)
F. 1 tablespoon chopped scallion
G. 1 teaspoon chopped ginger
H. 1 clove garlic, minced
I. 2 teaspoons light soy sauce

J. 2 teaspoons brown bean sauce
K. ½ teaspoon salt
L. 2 teaspoons sherry
M. 2 teaspoons vinegar
N. 1 teaspoon sugar
O. 2 teaspoons cornstarch mixed with ¼ cup water
P. Chinese hot sauce or anise pepper to taste (optional)

PREPARATION:

I. Slice B thin, shred, mix with C, D and 1 teaspoon A.

II. Cut E into 1- to 1½-inch-long pieces.

III. Bring 1 qt. water to boil, add asparagus and parboil 2 to 4 minutes depending on thickness of pieces. Drain. Mix I, J, K, L, M, N, O.

COOKING:

1. Heat remaining A, add B–D mixture, stir-fry 1 to 2 minutes. Remove to a dish, pour excess oil back to pan.

2. Add E, F, G, H, stir-fry 1 minute.

3. Return B–D to pan, stir-fry 1 to 2 minutes.

4. Add I–O mixture, stir until thickened.

5. Add P to taste.

KOHLRABI WITH SHREDDED PORK
Ro Si Da To Tsai: Adapted

A. 3 tablespoons peanut oil
B. ½ lb. pork (or beef), shredded
C. 1 tablespoon chopped scallion
D. ½ teaspoon sugar

E. 2 teaspoons light soy sauce
F. 1½ teaspoons cornstarch
G. 1 bunch kohlrabi (about 4)
H. 1 teaspoon salt

PREPARATION:

I. Peel G, slice, then shred.

II. Mix B, C, D, E, F.

COOKING:

1. Heat A, add B–F mixture, stir-fry 1 minute.

2. Add G, H, stir-fry 2 or 3 more minutes.

STIR-FRIED BEAN SPROUTS WITH PORK
Loh Dow Ya Tsao Ro Si: Shanghai

A. 3 tablespoons peanut oil
B. ½ lb. pork loin (or shredded chicken)
C. 3 teaspoons light soy sauce
D. 1 teaspoon sugar
E. 2 teaspoons cornstarch

F. ½ teaspoon sesame oil
G. 2 scallions
H. salt to taste
I. 1 lb. bean sprouts

PREPARATION:

I. Wash, clean and drain I; parboil in boiling water ½ minute, drain, and set aside.
II. Slice G into thin shreds.

III. Cut B into 1- to 2-inch shreds.
IV. Mix B, C, D, E, F.

COOKING:

1. Heat A, add B–F mixture, stir-fry 1 to 2 minutes.

2. Add G and stir ½ minute.
3. Add H, mix well, and serve hot over I.

SHREDDED PORK WITH BEAN SPROUTS AND SCALLIONS
Nying Ya Ro Si: Hunan

A. 4 tablespoons peanut oil
B. 1 lb. bean sprouts
C. 2 scallions
D. 4 slices ginger, shredded
E. 1 teaspoon salt

F. ½ lb. pork (or veal or beef), shredded
G. 1 tablespoon light soy sauce
H. 1 teaspoon sherry
I. 1 teaspoon cornstarch
J. ½ teaspoon sugar

PREPARATION:

I. Mix F thoroughly with G, H, I, J.
II. Wash B, drain. Trim and discard tail roots.

III. Slice C into 1½-inch pieces

COOKING:

1. Heat 1 tablespoon A. Add B, C, D, stir-fry a few seconds.
2. Add E, stir-fry 1 minute. Drain off liquid, place B–E mixture on plate for later use.

3. Heat remaining A until very hot. Add F–J, stir-fry 2 minutes.
4. Add B–E mixture, mix well, and serve hot.

STIR-FRIED PORK WITH TOMATO
Fan Cheh Ro Pien: Shanghai

A. 3 tablespoons peanut oil
B. 1 clove garlic
C. 1 scallion
D. ½ lb. pork
E. 1 tablespoon light soy sauce
F. ½ teaspoon sugar
G. ½ teaspoon salt

H. ½ teaspoon sesame oil
I. 2 teaspoons cornstarch
J. 2 to 3 tomatoes
K. ½ teaspoon sugar
L. ½ teaspoon salt
M. 1 teaspoon cornstarch

PREPARATION:

I. Slice D into thin pieces 2- by ½-inch.
II. Mix D with E, F, G, H, I.
III. Pound B with side of cleaver, discard skin.
IV. Cut C into 1- to 2-inch pieces.

V. Place J in boiling water for few seconds, remove skin. Slice each J into 8 to 10 pieces, mix with K, L, M.

COOKING:

1. Heat A, brown B, C, lightly, add D–I mixture, stir-fry 1 to 2 minutes or until D is done.

2. Add J–M mixture, mix well. Serve.

PORK WITH CUCUMBERS
Hwang Gwa Ro Pien: Shanghai

A. 3 tablespoons peanut oil
B. 1 clove garlic
C. 1 scallion
D. ½ lb. pork
E. 1 tablespoon light soy sauce
F. ½ teaspoon sugar
G. ¼ teaspoon salt

H. ½ teaspoon sesame oil
I. 2 teaspoons cornstarch
J. 1 cucumber
K. ½ teaspoon sugar
L. salt to taste
M. 1 teaspoon cornstarch

PREPARATION:

I. Slice D into thin pieces 2- by ½-inch.
II. Mix D with E, F, G, H, I.
III. Pound B with side of cleaver, discard skin.

IV. Cut C into 1- to 2-inch pieces.
V. Peel J, split into halves, remove seeds. Cut diagonally into ¼-inch pieces.

COOKING:

1. Heat A, brown B, C, lightly, add D–I mixture, stir-fry 1 to 2 minutes or until D is done.
2. Remove D–I mixture to a dish, pour excess oil back into pan; turn on heat and stir-fry J

2 to 3 minutes or until it looks transparent; add K and L.
3. Add D–I mixture, stir well and serve.

STIR-FRIED PORK WITH KOHLRABI
Da To Tsai Tsao Ro Si: Szechuan

A. 3 tablespoons peanut oil
B. 8 dried shrimp
C. ¼ lb. pork, shredded
D. 2 teaspoons light soy sauce
E. ¼ teaspoon sugar
F. 1 teaspoon cornstarch

G. 2 slices ginger, shredded
H. 1 teaspoon chopped scallion
I. 1 bunch kohlrabi
J. ½ to 1 teaspoon sesame oil
K. salt to taste

PREPARATION:

I. Peel I, slice thin, shred. II. Mix C, D, E, F, G, H. III. Wash B and soak in water 15 minutes, chop.

COOKING:

1. Heat A, add B and C–H, stir-fry 1½ minutes.
2. Add I and stir-fry another 2 to 3 minutes.

3. Add J, K to taste.

STIR-FRIED BEEF WITH KOHLRABI
Da Tow Tsai Tsao Niu Ro Si: Szechuan

Substitute beef (or shredded lamb) for C, omit B, and add a few drops of Chinese hot sauce in Step 3.

STIR-FRIED PORK WITH SNOW PEAS
Shieh Do Ro Pien: Peking

A. 3 tablespoons peanut oil
B. ¼ lb. pork, thinly sliced
C. ½ egg white
D. 1 teaspoon cornstarch
E. ¼ teaspoon sesame oil
F. 1 clove garlic, minced

G. 1 tablespoon chopped scallion
H. ½ cup thinly sliced bamboo shoots
I. 6 Chinese mushrooms
J. ¼ lb. snow peas
K. ½ teaspoon sugar
L. salt to taste

PREPARATION:

I. Mix B, C, D, E.
II. Wash I and soak in warm water 15 minutes, drain (save water), discard stems, slice each into 4 to 6 pieces. Discard tips of J.

COOKING:

1. Heat A, add B–E mixture, stir-fry 2 minutes.
2. Add F, G, H, I, stir-fry 1 minute.
3. Add J, stir ½ minute, add K, L, and 2 tablespoons I liquid, mix well, cover and cook 1 minute.

YU SIANG* SHREDDED PORK
Yu Siang Ro Si: Szechuan

A. 3 tablespoons peanut oil
B. ½ lb. pork (or beef)
C. 2 teaspoons light soy sauce
D. 1 teaspoon cornstarch
E. 8 water chestnuts
F. 1 cup shredded bamboo shoots
G. 4 Chinese mushrooms
H. 1 tablespoon chopped scallion
I. 1 teaspoon chopped ginger
J. 1 clove garlic, minced

K. 2 teaspoons light soy sauce
L. 2 teaspoons brown bean sauce
M. ½ teaspoon salt
N. 2 teaspoons sherry
O. 2 teaspoons vinegar
P. 1 teaspoon sugar
Q. 2 teaspoons cornstarch mixed with ¼ cup water
R. Chinese hot sauce to taste (optional)

PREPARATION:

I. Slice B thin, then shred, mix with C, D and 1 teaspoon A.
II. Slice E thin, then shred.
III. Wash G and soak 15 minutes in warm water; shred.
IV. Mix K, L, M, N, O, P, Q (fish sauce).

COOKING:

1. Heat A. Add B–D, stir-fry 1 to 2 minutes. Remove to dish, pour excess oil back into pan.
2. Stir-fry E, F, G 1 minute, add H, I, J and mix well.
3. Return B–D mixture to pan, stir half a minute.
4. Add K–Q, stir until thickened.
5. Add R to taste.

* "Fish sauce" highly desired in cooking fish. It also combines well with meats.

YU SIANG SHREDDED PORK
Yu Siang Ro Si: Szechuan

Substitute 1 to 1½ cups asparagus for E, F, G. Cut asparagus into 1- to 1½-inch pieces. Bring 1 qt. water to boil, add asparagus, parboil 2 to 4 minutes, depending on thickness of pieces. Drain. In Step 2, add asparagus and H–J; stir-fry 1 minute. Add sauce mixture, stir until thickened, serve with rice.

STIR-FRIED PORK WITH BEAN CURD
Ro Sih Dow Fu: General

A. 1½ tablespoons peanut oil
B. ½ teaspoon salt
C. 1½ cloves garlic
D. ½ slice ginger, minced
E. 1 lb. fresh pork loin, sliced or ground
F. 4 cakes bean curd, cubed
G. 1 teaspoon light soy sauce
H. 1 teaspoon sugar

I. 1 teaspoon rice wine or
   1 tablespoon gin
J. 1 cup soup stock
K. ½ cup soup stock
L. 1 tablespoon cornstarch
M. 3 drops sesame oil
N. 1 teaspoon heavy soy sauce
O. 2 scallions, sliced

PREPARATION:

I. Mix B, C, D.   II. Mix G, H, I.   III. Mix K, L, M, N. Stir well before using.

COOKING:

1. Preheat skillet. Add A and heat until oil begins to smoke.
2. Add B–D and stir-fry rapidly 15 seconds.
3. Add E and fry until nearly done (brown), about 5 minutes.
4. Add F and stir-fry 1 minute.
5. Add G–I and stir-fry 30 seconds.
6. Add J. Cover and cook over moderate heat 5 minutes.
7. Add K–N. Stir-fry until gravy thickens. Add half of O and mix.
8. Serve with garnish of remaining half of O.

STIR-FRIED PORK WITH GREEN PEPPERS
Chu Ro Tsao Ching Jiao: General

Substitute 2 cups thinly sliced green peppers, with seeds removed, for F. Parboil in water 3 minutes; rinse in cold water; drain; add just before Step 5.

STIR-FRIED PORK WITH MUSTARD GREENS
Tsu Ro Tsao Gai Tsai: General

Substitute 2 cups mustard greens for F and add just before Step 5.

STIR-FRIED PORK WITH ONIONS
Tsu Ro Tsao Yang Tsung: General

Substitute 2 cups chopped onions for F and add just before Step 5.

STIR-FRIED PORK WITH CAULIFLOWER
Tsu Ro Tsao Hwa Tsai: General

Substitute 2 cups cauliflower flowerets for F; parboil 3 minutes, drain and add just before Step 5.

STIR-FRIED ROAST PORK WITH BEAN CURD AND OYSTER SAUCE
Ho Yow Cha Shiu Dow Fu: Canton

A. 3 tablespoons peanut oil
B. 1 scallion, minced
C. 2 slices ginger, minced
D. 1 clove garlic, minced
E. 1 cup bite-size pieces of roast pork (see Index)
F. 4 pieces bean curd
G. 1 tablespoon light soy sauce
H. ½ teaspoon sugar
I. 2 teaspoons oyster sauce
J. ¼ cup water
K. salt to taste

PREPARATION:

I. Cut each F into 16 pieces.
II. Mix G, H, I, J.

COOKING:

1. Heat A in frying pan over high heat.
2. Stir-fry B, C, D ½ minute.
3. Add E, stir-fry a few seconds, turn heat to medium, add F, brown slightly.
4. Add G–J mixture, cook 2 minutes, add K, and serve hot.

STIR-FRIED PORK WITH CLOUD EARS AND EGGS
Ywing Er Ro Sih Tsao Don: General

A. 2 tablespoons peanut oil
B. ½ lb. pork loin, sliced
C. 1 teaspoon cornstarch
D. ½ teaspoon salt
E. 1 tablespoon sherry
F. 3 tablespoons light soy sauce
G. 2 teaspoons heavy soy sauce
H. 1 slice ginger, minced
I. 12 cloud ears
J. 2 tablespoons peanut oil
K. 4 eggs
L. 3 tablespoons water
M. 4 scallions, sliced

PREPARATION:

I. Soak I in warm water 15 minutes. Drain. Discard water. Wash well. Cut into small pieces.
II. Marinate B in mixture of C, D, E, F, G, H.
III. Beat K lightly. Set aside.

COOKING:

1. Put A in very hot skillet and bring to high heat.
2. Add B and C–H marinade; add I. Stir-fry until pork is done. Remove from skillet and set aside.
3. Add J to skillet and heat over high heat.
4. Add K. Scramble until set.
5. Return B–I (from Step 2) to skillet. Mix well.
6. Add L (add more L if desired) and half of M and stir-fry 1 minute.
7. Serve with garnish of remaining M.

STIR-FRIED PORK WITH LOTUS ROOTS
Gno Tsao Tsu Ro: Hupeh

A. 2 tablespoons peanut oil
B. 1 clove garlic, minced
C. ½ slice ginger, minced
D. ½ lb. pork loin, sliced
E. 1 tablespoon gin or sherry
F. 1 tablespoon light soy sauce
G. ½ lb. lotus roots
H. 1 cup soup stock or water
I. 1 tablespoon cornstarch or water chestnut flour
J. 1 tablespoon heavy soy sauce
K. 2 scallions, cut in 1-in. pieces

PREPARATION:

I. Scrape G with potato peeler. Halve roots lengthwise and slice into thin slivers along the grain.

II. Mix B, C. Set aside.

III. Mix E, F. Set aside.

IV. Mix H, I, J and add 3 tablespoons water. Set aside. Stir well before using.

COOKING:

1. Put A in very hot skillet and bring to high heat.
2. Add B, C. Stir-fry rapidly 15 seconds to brown B slightly.
3. Add D and stir-fry 2 minutes.
4. Add E, F and stir-fry 15 seconds.
5. Add G and stir-fry 30 seconds.
6. Cover and cook 8 minutes.
7. Add H–J mixture slowly. Stir-fry until sauce thickens and coats all ingredients well. (If water chestnut flour (I) is used, sauce will thicken almost immediately.)
8. Serve with garnish of K.

STIR-FRIED BEEF WITH LOTUS ROOTS
Ngo Yoke Tsao Ngo Si: Canton

Substitute ½ lb. flank steak, thinly sliced, for D. Also add ½ teaspoon salt to B, C mixture in Step III.

PORK WITH BITTER MELON AND SALTED BLACK BEANS
Fu Gwa Yoke Si: Canton

A. 2 tablespoons peanut oil
B. 2 tablespoons salted black beans
C. 2 cloves garlic, minced
D. ½ lb. pork loin
E. 1 teaspoon cornstarch
F. 1 teaspoon light soy sauce
G. 2 teaspoons sherry
H. ¼ teaspoon sugar

I. ¼ teaspoon peanut oil
J. 1 bitter melon
K. 1 teaspoon light soy sauce
L. ½ teaspoon sugar
M. 2 scallions, sliced
N. 1 tablespoon cornstarch
O. 1 cup soup stock

PREPARATION:

I. Slice D into thin, bite-sized pieces. Mix E, F, G, H, I and use as marinade for D. Soak 15 minutes.

II. Wash J, halve lengthwise and discard seeds. Cut into 1/16-inch slices and parboil 3½ minutes with ½ teaspoon baking soda. Drain, rinse well; discard water. This step is very important to avoid undesired bitterness.

III. Wash B and mash.

IV. Mix B, C. Set aside.

V. Mix N, O. Set aside. Stir well before using.

VI. Mix K, L, M. Set aside.

COOKING:

1. Put A in very hot skillet and bring to high heat.
2. Add B–C mixture. Stir-fry rapidly 15 seconds to brown garlic slightly.
3. Add D and E–I marinade. Stir-fry until pork is just done.
4. Add J, stir-fry 2 minutes and add K–M mixture; stir-fry well.
5. Cover and cook 2 minutes.
6. Add N–O slowly. Stir-fry until sauce thickens and coats all ingredients well.

SHRIMP WITH BITTER MELON AND SALTED BLACK BEANS
Fu Gwa Dow Si Har: Canton

Substitute ½ lb. fresh shrimp for D. In Step 3, stir-fry shrimp about 3 minutes (so as to be just under-cooked).

TEN-IN-ONE
Tsao Sih Jing: General

A. 3 tablespoons vegetable oil
B. ½ lb. lean pork
C. ¼ cup diced Smithfield ham
D. 4 chicken wings
E. ½ to 1 cup chicken or meat soup
F. 6 dried mushrooms

G. 2 to 3 cloves star anise
H. 1 scallion, shredded
I. 1 clove garlic, chopped
J. 1 tablespoon sherry
K. 1 cup sliced bamboo shoots
L. 1 tablespoon light soy sauce

PREPARATION:

I. Cut B into bite-size pieces.
II. Soak F 20 minutes in hot water. Drain, save water.

III. Cut each F into thirds.
IV. Disjoint D.

COOKING:

1. In Dutch oven, heat A. Add B, C, D, stir-fry 5 minutes.
2. Add E, F water, G, H, I, J, K, L. Simmer 35 minutes.

3. When all ingredients are tender, season with salt.

TEN-IN-ONE
Tsao Sih Jing: General

Substitute lily flowers for K. Prepare by soaking in hot water, draining, and discarding water.

TEN-IN-ONE
Tsao Sih Jing: General

Substitute 4-oz. can button mushrooms for F and 1 cup tender asparagus shoots for K. Omit Step II. In Step 2, do not add asparagus until last 5 minutes of simmering.

SWEET AND SOUR PORK CUBES
Gu Lau Yoke: Canton

A. peanut oil for deep frying
B. 1 lb. pork tenderloin
C. ½ teaspoon salt
D. 2 teaspoons sherry
E. ¼ teaspoon sesame oil
F. 1 egg white
G. 2 tablespoons cornstarch

H. 2 tablespoons tomato sauce
I. ¼ cup vinegar
J. ¼ cup sugar mixed with 1 teaspoon corn-starch and 2 tablespoons water
K. 1 green pepper
L. 1 red pepper
M. salt to taste

PREPARATION:

I. Cut B into 1-inch cubes. Cook 5 minutes in boiling water. Drain.

II. Mix B, C, D, E; marinate 15 minutes.

COOKING:

1. Heat A to 325°. Deep-fry B–G 2 minutes. When B–G floats, remove, drain on paper towels.

2. Mix H, I, J thoroughly in saucepan. Add

III. Beat F, G until a smooth paste is formed. Add to B–E mixture, mix well.

IV. Cut K, L into bite-size pieces.

K, L, bring to boil. Add M.

3. When H–M sauce mixture is thick, add B–G, mix well, and serve hot.

SNOWBALL PORK
La-ee-tzee Yoke Kew: Canton

A. 2 cups peanut oil
B. ½ lb. pork tenderloin
C. 2 tablespoons sugar
D. 2 tablespoons catsup
E. 2 tablespoons vinegar
F. 2 teaspoons cornstarch
G. ½ cup litchi juice
H. 20-oz. can whole litchis

I. 1 teaspoon sherry
J. 2 teaspoons light soy sauce
K. ½ teaspoon anise pepper
L. 1 tablespoon chopped scallion
M. 1 egg white
N. 2 tablespoons cornstarch
O. salt to taste

PREPARATION:

I. Cook B in boiling water 5 minutes, then cut into cubes.

II. Mix I, J, K, L. Marinate B in mixture 30 minutes.

III. Mix M and N; add to B.

IV. Drain H, reserving juice for G.

COOKING:

1. Heat A to 325°. Deep fry B 5 minutes, stirring constantly to prevent sticking together. Drain on paper towels.

2. Mix C, D, E, F, G in a saucepan, bring to boil, stir until sauce is thickened.

3. Add H and B; mix well; add O; and serve.

SWEET AND SOUR PORK
Tien Swan Ro Jiu: General

A. peanut oil for deep frying
B. 2 eggs, beaten
C. ¾ teaspoon salt
D. ½ teaspoon garlic powder
E. ½ cup all-purpose flour

F. ¼ cup cornstarch
G. ½ cup milk
H. 2 tablespoons sherry
I. 1 lb. fresh pork, sliced thin
J. sweet and sour sauce (see Index)

PREPARATION:

I. Mix B, C, D, E, F, G, H to make a smooth batter.

II. Dredge I in batter.

COOKING:

1. Heat A to 375° and deep fry B–I until golden brown.

2. Remove, drain on paper towel and place in deep bowl.

3. Heat J and pour over I. Serve hot.

PINEAPPLE PORK
Bo Lo Yoke: Canton

A. 4 tablespoons vegetable oil
B. 1 lb. lean pork
C. 2 cups pineapple chunks
D. ½ cup pineapple juice
E. 1 tablespoon sugar
F. 2 stalks celery

G. 2 carrots
H. 1 medium green pepper
I. 1 tablespoon cornstarch, mixed with ¼ cup water
J. 1 teaspoon sherry
K. 5 slices ginger

PREPARATION:

I. Cut B into bite-size pieces, add I, J, K; mix thoroughly.
II. Mix C with D, E.
III. Slice F diagonally into ½-inch pieces.

IV. Skin G, then slice into ½-inch pieces.
V. Split H endwise. Remove core and seeds. Slice into pieces.

COOKING:

1. Heat A in skillet.
2. Add B mixture and stir-fry 4 minutes.
3. Add C–E, bring to boil and simmer 5 minutes.

4. Add F, G, cook 5 minutes.
5. Add H and salt to taste. Mix well for a minute.
6. Thicken with I.

PORK IN PLUM SAUCE
Mwei Jiong Yoke: Canton

A. ¼ cup vegetable oil
B. 1 clove garlic
C. 1 lb. boned pork
D. ⅓ cup plum sauce
E. 2 celery stalks, diced
F. 4 slices ginger
G. 1 tablespoon sherry

H. 2 carrots
I. 2 teaspoons sugar
J. 1 teaspoon salt
K. ⅓ cup Chinese pickled scallions
L. ¼ cup water
M. 2 teaspoons cornstarch
N. 2 tablespoons water

PREPARATION:

I. Cut C into bite-size pieces.
II. Peel H, cut into cubes.

III. Crush B with flat side of cleaver; remove skin.

COOKING:

1. Place A, B in skillet. Using high heat, brown C. Stir 5 minutes.

2. Add D, E, F, G, H, I, J, K, L. Simmer, covered, 12 minutes.
3. Add M mixed with N to thicken gravy.

LION'S HEAD
Sih Tze Do: Shanghai

A. 3 tablespoons peanut oil
B. ½ lb. hearts of celery cabbage
C. 1 cup soup stock
D. 3 dried black mushrooms
E. ⅔ small onion, chopped
F. 2 teaspoons heavy soy sauce

G. 2 tablespoons sherry
H. 2 tablespoons light soy sauce
I. 1 teaspoon salt
J. 1½ teaspoons sugar
K. 1 lb. ground pork
L. 2 slices ginger, minced

PREPARATION:

I. Cut B into quarters (lengthwise).

II. Soak D in warm water 15 minutes. Discard water. Cut into small pieces.

III. Mix F, G, H, I, J. Marinate K in F–J.

IV. Mix D, E, L well. Add F–K mixture. Stir well. Let stand for 5 minutes.

V. Form into 5 meatballs.

COOKING:

1. Put A in very hot skillet and bring to high heat.

2. Add B and stir-fry 2 minutes. Distribute leaves evenly on bottom of skillet.

3. Place meatballs on B. Add C.

4. Bring to boil. Cover. Simmer over low heat 15 minutes.

PORK BUTT STEWED WITH MUSHROOMS AND BAMBOO SHOOTS
Tsu Ro Sao Er Dung: General

A. 3 tablespoon peanut oil

B. 1 scallion

C. 2 slices ginger

D. 1 lb. pork butt

E. 8 dried Chinese mushrooms

F. ¼ cup light soy sauce

G. ½ teaspoon salt

H. 1 teaspoon sugar

I. 2 cups mushroom soak water

J. 1 cup bite-size pieces bamboo shoots

PREPARATION:

I. Cut D into bite-size pieces.

II. Wash E, soak 15 minutes in 1 cup water. Drain, saving water. Cut E in quarters.

III. Cut B into 1-inch pieces.

IV. Mix F, G, H.

COOKING:

1. Heat A in frying pan, add B, C, stir-fry 1 minute.

2. Add D, E, stir-fry 2 to 3 more minutes.

3. Add F–H, I. Bring to boil.

4. Simmer 15 minutes. Add J, cook another 30 to 45 minutes. Serve.

BRAISED PORK HOCK WITH ASPARAGUS
Lu Sun Tsu Ti: Adapted

A. 1 lb. pork hock

B. 2 scallions

C. 3 slices ginger (or ½ tsp. ginger powder)

D. ⅓ cup light soy sauce

E. 1 teaspoon sugar

F. 2 tablespoons sherry

G. 1 to 2 cups water

H. salt to taste

I. ½ lb. asparagus

PREPARATION:

I. Wash A.

II. Tie B into 2 bundles.

III. Break tender shoots of I and cut into 1½-inch pieces. Mix C, D, E, F.

COOKING:

1. Place A, B, and C–F in heavy 3-qt. saucepan. Add G and bring to boil, cover and simmer for 1½ to 2 hours or until A is chopstick-tender. Add more water if necessary.

2. When A is done, adjust with H, add I and simmer 5 more minutes; serve hot.

PORK WITH CELLOPHANE NOODLES
Ro Sih Fun See: General

A. 1 tablespoon peanut oil
B. 1 lb. pork loin, sliced
C. 1 yellow onion, chopped
D. 1 tablespoon sherry
E. 2 tablespoons light soy sauce
F. ½ teaspoon sugar
G. ½ teaspoon salt

H. ½ cup water chestnuts, sliced
I. 8 dried black mushrooms
J. 1 slice ginger, minced
K. 3 scallions, sliced
L. 2 tablespoons peanut oil
M. 1 oz. cellophane noodles
N. 1½ cups cold water

PREPARATION:

I. Soak M in hot water 20 minutes. Drain.
II. Mix D, E, F, G. Set aside.
III. Mix H, I, J, K. Set aside.

COOKING:

1. Put A in very hot skillet and bring to high heat.
2. Add B and stir-fry 2 minutes.
3. Add C and continue to stir-fry 4 more minutes.
4. Add D–G. Stir well.
5. Add H–K. Stir well.
6. Remove from pan. Set aside.
7. Put L in very hot skillet and bring to high heat.
8. Add M. Stir well.
9. Add A–K.
10. Add N. Bring to boil. Turn heat to medium. Cook 5 minutes or until all water is absorbed.

PORK LO MEIN
Tsu Ro Lo Mein: General

A. 3 tablespoons peanut oil
B. 4 Chinese mushrooms
C. 1 tablespoon chopped scallions
D. ¼ lb. pork (or beef or chicken)
E. 2 tablespoons light soy sauce
F. 1 teaspoon salt
G. 1 cup shredded celery cabbage

H. 1 cup thinly shredded bamboo shoots
I. 1 cup thinly shredded celery
J. ¼ cup mushroom water
K. 10 snow peas
L. 1 teaspoon cornstarch mixed with 1 tablespoon water
M. ½ lb. fresh or dried thin noodles

PREPARATION:

I. Cook M in 2 qts. boiling water 5 to 8 minutes. Drain and run under cold water a few seconds; drain again.
II. Mix cooked M with ½ E, ⅓ A, and ½ teaspoon F. Put mixture in baking dish and bake in 375° oven 25 minutes.
III. Wash B and soak in warm water 15 minutes. Cut in thin shreds 2 inches long.
IV. Cut D in thin shreds 2 inches long.

COOKING:

1. Heat A in frying pan until hot, stir in B, C, add D and stir-fry 2 minutes. Add E, F, stir-fry 1 minute.
2. Add G, H, I and mix well. Add J, cover and cook 2 minutes. Add K and continue to stir-fry 1 minute.
3. Add L, stir well.
4. Pour over baked crispy M and serve.

PORK LO MEIN   *Approved Ulcer Recipe*
Ro Si Lo Mein: Canton

A.   2 tablespoons vegetable oil
B.   ¼ lb. ground pork
C.   2 tablespoons light soy sauce
D.   1 teaspoon salt
E.   1 teaspoon cornstarch

F.   ¼ cup chicken soup
G.   1 cup finely chopped celery cabbage
H.   1 cup canned mushrooms
I.   ¼ cup mushroom water
J.   ½ lb. fresh (or ⅓ lb. dried) noodles

PREPARATION:

I.   Cook J in 2 qts. boiling water 8 minutes. Drain, run cold water over it until cool.
II. Place cooked J in baking dish. Add one-half of A, C, D; mix well. Bake 10 minutes in 375° oven.

III. Drain H, saving water.
IV. Mix B with remaining C, D and E moistened with a little F.

COOKING:

1. Place remaining A in frying pan; heat. Add B–F mixture and break into spoon-size pieces. Stir-fry 2 minutes.
2. Add G, cook 10 more minutes or until all ingredients are soft.

3. Mix in H, additional liquid from F and I as needed.
4. Pour over J; serve.

CHICKEN LO MEIN   *Approved Ulcer Recipe*
Gai Si Lo Mein: Canton

Substitute chopped chicken breasts for B.

PORK SOONG
Soong Yoke: Canton

A.   3 tablespoons peanut oil
B.   ½ lb. pork tenderloin
C.   1 scallion, chopped
D.   ½ cup shredded bamboo shoots
E.   ½ cup thinly sliced water chestnuts
F.   ¼ lb. snow peas
G.   ½ cup chicken broth

H.   2 teaspoons sherry
I.   1 tablespoon light soy sauce
J.   ½ tablespoon oyster sauce
K.   ½ teaspoon sugar
L.   2 teaspoons cornstarch
M.   ½ teaspoon salt
N.   fried cellophane noodles (see Index)

PREPARATION:

I.   Mince B.
II. Remove and discard tips of F, then wash F.

III. Mix G, H, I, J, K, L, M.

COOKING:

1. Heat A, add B, C; stir-fry until meat turns white (about 1 to 2 minutes).
2. Add D, E, stir-fry for 1 minute.

3. Add F, stir-fry ½ minute.
4. Add G–M mixture, stir until it is thickened.
5. Spread N on top and serve.

PORK SLICE WITH ANISE PEPPER SALT
Jiao Yen Ro Pien: Peking

A. 2 cups peanut oil
B. ½ lb. pork tenderloin
C. 1 egg white

D. 2 tablespoons flour
E. anise pepper salt for dipping (see Index)

PREPARATION:

I. Slice B in pieces about ⅛ inch thick.   II. Beat C, mix with D.   III. Dip each B slice into B–D mixture.

COOKING:

1. Heat A in saucepan.
2. Deep fry B–D until golden brown, about 30

to 60 seconds.
3. Serve with E.

RED BEAN CURD CHEESE PORK WITH POTATOES
Shu Tzai Nam Yu Yoke: Canton

A. 1 lb. boneless pork butt
B. 2 cups water
C. 1 tablespoon sherry
D. 2 slices ginger

E. 2 tablespoons mashed red bean curd cheese
F. 2 teaspoons light soy sauce
G. 1 teaspoon sugar
H. 2 medium potatoes

PREPARATION:

I. Cut A into bite-size pieces.
II. Peel H, cut into bite-size pieces. (To avoid

discoloration, either cook immediately or cover with cold water until ready to cook.)

COOKING:

1. Place A in pot, cover with B, bring to boil. Skim off fatty foam.
2. Add C, D, reduce heat, cover, cook 30 minutes.

3. Add E, F, G, mix well, bring to boil again. Reduce heat, simmer 30 more minutes.
4. During final 15 minutes of simmering, add H.

SPICED PORK WITH SOY SAUCE
Jiang Ro: Shanghai

A. 1- to 1½-lb. pork butt
B. 1 teaspoon salt
C. 1 scallion
D. 3 slices ginger
E. 1 piece stick cinnamon, ½ inch long

F. 1 star anise
G. 1 cup chicken broth
H. 2 tablespoons sherry
I. 3 tablespoons light soy sauce
J. 1 teaspoon rock sugar

PREPARATION:

I. Clean and wash A, dry with paper towel, rub with B, let stand 2 hours.

II. Place C, D, E, F in piece of clean cloth, gather corners and tie with string. Mix H, I, J.

COOKING:

1. Place A–B in pot.
2. Place C–F in G, bring to boil, add to A, bring to boil, cook 2 to 3 minutes.

3. Add H–J, simmer 1 to 1½ hours (until pork is tender). Turn A once or twice during cooking.
4. Cool, slice, and serve.

PORK CONCENTRATE
Ro Sung: Fukien

A. 4 lbs. pork loin
B. 4 cups chicken soup
C. 2½ tablespoons lard or vegetable oil
D. ½ teaspoon meat tenderizer

E. 3 tablespoons sugar
F. 4 tablespoons sherry
G. 3 tablespoons light soy sauce

PREPARATION:

I. Bone A, remove fat and gristle. About 2 to 2¼ lbs. of lean meat should remain. Bones and gristle can be used for soup stock. Cut A across the grain into pieces ¼ inch thick.

II. Thoroughly mix D with A; allow mixture to stand at room temperature for ½ hour. (If D is not used, cooking time must be doubled).

III. Mix E, F, G with A in heavy 3-qt. saucepan.

COOKING:

1. Heat A, using high heat, stirring constantly ½ minute.

2. Add B, bring to boil, cover, lower heat and simmer 2 hours or until pieces of A disintegrate on stirring. About ½ cup of liquid should be left.

3. Add C, cook uncovered over low heat, stirring constantly. Mixture will become lumpy with no visible moisture. Constant stirring is crucial at this stage to prevent scorching. Although mixture is lumpy, it will become fluffy when cold. Serve hot or cold.

GOLDEN STRIPS WITH PRESSED BEAN CURD
La Jiao Tsao San Sih: Hupeh

A. ¼ cup peanut oil
B. 3 medium pork chops
C. 2 to 3 hot green Italian peppers or
    1 to 2 large sweet green peppers
D. 4 eggs
E. 4 cakes pressed bean curd

F. ¼ cup chicken soup
G. salt, to taste
H. ½ teaspoon salt
I. 2 teaspoons light soy sauce
J. 2 teaspoons sherry

PREPARATION:

I. Beat D, add H, heat just enough A in skillet to oil pan. Add 2 tablespoons D mixture and tip pan to ensure making thin egg skins without holes. Turn skins over, being careful not to scorch them. Cut skins into strips ¼-inch wide by 2 inches long. Continue procedure until all D has been used.

II. Cut E into ¼-inch strips.

III. Bone B, discard bones; cut meat into ½-inch by 2¼-inch strips.

IV. Split C, discard seeds and stems; cut into ¼-inch by 2-inch strips.

V. Mix B with I, J.

COOKING:

1. Heat rest of A in skillet; add B mixture; stir-fry 1 minute.

2. Add C, continue to stir-fry 1 minute.

3. Add D, E strips and F. Cover and simmer for 3 to 4 minutes; adjust with G.

SIMPLE SPICY PORK CHOPS
Jien Dan Tsu Pai: General

A. 3 tablespoons vegetable oil
B. 3 lbs. pork chops
C. 2 onions
D. 5 to 10 drops tabasco

E. ¼ cup light soy sauce
F. 1 teaspoon sugar
G. dash paprika (optional)

PREPARATION:

I. Cut B into 12 to 15 pieces.
II. Slice C.
III. Mix D, E.

IV. Marinate B in D–E 20 minutes. Drain, saving liquid.

COOKING:

1. Heat A in large frying pan.
2. Using high heat, stir-fry B 10 minutes.
3. Add C, cook 3 minutes, cover pan, lower heat to medium.

4. Add D–E, F, G. Continue cooking 15 to 25 minutes (depending on thickness of chops) until done. Salt to taste.

SPICY PORK CHOPS
Yong Chung Pai Gwut: Canton

A. ¼ cup peanut oil
B. 6 medium pork chops
C. 2 onions, cut into rings
D. ¼ cup flour
E. dash black pepper
F. ½ teaspoon salt

G. 3 tablespoons catsup
H. Chinese hot sauce (optional)
I. 2 tablespoons sherry
J. 1 tablespoon light soy sauce mixed with 2 tablespoons water

PREPARATION:

I. Place D, E, F in paper bag. Add B and shake.

II. Mix G, H, I, J.

COOKING:

1. Heat A in frying pan. Fry B until brown on both sides. Add C, cook 5 more minutes. Adjust heat so that B does not scorch.

2. Add G–J, simmer, covered, 10 more minutes. Serve hot.

BARBECUED PORK
Jiang Yo Sao Ro: Shanghai

A. 4 lbs. pork chops
B. ½ cup light soy sauce

C. 2 tablespoons sherry
D. ¼ teaspoon paprika

PREPARATION:

I. Mix B, C, D and marinate A in mixture 30 minutes.

COOKING:

1. Place A on horizontal grill over red-hot coals. Cover A with 18″ wide aluminum foil to retain juices. If half hood is on grill, place one end of foil on top of hood (with weights) and allow foil to hang extended over edge of grill. When A browns, turn over. Cooking time: 40 to 60 minutes.

RED-COOKED PORK CHOPS WITH BEAN CURD
Hung Sao Tsu Pai Dow Fu: General

A. 3 tablespoons peanut oil
B. 2 scallions, sliced
C. 2 slices ginger, slivered
D. 2 medium pork chops
E. 6 dried black mushrooms

F. 4 cakes bean curd
G. 12 cloud ears (optional)
H. 2 tablespoons light soy sauce
I. ½ teaspoon sugar
J. ½ cup water from E

PREPARATION:

I. Soak E in warm water 15 minutes; drain, saving water, and slice.
II. Soak G in cold water 15 minutes; wash and drain.

III. Cut each F into 16 pieces.
IV. Slice D into strips.
V. Mix B, C.

COOKING:

1. Put A into very hot skillet and bring to high heat.
2. Fry B, C ½ minute.

3. Add D, E. Cook until D is thoroughly done (pork will turn white).
4. Add F, G, H, I, J. Cook 5 minutes.
5. Serve hot on rice.

PORK CHOP WITH ONIONS
Yong Chung Ju Pai: Adapted

A. 1 tablespoon vegetable oil
B. 6 medium pork chops
C. 2 medium onions
D. 2 tablespoons light soy sauce

E. 2 teaspoons sugar
F. 1 tablespoon sherry
G. 3 slices ginger, minced
H. Salt to taste

PREPARATION:

I. Marinate B in mixture of D, E, F, G.

II. Cut C into rings.

COOKING:

1. Heat frying pan, add A. Remove B from sauce, brown both sides about 15 minutes, remove excess fat. Lower heat, add C. Add D–G mixture and ⅓ cup water. Add more water when needed. Add H.
2. Simmer covered 45 minutes or until chops are well done, turning them several times during cooking. Serve hot.

PORK CHOPS WITH ONION AND NOODLES
Yong Chung Ju Pai Mein: Adapted

Add Step III: Cook ½ lb. thin noodles until soft. Drain, rinse with cold water, drain again. Add Step 3: Remove B from pan. Add noodles, 2 cups meat or chicken stock. Bring to boil, spread B and sauce over noodles. Serve hot.

PORK CHOPS WITH ONION AND CELLOPHANE NOODLES
Yong Chung Ju Pai Fun See: Adapted

Add Step III: Soak 1 oz. (dried) cellophane noodles in warm water 30 minutes. Drain. Add Step 3: Remove B from pan; add noodles and 1 cup meat or chicken stock to pan. Boil, spread B and sauce on top, and serve hot.

STUFFED PORK CHOPS
Yeon Ju Pai: Adapted

A. 8 to 10 loin pork chops
B. 3 tablespoons peanut oil
C. 8 Chinese mushrooms
D. 1 cup shredded Smithfield ham
E. 1 cup shredded water chestnuts

F. 1 cup shredded bamboo shoots
G. 1 cup glutinous rice
H. 1 tablespoon light soy sauce
I. 2 teaspoons sherry
J. ⅔ teaspoon salt

PREPARATION:

I. Wash G several times (discard water) and place in pot.

II. Cover G with 1½ cups water, bring to boil; reduce liquid slightly by continuing to boil.

III. Cover pot tightly, reduce heat, simmer 20 minutes, remove from heat and drain.

IV. Wash C, soak 15 minutes in warm water. Drain, and cut into long, thin slices.

COOKING:

1. Brown A lightly in 1 tablespoon B, remove from pan, and set aside.
2. Add 2 tablespoons B to pan, stir-fry C, D 1 minute.
3. Add E, F; stir 1 more minute.
4. Add G, H, I, J and mix well.
5. Divide mixture into portions 1 less than total number of A used (e.g., for 8 chops, make 7 portions of stuffing).
6. Place single A in baking pan, add 1 portion stuffing; add 1 more chop, then 1 more portion stuffing. Continue stacking balance of chops and stuffing. Then, using 4 skewers, skewer entire stack together.
7. Bake in 325° oven 1 hour and 15 minutes.

STEAMED PORK CHOPS WITH RICE FLOUR
Fun Tsen Tsu Pai: General

A. 4 medium pork chops
B. 2 teaspoons sherry
C. 2 teaspoons light soy sauce
D. ¾ teaspoon salt

E. ½ cup Cream of Rice
F. 2 scallions
G. 2 slices ginger, shredded

PREPARATION:

I. Marinate A with B, C, D.
II. Mix in E and place in shallow bowl.

III. Slice F. Scatter F and G over chops.

COOKING:

1. Place bowl in steamer and steam 45 minutes. Serve hot.

BRAISED SPARERIBS I
Hung Sao Pai Gu: Shanghai

A. 2 tablespoons peanut oil
B. 1 scallion
C. 2 slices ginger
D. 1 lb. spareribs

E. 2 tablespoons light soy sauce
F. 1 tablespoon sherry
G. 1 teaspoon sugar
H. salt to taste

PREPARATION:

I. Cut D into 1½-inch pieces.
II. Cut B, C into 1-inch pieces.
III. Mix E, F, G.

COOKING:

1. Heat A. Add B, C, stir-fry a few seconds.
2. Add D, stir-fry 1 minute.
3. Add E–G; mix well.

4. Add about 1 cup boiling water, bring to boil, then simmer 30 to 45 minutes or until D is tender and very little gravy is left. Add H.

BRAISED SPARERIBS II
Dow Si Shiu Pai Gwut: Canton

A. 2 tablespoons peanut oil
B. 1½ tablespoon fermented, salted black beans
C. 1 to 2 cloves garlic
D. 2 slices ginger

E. 1 lb. spareribs
F. 1 tablespoon light soy sauce
G. 1 teaspoon sugar
H. ¾ cup water

PREPARATION:

I. Cut E into 1-inch pieces.

II. Chop and mix B, C, D.

COOKING:

1. Heat A. Add B–D mixture, stir-fry a few seconds.
2. Add E, stir-fry 1 minute.

3. Add F, G, mix well.
4. Add H, bring to boil, simmer 45 minutes, or until E is tender.

SPARERIBS WITH ANISE PEPPER SALT
Jiao Yen Pai Gu: Shanghai

A. peanut oil for deep frying
B. 1 lb. spareribs
C. 1 teaspoon anise pepper salt (see Index)

D. 1 egg white
E. 3 tablespoons cornstarch

PREPARATION:

I. Cut B in 1-inch to 2-inch pieces. Mix thoroughly with C.

II. Mix D, E, F.
III. Dip B in E–F.

COOKING:

1. Heat A to 325°, deep fry B–F mixture until golden brown (about 2 to 3 minutes).

ONION SPARERIBS
Yang Tsung Tsu Pai: Wushih

A. ⅓ cup peanut oil
B. 1 lb. spareribs
C. 1 lb. onions

D. 1 tablespoon sherry
E. ¼ cup catsup
F. 1½ tablespoons vinegar

G. 1½ tablespoons sugar
H. 1 tablespoon light soy sauce
I. ¼ cup water

PREPARATION:

I. Pound B with back of cleaver several times; cut each rib into 2-inch pieces.

II. Peel C and slice into ½-inch pieces.
III. Mix E, F, G, H, I.

COOKING:

1. Heat A, add B and brown 1 to 2 minutes; remove B to dish.
2. Heat 2 tablespoons A, add C, and brown 1 minute.

3. Return B, add D, stir well.
4. Add E–I, bring to boil, lower heat and simmer for 10 to 15 minutes, depending on the tenderness of the ribs.

SPARERIBS WITH BAMBOO SHOOTS
Dung Sun Pai Gu: Shanghai

A. 2 tablespoons peanut oil
B. 1 lb. spareribs
C. 1 tablespoon sherry
D. 1 cup diced bamboo shoots
E. 1 tablespoon chopped scallion

F. 2 tablespoons light soy sauce
G. 1 teaspoon sugar
H. ½ cup chicken broth
I. 2 teaspoons cornstarch mixed with ¼ cup water

PREPARATION:

I. Cut B into 1- to 2-inch pieces.

II. Mix D, E, F, G.

COOKING:

1. Heat A, add B, stir-fry 1 minute.
2. Add C, stir well, cover a few seconds.
3. Add D–G, mix well.

4. Add H, bring to boil, lower heat and simmer 30 minutes.
5. Thicken with I.

STEAMED SPARERIBS
Swan Tsai Tsen Pai Gu: Szechuan

A. 1 lb. spareribs
B. 3 teaspoons brown bean sauce
C. 1 tablespoon water
D. ½ teaspoon salt

E. 1 cup shredded pickled mustard greens
F. ½ teaspoon sugar
G. ½ cup rice flour
H. 1 or 2 red-hot peppers (optional)

PREPARATION:

I. Cut A into 1-inch pieces.
II. Mix A, B, C, D, marinate 30 to 60 minutes.
III. Chop E, mix with F and 1 tablespoon G. Add H.

IV. Place rest of G in paper bag. Add marinated A, and shake, coating each piece with G.
V. Line soup dish with E, top with A mixture.

COOKING:

1. Steam A over boiling water in steamer 1 hour, or until meat is tender.

STEAMED SPARERIBS   *Approved Diabetic Recipe*
Ching Tsen Pai Gu: General

A. 1 lb. spareribs
B. 2 teaspoons brown bean sauce
C. 1 tablespoon water

D. ½ teaspoon salt
E. ½ cup rice flour

PREPARATION:

I. Cut A into 1-inch pieces.
II. Mix A, B, C, D and let stand 30 to 60 minutes. Remove.

III. Add E and place mixture in dish.

COOKING:

1. Steam over boiling water in steamer 1 hour.

STEAMED SPARERIBS WITH RICE FLOUR
Fun Tsen Woo Siang Pai Gu: Anhwei

A. 1½ lbs. spareribs
B. 2 teaspoons light soy sauce
C. ½ teaspoon sugar
D. 1 teaspoon salt
E. ⅛ teaspoon five spices powder
F. 1 teaspoon sherry
G. 2 tablespoons chopped scallion
H. 1 teaspoon chopped ginger
I. ¼ cup rice flour

PREPARATION:

I. Cut A into 1½-inch pieces.
II. Mix A, B, C, D, E, F, G, H, let stand 1 hour.
III. Add I to A–H mixture, arrange on dish.

COOKING:

1. Steam over boiling water 45 to 60 minutes.

SPARERIBS CREAM OF RICE
Fun Tsen Pai Go: General

A. 3 lbs. spareribs
B. 1 teaspoon salt
C. 1 tablespoon sherry
D. ¼ teaspoon five spices powder (optional)
E. 2 tablespoons light soy sauce
F. 4 slices ginger, minced
G. ½ cup Cream of Rice
H. 3 scallions, minced
I. 2 teaspoons vegetable oil
J. ¼ teaspoon sesame oil (optional)

PREPARATION:

I. Cut A into bite-size pieces; steam 1 hour.
II. Mix B, C, D, E, F with A.
III. Place G in paper bag and shake prepared A.
IV. Place A mixture in large bowl and garnish with H. Pour I, J over and place in steamer.

COOKING:

1. Cover bowl with aluminum foil and steam 40 minutes. Serve.

STEAMED SPARERIBS WITH PUMPKIN
Nan Gwa Pai Gu: General

A. 1 to 1½ lbs. spareribs
B. 1 tablespoon light soy sauce
C. 2 teaspoons sherry
D. 1 teaspoon salt
E. ½ teaspoon sugar
F. ½ cup rice flour
G. 1½ cups pumpkin meat, sliced 1½ by ¾ inches
H. ½ teaspoon salt

PREPARATION:

I. Cut A into 1½-inch pieces; mix with B, C, D, E, and let stand 1 hour.
II. Mix A–E with F.
III. Mix G, H and place in dish.
IV. Arrange A–F mixture on top of G–H mixture.

COOKING:

1. Steam A–H in steamer over boiling water 1 hour.

STEAMED SPARERIBS WITH SALTED BLACK BEANS
Dow Si Pai Gwut: Canton

A. 2 tablespoons peanut oil
B. 2 tablespoons salted black beans
C. 1 clove garlic, minced
D. 1 lb. spareribs

E. 1 teaspoon sherry
F. 1 teaspoon sugar
G. 1 tablespoon light soy sauce

PREPARATION:

I. Cut D into 1-inch pieces.

COOKING:

1. Heat A in skillet until hot.
2. Add B, C, fry 1 minute.
3. Add D, E, F, G. Mix well; place on platter

suitable for steaming.
4. Steam 30 minutes.
5. Serve hot.

FRIED SPARERIBS
Jien Pai Gwut: Canton

A. peanut oil for deep frying
B. 1½ lbs. spareribs
C. 1 tablespoon chopped scallion

D. 2 slices ginger, chopped
E. 1 tablespoon light soy sauce
F. ¼ teaspoon salt

G. 1 teaspoon sherry
H. 1 egg white
I. 2½ tablespoons cornstarch

PREPARATION:

I. Cut B into bite-size pieces. Cook 10 minutes in boiling water, drain, and save stock for other uses.
II. Mix C, D, E, F, G. Let B stand in mixture 15 minutes, turning several times so that

meat is well mixed and soaks up most of sauce.
III. Beat H, add I, and make a smooth paste. Pour over B, mix well.

COOKING:

1. Heat A to 325°. Deep-fry marinated B 2 minutes. Drain on paper towels.
2. Serve with oyster sauce, or sweet and sour sauce.

SPARERIBS WITH FROZEN BEAN CURD
Pai Gwut Shiu Dung Dow Fu: Adapted

A. 1 lb. spareribs
B. 2 slices ginger
C. 2 tablespoons light soy sauce
D. 1 tablespoon sherry

E. 1 tablespoon brown bean sauce
F. 1 teaspoon sugar
G. 1 cup boiling water
H. 4 cakes frozen bean curd

PREPARATION:

I. Cut A into 1-inch pieces.
II. Cut each H into 16 pieces.

COOKING:

1. Place A, B, C, D, E, F in saucepan. Add G, mix well.
2. Bring to boil, cook 2 minutes.
3. Lower heat, simmer 45 minutes.
4. Add H, cook 10 more minutes.

SPARERIBS WITH DRIED BEAN CURD
Pai Gwut Shiu Tiem Jook: Adapted

Substitute ¼ lb. (about 20 sheets) dried bean curd for H. In Step II, soak curd 30 minutes in hot water, drain, and cut each sheet into 5 or 6 pieces. In Step 4, cook 25 to 30 minutes.

SPARERIBS WITH CELLOPHANE NOODLES
Pai Gwut Shiu Fun See: Adapted

Substitute 1 oz. cellophane noodles for H. In Step II, soak noodles 30 minutes in hot water. In Step 4, cook 15 minutes.

BAKED SPARERIBS WITH HOISIN SAUCE
Hoisin Jiong Siu Pai Gwut: Canton

A. 1 to 2 lbs. spareribs
B. 1 clove garlic, minced
C. 2 tablespoons hoisin sauce
D. ½ teaspoon salt

E. 2 tablespoons light soy sauce
F. 1 tablespoon sherry
G. 2 tablespoons water

PREPARATION:

I. Mix B, C, D, E, F, G.
II. Marinate A in B–G mixture a few hours (or overnight).

III. Line shallow pan with aluminum foil, spread ribs in pan, cover with another single layer of aluminum foil.

COOKING:

1. Bake in 375° oven one hour.

2. Serve hot or cold.

SWEET AND PUNGENT SPARERIBS
Tiem Shwin Pai Gwut: Canton

A. 2 lbs. spareribs
B. 1 tablespoon light soy sauce
C. 1 tablespoon sherry
D. 1 teaspoon cornstarch
E. peanut oil for deep frying
F. 2 tablespoons peanut oil
G. 1 green pepper

H. 1 large tomato
I. 8-oz. can pineapple chunks, with juice
J. 3 tablespoons sugar
K. 3 tablespoons vinegar
L. 1 tablespoon light soy sauce
M. 2 teaspoons cornstarch

PREPARATION:

I. Cut A into 1½-inch pieces; cook 10 minutes with just enough water to cover; salt to taste; drain.
II. Mix B, C, D.

III. Add A, let stand 1 hour.
IV. Cut G into small pieces.
V. Cut H into 8 wedges.
VI. Mix I, J, K, L, M and set aside in bowl.

COOKING:

1. Deep-fry A–D mixture in E until golden brown; drain.
2. Heat F; stir-fry G 1 minute.
3. Add H, stir-fry 1 minute.

4. Add A, I–M and stir well; cook until mixture thickens.
5. Serve hot with rice.

SWEET AND SOUR SPARERIBS
Tang Tsu Pai Gu: Shanghai

A. 2 to 3 cups peanut oil
B. 1 to 2 lbs. spareribs
C. 1 tablespoon sherry
D. 3 tablespoons sugar
E. 3 tablespoons vinegar

F. 3 tablespoons catsup
G. 1 tablespoon light soy sauce
H. 1 teaspoon cornstarch mixed with
   ¼ cup water
I. 2 teaspoons light soy sauce

PREPARATION:

I. Cut B into 1½-inch pieces, mix with C, I.

II. Mix D, E, F, G, H thoroughly.

COOKING:

1. Heat A to 325°, deep fry B pieces until golden brown (about 2 to 3 minutes or until ribs are done).

2. Pour off excess A, leave B in pot.
3. Add C–H mixture, bring to boil, cook over low heat 3 to 5 minutes.

SWEET AND SOUR PINEAPPLE SPARERIBS
Tien Swan Bo Lo Pai Gu: Peking

A. 2 cups peanut oil
B. 1 to 1½ lbs. spareribs
C. 2 cloves garlic
D. 1 red-hot pepper
E. 2 small green peppers
F. ½ teaspoon salt
G. 1 cup pineapple chunks

H. 2 tablespoons brown sugar
I. 3 tablespoons vinegar
J. 2 tablespoons light soy sauce
K. ½ cup G pineapple juice
L. 1 tablespoon cornstarch
M. ½ teaspoon salt
N. ⅓ cup cornstarch

PREPARATION:

I. Cut each B into 1½-inch pieces, cover with boiling water and cook 5 minutes; drain, dry with paper towel, mix with M and coat with N.

II. Pound C with side of cleaver, discard skin.
III. Wash D, E, discard stems and seeds, cut into cubes.

COOKING:

1. Heat A to 325°, deep fry B until golden brown (about 2 minutes), arrange on platter.
2. Leave 1 tablespoon A in pan, add C and brown.

3. Add D, E, stir-fry 1 minute, add F.
4. Add G, mix well and place around B.
5. Mix H, I, J, K, L, stir over heat until thickened. Pour over B and serve.

SPARERIBS WITH SZECHUAN SAUCE
Yu Shiang Pai Gu: Szechuan

A. 1 tablespoon peanut oil
B. 1 lb. spareribs
C. 1 tablespoon brown bean sauce
D. 2 teaspoons light soy sauce
E. 1 tablespoon sherry
F. 2 teaspoons vinegar

G. 1 teaspoon sugar
H. 1 tablespoon chopped scallion
I. 1 teaspoon chopped ginger
J. 1 tablespoon light soy sauce
K. 1 clove garlic, minced
L. 1 teaspoon cornstarch

PREPARATION:

I. Cut B into 1½-inch pieces, mix with J, K, L.

II. Mix C, D, E, F, G, H, I for sauce.

COOKING:

1. Heat A, stir-fry B 1 to 2 minutes.
2. Add 1 cup water, bring to boil 1 minute, lower heat, and simmer 45 minutes or until B is tender.
3. Add C–I, turn up heat and stir well 1 minute or until gravy is almost gone.

BITTER MELON SPARERIBS
Fu Gwa Mun Pai Gwut: Canton

A. 2 cups peanut oil
B. ½ lb. spareribs
C. 2 tablespoons cornstarch
D. 2 cloves garlic, chopped
E. 1 tablespoon fermented salted black beans
F. 1 medium bitter melon
G. ½ teaspoon baking soda
H. 1 tablespoon light soy sauce
I. 1 tablespoon sherry
J. 1 teaspoon sugar
K. 1 teaspoon salt
L. ½ cup water
M. 2 teaspoons cornstarch mixed with 2 tablespoons water

PREPARATION:

I. Cut B into 1- to 2-inch pieces; coat each with C.
II. Cut F into halves, discard seeds and pods; cut diagonally into slices ½-inch thick.
III. Place F, G in 3 cups boiling water, let cook 1 minute; drain. Place in cold water 15 minutes; drain. Mix H, I, J, K, L.

COOKING:

1. Heat A to 325°, add B–C, deep fry 1 minute. Remove from oil onto dish.
2. Drain A from pot, leaving 1 tablespoonful. Heat remaining A, add D, E and stir-fry a few seconds.
3. Add B and F, continue stirring ½ minute longer.
4. Add H–L. Stir well. Cover and simmer 15 to 20 minutes or until meat is tender.
5. Thicken with M.

STEAMED PORK BALLS
Tsen Ro Jiu: General

A. ¾ lb. ground pork
B. ½ teaspoon salt
C. 1 slice ginger, minced
D. 3 scallions, sliced
E. 2½ tablespoons peanut oil
F. 4 dried black mushrooms
G. 6 water chestnuts
H. 1½ tablespoons sherry
I. 1 teaspoon sugar
J. 2 tablespoons light soy sauce
K. 2 teaspoons cornstarch
L. 1 teaspoon heavy soy sauce
M. 2 egg yolks, beaten

PREPARATION:

I. Soak F in warm water 15 minutes. Drain, chop fine.
II. Chop G.
III. In large bowl, mix all ingredients except M.
IV. Form into meatballs about 1 inch in diameter. Brush top of each with small quantity of M.
V. Set each on serving platter suitable for steaming.

COOKING:

1. Place platter of meatballs in steamer and steam 30 minutes.
2. Remove and serve with dish of light soy sauce.

PORK BALLS WITH GLUTINOUS RICE (Pearl Balls) I
Tsen Tsu Ro Chiu: Hupeh

A. 1½ cups glutinous rice
B. 2 eggs
C. 1 lb. ground pork

D. 1 teaspoon salt
E. 1 teaspoon sugar
F. 2 tablespoons light soy sauce

G. 3 scallions, sliced
H. 2 teaspoons cornstarch
I. 3 slices ginger, minced
J. 1 tablespoon sherry

PREPARATION:

I. Wash A. Parboil in boiling water 5 minutes. Drain.
II. Beat B slightly.
III. Mix B, C, D, E, F, G, I, J.
IV. Spread A on large plate.

V. Divide B–J mixture into small balls about 1¼ inch in diameter.
VI. Roll each over A so that A adheres to and coats it completely.
VII. Set meatballs on serving platter suitable for steaming.

COOKING:

1. Place platter of meatballs in steamer and steam 1 hour.

2. Remove platter and serve on trivet.

PORK BALLS WITH GLUTINOUS RICE (Pearl Balls) II
Tsen Tsu Ro Chiu: Hupeh

A. 1 cup glutinous rice
B. ½ lb. ground pork
C. 6 dry shrimp

D. 1 tablespoon light soy sauce
E. ½ teaspoon sugar
F. ½ teaspoon cornstarch

G. 1 egg
H. ¼ teaspoon salt

PREPARATION:

I. Wash A and soak in cold water 25 minutes. Drain.
II. Wash and soak C in hot water 15 minutes; chop fine.

III. Mix B, C, D, E, F, G, H.
IV. Take 1 teaspoonful B–H mixture and roll into ball; roll over A until well covered. Repeat until all of B–H is used.

COOKING:

1. Arrange meatballs on a plate and steam about one hour.

2. After steaming, the rice should have a pearl-like appearance.
3. Serve hot or cold.

PEARL MEATBALLS   Approved Ulcer Recipe
Tsen Tsu Ro Jiu: Hupeh

Omit C.

MEATBALLS WITH VEGETABLES
Ju Yoke Yuan Ju Shiu Tsoi: Adapted

A. ¼ cup vegetable oil
B. ½ lb. ground pork
C. 1 egg
D. 7 water chestnuts, chopped (or 4 tablespoons bread crumbs)
E. 2 teaspoons sherry

F. ½ cup chicken broth
G. 6 dried mushrooms
H. 3 slices fresh ginger
I. ¾ lb. Chinese celery cabbage
J. 2 tablespoons minced scallions
K. salt to taste

PREPARATION:

I. Mix B, C, D, E. Make spoon-size balls.

II. Soak G in hot water 20 minutes. Drain, saving water. Remove stems; shred.

III. Cut I into 2-inch pieces.

COOKING:

1. Heat A in deep frying pan, add B–E mixture. Stir-fry 1 to 2 minutes.

2. Add F, G, H, simmer covered 10 to 15 minutes.

3. Add I, J. Cook 5 minutes covered. Add K. Serve hot.

SHRIMP MEATBALLS WITH VEGETABLES
Har Yoke Yuan Ju Bok Tsoi: Canton

Substitute mixture of ¼ lb. ground pork and ¼ lb. ground shrimp for B.

SCALLOP MEATBALLS WITH VEGETABLES
Kong Yu Chi Ju Bok Tsoi: Canton

Substitute mixture of ¼ lb. ground pork and ¼ lb. ground scallops for B; add ¼ teaspoon ginger juice.

MEATBALL PUFFS WITH SWEET AND PUNGENT SAUCE
Tien Swan Ro Jiu: Shanghai

A. ½ lb. pork tenderloin
B. ¼ cup glutinous rice flour
C. 2 cups peanut oil for deep frying
D. 1 large green pepper
E. 1 cup pineapple chunks
F. 3 tablespoons vinegar
G. 1½ tablespoons sugar
H. 3 tablespoons catsup
I. 2 teaspoons cornstarch
J. ½ cup E pineapple juice
K. 2 teaspoons light soy sauce
L. 2 teaspoons sherry
M. ¼ teaspoon ground anise pepper
N. ¼ cup flour
O. 1 teaspoon baking powder
P. dash salt
Q. 5 tablespoons water

PREPARATION:

I. Cut A into cubes, steam over boiling water 5 minutes, drain. Mix with K, L, M and marinate 15 minutes.

II. Mix B and N, O, P, Q, stir into a batter.

III. Wash D, discard seeds and stem, cut into cubes.

IV. Mix F, G, H, I, J.

COOKING:

1. Dip A mixture into B batter and deep fry at 350° until golden brown (about 2 to 3 minutes); drain on paper towel.

2. Heat 1 tablespoon C, add D, stir-fry 15 seconds, add dash of salt.

3. Add E, F–J, stir until thickened.

4. Add A mixture, stir well and serve with rice.

PORK WITH PRESERVED KOHLRABI
Tsu Ro Si Tza Tsai: Szechuan

A. 3 tablespoons peanut oil
B. ½ lb. shredded pork
C. 2 teaspoons cornstarch
D. 2 slices ginger
E. 1 tablespoon chopped scallion
F. 1 teaspoon light soy sauce
G. ½ cup shredded preserved kohlrabi
H. 1 cup shredded bamboo shoots
I. 1 teaspoon sugar
J. ¼ teaspoon salt

PREPARATION:

I. Chop D fine.   II. Mix B, C, D, E, F well.   III. Combine I, J.   IV. Rinse and clean G.

COOKING:

1. Heat A and B–F mixture. Stir-fry about 3 minutes.
2. Put G, H into same pan. Stir-fry 1 minute.
3. Add I, J to cooked mixture. Mix well and serve.

PORK ROLLS ON SPINACH
Ro Guen Bo Tsai: Peking

A. ½ cup vegetable oil
B. 6 eggs
C. 2 scallions
D. 3 slices ginger
E. 1 lb. ground pork
F. 2 teaspoons sherry
G. ½ teaspoon salt
H. dash black pepper
I. 2 teaspoons cornstarch
J. ½ teaspoon salt
K. 1 qt. soup stock
L. 10-oz. package spinach
M. ½ teaspoon salt

PREPARATION:

I. Mince C, D; mix with E, F, G, H, I.

II. Break B into bowl, add J, beat mixture slightly.

COOKING:

1. Put 2 tablespoons A in 8-inch nonstick skillet, heat and spread; using low heat, add a cooking ladle of B, J mixture to form a skin about 8 inches in diameter. Make 6 such skins.
2. Take C–I mixture and divide into 6 equal portions; put 1 portion onto each egg skin and roll 6 pork rolls.
3. Using medium heat, fry rolls in remaining A, turning to ensure even cooking. Add ½ cup K, cover and simmer 10 minutes; remove from skillet and allow to cool.
4. Place rest of K in skillet; bring to boil, add L, M. Be sure that L is completely covered. Scoop out L, drain; place in shallow bowl.
5. Slice rolls diagonally ¼ inch thick, place neatly over L.

FRIED PORK MEAT CAKES
Jien Tsu Ro Bing: General

A. 1 cup peanut oil
B. 1 lb. ground pork
C. 3 water chestnuts
D. 1 egg
E. 3 scallions, sliced
F. 1 slice ginger, minced
G. ½ teaspoon salt
H. 4½ teaspoons cornstarch
I. 1 tablespoon light soy sauce
J. ¼ teaspoon garlic powder

PREPARATION:

I. Place B in mixing bowl.

II. Chop C fine.

III. Mix C, D, E, F, G, H, I, J and add to B. Combine thoroughly.

IV. Form mixture into patties, each containing a heaping tablespoon of ingredients.

COOKING:

1. Heat A in skillet to 375°.

2. Add patties and cook until golden brown (about 10 minutes). Turn repeatedly so that they are well done.

3. Serve with duck sauce or light soy sauce.

PORK STUFFED PEPPERS
La Jiu Yiang Ju Yoke: Canton

A. 3 tablespoons peanut oil
B. 6 to 8 small green peppers
C. 1 lb. ground pork
D. 1 tablespoon chopped scallion
E. 2 slices ginger, chopped
F. 1 egg

G. 1 teaspoon salt
H. 1 teaspoon cornstarch
I. 1 teaspoon sherry
J. 2 tablespoons light soy sauce
K. 1 teaspoon sugar
L. ½ cup chicken broth

PREPARATION:

I. Make a hole on top of each B; scoop out and discard seeds, and stems.

II. Beat F slightly.

III. Combine and mix C, D, E, F, G, H, I and 1 tablespoon J.

IV. Stuff B with C–J mixture.

COOKING:

1. Heat A. Add B stuffed with C–J, stir-fry 1 minute.

2. Add K, L and remaining J.

3. Remove to saucepan, bring to boil.

4. Simmer 30 to 45 minutes.

STEAMED CHINESE SAUSAGE WITH RICE
Shang Tsong Fan: General

A. 2 cups cooked rice
B. 2 Chinese pork sausages

C. 4 teaspoons light soy sauce
D. 1 teaspoon heavy soy sauce

PREPARATION:

I. Slice B into thin slivers.

II. Mix C, D.

COOKING:

1. Place A in serving bowl suitable for use in steamer. Steam 15 minutes. Remove.

2. Distribute B evenly over A. Replace in steamer and steam 15 minutes over high heat, steam an additional 15 minutes over reduced heat.

3. Remove from steamer; add C–D; mix all ingredients well. Serve.

STEAMED CHINESE PORK SAUSAGE WITH MINCED PORK AND WATER CHESTNUTS
Lap Tsong Tsing Ju Yoke: Canton

A. ½ lb. ground pork
B. 9 water chestnuts, chopped
C. 1 teaspoon cornstarch
D. 2 tablespoons water
E. 3 drops sesame oil (optional)

F. 1 tablespoon light soy sauce
G. ½ teaspoon sugar
H. ½ teaspoon salt
I. 1 Chinese pork sausage, minced

PREPARATION:

I. Mix A, B, C, D, E, F, G, H well.

COOKING:

1. Flatten A–H in a flat serving dish suitable for steaming.
2. Sprinkle I on top.
3. Place dish in steaming utensil and steam 25 minutes.
4. Remove from steaming utensil. Serve.

PEKING SMOKE ROLL
Chuen Jien: Peking

A. 1 teaspoon peanut oil
B. 3 eggs
C. 2 teaspoons cornstarch mixed with 2 tablespoons water
D. ½ teaspoon salt
E. ½ lb. ground pork
F. 1 egg white

G. 1 tablespoon chopped scallion (white only)
H. ½ teaspoon chopped ginger
I. 1 teaspoon light soy sauce
J. ⅛ teaspoon five spices powder
K. ½ teaspoon salt
L. sesame oil, as needed

PREPARATION:

I. Mix E, F, G, H, I, J, K well.

II. Beat B, add C, D, mix thoroughly (makes about 1 cup mixture).

COOKING:

1. Grease bottom of 10-inch frying pan with A.
2. Heat over medium heat, add ¼ cup B–D; tip pan so that egg mixture covers it evenly; when skin is done (about 1 to 2 minutes), skin will slide off the pan. Make 4 egg skins; add more oil to frying pan if necessary.
3. When skins cool completely, place ¼ of E–K mixture on each, fold skin, and make into a 5-inch roll.
4. Place rolls on round cake rack and steam over boiling water 8 to 10 minutes.
*5. Smoke rolls over sawdust for 5 to 10 minutes, brush L on rolls, slice each into 4 or 5 pieces and serve.

* Fire should burn in grill until only red coals (charcoal) remain. Cover coals with ashes. Sprinkle sawdust on coals so that it smokes but does not catch fire. If a flame appears extinguish it with a few drops of water. If not enough smoke is produced, add more sawdust. Place rolls on a wire rack and hold rack over smoke. If a charcoal grill is used, place aluminum foil so that it hangs down from hood, thereby cutting out air and allowing more concentrated smoking.

SEARED PORK LIVER
Sun Pien Tsao Tsu Gahn: General

A. 6 tablespoons peanut oil
B. ½ lb. pork liver
C. 1 teaspoon cornstarch
D. 1 teaspoon sherry
E. ⅛ teaspoon pepper
F. ½ teaspoon salt
G. ½ cup sliced bamboo shoots
H. 1 scallion, chopped

I. 3 slices ginger, shredded
J. 1 tablespoon light soy sauce
K. 1 clove garlic, chopped
L. 2 teaspoons sherry
M. 1 teaspoon sugar
N. 2 teaspoons cornstarch
O. several drops sesame oil (optional)

PREPARATION:

I. Wash and clean B, remove any white veins and spots, slice B into long, thin pieces.

II. Mix B, C, D, E, F, thoroughly.
III. Mix J, K, L, M, N.

COOKING:

1. Heat A, stir-fry B–F 1 minute. Remove to a plate, leaving 2 tablespoons A in pan.
2. Stir G, H, I in same pan 1 minute.

3. Return cooked B–F to pan, add J–N, and stir 1 to 2 more minutes. Add O.

PORK LIVER WITH PEAS AND CLOUD EARS
Ning Er Tsao Tsu Gahn: General

Substitute 1 cup frozen peas and 2 tablespoons cloud ears for G. Wash cloud ears and soak in hot water 15 minutes (or until soft) ; discard water, and wash thoroughly.

STIR-FRIED PORK LIVER
Tsao Tsu Gahn: Shanghai

A. 1 tablespoon peanut oil
B. 2 scallions
C. 1 cup sliced bamboo shoots
D. 4 to 6 Chinese mushrooms
E. ¼ cup peanut oil
F. ½ lb. pork liver

G. 1 tablespoon light soy sauce
H. 2 teaspoons sherry
I. 1½ teaspoons cornstarch
J. ½ teaspoon sugar
K. ¼ teaspoon salt (or to taste)
L. dash pepper

PREPARATION:

I. Wash and clean F, remove any white veins and spots, cut into slices about ⅛ inch thick, dip in boiling water 30 seconds, drain.

II. Mix F with G, H, I, J, K, L.

III. Cut B into 1½-inch pieces (white part only).
IV. Wash D and soak in warm water 15 minutes or until soft, drain; discard stems, cut each into 3 or 4 pieces.

COOKING:

1. Heat A; add B, C, D, stir-fry ½ minute, remove to dish.
2. Heat E until smoking, add F–L, stir-fry 1 minute, return B–D, mix well, and serve.
Note: When stir-frying liver, the oil has to be very hot. As a safety measure, either turn off heat when adding liver (turning heat on again right away), or cover frying pan as soon as liver is added, and shake pan over heat.

PORK LIVER WITH ONIONS
Yong Tsung Ju Gohn: Canton

A. 6 tablespoons peanut oil
B. ½ lb. pork liver
C. 1 teaspoon sherry
D. 1 teaspoon cornstarch
E. ⅛ teaspoon pepper
F. ½ teaspoon salt

G. ½ lb. onions
H. 1 clove garlic, chopped
I. 1 tablespoon light soy sauce
J. 2 teaspoons sherry
K. 1 teaspoon sugar
L. 2 teaspoons cornstarch

PREPARATION:

I. Wash and clean B, remove any white veins and spots, slice B into long, thin pieces.
II. Mix B, C, D, E, F thoroughly.

III. Slice each G ⅛-inch thick.
IV. Mix H, I, J, K, L.

COOKING:

1. Heat A, stir-fry B–F 1 minute. Remove to dish, leaving 2 tablespoons A in pan.
2. Stir-fry G 2 minutes.

3. Return cooked A–F mixture to pan, add H–L mixture, and cook 1 to 2 more minutes.

YU SIANG KIDNEY
Yu Siang Yao Hwa: Szechuan

A. ¼ cup peanut oil
B. 4 pork kidneys
C. 1 teaspoon salt
D. ½ cup shredded bamboo shoots
E. 4 Chinese mushrooms
F. 1 tablespoon chopped scallions
G. 1 teaspoon chopped ginger
H. 1 clove garlic, minced
I. 2 teaspoons light soy sauce

J. 3 teaspoons brown bean sauce
K. 2 teaspoons sherry
L. 1 teaspoon sugar
M. ½ teaspoon salt
N. 2 teaspoons cornstarch mixed with ⅓ cup water
O. 2 teaspoons vinegar
P. Chinese hot sauce to taste (optional)
Q. 2 to 3 tablespoons cornstarch

PREPARATION:

I. Wash and remove any outer membranes of B. Split lengthwise and with sharp scissors remove all the white veins; make tiny crisscross patterns on top, then cut each B into 8 to 10 slices.
II. Rub with C, squeeze out any blood and rinse thoroughly with water. Drain. Add B to 1 qt. boiling water. Cook 1 minute. Drain. Dry between paper towels.

III. Mix B with 1 teaspoon K, dash salt and pepper.
IV. Place Q in paper bag, add B mixture and shake until B pieces are coated with Q.
V. Wash D and soak in water 15 minutes; drain and shred.
VI. Mix I, J, K, L, M, N, O.

COOKING:

1. Heat A until smoking, then lower heat, add B, stir-fry 1 minute, remove to dish.
2. Heat excess oil in same pan, add D, E, F, G, H, stir-fry 1 minute.
3. Add I–O, stir in B until all is mixed and gravy has thickened. Add P if desired.

STIR-FRIED KIDNEY
Tsao Yao Hwa: Shanghai

A. 4 tablespoons peanut oil
B. 1 cup sliced bamboo shoots
C. 2 tablespoons dried cloud ears
D. 1 to 2 cloves garlic
E. 2 pairs pork kidneys
F. 1 teaspoon salt
G. 2 teaspoons light soy sauce

H. 2 teaspoons sherry
I. ½ teaspoon salt
J. 1 teaspoon sugar
K. 1 teaspoon cornstarch
L. ½ teaspoon sesame oil
M. dash pepper
N. 2 scallions

PREPARATION:

I. Split E lengthwise, wash, remove all white veins and any outer membranes; make tiny crisscross patterns on top of E, then cut each into 6 to 8 slices. Rub with F, squeeze out any blood; rinse thoroughly with water, drain.

II. Dip E in boiling water ½ minute, drain dry between paper towels.

III. Mix E with G, H, I, J, K, L, M.

IV. Cover C with hot water 30 minutes, discard water, and wash and clean C thoroughly. Then slice each into several pieces.

V. Using white part of N only, cut into 1- to 1½-inch pieces.

VI. Pound D with side of cleaver, discard skin.

COOKING:

1. Heat 1 tablespoon A, add B, C, N, stir-fry ½ to 1 minute, remove to dish.

2. Heat rest of A to smoking. Add D, stir once or twice, add E–M, stir-fry 1 minute.

3. Add B, C, N, mix well; serve hot.

STIR-FRIED KIDNEY WITH WALNUTS
Heh Tao Yao Hwa: Peking

A. 2 cups peanut oil
B. 4 pork kidneys
C. ½ to 1 cup shelled walnuts
D. 1 teaspoon salt

E. 1 egg
F. ½ teaspoon salt
G. dash pepper
H. 2 tablespoons cornstarch

PREPARATION:

I. Split B lengthwise, wash, remove all white veins and any outer membranes. Make tiny crisscross patterns on top of B, then cut each into 8 to 10 slices.

II. Rub with D, squeeze out any blood; rinse thoroughly with water, drain.

III. Add B to 1 qt. boiling water, cook 1 minute, drain and dry between paper towels.

IV. Beat E, mix thoroughly with F, G, H.

V. Add B to E–H and coat each piece well.

VI. Pour boiling water over C, let soak 1 to 2 minutes, peel off skins to avoid bitter taste, and dry completely before frying.

COOKING:

1. Heat A to 375°, deep fry prepared B until golden brown, drain on paper towel.

2. Deep fry C until golden brown (about ½ to 1 minute) in 325° oil; do not burn by over-frying.

3. Mix fried B and C. May be served with Szechuan ground pepper.

KIDNEY IN PEANUT BUTTER SAUCE
Hwa Sun Jiang Yaw Pien: Szechuan

A. 3 slices ginger
B. 1 scallion
C. 2 tablespoons sherry
D. 2 pairs pork kidneys
E. 2 cups shredded iceberg lettuce hearts
F. 1 tablespoon sesame sauce from Chinese grocery
G. 2 tablespoons peanut butter

H. 1 teaspoon Chinese hot sauce or to taste
I. 1 tablespoon light soy sauce
J. 1½ teaspoons sugar
K. 3 teaspoons salt
L. 1 tablespoon vinegar
M. 1 teaspoon sesame oil
N. 3 tablespoons water

PREPARATION:

I. Split D lengthwise, wash, remove any white veins and outer membranes; rub with 1 teaspoon K, rinse with water; cover with cold water and soak 1 to 2 hours; drain, slice into thin pieces, rub with 1 to 1½ teaspoons K, rinse well and drain.

II. Mix F, G, H, I, J, L, M, N and steam over boiling water 5 minutes to soften into paste.

COOKING:

1. Add A, B, C to 1 qt. boiling water; boil 2 minutes.
2. Add D slices, continue stirring. When water boils, turn off heat and drain.

3. Arrange E on a plate, spread D on top.
4. Pour F–N over D and serve.

RED-COOKED PORK STOMACH
Hung Sao Tsu Du: Adapted

A. 1 pork stomach
B. 4 tablespoons light soy sauce
C. 2 tablespoons heavy soy sauce
D. ⅛ teaspoon five spices powder

E. 2 teaspoons sugar
F. 1 scallion
G. 2 slices ginger
H. ½ cup water

PREPARATION:

I. If A is not ready to cook, wash well with 3 tablespoons salt and ½ cup vinegar; rinse with hot water; repeat 2 or 3 times until clean.

COOKING:

1. Put A in pot, add B, C, D, E, F, G, H. Bring to boil.
2. Lower heat, simmer 2½ hours. Add more water if necessary.

3. Slice into bite-size pieces. Serve hot or cold with Chinese hot sauce (optional).

GINGER PIGS' FEET
Siu Ju Gyok: Canton

A. 1 to 2 lbs. pigs' feet
B. 1 clove garlic
C. 1 chunk ginger, ¾ inch long
D. 3 tablespoons wine vinegar

E. 2 tablespoons sugar
F. ⅓ cup light soy sauce
G. 1½ cups boiling water

PREPARATION:

I. Wash A and cover with water. Bring to boil and cook 1 minute. Discard water and wash A again.

II. Pound B, C with back of cleaver. Discard B skin.

COOKING:

1. Put all ingredients together in cleaned pot. Bring to boil, turn heat down and simmer 2½ hours or until tender. Add more boiling water as needed. Serve. Add gravy on rice.

RED-COOKED PIGS' FEET
Hung Shiu Ju Giok: Adapted

A. 2 to 2½ lbs. pigs' feet cut as below
B. 1 scallion (tied in a knot)
C. 1 clove garlic
D. 1 slice ginger, ½ inch thick
E. ¼ cup light soy sauce

F. 2 tablespoons sherry
G. 1 teaspoon sugar
H. 2 cups chicken broth mixed with ½ cup water
I. 1 square red bean curd cheese (optional)

PREPARATION:

I. Have butcher cut A into 1½-inch pieces.
II. Pound C with side of cleaver, discard skin.

III. Wash D and pound with side of cleaver.
IV. Break up I.

COOKING:

1. Combine A, B, C, D, E, F, G, H in pot, bring to boil, stir well; lower heat and cook 1 hour.
2. Add I, stir well and cook over low heat 1 hour longer.

3. Serve with rice or noodles and plenty of gravy.

PICKLED PIGS' FEET
Ba Wun Ju Sow: Canton

A. 2 lbs. pigs' feet
B. 1 cup sugar

C. 2 cups distilled vinegar
D. 2 tablespoons salt

PREPARATION:

I. Cut each A in half.

II. Mix B, C, D, place in saucepan and bring to boil. Cool. When cold, pour into jar.

COOKING:

1. Put A in pot, cover with water and boil 1½ hours.
2. Rinse in cold water and then soak in ice water (enough cold water to cover A, plus a tray of ice cubes) 3 hours. Change ice water once.
3. Dry with paper towels.
4. Put cooked cold A in B–D jar. Cover, refrigerate 2 days. Serve.

HOT PICKLED PIGS' FEET
Shwin La Ju Giok: Canton

In Step II, add to B–D 4 pieces dried red-hot pepper, 1 clove garlic, 3 slices ginger.

JELLIED PIGS' KNUCKLES
Dung Tee: General

A.   2 pigs' knuckles (1½ lbs.)
B.   2½ cups water
C.   1 chunk ginger, ¾ inch long
D.   2 tablespoons sherry
E.   ½ cup light soy sauce
F.   1 tablespoon rock sugar

PREPARATION:

I.   Cover A with cold water, bring to boil; continue boiling several minutes. Discard water, rinse A and pot under cold water.

II.   Peel C skin; pound with back of cleaver.

COOKING:

1.   Cover A with B, bring to boil.
2.   Add C, D, cook 30 minutes. Scoop froth off top, discard.
3.   Add E, F, lower heat, simmer 2 hours. During this time, turn A over every 30 minutes.

Remove A from pot, saving gravy (there should be about 1 cup gravy left).
4.   Bone A, chop very fine. Remove fat from gravy and add gravy to meat, mix well.
5.   Pour into loaf pan, refrigerate until jelled. Slice and serve.

RED-COOKED PORK TONGUE
Hung Sao Tsu Suh: General

A.   2 pork tongues (about 1 lb.)
B.   1 tablespoon whiskey
C.   1 star anise
D.   ½ teaspoon anise pepper
E.   3 teaspoons sauterne
F.   2 tablespoons light soy sauce
G.   1 tablespoon heavy soy sauce
H.   2 teaspoons sugar
I.   ¼ cup water

PREPARATION:

I.   Place A in cold water and clean. Drain; place in pot; add boiling water to cover. Bring to boil, add B, boil 5 to 7 minutes. Drain and let it stay in cold water 1 minute. Slice off white skin. Wash and drain.

COOKING:

1.   Place prepared A in pot, add C, D, E, F, G, H, I, bring to boil, lower heat and simmer 45 minutes.
2.   Turn A over and simmer another 45 minutes, adding water if necessary.
3.   Chill, slice, and serve.

BRAISED PORK TONGUE WITH BAMBOO SHOOTS
Tsu Suh Sao Sun Pien: General

A.   1 pork tongue (about ½ lb.)
B.   1 tablespoon whiskey
C.   2 tablespoons peanut oil
D.   1 cup sliced bamboo shoots
E.   3 slices ginger
F.   1 scallion
G.   1 tablespoon sherry
H.   1 teaspoon sugar
I.   2 tablespoons light soy sauce
J.   ¼ cup tongue stock

PREPARATION:

I. Place A in cold water and clean. Drain; place in pot; add boiling water to cover. Bring to boil, add B, boil 5 to 7 minutes. Drain and

let stay in cold water 1 minute. Slice off white skin. Wash and drain.

II. Set aside J.

COOKING:

1. Cover prepared A with water, bring to boil, lower heat and simmer 1 to 1¼ hours. Remove A from pot and cut into thin slices. Serve soup.

2. Heat C, add sliced A, and D, E, F, G, H, I, stir well.

3. Add J, mix well, cover and cook over low heat 25 to 30 minutes. Serve hot.

SWEET AND SOUR BRAISED PORK TAIL
Tiem Shwin Ju Mei: Canton

A. 1 lb. pork tail
B. 2 tablespoons light soy sauce
C. 2 tablespoons vinegar
D. 1 tablespoon brown sugar
E. 1 clove garlic, minced

F. 4 slices ginger, slivered
G. 1 tablespoon sherry
H. 1 tablespoon chopped scallion
I. ⅔ cup water

PREPARATION:

I. Wash A well, cut into 1-inch pieces.

COOKING:

1. Combine all ingredients in cooking pot, bring to boil.

2. Reduce heat, simmer 30 minutes or until A is tender.

RED-COOKED FRESH HAM I
Hung Sao Bing Tang Ti Pong: Shanghai

A. ½ cup heavy soy sauce
B. 2 tablespoons sherry
C. 1 star anise

D. 1 tablespoon rock sugar
E. 2½ lbs. fresh ham
F. salt to taste

PREPARATION:

I. Clean and wash E thoroughly.

COOKING:

1. Bring 3 cups water in cooking pan to boil.
2. Add A, B, C, D. Keep boiling.
3. Add E, bring back to boil and cook in bubbling A–D sauce 5 to 10 minutes; lower heat and simmer 2 hours (or until E is tender).

4. Turn E over 2 or 3 times during cooking so that it will absorb A–D sauce evenly. Add boiling water if necessary.
5. Add F, if necessary, after first hour of cooking.

RED-COOKED FRESH HAM II
Nam Yu Ju Gyok: Canton

A. 4 tablespoons peanut oil
B. 1 scallion
C. 2 slices ginger
D. 1 clove garlic
E. 2½ lbs. fresh ham
F. ½ cup light soy sauce
G. 2 teaspoons sugar
H. 1 tablespoon sherry
I. 1 square red bean curd cheese

PREPARATION:

I. Cut B into 1-inch pieces.
II. Pound D with back of cleaver, remove skin.
III. Mix F, G, H, I well.

COOKING:

1. Heat A in saucepan. Stir-fry B, C, D a few seconds.
2. Add E, F–I mixture, and brown a few minutes.
3. Add 2 to 3 cups water, bring to boil. Lower heat, simmer 2 hours.

COOKED HAM IN FRIED RICE
Ho Twei Tsao Fan: General

A. 2 eggs
B. 5 tablespoons peanut or vegetable oil
C. 1 clove garlic, diced
D. ¼ cup diced onion
E. 1 cup diced cooked ham
F. 1 cup frozen peas
G. 4 cups cold cooked rice
H. 2 tablespoons light soy sauce

PREPARATION:

I. Run hot water over F 1 minute, drain.

COOKING:

1. Scramble A in 2 tablespoons B. Remove from pan.
2. Heat remaining B in same pan, stir-fry C, D ½ minute.
3. Add E, stir-fry 1 minute.
4. Add F, G, H. Stir 2 minutes.
5. Add A and mix well, serve hot.

FRIED FRESH HAM
Go Sao Ti Pong: Peking

A. 2 lbs. fresh ham
B. 1 tablespoon chopped scallion
C. 1 teaspoon chopped ginger
D. 1 clove garlic, chopped
E. 1 tablespoon light soy sauce
F. 1 egg
G. 1 tablespoon cornstarch
H. 1 qt. vegetable oil
I. anise pepper salt for dipping (see Index)

PREPARATION AND COOKING:

I. Cover A with boiling water, simmer 1 hour; remove to dish, save water for soup.
II. Mix B, C, D, E and rub over A.
III. Steam over boiling water until meat is tender (about 1 hour); remove A from juice and remove bone, if any.
IV. Mix F, G well and dip A in mixture.
V. Deep fry in H at 350° until A is golden brown (about 5 to 10 minutes).
VI. Cut into 2½-inch by 1-inch strips; serve with I.

SPICED FRESH PICNIC HAM
Hung Sao Wu Siang Ro: General

A.   2 tablespoons peanut oil
B.   2½-lb. fresh picnic ham (shank half)
C.   2 tablespoons heavy soy sauce
D.   ½ star anise
E.   ½ teaspoon anise pepper

F.   1 teaspoon sugar
G.   1 scallion
H.   4 slices ginger
I.   1 cup water (or meat broth)
J.   salt to taste

COOKING:

1. Heat A in 3-qt. saucepan. Brown all sides of B.
2. Add C, D, E, F, G, H, turn B in this mixture a few times.

3. Add I, bring to boil; lower heat, simmer until B is tender (about 2 hours). During this time, turn B over 2 or 3 times so that it will absorb juice evenly. Add water or broth if needed. Adjust with J.

SPICED FRESH PICNIC HAM WITH HARD-COOKED EGGS
Hung Sao Wu Siang Dan: General

During last hour of simmering in Step 3, add to B 6 to 10 peeled, hard-cooked eggs in which several 1½-inch slashes have been made around the middle portions. The eggs may be served as hors d'oeuvres.

HOT SPICED FRESH HAM
Swan La Ti Pong: Szechuan

A.   3 tablespoons peanut oil
B.   3 slices ginger
C.   1 or 2 cloves garlic
D.   1 or 2 red-hot peppers
E.   2 green peppers
F.   2½-lb. fresh ham, with skin (or ½ ham)
G.   ¼ cup light soy sauce

H.   1 teaspoon salt
I.   1 cup chicken soup
J.   1 scallion (white part only), chopped
K.   3 tablespoons sugar
L.   ¼ cup vinegar
M.   2 teaspoons cornstarch mixed with ¼ cup water

PREPARATION:

I.   Place F in 2 qts. boiling water, bring back to boil, lower heat and simmer 1½ hours or until skin is tender. Remove from pot and cool.
II. Bone cooked F and cut into ½-inch pieces with skin on.

III. Cut each B into 4 pieces.
IV. Pound C with side of cleaver, discard skin and chop.
V.   Wash D, E, split open, discard seeds and cut into cubes.
VI. Mix J, K, L, M.

COOKING:

1. Heat A to smoking, add B, C, stir-fry ½ to 1 minute.
2. Add D, E, stir-fry ½ minute, then remove to dish.
3. Heat excess oil, stir-fry F pieces, add G, H,

stir 2 to 3 minutes longer.
4. Add I, bring to boil, cover and cook 3 to 5 minutes.
5. Return B–E mixture, mix well.
6. Thicken with J–M; serve hot.

FRESH HAM WITH SPINACH
Bo Tsai Ti Pong: Shanghai

A. ½ cup light soy sauce
B. 2 tablespoons sherry
C. 1 star anise
D. 1 tablespoon rock sugar
E. 2½ lbs. fresh ham

F. salt to taste
G. 1½ lbs. spinach, washed
H. 2 teaspoons cornstarch mixed with ⅓ cup water

PREPARATION:

COOKING:

1. Bring 3 cups of water to boil in medium-sized pan.
2. Add A, B, C, D, and continue boiling 2 to 3 minutes.
3. Add E, bring back to boil and cook in bubbling sauce for 5 to 10 minutes; lower heat and simmer 2 hours or until E is tender.
4. Turn E over 2 or 3 times during cooking

I. Clean and wash E thoroughly.

so that meat will absorb sauce evenly; add boiling water if necessary.
5. Add F after first hour of cooking.
6. Bring 2 to 3 qts. of water and 1 tablespoon salt to boil in another pot.
7. Add G and turn off heat.
8. Drain immediately.
9. Arrange G in dish and place E on top.
10. Thicken meat gravy with H. Pour over meat and serve.

HAM STEAMED WITH WINTER MELON
Ho Twei Tsen Dung Gwa: General

A. 1-lb. slice winter melon
B. ½ lb. cooked Virginia ham

C. 2 slices ginger, minced
D. 2 scallions, minced

E. Chinese parsley (optional)

PREPARATION:

I. Cut A into sections 1¼ inches long by 1¼ inches thick. Remove skin. Make slit in back of each section but do not cut through.

II. Slice B thin and cut into 1-inch strips. Slip B strips into slits in A pieces. Place on deep platter and sprinkle with C, D, E.

COOKING:

1. Steam prepared A for at least 20 minutes or until melon becomes translucent. Serve hot.

STEAMED LITCHI HAM
Tsing La-ee-tzee Fo Twei: Canton

A. 2 lbs. Smithfield ham
B. 2 tablespoons sugar

C. 2 tablespoons cornstarch
D. 20-oz. can litchis

PREPARATION:

I. Remove dark crust, and exterior fat from A; wash and clean A.

II. Cover A with water and boil 10 to 15 minutes to remove saltiness; drain.

COOKING:

1. Place A in bowl; spread B over A; steam 30 minutes or until large bone is loosened.

2. Mix C with D; cook until sauce has thickened; pour over A and serve.

VIRGINIA HAM WITH CHICKEN BREASTS
Ring Twei Gee Pien: Peking

A. 3 tablespoons peanut oil
B. 1 lb. chicken breasts
C. 3 Chinese mushrooms
D. 1 oz. Virginia ham
E. ½ cup diced bamboo shoots
F. 2 scallions
G. 3 slices ginger, chopped

H. dash pepper
I. 1 teaspoon sugar
J. salt to taste
K. 2 egg whites
L. 2 tablespoons cornstarch
M. 2 teaspoons sherry

PREPARATION:

I. Soak C in hot water 15 minutes. Drain, reserving water. Remove and discard stems; cut C into 3 pieces each.

II. Bone and slice B into pieces 2 by 2 by ⅛ inches.

III. Mix K, L, M with some C soak water; coat B with mixture.

IV. Cut D about size of B. Cut E similarly.

COOKING:

1. Heat A in frying pan; add prepared B, stir-fry 1 minute, add C, D, E, F, G, stir-fry 1 more minute. Then add H, I and C water so that meat does not scorch. Adjust with J.

GOLDEN HAM ROLLS
Ho Twei Don Chuen: Hupeh

A. ¼ cup vegetable oil
B. 8 eggs
C. ½ lb. lean pork, minced
D. ½ lb. ham, minced
E. 3 slices ginger, minced
F. 2 scallions, minced

G. dash pepper
H. 1½ teaspoons cornstarch
I. 2 teaspoons sherry
J. 1 lb. celery cabbage
K. 1 qt. soup stock
L. 1 teaspoon salt

PREPARATION:

I. Cut J, separating stems from leaves, shred stems, and cut leaves into 1½-inch squares; keep separate.

II. Mix C, D, E, F with G, H, I and stems of J.

III. Break B into bowl, add ½ of L; beat mixture slightly.

COOKING:

1. Put 2 tablespoons A in 8-inch nonstick skillet, heat and spread, using low heat; add a cooking ladle of B mixture to form a skin about 8 inches in diameter. Make 8 such skins.

2. Divide C–J into 8 equal portions; put 1 portion onto each egg skin and roll 8 ham rolls.

3. Using medium heat, fry rolls in remaining A, turning to ensure even cooking.

4. Add ½ cup K, cover and simmer 10 minutes. Remove from skillet and allow to cool.

5. Place rest of K in skillet; bring to boil, add saved J leaves and rest of L; bring to boil again 1 minute, or until J is just done. Spoon out pieces of J and drain; place in shallow bowl.

6. Slice B–I diagonally in pieces ¼ inch thick; place neatly over J. (B–I pieces should be golden-edged, with pink centers set over light green J base.)

BEEF WITH BITTER MELON AND SALTED BLACK BEANS
Fu Gwa Gno Yoke Do Si Jiong: Canton

A. 2 tablespoons peanut oil
B. 2 tablespoons salted black beans
C. 2 cloves garlic, minced
D. ½ lb. beef
E. 1 teaspoon cornstarch
F. 1 teaspoon light soy sauce
G. 2 teaspoons sherry
H. ¼ teaspoon sugar

I. ¼ teaspoon peanut oil
J. ¼ teaspoon salt
K. 1 bitter melon
L. 1 teaspoon light soy sauce
M. ½ teaspoon sugar
N. 2 scallions, sliced
O. 1 teaspoon cornstarch
P. 1 cup soup stock

PREPARATION:

I. Slice D into thin, bite-size pieces. Mix E, F, G, H, I, J and marinate D in E–J 15 minutes.
II. Wash K, cut in half lengthwise and discard seeds and pods. Cut K into 1/16-inch slices and parboil 3½ minutes with ½ teaspoon baking soda. Drain, rinse well; discard water.
III. Wash B and mash.
IV. Mix B, C. Set aside.
V. Mix O, P. Set aside. Stir well before using.
VI. Mix L, M, N. Set aside.

COOKING:

1. Put A in very hot skillet and bring to high heat.
2. Add B–C mixture. Stir-fry rapidly 15 seconds to brown C.
3. Add D and E–J. Stir-fry until D is browned slightly.
4. Add K, stir-fry 2 minutes and add L–N; stir-fry well 2 minutes longer.
5. Add O, P slowly. Stir-fry until sauce thickens and coats all ingredients well.

BEEF WITH NOODLES AND BROWN BEAN SAUCE
Jiang Bao Niu Ro Mein: Shanghai

A. 1 lb. fresh noodles
B. 4 tablespoons peanut oil
C. 2 tablespoons yellow (or brown) bean sauce
D. 1 clove garlic, minced
E. ½ teaspoon salt
F. 1 slice ginger, minced
G. 1 lb. thinly sliced flank steak

H. 1½ tablespoons hoisin sauce
I. ½ teaspoon sugar
J. 1 tablespoon heavy soy sauce
K. ¼ teaspoon salt
L. 5 dried black mushrooms
M. ¾ cup water

PREPARATION:

I. Soak L in warm water 15 minutes; drain and slice thin.
II. Mash C to a paste.
III. Mix C, D, E, F. Set aside.
IV. Mix G, H, I, J, K. Set aside 15 minutes.

COOKING:

1. Boil A 3 to 4 minutes. Drain.
2. Put B in very hot skillet and bring to high heat.
3. Add C–F and stir-fry rapidly 15 seconds to brown garlic slightly.
4. Add G–K and sliced L. Stir-fry well, until beef is fully done (2 minutes).
5. Add M. Cover and cook 5 minutes over medium heat.
6. Pour very hot tap water over A to heat. Drain well.
7. Place A in serving dish and pour meat sauce over noodles.

STIR-FRIED BEEF WITH SAUCE
Tsao Niu Ro: General

A. 2 tablespoons peanut oil
B. 1 clove garlic, minced
C. ½ slice fresh ginger, minced
D. ¼ teaspoon salt
E. ½ lb. flank steak
F. 1 teaspoon light soy sauce
G. 1 teaspoon sugar

H. 2 tablespoons sherry or gin
I. 1 tablespoon water
J. 1 tablespoon cornstarch
K. 1 tablespoon heavy soy sauce
L. 1 cup soup stock
M. 2 scallions, sliced

PREPARATION:

I. Slice E very thin.
II. Mix B, C, D. Set aside.
III. Mix F, G, H. Set aside.
IV. Mix I, J, K, L. Set aside. Stir well before using.

COOKING:

1. Put A in very hot skillet and bring to high heat.
2. Add B–D. Stir-fry rapidly 15 seconds to brown B slightly.
3. Add E. Stir-fry 1 minute.
4. Add F–H and stir-fry 1 minute.
5. Add I–L slowly. Stir-fry until sauce thickens and coats all ingredients well. Do not cover.
6. Serve, garnished with M.

STIR-FRIED BEEF WITH BLACK MUSHROOMS
Niu Ro Dung Gu: General

Add 8 black mushrooms soaked in warm water for 15 minutes; drain, slice; add before Step 4.

STIR-FRIED BEEF WITH GREEN PEPPERS
Ching Jiao Tsao Niu Ro: Canton

Parboil 2 cups thinly sliced green peppers, with seeds removed, in water for 3 minutes; rinse in cold water; drain; add before Step 4.

STIR-FRIED BEEF WITH TOMATOES
Niu Ro Tsao Fan Chieh: General

Omit L; add 2 cups tomatoes (sliced diagonally into eighths) before Step 4.

STIR-FRIED BEEF WITH BEAN SPROUTS
Niu Ro Ya Tsai: General

Add 4 cups bean sprouts before Step 4.

STIR-FRIED BEEF WITH MUSTARD GREENS
Niu Ro Gai Lan: General

Add 2 cups mustard greens before Step 4.

STIR-FRIED BEEF WITH SNOW PEAS
Niu Ro Sheh Do: General

Add 1½ cups pea pods before Step 4.

STIR-FRIED BEEF WITH GREEN PEAS
Niu Ro Ching Do: General

Add 1 cup peas, fresh or frozen, before Step 4.

STIR-FRIED BEEF WITH CAULIFLOWER
Niu Ro Hwa Tsai: General

Parboil 2 cups cauliflower in water for 3 minutes; add before Step 4.

STIR-FRIED BEEF WITH OYSTER SAUCE
Ho Yow Tsao Ngo Yoke: Canton

Add 2 tablespoons oyster sauce and M to F–H mixture in Step 4.

STIR-FRIED BEEF WITH ONIONS
Niu Ro Yang Tsung: General

Add 2 cups sliced onions before Step 3.

STIR-FRIED BEEF WITH BAMBOO SHOOTS
Niu Ro Dung Sun: General

Add 1 cup finely sliced bamboo shoots before Step 4.

RED-COOKED BEEF WITH CELLOPHANE NOODLES
Hung Sao Ngo Yoke Fun See: Canton

A. 4 lbs. beef shin (including bone)
B. 6 tablespoons light soy sauce
C. ¼ cup sherry
D. 5 slices ginger, minced
E. 1 cup water
F. water to cover ⅓ of meat
G. 2 oz. cellophane noodles

PREPARATION:

I. Precook G by soaking in hot water 20 minutes.
II. Mix B, C, D, E. Set aside.

COOKING:

1. Place A in heavy cooking utensil with cover.
2. Add B–E mixture. Cook over high heat 10 minutes. Stir.
3. Add F. Bring to boil. Turn heat to low and cook until tender (about 2½ hours). Stir occasionally to prevent sticking.
4. Add G. Simmer 10 minutes. Serve.

RED-COOKED SHANK OF BEEF
Hung Sao Niu Ro: General

A. 2 tablespoons peanut oil
B. 2-lb. shank of beef
C. 1 scallion
D. 3 slices ginger
E. 2 cloves garlic

F. ⅓ cup light soy sauce
G. 1 teaspoon sugar
H. 1 tablespoon sherry
I. salt, pepper to taste
J. water to cover B

PREPARATION:

I. Cut B into bite-size pieces.
II. Cut C into 1-inch pieces.

III. Pound E with side of cleaver, remove skin.

COOKING:

1. Heat A in saucepan. Stir-fry B, C, D, E 1 minute.
2. Add F, G, H, I, stir well.
3. Add J. Bring to boil, lower heat, and simmer until tender (about 2 to 3 hours.) Add more boiling water if necessary.

COLD CUT SHANK OF BEEF
Hung Sao Niu Ro: General

Place whole, uncut B in saucepan, cook with other ingredients until done. Then cool, slice thin, and serve cold.

RED-COOKED SHANK OF BEEF WITH CARROTS
Hung Lo Bo Hung Sao Niu Ro: General

Wash and peel 1 bunch carrots. Cut into bite-size pieces. In Step 3, after B has cooked 2½ hours, add carrots, cook another 30 minutes. Serve with gravy on rice.

RED-COOKED SHANK OF BEEF WITH POTATOES
Yang Yu Hung Sao Niu Ro: General

Substitute 1 lb. potatoes for carrots immediately above. Peel potatoes, cut into bite-size pieces, and cook 15 minutes.

STEAMED BEEF
Fun Tsen Niu Ro: Szechuan

A. 1 lb. beef tenderloin
B. 1½ tablespoons light soy sauce
C. 1 tablespoon brown bean sauce
D. 1 teaspoon sugar
E. 1 tablespoon sherry

F. 1 teaspoon sesame oil
G. 1 teaspoon chopped ginger
H. ½ teaspoon salt
I. 2 tablespoons water
J. ⅓ cup rice flour

PREPARATION:

I. Slice A against the grain into thin pieces, mix with B, C, D, E, F, G, H, I and marinate 30 minutes.
II. Mix A–I well with J in dish.

COOKING:

1. Steam in steamer over boiling water 30 to 45 minutes or until beef is tender and soft. Serve hot.

STEAMED BEEF WITH PUMPKIN
Nan Gwa Niu Ro: Szechuan

Add 1½ cups peeled, sliced pumpkin in 1½- by ¾-inch pieces, mixed with ½ teaspoon salt and 2 teaspoons butter or margarine. Arrange pumpkin pieces in dish and place A–J mixture on top of pumpkin. In Step 1, steam in steamer 30 to 45 minutes or until pumpkin is soft.

STEAMED BEEF WITH SWEET POTATO
Fun Tsen Tien Sao Niu Ro: Szechuan

Add 2 sweet potatoes (about ½ to 1 lb.), peeled and cut into bite-size pieces. Mix with ½ teaspoon salt and 2 teaspoons margarine, arrange on dish and place A–J mixture on top of sweet potato.

BROILED STEAK, MANDARIN STYLE
Sao Niu Pa: Peking

A. 2 cloves garlic
B. 6 slices ginger
C. 2 scallions
D. 3 tablespoons light soy sauce

E. 1 tablespoon sugar
F. 1 teaspoon peanut oil
G. salt, pepper to taste
H. 1 flank or sirloin steak

PREPARATION:

I. Chop A, B, C very fine.
II. Combine A, B, C, D, E, F, G, mix well.

III. Marinate H in sauce mixture half a day.
IV. Preheat broiler.

COOKING:

1. Broil H 5 to 8 minutes on each side.

STEAK KEW
Ngo Pa Kew: Canton

A. 3 tablespoons peanut oil
B. 8 to 10 Chinese mushrooms
C. ½ lb. filet mignon or other steak (if less expensive cut is used, sprinkle with ¼ teaspoon meat tenderizer and let stand for 5 minutes before cutting)
D. 1 clove garlic, chopped
E. 2 slices ginger, shredded

F. 1 tablespoon chopped scallion
G. 1 tablespoon oyster sauce
H. 1 tablespoon light soy sauce
I. ½ teaspoon sugar
J. 2 teaspoons cornstarch
K. ¼ lb. snow peas
L. ½ teaspoon salt

PREPARATION:

I. Cut C into 1-inch cubes; mix with D, E, F, G, H, I, J; marinate 15 to 30 minutes.
II. Rinse B; cover with warm water and soak for 15 minutes or until soft. Drain and quarter.

III. Remove and discard tips of K; wash and drain.
IV. Add K to 1 quart of boiling water, stir well. When water boils again, remove from heat, drain, and run cold water over pea pods.

COOKING:

1. Heat A, add B, stir-fry ½ to 1 minute.
2. Add C–J, stir-fry 1 to 2 minutes.
3. Add K, mix well.
4. Stir in L.
5. Pour onto dish and serve hot.

STEAK WITH ONIONS
Yang Tsung Niu Ro: General

A.   3 tablespoons peanut oil
B.   1 medium onion, sliced
C.   1 clove garlic, minced
D.   3 slices ginger, minced

E.   1 teaspoon salt
F.   1 tablespoon light soy sauce
G.   ½ lb. flank steak
H.   2 teaspoons cornstarch

PREPARATION:

I. Slice G into thin, bite-size pieces.   II. Mix B, C, D, E.   III. Mix F, G, H.

COOKING:

1. Put A in very hot skillet and bring to high heat.
2. Add B–F and stir-fry until onions are tender.

3. Add F–H. Stir-fry until brown on outside but slightly rare inside. Serve.

BROILED STEAK WITH PEPPER
Kow Ngo Pai: Adapted

A.   1 to 1½ lbs. boneless top sirloin steak
B.   1 clove garlic, chopped
C.   4 slices ginger, chopped
D.   2 scallions (white part only), chopped
E.   3 tablespoons light soy sauce
F.   2 teaspoons sugar

G.   1 teaspoon peanut oil
H.   2 teaspoons peanut oil
I.   1 to 2 green peppers
J.   dash salt
K.   ¼ teaspoon meat tenderizer

PREPARATION:

I. Sprinkle K on A; rub in.
II. Mix B, C, D, E, F, G. Pour over A, marinate 2 to 3 hours.

III. Line pan with aluminum foil, place A on foil.
IV. Cut I diagonally in ½-inch slices. Discard seeds.

COOKING:

1. Place marinated A 1 inch below broiler, broil 5 to 7 minutes each side, remove to dish.
2. Heat H, add I, stir-fry ½ to 1 minute, add J

and mix with juice of A.
3. Cut A into 8 to 10 pieces, place around plate with I in middle.

PINEAPPLE STEAK
Bo Lo Niu Ro: General

A.   3 tablespoons peanut oil
B.   ½ lb. beefsteak
C.   1 teaspoon peanut oil
D.   2 teaspoons cornstarch
E.   1 tablespoon light soy sauce
F.   ½ teaspoon sugar

G.   6 slices ginger, shredded
H.   1 scallion
I.   2 8¼-oz. cans sliced pineapple
J.   1 tablespoon sherry
K.   salt to taste
L.   12 toasted almonds

PREPARATION:

I. Cut B into thin slices; mix well with C, D, E, F.

II. Cut H into 1½-inch pieces.
III. Drain I and cut each ring into 6 pieces.

COOKING:

1. Heat A; add B–F and G, H; stir-fry 1 to 1½ minutes.

2. Add I, J; stir well.
3. Add K; garnish with L and serve.

PAPER-WRAPPED STEAK
Tze Bao Ngo Pa: Canton

A. 1 lb. sirloin or porterhouse steak
B. 6 scallions
C. 2 cups peanut oil
D. ½ slice ginger, minced
E. 3 tablespoons light soy sauce
F. 1 teaspoon heavy soy sauce

G. 1 teaspoon duck sauce
H. 1 teaspoon salt
I. 1 teaspoon sugar
J. ¼ teaspoon garlic powder
K. 1 tablespoon gin

PREPARATION:

I. Slice A into 1-inch cubes; place in bowl.
II. Mix D, E, F, G, H, I, J, K and pour over A

in bowl; mix well; set aside 30 minutes.
III. Cut B into thirds.

COOKING:

1. Wrap 2 or 3 pieces of A in aluminum foil with 2 or 3 sections of B.
2. Heat C to 370° and deep fry packages 5 to 7 minutes.

3. Serve hot in foil wrapping (to be unwrapped at table).

PEPPER STEAK
Ching Jao Tsao Niu Ro: General

A. 3 tablespoons peanut oil
B. 1 lb. flank steak
C. 2 green peppers
D. 2 tablespoons water
E. 1 tablespoon light soy sauce
F. 1 teaspoon oyster sauce

G. 1 tablespoon sherry
H. 2 teaspoons cornstarch
I. ½ teaspoon sugar
J. 1 scallion, chopped
K. 4 slices ginger, shredded

PREPARATION:

I. Cut B into narrow strips about 2 inches by ¼ inch, against the grain.
II. Cut C into strips. Discard seeds.

III. Mix B with E, F, G, H, I, J, K. Let stand 15 minutes.

COOKING:

1. Heat A in skillet until hot.
2. Add B and stir-fry 1 minute. Remove and set aside.

3. Using the same pan, add C and stir.
4. Add D, cover and simmer ½ minute.
5. Add E–K mixture, stir 1 minute and serve.

TOMATO SAUCE STEAK
Kieh Tsup Ngo Yoke: Canton

A. ¼ cup peanut oil
B. ½ lb. beefsteak, shredded
C. 1 onion
D. 1 cup peas
E. 2 teaspoons sherry
F. 3 tablespoons catsup
G. 1 teaspoon sugar

H. ½ teaspoon salt
I. ¼ to ½ teaspoon sesame oil, or to taste
J. 1 egg white
K. 2 teaspoons cornstarch
L. ½ teaspoon salt
M. ½ teaspoon sugar
N. 1 teaspoon peanut oil

PREPARATION:

I. Mix B with J, K, L, M, N.   II. Peel C and dice into ½-inch cubes.   III. Mix F, G, H, I.

COOKING:

1. Heat 3 tablespoons A, add prepared B, stir-fry 2 minutes, remove to dish.

2. Heat 1 tablespoon A, add C, D, stir-fry 1 minute, add E, stir well.

3. Return B and add F–I; mix well and serve.

FLANK STEAK WITH OYSTER SAUCE
Ho Yow Ngo Yoke: Canton

A. 2 tablespoons peanut oil
B. ½ lb. flank steak
C. 1 tablespoon oyster sauce
D. 1 tablespoon sherry
E. ½ teaspoon sugar
F. 1 clove garlic, minced

G. 2 teaspoons cornstarch
H. ½ slice ginger, minced
I. ½ teaspoon salt
J. 1½ teaspoons light soy sauce
K. 1 teaspoon heavy soy sauce
L. 2 scallions, sliced

PREPARATION:

I. Cut B into bite-size pieces ⅛ inch thick.
II. Mix C, D, E, F, G, H, I. Set aside.

III. Mix J, K. Set aside.

COOKING:

1. Put A in very hot skillet and bring to high heat.
2. Add B. Stir-fry until meat turns light gray color.

3. Add C–I and stir-fry until B is nearly done (center remains rare).
4. Add J, K. Stir well.
5. Serve with garnish of L.

GRILLED STEAK WITH OYSTER SAUCE
Ho Yow Shiu Ngo Pa: Canton

A. 2 lbs. steak
B. 1 to 2 cloves garlic

C. 1 tablespoon oyster sauce
D. 3 tablespoons light soy sauce

E. 1 teaspoon sherry

PREPARATION:

I. Preheat broiler.
II. Place A on aluminum foil.
III. Crush B with press or cleaver, remove skin, and mince.

IV. Mix B, C, D, E. Smear half on one side of A, using a fork to scratch surface. Repeat on other side.

COOKING:

1. Broil each side of A 6 to 7 minutes. For very thick steaks, broil each side 1 more minute.

If broiled in oven, remove oil accumulation to avoid flash fires.

GRILLED CHICKEN WITH OYSTER SAUCE
Ho Yow Shiu Gai: Canton

Substitute chicken for A, and add 2 tablespoons peanut oil to B–E in Step IV.

STEAK LO MEIN
Ngo Yoke Lo Mein: Canton

A. 4 tablespoons peanut oil
B. ½ lb. flank steak
C. 2 slices ginger, minced
D. 1 scallion, minced
E. 2 teaspoons cornstarch
F. ½ teaspoon sugar
G. 1 tablespoon light soy sauce

H. 1 large carrot, shredded
I. 2 stalks celery, shredded
J. 1½ cups bean sprouts
   (or shredded cabbage)
K. ½-lb. package thin spaghetti
L. 1 tablespoon light soy sauce
M. ½ teaspoon salt

PREPARATION:

I. Cook K as directed on package. Drain.
II. Slice B against the grain in thin pieces 2 inches long.

III. Shred H, I.
IV. Mix B, C, D, E, F, G.
V. Mix L, M.

COOKING:

1. Heat A in frying pan. Stir in B–G mixture, stir-fry 1 to 2 minutes. Remove from pan.
2. Put H, I in same pan. Stir and add ¼ cup water, lower heat and cover. Cook 2 minutes.
3. Add J, stir a few seconds. (If cabbage is used, add in Step 2 with H, I.)
4. Add cooked K. Stir well and cook 2 minutes.
5. Add L, M and B mixture. Mix well and serve.

YU SIANG STEAK
Yu Siang Niu Ro Si: Szechuan

A. 6 tablespoons peanut oil
B. 1-lb. flank steak
C. 6 stalks asparagus, chopped
D. 1 scallion, chopped
E. 2 slices ginger, chopped
F. 1 clove garlic, minced
G. 4 teaspoons light soy sauce
H. 2 teaspoons brown bean sauce
I. ½ teaspoon salt

J. 1½ tablespoons sherry
K. 4 teaspoons vinegar
L. 2 teaspoons sugar
M. 1½ tablespoons cornstarch mixed with
   ¼ cup water
N. ¼ teaspoon meat tenderizer
O. 1 tablespoon light soy sauce
P. 2 teaspoons cornstarch
Q. Chinese hot sauce (optional)

PREPARATION:

I. Slice B across grain, 3/16-inch thick, sprinkle on N and mix well; let stand at room temperature ½ hour, then mix with O, P and 2 teaspoons A.
II. Bring 1 quart water to boil, add C and parboil 2 or 3 minutes, drain.
III. Mix G, H, I, J, K, L, M.

COOKING:

1. Heat remaining A, add prepared B, stir-fry 1 to 2 minutes; remove to dish and pour excess oil back.
2. Add C, D, E, F, stir-fry 1 minute.
3. Return prepared B to pan, stir-fry 1 minute.
4. Add G–M mixture, stir until thickened.
5. Add Q to taste; serve hot.

STIR-FRIED STEAK WITH GREEN PEPPERS AND TOMATOES
Jiao Cheh Niu Ro: General

A. 3 tablespoons peanut oil
B. 1 clove garlic
C. 1 scallion, white part only, chopped
D. 4 slices ginger
E. ¼ teaspoon salt
F. ½ lb. flank steak
G. 2 medium tomatoes
H. 2 medium green peppers

I. 1 medium onion
J. ½ teaspoon sugar
K. 2 teaspoons sherry
L. 2 teaspoons light soy sauce
M. ⅛ teaspoon black pepper
N. ¼ cup bouillon
O. 1 tablespoon cornstarch

PREPARATION:

I. Slice F into strips ⅛ inch by 1½ inches.
II. Cut each G into 10 wedges. Slice each H diagonally after discarding seeds.
III. Peel I, cut in half, slice thin.
IV. Pound B with back of cleaver, discard skin; then chop.
V. Slice D into long, thin pieces.
VI. Mix J, K, L, M, N.
VII. Mix O with 2 tablespoons cold water.

COOKING:

1. Heat A. Add B, C, D, E, stir-fry a few seconds.
2. Add F slices, stir-fry 1 minute.
3. Add G–I, stir-fry 1 more minute.
4 Add J–N. Keep stirring until all ingredients are well mixed.
5. Add O, stir until gravy thickens. Serve hot with rice.

STIR-FRIED STEAK WITH CARROTS, PEAS, MUSHROOMS, AND PEPPERS
Niu Ro Tsao Ching Tsai: General

A. 3 tablespoons peanut oil
B. ½ lb. flank steak
C. ½ teaspoon sugar
D. 2 teaspoons sherry
E. 2 teaspoons light soy sauce
F. 1 carrot, diced

G. 1 cup frozen peas
H. 1 green pepper, diced
I. ¼ cup canned sliced mushrooms
J. salt, pepper to taste
K. 3 teaspoons cornstarch

PREPARATION:

I. Slice B into pieces ⅛ inch by 1½ inches.
II. Mix B thoroughly with C, D, E, and 1 teaspoon K.
III. Parboil F 2 minutes.
IV. Defrost G.
V. Drain I. Save I water, and mix with remaining K.

COOKING:

1. Heat A. Add B–E, stir-fry 1 minute. Remove to dish, pouring excess oil back into pan.
2. Add F, G, H, I, stir-fry 2 minutes. Add J.
3. Return B–E mixture to pan, mix well. Stir 1 minute. Thicken with I water and K mixture.

BEAN SAUCE STEAK WITH PUMPKIN
Fun Tsen Nan Gwa Niu Ro: Szechuan

A. 1 lb. beef flank steak
B. 1½ tablespoons light soy sauce
C. 1 tablespoon brown bean sauce
D. 1 teaspoon sugar
E. 1 tablespoon sherry
F. 1 teaspoon sesame oil
G. 1 teaspoon chopped ginger

H. ½ teaspoon salt
I. 2 tablespoons water
J. ⅓ cup rice flour
K. 1 pumpkin
L. ½ teaspoon salt
M. 2 teaspoons butter or margarine

PREPARATION:

I. Slice A against the grain into thin pieces, mix with B, E, F, G, H, I and marinate 30 minutes.

II. Mix A–I well with J in a dish.

III. Peel K and discard skin; cut K into 1½- by ¾-inch slices until 1½ cups are obtained; mix with L and M.

IV. Arrange K pieces in a dish.

V. Place A mixture on top of pumpkin.

COOKING:

Steam in steamer 30 to 45 minutes or until K is soft.

PAPER-WRAPPED BEEF
Tze Bao Niu Ro: Szechuan

A. ½ lb. beef tenderloin or steak
B. 4 slices ginger, chopped
C. 2 tablespoons oyster sauce

D. ¼ cup Cream of Rice
E. Chinese hot sauce to taste

PREPARATION:

I. Slice A into small pieces.

II. Mix B, C, D, E, add A, and marinate 30 minutes.

III. Divide mixture into several portions. Wrap each in waxed paper (shaped like small envelope).

COOKING:

1. Steam 30 to 45 minutes over hot water. Serve.

PAPER-WRAPPED BEEF   *Approved Diabetic Recipe*
Tze Bao Niu Ro: Szechuan

A. ¼ lb. steak
B. 2 teaspoons oyster sauce
C. ½ teaspoon chopped pickled or fresh ginger

D. ½ teaspoon salt
E. Chinese hot sauce to taste
F. 2 tablespoons rice flour or Cream of Rice

PREPARATION:

I. Slice A into small pieces.

II. Mix all ingredients and marinate ½ hour.

III. Divide into 4 portions. Wrap each in waxed paper (shaped like small envelope).

COOKING:

Steam over boiling water 45 minutes. Serve.

BEEF WITH GINGER
Jiang Sih Niu Ro: General

A. 2 tablespoons peanut oil
B. 1½ cloves garlic, mashed
C. 1 lb. flank steak
D. 2 tablespoons peanut oil
E. ½ cup thin slices fresh ginger root
F. 1 tablespoon salt
G. 2 tablespoons light soy sauce

H. 1 teaspoon rice wine or
   1 tablespoon sherry
I. 2 teaspoons sugar
J. 2 teaspoons cornstarch
K. ⅔ cup soup stock
L. 2 teaspoons heavy soy sauce
M. 4 scallions, sliced

PREPARATION:

I. Slice C into thin, bite-size pieces.
II. Mix E and F. Stir well. Let mixture stand 15 minutes. Wash ginger thoroughly under cold water (to remove "hotness"). Drain. Set aside.
III. Mix G, H, I, J, K, L. Set aside. Stir well before using.

COOKING:

1. Put A in very hot skillet and bring to high heat.
2. Add B. Stir-fry rapidly 15 seconds to brown B slightly.
3. Add C. Stir-fry until nearly done—leaving center rare.
4. Remove B–C from skillet to another container. Set aside.
5. Add D and heat well.
6. Add E–F. Stir-fry 3 minutes.
7. Add G–L mixture and stir until sauce thickens.
8. Replace B–C and mix well to be sure sauce coats all ingredients well.
9. Garnish with M.

ROAST BEEF FRIED RICE
Niu Ro Tsao Fan: General

A. 2 eggs
B. 3 tablespoons peanut or vegetable oil
C. 1 clove garlic, diced
D. 1 small onion, diced
E. 1 cup diced roast beef

F. 1 cup frozen peas
G. 4 cups cold cooked rice
H. 2 tablespoons light soy sauce
I. Salt and pepper to taste

PREPARATION:

I. Pour hot water over F for 1 minute, drain.

COOKING:

1. Scramble A in 2 tablespoons B; set aside.
2. Heat remaining B in same pan, stir-fry C, D ½ minute.
3. Add E, stir-fry 1 minute.
4. Add F, G, H, I. Stir 2 minutes.
5. Add A and mix well, serve hot.

ROAST TURKEY OR CHICKEN FRIED RICE
Gee Si Tsao Fan: General

Substitute leftover roast turkey or chicken for E. In Step 4 add ¼ cup canned sliced mushrooms, drained.

BAKED CHUCK STEAK
Koiv Tsung Shiang Niu Ro: General

A. 1½- to 2-lb. chuck steak (center cut)
B. 2 medium onions
C. 4 to 6 carrots
D. 1 lb. potatoes

E. 1 tablespoon light soy sauce
F. 1½ tablespoons oyster sauce
G. 1½ tablespoons sauterne
H. 1 teaspoon sugar

PREPARATION:

I. Line a rectangular cake pan with a piece of aluminum foil. Place A on foil.
II. Peel B and cut into slices.
III. Peel C and cut into bite-size pieces.
IV. Peel D and cut each into 8 pieces.

V. Mix E, F, G, H and pour over A. Marinate 15 minutes, turning A over 2 or 3 times. Arrange B on top of A; place C, D around A. Cover the pan with another piece of foil.

COOKING:

1. Preheat oven to 350°. Bake 1 hour 45 minutes or until meat is tender. Remove foil during last 15 minutes. Serve.

CURRIED BEEF
Ja Li Niu Ro: General

A. 3 tablespoons peanut oil
B. 1 medium onion, chopped
C. 1 to 2 teaspoons curry powder
D. 1 lb. beef chuck

E. 2 cups water
F. 2 medium potatoes
G. 1 teaspoon salt
H. ½ teaspoon sugar

PREPARATION:

I. Cut D into bite-size pieces.

II. Cut F into bite-size pieces (cover with cold water until ready to cook).

COOKING:

1. Heat A, add B, stir-fry 1 minute.
2. Add C, mix well.
3. Add D, stir 1 to 2 minutes.

4. Add E, bring to boil. Lower heat, simmer until D is tender (1 to 2 hours).
5. Add F, G, H, mix well, and cook 15 more minutes.

CURRIED BEEF   *Approved Diabetic Recipe*
Ga Li Gno Yoke: Canton

A. 1 tablespoon peanut oil
B. 2 teaspoons chopped onion
C. 1 teaspoon curry powder
D. ½ lb. beef chuck

E. 1 cup water
F. 1 medium potato
G. ½ teaspoon salt

PREPARATION:

I. Cut D into bite-size pieces.

II. Peel F and cut into bite-size pieces.

COOKING:

1. Heat A, stir-fry B 1 minute.
2. Add C, mix well; add D and continue stirring 1 to 2 minutes.

3. Add E, bring to boil, lower heat and simmer until D is tender (1 to 2 hours).
4. Add F, G and cook 15 minutes. Add a bit of water, if necessary.

CURRIED LAMB   *Approved Diabetic Recipe*
Ga Li Yang Yoke: Canton

Substitute lamb for D.

CURRIED CHICKEN   *Approved Diabetic Recipe*
Ga Li Gai Yoke: Canton

Substitute ¼ chicken cut into bite-size pieces for D. In Step 3, cook only 30 minutes.

RED BEAN CURD CHEESE BEEF
Nam Yu Ngo Yoke: Canton

A. 1 lb. beef chuck
B. 2½ cups water
C. 1 tablespoon sherry
D. 2 slices ginger

E. 2 mashed tablespoons red bean curd cheese
F. 2 teaspoons light soy sauce
G. 1 teaspoon sugar

PREPARATION:

I. Cut A into bite-size pieces.

COOKING:

1. Place A in pot, cover with B, bring to boil. Skim fatty foam from top.
2. Add C, D, lower heat, cover and cook 45 minutes.

3. Add E, F, G, mix well, bring to boil again. Reduce heat, simmer 1 more hour. Serve with rice.

HOME-STYLE BEEF CONCENTRATE
Jia Shang Niu Ro Sung: General

A. 3 lbs. round steak
B. ½ teaspoon meat tenderizer
C. 1½ teaspoons sugar
D. 4 tablespoons sherry

E. 2 tablespoons light soy sauce
F. 1 qt. beef stock
G. 1 to 2 tablespoons vegetable oil

PREPARATION:

I. Remove bones, gristle, and fat from A; cut A across grain into ¼-inch-thick pieces.
II. Mix B with A thoroughly; allow mixture to stand at room temperature 30 to 60 minutes.

(If B is not used, cooking time must be doubled.)
III. Mix C, D, E with A in heavy 3-qt. saucepan.

COOKING:

1. Using high heat, cook A–E mixture, stirring constantly, ½ minute.
B. Add F, bring to boil, cover, lower heat and simmer 2 hours or until pieces of A disintegrate on stirring. If more than two cups of liquid remain, remove cover and allow liquid to boil off.

3. Add G, keep lid off, stir constantly over low heat to prevent scorching. Continue stirring over very low heat until all liquid is gone. When concentrate appears to be quite dry, it is done. Serve hot or cold, for sandwiches or in congee.

FRAGRANT GROUND CHUCK BALLS
Shang Ching Niu Ro Ruan: Shanghai

A. 3 tablespoons peanut oil
B. 1 clove garlic
C. ½ lb. ground chuck beef
D. salt to taste
E. 2 teaspoons light soy sauce
F. 2 teaspoons cornstarch
G. 1 egg

H. 1 tablespoon sherry
I. ½ teaspoon sugar
J. dash pepper
K. ¼ teaspoon vinegar
L. 1 lb. celery hearts with leaves
M. ½ cup chicken soup

PREPARATION:

I. Mash B with flat side of cleaver; discard skin.
II. Mix C thoroughly with D, E, F, G, H, I, J, K, roll into 10 meatballs.
III. Shred L; parboil in M 1 to 2 minutes; drain and set aside; save M.

COOKING:

1. Place A in frying pan, brown B, remove.
2. Add C–K to pan with A, brown 1 to 2 minutes.
3. Add L, M; cover and simmer 3 minutes or until meatballs are done.

STEAMED GROUND CHUCK WITH WATER CHESTNUTS
Ma Tie Ngo Yoke Bang: Canton

A. 1 cup water chestnuts, chopped
B. 1 scallion, chopped
C. 4 slices ginger, chopped
D. 1 lb. ground chuck
E. 1 tablespoon light soy sauce

F. 1 teaspoon sugar
G. 1 teaspoon salt
H. 1 teaspoon sesame oil
I. 1 tablespoon cornstarch

PREPARATION AND COOKING:

I. Mix all ingredients in dish and steam over boiling water 30 to 35 minutes.

SWEET AND SOUR MEATBALLS
Tien Swan Ro Jieu: General

A. 2 tablespoons peanut oil
B. 1 large onion, sliced
C. 1 green pepper
D. 2 tomatoes
E. ½ cup canned pineapple chunks
F. ½ cup sweet pickles
G. ½ cup pineapple juice
H. ¼ cup sweet pickle juice
I. 2 tablespoons vinegar
J. 2 tablespoons sugar
K. 1 tablespoon light soy sauce

L. 1 tablespoon cornstarch, dissolved in 3 tablespoons water
M. 2 slices ginger
N. 1 scallion
O. 1 lb. ground chuck
P. 1 egg
Q. 1 tablespoon light soy sauce
R. ½ teaspoon salt
S. ½ teaspoon sugar
T. 1 tablespoon cornstarch
U. salt to taste

PREPARATION:

I. Chop M, N very fine. Mix thoroughly with O, P, Q, R, S, T.

II. Make M–T into balls 1 inch in diameter. Brown in frying pan with 1 tablespoon A.

COOKING:

1. Heat 1 tablespoon A in frying pan. Stir-fry B 2 minutes. Add C–K mixture and bring to

Remove to bowl.

III. Cut C in 16 pieces. Cut D in 8 pieces. Mix C, D, E, F.

IV. Mix G, H, I, J, K; add C–F.

boil. Thicken with L.

2. Add M–T. Add U. Mix well and serve hot.

CHANG FAMILY BURGER
Ngo Yoke Bang: Adapted

A. 1 lb. ground chuck
B. 1 egg
C. 1½ tablespoons light soy sauce
D. 1 scallion, chopped
E. 2 slices ginger, chopped
F. ½ teaspoon salt
G. ½ teaspoon sugar

PREPARATION:

I. Mix all ingredients; make 8 to 10 hamburger patties.

COOKING:

1. Grease frying pan with peanut oil; cook as hamburgers.

CHANG FAMILY BURGER
Ngo Yoke Bang: Adapted

Add 10 dried shrimp, shredded very fine, to burger mix.

CHANG FAMILY BURGER WITH OYSTER SAUCE
Ho Yu Ngo Yoke Bang: Adapted

Substitute 1 tablespoon oyster sauce for C.

PEAS WITH GROUND BEEF
Niu Ro Ching Do: General

A. 2 tablespoons peanut oil
B. 1 tablespoon chopped scallion
C. 2 slices ginger, chopped
D. ½ lb. ground beef
E. 2 teaspoons cornstarch
F. 1 teaspoon sherry
G. 1 teaspoon light soy sauce
H. 1 pkg. frozen peas
I. 1 teaspoon salt

PREPARATION:

I. Defrost H and drain.

II. Mix D, E, F, G well.

COOKING:

1. Heat A in frying pan.
2. Add B, C, stir-fry several seconds.
3. Add D–G, stir-fry until it changes color

(about 2 to 3 minutes).

4. Add H, I. Stir thoroughly 1 minute. Serve hot.

BEEF STUFFED PEPPERS
La Jiu Yiang Ngo Yoke: Canton

A. 3 tablespoons peanut oil
B. 6 to 8 small green peppers
C. ½ lb. ground chuck
D. 1 tablespoon chopped scallion
E. 2 slices ginger, chopped
F. 1 egg

G. 1 teaspoon salt
H. 1 teaspoon cornstarch
I. 1 teaspoon sherry
J. 2 tablespoons light soy sauce
K. 1 teaspoon sugar
L. 1 cup chicken broth

PREPARATION:

I. Make a hole on top of each B; scoop out and discard seeds and stem.
II. Beat F slightly.

III. Mix C, D, E, F, G, H, I with 1 tablespoon J.
IV. Stuff B with C–J mixture.

COOKING:

1. Heat A. Add stuffed B–J, stir-fry 1 minute.
2. Add K, L and remaining J.

3. Remove to saucepan, bring to boil.
4. Simmer 25 to 30 minutes.

BEEF STEWED IN FRUIT SAUCE
Go Tsup Ngo Yoke: Canton

A. 3 tablespoons peanut oil
B. 2 lbs. stewing beef, cut in 1-inch cubes
C. 4 cloves garlic, minced
D. 2 teaspoons brown bean sauce
E. 1 slice ginger, minced
F. 1 tablespoon sugar
G. ½ cup sherry

H. ⅛ teaspoon cinnamon
I. 1 star anise
J. juice of 1 large orange
K. juice of 1 lemon
L. 1½ cups boiling water
M. 1½ teaspoons salt

PREPARATION:

I. Squeeze J. Set juice aside.

II. Mix C, D, E.

III. Mix F, G, H, I.

COOKING:

1. Put A in very hot skillet and bring to high heat.
2. Brown B with C–E.
3. Add F–I. Stir-fry 2 minutes.

4. Add J, K. Stir-fry 15 seconds.
5. Add L. Stir well.
6. Cover tightly. Simmer gently 2 to 3 hours until beef is very tender. Add M. Serve.

STEAMED BEEF WITH BEAN CURD
Niu Ro Tsen Dow Fu: General

A. ½ lb. beefsteak, shredded
B. 2 teaspoons light soy sauce
C. ¼ teaspoon ginger juice (see Index)
D. 1 teaspoon cornstarch
E. 4 cakes bean curd, cubed

F. 1 teaspoon light soy sauce
G. 1 teaspoon sherry
H. 1 tablespoon chopped scallion
I. 1 tablespoon cornstarch

PREPARATION:

    I. Mix B, C, D, marinate A in it 15 minutes.

    II. Mix E, F, G, H, place in dish.

    III. Mix I with 2 tablespoons water.

    IV. Spread A–D over E–H.

COOKING:

1. Steam A–H 15 minutes over boiling water.
2. Pour gravy into small saucepan, thicken with I mixture.
3. Return thickened gravy to main dish, add pepper to taste, serve with rice.

PRESSED BEAN CURD AND CELERY WITH STIR-FRIED BEEF
Dow Fu Gahn Ching Tsai Ro Si: Shanghai

A. 3 tablespoons peanut oil
B. ½ lb. beef (or lamb)
C. 1 clove garlic, chopped
D. 2 slices ginger, chopped
E. 1 tablespoon light soy sauce
F. 2 teaspoons sherry
G. 2 teaspoons cornstarch
H. 1 teaspoon peanut oil
I. 3 stalks celery
J. 2 cakes pressed bean curd
K. 1 teaspoon sugar
L. ½ teaspoon salt

PREPARATION:

    I. Slice B, then shred very thin.

    II. Mix B, C, D, E, F, G, H and marinate 20 to 30 minutes.

    III. Slice I diagonally 2½ by ¼ inches.

    IV. Slice J into thin pieces.

COOKING:

1. Heat A, add B–H, stir-fry 1 to 1½ minutes.
2. Remove to dish, pour excess A back into pan.
3. Reheat A, add I, J, stir-fry 1 to 2 minutes; add K, L; mix well with B–H and serve.

BEEF WITH BEAN SPROUTS
Niu Ro Loh Do Ya: General

A. 4 tablespoons peanut oil
B. 1 clove garlic
C. ½ teaspoon salt
D. 1 slice ginger, minced
E. 1 lb. flank steak
F. 2 tablespoons sherry
G. 1 tablespoon light soy sauce
H. 1 teaspoon sugar
I. 1 tablespoon cornstarch
J. ½ cup cold water
K. 2 scallions, sliced
L. 1½ teaspoons heavy soy sauce
M. 1 lb. fresh bean sprouts
N. 2 scallions, sliced

PREPARATION:

    I. Cut E into very thin, bite-size slices.

    II. Mix B, C, D. Set aside.

    III. Mix F, G, H, I, J, K, L. Set aside. Stir well before using.

COOKING:

1. Put A in very hot skillet and bring to high heat.
2. Add B–D and stir-fry rapidly 15 seconds to brown slightly.
3. Add E and brown lightly, leaving center of meat rare.
4. Remove E from skillet and set aside.
5. Add F–L to skillet, stir continuously and heat until sauce thickens.
6. Add M. Stir-fry in sauce 1 minute.
7. Return E to skillet and cook 1 minute, mixing well to be sure that it is well coated by sauce.
8. Serve with garnish of N.

STIR-FRIED BEEF WITH CELERY
Szechuan Ching Tsai Niu Ro Si: Szechuan

A. ¼ cup peanut oil
B. ½ lb. beef tenderloin
C. 2 teaspoons brown bean sauce
D. 2 teaspoons light soy sauce
E. ½ teaspoon salt
F. 2 teaspoons sherry

G. 1 teaspoon sugar
H. 4 stalks celery
I. 1 tablespoon chopped scallion
J. 1 teaspoon chopped ginger
K. ½ teaspoon Szechuan ground pepper

PREPARATION:

I. Cut B into thin slices, then shred.   II. Mix C, D, E, F, G.   III. Cut H diagonally into thin pieces.

COOKING:

1. Heat A, add B and stir until almost dry. (If too much water comes out of B, remove to another pan and stir-fry until dry.)

2. Add C–G, mix well.
3. Add H and stir-fry 1 or 2 minutes.
4. Add I, J, K, mix well and serve.

STIR-FRIED BEEF WITH BROCCOLI
Niu Ro Gai Lan: General

A. 2 tablespoons peanut oil
B. 2 tablespoons salted black beans
C. ½ clove garlic, minced
D. 1 to 2 slices ginger, minced
E. ½ teaspoon salt
F. 1 lb. flank steak
G. 1 teaspoon peanut oil

H. 1 teaspoon cornstarch
I. 1 teaspoon light soy sauce
J. 2 teaspoons sherry
K. ½ teaspoon sugar
L. 1 bunch fresh broccoli
M. 2 teaspoons cornstarch
N. 2 tablespoons heavy soy sauce

PREPARATION:

I. Slice F into ⅛-inch, bite-size pieces.
II. Mix G, H, I, J, K and marinate F in mixture 15 minutes.
III. Mix B, C, D, E. Set aside.

IV. Slice stems of L diagonally into 1½ inch segments, splitting heavier stems. Parboil stems 2 minutes and set aside.
V. Mix M, N. Stir well before using.

COOKING:

1. Put A in very hot skillet and bring to high heat.
2. Add B–E mixture and stir-fry rapidly 15 seconds to brown garlic slightly.

3. Add F and G–K and stir-fry until F is nearly done but remains rare on inside.
4. Add L. Stir-fry 15 seconds.
5. Add M–N mixture slowly. Stir-fry until sauce thickens and coats all ingredients well.

STIR-FRIED BEEF WITH BROCCOLI   *Approved Diabetic Recipe*
Gai Lan Niu Ro: General

A. 1½ tablespoons peanut oil
B. 1 teaspoon chopped scallion
C. 1 to 2 slices pickled ginger (unsweetened)
D. ¼ lb. beef tenderloin steak, shredded

E. 1 teaspoon light soy sauce
F. ½ teaspoon cornstarch
G. 2 cups cut-up broccoli flowerets
H. ½ teaspoon salt

PREPARATION:

i. Mix D with E, F, and 1 teaspoon A.

ii. Put G in boiling water; when water boils

again turn off heat. Drain and run under cold water.

COOKING:

1. Heat remaining A, stir-fry B, C a few seconds.
2. Add D–F mixture; stir-fry 1 to 1½ minutes.

3. Add G, H and continue stir-frying 1 minute.

STIR-FRIED BEEF WITH CHINESE CABBAGE, CABBAGE HEART, OR CHINESE CELERY CABBAGE *Approved Diabetic Recipe*
Niu Ro Bai Tsai: General

Substitute any of various cabbages for G.

STIR-FRIED LAMB WITH BROCCOLI *Approved Diabetic Recipe*
Yang Ro Gai Lan: General

Substitute shredded lamb for D.

STIR-FRIED BEEF, LAMB, OR CHICKEN WITH KOHLRABI *Approved Diabetic Recipe*
Ro Si Tsao Da To Tsai: Szechuan

Substitute ½ lb. kohlrabi for G. Peel kohlrabi and shred.

BEEF WITH PRESERVED KOHLRABI
Niu Ro Tza Tsai: Szechuan

A. 3 tablespoons peanut oil
B. ½ lb. boneless beef
C. 2 teaspoons cornstarch
D. 2 slices ginger
E. 1 tablespoon chopped scallion
F. 1 teaspoon light soy sauce

G. 1 teaspoon peanut oil
H. 1 cup shredded bamboo shoots
I. ½ cup preserved kohlrabi
J. 1 teaspoon sugar
K. ½ teaspoon salt

PREPARATION:

i. Shred B very fine.

ii. Chop D fine.

iii. Mix B, C, D, E, F, G. Mix well.

iv. Combine J, K.

v. Wash and clean I; slice thin and shred.

COOKING:

1. Heat A and add B–G. Stir-fry about 1½ minutes. Remove from pan.
2. Put H, I into same pan. Stir-fry 1 minute.

3. Return cooked B–G and J–K. Mix well and serve.

BEEF WITH PRESERVED KOHLRABI AND FRIED CELLOPHANE NOODLES
Niu Ro Tza Tsai Fun See: Canton

Thicken sauce in Step 3 with 2 teaspoons cornstarch mixed with ½ cup soup stock. Pour over fried cellophane noodles (see Index) and serve.

BEEF WITH FRESH MUSHROOMS
Tsao Gu Niu Ro: General

A.	3 tablespoons peanut oil	F.	2 teaspoons cornstarch
B.	½ lb. flank steak	G.	½ teaspoon sugar
C.	3 slices ginger	H.	1 teaspoon light soy sauce
D.	2 scallions	I.	½ lb. fresh mushrooms
E.	1 tablespoon sherry	J.	1 teaspoon salt

PREPARATION:

I. Cut B against grain into slices 1½ inches long and ¼ inch thick.

II. Wash I, slice each in halves or thirds.

III. Cut C into long shreds. Cut D into 1-inch pieces.

IV. Mix B, C, D, E, F, G, H.

COOKING:

1. Heat A in frying pan.
2. When hot, add B–H mixture, stir-fry 1 minute.
3. Add I, stir-fry 1 minute.
4. Add J and mix well over high heat. Total cooking time: about 3 minutes. Serve hot.

STIR-FRIED BEEF WITH SPINACH
Niu Ro Bo Tsai: General

A.	3 tablespoons peanut oil	G.	½ teaspoon sugar
B.	½ lb. beef	H.	1 tablespoon peanut oil
C.	2 slices ginger, chopped	I.	10-oz. pkg. spinach
D.	1 tablespoon chopped scallion	J.	½ teaspoon salt
E.	2 teaspoons cornstarch	K.	2 teaspoons cornstarch
F.	1 tablespoon light soy sauce	L.	1 tablespoon water

PREPARATION:

I. Shred B very fine.   II. Mix B, C, D, E, F, G.   III. Mix J, K, L.

COOKING:

1. Heat A. Add B–G, stir-fry 1½ minutes. Remove from pan and place on plate.
2. Add H to same pan.
3. Add I, stir well, add ½ tablespoon hot water, cover and cook 1 minute.
4. Return B–G to H–I, stir a few seconds, add J–L. Stir well until gravy is thickened. Serve with fried cellophane noodles (see Index).

STIR-FRIED BEEF WITH SPINACH *Approved Ulcer Recipe*
Niu Ro Bo Tsai: General

Omit C and D; chop I very fine.

BEEF SHANK WITH BROWN ONIONS
Dzao Tze Mun Yang Chung: Shanghai

A. 1 lb. beef shank
B. 3 tablespoons peanut oil
C. 1 lb. onions
D. 3 tablespoons light soy sauce

E. 1 teaspoon sugar
F. dash pepper
G. salt to taste

PREPARATION:

I. Cut A across grain into bite-size pieces.

II. Skin C, cut into rings.

COOKING:

1. Heat heavy saucepan. Brown A (using no fat), stirring vigorously. Add 1 cup water and cover. Over low heat, simmer until A is tender (1½ to 2 hours); add water when needed. When A is done, there should not be much gravy in pot. If too much gravy remains, remove A and cook gravy down.

2. Put B in large frying pan, heat to smoking, add C, stir-fry 1 to 2 minutes, then add D, E and stir-fry 1 minute.

3. Combine C–E with A, simmer 40 minutes; adjust flavor with F, G.

BEEF WITH TOMATO
Niu Ro Fan Chieh: General

A. 4 tablespoons peanut oil
B. 2 cloves garlic, minced
C. 1 tablespoon salted black beans
D. ¾ teaspoon salt
E. 3 teaspoons sugar
F. 2 teaspoons light soy sauce
G. 1 tablespoon sherry

H. 1 lb. flank steak
I. 2 tablespoons peanut oil
J. 1 cup sliced onions
K. 1 to 2 teaspoons cornstarch
L. 1 tablespoon heavy soy sauce
M. 3 tablespoons water
N. 1 cup stewed or canned tomatoes

PREPARATION:

I. Cut H into thin slices.
II. Mix B, C.
III. Mix K, L and add M.

IV. Mix D, E, F, G and marinate H in mixture 15 minutes.

COOKING:

1. Put A in very hot skillet and bring to high heat.
2. Add B–C and stir-fry rapidly 15 seconds to brown slightly.
3. Add D–G and stir-fry 15 seconds.
4. Add H and stir-fry 1 minute. Remove contents from skillet and set aside.

5. Reheat skillet. Add I and bring to high heat.
6. Add J and stir-fry 2 minutes.
7. Return B–H and stir-fry 1 minute.
8. Add K–L slowly. Stir-fry until sauce thickens and coats all ingredients well.
9. Add N. Cook 1 minute. Serve.

BEEF WITH TOMATO AND OYSTER SAUCE
Fan Chieh How Yo Niu Ro: General

Add 2 tablespoons oyster sauce in Step 9. Omit L in III.

BEEF WITH TOMATOES AND ONION
Niu Ro Tsao Fan Chieh: General

A. 3 tablespoons peanut oil
B. 1 lb. flank steak or beef tenderloin
C. 1 teaspoon cornstarch
D. 2 tablespoons light soy sauce
E. 1 tablespoon sherry
F. 2 tablespoons chopped scallions

G. 3 slices ginger
H. ½ teaspoon sugar
I. dash pepper
J. 1 medium onion, sliced
K. 2 medium tomatoes
L. ½ teaspoon salt

PREPARATION:

I. Cut B into strips about 2 inches by ¼ inch, against the grain.
II. Mix with C, D, E, F, G, H, I.

III. Soak K in boiling water ½ minute until skin is easy to peel off; cut K into 10 wedges each.

COOKING:

1. Heat A in skillet until hot.
2. Stir-fry B–I in A for about 1½ minutes. Remove B.

3. Add J; stir until tender.
4. Add K; stir until heated through.
5. Add L, B–I, mix well and serve hot.

RED-COOKED OXTAIL
Hung Sao Niu Wei: General

A. 2 tablespoons peanut oil
B. 1 scallion
C. 1 piece fresh ginger (size of a marble)
D. 1 oxtail (about 1½ lbs.)
E. ¼ cup light soy sauce

F. 3 tablespoons sherry
G. 2 teaspoons sugar
H. 1 teaspoon whole black pepper
I. 2 cups water
J. 1 lb. tomatoes

PREPARATION:

I. Cut D into 1½-inch pieces.
II. Cut B into 1-inch pieces.
III. Peel C and pound with side of cleaver.

IV. Mix E, F, G, H.
V. Dip J into boiling water and peel off skin. Quarter each.

COOKING:

1. Heat A, add B, C, stir-fry 30 seconds.
2. Add D and brown.
3. Add E–H, continue stirring 1 minute.

4. Add I, bring to boil, lower heat, simmer 1½ hours, adding water if necessary.
5. Add J and simmer 1 more hour until D is tender. Serve with rice.

OXTAIL STEW
Hung Sao Niu Wei: General

A. 4 tablespoons peanut oil
B. 2 lbs. disjointed oxtails
C. 2 onions, sliced
D. 2 cloves garlic, minced
E. 2 slices ginger, minced
F. 2 tablespoons tomato catsup
G. ¼ teaspoon vinegar

H. 1 tablespoon duck sauce
I. 1 teaspoon sugar
J. 1 teaspoon salt
K. 3 tablespoons cornstarch
L. ½ cup water
M. 2 scallions, sliced

PREPARATION:

I. Put B into boiling water and cook over moderate heat 15 minutes. Drain. Set aside.

II. Mix C, D, E. Set aside.

III. Mix F, G, H, I, J. Set aside.

IV. Mix K, L. Set aside. Stir well before using.

COOKING:

1. Put A in very hot skillet and bring to high heat.

2. Add B and then C–E. Stir-fry until B is brown.

3. Add F–J and enough water to cover B in saucepan.

4. Cover pot and simmer 2 to 3 hours—until oxtails are tender. Add more water, if needed, while simmering.

5. Slowly add as much of K–L mixture as is necessary to thicken sauce and coat B evenly.

6. Serve with garnish of M.

Note: This dish may taste even better if prepared the day before and reheated.

SAVORY BEEF LIVER WITH ONIONS
Yang Tsung Mun Niu Gan: Shantung

A. ¼ cup vegetable oil

B. 1 lb. beef liver

C. 3 slices ginger, minced

D. 2 tablespoons light soy sauce

E. 1 tablespoon sherry

F. ½ teaspoon salt

G. dash black pepper

H. ⅓ cup flour

I. 2 stalks celery, diced

J. 1 onion

K. ½ teaspoon sugar

PREPARATION:

I. Dice B, removing membrane and tough fibers.

II. Cut J in half and slice into rings.

III. Marinate B in C, D, E, F, G 30 minutes. Mix in H.

COOKING:

1. Heat A in frying pan. Add B–H, fry 5 to 7 minutes over medium heat until browned.

2. Add I, J, K, lower heat, cover, and simmer 12 to 15 minutes. Gradually add ⅓ cup water while simmering. Serve hot.

RED-COOKED BEEF TONGUE
Hung Sao Niu Seh To: General

A. 4- to 5-lb. beef tongue (fresh, not pickled)

B. ½ cup light soy sauce

C. 2 cloves star anise

D. 1 tablespoon sugar

E. 3 tablespoons sherry

F. salt to taste

PREPARATION AND COOKING:

I. In Dutch oven, boil water. Add A, boil 10 to 15 minutes. Remove, cool in cold water. Trim gristle and bone off thick end. A may now be skinned easily. Discard water.

II. Place A, B, C, D, E in Dutch oven. Bring to boil. Cover and simmer about 3 to 3½ hours —until chopstick can puncture A. Add water when needed.

III. Adjust with F, slice and serve.

BEEF TONGUE WITH TOMATO SAUCE
Cheh Tze Niu Suh: Shanghai

A. 3 tablespoons peanut oil
B. 2 large onions
C. 1 cup catsup
D. 3 teaspoons salt
E. ½ to 1 teaspoon black pepper
F. 6 cloves
G. 2 tablespoons white vinegar
H. 4- to 5-lb. beef tongue (fresh, not pickled)
I. 2 qts. soup stock

PREPARATION:

I. In Dutch oven, boil water. Add H, boil 10 to 15 minutes. Remove, cool in cold water. Trim gristle and bone off thick end. H may now be skinned easily. Discard water.

II. Peel B and shred.
III. Mix C, D, E, F, G.

COOKING:

1. Put A into Dutch oven and heat; stir-fry B until brown.
2. Add C–G, simmer 1 minute.
3. Add H and half of I; cover tightly and simmer 3 to 3½ hours or until H is chopstick tender. Add more soup when needed.
4. Slice and serve.

FRIED TRIPE
Tza Ngo Ba Yip: Canton

A. 1 lb. beef tripe
B. 1 clove garlic, chopped
C. 1 tablespoon light soy sauce
D. 1½ teaspoons salt
E. ½ teaspoon ginger powder

PREPARATION:

I. Cut A into pieces 1½ inches by 2½ inches.

II. Combine B, C, D, E, add A, mix well, and marinate A in mixture 15 minutes.

COOKING:

1. Steam 30 minutes over boiling water. Drain and dry with paper towel.
2. Deep fry at 350° 2 minutes.

BRAISED TRIPE WITH CATSUP
Si Tsup Ngo Ba Yip: Canton

A. 3 tablespoons peanut oil
B. 4 slices ginger, sliced
C. 1 small onion, sliced
D. 1 clove garlic
E. 1 lb. beef tripe
F. 1 tablespoon sherry
G. 1 tablespoon light soy sauce
H. ⅓ cup catsup
I. ¼ teaspoon salt
J. dash pepper
K. 1 cup water

PREPARATION:

I. Cut E into pieces ¾ inch by 2 inches.

II. Pound D, discard skin.

COOKING:

1. Heat A. Brown B, C, D 30 seconds.
2. Add E, stir-fry 1 minute.
3. Add F, G, H, I, J, stir well.
4. Add K, bring to boil, and simmer 1½ hours.

MUTTON GELATIN
Yang Gow: Peking

A. 2½-lb. leg of lamb, shank half
B. 2 qts. water
C. 3 cloves garlic
D. ¼ cup light soy sauce

E. dash black pepper
F. 1 teaspoon salt
G. salt to taste

PREPARATION AND COOKING:

I. Bone A, cut into 2-inch squares. Place bone and meat in Dutch oven and add B.
II. Add C, D, E, F. Bring to boil. Lower heat and simmer 3 hours.
III. Remove bones and C.

IV. Shred A chunks. Meat juice at this time should be around 1 qt.; add G.
V. Mix shredded A and juice. Place in mold. Allow to cool, then place in refrigerator to jell.
VI. Skim off fat. Cut gelatin into squares.

MUTTON GELATIN   *Approved Ulcer Recipe*
Yang Ro Dung: Peking

Omit E and substitute 1 tablespoon oyster sauce for C.

STIR-FRIED LAMB (SZECHUAN)
Jiang Bao Yang Ro Pien: Szechuan

A. ½ cup peanut oil
B. 1 lb. lean lamb meat
C. 1 teaspoon cornstarch
D. ½ teaspoon salt
E. 1 clove garlic
F. 1 scallion
G. 3 slices ginger, shredded
H. 2 teaspoons light soy sauce

I. 1 teaspoon sugar
J. 2 teaspoons brown bean sauce
K. 2 teaspoons sherry
L. ½ teaspoon sesame oil
M. 2 teaspoons cornstarch mixed with ¼ cup water
N. ½ teaspoon meat tenderizer

PREPARATION:

I. Slice B into thin pieces 2 inches long, mix with N, let stand 15 minutes.
II. Mix B with C, D.

III. Pound E with side of cleaver, discard skin.
IV. Cut F in 1½-inch pieces.
V. Mix H, I, J, K, L, M.

COOKING:

1. Heat A until smoking, add B–D, stir-fry 1 minute, remove to dish.
2. Heat 2 tablespoons A in frying pan, add E, F, G, stir-fry a few seconds.

3. Return B–D, stir-fry ½ minute.
4. Add H–M, stir until sauce is thickened.

STIR-FRIED LAMB WITH SCALLIONS
Chung Bao Yang Ro: Peking

A. 2 tablespoons peanut oil
B. 2 teaspoons sesame oil
C. 1 clove garlic
D. 1 lb. lean lamb
E. 4 to 6 scallions, white part only
F. 2 teaspoons sherry

G. 1 tablespoon light soy sauce
H. ¼ teaspoon ground anise pepper
I. 1 teaspoon peanut oil
J. 2 teaspoons vinegar
K. few drops sesame oil
L. salt to taste

PREPARATION:

I. Pound C with side of cleaver, discard skin.
II. Cut D into very thin slices 2 inches by 1 inch.

III. Split E lengthwise, then cut into 1- to 2-inch pieces.
IV. Mix D, E, F, G, H, I, and marinate 15 minutes.

COOKING:

1. Heat A, B, C in pan until very hot.
2. Add D–I, stir-fry 2 to 3 minutes.

3. Add J, K, L and serve.

THE DOWAGER'S FAVORITE OR SWEET LIKE HONEY
Ta Sih Mi: Peking

A. ⅓ cup sesame oil
B. ½ lb. meat from leg of lamb
C. 1 tablespoon sugar
D. 1 tablespoon brown bean sauce
E. ½ tablespoon sugar
F. 2 teaspoons cornstarch

G. 2 teaspoons vinegar
H. 2 teaspoons light soy sauce
I. 2 teaspoons sherry
J. ½ teaspoon ginger juice (see Index)
K. 2 teaspoons cornstarch mixed with ½ cup water

PREPARATION:

I. Cut B into thin pieces 2 inches long, mix well with D, E, F. Mix G, H, I, J, K.

COOKING:

1. Heat A and stir-fry B mixture 2 minutes; remove to a dish and drain off A.
2. In a saucepan, heat 1 tablespoon A, and C, stir until it boils; add G–K, stir until thickened.

3. Return B mixture, cook 1½ minutes; serve with Man To bread (see Index) or rice.

MONGOLIAN BARBECUED LAMB (OR BEEF)
Kow Yang Ro: Adapted

A. 2 lbs. boneless lamb (or beefsteak)
B. 2 or 3 leeks or scallions
C. 2 or 3 stalks Chinese parsley
D. 3 tablespoons light soy sauce

E. 2 teaspoons sugar
F. 2 tablespoons mashed fermented bean cake
G. 2 tablespoons sherry

PREPARATION:

I. Slice A into very thin slices 4 inches long.

II. Mix all ingredients and marinate 6 hours.

COOKING:

1. Cook on grill 3 to 5 minutes, turning frequently. Each person may grill his own pieces.

BARBECUED LAMB
Jiang Yo Sao Yang Pai: Shanghai

A. 3- to 4-lb. leg of lamb
B. ½ cup light soy sauce

C. 1 tablespoon sherry
D. ¼ teaspoon paprika

PREPARATION:

I. Mix B, C, D.

II. Marinate A 1 to 2 hours.

COOKING:

1. Place A on horizontal grill over red-hot coals. Cover A with 18-inch-wide aluminum foil to retain juices. If half hood is on grill, place one end of foil on top of hood (with weights) and allow foil to hang extended over edge of grill. When A browns, turn over. Cooking time: 1 to 1½ hours.

SPICED LEG OF LAMB
Wei Yang Ro: Shanghai

A. ½ leg of lamb (about 2 lbs.)
B. 1 star anise
C. ½-inch piece cinnamon
D. 1 scallion
E. 3 slices ginger
F. 1 tablespoon sherry

G. 2 cups water
H. ¼ tablespoon heavy soy sauce
I. 2 tablespoons light soy sauce
J. 1 teaspoon sugar
K. ½ teaspoon sesame oil
L. 1 tablespoon chopped scallion

PREPARATION AND COOKING:

I. Bone A, clean and wash. Place in Dutch oven.

II. Wrap B, C in cloth, tie tightly with string, add to A.

III. Add D, E, F, G to A, bring to boil; skim froth off top and discard.

IV. Lower heat and simmer 1 hour.

V. Add H, I, J, bring to boil, simmer another hour or until meat is tender and gravy becomes thick. Turn meat over once or twice during cooking and add more water if necessary.

VI. Discard B, C, D, E; add K, stir in well.

VII. Slice A on platter, pour gravy over slices, garnish with L and serve.

ROAST LEG OF LAMB WITH OYSTER SAUCE
How Yo Yang Twei: Adapted

A. ½ leg of lamb (about 3 lbs.)
B. 2 scallions, chopped
C. 2 cloves garlic, chopped
D. 2 tablespoons oyster sauce

E. 1 tablespoon light soy sauce
F. 1 teaspoon sugar
G. 1 tablespoon sherry

PREPARATION:

I. Mix B, C, D, E, F, G.

II. Make 4- to 5-inch gashes on surface of A.

III. Rub B–G over A and into all gashes and cavities; marinate overnight; turn lamb over once or twice during marinating process.

COOKING:

1. Preheat oven to 425°, roast A ½ hour, turn over and roast two hours at 325°.

SHREDDED LAMB WITH VEGETABLES *Approved Diabetic Recipe*
Tsao Yang Ro Si: Shanghai

A. 1 tablespoon peanut oil
B. 1 teaspoon chopped leek or scallion
C. ½ lb. lamb, shredded
D. 1 teaspoon light soy sauce
E. ½ to 1 teaspoon salt

F. 2 Chinese black mushrooms
G. ¼ cup shredded bamboo shoots
H. ¼ cup shredded water chestnuts
I. 8 to 10 snow peas
J. ½ teaspoon cornstarch

PREPARATION:

I. Wash F and soak in hot water 15 minutes. Drain; save water. Remove stems and cut each into 5 to 6 pieces.

II. Mix J with 2 tablespoons mushroom water.

COOKING:

1. Heat A add B, stir-fry a few seconds.
2. Add C, stir-fry only long enough to lose pink color (1 to 2 minutes). Stir in D, E, mix well.

3. Add F, G, H, I, stir 1 to 2 more minutes.
4. Thicken with J.

LAMB STEW
Hung Sao Yang Ro: Peking

A. 2 tablespoons vegetable oil
B. 1 scallion
C. 1 teaspoon chopped ginger
D. 1 clove garlic, chopped
E. 1½ lbs. leg of lamb

F. 1 teaspoon sugar
G. ½ teaspoon sesame oil
H. 2 tablespoons heavy soy sauce
I. 2 tablespoons light soy sauce
J. 5 carrots (optional)

PREPARATION:

I. Cut E into small pieces.
II. Cut B into 1-inch pieces.

III. Crush D with back of knife. Remove skin.
IV. Cut J into 1-inch pieces.

COOKING:

1. Heat A; stir-fry B, C, D a few seconds.
2. Add E, stir.
3. Add F, G, H, I. Mix well.

4. Bring to boil; simmer 1½ hours or until E is tender. Add J half an hour before E is done. Add chicken broth if necessary.
5. Serve hot or cold.

LAMB STEW *Approved Ulcer Recipe*
Sao Yang Ro: General

Omit C and D; tie B into bundle, uncut; remove B before serving.

WOOLLY LAMB
Tsao Yang Ro: Adapted

A. 2 cups peanut oil
B. 1 oz. cellophane noodles
C. 1 medium onion, shredded
D. 1½ lbs. lean lamb, shredded

E. 1 black mushroom
F. 1 teaspoon sherry
G. 1 tablespoon light soy sauce
H. ½ teaspoon salt

I. 1 teaspoon sugar

J. 1 cup canned bamboo shoots, shredded

K. 4 water chestnuts, shredded

L. ¼ lb. snow peas, shredded

M. 2 teaspoons cornstarch mixed with 1 tablespoon cold water

PREPARATION:

I. Wash E, soak 15 minutes in warm water. Drain. Discard stem, shred E fine.

II. Arrange B loosely on a plate.

COOKING:

1. Heat A in deep skillet to 400°. Slide in B, which will puff up almost instantly. Remove, set aside.

2. Pour off A, leaving 3 tablespoons in skillet.

3. Add C, stir-fry until barely wilted.

4. Add D, stir-fry only until it loses pink color. Stir in E, F, G, H, I.

5. Add J, K, L, stir until heated (½ to 1 minute).

6. Stir in M paste. Cook until sauce thickens.

7. Serve on large plate, topped with fried B.

LAMB CHAFING DISH (FONDUE)
Sa Yang Ro: Peking

A. 10 cups chicken stock

B. 2 lbs. leg of lamb

C. 1 lb. celery cabbage

D. 10-oz. package spinach

E. 10 to 20 cakes bean curd (optional)

F. 1 oz. cellophane noodles

G. 2 or 3 scallions, minced

H. 3 tablespoons light soy sauce

I. ½ teaspoon sesame oil (optional)

J. vinegar*

K. peanut butter*

L. 2 slices ginger

M. 3 tablespoons Chinese parsley, minced (optional)

N. 4 cups soup stock from lamb bones or additional chicken stock

PREPARATION:

This recipe requires a fondue dish or an electric hot plate or an electric deep frying pan. (Each guest is supplied with a porcelain spoon and chopsticks, and will cook his own food at the table.)

I. Cut lamb off bone and slice paper thin.

II. Cut C into 1½-inch strips.

III. Cut E into 1-inch squares.

IV. Soak F in hot water 20 minutes.

V. Place each of the above ingredients in separate bowls on the table.

VI. Prepare sauces by mixing G, H, I or by using J or K, individually or blended together, in any desirable mixture.

COOKING:

1. Place A in deep frying pan or fondue dish as described above. Add L, cover with lid and use high heat to bring to boil.

2. Each guest cooks his own ingredients in a corner of the cooking utensil. When the soup boils again, the cooked food and some of the soup should be ladled out into a bowl and garnished with M.

3. Whenever required, N should be added to cooking utensil.

---

* Amounts to be determined by individual preference at the table. However, one cup of each should suffice.

VEAL CUTLET WITH LETTUCE AND SCALLIONS
Sun Tsai Shiao Niu Ro Pien: Shanghai

A. 4 tablespoons peanut oil
B. 2 to 3 scallions
C. 1 small head iceberg lettuce
D. 4 slices ginger, shredded
E. 1 teaspoon salt
F. ½ lb. veal cutlet

G. 2 teaspoons light soy sauce
H. 1 teaspoon sherry
I. 2 teaspoons cornstarch
J. ½ teaspoon sugar
K. dash pepper
L. 1 teaspoon peanut oil

PREPARATION:

I. Slice F thin, then shred; mix with G, H, I, J, K, L.

II. Cut B into 2-inch pieces.
III. Quarter C, then shred.

COOKING:

1. Heat 2 tablespoons A, add B, C, D, stir-fry ½ to 1 minute, add E, stir-fry 1 minute. Drain, remove to dish.

2. Heat remaining A, add F–L, stir-fry 2 to 3 minutes.
3. Return A–E, mix well and serve hot.

STIR-FRIED VEAL CUTLET WITH BROCCOLI
Gai Lan Shiao Niu Ro: General

A. 3 tablespoons peanut oil
B. 1 tablespoon chopped scallion
C. 1 clove garlic, chopped

D. ½ lb. veal cutlet
E. 2 teaspoons light soy sauce
F. 2 teaspoons cornstarch

G. ½ teaspoon sugar
H. few drops sesame oil
I. 1 bunch broccoli

PREPARATION:

I. Slice D thin into about 1- by 2-inch pieces, mix with E, F, G, H.

II. Cut flowerets of I about 1½ inches long. (Save stems for other dishes.) Drop into boiling water; when water returns to boil, turn off heat, drain, and let cold water run over it several seconds.

COOKING:

1. Heat A, add B, C, stir-fry ½ to 1 minute; add D, E–H; stir-fry 2 minutes.

2. Add I, mix well and serve.

VEAL CUTLET WITH SPINACH
Bo Tsai Shiao Niu Ro Pien: Shanghai

A. 10 oz. fresh spinach
B. few drops sesame oil
C. 2 tablespoons peanut oil
D. ½ lb. veal cutlet
E. 1 teaspoon chopped ginger
F. 1 tablespoon chopped scallion

G. 1 clove garlic, chopped
H. 2 teaspoons light soy sauce
I. 2 teaspoons cornstarch
J. ½ teaspoon sugar
K. 2 teaspoons sherry
L. 1 teaspoon peanut oil

PREPARATION:

I. Slice D into thin pieces, then shred. Mix with E, F, G, H, I, J, K, L.

II. Wash and clean A, drain.

COOKING:

1. Add 1 teaspoon salt to 2 qts. boiling water; stir.
2. Add A, turn off heat, stir well, and drain A in colander immediately.

3. Mix drained A with B; place on plate.
4. Heat D, add E–L and stir-fry 2 to 3 minutes; add 1 to 2 tablespoons water, if necessary.
5. Arrange on top of A and serve.

STIR-FRIED VEAL STEAK WITH VEGETABLES
Tsao Shiao Niu Ro Pien: Adapted

A.   3 tablespoons peanut oil
B.   2 tablespoons chopped scallion
C.   1 teaspoon chopped ginger
D.   2 stalks celery
E.   ½ lb. veal steak
F.   2 teaspoons light soy sauce
G.   2 teaspoons cornstarch

H.   1 teaspoon peanut oil
I.   4 to 6 Chinese mushrooms
J.   ¼ lb. Chinese cabbage heart
K.   ¼ cup mushroom water
L.   ½ teaspoon salt
M.   ½ teaspoon sugar

PREPARATION:

I. Cut E into thin slices against the grain, mix with F, G, and dash of pepper.

II. Wash I, and soak in warm water 15 minutes or until soft; drain, save ¼ cup mushroom water, discard stems, and slice each into 4 pieces.

III. Wash D and J; cut on the diagonal into ½-inch pieces.

COOKING:

1. Heat 2 tablespoons A, add B, C, stir-fry a few seconds; add E–H, stir-fry 2 minutes, remove to dish.
2. Using same pan, heat 1 tablespoon A, add D, I, J, stir-fry ½ minute; add K. Mix well, cover and cook 1 to 2 minutes.
3. To A–K add E–H, L, M, continue stirring 1 minute. Serve.

PEPPER VEAL STEAK
Ching Jiao Shiao Niu Ro: General

A.   4 tablespoons peanut oil
B.   2 green peppers
C.   1 lb. veal steak
D.   1 tablespoon chopped scallion

E.   4 slices ginger, shredded
F.   1 tablespoon light soy sauce
G.   2 teaspoons sherry
H.   1 teaspoon sugar

I.   2 teaspoons cornstarch
J.   ½ teaspoon sesame oil
K.   salt to taste

PREPARATION:

I. Cut C into 1½- by ½-inch strips, mix with D, E, F, G, H, I.

II. Wash B, discard stems and seeds, cut diagonally in ½-inch strips.

COOKING:

1. Heat 1 tablespoon A, add B, stir-fry ½ minute, add a dash of K. Remove to dish.
2. Using same pan, heat the rest of A, add C–I, stir-fry 2 minutes.
3. Add J and B; mix well.
4. Add K and serve.

DICED VEAL CUTLET WITH SWEET SAUCE
Jiang Bao Shiao Niu Ro: Adapted

A. 3 tablespoons peanut oil
B. ½ lb. veal cutlet
C. 1 egg white
D. 2 teaspoons cornstarch
E. dash salt
F. 1 cup diced asparagus
G. 1 sweet red pepper

H. 2 tablespoons brown bean sauce
I. 1 teaspoon sugar
J. 2 teaspoons sherry
K. 1 teaspoon light soy sauce
L. 2 teaspoons chopped scallions
M. 1 teaspoon chopped ginger
N. 1 teaspoon cornstarch

PREPARATION:

I. Dice B and mix with C, D, E.
II. Cut G in halves, remove seeds and stem and dice.

III. Mix H, I, J, K, L, M, N.

COOKING:

1. Heat A, add B–E, stir-fry 3 minutes.
2. Add F, G; continue stirring 2–3 minutes.

3. Add H–N, stir few seconds to mix well, serve.

DICED VEAL CUTLET WITH HOT PEPPERS
La Tze Shiao Niu Ro Ding: Szechuan

A. 4 tablespoons peanut oil
B. 1 lb. veal cutlet, diced
C. 1 egg white
D. 2 teaspoons cornstarch
E. ½ teaspoon salt

F. 2 cloves garlic, chopped
G. 1 green pepper
H. 2 red-hot peppers
I. 1 teaspoon chopped ginger
J. 1 tablespoon chopped scallion

K. 1 teaspoon salt
L. 2 tablespoons light soy sauce
M. 1 tablespoon vinegar
N. 2 teaspoons sugar
O. sesame oil to taste

PREPARATION:

I. Mix B, C, D, E.
II. Wash and discard stems and seeds of G, H; dice.

III. Mix I, J, K.
IV. Mix L, M, N.

COOKING:

1. Heat 3 tablespoons of A; add B–E; stir-fry 3 to 5 minutes or until meat is done; remove from pan.
2. Add 1 tablespoon A, add F, G, H, stir-fry ½ minute.
3. Add I–K, stir a few seconds.
4. Return B to pan, add L–O, mix well and serve.

STIR-FRIED VEAL CUTLET WITH TOMATO AND PEPPERS
Jiao Chieh Shiao Niu Ro Pien: Shanghai

A. 3 tablespoons peanut oil
B. 1 clove garlic, chopped
C. 1 tablespoon chopped scallion
D. ½ lb. veal cutlet
E. 2 teaspoons light soy sauce
F. ½ teaspoon sugar

G. 2 teaspoons cornstarch
H. few drops sesame oil
I. 1 large green pepper
J. 2 tomatoes
K. ½ teaspoon sugar
L. ½ teaspoon salt

PREPARATION:

I. Slice D thin into 2- by ¼-inch strips. Mix well with E, F, G, H.

II. Slice I diagonally into ½-inch strips, discarding seeds.

III. Place J in boiling water a few seconds, remove skin and cut each into 8 to 10 wedges.

IV. Mix K, L.

COOKING:

1. Heat 2 tablespoons A, add B, C, stir-fry a few seconds.

2. Add D–H, stir-fry 2 minutes, remove to dish.

3. Heat 1 tablespoon A, add I, stir-fry 1 minute.

4. Add D–H, J, K, L, continue stirring until everything is well mixed, serve hot.

STIR-FRIED VEAL STEAK WITH OYSTER SAUCE
How Yu Shiao Niu Ro: General

A. 3 tablespoons peanut oil
B. ½ lb. veal steak
C. 1 clove garlic, chopped
D. 1 tablespoon chopped scallion
E. 1 teaspoon chopped ginger
F. 2 teaspoons oyster sauce

G. 2 teaspoons cornstarch
H. ½ teaspoon sugar
I. 6 Chinese mushrooms
J. ¼ lb. snow peas
K. ½ cup sliced bamboo shoots
L. dash salt

PREPARATION:

I. Cut B into 1½- by ½-inch strips and mix with C, D, E, F, G, H.

II. Wash I and soak in warm water 15 minutes, drain, discard stems; quarter each.

III. Discard tips of J.

COOKING:

1. Heat 2 tablespoons A, add B–H, stir-fry 2 minutes; remove to dish.

2. Heat the rest of A, add I, J, K, L, stir-fry 1 minute; add B–H mixture, stir well, add 1 to

2 tablespoons water if necessary; cover and cook 1 minute.

3. Mix well and serve.

VEAL CHOPS WITH OYSTER SAUCE
How Yu Shiao Niu Pai: Adapted

A. 3 tablespoons peanut oil
B. 2 slices ginger
C. 1 scallion
D. 4 veal chops
E. 2 tablespoons oyster sauce

F. 1 tablespoon light soy sauce
G. 2 tablespoons sherry
H. 1 teaspoon sugar
I. ⅓ cup water
J. salt to taste

PREPARATION:

I. Cut B into long, thin pieces.

II. Cut C into 1½-inch pieces.

III. Mix E, F, G, H, I.

COOKING:

1. Heat A, add B, C. Stir-fry a few seconds.

2. Add D, brown each side 2 to 3 minutes.

3. Add E–I, bring to boil. Add J. Lower heat, simmer each side 15 minutes.

4. Serve hot with rice.

VEAL CUTLET WITH SZECHUAN SAUCE
Yu Shiang Shiao Niu Ro Pien: Szechuan

A. 3 tablespoons peanut oil
B. ½ lb. veal cutlet
C. 2 teaspoons light soy sauce
D. 1 teaspoon cornstarch
E. 1 teaspoon peanut oil
F. ½ lb. asparagus
G. 1 or 2 cloves garlic, chopped
H. 1 teaspoon chopped ginger
I. 1 tablespoon chopped scallion

J. 2 teaspoons brown bean sauce
K. 1 teaspoon sugar
L. 2 teaspoons light soy sauce
M. 2 teaspoons sherry
N. 2 teaspoons vinegar
O. ½ teaspoon salt
P. 2 teaspoons cornstarch mixed with ¼ cup water

PREPARATION:

I. Slice B thin, then shred, mix with C, D, E.
II. Break F into 1- to 1½-inch pieces; wash well.

III. Bring 1 to 2 qts. water to boil, add F, parboil 2–3 minutes, drain. Mix J, K, L, M, N, O, P.

COOKING:

1. Heat A, add B–E, stir-fry 2 minutes, remove to a dish, pour excess oil back into pan.
2. Turn on heat, stir-fry F, G, H, I 1 minute.
3. Return B to pan, stirring 1 to 2 minutes.

4. Add J–P, stir until mixture is thickened.
5. Add Szechuan pepper or Chinese hot sauce to taste.

STIR-FRIED VEAL CUTLET WITH WALNUTS
Heh Tao Shiao Niu Ro Ding: Peking

A. 1 cup shelled walnut halves
B. 2 cups peanut oil
C. 1 egg white

D. ½ teaspoon salt
E. 2 teaspoons light soy sauce
F. 2 teaspoons sherry
G. ½ teaspoon sugar

H. ¼ to ½ teaspoon sesame oil
I. 2 teaspoons cornstarch
J. 1 lb. veal cutlet, diced

PREPARATION:

I. Pour boiling water over A, let stand 1 to 2 minutes or until skin is easy to peel off. After skin is off, spread out on paper towel; dry completely before frying.
II. Beat C and mix well with D, E, F, G, H, I.
III. Add J and mix well.

COOKING:

1. Deep fry A in B at 325° until golden brown, about ½ to 1 minute (do not overfry and burn walnuts); drain on paper towel.
2. Heat 3 tablespoons B, add C–J, stir-fry 3 to 5 minutes or until J is tender.
3. Add A. Mix well, and serve hot.

VEAL CHOPS WITH CATSUP
Chieh Tze Shiao Niu Pai: Adapted

A. 3 tablespoons peanut oil
B. 1 small red onion, sliced
C. 1 to 2 cloves garlic, sliced

D. 4 veal chops
E. 2 tablespoons catsup
F. 2 tablespoons light soy sauce
G. 2 tablespoons sherry

H. 1 teaspoon sugar
I. ⅓ cup water
J. salt to taste

PREPARATION: I. Mix E, F, G, H, I.

COOKING:

1. Heat A, brown B, C.
2. Add D, brown each side 2 minutes.

3. Add E–I, bring to boil. Lower heat, simmer each side 15 minutes. Add J.

PAPER-WRAPPED VEAL CUTLET
Tze Bao Shiao Niu: Shanghai

A. 2 cups peanut oil
B. ½ lb. veal cutlet
C. 2 teaspoons light soy sauce
D. 2 teaspoons sherry
E. ½ teaspoon sugar
F. ½ teaspoon salt
G. ¼ teaspoon ground white pepper
H. ½ to 1 teaspoon sesame oil (to taste)

PREPARATION:

I. Slice B into 1- by 2-inch paper-thin slices.
II. Mix C, D, E, F, G, H well and pour over B, marinate 1 hour.
III. Wrap B slices individually in waxed paper.

COOKING:

1. Heat A to 375°, deep fry B 1 minute on each side.
2. Serve hot in waxed paper wrapping (to be unwrapped at the table).

CALF BRAIN TOSSED WITH BEAN CURD
Shiao Niu Nao Ban Dow Fu: General

A. 1 calf brain
B. 3 slices ginger
C. 1 tablespoon dry sherry
D. 2 to 3 cakes bean curd
E. 1 to 2 teaspoons sesame oil
F. salt to taste

PREPARATION AND COOKING:

I. Place A in cold water, remove thin membrane and blood vessels with a toothpick; rinse thoroughly until water is clear; drain.
II. Boil 1 cup water, add A, B, C and boil 5 to 7 minutes; drain.
III. Cut D into cubes and rinse under cold water a few seconds; drain.
IV. Mix A–C with D; cut into tiny pieces with a fork.
V. Add E, F and mix well. Serve.

CALF BRAIN WITH FRESH MUSHROOMS
Shien Gu Niu Nao: General

A. 2 tablespoons lard
B. ¼ cup thin sliced Smithfield ham
C. 1 calf brain
D. 2 teaspoons whiskey
E. ¼ cup sliced bamboo shoots
F. 6 oz. fresh mushrooms
G. 4 slices ginger
H. 2 teaspoons light soy sauce
I. ¼ cup chicken broth
J. ¼ teaspoon sugar
K. 2 teaspoons cornstarch mixed with 2 tablespoons water
L. 1 scallion, chopped

PREPARATION:

I. Place C in cold water, remove thin membrane and blood vessels with a toothpick; rinse until water is clear. Drain and mince.
II. Add D and mix well.
III. Wash F and cut each into 2 or 3 slices.
IV. Mix H, I, J.

COOKING:

1. Heat A, add B, stir-fry a few seconds; add C–D and stir-fry ½ minute.
2. Add E, F, G, H–J, stir well, bring to boil; lower heat and cook 10 minutes.
3. Thicken with K.
4. Garnish with L and serve hot.

ASPARAGUS WITH ALMONDS
Shing Ren Lu Shun: Adapted

A. 4 tablespoons peanut oil
B. 2 scallions
C. 1 lb. asparagus (or cauliflower)

D. 1 teaspoon salt
E. ½ teaspoon sugar
F. ⅓ cup sliced almonds

PREPARATION:

I. Using only tips of C, French-cut each into 1½- to 2-inch pieces.
II. Cut B in same manner as C.

III. Stir-fry F in 1 teaspoon A over low heat until golden brown.

COOKING:

1. Heat remaining portion of A. Stir-fry B a few seconds.
2. Add C, stir-fry over high heat until color turns bright green (about 4 or 5 minutes).

3. Add D, E, mix well.
4. Place B–E in serving dish. Sprinkle with fried F.

GREEN BEANS WITH ALMONDS
Shing Ren Ching Do: Adapted

Substitute 1 lb. string beans for C and add 2 tablespoons light soy sauce. To prepare strings beans, cut into 1½-inch lengths, parboil 3 minutes. Drain, run under cold water before stir-frying in Step 2; cook 3 additional minutes.

BRAISED BAMBOO SHOOTS
Hung Mun Sun: Szechuan

A. 2 tablespoons peanut oil
B. 1 cup sliced bamboo shoots
C. 1½ tablespoons brown bean sauce
D. 1 teaspoon sugar
E. ½ cup chicken broth

F. 2 teaspoons sherry
G. 1 teaspoon cornstarch mixed with 2 tablespoons water
H. sesame oil
I. salt to taste

COOKING:

1. Heat A, add B, stir-fry 1 to 2 minutes.
2. Add C, D, E, continue stirring 1 minute.

3. Add F, mix well, cover and cook 2 to 3 minutes.
4. Thicken with G, add H, I.

BRAISED SOYBEAN SPROUTS
Hung Sao Hwang Do Ya: Shanghai

A. 2 tablespoons peanut oil
B. 1 tablespoon chopped scallion
C. ¼ cup diced Virginia ham
D. 1 lb. soybean sprouts

E. 1 tablespoon light soy sauce
F. 1 teaspoon sugar
G. ½ teaspoon salt
H. ½ cup water

PREPARATION:

I. Remove tail part of D. Wash well, drain.

II. Mix E, F, G, H.

COOKING:

1. Heat A, add B, stir-fry a few seconds.
2. Add C, stir-fry ½ minute, add D, mix well.

3. Add E–H, bring to boil, lower heat and simmer 35 minutes.

ONE-MINUTE BEAN SPROUTS
Ching Tsao Do Ya: Adapted

A. 3 tablespoons peanut oil
B. 4 slices ginger, shredded
C. 1 scallion

D. 1 lb. bean sprouts
E. 1 teaspoon salt
F. ½ teaspoon sugar

PREPARATION:

I. Remove tail part of D. Wash well, drain.

II. Cut C into 1-inch pieces.

COOKING:

1. Heat A, add B, C, and stir-fry several seconds.
2. Add D, stir-fry 30 seconds.

3. Add E, F, stir well several times. D will be crisp and ready to serve in exactly 1 minute.

BROCCOLI WITH MUSHROOMS
Gai Lan Dung Gu: Adapted

A. 1 bunch broccoli
B. 4 tablespoons peanut oil

C. 8 to 10 Chinese mushrooms
D. 2 tablespoons chopped scallion

E. 1½ teaspoons salt
F. 1 teaspoon sugar

PREPARATION:

I. Use only flower parts of A cut into pieces 1 to 2 inches long. Marinate stems and save for other recipes.

II. Wash C, soak in warm water 15 minutes. Drain, saving water.
III. Cut each C into 2 or 3 pieces.

COOKING:

1. Drop tips of A into boiling water. When water boils again, remove from heat. Drain, and let cold water run over.

2. Heat B, stir-fry C, D 1 minute.
3. Add A, E, F, and ¼ cup C water. Continue stir-frying 1 to 2 minutes. Serve hot.

CAULIFLOWER WITH AMERICAN MUSHROOMS
Tsao Gu Hwa Tsai: General

Substitute ¼ cup canned American button mushrooms for C. Add mushrooms, during Step 3, to A, E, F, omit ¼ cup water. After stir-frying 1 to 2 minutes, thicken with 1 teaspoon cornstarch mixed with 2 tablespoons water.

BROCCOLI WITH MUSHROOMS AND BAMBOO SHOOTS
Er Dung Tsao Gai Lan: General

Add ½ cup thinly sliced bamboo shoots to C, D.

BROCCOLI WITH MUSHROOMS *Approved Diabetic Recipe*
Dung Gu Bai Tsai: General

A. ½ bunch broccoli
B. 1 tablespoon peanut oil
C. 3 to 4 Chinese mushrooms

D. 1 teaspoon chopped scallion
E. ½ teaspoon salt

PREPARATION:

I. Use flowers of A cut into 1- to 2-inch pieces.
II. Wash C, soak in warm water 15 minutes. Drain and remove stems; cut into 4 pieces. Save 2 tablespoons C water.

COOKING:

1. Drop tips of A into boiling water, when water boils again remove from heat, drain and run under cold water for a few seconds.
2. Heat B, stir-fry C, D 1 minute.
3. Add A, E, and 2 tablespoons C water and stir-fry 1 to 2 more minutes.

CABBAGE OR CABBAGE HEART WITH MUSHROOMS *Approved Diabetic Recipe*
Dung Gu Bai Tsai: General

Substitute 1 lb. Chinese cabbage for A.

STIR-FRIED BROCCOLI
Ching Tsao Gai Lan: General

A. 2 tablespoons peanut oil
B. ½ teaspoon salt
C. 1 clove garlic, minced
D. 1 bunch broccoli
E. ½ cup soup stock
F. 2 teaspoons heavy soy sauce

G. 1 teaspoon light soy sauce
H. 1 teaspoon sugar
I. ½ to 1 teaspoon ginger, minced
J. 1 teaspoon rice wine or sherry
K. 1½ teaspoons cornstarch

PREPARATION:

I. Wash D thoroughly and drain in colander.
II. Cut D diagonally into 1-inch sections.
III. Mix B, C.

IV. Mix E, F, G, H, I, J, K. Set aside. Stir well before using.

COOKING:

1. Heat skillet; add A and bring to smoking point. Lower heat for 1 minute.
2. Add B–C, stir-fry 15 seconds. Raise heat again to high.
3. Add D, stir-fry 3 minutes.
4. Add E–K. Stir well 1 minute.
5. Cover. Cook 2 minutes or until sauce thickens and coats vegetable well. Serve.

MARINATED BROCCOLI STEMS
Pao Gai Lan: Adapted

A. 3 to 4 broccoli stems
B. 1 teaspoon salt

C. 1 clove garlic, minced
D. 1 teaspoon olive oil

E. 2 teaspoons distilled white vinegar

PREPARATION:

I. Peel skin from A; slice thin, diagonally.
II. Place A, B in a jar and shake well. Let stand overnight.
III. Mix C, D, E.

IV. Drain salt water from A.
V. Add C–E mixture. Shake well.
VI. Let stand several hours before serving.

STIR-FRIED CHINESE BROCCOLI WITH WINE
Tsao Gai Lan: Adapted

A. 4 tablespoons peanut oil
B. 2 slices ginger
C. 1 to 2 lbs. Chinese broccoli
D. 1 tablespoon wine

E. 1 teaspoon sugar
E. 1 teaspoon salt
G. 1 tablespoon light soy sauce

PREPARATION:

I. Cut C diagonally into 2- to 3-inch segments.

II. Mix D, E, F, G.

COOKING:

1. Heat A. Add B, stir-fry a few seconds.
2. Add C, stir well for 1 minute.

3. Add D–G, and stir-fry over high heat 2 to 3 minutes.

CHINESE CABBAGE IN CREAM SAUCE
Nye Yow Box Tsoi Sum: Canton

A. 2 tablespoons butter
B. 2 tablespoons flour
C. 1 cup milk
D. 1 teaspoon salt

E. ½ teaspoon sugar
F. 1 lb. Chinese cabbage hearts
G. 1 cup chicken broth

PREPARATION:

I. Cut F lengthwise. Parboil until tender (about 1 minute). Drain, dry between paper towels.

II. Cut F into still thinner strips lengthwise, soak in G 30 minutes.

COOKING:

1. Melt A, add B slowly, and make into a paste.
2. Add C, D, E; heat until thickened.

3. Remove F from G, add to sauce, cook ½ minute.

CABBAGE HEARTS WITH CHICKEN FAT
Gee Yo Tsai Shing: Szechuan

A. 2 tablespoons peanut oil
B. 1½ lbs. Chinese cabbage hearts
C. ½ cup chicken broth
D. ½ teaspoon sugar

E. ½ to 1 teaspoon salt (to taste)
F. 1 tablespoon cornstarch mixed with ¼ cup water
G. 1 teaspoon chicken fat

PREPARATION:

I. Remove tough leaves of B, cut tender part in 1½-inch lengths, and parboil in boiling water 1 minute. Drain and squeeze out water.

COOKING:

1. Heat A, stir-fry B a few seconds.
2. Add C, cook 2 to 3 minutes.
3. Add D, E and stir well.

4. Thicken with F.
5. Heat G, pour over B, and serve.

CABBAGE HEARTS WITH BAMBOO SHOOTS
Sun Sih Tsai Shing: Yangchow

A. 4 tablespoons vegetable oil
B. 2 lbs. Chinese cabbage hearts
C. 1 cup sliced bamboo shoots
D. 1 teaspoon salt

E. 1 tablespoon sherry
F. 1 teaspoon sugar
G. ¼ cup chicken soup mixed with 2 teaspoons cornstarch

PREPARATION:

I. Wash and clean B, cut into 1½-inch segments.

II. Slice C into pieces ¼ inch thick, ½ inch wide and 1½ inches long.

COOKING:

1. Place A in frying pan; when hot, add B, C; stir-fry 1 minute.

2. Add D, E, F and stir-fry 1 minute.
3. Add G and simmer 1 to 2 minutes.

STIR-FRIED CHINESE CABBAGE
Ching Tsao Bai Tsai: General

A. 2 tablespoons peanut oil
B. ½ teaspoon salt
C. 1 clove garlic, minced
D. 1 lb. Chinese cabbage
E. ½ cup soup stock
F. 2 teaspoons heavy soy sauce

G. 1 teaspoon light soy sauce
H. 1 teaspoon sugar
I. ½ to 1 teaspoon ginger, minced
J. 1 teaspoon rice wine or sherry
K. 1½ teaspoons cornstarch

PREPARATION:

I. Wash D; cut leaves and stem into 1-inch sections; keep white stems separate.
II. Mix B, C.

III. Mix E, F, G, H, I, J, K. Set aside. Stir well before using.

COOKING:

1. Heat skillet; add A and bring to smoking point. Lower heat 1 minute.
2. Add B, C, stir-fry 15 seconds. Raise heat again to high.
3. Immediately (before C burns), add white

stem of D. Stir-fry 2 minutes; add green parts of D; stir-fry 1 minute.
4. Add E–K mixture. Stir well 1 minute.
5. Cover. Cook 2 minutes or until sauce thickens and coats vegetable well. Serve.

SWEET AND SOUR CABBAGE
Tiem Swan Bai Tsai: Adapted

A. 1 tablespoon peanut oil
B. ½ teaspoon pepper flakes
C. 5 tablespoons sugar

D. ½ cup vinegar
E. 1½ teaspoons salt
F. 1 lb. American cabbage

PREPARATION:

I. Mix C, D, E thoroughly.

II. Cut F into bite-size pieces, wash, drain, and put into a jar.

COOKING:

1. Heat A, add B, stir-fry a few seconds, turn off heat.
2. Add C–E (be careful that oil does not spatter), bring to a boil.
3. Pour hot mixture over F, let stand overnight before serving. Shake the jar a few times so that the juice is absorbed evenly.

STEAMED CELERY CABBAGE
Tsen Bai Tsai: General

A.   1- to 2-lb.-head celery cabbage
B.   12 dried shrimp or scallops
C.   1 teaspoon salt

PREPARATION:

I. Remove tough outside leaves of A. Wash remaining A free of dirt. Cut into 2-inch pieces, and place in large shallow bowl.
II. Wash B in cold water; chop, and spread over A.
III. Sprinkle C over A–B.

COOKING:

1. Steam 30 minutes.

STEAMED CELERY CABBAGE HEARTS
Tsen Sha Mi Bai Tsai Shing: General

A.   3 large heads celery cabbage
B.   12 dried shrimp
C.   1 teaspoon salt

PREPARATION:

I. Use hearts of A only. Remove outside leaves. Wash remainder with cold water, place in large shallow bowl.
II. Wash B in cold water. Chop.
III. Spread B, C on A.

COOKING:

1. Steam 30 minutes.

CELERY CABBAGE HEARTS IN CREAM SAUCE   *Approved Ulcer Recipe*
Nye Yow Shu Tsoi: Canton

A.   ½ cup chicken broth
B.   1 lb. celery cabbage hearts
C.   ½ cup milk
D.   ½ tablespoon margarine
E.   salt to taste
F.   1 tablespoon cornstarch
G.   ¼ cup finely chopped white meat chicken

PREPARATION:

I. Chop B very fine.
II. Mix C, D, E, F.

COOKING:

1. Bring A to boil. Add B, cook over medium heat about 3 to 5 minutes, or until tender. Drain.
2. Heat C–F, stir until thickened.
3. Add B to C–F mixture, heat thoroughly.
4. Place in bowl, garnish with G.

STEAMED CELERY CABBAGE CASSEROLE
Chien Tsen Bai Tsai: Peking

A. 2 lbs. celery cabbage
B. 4 oz. flounder fillet
C. 4 oz. chicken white meat
D. 2 oz. ham
E. 2 eggs
F. 4 slices ginger

G. 2 scallions
H. 1 tablespoon cornstarch
I. ¼ cup flour
J. 1 teaspoon salt
K. 1 teaspoon sherry

PREPARATION:

I. Remove leaves of A from main stem. Wash and clean leaves.
II. Chop B, C, D very fine.
III. Chop F, G very fine.

IV. Mix B, C, D, E, F, G, H, I, J, K. Place layer of A on bottom of shallow bowl. Coat A with layer of B–K mixture. Alternate layers. Cover with aluminum foil.

COOKING:

1. Steam dish 30 minutes, remove. Cut with knife and serve.

STIR-FRIED CELERY HEARTS WITH BEEF
Ching Tsai Niu Ro: General

A. 4 tablespoons peanut oil
B. ½ lb. beefsteak
C. 1 tablespoon light soy sauce
D. 2 teaspoons sherry
E. ½ teaspoon sugar
F. 2 teaspoons cornstarch

G. 3 slices ginger
H. 1 tablespoon chopped scallion
I. 4 celery hearts
(about 2 cups after slicing, below)
J. ¼ teaspoon salt

PREPARATION:

I. Cut B into thin slices. Mix with C, D, E, F, G, H. Cut I diagonally into ½-inch-thick slices.

COOKING:

1. Heat A, add B–H, stir-fry 1 minute, remove to dish. Return excess oil to pan.
2. Turn up heat, add I to same pan, stir-fry a few seconds, add 2 tablespoons water, mix well; cover and cook ½ minute.
3. Return B to pan, stir well, add J. Mix well and serve.

BRAISED CHESTNUTS WITH CELERY CABBAGE
Hung Sow Li Tze Bai Tsai: Shanghai

A. ¼ cup peanut oil
B. 4 cups, 1-inch-wide pieces, center portion celery cabbage
C. 12 Chinese mushrooms
D. 2 teaspoons sugar

E. 3 tablespoons soup stock (or mushroom water)
F. 2 tablespoons light soy sauce
G. 1 cup chestnuts
H. salt to taste

PREPARATION:

I. Make slits in G, cover with water. Boil 10 minutes, then shell and cut into halves.

II. Wash C, and soak 15 minutes in warm water. Drain, saving water. Cut each C in half.

COOKING:

1. Heat A, add B, C, stir-fry about 5 minutes.
2. Add D, E, F, cover, cook over low heat 5 min-utes.
3. Add G, cook another 5 minutes. Add H.

ONE-TWO-THREE VEGETARIAN DISH
I Er San Lo Han Chai: Adapted

A. 13¾-oz. can chicken broth
B. 2-oz. pkg. cellophane noodles
C. 4 to 5 cups celery cabbage
D. 13-oz. can vegetarian chop suey

PREPARATION:

I. Wash C well, cut crosswise into 1-inch pieces.
II. Soak B 30 minutes in hot water, drain.

COOKING:

1. Empty A into 3-qt. saucepan, add 1 can water, bring to boil.
2. Add B, bring to boil again, simmer 10 minutes.
3. Add C, cook 5 minutes.
4. Add D, mix well, cook 2 to 3 minutes. Serve hot.

CELERY CABBAGE WITH MUSTARD
Suen La Bai Tsoi: Canton

A. 2½ lbs. celery cabbage
B. 2 teaspoons mustard
C. ½ teaspoon salt
D. 2 tablespoons light soy sauce
E. 1 tablespoon cider vinegar

PREPARATION:

I. Peel off outside leaves of A to leave only the tender center. Cut each center leaf into 3 or 4 pieces.
II. Mix B, C, D, E to form paste.

COOKING:

1. Parboil A by keeping leaves in boiling water about 30 seconds. Drain and cool.
2. Mix A with B–E paste.

CHINESE COLE SLAW
Lun Ban Bai Tsai Si: Tientsin

A. ½ cup shredded carrots
B. 2 cups shredded celery cabbage
C. 15 to 20 whole peppercorns
D. 1 to 2 teaspoons salt
E. 1 handful Chinese parsley
F. ¼ teaspoon sesame oil

PREPARATION:

I. Combine A, B, C, D and mix well. Place in jar and allow to stand 6 hours.
II. Cut E into 1-inch pieces.
III. Drain water from A–D; add E, F, mix and serve.

CHINESE COLE SLAW
Lun Dan Juan Shing Tsai: Tientsin

Substitute American cabbage for B in Step I, allow to stand in refrigerator 1 to 2 days.

HOT AND SOUR CELERY CABBAGE I
Swan La Tsai: Szechuan

A. 4 tablespoons peanut oil
B. 1 teaspoon anise pepper
C. 3 red-hot peppers
D. 1 lb. center portion celery cabbage
E. ⅓ cup white vinegar

F. ½ teaspoon salt
G. 1 tablespoon light soy sauce
H. ½ to 1 teaspoon sesame oil
I. 1 teaspoon cornstarch

PREPARATION:

I. Cut D into pieces 1 to 1½ inches wide.
II. Cut C endwise, discard seeds and stem, then slice diagonally in thin pieces.
III. Mix E, F, G, H, I.

COOKING:

1. Heat A. Add B, stir-fry 1 minute, remove B from pan. Discard.
2. Add C, stir-fry a few seconds, add D. Continue stir-frying 2 to 3 minutes.
3. Add E–I, mix well. Cover, cook 2 minutes. Serve hot.

HOT AND SOUR CELERY CABBAGE II
Swan La Tsai: Shanghai

A. 2 teaspoons sesame oil
B. 1 hot chili pepper, chopped
C. ¼ cup vinegar

D. 1 tablespoon sugar
E. 1 to 2 lbs. celery cabbage
F. 1 to 2 teaspoons salt

PREPARATION:

I. Using center stalk portion of E (removing top leafy part), cut into 2-inch cross-section pieces. Pour boiling water over E, drain. Repeat pouring and draining process 4 times, then cool. When cold, mix with F.
II. Mix C, D.

COOKING:

1. Heat A. Add B, fry until golden brown.
2. Add C–D, mix well.
3. Pour A–D over cold E. Serve as hors d'oeuvres.

PEKING PICKLES
La Bai Tsai: Peking

A. 1 tablespoon peanut oil
B. ½ teaspoon anise pepper
C. ¼ cup sugar
D. ¼ cup vinegar
E. 1 to 2 lbs. celery cabbage

F. 1½ tablespoons salt
G. 4 slices ginger
H. ½ to 1 teaspoon red pepper flakes (to taste)

PREPARATION:

I. Remove E leaves from main stem. Rub each with F, and spread out uniformly in an 8- by 12-inch cake pan. Cover with waxed paper topped by another 8- by 12-inch pan. Place a heavy weight over second pan. Let stand at least 6 hours.
II. Remove E leaves from pan, squeeze out water. Cut each into 2-inch pieces, place in a bowl, and add G, H.

COOKING:

1. Heat A, stir-fry B a few seconds. Add C, D, bring to boil.
2. Pour A–D over E–H mixture, mix well, and marinate 2 hours.
3. Pour juice back in pot, bring to boil. Pour over E–H again; marinate 4 more hours.
4. To serve, discard B (it is easily visible), drain, and arrange pickles on a dish.

SZECHUAN PICKLES
Pow Tsai: Szechuan

A. 6 cups bite-size American cabbage pieces, from center portion
B. 2 carrots
C. 1 red-hot pepper
D. 1 slice ginger (about ½-inch)

E. 2 cloves garlic
F. 3 tablespoons salt
G. 6 cups boiling water
H. 2 tablespoons dry sherry

PREPARATION:

I. Peel B; cut into sticks 1 to 2 inches long.
II. Discard C seeds and stem, cut C into long, thin diagonal pieces.
III. Slice D into 4 to 5 pieces.
IV. Peel E, discard skin.
V. Wash A, B, drain. Dry thoroughly with paper towels. Place in a 2-qt. jar with C, D, E.

VI. Dissolve F in G, cool thoroughly, and add to mixture.
VII. Add H, cover jar tightly. Let stand 3 days, when pickle will be ready to serve. Pickle juice may be reused indefinitely. With each use, add ½ tablespoon salt, and pickle will be ready to serve in one day.

CARROTS WITH SHRIMP SAUCE
Har Yung Ju Hung Lo Ba: Canton

A. 13¾-oz. can chicken broth
B. 1 bunch carrots
C. ¼ lb. shrimp

D. 2 teaspoons sherry
E. 2 tablespoons cornstarch mixed with ¼ cup water

PREPARATION:

I. Wash, peel B; grate.

II. Shell C, devein, wash. Mince, mix with D.

COOKING:

1. Empty A into saucepan. Add B, bring to boil, cook 5 minutes.
2. Add C–D, cook 2 to 3 minutes.
3. Add E to thicken. Serve with rice.

CAULIFLOWER WITH HAM SAUCE
Yung Twei Hwa Tsai: Shanghai

A. 4 cups bite-size pieces cauliflower
B. ⅔ cup soup stock
C. ½ teaspoon salt
D. ½ cup chopped Virginia ham

E. 4 slices ginger
F. 1 tablespoon chopped scallion
G. 2 teaspoons cornstarch mixed with ¼ cup water

COOKING:

1. Mix A, B in saucepan, bring to boil; cook covered 5 minutes.
2. Add C, stir well.
3. Remove A to dish, leaving liquid in saucepan.
4. Add D, E, F, bring to boil.
5. Thicken with G.
6. Pour sauce over cooked A.

CAULIFLOWER WITH MUSHROOMS
Dung Gu Hwa Tsai: General

A. 1 medium cauliflower
B. 4 tablespoons peanut oil
C. 2 tablespoons chopped scallion

D. 4 oz. canned American button mushrooms
E. 1½ teaspoons salt
F. 1 teaspoon sugar

PREPARATION:

I. Cut A into 1-inch cubes.
II. Drain D, save liquid.

III. Mix E, F.

COOKING:

1. Drop A into boiling water. When water boils again, remove from heat. Drain and rinse under cold water.

2. Heat B in pan, stir-fry C ½ minute.
3. Add A, D and D liquid and E and F.
4. Stir-fry 1 to 2 minutes. Serve.

STUFFED CUCUMBER
Rong Hwong Gwa: General

A. 2 large cucumbers
B. ½ lb. ground pork
C. ½ teaspoon sesame oil
D. 1 slice ginger, minced
E. 10 water chestnuts, chopped

F. 2 tablespoons light soy sauce
G. 1 scallion, sliced
H. 1 tablespoon lard
I. ¼ teaspoon salt
J. 1 teaspoon chopped Chinese parsley

PREPARATION:

I. Peel A; cross-cut into 2-inch slices; scoop out seeds.
II. Mix B, C, D, E, F, G, H, I.

III. Fill centers of A with B–I mixture. Arrange on a plate.

COOKING:

1. Steam A–I 20 minutes in a steamer.
2. Garnish with J.

3. Serve hot.

SWEET AND SOUR CUCUMBERS I
Tien Swan Hwang Gwa: Peking

A. 2 tablespoons vegetable oil
B. 3 medium cucumbers
C. 4 slices ginger
D. 4 tablespoons cider vinegar

E. 1 teaspoon light soy sauce
F. ½ teaspoon sesame oil (optional)
G. 3 tablespoons sugar
H. 1 teaspoon salt

PREPARATION:

I. Wash and cut B in half lengthwise. Remove seeds. Cut into 1- to 1½-inch slices.

II. Mix C, D, E, F, G, H.

COOKING:

1. Heat A in skillet. Stir-fry B one minute (do not cook thoroughly).
2. Add C–H, allow mixture to boil.

3. Remove to bowl and cool.
4. Marinate 30 minutes or more and serve.

SWEET AND SOUR CUCUMBERS II
Tien Swan Huang Gwa: Szechuan

A. 1 tablespoon sesame oil
B. 2 to 3 medium cucumbers
C. 1 teaspoon light soy sauce
D. 4 tablespoons cider vinegar

E. 3 tablespoons sugar
F. 1 teaspoon salt
G. 1 to 2 red-hot peppers

PREPARATION:

I. Wash and cut B in half lengthwise. Remove seeds. Cut each half into 3 cross-sections, dry with paper towels.

II. Halve G, discard seeds and stems, and shred diagonally.

COOKING:

1. Heat A, stir-fry B 1 minute.
2. Add C, D, E, F, stir well, and bring to boil.
3. Add G, stir a few seconds.

4. Remove mixture to a bowl, cover, and let stand 3 to 4 hours.
5. Before serving, remove B and G from mixture. Shred B, garnish with G.

BARBECUED EGGPLANT
Kow Cheh Tze: Szechuan

A. 1-lb. eggplant
B. ¼ cup peanut butter
C. 1 teaspoon salt

D. dash garlic salt or 1 clove garlic, chopped
E. ⅓ cup water

PREPARATION AND COOKING:

I. Skin A, cut into 8 lengthwise pieces and place on aluminum foil.

II. Mix B, C, D, E to form paste. Paint mixture on A. Wrap with the foil. Grill 15 minutes on medium heat, 7½ minutes on each side.

BRAISED EGGPLANT I
Mun Keh: Canton

A. 3 tablespoons peanut oil
B. 10 dried shrimp
C. 1 clove garlic, chopped
D. 1 tablespoon chopped scallion
E. 2 slices ginger
F. ½ lb. pork, shredded

G. 1- to 1½-lbs. eggplant
H. 2 tablespoons light soy sauce
I. 1 teaspoon sugar
J. ½ teaspoon salt
K. ½ cup B water

PREPARATION:

I. Wash B and soak in water 15 minutes. Drain, chop, saving water (K).

II. Peel G, cut into 6 long sections; cut each section diagonally into bite-size pieces.
III. Mix H, I, J, K.

COOKING:

1. Heat A. Add B, C, D, E, stir-fry a few seconds.
2. Add F, stir-fry over high heat 2 minutes.
3. Add G, mix well.

4. Add H–K, bring to boil, cover, and cook over low heat until G is soft (about 10 to 15 minutes).

BRAISED EGGPLANT II
Hung Sao Chieh Tze: General

A. 3 tablespoons peanut oil
B. 1 clove garlic, chopped
C. 4 slices ginger, chopped
D. 1-lb. eggplant

E. 3 tablespoons light soy sauce
F. 1 teaspoon sugar
G. ¼ cup chicken broth or water

PREPARATION:

I. Peel D, slice into 8 lengthwise pieces. Halve each.

COOKING:

1. Heat A, stir-fry B, C several seconds.
2. Add D, stir-fry 2 minutes.
3. Add E, F, G, mix well, bring to boil.

4. Reduce heat, simmer until D is tender (about 15 minutes).

EGGPLANT BUTTER
Tsen Chieh Nee: Shantung

A. 1-lb. eggplant
B. 1 tablespoon sesame sauce or peanut butter
C. 1 clove garlic, minced

D. ¼ teaspoon sesame oil
E. ½ teaspoon salt

PREPARATION:

I. Peel A and remove stem. Cut into small pieces. Place in deep platter.

COOKING:

1. Steam A 20 minutes or until it is soft and breaks up easily. Mix with B, C, D, and E to taste. Serve.

EGGPLANT BUTTER *Approved Ulcer Recipe*
Tsen Chieh Nee: Shantung

Steam A 30 minutes, mash, remove skin; omit C; mix with sesame sauce. Salt to taste.

FRIED EGGPLANT CAKES
Jien Cheh Bing: General

A. 2 to 3 tablespoons salad oil
B. 1-lb. eggplant
C. 1 or 2 eggs
D. 3 tablespoons flour

E. dash garlic powder
F. dash pepper
G. ½ teaspoon salt

PREPARATION:

I. Skin B and slice into pieces ¼ inch thick.
II. Break C into bowl.

III. Add E, F; then add D gradually until a smooth, thick batter is formed.
IV. Soak B slices in C–G.

COOKING:

1. Place A in hot skillet; fry coated B in A until tender.

GINGER JUICE EGGPLANT
Jiang Tze Chieh Tze: Shanghai

A. 3 tablespoons peanut oil
B. 1-lb. eggplant
C. 2 teaspoons ginger juice (see Index)

D. 3 tablespoons shrimp-flavored soy sauce (see Index)
E. 1 teaspoon sugar
F. ½ cup water

PREPARATION:
I. Peel B. Slice B in 8 lengthwise pieces, then halve each.

COOKING:
1. Heat A, stir-fry B 2 minutes.
2. Add C, stir-fry a few seconds.

3. Add D, E, F, mix well, and bring to boil. Reduce heat, simmer until B is tender (about 15 to 20 minutes).

LIMA BEANS WITH EGGPLANT
Tsan Do Chieh Tze: General

A. 3 tablespoons vegetable oil
B. 1-lb. eggplant
C. 2 teaspoons minced scallion
D. 1 clove garlic, minced
E. 1 cup water
F. ½ pkg. (5 oz.) frozen baby lima beans

G. 2 to 3 slices ginger
H. ½ teaspoon sugar
I. ½ teaspoon salt
J. 2 teaspoons light soy sauce
K. ¼ cup ground pork
L. 1 teaspoon cornstarch

PREPARATION:
I. Peel B and slice into round sections ¼ inch thick.

II. Mix J, K, L in small bowl.

COOKING:
1. Heat 2 tablespoons A in large frying pan. Add B, C, D, stir-fry 1 minute.
2. Add ¼ cup E, simmer 15 minutes. Remove B–D from pan.

3. Add remaining A, heat. Add F, G, H, I, stir-fry a little longer.
4. Add J–L. Continue stir-frying 5 minutes. Return B–D, and gradually add rest of E. Cook for 5 to 10 minutes, until B is soft.

STEAMED EGGPLANT WITH MINCED MEAT
Chieh Nee: Szechuan

A. 2 tablespoons peanut oil
B. ½ cup ground pork
C. 1 small hot pepper
D. 1 clove garlic, chopped

E. 1 tablespoon preserved celery cabbage
F. 1-lb. eggplant
G. 1 teaspoon salt

PREPARATION:
I. Peel F, split in half, steam over boiling water 20 minutes or until soft; mash.
II. Discard stem and seeds of C, chop.

III. Cover E with cold water, stir so that any sediment will sink to bottom; remove E from water.

COOKING:
1. Heat A, add B, C, D, E, stir-fry 1 to 2 minutes.

2. Add F, G, stir well and serve.

EGGPLANT SANDWICH
Chieh Pien Ja Ro: Shanghai

A. peanut oil for deep frying
B. 1-lb. eggplant
C. 10 dried shrimp
D. 1 scallion, chopped (white part only)
E. ½ lb. ground pork
F. 2 teaspoons light soy sauce

G. 1 teaspoon sugar
H. 3 teaspoons cornstarch
I. ¼ teaspoon pepper
J. 1 teaspoon salt
K. 1 large egg
L. bread crumbs

PREPARATION:

I. Peel B and cut diagonally in thin slices.
II. Soak C in water 15 minutes or until soft, drain and mince.
III. Mix C, D, E, F, G, H, I, J thoroughly.

IV. Make sandwich with B pieces by spreading them with C–J mixture.
V. Beat K well, mix with additional ½ teaspoon salt.
VI. Dip each B sandwich in K, then coat with L.

COOKING:

1. Heat A to 350°, deep fry B sandwiches until golden brown, and serve.

STUFFED EGGPLANT
Rahng Chieh Tze: General

A. 1- to 1½-lb. eggplant
B. 8 water chestnuts, chopped
C. 1 scallion, chopped
D. 2 slices ginger, chopped
E. 2 teaspoons sherry

F. ½ lb. ground pork
G. 2 teaspoons light soy sauce
H. 1 teaspoon sugar
I. ½ teaspoon salt
J. ¼ cup chicken broth

PREPARATION:

I. Peel A, cut in half, remove seeds.
II. Mix B, C, D, E, F, G, H, I.

III. Stuff A with B–I.
IV. Place stuffed A in bowl; pour J over it.

COOKING:

1. Place in steamer and steam over boiling water 45 minutes.

SWEET AND SOUR EGGPLANT
Tong Tsu Chia Nee: Peking

A. 1-lb. eggplant
B. 1 teaspoon salt
C. 1 clove garlic, chopped

D. ¾ teaspoon sesame oil
E. 2 teaspoons sugar
F. 1½ tablespoons vinegar

PREPARATION:

I. Peel A, cut into 16 pieces.

II. Mix B, C, D, E, F.

COOKING:

1. Place A in dish, steam over boiling water 30 minutes or until soft.
2. Break up A with fork.
3. Add B–F, mix well.

STIR-FRIED GREEN BEANS WITH FERMENTED BEAN CAKE
Fu Yu Tsang Dow: Canton

A. 3 tablespoons peanut oil
B. 1 to 2 cloves garlic
C. 1 lb. green beans
D. ½ cup water

E. 1 tablespoon fermented bean cake, mashed
F. ½ teaspoon sugar
G. ½ teaspoon salt

PREPARATION:

I. Trim and discard ends of C. Wash, break C into 1-inch pieces.

II. Pound B with back of cleaver; discard skin.

COOKING:

1. Heat A, stir-fry B a few seconds.
2. Add C pieces, stir 1 minute.
3. Add D, bring to boil. Lower heat, cover, and cook 3 minutes.

4. Add E, F, G and mix thoroughly. Cook 3 more minutes or until liquid is almost absorbed.

STIR-FRIED GREEN BEANS WITH FERMENTED BEAN CAKE *Approved Diabetic Recipe*
Fu Yu Tsang Dow: Canton

A. 1 tablespoon peanut oil
B. 1 small clove garlic
C. ½ lb. green beans

D. ¼ cup water
E. 2 teaspoons fermented bean cake, mashed
F. ½ teaspoon salt

PREPARATION:

I. Trim and discard ends of C. Wash, break C into 1¼-inch pieces.

II. Pound B with back of cleaver; discard skin.

COOKING:

1. Heat A, stir-fry B a few seconds; add C pieces, continue stirring 1 minute.
2. Add D, bring to boil. Lower heat, cover, and cook 3 minutes.

3. Add E, F, mix thoroughly. Cook 3 more minutes or until liquid is almost absorbed.

STIR-FRIED GREEN BEANS WITH GARLIC
Shuin Tow Chan Dow: Adapted

A. 3 tablespoons peanut oil
B. 2 or 3 cloves garlic

C. 1 lb. green beans
D. 2 tablespoons light soy sauce

E. ½ teaspoon sugar
F. salt to taste

PREPARATION:

I. Trim and discard ends of C. Wash, break C into 1½-inch pieces, parboil 3 minutes. Drain and rinse with cold water.

II. Pound B with back of cleaver, discard skin.
III. Mix D, E.

COOKING:

1. Heat A, add B, brown slightly.
2. Add C and stir-fry 3 minutes. Add 1 to 2 tablespoons water, if necessary.

3. Add D, E, continue stirring 1 minute.
4. Discard B, add F and serve.

KOHLRABI OR CABBAGE PICKLES
Pow Tsai: Szechuan

A. 1 lb. kohlrabi or cabbage
B. 1 red-hot pepper (optional)
C. 4 slices ginger

D. 2 cloves garlic
E. 1 tablespoon salt

F. 2 cups boiling water
G. 1 tablespoon wine

PREPARATION:

I. Peel A and discard skin. Slice A into bite-size pieces or use center portion of cabbage and cut into bite-size pieces.

II. Discard B seeds and stem. Cut B diagonally into thin, long pieces.
III. Peel D, discard skin.

COOKING:

1. Mix A, B, C, D, place in jar.
2. Dissolve E in F. Cool thoroughly, add to jar.
3. Add G, cover jar tightly, and let stand 2 to 3 days, when pickle will be ready to serve.

Pickle juice can be used over and over, each time, adding ½ tablespoon salt, and pickle will be ready to serve in only one day. Refrigerate between use.

KOHLRABI OR CABBAGE PICKLES *Approved Diabetic Recipe*
Pow Tsai: Szechuan

A. 1 lb. kohlrabi or cabbage
B. 1 to 2 red-hot peppers, according to taste
C. 1 to 2 slices pickled ginger or fresh ginger shoots

D. 1 small clove garlic
E. 1 tablespoon salt
F. 2 cups boiling water

PREPARATION:

I. Peel A and discard skin. Slice A into bite-size pieces or use center portion of cabbage and cut into bite-size pieces.

II. Discard B seeds and stems. Cut B diagonally into thin, long pieces.
III. Peel D, discard skin.

COOKING:

1. Mix A, B, C, D, place in jar.
2. Dissolve E in F. Cool thoroughly, add to jar. Cover jar tightly. Pickle will be ready to serve in 2 days. After first day refrigerate jarred

pickle. Pickle juice can be used over and over, each time adding ½ tablespoon salt, and pickle will be ready to serve in only one day. Refrigerate between use.

LETTUCE AND FERMENTED BEAN CAKE
Fu Yu Sang Tsoi: Canton

A. 2 tablespoons peanut oil
B. 1 clove garlic, minced
C. 1 head iceberg lettuce

D. 1 tablespoon fermented bean cake, mashed
E. 1 tablespoon soup stock

PREPARATION:

I. Separate leaves of C. Wash, drain well.

II. Mix D, E into smooth paste.

COOKING:

1. Put A in very hot skillet and bring to high heat.
2. Add B. Stir-fry 10 seconds to brown slightly.

3. Add C and stir-fry about 3 minutes or until soft.
4. Add D–E. Stir well. Heat thoroughly. Serve.

STUFFED BITTER MELON
Yeong Fu Gwa: Canton

A. 2 tablespoons peanut oil
B. 2 medium bitter melons
C. ½ teaspoon baking soda
D. 2 cloves garlic, chopped
E. 1 tablespoon fermented salted black beans
F. 1 tablespoon sherry
G. 2 teaspoons light soy sauce
H. ½ teaspoon salt
I. 1 teaspoon sugar
J. ½ cup water

K. ½ lb. ground pork
L. 12 dried shrimp
M. 1 scallion, chopped
N. 1 teaspoon light soy sauce
O. 1 teaspoon cornstarch
P. ½ teaspoon sugar
Q. dash pepper and salt
R. 2 teaspoons cornstarch mixed with 2 tablespoons water

PREPARATION:

I. Cut B into 2-inch cross sections; remove seeds, pods, and pulp, leaving a hollow shell. Place B, C in 1 qt. boiling water and cook 2 minutes; rinse in cold water and cover with cold water. Let stand for ½ hour, then drain.

II. Soak L in water 15 to 30 minutes or until soft, drain and chop.
III. Mix K, L, M, N, O, P, Q well and stuff into B rings.
IV. Mix F, G, H, I, J.

COOKING:

1. Heat A; add stuffed B and brown both ends.
2. Add D, E; stir-fry a few seconds.
3. Add F–J; mix well, lower heat and simmer 15 to 20 minutes. Remove stuffed B to a dish.
4. Thicken gravy with R and pour over B. Serve hot.

STIR-FRIED BITTER MELON WITH BEEF
Fu Gwa Tsao Ngo Yoke: Canton

A. 3 tablespoons peanut oil
B. 1 to 2 cloves garlic
C. 1 tablespoon fermented salted black beans
D. ½-lb. bitter melon
E. ½ teaspoon baking soda
F. ½ lb. beefsteak
G. 1 teaspoon chopped ginger

H. 1 tablespoon sherry
I. 1 tablespoon light soy sauce
J. 1 teaspoon sugar
K. 2 teaspoons cornstarch
L. 1 teaspoon peanut oil
M. salt to taste

PREPARATION:

I. Cut D into halves, discard seeds and pods. Cut diagonally into ⅜-inch pieces. Cover D, E with boiling water and cook 2 minutes. Drain; leave in cold water 15 minutes. Drain.

II. Discard skin of B and mince.
III. Cut F into thin slices and shred. Mix with G, H, I, J, K, L.

COOKING:

1. Heat, A, add B, C; stir-fry a few seconds.
2. Add D, continue stirring 1 minute.
3. Add F–L mixture, stir-fry 1 to 2 minutes.
4. Add M and serve.

STUFFED HAIRY MELON
Yeong Mo Gwa: Canton

A. 1-lb. hairy melon
B. ¼ lb. pork, minced
C. 3 Chinese mushrooms
D. 6 dried shrimp
E. 1 tablespoon chopped scallion
F. ½ teaspoon chopped ginger

G. 2 teaspoons light soy sauce
H. ¼ teaspoon sugar
I. 1 teaspoon lard
J. ½ teaspoon salt
K. 2 teaspoons cornstarch

PREPARATION:

I. Peel A, cut into 1-inch segments; with a sharp knife, cut out the middle, seedy part.
II. Rinse C and soak in warm water 15 minutes; drain and mince.
III. Clean D; soak in cold water 10 minutes; drain and chop.
IV. Mix B, C, D, E, F, G, H, I, J, K.
V. Stuff A pieces with B–K and arrange on a dish.

COOKING: 1. Steam A pieces 20 to 25 minutes.

STEAMED MUSHROOMS
Ching Tsen Dung Gu: Peking

A. 2 oz. Chinese mushrooms
B. 2 scallions, chopped

C. 3 slices ginger, chopped
D. 1 teaspoon sherry

E. 1 teaspoon sugar
F. salt to taste

PREPARATION:

I. Soak A in warm water 20 minutes. Drain and cut off stems. Place in deep dish for steaming.
II. Mix A, B, C, D, E.

COOKING:

1. Place dish in steamer and steam 35 minutes. Add F and serve.

STUFFED MUSHROOM SANDWICH
Dung Gu Heh Tze: Suchow

A. 20 large Chinese mushrooms
B. 2 tablespoons light soy sauce
C. 2 teaspoons sherry
D. 1 teaspoon sugar
E. ⅓ cup chicken broth
F. 1 lb. any fresh green vegetable (Chinese cabbage, spinach, etc.)

G. 1 tablespoon peanut oil
H. salt to taste
I. 2 teaspoons cornstarch mixed with ¼ cup water
J. ¼ lb. ground pork
K. 1 teaspoon sherry
L. 2 teaspoons cornstarch

PREPARATION:

I. Wash A in cold water and soak in warm water 15 minutes; drain (if chicken broth or soup stock are not available, use mushroom water); discard stems, dry between paper towels; sprinkle A with ½ L.
II. Slice F diagonally in 1-inch lengths.
III. Mix H, J, K and rest of L well, divide into 10 portions.
IV. Stuff ½ A with H, J, K, L mixture, cover stuffing with remaining A to make 10 sandwiches.

COOKING:

1. Place stuffed A in saucepan; add B, C, D, E, bring to boil and cook 3 to 5 minutes until meat is done.
2. Parboil F, stir-fry in G 1 minute; add rest of H. (If spinach is used, heat should be turned off as soon as spinach is dropped into boiling water, and the spinach stirred well and then drained.)
3. Arrange F on dish, place stuffed A on top.
4. Thicken sauce with I and pour over A.

MUSHROOMS WITH BAMBOO SHOOTS
Yang Chow Tsao Er Dung: Yangchow

A. 3 tablespoons peanut oil
B. 2 cups sliced bamboo shoots
C. 12 large Chinese mushrooms
D. 1½ tablespoons light soy sauce
E. 1 teaspoon sugar
F. 2 teaspoons sherry
G. ½ teaspoon ginger juice (see Index)
H. ⅓ cup chicken broth or mushroom water
I. 2 teaspoons cornstarch mixed with ¼ cup water
J. few drops sesame oil

PREPARATION:

I. Wash C in cold water, then soak in warm water 15 minutes; drain, save water; cut each C into halves.

II. Mix D, E, F, G.

COOKING:

1. Heat A, add B, C, stir-fry 1 minute.
2. Add D–G and H, cook 1 to 2 minutes.
3. Thicken with I.
4. Add J and serve.

MUSTARD GREENS WITH PORK SAUCE
Gai Lan Ju Yoke Jeong: Canton

A. 1½ tablespoons peanut oil
B. 1 clove garlic, minced
C. ½ lb. ground pork
D. 1 tablespoon light soy sauce
E. 1 tablespoon sherry
F. 1 teaspoon heavy soy sauce
G. 1¾ cup soup stock
H. 2 tablespoons cornstarch
I. 1 lb. mustard greens

PREPARATION:

I. Wash I. Cut into 1½-inch segments. Parboil by dropping into 3 qts. vigorously boiling water and cooking uncovered for 3 minutes. Drain. Wash in cold water. Drain.

II. Mix D, E. Set aside.
III. Mix F, G, H. Set aside. Stir well.

COOKING:

1. Put A in very hot skillet and bring to high heat.
2. Add B. Stir-fry rapidly 15 seconds to brown B slightly.
3. Add C and stir-fry 3 minutes.
4. Add D–E. Stir-fry 1 minute.
5. Add F–H and bring to boil. Stir constantly as sauce thickens.
6. Add I. Serve when piping hot and all ingredients are well coated with sauce.

TOSSED PRESERVED MUSTARD GREENS
Swan Tsai Ban Sha Mi: Hunan

A. 1 cup preserved mustard greens (center part only)

B. 1 cup diced bamboo shoots

C. 1½ tablespoons sugar

D. 1 tablespoon vinegar

E. 2 teaspoons light soy sauce

F. 20 dried shrimp

G. ½ to 1 teaspoon sesame oil (to taste)

PREPARATION:

I. Wash A, squeeze out water and dice.

II. Wash F well, soak 15 minutes in warm water, drain, dice.

III. Mix A with B; mix in C, let stand 30 minutes.

IV. Add D, E, mix well, and let stand 15 minutes. Add F, G, mix well, and serve.

MUSTARD GREEN PICKLES
Kwangtung La Tsoi: Canton

A. 2 tablespoons salt

B. 3 qts. boiling water

C. 1 lb. mustard green hearts

D. ¼ cup sugar

E. ½ cup vinegar

PREPARATION AND COOKING:

I. Add A to B.

II. Wash and clean C (if they are large, halve lengthwise); add to A–B.

III. Turn off heat, leave C in B until soft (about 4 to 5 minutes).

IV. Remove C from B and drain; squeeze out excess B.

V. Shred, add D and E; marinate for two days. If kept in a tightly covered jar and refrigerated for a week or two, mustard flavor will become stronger. Pickles may be served as is or mixed with other salad vegetables.

SWEET GREEN PEPPER STUFFED WITH MEAT
Ching Jiu Yeong Ju Yoke: Canton

A. 1 tablespoon peanut oil

B. ½ lb. ground pork

C. 10 dried shrimp

D. 2 teaspoons sherry

E. 3 tablespoons light soy sauce

F. ½ teaspoon salt

G. 2 teaspoons cornstarch

H. ½ teaspoon sugar

I. 6 small sweet green peppers

J. 1 tablespoon sherry

K. 1 tablespoon light soy sauce

L. 2 tablespoons dried shrimp water or soup stock

PREPARATION:

I. Clean and wash C; soak in water 15 minutes; drain and mince. Save water.

II. Mix B, C, D, E, F, G, H.

III. Wash I, split lengthwise, discard stems and seeds. Stuff with B–H.

IV. Mix J, K, L.

COOKING:

1. Heat A over medium heat.

2. Brown meat side of B–I 3 minutes.

3. Turn B–I over and brown 1 more minute.

4. Add J–L. Cover and cook 5 to 7 minutes or until meat is done.

SHREDDED THREE: GREEN, RED, AND WHITE
Tsao Sam Sic: Adapted

A. 3 tablespoons peanut oil
B. 1 medium sweet red pepper
C. 1 medium sweet green pepper
D. 1 chicken breast
E. 2 teaspoons cornstarch

F. 1 tablespoon sherry
G. 1 teaspoon peanut oil
H. 1 teaspoon sugar
I. 1 teaspoon salt
J. 1 tablespoon brown bean sauce

PREPARATION:

I. Wash B, C, quarter and discard stems and seeds, then cut diagonally into ¼-inch slices.

II. Bone D and shred, mix with E, F, G.
III. Mix H, I, J.

COOKING:

1. Heat A, stir-fry B, C a few seconds.
2. Add D–G, continue stirring 2 to 3 minutes.

3. Add H–J, stir ½ minute; serve.

BRAISED POTATOES
Hung Sao Yang Yu: General

A. 3 tablespoons peanut oil
B. 1 lb. potatoes
C. 3 tablespoons light soy sauce

D. 1 teaspoon sugar
E. ½ cup boiling water

PREPARATION:

I. Peel B, cut into bite-size pieces.

COOKING:

1. Heat A, stir-fry B 2 minutes.
2. Add C, D, stir well.

3. Add E, mix well; bring to boil. Reduce heat, simmer until B is tender (about 15 minutes).

FRIED SALTY PUMPKIN STICKS
Tza Nahn Gwa: General

A. 1 qt. peanut oil
B. ½- to 1-lb. pumpkin
C. ½ cup flour
D. 5 tablespoons water

E. 1 teaspoon salt
F. 2 teaspoons light soy sauce
G. pepper to taste

PREPARATION:

I. Peel B and discard seeds and soft pulp and strings; cut into finger-size sticks.

II. Mix C, D, E, F into a paste.
III. Add B sticks to C–F until each is coated well.

COOKING:

1. Heat A to 350°.
2. Deep fry B–F, ⅓ at a time, until golden brown (about 2 minutes). The pumpkin sticks

will float when they are done. Serve hot or cold, with or without G.

RED-IN-SNOW WITH PORK
Shieh Li Hung Ro Si: Shanghai

A. 3 tablespoons peanut oil
B. ½ lb. pork, shredded
C. 1 teaspoon cornstarch
D. 2 teaspoons light soy sauce
E. ½ teaspoon sugar
F. 1 tablespoon chopped scallion

G. 1½ cups shredded bamboo shoots
H. ½ (5-oz.) can preserved red-in-snow
I. ½ teaspoon salt
J. ½ teaspoon sugar
K. ¼ cup water

PREPARATION:

I. Mix B, C, D, E, F.

II. Mix I, J, K.

COOKING:

1. Heat A, stir-fry B–F 2 minutes.
2. Add G, H, and I–K. Mix well.

3. Cover, lower heat, and cook 3 minutes.

PRESERVED RED-IN-SNOW
Yen Shieh Li Hung: Shanghai

Wash 1 to 2 lbs. fresh red-in-snow well, dry with paper towels, and let stand 2 days in an airy place. Rub thoroughly with ½ cup salt, place in a clean jar, and cover tightly. Let stand 2 weeks before cooking. Stir-fry with pork, beef, or veal, or cook in meat soup.

RED-IN-SNOW WITH PORK AND CARROTS
Shieh Tsai Ro Si Hu Lo Bo: Shanghai

Add 2 carrots, peeled and shredded, and reduce G to 1 cup. Stir-fry B–F 1 minute in A. Add shredded carrots, stir-fry 2 minutes. Add rest of ingredients, mix well. Cover, lower heat, and cook 2 to 3 more minutes.

RED-IN-SNOW WITH VEAL
Shieh Tsai Tsao Shiao Niu Ro Si: Shanghai

Substitute 4 veal chops (about 1 cup shredded) for B.

RED-IN-SNOW WITH BEEF
Shieh Tsai Niu Ro Si: Shanghai

Substitute ½ lb. beef, shredded, for B.

RED-IN-SNOW WITH PORK RICE
Shieh Tsai Ro Si Fan: Shanghai

A. 1 to 1½ cups cooked rice
B. ½ cup Red-in Snow with Pork (see Index)

C. ½ cup boiling water
D. salt to taste

COOKING:

1. Place A in a pot.
2. Add B, C, mix well, and bring to boil.

3. Lower heat, simmer 5 minutes.
4. Add D.

STIR-FRIED SNOW PEAS
Bi Yur Twei Pien: Adapted

A. 2 tablespoons peanut oil
B. 1 clove garlic, chopped
C. 1 tablespoon chopped scallion
   (white part only)
D. ½ cup sliced ham

E. 6 Chinese mushrooms
F. 1 cup thinly sliced bamboo shoots
G. ¼ lb. snow peas
H. ½ teaspoon sugar
I. ½ teaspoon salt

PREPARATION:
I. Discard G tips.
II. Wash E and soak in warm water 15 minutes. Drain (save mushroom water), discard stems, cut each into 4 to 6 slices.

COOKING:
1. Heat A, add B, C, stir-fry a few seconds, add D, stir-fry 1 minute.
2. Add E, F, continue stirring 1 or 2 minutes.
3. Add G mix well, add H, I, and 2 tablespoons E water, stir well, cover, cook 1 minute and serve.

STIR-FRIED SPINACH WITH DRIED SHRIMP
Sha Mi Bo Tsai Nee: Shanghai

A. 3 tablespoons vegetable oil
B. 12 dried shrimp
C. 1 tablespoon minced scallion
D. 10 oz. pkg. fresh spinach

E. ½ teaspoon sugar
F. 1 teaspoon salt
G. ½ teaspoon sesame oil (optional)

PREPARATION:
I. Wash D, drain.

II. Soak B in hot water 20 minutes. Drain and chop, saving water.

COOKING:
1. Heat A in skillet.
2. Add B, C, stir-fry 30 seconds.
3. Add B water and D; stir continuously 1 to 2 minutes.
4. Add E, F; mix well. Remove to bowl.
5. Add G, and mix in bowl. Serve hot.

SPINACH AND FERMENTED BEAN CAKE
Dow Fu Bo Tsai: General

A. 2 tablespoons peanut oil
B. ⅛ teaspoon garlic powder
C. 1 lb. spinach

D. 1 tablespoon fermented bean cake, mashed
E. 1 tablespoon soup stock

PREPARATION:
I. Wash C. Cut off large, tough stems. Drain well.

II. Mix D, E into smooth paste.

COOKING:
1. Put A in very hot skillet and bring to high heat.
2. Add B. Stir-fry 10 seconds.
3. Add C and stir-fry in hot oil until leaves turn bright green (about 2 to 3 minutes) and are just fully soft ("collapsed").
4. Add D–E. Stir well. Heat thoroughly. Serve.

WATERCRESS AND FERMENTED BEAN CAKE
Fu Yu Sai Yong Tsoi: Canton

Substitute ½ pound watercress (1 bunch) for C and reduce D to 1½ teaspoons.

STEAMED SPINACH CAKE
Bo Tsai Gao: General

A. 10-oz. pkg. fresh spinach
B. 1½ tablespoons butter or lard
C. 3 tablespoons flour
D. 2 eggs

E. 2 tablespoons chopped Smithfield ham
F. 1 cup chopped bamboo shoots
G. 1 teaspoon salt
H. ½ teaspoon sugar

PREPARATION:

I. Discard tough part of A stems; soak and rinse leaves with cold water; drain.
II. Add A to 2 qts. boiling water, stir 30 seconds. Drain, cool, squeeze out water, and chop.
III. Melt B, add C and mix well; add to A and blend.

IV. Separate D, beat whites until fluffy. Beat yolks, add E, F, G, H, mix well.
V. Combine A–C with D–H. Mix thoroughly, fold in D whites.
VI. Place in a well-greased 8-inch round cake pan.

COOKING:

1. Steam over boiling water 25 minutes. Cool and turn cake over onto plate. Cut into pieces and serve as snack or garnish with sliced tomato. Can also be served as side dish.

CHOPPED SPINACH IN CREAM SAUCE   *Approved Ulcer Recipe*
Nye Yao Bo Tsai: Canton

A. ½ cup chicken broth
B. 10 oz. frozen chopped spinach
C. ½ cup milk
D. ½ tablespoon margarine

E. salt to taste
F. 1 tablespoon cornstarch
G. ¼ cup finely chopped white meat chicken

PREPARATION:

I. Mix C, D, E, F.

COOKING:

1. Bring A to boil. Add B, cook over medium heat about 5 to 10 minutes or until tender.
2. Heat C–F, stir until thickened.

3. Add B to C–F, heat thoroughly.
4. Place in bowl, garnish with G.

STIR-FRIED YELLOW SQUASH
Ching Tsao Nan Gwa: General

A. 2 tablespoons peanut oil
B. 1 scallion
C. 1-lb. yellow squash

D. 1 teaspoon salt
E. ½ teaspoon sugar
F. 2 tablespoons water

PREPARATION:

I. Peel C, split in half, then cut diagonally in ¼-inch slices.

II. Chop B.

COOKING:

1. Heat A, add B, stir-fry a few seconds.
2. Add C, continue stirring 1 minute.
3. Add D, E, mix well.

4. Add F, cover and cook over medium heat 3 minutes or until C is tender but not mushy.

STIR-FRIED MIXED CHINESE VEGETABLES
Ching Tsao Su Tsai: Adapted

A. 3 tablespoons peanut oil
B. 6 Chinese mushrooms
C. 1 tablespoon chopped scallion
D. 2 cups sliced celery cabbage
E. ½ cup sliced water chestnuts

F. ½ cup sliced bamboo shoots
G. 24 snow peas
H. ½ teaspoon sugar
I. 1 teaspoon salt

PREPARATION:

I. Rinse B under cold water; soak in warm water 15 minutes or until soft.

II. Discard tips of G.

COOKING:

1. Heat A, add B, C; stir-fry a few seconds.
2. Add D, stir-fry 1 minute.

3. Add E, F, G, mix well. Add 1 tablespoon water, cover and cook for 1 minute.
4. Add H, I, stir well and serve.

WHITE TURNIP PICKLES
Yen Lo Bo: Peking

A. 1-lb. Chinese white turnip
B. 1½ tablespoons salt
C. 2½ cups boiling water

D. 1 red-hot chili pepper or dried red-hot pepper
E. 2 slices ginger

PREPARATION:

I. Peel A and cut into finger-length strips.
II. Place B, C in clean qt. jar. Cool thoroughly.

III. Add A, D, E and cover tightly.
Note: Pickle may be served after marinating 1 day. Juice may be reused; add salt to taste.

SWEET AND SOUR WHITE TURNIP PICKLES
Yen Lo Bo Si: General

A. 1-lb. white turnip
B. 2 teaspoons salt
C. 1 red chili pepper

D. 2 tablespoons vinegar
E. 2 tablespoons sugar

PREPARATION:

I. Peel A; slice, then shred, rub with B and let stand 30 to 60 minutes.
II. Discard C stem and seeds, shred.

III. Discard A water; mix A, C.
IV. Add D, E, mix well. Let stand 1 hour before serving.

VEGETARIAN ROAST DUCK
Sue Sao Ya: Shanghai

A. 1 tablespoon peanut oil
B. 4 large mushrooms
C. 1 cup finely shredded bamboo shoots
D. 2 teaspoons light soy sauce
E. ½ teaspoon sugar
F. ½ teaspoon salt
G. 1 tablespoon mushroom water
H. 1½ teaspoons cornstarch

I. 1 teaspoon sugar
J. 2 teaspoons light soy sauce
K. ½ teaspoon sesame oil
L. ½ teaspoon salt
M. 2 tablespoons mushroom water
N. 4 pieces fresh bean curd skin
O. 2 cups peanut oil

PREPARATION:

I. Wash B and soak in warm water 15 minutes; drain and save water; shred B very fine.

II. Mix D, E, F, G.

III. Mix H, I, J, K, L, M.

COOKING:

1. Heat A, add B, stir-fry a few seconds, add C, mix well.

2. Add D–G, stir well and cook 1 minute.

3. Dip pastry brush into H–M and brush 1 piece of N generously.

4. Spread ¼ of A–G on top; place second piece of N over this; brush again with H–M and spread ¼ A–G over this.

5. Repeat procedure until fourth layer is finished.

6. Fold into a 2- to 3-inch roll; place on a plate and steam over boiling water 10 minutes; cool completely.

7. Heat O to 375°, deep fry A–N until golden brown (1 to 2 minutes), cool. Slice and serve as hors d'oeuvres or serve with rice.

VEGETARIAN STEAK WITH MUSHROOMS AND BAMBOO SHOOTS
Mien Jing Tsao Er Dung: Shanghai

A. 3 tablespoons peanut oil
B. 1 scallion, chopped
C. 2 slices ginger, chopped
D. 10-oz. can vegetarian steak
E. 1 cup diced bamboo shoots
F. 6 Chinese mushrooms
G. ¼ cup dry lily flowers

H. ¼ cup cloud ears
I. 2 tablespoons light soy sauce
J. ½ teaspoon sugar
K. ½ teaspoon salt
L. 1 teaspoon cornstarch mixed with ¼ cup water
M. ½ teaspoon sesame oil

PREPARATION:

I. Cut D into bite-size pieces.

II. Wash F, soak 15 minutes in warm water. Drain, saving water; cut each F in quarters.

III. Soak G 15 to 20 minutes in cold water; discard water. Remove hard tips, cut each G in half.

IV. Place H in pan large enough to allow it to double when expanded. Cover with 1 cup hot water, soak 15 to 30 minutes. Discard water; wash H well.

COOKING:

1. Heat A, stir-fry B, C a few seconds. Add D, E, F, G, H, stir-fry 2 minutes.

2. Add I, J, K and 3 tablespoons F water; cover, cook 5 minutes over low heat.

3. Stir in L until gravy is thick.

4. Remove from heat, add M, and mix thoroughly.

VEGETARIAN STEAK WITH CELLOPHANE NOODLES
Fun See Tsai Tsoi: Canton

Omit G, H, L and add 1-oz. package cellophane noodles. Soak noodles 30 minutes in hot water; drain. Cook noodles in 1 cup chicken broth until broth is nearly absorbed; add to Step 4.

VEGETARIAN SWEET AND SOUR MEATBALLS
Tien Swan Sue Ro Jiu: Shanghai

A. 1 cup peanut oil
B. 1 cup walnut halves
C. ¼ cup glutinous rice flour
D. ¼ cup flour
E. 1 teaspoon baking powder
F. dash salt
G. 1 green pepper
H. 1 red pepper

I. 1 scallion, chopped
J. 2 tablespoons vinegar
K. 2 tablespoons sugar
L. 2 tablespoons catsup
M. 1 tablespoon light soy sauce
N. ½ teaspoon salt
O. 2 teaspoons cornstarch mixed with ¼ cup water

PREPARATION:

I. Pour boiling water over B, let stand 2 minutes; peel, dry completely on paper towel.
II. Mix C, D, E, F with 5 tablespoons water to make batter.
III. Wash G, H; discard stems and seeds; cut G, H into cubes.

COOKING:

1. Heat A to 325°; deep fry B 15 to 30 seconds until golden brown; do not burn; drain on paper towel.
2. Dip fried B in C–F batter; then deep fry again in A until golden brown; drain on paper towel.
3. Heat 1 tablespoon A, add G, H, I, stir-fry ½ minute, add salt to taste.
4. Mix J, K, L, M, N, O in a saucepan over medium heat, stirring until thickened.
5. Add B and G–I, stir well and serve.

VEGETARIAN STIR-FRIED SLICED FISH
Tsao Sue Yu Pien: Shanghai

A. 1 cup peanut oil for deep frying
B. 12 wood ears
C. ¼ lb. snow peas
D. 1 medium tomato
E. 1 teaspoon salt

F. ½ teaspoon sugar
G. 1 teaspoon cornstarch mixed with ⅓ cup water
H. 1 large cooked potato (about ½ lb.)
I. 1½ tablespoons flour

PREPARATION:

I. Peel H, cut in half, then into ¼-inch slices; coat with I, deep fry in A at 375° until golden brown (1 to 2 minutes); drain on paper towel.
II. Wash B thoroughly and cook in boiling water ½ hour; drain and shred.
III. Remove tips of C.
IV. Cut D into 8 to 10 pieces.

COOKING:

1. Heat 2 tablespoons A, add B, C, stir-fry 1 minute; add 1 tablespoon water, cover and cook 1 minute.
2. Add D, stir-fry ½ minute.
3. Add E, F, G and stir until thickened.
4. Add H, mix well and serve.

VEGETARIAN STIR-FRIED CRAB MEAT
Tsao Sue Pong Sha Ro: Shanghai

A. ½ cup peanut oil
B. ½ cup mashed cooked carrot
C. ⅔ cup mashed potato
D. 1 cup finely shredded bamboo shoots
E. 8 Chinese mushrooms

F. ¼ lb. snow peas
G. ½ teaspoon sugar
H. 1½ teaspoons salt
I. 2 teaspoons wine vinegar

PREPARATION:

I. Wash E and soak in warm water 15 minutes; shred very fine.

II. Discard tips of F, shred.
III. Mix G, H.

COOKING:

1. Heat A, add B, C, stir-fry until crispy (about 4 minutes).
2. Add D, E, F, stir-fry 2 minutes.

3. Add G, H, mix well.
4. Add I and serve.

VEGETARIAN CHOP SUEY
Lo Han Chai: General

A. 1 cup chicken broth
B. 2-oz. package cellophane noodles
C. ½ lb. romaine lettuce

D. 10-oz. can vegetarian chop suey
E. 1 tablespoon Fu Yu juice

PREPARATION:

I. Soak B in hot water 30 minutes.
II. Wash C and break each leaf in half.

III. Cut D into bite-size pieces.

COOKING:

1. Bring A to boil, add B and cook 5 minutes or until broth is absorbed.

2. Add C, D, E; stir and cook 2 to 3 minutes.

VEGETARIAN CHOP SUEY WITH ASSORTED VEGETABLES
Lo Han Chai: Adapted

A. 2 tablespoons peanut oil
B. 2 slices ginger
C. 1 scallion, chopped
D. 6 Chinese mushrooms

E. ½ head celery cabbage
F. ¼ lb. snow peas
G. ½ teaspoon salt
H. 13-oz. can vegetarian chop suey

PREPARATION:

I. Wash D and soak 15 minutes. Drain, save 2 tablespoons water; quarter each D.
II. Shred B.

III. Remove tips of F.
IV. Cut E into 1½-inch pieces.

COOKING:

1. Heat A, add B, C, stir-fry a few seconds; add D, E, stir-fry 3 minutes.
2. Add F, G, and 2 tablespoons D water; stir-fry ½ minute.

3. Add H, mix well, cover and cook for 1 to 2 minutes.

FRIED WALNUTS
Tza Heh Tao: Hunan

A. 2 cups peanut oil
B. 2 cups shelled walnuts

C. 1 cup sugar
D. ⅔ cup water

PREPARATION:

I. Pour boiling water over B. Let stand 1 to 2 minutes. Peel off skin and dry on paper towels.

II. Mix C, D. Add to B, stir until B is well coated.
III. Remove to plate and let cool.

COOKING:

1. Heat A to 300°. Add B–D mixture, stir-fry until golden brown (about ½ to 1 minute).

2. Drain on paper towels, let cool, and serve.

LONGEVITY NUTS
Ming Sun Kwoh: Fukien

A. 1 qt. peanut oil
B. 2 cups shelled, skinless raw peanuts
C. 1 teaspoon lard (or peanut oil)

D. 2 teaspoons sugar
E. ¼ teaspoon five spices powder
F. ½ teaspoon anise pepper salt (see Index)

PREPARATION:

Mix D, E, F.

COOKING:

1. Heat A to 350°.
2. Add B, stir-fry until golden brown, about 1 to 2 minutes; avoid overfrying and resultant bitter taste.
3. Remove B, drain and cool on paper towel.

4. Mix B with C (for distinctive fragrance).
5. Add D–F and mix thoroughly. Keep in tightly covered jar. Nuts may be kept 1 to 2 weeks.

PEANUTS COOKED WITH RED BEAN CURD CHEESE
Nam Yu Fa Sun: Adapted

A. 3 cups shelled, skinless raw peanuts
B. 3 tablespoons mashed red bean curd cheese

C. 1 tablespoon sugar
D. ½ cup water

PREPARATION:

I. Wash A, drain.

COOKING:

1. Place all ingredients in saucepan, bring to boil. Cook, stirring constantly until liquid is absorbed (about 2 minutes).
2. Spread A on a cooky sheet.

3. Preheat oven to 300°. Bake 40 minutes, turning A over every 10 minutes.
4. Cool, store in jar.

FRIED PEANUTS WITH ONION AND GARLIC
Yow Tza Fa Sun: Adapted

A. 2 cups peanut oil
B. 1 medium Spanish onion
C. 1 to 2 cloves garlic

D. 3 cups shelled, skinless raw peanuts
E. 1 to 2 teaspoons salt

PREPARATION:

I. Peel skin from B and C; cut both into thin slices.

COOKING:

1. Heat A to 350°.
2. Add B; stir-fry 1 minute.
3. Add C; brown 1 minute.
4. Add D; continue stirring 3 minutes.
5. Remove B, C, then remove pan from heat; continue stirring ½ minute until golden brown.
6. With slotted spoon remove D and drain on paper towel.
7. Mix D well with B, C; add E to taste. When cool, store in a tightly covered jar.

ROAST PEANUTS
Ham So Fa Sun: Adapted

A. 3 cups shelled skinless raw peanuts

B. 1 teaspoon salt

PREPARATION:

I. Wash and drain A.
II. Add B, mix well.

III. Line 12- by 18-inch cooky sheet with aluminum foil.
IV. Spread single layer of A over foil.

COOKING:

1. Preheat oven to 325°.
2. Bake prepared A 25 minutes, turn over gently, bake 5 more minutes.
3. Turn over once more, bake 5 minutes.
4. Wait until peanuts are completely cool before storing in jar.

FRAGRANT ROAST PEANUTS
Ng Hiong Fa Sun: Adapted

Add ½ teaspoon five spices powder to A–B in Step II, mixing thoroughly.

NOODLES, PANCAKES, BREAD

In Northern China, noodles are a common food staple. They are cheaper than rice and need few meat or vegetable dishes to accompany them; also a small quantity of meat can be added to produce a complete dish. The Chinese have always regarded noodles as a symbol of longevity because of their great length, and therefore never cut them. Noodles frequently are served at birthday celebrations and festivals because of their symbolic nature.

Like all noodles, the Chinese types come in a variety of shapes and sizes; some are small, often as fine as thread. Various kinds of American egg noodles are reasonably good substitutes.

Dry noodles should never be washed before cooking and should be stored in a cool, dry place. Both dry and fresh noodles should be added slowly to rapidly boiling water, separated with a fork, and cooked until they are barely tender (4 to 6 minutes), never overcooked. If other ingredients are to be added just before serving, the noodles should be set aside before they are fully cooked and then re-heated when the final ingredients are incorporated into the dish. The boiled noodles should then be drained and rinsed with cold water in a colander, and separated with a fork. Leftover noodles can be used in many noodle dishes, including noodle soup and chao (or chow) mein. "Chao mein" means "fried noodles." Authentic Chinese chao mein recipes require cold cooked noodles, which are then quick-fried with other ingredients; leftover spaghetti may be substituted.

EGG NOODLES
Gee Don Mein: General

A. 4 eggs

B. 2 cups flour

C. cornstarch

PREPARATION:

I. Beat A slightly with fork. Add B gradually, mix well.

II. Knead mixture into a soft dough. Cover with damp dish towel, let stand 10 to 12 minutes. Knead again several minutes.

III. Sprinkle board and rolling pin with C. Roll dough out as thin as possible.

IV. Fold thin dough over several times. Cut across folds, slicing noodles as narrow (or as broad) as desired.

COOKING:

1. Bring 2 to 3 quarts water to boil.

2. Add prepared A–C, cook 2 minutes. Drain, run under cold water until cold. Can be used for any noodle dish.

SIMPLE EGG NOODLES
Jia Sang Don Mein: General

A.   3 tablespoons vegetable oil
B.   ½ lb. celery cabbage
C.   2 scallions, minced
D.   ½ cup shredded cooked meat (leftover)
E.   1 teaspoon light soy sauce

F.   1 teaspoon salt
G.   ½ cup soup stock
H.   ½ lb. egg noodles (see Index)
I.   ½ cup meat concentrate
     (see Home-Style Beef Concentrate)

PREPARATION:

I.   Wash B and cut into ½-inch pieces.
II. Mix C, D, E.

III. Boil 3 qts. water, add H and bring to boil; boil 6 minutes, drain, and place under running cold water to cool. Set aside.

COOKING:

1.   Heat A in large frying pan, add B, stir-fry 1 to 2 minutes; add C–E, stir-fry 1 minute.
2.   Add F, G, half of H and cover. Simmer 5 minutes.

3.   Place remaining H in shallow bowl, cover with B–H and garnish with I.

FRAGRANT NOODLES
Chung Yo Mein: Shanghai

A.   ¼ cup peanut oil
B.   ½ lb. (or 3 medium) onions, diced
C.   20 dried shrimp
D.   1 teaspoon dark soy sauce

E.   2 teaspoons light soy sauce
F.   2 teaspoons sherry
G.   1 lb. egg noodles, ¼-inch wide (see Index)

PREPARATION:

I.   Soak C in cold water 10 minutes; clean, and cut each C into 3 pieces.

II. Mix E, F.

COOKING:

1.   Heat half of A in frying pan, add B, stir-fry 1 to 2 minutes, lower heat, and brown B slightly.
2.   Add C, continue to simmer at low heat, stirring until only residual moisture is left and oil spatters when in contact with moisture; remove cooked C from pan. Set aside.

3.   In small pot, heat rest of A, add C, D, E, F, stir-fry 1 to 2 minutes; add 2 cups water and simmer 30 minutes or until water has nearly evaporated.
4.   Cook G in water as directed on package, then rinse quickly under cold water and drain. (G should still be warm when ready to serve.)
5.   Mix all ingredients together and serve.

STIR-FRIED PLAIN NOODLES
Ching Chao Mein: General

A.   2 tablespoons peanut oil
B.   1 lb. fresh noodles
C.   2 tablespoons light soy sauce

D.   1 tablespoon heavy soy sauce
E.   ½ teaspoon garlic powder
F.   4 scallions, sliced

PREPARATION:

I.   Parboil B.

II. Mix C, D, E, and half of F.

COOKING:

1. Put A in very hot skillet and bring to high heat.
2. Add B. Stir-fry until hot.
3. Add C–F mixture. Mix well. Heat thoroughly.
4. Serve with garnish of remaining F.

STIR-FRIED NOODLES WITH SMOKING PEANUT OIL
Chao Su Mein: Canton

A. 1 lb. fresh noodles
B. ½ teaspoon garlic powder
C. 2 tablespoons heavy soy sauce
D. 1 tablespoon light soy sauce
E. 1 slice ginger, minced
F. 5 tablespoons peanut oil
G. 4 scallions, sliced

PREPARATION:

I. Parboil A; drain, rinse in cold water. Set aside.
II. Mix B, C, D, E. Set aside.

COOKING:

1. Warm A under hot running tap water; drain; place in large deep skillet.
2. Pour B–E mixture over A and stir thoroughly.
3. Heat F in small skillet until smoking.
4. Pour F over A–E in large skillet. Mix well. Heat until piping hot.
5. Add half of G. Mix well again.
6. Serve with garnish of remaining G.

NOODLES WITH PORK AND SALTED BROWN BEAN SAUCE
Jiang Bao Tsu Ro Mein: Shanghai

A. 1 lb. fresh noodles
B. 2 tablespoons peanut oil
C. 2 tablespoons brown (or yellow) bean sauce
D. 1 clove garlic, minced
E. ½ teaspoon salt
F. 1 slice ginger, minced
G. 1 lb. ground pork
H. 1½ tablespoons hoisin sauce
I. ½ teaspoon sugar
J. 1 tablespoon heavy soy sauce
K. 5 dried black mushrooms
L. ¾ cup water

PREPARATION:

I. Soak K in warm water 15 minutes, drain. Slice thin.
II. Mash C to a paste.
III. Mix C, D, E, F. Set aside.
IV. Mix G, H, I, J. Set aside 15 minutes.

COOKING:

1. Boil A 3 to 4 minutes. Drain.
2. Put B in very hot skillet and bring to high heat.
3. Add C–F and stir-fry rapidly 15 seconds to brown D slightly.
4. Add G–J and K. Stir-fry well until G is fully done.
5. Add L. Cover and cook 5 minutes over medium heat.
6. Pour very hot tap water over A to heat. Drain well.
7. Place A in serving dish and pour B–L over.

NOODLES IN THICK GRAVY
Nung Tong Mein: General

A. 1 tablespoon peanut oil
B. ½ lb. pork loin, sliced
C. 5 dried black mushrooms
D. 4 pieces wood ears or cloud ears
E. 2 scallions, sliced
F. ½ teaspoon salt
G. 1 tablespoon light soy sauce
H. 1 tablespoon sherry

I. 1 tablespoon oyster sauce
J. 4 cups chicken stock
K. 4 tablespoons cornstarch
L. 6 tablespoons water
M. 1 tablespoon heavy soy sauce
N. 2 eggs
O. 1 lb. fresh noodles
P. 2 scallions, sliced

PREPARATION:

I. Parboil O. Set aside.
II. Soak C in warm water 15 minutes. Reserve soak water to substitute for L. Shred C.
III. Soak D 15 minutes in warm water. Discard water. Cut each in two or more pieces.
IV. Mix C, D, E. Set aside.
V. Mix F, G, H, I.
VI. Mix K, L, M.

COOKING:

1. Put A in very hot skillet and bring to high heat.
2. Add B; stir-fry 2 minutes.
3. Add C–E. Stir-fry ½ minute.
4. Add F–I. Stir-fry ½ minute.
5. Add J and bring to boil. Simmer 20 minutes.
6. Add K–M slowly. Stir-fry until sauce thickens and coats all ingredients well. Sauce should be as thick as heavy cream. Turn off heat.
7. Begin at once to pour N into sauce slowly, stirring continuously to achieve egg-drop effect.
8. Warm O under hot water tap and place in large serving bowl.
9. Pour piping hot sauce over O and serve with garnish of P.

SWEET AND SOUR FRIED NOODLES
Tiem Shwin Mien: Canton

A. 2 tablespoons peanut oil
B. ½ cup subgum ginger and juice to cover (or mixed sweet pickles)
C. ¼ teaspoon garlic powder
D. 4 tablespoons vinegar
E. 4 tablespoons sugar

F. ⅛ teaspoon red food coloring (optional)
G. 2 tablespoons heavy soy sauce
H. 1 cup soup stock
I. 2 tablespoons cornstarch
J. 3 tablespoons peanut oil
K. 1 lb. fresh boiled, drained noodles

PREPARATION:

I. Heat A to smoking hot. Set aside to cool.

II. Mix C, D, E, F, G.   III. Mix H, I.

COOKING:

1. Warm A.
2. Add B and juice. Stir-fry 30 seconds.
3. Add C–G. Stir well and bring to boil. Cook 2 minutes.
4. Add H, I slowly. Stir-fry until sauce thickens.
5. Bring J to smoking in small skillet.
6. Place K in large skillet.
7. Pour J over K, mix well and stir-fry over high heat until piping hot.
8. Transfer to serving dish. Pour A–I sweet and sour sauce over noodles. Serve.

INSTANT NOODLE LUNCH
Yee Fu Mein: Canton

A. 1 qt. water

B. 1 cup shredded cooked meat
(pork, chicken, beef, duck, or other)

C. 2 pkgs. yee fu mein noodles, with soup base
(or 2 cups chicken broth)

D. 1 scallion

E. 3 to 4 cups chopped lettuce leaves

F. pepper to taste

COOKING:

1. Bring A to boil, add B.

2. Add C, separating with chopsticks; cook 3
minutes.

3. Add C soup base and D, E; mix well, turn off
heat.

4. Add F.

NOODLE SALAD
Liang Ban Mein: Adapted

A. ½ lb. fresh noodles

B. 2 medium carrots

C. 2 cups shredded iceberg lettuce hearts

D. 1 scallion

E. 1 tablespoon chopped pickled ginger

F. 3 tablespoons vinegar

G. 2 tablespoons light soy sauce

H. 2 teaspoons sugar

I. 1 teaspoon salt

J. 2 to 3 teaspoons sesame oil

PREPARATION AND COOKING:

I. Cook A in 2 qts. boiling water 5 to 8 minutes, drain and rinse under cold water.

II. Peel B and shred, cook in boiling water for
1 to 2 minutes.

III. Cut D into thin diagonal shreds.

IV. Mix all ingredients and serve cold.

OYSTER SAUCE NOODLES
How Yo Ban Mein: General

A. 1 cup water

B. 1 pkg. yee fu mein noodles

C. ½ teaspoon lard

D. 1 teaspoon oyster sauce

E. 1 or 2 teaspoons chopped scallion

COOKING:

1. Bring A to boil in a saucepan.

2. Add B, stir with chop sticks; cook about 2 to
3 minutes or until water is absorbed.

3. Add C, D, mix well; garnish with E and serve.

SHREDDED HAM NOODLES
Yuin Twei Si Mein: General

A. 1 cup water

B. 1 pkg. yee fu mein noodles

C. ¼ cup shredded baked Virginia ham

D. ½ teaspoon sesame oil

COOKING:

1. Bring A to boil in saucepan.

2. Add B, stir with chopsticks; cook about 2 or
3 minutes or until water is absorbed.

3. Add C, D, mix well and serve.

SHREDDED TURKEY OR CHICKEN NOODLES
Gee See Yee Fu Mein: General

A. 1 cup water
B. 1 pkg. yee fu mein noodles
C. 1 teaspoon peanut oil
D. 1 teaspoon peanut butter

E. ¼ cup cooked chicken or shredded turkey white meat
F. ¼ cup shredded celery heart

COOKING:

1. Bring A to boil in saucepan.
2. Add B, stir with chopsticks; cook about 2 to 3 minutes or until water is absorbed.

3. Add C, D, blend.
4. Add E, F, mix well and serve.

FRIED CELLOPHANE NOODLES
Tza Fun See: Fukien

A. 1 qt. vegetable oil

B. 1 oz. cellophane noodles

PREPARATION:

I. Separate B into four portions.

COOKING:

1. Heat A in skillet to 375°.
2. Add B, a portion at a time. As soon as each expands, remove and place on paper towel.

B is ready to serve as base for meat and vegetable dishes.

CELLOPHANE NOODLES STEAMED EGG
Fun See Tsin Dan: Canton

A. 1 oz. cellophane noodles
B. 12 dried shrimp
C. 2 tablespoons dry sherry
D. 4 eggs

E. 1 teaspoon salt
F. 1½ cups cold water
G. 2 teaspoons light soy sauce
H. few drops sesame oil

PREPARATION:

I. Cut A into 1½-inch segments; soak in hot water for 30 minutes.
II. Clean and rinse B under cold running water;

soak in C 15 minutes. Remove and chop.
III. Beat D well in a bowl; add E, F.
IV. Add A, B–C and mix thoroughly.

COOKING:

1. Steam A–F over boiling water 15 minutes.

2. Sprinkle G, H on top and serve hot.

CELLOPHANE NOODLES WITH SHREDDED BEEF
Fun See Niu Ro: Hunan

A. 5 tablespoons peanut oil
B. ½ lb. beef
C. 2 teaspoons brown or yellow bean sauce
D. 2-oz. pkg. cellophane noodles
E. 1½ tablespoons light soy sauce
F. 1 scallion, chopped

G. ½ teaspoon sesame oil
H. ½ beaten egg
I. 1 teaspoon cornstarch
J. ¼ teaspoon salt
K. ¼ teaspoon sesame oil

PREPARATION:

I. Pour boiling water over D, soak until soft; drain.

II. Shred B and mix with H, I, J, K.

COOKING:

1. Heat 3 tablespoons A, add B mixture and stir-fry 2 minutes, remove to a dish.
2. Heat 2 tablespoons A, add C, stir-fry ½ minute, add D, stir well.

3. Add E, mix well.
4. Add B mixture and F, continue stirring until mixture is quite dry; remove to a dish; add G and serve.

CELLOPHANE NOODLES WITH MINCED MEAT
Ma Yee Song Sue: Szechuan

A. 1 qt. peanut oil
B. ½ lb. ground pork (or beef)
C. 2 teaspoons brown or yellow bean sauce
D. 2 teaspoons sherry
E. 2 teaspoons light soy sauce
F. ½ teaspoon sugar

G. 1 red-hot pepper
H. ½ cup chicken broth
I. 2 teaspoons cornstarch
J. 2-oz. pkg. cellophane noodles
K. 1 tablespoon chopped scallion
L. 1 teaspoon chopped ginger

PREPARATION:

I. Divide J into 4 portions; deep fry in A at 375°. As soon as J expands (in a few seconds), remove to plate.

II. Mix B, C, D, E, F.
III. Discard seeds and stem of G, chop.
IV. Mix H, I well.

COOKING:

1. Reheat 2 tablespoons A, stir-fry B–F and G 2 or 3 minutes.
2. Add H, I, mix well, and cook until thickened; place in dish.

3. Just before serving, spread B–F over J and garnish with K, L.

COLD SAVORY NOODLES WITH HAM
Lun Ban Ho Twei Mein: General

A. 2 cups shredded carrots
B. ½ cup chicken broth
C. ½ cup shredded bamboo shoots
D. ¼ cup chopped preserved kohlrabi
E. 10 dried shrimp

F. ½ lb. fresh noodles
G. 2 tablespoons light soy sauce
H. 1 teaspoon sesame oil
I. salt to taste
J. 1 to 2 cups shredded ham

PREPARATION:

I. Cook F in 2 qts. boiling water 5 to 8 minutes. Drain and run under cold water, gently, a few seconds.

II. Wash E and soak in warm water 10 minutes. Drain. Chop.
III. Mix G, H, I.

COOKING:

1. Cook A in B 1 minute. Add C, D, E and cook 1 minute.

2. Mix in F, G–I, and J, refrigerate, and serve cold.

COLD SAVORY NOODLES WITH CHICKEN
Lun Ban Gee Se Mein: General

A. ½ lb. spaghetti
B. ½ cup chicken broth
C. 1 cup shredded carrot
D. 1 cup shredded asparagus or celery
E. 1 cup shredded cooked white meat of chicken

F. 2 tablespoons light soy sauce
G. 1 teaspoon Chinese hot sauce (optional)
H. salt and pepper to taste
I. 2 scallions, chopped

COOKING:

1. Cook A as directed on package.
2. Bring B to boil and cook C in it 1 minute, add D, cook 1 more minute. Drain.
3. Mix in E, F, G, H, I, add A, refrigerate and serve cold.

PANCAKES
Bo Bing: General

A. 2 cups flour
B. 1 teaspoon salt

C. ¾ cup boiling water
D. ¼ cup peanut oil

PREPARATION:

I. Sift A, B into bowl.
II. Add C, stir well with chopsticks.
III. Knead A–C on floured board until dough is smooth.
IV. Roll A–C with hands into a long roll, divide into 12 to 15 parts.
V. Take one part only, shape into a ball. Roll it into a very thin round piece about 8 inches in diameter.
VI. Brush A–C piece with D; then make into a long roll; again shape it into a ball.
VII. Again roll A–C ball into 8-inch thin piece. Brush with D. Put 2 pieces together.
VIII. Repeat with each of 12 to 15 parts.

COOKING:

1. Heat frying pan over low heat, grease, and fry each pancake until done (3 to 5 minutes); turn each over 2 or 3 times. Separate two pieces when done. Serve with Peking Duck, Szechuan Yu-Siang Shredded Pork or Szechuan Double Cooked Pork with Hoisin Sauce.

SCALLION PANCAKES
Chung Yo Bing: Peking

A. 2 eggs
B. milk
C. 1½ cups flour

D. ⅓ cup peanut oil
E. 1 teaspoon salt
F. 4 scallions, minced

PREPARATION:

I. Beat A and add enough B to make 2 cups.
II. Place C in large bowl.
III. Add A–B mixture, stirring so no lumps form.
IV. Add D, E, F. Mix well.

COOKING:

1. Heat skillet and grease it.
2. Add one ladleful of A–F batter to hot pan and spread as thin as possible.
3. Use medium heat and brown pancake on both sides. Serve hot with eggs and bacon or with meat dishes.

CHINESE BREAD
Man To: Peking

A. 4 cups flour
B. 1 teaspoon salt
C. ¼ cup sugar
D. 1¼ cups warm water
E. 2 tablespoons sugar
F. 1 pkg. dry yeast
G. 2 tablespoons melted butter or margerine

PREPARATION:

I. Sift A, B, C in large bowl.
II. Mix D, E in measuring cup.
III. Stir in F slowly. Mix well.
IV. Add G to D–F.
V. Hollow out center of A–C. Add D–G. Mix thoroughly.
VI. Knead lightly on floured board until dough is smooth and elastic.
VII. Place in greased bowl, cover, and let dough rise at room temperature until it doubles in bulk, about 1 to 1½ hours.
VIII. Divide dough into 24 parts. Shape each into a rectangular bun and let rise once more.

COOKING:

1. Steam in steamer 20 minutes. Serve with Chinese red-cooked pork or use as bread spread with peanut butter or jam.

SNOW-WHITE STEAMED BREAD
Shwieh Bai Man To: General

A. 1 pkg. dry yeast
B. ¼ cup warm water
C. ½ tablespoon sugar
D. ½ cup warm milk
E. ¼ cup warm water
F. ¼ cup peanut oil
G. ¼ cup sugar
H. ½ teaspoon salt
I. 4 cups cake flour
J. ½ teaspoon vegetable oil

PREPARATION:

I. Combine A, B, C in large bowl; let stand until spongy (about 10 minutes).
II. Add D, E, F, G, H, blend well.
III. Stir in 3½ cups I, knead, adding remaining I until dough is smooth and firm. Brush top of dough with J; cover with wet clean dish towel. Let stand until doubled in size (about 45 to 60 minutes).
IV. Punch dough down with fist and let it stand a few more minutes; then turn dough onto lightly floured board and knead.
V. Divide into 2 parts; then divide each part into 10 to 12 pieces.
VI. Place each piece on top of a 2-inch-square piece of waxed paper; cover with a clean towel and let rise about 1½ hours before steaming.

COOKING:

1. Steam over boiling water 15 minutes. Bread can replace rice and is particularly good with red-cooked dishes. Also, it can be sliced and served with peanut butter or jam.

There are two kinds of rice: long grain and short grain. Long grain rice is long and narrow, absorbs more water, is fluffier after cooking, and is the best kind to use for fried rice. Short grain rice is short and wide, absorbs less water, and is softer after cooking. Soft rice, which is easier to digest, is preferred by most Chinese. In this country, a dried, fluffier rice is preferred. Sweet rice, also known as glutinous rice, is used primarily in pastries and special festival dishes.

When properly cooked, a grain of rice is about twice its uncooked size, fluffy and white, and somewhat translucent. Each grain should be separated. If an insufficient amount of water has been used, the inside of the grain remains hard and white, whereas if too much water has been used, the outside of the rice becomes soft and mushy. The Cantonese prefer hard rice, with each grain separated from the other; the Shanghailanders prefer softer, more glutinous rice. Rice goes particularly well with salty dishes or those cooked with large amounts of soy sauce.

Rice may be cooked three ways. The first is a congee, a soup, essentially, in which a small amount of rice has been cooked in a large quantity of water for several hours. Congee prepared in advance is eaten for breakfast with salted eggs or other highly flavored foods, also as a late evening snack when bits of beef, chicken, pork, or sliced raw fish are added. The second method is to make a thicker, more chowderlike soup by boiling it in slightly less water and adding other ingredients. This method gives the greatest bulk of food for the least amount of rice. In the third technique, boiled or steamed rice is made with even less water, the amount being a matter of personal preference, until all the moisture has been evaporated. A general rule is for the water level to be approximately one inch above the rice level in the pot; also, a standard recipe cup of rice will require 1½ cups of water and will serve three people. The pot should never be more than half filled with raw rice; if more is needed, a larger pot should be used. Once the proper technique for obtaining the desired consistency has been established, a little experience will readily produce the same kind of rice each time.

The cooking procedure should begin with the use of high heat and an uncovered pot. If foaming occurs, the heat should be adjusted so that the contents of the pot do not foam over the stove. Allow the rice to swell; when the liquid is almost completely absorbed, cover the pot and lower the heat. Allow to cook for 15 more minutes.

The type of pot used is important. It should have a snug lid and be made of aluminum so that if the rice is left on low heat for too long, it will not burn. Rice has a tendency to burn in copper-bottomed pots, and charred rice is difficult to remove. Always use the same pot for cooking rice since it will then be easier to judge how much water to add each time. Recently, automatic electric rice cookers have been introduced here and abroad which produce rice of just the desired consistency—uniformly and effortlessly, and ready to serve.

If cooked rice is not to be served immediately, it may be kept warm in a pot over the very lowest possible heat or in a warm oven at very low heat. If necessary, several tablespoons of water may be sprinkled around the edge of the pot.

It is better to cook too much rice, rather than too little, since it is served with almost every dish, and any that is left over may be reused. Leftover rice should be loosened with a lifting motion of a fork or chopstick and not stirred, to avoid breaking up the grains. It should be refrigerated in a covered container (it is preferable for fried rice to be hard), and thoroughly chilled before refrying, otherwise the rice grains will stick together in a gluey mess.

To warm cooked rice, add 1 tablespoon of hot water for each cup of cold cooked rice, then loosen the grains with a fork, cover the pot tightly, and warm over low heat for 8 to 10 minutes, allowing the rice to steam until it is hot. Cold cooked rice that is lumpy can best be separated with wet hands.

Leftover boiled or steamed rice that sticks to the bottom and sometimes the sides of the pan can be removed and refrigerated; it makes a delicious dish—sizzling rice.

PLAIN FRIED RICE
Ching Chao Fan: Canton

A. 4 cups cold cooked rice

B. 3 tablespoons peanut oil

C. 2 tablespoons light soy sauce

D. 4 scallions, sliced

COOKING:

1. Place A in large deep skillet.
2. Heat B over high heat until it smokes.
3. Pour at once over A. Stir-fry 2 minutes over moderate heat.

4. Add C. Stir-fry until mixture is piping hot.
5. Mix in half of D. Serve with garnish of remaining D.

FRIED RICE I
Chao Fan: General

A. 3 tablespoons peanut oil

B. 6 cups cold cooked rice

C. 2 tablespoons cold water

D. 2 tablespoons light soy sauce

E. 1 tablespoon heavy soy sauce

F. 1 tablespoon sherry

G. 1 tablespoon brown bean sauce

H. 2 eggs

I. 3 scallions, sliced

J. 1 slice ginger, minced

K. 2 tablespoons peanut oil

L. 3 scallions, sliced

M. 1 tablespoon peanut oil

PREPARATION:

I. Beat H lightly. Fry 1 ladleful at a time, spreading thin in skillet with M until set. Repeat until all is used up. Allow to cool. Sliver into thin shreds. Set aside.

II. Separate grains of B, adding C if necessary.

III. Mix D, E, F, G. Set aside.

COOKING:

1. Put A in very hot skillet and bring to high heat.
2. Add B. Stir-fry 2 minutes, stirring continuously.
3. Add D–G mixture and stir-fry 1 minute.

4. Add H. Stir-fry 15 seconds.
5. Add I, J. Stir well 15 seconds.
6. Heat K in separate saucepan until smoking hot. Pour over fried B–J. Stir well 30 seconds.
7. Serve with garnish of L.

FRIED RICE II
Chao Fan: General

A. 2 eggs
B. 3 tablespoons peanut oil
C. 1 small onion, sliced
D. 1 clove garlic, minced
E. ¼ lb. shrimp
F. ½ cup frozen peas

G. ½ cup diced cooked ham (or pork)
H. 4 cups cold cooked rice
I. 1 tablespoon light soy sauce
J. salt and pepper to taste
K. 1 scallion

PREPARATION:

I. Beat A.
II. Shell and clean E; cut into small pieces.

III. Slice K bulb thin; cut stalk in ½- to 1-inch lengths.

COOKING:

1. Scramble A in 1 tablespoon B. Set aside.
2. Put remaining B into very hot skillet and heat. Fry C, D until golden brown.
3. Add E; cook ½ minute.
4. Add F, G; stir continuously and cook until F is heated through.

5. Add A; stir well.
6. Add H, I, J. Mix well; cook until H is heated through.
7. Garnish with K.
8. Serve hot.

FRIED RICE III
Chao Fan: Yangchow

A. 5 tablespoons peanut oil
B. ½ cup diced medium frozen shrimp
C. ½ cup diced cooked chicken
D. ½ cup diced cooked ham or Cantonese roast pork
E. ½ cup frozen peas
F. ½ cup diced bamboo shoots

G. 4 Chinese mushrooms
H. 2 eggs
I. 4 cups cold cooked rice
J. 1 tablespoon sherry
K. 2 tablespoons light soy sauce
L. salt, pepper to taste

PREPARATION:

I. Add dash of L and 1 teaspoon J to B.
II. Wash G, soak in warm water 15 minutes; drain and dice.

III. Mix C, D, E, F, G.
IV. Beat H.
V. Mix remaining J, K.

COOKING:

1. Heat 3 tablespoons A in frying pan. When hot, stir-fry B 30 seconds.
2. Add C–G, stir-fry 2 to 3 minutes; put aside.

3. Heat remaining A, add H, and scramble.
4. Add I, J, K and stir over low heat.
5. Add B–G, mix thoroughly. Add L. Serve hot.

GLUTINOUS RICE CHICKEN ROLLS
Noh Mai Gai Guen: Canton

A. 3 tablespoons peanut oil
B. 6 Chinese mushrooms
C. 8 dried shrimp
D. ½ cup diced Virginia ham

E. 2 Chinese sausages
F. 1 chicken breast, boned
G. 2 cups glutinous rice
H. 2 teaspoons salt

PREPARATION:

I. Wash G, add 2½ cups water, bring to boil. Lower heat, simmer 20 minutes. Drain.

II. Wash B, C. Soak in warm water 10 minutes, drain, and dice.

III. Chop E into small pieces.

IV. Dice F.

COOKING:

1. Heat A; stir-fry B,C, D, E 1 minute.
2. Add F, stir-fry 2 minutes.
3. Add cooked G and H, mix well.
4. Make into 20 rolls, wrap with aluminum foil, and bake in 375° oven 15 minutes. Rolls may be left in refrigerator for several days; just warm and serve.

FRIED GLUTINOUS RICE CHICKEN ROLLS
Yow Tza Noh Mai Gai Guen: Canton

Beat 2 egg whites lightly, coat each chicken roll. Roll each in cornstarch. Instead of baking in Step 4, deep fry at 400° until golden brown (about 2 minutes each side).

GLUTINOUS RICE CHICKEN ROLLS   *Approved Diabetic Recipe*
Noh Mai Gai Guen: Canton

A. 1 cup glutinous rice
B. 1¼ cups water
C. 1 tablespoon peanut oil
D. 1 teaspoon chopped onion
E. 1 small clove garlic, chopped
F. 1 teaspoon curry powder
G. 1 chicken breast
H. 1 teaspoon salt

PREPARATION:

I. Wash A a couple of times, drain.

II. Bone and shred G.

COOKING:

1. Add A to B, bring to boil, lower heat, let water boil down a little. Cover and simmer 20 minutes.
2. Heat C, add D, E, stir-fry a few seconds and add F; continue stirring 1 minute.
3. Add G and stir-fry 2 minutes.
4. Add H, mix thoroughly and add A, mix well.
5. Make into 6 to 8 rolls, wrap with aluminum foil, and bake in 375° oven 15 minutes. Rolls may be left in refrigerator for several days; just warm and serve.

GLUTINOUS RICE WITH DICED CHINESE SAUSAGE
Heong Tsong Noh Mai: Canton

A. 2 cups glutinous rice
B. 1½ cups boiling water
C. ¼ teaspoon salt
D. 1 tablespoon heavy soy sauce
E. 2 teaspoons light soy sauce
F. 1 cup chopped Chinese sausage
G. 8 dried black mushrooms
H. 2 scallions, sliced

PREPARATION:

I. Wash A a couple of times and drain.

II. Soak H in hot water. Drain. Reserve water for B. Slice thin.

III. Mix C, D, E. Set aside.

COOKING:

1. Place A, B and C–E in a heavy pot and cook covered until water boils. Remove cover.
2. Place F, G on top of A–E. Re-cover pan.
3. Reduce heat to low and continue to cook 20 minutes. Stir well.
4. Serve with garnish of H.

STIR-FRIED RICE STICKS I
Chao Mi Fun: Fukien

A. 2 tablespoons peanut oil
B. 1 scallion
C. 8 Chinese mushrooms
D. 12 dried shrimp
E. ½ lb. pork

F. 2 tablespoons light soy sauce
G. ½ teaspoon sugar
H. 13¾-oz. can chicken broth
I. 1 lb. rice sticks
J. 1 scallion, chopped, or Chinese parsley

PREPARATION:

I. Slice E, shred.
II. Wash C, soak in warm water 15 minutes. Drain, saving mushroom water, and shred.
III. Wash D under cold water, soak 15 minutes.

IV. Soak I in cold water a few minutes. Drain, just before adding to A, B, C, D, E, F, G, H below.

COOKING:

1. Heat A, add B, stir-fry a few seconds.
2. Add C, D, stir-fry 1 minute.
3. Add E, stir-fry 2 minutes.
4. Add F, G, mix well.
5. Add H plus 1 can water and mushroom water, bring to boil. Cover, cook over low heat 5 minutes.
6. Add I, cook until all liquid is absorbed. Stir with chopsticks or fork.
7. Garnish with J.

STIR-FRIED RICE STICKS II
Kwangtung Chao Mi Fun: Canton

A. 3 tablespoons peanut oil
B. 1 scallion, chopped
C. 1 clove garlic, chopped
D. ½ lb. pork
E. 6 Chinese mushrooms
F. 2 tablespoons light soy sauce

G. 1 cup shredded bamboo shoots
H. 1 cup 1- to 2-inch strips Chinese cabbage
I. ¼ cup mushroom water from II
J. 1 lb. rice sticks
K. 1 teaspoon salt

PREPARATION:

I. Slice D and shred.
II. Wash E, soak in warm water 15 minutes. Drain, saving water. Cut into long, thin strips.

III. Soak J in hot water until soft; drain.

COOKING:

1. Heat A in frying pan, then stir-fry B, C a few seconds.
2. Add D, E; stir-fry 2 minutes.
3. Add F; stir-fry another minute.
4. Add G, H; stir-fry thoroughly. Add I, cook over low heat 2 minutes.
5. Add J, stir well, add K, stir-fry 2 to 3 minutes. Serve hot with Chinese hot sauce.

STIR-FRIED SHRIMP RICE STICKS
Sien Ha Mi Fun: Canton

Substitute shrimp for D, and use snow peas or pea pods instead of H. Add dash pepper and salt and 1 teaspoon sherry to shrimp before stir-frying in Step 2.

STIR-FRIED RICE STICKS WITH BEEF
Ngo Yoke Chao Mi Fun: Canton

A. 4 tablespoons peanut oil
B. 1 clove garlic, chopped
C. ½ lb. flank steak
D. 2 slices ginger, chopped
E. 1 scallion, chopped
F. 1 tablespoon light soy sauce
G. ½ teaspoon sugar

H. 2 teaspoons cornstarch
I. 8 Chinese mushrooms
J. 1 cup snow peas
K. 1 tablespoon light soy sauce
L. ¼ cup mushroom water
M. 1 lb. rice sticks
N. salt, pepper to taste

PREPARATION:

I. Slice C against grain into strips 2 inches long.
II. Mix C, D, E, F, G, H.
III. Wash I, soak in warm water 15 minutes.

Drain. Save mushroom water. Shred.
IV. Cut each J into 2 or 3 strips.
V. Mix K, L.
VI. Soak M in hot water until soft. Drain.

COOKING:

1. Heat A in frying pan, stir in B, stir-fry a few seconds.
2. Add C–H mixture and I. Stir-fry 1 to 1½

minutes.
3. Add J, K, L, M. Stir-fry thoroughly. Add N to taste. Serve hot.

RICE PATTY OR RICE CRUST I
Go Ba: General

A. 2 cups rice

B. 3 cups water

COOKING:

1. Place A in cooking pot. Wash and drain.
2. Add B to drained, wet rice. Bring to boil. Lower heat and cook until very little water is left. Cover and allow to simmer. Rice is generally cooked in 15 minutes; however, in order to form crust, allow to simmer for a longer period, until a thick brown crust forms on bottom of pot. Take care not to char crust.

3. Scoop out all the soft rice. The remaining crust may be dried by maintaining low heat while turning crust a few times (crust must be hard and crispy) or by removing crust from pot and placing it in the oven at a very low heat until it is crispy.
4. Cut crispy crust into 2- to 3-inch squares. Crust in this form may keep in tightly covered jar 1 to 2 months.

RICE PATTY OR RICE CRUST II
Go Ba: General

A. 2 cups cooked rice

PREPARATION:

I. Hand pat A into a 10-inch flat-bottom pan until it contains rice (moisten hand so that rice does not stick) approximately two grains thick.

COOKING:

1. Heat under low heat in oven 30 minutes or until a rice crust forms. Then turn over patty and brown on other side 20 minutes. If not to

be used immediately, patty can be stored in a tightly covered jar 2 to 3 months.

STIR-FRIED FROZEN BEAN CURD
Tsao Dung Dow Fu: Peking

A. 2 tablespoons vegetable oil
B. 6 cakes frozen bean curd*
C. 2 slices ginger, shredded

D. 2 tablespoons mashed fermented bean cake
E. 1 tablespoon light soy sauce
F. few drops sesame oil

PREPARATION:

I. Cover B with warm water several hours ahead of cooking until defrosted. Squeeze out water; shred.

COOKING:

1. Heat A. Add B, C, stir-fry over high heat 1 to 2 minutes.

2. Add D, E, stir, mix well.
3. Remove to serving dish, add F; serve.

BEAN CURD WITH PICKLED MUSTARD GREENS
Ham Tsoi Dow Fu: Canton

A. 3 tablespoons peanut oil
B. 8 cakes bean curd

C. ½ cup chopped preserved mustard greens
D. ½ cup chicken broth

PREPARATION:

I. Slice B into long, thin strips.

COOKING:

1. Heat A. Stir-fry B 1 minute.
2. Add C, stir 1 minute.

3. Add D, cover, and heat 10 minutes over low heat. Serve.

BEAN CURD WITH MUSTARD GREEN SOUP
Dow Fu Gai Tsai Tong: General

A. 13¾-oz. can chicken broth
B. 2 slices ginger

C. ½ lb. mustard greens
D. 4 cakes bean curd (or frozen)

PREPARATION:

I. Cut each D into 6 to 7 strips.
II. Wash, clean C, and cut diagonally into

pieces 2½ inches by ½ inch.
III. Cut B into strips.

COOKING:

1. Empty A into pot, dilute with 1 can water.
2. Add B, bring to boil.
3. Add C, cook until it turns jade green in color

(about 3 to 5 minutes).
4. Add D. As soon as mixture comes to boil again, turn off heat and serve.

* Wrap 2 to 3 pieces fresh bean curd together in waxed paper, freeze until hard.

BEAN CURD WITH BLACK MUSHROOMS
Dung Gu Dow Fu: General

A. 2 tablespoons peanut oil
B. 8 Chinese black mushrooms
C. ½ cup mushroom water
D. 6 cakes bean curd
E. ½ teaspoon salt

F. ½ teaspoon sugar
G. 1 tablespoon sherry
H. ⅛ teaspoon sesame oil
I. 1 tablespoon light soy sauce
J. 2 teaspoons cornstarch

PREPARATION:

I. Wash B and soak 15 minutes in warm water. Drain, cut each into 5 to 6 pieces.

II. Cut each D into 8 pieces.

III. Mix I, J.

COOKING:

1. Heat A. Add B, stir-fry a few seconds. Add C, bring to boil.

2. Add D. Continue cooking 2 minutes.

3. Add E, F, G, H and I–J to thicken.

STIR-FRIED BEAN CURD WITH OYSTER SAUCE
How Yo Dow Fu: General

A. 2 tablespoons peanut oil
B. ½ teaspoon salt
C. 4 cakes bean curd
D. 1 tablespoon oyster sauce
E. 3 scallions, sliced
F. 1 tablespoon light soy sauce

G. 1 tablespoon heavy soy sauce
H. 1 teaspoon sugar
I. ½ cup soup stock
J. 1 teaspoon cornstarch
K. 1 scallion, sliced

PREPARATION:

I. Cut each C into 8 cubes.

II. Mix D, E, F, G, H, I, J. Set aside.

COOKING:

1. Put A in very hot skillet and bring to high heat.

2. Add B.

3. Add C and stir-fry gently until light brown.

4. Add D–J. Stir-fry until sauce thickens and coats bean curd sections well.

5. Serve with garnish of K.

BEAN CURD WITH SOY SAUCE   *Approved Ulcer Recipe*
Jiang Yo Dow Fu: General

A. 3 tablespoons vegetable oil
B. 6 cakes bean curd
C. 2 tablespoons light soy sauce

D. 1 scallion
E. ½ cup chicken stock

PREPARATION:

I. Cut each B into 6 pieces.

II. Tie D into a bundle.

III. Mix B, C.

COOKING:

1. Heat A in heavy skillet; add B–C, then D, stir-fry 30 seconds.

2. Add E; steam, covered, 3 to 5 minutes.

3. Remove D. Serve hot.

BEAN CURD WITH OYSTER SAUCE   *Approved Ulcer Recipe*
How Yo Dow Fu: General

Substitute oyster sauce for C.

BEAN CURD WITH SOY SAUCE AND SCALLIONS
Jiang Yo Dow Fu: General

A. 4 tablespoons peanut oil
B. 6 cakes bean curd, cubed
C. 2 to 3 tablespoons light soy sauce
D. 2 tablespoons water or soup stock

E. 1 tablespoon heavy soy sauce
F. ⅛ to ¼ teaspoon garlic powder
G. 1 to 2 slices ginger, minced
H. 4 scallions, sliced

PREPARATION:

I. Mix C, D, E, F, G.
II. Pour C–G over B in deep bowl and mix well by shaking contents of bowl with plate covering the top.

COOKING:

1. Heat A to smoking and pour at once over B–G.
2. Put half of H into above and mix carefully by shaking contents of bowl (with plate cover).
3. Serve at room temperature or after refrigeration; garnish with remaining half of H.

BEAN CURD WITH OYSTER SAUCE AND SCALLIONS
How Yo Dow Fu: Canton

Add 1 to 2 tablespoons oyster sauce to C–G, in Step I.

DRIED BEAN CURD STRIPS WITH SOY SAUCE
Hung Shu Tiem Jook: General

Precook ½ pound dried soy bean curd strips in 2 qts. rapidly boiling water until just soft (several minutes). Drain (discard water). Rinse well with cold water. Cut into pieces roughly 1 by 2 inches. Substitute for F ½ teaspoon garlic powder.

BEAN CURD WITH TOMATO
Dow Fu Fan Keh: Adapted

A. 3 tablespoons peanut oil
B. 1 scallion, chopped
C. 3 slices ginger, chopped
D. 6 cakes bean curd, cubed

E. 2 to 3 tomatoes
F. ½ teaspoon sugar
G. 1 teaspoon salt

PREPARATION:

I. Soak E in boiling water a few seconds. Discard skin, cut E into cubes.

COOKING:

1. Heat A. Stir-fry B, C a few seconds over high heat.
2. Add D, E; keep stirring 2 minutes.
3. Add F, G, mix well, and serve hot.

BLACK AND WHITE BEAN CURD
Heh Bai Dow Fu: Shanghai

A. 2 cups chicken broth
B. 1 cup water
C. 8 to 10 pieces dried sea cucumber
D. 3 cakes bean curd

E. 2 teaspoons cornstarch mixed with ¼ cup water
F. 1 egg
G. 1 tablespoon sherry
H. salt to taste

PREPARATION:

I. Place C in bowl, cover with cold water, soak 4 to 6 days changing water 3 to 4 times a day. Drain and cut into cubes.

II. Cut D same size as C.
III. Beat F well.

COOKING:

1. Place A in cooking pot, add B; bring to boil, add C and cook over medium heat 10 minutes.
2. Add D, bring to boil. Remove from heat.
3. Stir in E slowly.

4. Return to heat, stirring constantly until it boils again. Remove from heat.
5. Stir in F gradually and add G. Mix well.
6. Add H.

BUDDHA'S DELIGHT
Fat Yow Yuen: Adapted

A. ¼ cup peanut oil
B. 4 slices ginger
C. 6 Chinese black mushrooms
D. 8 sheets dried bean curd skin
E. ¼ cup cloud ears
F. ¼ cup lily flowers
G. 1 cup sliced bamboo shoots
H. 2 stalks celery

I. ½ lb. celery cabbage
J. 1 cup sliced vegetarian steak
K. 2 tablespoons light soy sauce
L. ½ teaspoon sugar
M. ½ teaspoon salt
N. 2 teaspoons cornstarch mixed with ¼ cup water
O. sesame oil to taste

PREPARATION:

I. Wash C and soak 15 minutes, drain and save water, cut C into quarters.
II. Soak D in hot water ½ hour or until soft; drain, cut into ½-inch slices.
III. Soak E in hot water 15 to 30 minutes, allow ample room for expansion; discard water, wash and clean E thoroughly.

IV. Soak F in cold water 15 to 20 minutes, discard water; remove hard tips and cut each in half.
V. Cut H into ½-inch diagonal slices.
VI. Split I in half, cut one half into ½- to 1-inch pieces; then repeat procedure with remaining half.

COOKING:

1. Heat A, add B, stir-fry ½ minute. Add C, D, E, F, G, H, I, J, continue stirring 1 to 2 minutes.
2. Add K, L, M and ⅓ cup mushroom water (C), stir well. Cover and cook over low heat 5 minutes.
3. Thicken with N.
4. Add O, mix well, and serve.

BEAN CURD WITH PRESERVED HORSE BEAN CHILI SAUCE
La Jiong Dow Fu: Adapted

A. ½ tablespoon preserved horse bean chili sauce (from Chinese grocery)
B. 3 tablespoons light soy sauce
C. 1 scallion
D. 2 slices ginger
E. 1 teaspoon sugar
F. 1 tablespoon cornstarch
G. 1 cup water
H. 6 cakes bean curd
I. salt to taste

PREPARATION:

I. Cut each H into 16 pieces.

II. Cut C, D into 1-inch pieces.

COOKING:

1. Combine ingredients A, B, C, D, E, F, G in saucepan, mix well, and bring to boil.

2. Add H, cook 1 minute, stirring constantly. Add I. Serve with rice.

BEAN CURD PORK WITH PRESERVED HORSE BEAN CHILI SAUCE
La Jiong Dow Fu Ju Yoke: Adapted

A. 3 tablespoons peanut oil
B. 1 scallion
C. 2 slices ginger
D. ¼ lb. pork, shredded
E. 4 cakes bean curd
F. 2 teaspoons preserved horse bean chili sauce (from Chinese grocery)
G. 3 tablespoons light soy sauce
H. 1 teaspoon sugar
I. 1 teaspoon cornstarch
J. ¼ cup water

PREPARATION:

I. Cut each E into eighths.

II. Cut B, C into 1-inch pieces.

III. Mix F, G, H, I, J.

COOKING:

1. Heat A, add B, C, stir-fry a few seconds.
2. Add D, stir-fry 1 to 2 minutes.
3. Add E, mix well.

4. Add F–J, continue stirring until mixture thickens.

FLUFFY BEAN CURD
Fong Wo Dow Fu: Peking

A. 2 tablespoons peanut oil
B. ¼ lb. pork, shredded
C. 6 cakes bean curd
D. 6 Chinese black mushrooms
E. 10 dried shrimp
F. ½ cup chopped bamboo shoots
G. ¼ cup finely chopped preserved tea melon
H. 1 teaspoon salt

PREPARATION:

I. Cook C in boiling water until fluffy (about 25 minutes). Drain well, squeeze out water; shred.

II. Wash G and soak in warm water 15 minutes. Drain.

III. Wash E well, soak in water 15 minutes. Drain.

IV. Chop D, E fine.

COOKING:

1. Heat A. Add B, stir-fry 2 minutes.

2. Add C, D, E, F, G, H, stir-fry until gravy is almost absorbed.

STIR-FRIED PRESSED BEAN CURD WITH PORK
Dow Fu Gahn Tsao Ro Si: Shanghai

A. 2 tablespoons peanut oil
B. ½ lb. pork, shredded
C. 1 tablespoon light soy sauce
D. 1 teaspoon cornstarch
E. ½ teaspoon sugar
F. 1 scallion, chopped

G. 4 cakes pressed bean curd
H. 6 stalks celery
I. 1 teaspoon sherry
J. ½ teaspoon salt
K. 3 tablespoons water

PREPARATION:

I. Wash G; cut each into long, thin strips.
II. Cut H diagonally into long, thin strips.

III. Mix B, C, D, E, F.

COOKING:

1. Heat A. Stir-fry B–F over high heat 1 to 2 minutes.
2. Add G, H. Continue stirring until well mixed.

3. Add I, J, K, mix well. Cover, cook over low heat 5 minutes.

STIR-FRIED PRESSED BEAN CURD WITH CHICKEN
Dow Fu Gahn Tsao Gee Si: Shanghai

Substitute 1 boned chicken breast for B and in Step 2 add 6 Chinese black mushrooms which have been washed and soaked in water 15 minutes, drained, and cut into strips. Use mushroom water instead of K in Step 3.

STEAMED BEAN CURD WITH PORK
Dow Fu Tsen Tsu Ro: Peking

A. 6 cakes bean curd
B. ¼ lb. ground pork, shredded
C. 1 tablespoon chopped scallion
D. 2 slices ginger, chopped
E. 2 teaspoons sherry

F. ½ teaspoon sugar
G. 2 tablespoons light soy sauce
H. 1 teaspoon sesame oil
I. ½ teaspoon salt

PREPARATION:

I. Cover A with boiling water 1 to 2 minutes. Remove from water, arrange in large bowl.

II. Mix B, C, D, E, F, G, H, I thoroughly.
III. Spread over A.

COOKING:

1. Place bowl in steamer, cover. Steam over boiling water 20 minutes.

STEAMED BEAN CURD WITH BEEF
Dow Fu Tsen Niu Ro: Peking

Substitute beef for B. Steam over boiling water 15 minutes.

BRAISED BEAN CURD
Dow Fu Mun Ju Yoke: Adapted

A. 3 tablespoons peanut oil
B. 1 scallion, chopped
C. 3 slices ginger, chopped
D. ½ lb. pork, shredded
E. 6 Chinese black mushrooms

F. 4 cakes bean curd
G. ½ teaspoon sugar
H. 3 tablespoons light soy sauce
I. 1 teaspoon cornstarch mixed with
     3 tablespoons mushroom water

PREPARATION:

I. Wash E, soak 15 minutes. Drain, saving water; cut into strips.

II. Cut each F into 6 or 7 long strips.

III. Mix G, H, I.

COOKING:

1. Heat A. Add B, C, stir-fry a few seconds.
2. Add D, E, stir-fry until pork turns white (about 2 to 3 minutes).

3. Add F, stir well.
4. Add G–I, cover. Cook over low heat 3 to 5 minutes. Serve hot.

BRAISED BEAN CURD
Dow Fu Mun Ju Yoke: Szechuan

Add 2 fresh Italian hot peppers. Chop peppers into 1-inch pieces, discard stems and seeds. Mix with D–E.

NANKIANG BEAN CURD
Nankiang Dow Fu

A. 4 cakes bean curd
B. 1 teaspoon peanut oil
C. 3 dried scallops
D. ¼ cup sliced Virginia ham

E. ½ cup sliced bamboo shoots
F. 1 tablespoon chopped scallions
G. 1 cup chicken broth
H. salt, pepper to taste

COOKING:

1. Cut each A into 4 squares, brown in B. Cover with boiling water and cook for few seconds; discard water. Cut each square into 4 pieces.
2. Rinse C and steam over boiling water until

soft (about 25 to 30 minutes), break up C.

3. Mix A with B, C, D, E, F, G, bring to boil; lower heat and cook 10 minutes. Add H.
4. Serve with rice.

FRIED TRIPLE BEAN CURD
Sam Si Dow Fu: Adapted

A. ¼ cup peanut oil
B. 4 cakes bean curd
C. 1 clove garlic, chopped
D. 4 slices ginger, shredded
E. 4 to 6 Chinese black mushrooms
F. 1 cup shredded bamboo shoots
G. 1 scallion
H. ¼ lb. pork, shredded

I. 2 teaspoons light soy sauce
J. ½ teaspoon sugar
K. 1 teaspoon cornstarch
L. 1 cup mushroom water
M. 2 tablespoons light soy sauce
N. 1 tablespoon sherry
O. 2 teaspoons cornstarch mixed with
     2 tablespoons water

PREPARATION:

I. Cut each B into 4 long pieces, dry between paper towels.

II. Mix H, I, J, K.

III. Wash E, soak in warm water 15 minutes; drain and shred; save water.

IV. Cut G into 1½-inch pieces.

V. Mix L, M, N.

COOKING:

1. Heat A, add B, brown on all sides until golden (about 5 minutes).

2. Remove B to a dish leaving A in pan.

3. Reheat A, add C, D and stir-fry a few times; add H–K and E, stir-fry 1½ minutes.

4. Add F, continue stirring ½ minute.

5. Add B–G, and L–N, stir well, cover and cook 2 minutes.

6. Thicken with O.

VEGETARIAN HAM DRIED BEAN CURD
Sue Ho Twei Dow Fu: Shanghai

A. 1 tablespoon sugar

B. ¼ cup light soy sauce

C. 1 cup water

D. 20 sheets dried bean curd

E. 1 to 2 teaspoons sesame oil

F. 4 cakes bean curd skin

PREPARATION:

I. Soak D in water 2 minutes; drain, cut into 1-inch squares.

COOKING:

1. Place A, B, C in pot, bring to boil.

2. Add D and cook 15 minutes over medium heat.

3. Add E, mix well and cool.

4. Place ½ of A–E mixture in middle of 2 pieces of F.

5. Fold F over tightly and make into 5-inch roll.

6. Wrap 1 square foot waxed paper around the roll; tie with a string. Make 2 rolls like this.

7. Stand endwise on a plate.

8. Steam over boiling water 45 minutes.

9. Cool completely before unwrapping waxed paper; slice and serve.

BEAN CURD WITH CHICKEN GIBLETS
Dow Fu Gee Tza: General

A. 3 tablespoons peanut oil

B. 4 chicken giblets

C. 1 scallion, chopped

D. 2 slices ginger, chopped

E. 1 clove garlic, chopped

F. 2 teaspoons sherry

G. 2 teaspoons light soy sauce

H. 1 teaspoon cornstarch

I. ⅓ cup water

J. 3 to 4 cakes bean curd

K. 3 tablespoons vinegar

L. 3 tablespoons sugar

M. 1 teaspoon light soy sauce

N. ½ teaspoon salt

O. 1 teaspoon cornstarch

PREPARATION:

I. Cut each J into 16 cubes.

II. Slice each B thin.

III. Mix B, C, D, E, F, G, H thoroughly.

IV. Mix K, L, M, N, O.

COOKING:

1. Heat A, stir-fry B–H 2 minutes.

2. Add I, cook over low heat 3 minutes.

3. Add J, mix well, bring to boil.

4. Add K–O, stir until thick. Serve hot with rice.

STUFFED BEAN CURD
Yong Dow Fu: Canton

A. 1 tablespoon peanut oil
B. 4 cakes bean curd
C. ¼ lb. ground pork
D. 1 scallion, chopped
E. 4 slices ginger, chopped
F. 1 teaspoon cornstarch
G. ½ teaspoon salt

H. 1 teaspoon light soy sauce
I. 2 tablespoons chopped Chinese parsley (optional)
J. 10 dried shrimp
K. ¼ cup chicken broth
L. 2 teaspoons cornstarch mixed with 2 tablespoons water.

PREPARATION:

I. Cut each B into 2 triangles; scoop out a little in middle for stuffing.
II. Wash J, soak in water 10 minutes, then mince.

III. Mix C, D, E, F, G, H, I, J thoroughly.
IV. Fill each B center with C–J mixture.

COOKING:

1. Heat A in pot. Brown B–J on both sides.
2. Add K, bring to boil, then turn heat low and simmer 15 minutes.

3. Remove B–K. Thicken gravy with L.
4. Pour over B and serve.

STUFFED BEAN CURD   *Approved Ulcer Recipe*
Yong Dow Fu: Canton

Omit D, E, I; substitute 6 fresh shrimp for J. Wash J but do not soak; mince very fine.

STEAMED STUFFED BEAN CURD
Tsen Ho Yow Dow Fu: Canton

In Step 1, arrange stuffed B in single layer on a plate; in Step 2, pour oyster sauce (1 tablespoon oyster sauce diluted with ½ tablespoon water) over B; in Step 3, place in steamer and steam 15 minutes.

BEAN CURD WITH BEEF
Dow Fu Niu Ro: General

A. 3 tablespoons peanut oil
B. ½ lb. flank steak
C. 2 slices ginger, chopped
D. 1 scallion, chopped
E. 2 tablespoons sherry
F. 4 cakes bean curd

G. 3 teaspoons light soy sauce
H. 2 teaspoons cornstarch
I. ½ teaspoon sugar
J. 1 teaspoon salt
K. ¼ cup water

PREPARATION:

I. Cut each F into 10 pieces.
II. Slice B into pieces ⅛ by 1½ inches.

III. Mix B, C, D, E, 1 teaspoon G, 1 teaspoon H.
IV. Mix remaining G and H with I, J, K.

COOKING:

1. Heat A, add B–E, stir-fry 1 minute.
2. Add F, mix well, stir 1 minute.

3. Thicken with G–K, and serve with rice.

BEAN CURD WITH SHRIMP
Har Yen Dow Fu: Adapted

A. 3 tablespoons peanut oil
B. ½ lb. shrimp
C. 2 teaspoons sherry
D. 1 teaspoon light soy sauce
E. 1 teaspoon cornstarch
F. 1 teaspoon sugar

G. 1 scallion, chopped
H. 2 slices ginger, chopped
I. 6 cakes bean curd
J. 2 tablespoons brown bean sauce
K. ¼ cup water

PREPARATION:

I. Shell, devein, wash, and drain B. Cut each into 2 or 3 pieces.
II. Cut each I into 16 cubes.

III. Mix B, C, D, E, F, G, H thoroughly.
IV. Mix J, K.

COOKING:

1. Heat A. Add B–H, stir-fry over high heat 1 to 2 minutes.
2. Add I, mix well.

3. Add J, K, stir well, cover, and cook over low heat 5 minutes. Serve hot.

BEAN CURD MEAT CONCENTRATE
Dow Fu Ro Sung: Shanghai

A. 2 tablespoons peanut oil
B. 6 cakes bean curd
C. 2 scallions
D. 3 slices ginger
E. 1 tablespoon oyster sauce
F. 1 tablespoon sherry

G. 1 teaspoon sugar
H. ½ cup soup stock
I. 2 teaspoons cornstarch dissolved in 1 tablespoon water
J. ½ cup prepared meat concentrate (see Home-Style Pork or Beef Concentrate)

PREPARATION:

I. Cut each B into 4 pieces.
II. Chop C.
III. Mix C, D, E, F, G.

COOKING:

1. Heat A in pot; add B, fry on both sides 2 or 3 minutes.
2. Add C–G and H; simmer 6 minutes.

3. Thicken sauce with I.
4. Place in shallow bowl and sprinkle with J.

BEAN CURD TOSSED WITH PEANUT BUTTER
Liang Ban Dow Fu: Shanghai

A. 4 cakes bean curd
B. 1 tablespoon peanut butter
C. 1 tablespoon light soy sauce
D. 1 tablespoon vinegar
E. few drops sesame oil

F. ½ to 1 teaspoon sugar
G. ½ to 1 teaspoon salt (to taste)
H. 4 slices ginger, chopped
I. 2 tablespoons chopped Chinese parsley

PREPARATION:

I. Rinse A, cut each into 6 pieces.
II. Mix B, C, D, E, F, G thoroughly.

III. Mix A and B–G.
IV. Garnish with H, I.

SHREDDED BEAN CURD WITH MIXED MEATS I
Shih Jing Dow Fu: Shanghai

A. 3 tablespoons peanut oil
B. ¼ cup shredded Smithfield ham
C. 4 Chinese black mushrooms
D. ½ cup shredded bamboo shoots
E. 1 cup chicken broth
F. 2 cakes bean curd, shredded
G. ¼ cup peas

H. ¼ cup diced shrimp
I. ¼ cup diced crab meat
J. ¼ cup shredded chicken white meat
K. 1 teaspoon sherry
L. 1 teaspoon light soy sauce
M. 1 teaspoon salt
N. 1 tablespoon cornstarch

PREPARATION:

I. Wash C, soak 15 minutes in warm water. Drain (saving water to mix with N), and cut each C into 4 or 5 pieces.

II. Mix K, L, M.

III. Mix 2 tablespoons C water with N.

COOKING:

1. Heat A, stir-fry B, C, D 1 minute.
2. Add E, bring to boil.
3. Add F, G, cover, and cook 1 minute.

4. Add H, I, J and K–M, bring back to boil; boil several seconds.
5. Thicken with N mixture. Serve hot with rice.

SHREDDED BEAN CURD WITH MIXED MEATS II
Sih Gin Gahn Si: Shanghai

A. 3 tablespoons peanut oil
B. ¼ lb. pork, shredded, or
    ½ cup shredded ham
C. ½ cup diced frozen shrimp
D. 4 Chinese black mushrooms
E. ¼ cup shredded preserved kohlrabi

F. 1 teaspoon sugar
G. 1 tablespoon light soy sauce
H. 1 cup chicken broth
I. 3 cakes pressed bean curd
J. ½ cup shredded bamboo shoots
K. salt, pepper to taste

PREPARATION:

I. Slice I very thin, then shred.

II. Wash D and soak in warm water 15 minutes

or until soft. Drain, save mushroom water and add to H. Discard stems, shred very fine.

COOKING:

1. Heat A, add B, C, stir-fry 1 to 2 minutes, remove from pan.
2. In same pan add D, E, F, G, stir-fry 1 to 2

minutes, add H, bring to boil.
3. Add I, J, lower heat, cook 3 minutes.
4. Add K and garnish with B–C mixture.

SHREDDED BEAN CURD WITH CHICKEN AND HAM
Gai Si Dow Fu: Canton

A. 3 tablespoons peanut oil
B. 1 scallion, chopped
C. 2 slices ginger, chopped
D. 1 clove garlic, chopped
E. ½ cup shredded bamboo shoots
F. 6 shredded Chinese black mushrooms
G. 10 water chestnuts
H. 4 cakes bean curd

I. ½ cup shredded cooked chicken
J. ½ cup shredded cooked ham
K. 3 tablespoons light soy sauce
L. 1 teaspoon sugar
M. 1 tablespoon cornstarch
N. ½ cup chicken stock
O. ¼ cup mushroom water
P. salt, pepper to taste

PREPARATION:

I. Cut each H into 6 or 7 long strips.

II. Slice G into small pieces.

III. Wash F, soak in warm water 15 minutes. Cut into long strips.

IV. Mix K, L, M, N, O well.

COOKING:

1. Heat A. Add B, C, D, stir-fry 30 seconds. Add E, F, G, stir-fry 1 minute.

2. Add H, I, J, stir well.

3. Add K–O, stir well, cover, cook over medium heat a few minutes.

4. Add P; serve.

SHREDDED BEAN CURD WITH CHICKEN *Approved Ulcer Recipe*
Gai Si Dow Fu: Canton

A. 2 tablespoons vegetable oil

B. 1 scallion, tied in bundle

C. 1 teaspoon oyster sauce

D. 10 water chestnuts

E. 10 fresh mushrooms (or 4-oz. can, drained)

F. 4 cakes bean curd

G. 1 cup chopped cooked white meat chicken

H. 2 tablespoons light soy sauce

I. 1 teaspoon sugar

J. 1 tablespoon cornstarch

K. ½ cup chicken soup

L. salt to taste

M. 5 slices ham, minced very fine

PREPARATION:

I. Cut each F into 6 or 7 pieces.   II. Chop D and E into very small pieces.   III. Mix C, H, I, J, K.

COOKING:

1. Heat A in frying pan. Add B, stir-fry 30 seconds.

2. Add D, E, stir-fry 1 minute.

3. Add F, G, stir well.

4. Add C, H–K; continue stirring. Cook, covered, over medium heat 5 minutes. Discard B.

5. Add L and garnish with M; serve.

FRECKLED MA PO BEAN CURD
Ma Po Dow Fu: Szechuan

A. 3 tablespoons peanut oil

B. 2 cloves garlic, chopped

C. 2 teaspoons fermented salted black beans

D. ¼ lb. ground pork

E. 4 cakes bean curd

F. 2 tablespoons light soy sauce

G. 1 cup chicken broth

H. ½ teaspoon sugar

I. 1 scallion, chopped

J. 2 teaspoons yellow bean sauce

K. 1 teaspoon crushed red pepper

L. 3 slices ginger, chopped

M. 2 teaspoons cornstarch mixed with ¼ cup water

N. ½ to 1 teaspoon sesame oil

O. anise ground pepper to taste

PREPARATION:

I. Cut each E into 16 cubes.   II. Mix F, G, H.   III. Mix I, J, K, L.

COOKING:

1. Heat A in large frying pan. Add B, C, stir-fry a few seconds. Add D and stir-fry 2 minutes.

2. Add E and F–H mixture; cook 1 minute.

3. Add I–L mixture, mix well. Thicken with M, cook a few seconds.

4. Add N, stir.

5. Sprinkle with O to taste before serving.

BEAN CURD POTPOURRI
Gee Yung Dow Fu: Peking

A. 4 cakes bean curd
B. 4 oz. chicken white meat
C. 2 eggs
D. 1 oz. ham
E. 6 asparagus shoots
F. 10 fresh mushrooms
G. 2 teaspoons sherry
H. 1 scallion, chopped
I. 2 slices ginger
J. dash black pepper
K. 1 to 1½ qts. beef or chicken stock
L. salt to taste

PREPARATION:

I. Break off tough stems of E and save tender shoots.
II. Place A, B, C, D, E, F, G, H, I, J in blender and whirl 3 minutes; add small amount of water if needed. Then force mixture through coarse strainer.

COOKING:

1. Place A–J in bowl; cover with aluminum foil and steam 30 minutes; mixture should have firm texture; cut into 2- by 2-inch pieces.
2. Bring K to boil, float A–J pieces in it and adjust with L.

BEAN CURD WITH CRAB MEAT
Hai Yoke Dow Fu: Adapted

A. 3 tablespoons peanut oil
B. 1 scallion, chopped
C. 2 slices ginger, shredded
D. 1 clove garlic, chopped
E. 1 cup chicken broth
F. 3 cakes bean curd, diced
G. ¼ cup peas
H. 7½-oz. can crab meat
I. 4-oz. can mushrooms
J. 1 teaspoon sherry
K. 1 teaspoon salt
L. 1 tablespoon cornstarch

PREPARATION:

I. Drain I, saving liquid.
II. Mix 2 tablespoons I liquid with L.

COOKING:

1. Heat A, stir-fry B, C, D several seconds.
2. Add E, bring to boil.
3. Add F, G, reduce heat, cover, and cook 2 minutes.
4. Add H, I, J, K, bring back to boil, and cook 1 minute.
5. Thicken with L. Serve with rice.

BROWN GRAVY
Si Yow Nung Tsup: Canton

A. 1 cup soup stock
B. ½ teaspoon salt
C. 1 teaspoon heavy soy sauce

D. 1 teaspoon light soy sauce
E. 1 tablespoon cornstarch
F. 2 scallions, sliced

PREPARATION:

I. Combine A, B, C, D, E.

COOKING:

1. Bring A–E to boil in small saucepan, stirring constantly until sauce thickens.

2. Add hot water for thinner sauce, if desired.
3. Serve with garnish of F.

CREAM SAUCE
Ny Yow Tsup: Canton

A. 2 cups water
B. ½ cup half and half
C. 2 tablespoons cornstarch

D. 1 teaspoon salt
E. ¼ teaspoon garlic powder
F. 1 slice ginger, minced

PREPARATION:

I. Mix all ingredients in saucepan.

COOKING:

1. Bring to boil slowly and cook with continuous stirring until sauce becomes thick and smooth. Serve with chicken, mushrooms, seafood, etc.

BEAN PASTE
Dow Sha: General

A. ½ cup lard
B. 1 lb. red kidney beans

C. 1½ cups sugar

PREPARATION:

I. Wash B, place in pan, cover with water, and bring to boil. Lower heat, cook until B skins open up (2 to 3 hours).
II. Discard skins and drain resulting paste into a bowl.

III. Using piece of cheesecloth, squeeze excess water from B.
IV. Mix B with C.

COOKING:

1. Heat A, stir-fry B–C until thoroughly mixed.

BLACK BEAN SAUCE
Huk Dow Tsup: Canton

A. 1 tablespoon peanut oil
B. 2 cloves garlic
C. 1 slice ginger, minced
D. 2 tablespoons salted black beans
E. 1 teaspoon sugar
F. 2 tablespoons sherry

G. 1 teaspoon light soy sauce
H. 1 cup soup stock
I. 1 teaspoon heavy soy sauce
J. 1 tablespoon cornstarch
K. 2 scallions, sliced

PREPARATION:

I. Mix B, C, D.   II. Mix E, F, G.   III. Mix H, I, J. Set aside. Stir well before using.

COOKING:

1. Put A in very hot skillet and bring to high heat.
2. Add B–D. Stir-fry 15 seconds.
3. Add E–G. Stir-fry 15 seconds.

4. Slowly add H–J. Stir continuously and bring to boil as sauce thickens. Simmer 3 minutes.
5. Serve with garnish of K.

TOMATO SAUCE
Chieh Tze: General

A. 1 tablespoon peanut oil
B. 2 cloves garlic
C. 1 slice ginger, minced
D. 3 tablespoons catsup
E. 1 teaspoon sugar

F. 2 tablespoons sherry
G. 1 teaspoon light soy sauce
H. 1 cup soup stock
I. 1 teaspoon heavy soy sauce
J. 1 tablespoon cornstarch

PREPARATION:

I. Mix B, C.
II. Mix D, E, F, G.

III. Mix H, I, J. Set aside. Stir well before using.

COOKING:

1. Put A in very hot skillet and bring to high heat.
2. Add B–C. Stir-fry 15 seconds.

3. Add D–G. Stir-fry 15 seconds.
4. Slowly add H–J. Stir continuously and bring to boil as sauce thickens. Simmer 3 minutes.

SAUCE FOR RICE OR EGG FU YONG
Si Yow Tsup: Canton

A. 1 cup water
B. 1 tablespoon peanut oil
C. 1 teaspoon sugar
D. 1 teaspoon salt

E. 1 teaspoon light soy sauce
F. 2 teaspoons cornstarch
G. 2 tablespoons water

PREPARATION:

I. Mix B, C, D, E, F, G. Stir well before using.

COOKING:

1. Bring A to boil.
2. Slowly add B–G and stir continuously until

sauce thickens. Serve as all-purpose sauce, with meats, poultry, fish, etc.

SESAME OIL GRAVY
Ma Yo Jiang Tze: Szechuan

A.   2 tablespoons light soy sauce   D.   3 slices ginger, minced   F.   1 cup water
B.   2 tablespoons sesame oil   E.   1 tablespoon cornstarch   G.   ½ teaspoon salt
C.   1 clove garlic, minced

PREPARATION:

I.   Mix all ingredients in saucepan.

COOKING:

1.   Heat to boiling until gravy thickens and becomes smooth. Serve.

HOT OIL SAUCE
Hung Yo: Szechuan

A.   1 to 2 red-hot peppers   B.   ¼ cup salad oil

PREPARATION:

I.   Wash A, dry with paper towels. Remove A stems and seeds, cut into 1-inch pieces.

COOKING:

1.   Heat B to 375°, add A, cook 1 to 2 minutes.   The longer A remains, the hotter B will be. To
2.   Remove from heat, leaving A in B until cold.   use, remove A.

HOT SESAME OIL SAUCE
La Ma Yo: Szechuan

Substitute sesame oil for B and leave A in B 3 to 4 days.

RED OIL SAUCE
Hung Yo: Hunan

A.   2 lbs. red-hot peppers   B.   1½ qts. water

PREPARATION:

I.   Shred A, removing stems (do not discard seeds) ; chop A fine.

COOKING:

1.   Combine A, B, bring to boil, simmer until A   strainer and boil down sauce by continuous
     disintegrates. Strain mixture through fine   simmering until only red oil remains.

RED HOT PEPPER OIL
Hung La Yo: Szechuan

A.   ¼ cup peanut oil   B.   1 tablespoon ground cayenne (red pepper)   C.   2 teaspoons sesame oil

COOKING:

1.   Heat A to 375°, remove from heat.   place over a small jar. Pour A mixture in and
2.   Add B, stir well; cool.   let it drip into jar. It can be served with any
3.   Add C, mix thoroughly.   dish that requires a hot sauce, or add few
4.   Line funnel with a piece of tissue paper and   drops to a noodle dish or fried rice.

HOT SAVORY SAUCE
La Fu Jiang: Shanghai

A. 3 tablespoons vegetable oil
B. ¼ cup diced dried shrimp
C. 3 slices ginger, minced
D. 2 lbs. pork chops
E. 4 cakes pressed bean curd
F. 4- to 6-oz. can bamboo shoots
G. 8 Chinese black mushrooms

H. 3 tablespoons hoisin sauce
I. 1 tablespoon light soy sauce
J. 1 teaspoon hot red pepper, or to taste
K. 1 tablespoon sherry
L. 1 tablespoon cornstarch mixed with
   2 tablespoons water
M. salt to taste

PREPARATION:

I. Bone D, cut D, E, F into ½-inch cubes.

II. Wash B, G, soak in hot water 15 minutes or until soft; drain, combine waters and save.

Cut B and G into ½-inch pieces.

III. Mix H, I, J, K, adding ¼ cup water from B, G.

COOKING:

1. Heat A in casserole or heavy pot; stir-fry B, C 1 to 2 minutes. Add D and stir-fry 1 minute.

2. Add E, F, G, and H–K; cover and simmer 30 minutes, adding more water if needed.

3. Add L to thicken; sauce should be like gravy but not soupy. Adjust with M and serve with noodles or rice.

PEANUT OIL DIP PEPPER
Hwa Sun Yo Ching Jio: General

A. ½ cup peanut oil
B. 4 green peppers (about 1 lb.)
C. 2 tablespoons light soy sauce

D. 2 teaspoons sugar
E. 2 teaspoons vinegar
F. salt to taste

PREPARATION:

I. Wash B, discard stems and seeds, cut each into 8 pieces. Mix C, D, E.

COOKING:

1. Heat A to 375°, turn off heat; add B pieces, stir a few seconds until skin of B starts to wrinkle; pour off oil, leaving B in pot. Turn on heat.

2. Add C–E; stir a few seconds, add F and serve.

GINGER OIL
Giang Yo: Canton

A. 3 tablespoons vegetable oil
B. 1 piece ginger root (walnut size)

C. ¼ teaspoon salt
D. 1 teaspoon sugar

PREPARATION:

I. Peel B, wash, pound with side of cleaver until flat, then chop very fine.

COOKING:

1. Heat A until it almost smokes, remove from heat, add B, C, D, mix thoroughly. Serve with chicken, especially chicken roasted in salt (see Index) or salt-cured chicken (see Index).

SWEET AND SOUR SAUCE
Tiem Shwin Tsup: Canton

A. 2 tablespoons peanut oil
B. ½ cup sub gum ginger and juice to cover (or mixed sweet pickles)
C. ¼ teaspoon garlic powder
D. 4 tablespoons vinegar

E. 4 tablespoons sugar
F. ⅛ teaspoon red food coloring (optional)
G. 2 tablespoons heavy soy sauce
H. 1 cup soup stock
I. ½ tablespoon cornstarch

PREPARATION:

I. Heat A to smoking. Set aside to cool.

II. Mix C, D, E, F, G.   III. Mix H, I.

COOKING:

1. Bring A to high heat again.
2. Add B and juice. Stir-fry 30 seconds.
3. Add C–G. Stir well and bring to boil. Cook 2 minutes.
4. Add H, I slowly. Stir-fry until sauce thickens.

5. Pour over fried shrimp, pork, lobster, chicken. Also serve with hard-cooked eggs, fish, won ton, fried noodles, rice, litchis, pineapples, etc.

SWEET AND SOUR SUB GUM SAUCE
Sub Gum Tiem Shwin Tsup: Canton

A. 1 cup soup stock
B. ¾ cup sugar
C. ½ cup vinegar
D. 1 cup chopped imported (or

American) mixed pickles
E. 2 tablespoons duck sauce
F. 1 teaspoon heavy soy sauce
G. 4 teaspoons cornstarch

PREPARATION:

I. Mix E, F, G. Stir well before using.

II. Discard D liquid.

COOKING:

1. Boil A in saucepan.
2. Add B, C and cook, stirring constantly, until dissolved.

3. Add D. Cook 2 minutes.
4. Add E, F, G. Bring to boil until sauce thickens. Cool. Put in jar and refrigerate.

MEAT SAUCE
La Fu Jiang: Shanghai

A. 3 tablespoons peanut oil
B. 1 scallion, minced
C. 3 slices ginger, minced
D. 1 to 2 lbs. pork chops
E. 4 cakes pressed bean curd
F. ¼ cup cubed bamboo shoots

G. 8 Chinese black mushrooms, minced
H. 3 tablespoons hoisin sauce
I. 1 tablespoon light soy sauce
J. 2 teaspoons cornstarch
K. 1 tablespoon sherry
L. ¼ cup water

PREPARATION:

I. Cut D, E, into ⅜ inch cubes.
II. Wash G, soak in warm water 15 minutes or

until soft. Drain.
III. Mix H, I, J, K, L.

COOKING:

1. Heat A, stir-fry B, C a few seconds, add D, and stir constantly 1 minute.

2. Add E, F, G and H–L, simmer, covered, 30 minutes. Serve with noodles or rice.

MEAT SAUCE
La-Fu-Jiang: Shanghai

Add ¼ cup dried diced shrimp; soak in warm water 20 minutes. Add to other ingredients in Step 2.

MEAT SAUCE
La-Fu-Jiang: Shanghai

Add 1 tsp. hot red pepper powder to E–L. Decrease pepper for blander sauce.

STEAK SAUCE
Ngo Pa Tsup: Canton

A. 3 tablespoons peanut oil
B. ½ teaspoon salt
C. 1 to 2 large cloves garlic, minced
D. 1 to 2 slices ginger, minced
E. 1 teaspoon light soy sauce

F. 1 cup beef stock
G. 1 tablespoon cornstarch
H. 1½ tablespoons heavy soy sauce
I. 1½ tablespoons oyster sauce
J. 6 scallions, sliced

PREPARATION:
I. Mix B, C, D, E.

II. Mix F, G, H, I.

COOKING:
1. Put A in very hot skillet and bring to high heat.
2. Add B–E. Stir-fry 15 seconds.

3. Add F–I slowly until sauce thickens. Simmer 3 minutes.
4. Serve over (or as a dip for) meat, with garnish of J.

PLAIN FISH SAUCE
Lung Ha Jiang: General

A. 2 tablespoons peanut oil
B. 2 cloves garlic, minced
C. 1 slice ginger, minced
D. 2 tablespoons mashed salted black beans
E. ½ teaspoon salt
F. ½ lb. ground pork
G. 1 teaspoon sugar

H. 1½ tablespoons light soy sauce
I. 2 tablespoons sherry
J. 2 cups soup stock
K. 1 tablespoon heavy soy sauce
L. 2 tablespoons cornstarch
M. 2 eggs
N. 2 tablespoons soup stock

PREPARATION:
I. Mix B, C, D, E. Set aside.
II. Mix G, H, I. Set aside.

III. Mix K, L. Set aside.
IV. Beat M lightly. Add N. Set aside.

COOKING:
1. Put A in very hot skillet and bring to high heat.
2. Add B–E. Stir-fry rapidly 15 seconds to brown B slightly.
3. Add F. Stir-fry 2 minutes.
4. Add G–I. Stir-fry 1 minute.
5. Add J. Cover. Bring to boil. Cook 5 to 7 minutes.

6. Add K–L slowly. Stir-fry until sauce thickens.
7. Turn off heat and add ¾ of M–N at once. Do not stir, but let M set 30 seconds.
8. Remove entire contents of skillet at once to serving dish. Pour and distribute remainder of M–N on top of dish.
9. Serve with fish or shellfish.

FISH OR SHRIMP SAUCE
Yu Ha Tsup: Canton

A. 2 teaspoons ginger, minced

B. 2 teaspoons sugar

C. 2 teaspoons vinegar

D. 4 tablespoons light soy sauce

PREPARATION:

I. Mix all ingredients well. Serve as dip for shrimp or other fish.

SHRIMP-FLAVORED SOY SAUCE
Sha Tze Jiang Yo: General

A. ⅛ lb. shrimp

B. 1 cup light soy sauce

PREPARATION:

I. Shell and wash A under running water, dry with paper towels, and place in a bowl.

II. Add B, then cover tightly with a plate.

COOKING:

1. Steam 30 to 45 minutes over boiling water. Use for dipping, or in cooking.

DUCK SAUCE
Op Tsup: Canton

A. 4 cups peeled, pitted and mashed purple plums

B. 3 cups peeled, pitted and mashed peaches (or apricots)

C. 2 cups mashed strawberries

D. 1 cup red wine vinegar

E. 2 cups sugar

COOKING:

1. In 16-cup (at least) pot, mix A, B, C. Add D, E.

2. Simmer A–E 1½ hours.

3. Add additional vinegar, sugar, and water to taste when used. Serve.

CHICKEN SAUCE I
Siang Yo Tzan Gee Lu: General

A. 2 tablespoons peanut oil

B. 1 slice ginger, minced

C. ⅓ teaspoon salt

D. ⅛ teaspoon pepper

E. 5 drops sesame oil (optional)

PREPARATION:

I. Heat A to smoking. Set aside to cool.

II. Mix all ingredients. Serve as dip.

CHICKEN SAUCE II
Tien Swan Tzan Gee Lu: General

A. 2 tablespoons peanut oil
B. 2 tablespoons sherry
C. 1 teaspoon sugar

D. 1 tablespoon vinegar
E. 5 tablespoons light soy sauce

PREPARATION:

I. Heat A to smoking. Set aside to cool.

II. Mix all ingredients. Serve as dip.

STUFFING* (DRESSING) FOR TURKEY, CHICKEN, DUCK

A. 1½ tablespoons peanut oil
B. 6 dried Chinese black mushrooms
C. 1½ Chinese sausages
D. 1 cup diced bamboo shoots
E. 2 cups glutinous rice
F. 1 tablespoon peanut oil

G. 3 teaspoons salt
H. 2 cloves garlic, minced
I. 2 teaspoons light or heavy soy sauce
J. 1 teaspoon sugar
K. 1 teaspoon pepper (optional)

PREPARATION:

I. Wash E, drain; mix with 2½ cups water and bring to boil; simmer 15 to 20 minutes.
II. Soak B in warm water 15 minutes. Drain.

III. Mix B, C, D.
IV. Mix E, F, G, H, I, J, K well.

COOKING:

1. Put A in very hot skillet and bring to high heat.
2. Add B–D and stir-fry 1 minute.

3. Add E–K and stir-fry 30 seconds.
4. Use entire mixture to stuff poultry.

BATTER FOR FRYING SHRIMP, LOBSTER, CHICKEN, OR PORK IN DEEP FAT

Main ingredients prepared as follows may be served alone or garnished with a hot mixed vegetable sauce or sweet and sour sauce (both sauces prepared separately) just before serving.

A. 2 eggs, beaten
B. ¾ teaspoon salt
C. ½ teaspoon garlic powder
D. ½ cup all-purpose flour
E. ¼ cup cornstarch
F. ½ cup milk
G. 1 tablespoon honey
H. 1 teaspoon lemon juice

I. 2 tablespoons sherry
J. 1 teaspoon fresh ginger put through garlic press
K. 1 lb. fresh shrimp or
L. 1 lb. lobster meat, in cubes, or
M. 1 lb. chicken (boned) or
N. 1 lb. fresh pork, sliced thin

PREPARATION OF BATTER:

I. Mix A, B, C, D, E, F, to make a smooth batter.

II. Dredge prepared K, L, M or N (see separate instructions below) in batter. Proceed to Cooking.

* For an 11-pound turkey. Reduce proportions accordingly for smaller bird.

FRIED SHRIMP IN BATTER
Soo Tsao Har: Canton

I. Shell K and split slightly in back.

II. Mix G, H, I, J (see page 442).

III. Soak K in mixture 15 minutes.

IV. Proceed to Step II (Preparation of Batter).

FRIED LOBSTER IN BATTER
Soo Tsao Lung Har: Canton

I. Mix G–J (see page 442).

II. Soak L in mixture 15 minutes.

III. Proceed to Step II (Preparation of Batter).

FRIED CHICKEN IN BATTER
Soo Tsao Gai: Canton

I. Mix G–J (see page 442).

II. Cut M into pieces 1 by 2 inches.

III. Soak M in mixture 15 minutes.

IV. Proceed to Step II (Preparation of Batter).

FRIED PORK IN BATTER
Soo Tsao Ju Yoke: Canton

I. Mix G–J.

II. Soak N in mixture 15 minutes (see page 442).

III. Proceed to Step II (Preparation of Batter).

COOKING:

1. Fry dipped K, L, M, or N pieces in peanut oil at 375° until light brown. Serve with duck sauce.

2. Optional: Cool fried pieces after Step 1, refrigerate, if desired, and later redip in batter; refry until golden brown.

ANISE PEPPER SALT
Jiao Yen: Szechuan

A.   1 teaspoon anise pepper

B.   1 tablespoon salt

PREPARATION:

I. Brown A in ungreased pan over medium heat until the fragrance is strong and the color is dark brown (3 to 5 minutes).

II. Grind A with pepper grinder.

III. Mix with B and serve with meat and poultry dishes. Anise pepper salt can be kept indefinitely.

GROUND PEPPER
Hua Chiao Fun: Szechuan

Substitute 3 tablespoons anise pepper for A and B, place in ungreased pot over low heat, cook until very dry and dark brown (3 to 5 minutes).

SWEET AND SOUR COLD RADISHES
Lun Ban Shiao Lo Bo: Peking

A. 30 radishes

B. 3 tablespoons vinegar

C. 3 tablespoons light soy sauce

D. 1 tablespoon sugar

E. sesame oil to taste

PREPARATION:

I. Remove tops and tails of A.

II. Crush each A with blow from the side of a cleaver.

III. Mix B, C, D.

IV. Place A in deep serving bowl.

V. Add B–D. Mix well.

VI. Refrigerate 1 to 2 hours.

VII. Add E to taste (several drops to ½ teaspoon). Serve.

TOSSED SALAD
Lun Ban Tien Tsin Bai Tsai: Peking

A. 1 lb. celery cabbage

B. 2 teaspoons light soy sauce

C. 2 teaspoons vinegar

D. ½ to 1 teaspoon sesame oil

E. salt to taste

PREPARATION AND COOKING:

I. Split A in half lengthwise; use only half cut crosswise into 1-inch pieces.

II. Bring 1 qt. water with ½ teaspoon salt to boil; add A, stir in boiling water 2 minutes. Turn off heat and drain.

III. Mix B, C, D, E. Mix with A. Serve.

TOSSED HOT SALAD
La Bai Tsai: Szechuan

A. 1 lb. celery cabbage

B. ½ to 1 teaspoon hot pepper flakes (to taste)

C. ¼ to ½ teaspoon anise pepper salt (see Index)

D. 2 teaspoons sugar

E. 1½ tablespoons vinegar

F. ½ to 1 teaspoon sesame oil (to taste)

G. 4 slices ginger

PREPARATION:

I. Split A into half lengthwise; use only half cut crosswise into 1-inch pieces.

II. Bring 1 qt. water with ½ teaspoon salt to boil; add A stir in boiling water 2 minutes. Turn off heat and drain.

III. Shred G very thin.

IV. Mix B, C, D, E, F, G.

V. Mix A, B–G and serve.

PEKING SALAD
Ban San Si: Peking

A. 1 large kohlrabi

B. 1 carrot

C. ½ cup shredded celery cabbage

D. 1½ teaspoons salt

E. ½ teaspoon anise pepper

F. ½ teaspoon sesame oil

G. ½ cup chopped Chinese parsley

PREPARATION:

I. Peel A, B, slice very thin, then shred.

II. Wash G.

III. Mix A, B, C, D, E thoroughly, marinate vegetables 30 to 45 minutes.

IV. Pour off excess water, add F, G. Mix well and serve.

KOHLRABI SALAD
Pieh La (Liang Ban Da To Tsai) : Peking

A. 1 lb. kohlrabi

B. ¼ cup vinegar

C. 3 tablespoons sugar

D. 1 teaspoon salt

E. 1 teaspoon sesame oil

PREPARATION:

I. Peel A and shred.

II. Mix B, C, D, E thoroughly.

III. Add A to B–E, mix again, let stand a few minutes, and serve.

DRAGON WHISKERS SALAD
Lun Ban Lung Shu Tsai: Shanghai

A. 1 lb. asparagus

B. 1 tablespoon vinegar

C. 1 tablespoon sugar

D. 1 teaspoon salt

E. 1 teaspoon sesame oil

PREPARATION AND COOKING:

I. Break each green and tender (edible) part of A into 2-inch pieces. Wash.

II. Pour 1 qt. boiling water over A and cook 4 minutes, uncovered.

III. Drain, run under cold water a few seconds.

IV. Mix B, C, D, E well, add to A. Let stand a few minutes before serving.

SPINACH CHEESE SALAD
Liang Ban Bo Tsai: Adapted

A. 10-oz. pkg. fresh spinach

B. 1 oz. hickory smoked cheese, shredded

C. 1 teaspoon light soy sauce

D. 1½ tablespoons cider vinegar

E. ½ teaspoon sesame, olive, or salad oil

F. ¼ teaspoon salt (to taste)

PREPARATION AND COOKING:

I. Wash A, cut each leaf into 2 to 3 pieces.

II. Parboil A by dipping in boiling water 30 seconds. Drain and cool.

III. Place A, B in salad bowl. Flavor with C, D, E, F. Mix well; serve cold.

BEAN SPROUT SALAD I
Lun Ban Dow Ya: Shanghai

A. 1 lb. bean sprouts
B. 3 scallions, chopped
C. 1 teaspoon salt

D. ¼ cup vinegar
E. ¼ cup sugar
F. 1 teaspoon sesame oil

PREPARATION:

I. Wash A thoroughly.

II. Combine C, D, E, F, mix well.

COOKING:

1. Put A into 1 qt. boiling water. Let stand 30 seconds. Drain.
2. Rinse A under running cold water until thoroughly cold. Drain well.

3. Mix A, B. Just before serving, add C–F; mix well.

BEAN SPROUT SALAD II
Lun Ban Dow Ya: Adapted

A. 1 lb. bean sprouts
B. 1 tablespoon shredded pickled ginger
C. 2 tablespoons light soy sauce

D. 1 to 2 teaspoons sesame oil (to taste)
E. salt to taste

PREPARATION AND COOKING:

I. Bring 2 qts. water to boil. Add A, stir well, remove from heat, then drain.

II. Add B, C, D, E, mix well.

BEAN SPROUT SALAD   *Approved Diabetic Recipe*
Lun Ban Ya Tsai: General

A. ¼ lb. bean sprouts
B. 1 teaspoon light soy sauce

C. ½ teaspoon sesame oil
D. salt to taste

PREPARATION AND COOKING:

I. Bring 1 qt. water to boil. Add A, stir well, turn off heat. Drain.

II. Mix B, C, D thoroughly.
III. Mix A and B–D and serve.

BEAN SPROUT AND PICKLED GINGER SALAD   *Approved Diabetic Recipe*
Lun Ban Jiang Si Dow Ya: General

Add 1 teaspoon shredded pickled ginger in Step III.

SPICY BEAN SPROUT SALAD
Lun Ban La Chiao Dow Ya: Szechuan

A. 1 lb. bean sprouts
B. 2 red-hot peppers
C. 3 scallions, chopped
D. 4 slices ginger, chopped

E. 1 teaspoon salt
F. 2 tablespoons vinegar
G. 2 teaspoons sugar
H. 1 teaspoon sesame oil

PREPARATION:

I. Wash A thoroughly.

II. Shred B, discard seeds, and wash.

III. Combine C, D, E, F, G, H.

COOKING:

1. Mix A, B. Parboil 30 seconds in 1 qt. boiling water, drain.

2. Allow to cool or rinse under cold water. Drain well.

3. Mix with C–H just prior to serving.

HOT SPICY BEAN SPROUT SALAD
Lun Ban Dow Ya: Szechuan

Substitute 2 pickled hot peppers for B, 1 teaspoon hot oil sauce for H. In Step IV, combine B–H. In Step 1, B is not parboiled.

MUSTARD GREEN PICKLE SALAD
Kwangtung Leung Bon La Tsoi: Canton

A. 1 cup mustard green pickles (see Index)

B. 1 lb. bean sprouts

C. ½ cup packaged shredded jellyfish

D. 3 tablespoons vinegar

E. 2 tablespoons sugar

F. 1½ teaspoons salt

G. 1 teaspoon sesame oil

PREPARATION AND COOKING:

I. Wash and drain B, stir in boiling water ½ minute, turn off heat, drain and let cold water run over sprouts until they are cold.

II. Wash C well, cover and soak in water 30 minutes; drain.

III. Mix A, B, C.

IV. Mix D, E, F, G well.

V. Combine all ingredients, mix well, and serve.

HUNDRED-YEAR-OLD EGG SALAD
Hoi Git Pi Dan: General

A. 3 hundred-year-old eggs

B. 2 cups packaged shredded jellyfish

C. 12 dried shrimp

D. 2 tablespoons shredded pickled ginger

E. 3 tablespoons wine vinegar

F. 1½ tablespoons sugar

G. 1½ tablespoons light soy sauce

H. 2 teaspoons sesame oil

I. salt to taste

PREPARATION:

I. Crack A and shell; wash A under cold water to remove all ashes. Cut each into 4 to 6 pieces.

II. Rinse B thoroughly with cold water. Cover with cold water and soak 45 to 60 minutes; rinse and drain.

III. Clean and wash C; add just enough water to cover (about 2 tablespoons) and soak 15 minutes. Drain and chop.

IV. Mix E, F, G, H.

V. Combine A, B, C, add E–H, toss lightly; marinate 15 to 30 minutes. Toss once more before serving; add I and serve.

CUCUMBER SALAD
Lun Ban Huang Gwa: Hunan

A.   2 small cucumbers

B.   1 teaspoon salt

C.   1 teaspoon sugar

D.   2 tablespoons light soy sauce

E.   ½ to 1 teaspoon sesame oil

PREPARATION:

I.   Peel A, cut into pieces 1½ inches by ½ inch. Add B, let stand 1 to 2 hours.

II. Run A under cold water, drain.

III. Mix C, D.

IV. Marinate A with C–D 3 hours.

V.   Add E, serve cold.

MIXED VEGETABLE SALAD
Liang Bun Sub Gum: Canton

A.   2 medium tomatoes

B.   2 stalks celery heart

C.   1 cucumber

D.   2 oz. agar agar

E.   1 scallion

F.   3 tablespoons cider vinegar

G.   3 tablespoons sugar

H.   3 teaspoons sesame oil

I.   1 teaspoon salt

PREPARATION:

I.   Slice A into as many wedges as possible.

II. Slice B into thin pieces.

III. Peel C, cut lengthwise; discard seeds; cut remainder into 2-inch slices.

IV. Cut D into 2-inch pieces; wash in cold water. As soon as strips separate from each other, drain.

V.   Slice E into thin pieces. Combine F, G, H, I. Mix well.

VI. Combine A, B, C, D, E.

VII. Just before serving, pour F–I over A–E. Mix well.

AGAR AGAR SALAD I
Liang Bun Dung Yong Tsoi: Canton

A.   2 oz. agar agar

B.   1 medium cucumber

C.   1 cup cooked ham or chicken white meat

D.   3 tablespoons sugar

E.   1 tablespoon sesame oil

F.   1 teaspoon salt

G.   3 tablespoons cider vinegar

PREPARATION:

I.   Cut A into strips 2½ inches in length. Wash in cold water as soon as strips are separated from each other; drain.

II. Cut B lengthwise; discard seeds. Cut remainder into 2½-inch-long strips.

III. Cut C into 2½-inch strips.

IV. Mix A, B, C; refrigerate.

V.   Mix D, E, F, G, pour over A–C, mix well.

AGAR AGAR SALAD II
Lun Ban Liang Tsai: Peking

A.   2 tablespoons peanut oil

B.   1 chicken breast

C.   2 oz. agar agar

D.   1 to 2 small tender cucumbers

E.   2 tablespoons light soy sauce

F.   1 to 1½ tablespoons vinegar

G.   1 to 2 teaspoons sesame oil

H.   dash mustard

I.   ½ egg white

J.   1 teaspoon cornstarch

K.   ¼ teaspoon salt

PREPARATION:

I. Bone B, discard skin and shred, mix with I, J, K.

II. Wash D, cut diagonally in ⅛-inch slices, then shred.

III. Cut C into pieces 1 to 2 inches long. Wash in water, when strips are separated from each other, drain.

IV. Mix E, F, G, H.

COOKING:

1. Heat A, add B, stir-fry 1 to 2 minutes. Drain and cool.

2. Place C in dish, top with A–B.

3. Place D on top of A–B.

4. Pour E–H over all; serve.

BAKED VIRGINIA HAM AGAR AGAR SALAD
Ho Twei Ban Yang Tsai: General

A.   ½ cup shredded baked Virginia ham

B.   ¼ cup shredded cooked chicken or turkey white meat

C.   1 small cucumber

D.   3 to 4 cups 2½-inch strips agar agar

E.   1 cup bean sprouts

F.   3 tablespoons light soy sauce

G.   1 to 1½ teaspoons sesame oil

H.   salt to taste

PREPARATION AND COOKING:

I. Cut C lengthwise, remove and discard seeds. Then cut C lengthwise again; shred into 2½-inch strips.

II. Wash D in cold water until strips are separated, drain and rinse under cold water a few more seconds. Drain, squeeze out water, and dry between paper towels.

III. Add E to boiling water; stir well, then drain.

IV. Mix F, G.

V. Mix A, B, C, D, E in a bowl, pour F–G over, mixing well.

VI. Add H and serve.

SALAD À LA CHANG
Chang Jai Lun Ban: Adapted

A.   ½ cup shredded cooked Virginia ham

B.   ½ cup shredded cooked chicken white meat

C.   ½ cup shredded abalone

D.   1 cup bean sprouts

E.   1 small cucumber

F.   1 cup agar agar

G.   2 tablespoons light soy sauce

H.   ½ teaspoon mustard

I.   1 teaspoon sesame oil

J.   salt to taste

PREPARATION AND COOKING:

I. Place D in boiling water for several seconds, stirring well. Drain, then hold under running water to cool.

II. Peel E, discard seeds, shred.

III. Cut F into pieces 1½ by 2 inches, soak in cold water until soft, drain.

IV. Combine all ingredients; mix thoroughly. Serve.

CHICKEN SALAD À LA CHANG
Chang Jia Lun Ban Sun Si: Adapted

A. ½ chicken breast (or 1 cup cooked and shredded)

B. 1 cup shredded ham

C. 1 cup shredded abalone

D. 2 cups shredded lettuce hearts (or center portion)

E. 1 small cucumber

(or 2 stalks shredded celery)

F. 2 cups agar agar

G. 4 tablespoons vinegar

H. 3 tablespoons sugar

I. 1½ teaspoons salt

J. 1 teaspoon sesame oil

PREPARATION AND COOKING:

I. Place A in cooking pot, cover with boiling water, and let boil 5 minutes. Remove from heat, let stand in water 10 to 15 minutes, then shred. (If cooked and shredded A is used, eliminate Step 1.)

II. Cut F into 1½-inch pieces with kitchen shears. Soak in cold water until soft, drain.

III. Combine A, B, C, D, E, F.

IV. Mix G, H, I, J and pour over A–F; combine well. Serve.

LITCHI ROAST DUCK SALAD
Lun Ban La-ee-tzee Ya: Shanghai

A. ½ Cantonese roasted duck

B. 1 teaspoon sesame oil

C. 2 teaspoons light soy sauce

D. 20 fresh litchis

E. few leaves Chinese parsley

PREPARATION:

I. Bone A, shred, mix with B, C, place on a platter.

II. Discard skin and pits of D and cut in quar-

ters; spread on top of A.

III. Garnish with E.

KIDNEY SALAD
Liang Ban Yao Pien: Peking

A. 1 tablespoon sherry

B. 1 scallion

C. 1 to 2 slices ginger

D. 4 pork kidneys

E. 1 tablespoon light soy sauce

F. 1 tablespoon peanut butter

G. 1 teaspoon sesame sauce

from Chinese grocery

H. 1 teaspoon sugar

I. ½ to 1 teaspoon sesame oil

J. 2 teaspoons vinegar

K. salt, pepper to taste

L. 1 cucumber

PREPARATION:

I. Wash D and remove any outer membrane; split lengthwise; use sharp scissors to remove all white veins. Rub with salt and squeeze out any blood, rinse with water. Cover with cold water and soak 1 to 2 hours.

II. Drain, slice into thin pieces, rub again with salt, and rinse.

III. Split L, remove seeds, dip in boiling water mixed with 1 teaspoon salt for a few seconds. Cut into thin slices, drain.

IV. Arrange L in dish. (Pour off any excess water before serving.)

V. Mix E, F, G, H, I, J K thoroughly.

COOKING:

1. To 1 qt. water add A, B, C, bring to boil.
2. Add D, keep stirring, when water comes to boil again, turn off heat, drain.

3. Mix A–D with E–K, marinate 5 to 10 minutes.
4. Pour on top of L and serve.

CELERY TOSSED SHRIMP SALAD I
Sha Mi Ban Ching Tsai: Peking

A. 10 to 12 large dried shrimp
B. 1 tablespoon sherry
C. 1 small celery heart
D. 2 teaspoons sesame oil

E. ½ teaspoon anise pepper
F. 1 teaspoon salt
G. 1 teaspoon sherry

PREPARATION AND COOKING:

I. Clean and wash A, soak in B 20 to 30 minutes, drain.
II. Wash C, cut into 1-inch diagonal pieces, dip into boiling water for a minute; drain and cool.

III. Heat D very hot, fry E until dark brown, discard E; mix in F, G.
IV. Mix all ingredients and serve.

CELERY TOSSED SHRIMP SALAD II
Sha Tze Ban Ching Tsai: Peking

A. 2 teaspoons sesame oil
B. ½ cup diced shelled shrimp

C. 1 celery heart
D. 2 tablespoons light soy sauce

E. 1 tablespoon vinegar

PREPARATION AND COOKING:

I. Wash C and cut diagonally into 1-inch pieces. Parboil 1 minute, drain, cool.
II. Heat A and stir-fry B 1 to 2 minutes.

III. Add B to C.
IV. Add D, E, mix well and serve.

TOMATO-SHRIMP SALAD
Lun Ban Fan Keh Har: Canton

A. 12 shrimp
B. 1 egg white
C. 1 teaspoon cornstarch

D. ½ teaspoon salt
E. 4 tomatoes
F. ½ teaspoon sesame oil

PREPARATION:

I. Shell, clean and wash A; cut into small pieces to make 1 cup.
II. Mix B, C, D.

III. Coat A with B–D.
IV. Put E in boiling water until skin is easy to peel; peel and dice.

COOKING:

1. Drop A–D into boiling water. Cook until water again comes to a boil.
2. Drain A–D.

3. Mix all ingredients. Add more D if desired.
4. Serve.

SALMON SALAD
Ban Kwai Yu: General

A. 3¼-oz. can salmon
B. 1 to 2 tablespoons chopped scallion
C. 1 tablespoon pickled ginger

D. ½ teaspoon sesame oil
E. dash sugar

PREPARATION:

I. Drain A.

II. Mix all ingredients well. Use as sandwich spread or serve as salad on lettuce leaves.

TUNA FISH SALAD
Ning Mung Bun Gum Chong Yu: Canton

A. 4-oz. can tuna fish
B. 1 lemon
C. ½ teaspoon minced ginger

D. 1 tablespoon minced scallion
E. 1 cup bean sprouts
F. ½ teaspoon sugar

PREPARATION:

I. Cut B in half, peel, squeeze juice. Scrape and save yellow outer skin; chop skin very fine. Measure 1 teaspoon. (Scrapings should not include white rind.)

II. Wash E, dip into boiling water 30 seconds, remove, drain.

III. Mix A with B juice and minced B skin. Add C, D, E, F. Mix. Add salt to taste. Serve cold.

TUNA FISH SALAD
Kun Tsoi Bun Gum Chong Yu: Canton

Eliminate C; substitute ¼ cup minced celery for E. Serve on bread or toast.

TUNA FISH SALAD
Sun Tsoi Si Bun Gum Chong Yu: Canton

Substitute 1 cup shredded lettuce for E. In Step II, cut lettuce into shreds ¼ inch wide.

TUNA FISH SALAD
Fan Keh Bun Gum Chong Yu: Canton

Substitute 4 tomatoes for E. In Step II, drop tomatoes in boiling water 1 to 2 minutes. Remove, peel, and quarter, without separating quarters completely. Mix A, B, C, D, F. Stuff tomatoes with this mixture.

KING CRAB SALAD
Liang Ban Da Pong Sha: Adapted

A. few leaves of lettuce
B. 1 large tomato
C. 1 cucumber
D. ½ lb. frozen king crab meat
E. 1 teaspoon chopped ginger
F. 1 to 2 teaspoons powdered mustard mixed with 1 tablespoon boiling water

G. ¾ teaspoon salt
H. 2 teaspoons light soy sauce
I. 1 tablespoon sugar
J. 1 teaspoon sesame oil
K. 1 tablespoon vinegar

PREPARATION AND COOKING:

I. Defrost D and squeeze out liquid, steam over boiling water 5 minutes.

II. Dip B into boiling water a few seconds, remove skin, slice into 8 to 10 pieces.

III. Peel C, split into halves, discard seeds, cut diagonally into thin slices, mix with ½ teaspoon G. Let stand 20 to 30 minutes, drain.

IV. Arrange A on platter, place B slices around A.

V. Spread C over A.

VI. Place D on top of C and sprinkle E over D.

VII. Mix F, G, H, I, J, K, mix well and pour over D; serve.

JELLYFISH AND CUCUMBER SALAD
Wong Gwa Hoi Git Pey: Canton

A. ¼ lb. packaged shredded jellyfish

B. 1 cucumber

C. 3 tablespoons vinegar

D. 3 tablespoons sugar

E. 1 teaspoon salt

F. 1 teaspoon sesame oil

PREPARATION:

I. Cut A into 2- to 3-inch pieces, wash, soak in water ½ hour and drain. (If A comes unshredded, wash away salt, and shred very thin, about 2 to 3 inches long. Soak in water ½ hour before using.)

II. Peel skin of B, discard center part, shred into 2- to 3-inch pieces.

III. Mix C, D, E, F until D and E are dissolved.

IV. Mix A, B with C–F thoroughly, serve cold.

JADE ON SNOW SALAD
Tsung Fa Dow Fu: Adapted

A. 2 tablespoons olive or salad oil

B. 4 cakes bean curd

C. 2 scallions, chopped

D. 1 teaspoon salt

PREPARATION:

I. Wash B, cut into cubes, and place in bowl.

COOKING:

1. Heat A until very hot.

2. Pour A over B.

3. Add C, D, mix well, and chill. Serve cold.

PEANUT AND PRESSED BEAN CURD CAKE SALAD
Hwa Sun Mi Dow Fu Gahn: Shanghai

A. 8 ozs. roasted peanuts (in shell)

B. 2 cakes pressed bean curd, diced

C. 2 stalks celery, diced

D. 1 tablespoon light soy sauce

E. ½ to 1 teaspoon sesame oil

PREPARATION:

I. Shell and skin A.

II. Combine all ingredients, mix well, serve.

PRESSED BEAN CURD SALAD
Ching Tsai Ban Gahn Si: Shanghai

A. 6 cakes pressed bean curd
B. 1 celery heart
C. 2 tablespoons vinegar
D. 2 tablespoons sugar

E. 1 tablespoon light soy sauce
F. 1 teaspoon sesame oil
G. ½ teaspoon salt

PREPARATION:

I. Wash A, dry; cut into long, thin strips.
II. Wash B, cut diagonally into long, thin strips.
III. Mix A, B.

IV. Mix C, D, E, F, G.
V. Pour C–G over A–B. Combine well; serve.

PRESSED BEAN CURD SPINACH SALAD
Dow Fu Gahn Ban Bo Tsai: General

A. 10-oz. pkg. fresh spinach
B. 3 cakes pressed bean curd
C. 1 tablespoon light soy sauce

D. 1½ teaspoons sesame oil
E. 1 teaspoon sugar
F. salt to taste

PREPARATION:

I. Discard tough stems of A, wash leaves in clear water and drain.
II. Pour boiling water over B and let stand 30 seconds; remove from water and cut into halves, shred.
III. Mix C, D, E thoroughly.

COOKING:

1. Add A to 1½ qts. boiling water; stir when water starts to boil again. Turn off heat and drain; cool; squeeze out excess water.
2. Toss A, B in bowl.
3. Add C–E; mix well.
4. Add F to taste.

DESSERT

The Chinese generally do not serve dessert at the end of a meal but rather in the middle or sometimes as late as the second to the last dish. It is usually followed by a major dish, such as steamed duck or pork. The Chinese find that a sweet dish between courses serves as a change of pace from the salty and highly seasoned main dishes. However, this custom varies from region to region. In Szechuan, for example, dessert is sometimes served after a meal.

Few Chinese restaurants in America offer much in the way of authentic Chinese desserts. For this reason many Americans are unfamiliar with sweet Chinese dishes, and comparatively few such recipes are found in American-Chinese cookbooks.

During the Chinese New Year festival, it is customary to offer a guest tea with mixed, sweet preserved fruits, or with such other delicacies as kumquats, melon, lotus seeds, lotus roots, and dates—to wish him a year filled with sweetness.

ALMOND BEAN CURD WITH PINEAPPLE, CHERRIES, AND LITCHIS
Han Yen Dow Fu Bo Lo: Adapted

A. 1 envelope unflavored gelatin
B. 3 tablespoons cold water
C. ½ cup evaporated milk
D. 1¼ cups water
E. 3 tablespoons sugar
F. 2 teaspoons almond extract
G. 1 cup litchis with juice
H. ⅓ cup maraschino cherries
I. ½ cup pineapple chunks

PREPARATION AND COOKING:

I. Mix A, B well in a saucepan.
II. Place over low heat, stir until A is dissolved.
III. Add C, D, E, stir until E is completely dissolved.
IV. Add F, mix well.
V. Pour into 9- by 5- by 2½-inch dish and refrigerate.
VI. When set, cut into cubes, mix with G, H, I.

ALMOND BEAN CURD WITH MANDARIN ORANGES
Sing Jen Dow Fu: Shanghai

A. 1 envelope unflavored gelatin
B. 3 tablespoons cold water
C. ½ cup evaporated milk
D. 1¼ cups water
E. 3 tablespoons sugar
F. 2 teaspoons almond extract
G. ½ cup mandarin oranges

PREPARATION AND COOKING:

I. Mix A, B thoroughly in saucepan, place over low heat, stir until dissolved.
II. Add C, D, E, stir until E is completely dissolved.
III. Add F, mix well.
IV. Pour into 9- by 5- by 2½-inch dish and refrigerate.
V. When set, cut into cubes, mix with G. For more liquid, heat 1 cup water, add 3 tablespoons sugar, stir until dissolved. Cool and add at end.

ALMOND BEAN CURD WITH LOQUATS
Pi Pa Sing Jen Dow Fu: General

Substitute canned loquats for G, and cube.

ALMOND GEL WITH PEACHES   *Approved Ulcer Recipe*
Sing Jen Dow Fu: General

A. 1 envelope unflavored gelatin
B. 3 tablespoons sugar
C. ¾ cup water
D. 1 cup milk

E. 1 teaspoon almond extract
F. dash salt
G. 1-lb. can peaches

PREPARATION AND COOKING:

I. Mix A, B thoroughly in saucepan. Stir in C.
II. Cook over low heat, stirring until well mixed.
III. Remove from heat. Add D, E, F, mix well.
IV. Pour into bowl; refrigerate until set.

V. Cut into small cubes.
VI. Cut G into small pieces and mix with cubes. Serve cold.

FRIED ALMOND CUSTARD
Hong Yen Dan Ta: Canton

A. 1½ teaspoons almond extract
B. 3 egg yolks
C. 1 cup cold water
D. ½ cup flour
E. 1 tablespoon cornstarch

F. 1 tablespoon sugar
G. 3 tablespoons cornstarch
H. peanut oil for deep frying
I. 3 tablespoons sugar

PREPARATION:

I. Mix A, B, C, D, E, F well.

COOKING:

1. Cook A–F thoroughly in a saucepan; stir continuously until thick.
2. Pour into shallow dish or pan and allow to cool and set.
3. Cut into strips ½ inch wide and 1 inch long.

4. Coat each strip lightly with G.
5. Deep fry A–G strips in 390° oil to a golden brown. Drain well.
6. Sprinkle fried strips with I. Serve.

WHIPPED CREAM BEAN PASTE DELIGHT
Hey Bai Dow Sha: Adapted

A. sweet bean filling

B. whipped cream

C. 4 to 8 maraschino cherries

PREPARATION:

I. In each dessert dish place 2 to 3 tablespoons A.

II. Top each dish with B, to taste.
III. Add C to each dish, to taste.

SILVER EARS WITH TANGERINES
Jing Jiu Ning Erh: Szechuan

A. 15-oz. can white jelly fungus (silver ears) from Chinese grocery

B. 2 large fresh tangerines or oranges

PREPARATION:

I. Skin B, remove inside membrane and seeds; cut each segment into 2 to 3 pieces.

II. Open A and transfer to greaseless saucepan.

COOKING:

1. Bring A to boil.

2. Add B, bring to boil and serve.

DRAGON EYE AND LITCHI DESSERT
Mi Tong Lung Yien: Shanghai

A. ¼ cup rock sugar

B. 12 to 15 fresh (or canned) litchis

C. 24 fresh (or canned) longans

D. 1 cup rice

PREPARATION:

I. Wash and drain D. Cover with 1 qt. water, bring to boil, lower heat and cook 10 minutes. Pour about 2 cups rice water out and set aside. (Save rice for congee or serve with other dishes as is.)

II. Peel skins of fresh B, discard seeds, cut each in half. If canned litchis are used, simply cut each in half.

COOKING:

1. Bring rice water to boil, add A, stir until sugar dissolves.

2. Place A in bowl, add B, C, and serve.

APPLE FRITTERS
Ba Se Pin Goh: Peking

A. 2 cups peanut oil

B. 1 lb. apples (about 3)

C. ½ cup sugar

D. 2 tablespoons water

E. 1 tablespoon peanut oil

F. 3 tablespoons flour

G. 2 egg whites

H. 1 tablespoon cornstarch

I. 3 tablespoons flour

PREPARATION:

I. Peel B, discard seeds and cores, cut each into 8 pieces.

II. Place F in a paper bag, put in B and shake until B pieces are coated.

III. Mix G, H, I into a smooth batter.

IV. Coat each B with G–I.

COOKING:

1. Heat A to 375°, deep fry B until golden brown (about 2 to 3 minutes); remove to paper towel and drain.

2. Mix C, D, E in a saucepan, cook over medium heat until it forms long threads when dropped from spoon.

3. Add B, mix well.

4. Dip each piece in ice-cold water prior to eating.

STEAMED FRUIT NUT MIX
Ba Bao Yang Ping Go: Peking

A. 5 cooking apples
B. ¼ teaspoon salt
C. ¼ cup sugar
D. ¼ cup canned sliced peaches

E. 3 tablespoons raisins
F. 2 tablespoons shelled walnuts
G. 2 tablespoons sugared winter melon
H. 2 tablespoons blanched, shelled almonds

PREPARATION:

I. Core and peel A, place in large shallow bowl.
II. Sprinkle B on A. Then sprinkle on half of C.
III. Mix D, remaining C and E, F, G, H.

IV. Pour all over A.
V. Cover bowl with aluminum foil.

COOKING:

1. Steam dish in steamer 30 minutes.

STEAMED FRUIT NUT MIX
Ba Bao Yang Ping Go: Peking

Substitute 4 tablespoons dried seedless longans for E.

FRIED FRUIT PUFFS
Ruan Dza Go Jiu: Peking

A. 1 cup pitted dates
B. ½ cup raisins
C. ¼ cup dried apricots
D. ¼ cup peanut butter
E. ¼ teaspoon salt
F. 1 teaspoon sugar

G. 2 teaspoons sesame seeds
H. 2 egg whites
I. ½ cup cornstarch
J. red food coloring (few drops)
K. vegetable oil for deep frying

PREPARATION:

I. Chop or grind A, B, C.
II. Mix with D, E, F, G.

III. Mix H, I, J.
IV. Roll A–G into 30 to 40 balls; roll balls in H–J until coated.

COOKING:

1. Heat K to 375° and deep fry A–J.

HONEY WALNUTS
Mi Tze Hu Tao: Suchow

A. ½ lb. shelled walnut halves
B. ½ teaspoon salt
C. 2 tablespoons vegetable oil
D. 2 tablespoons honey

E. 2 teaspoons sugar
F. 1 teaspoon cornstarch mixed with 1 teaspoon water

PREPARATION AND COOKING:

1. Soak A in water with B until membrane peels easily; drain and air dry.
2. Heat C in frying pan; brown A in pan 2 minutes; drain oil from pan.
3. Mix D, E with A over medium heat. When well mixed, add F to thicken; serve hot or cold.

PEACH FRUIT PUDDING
Sun To Tseng Go: Canton

A. 1-lb. can sliced peaches

B. 2 tablespoons brown sugar
plus some to dust pan

C. 1¼ cups flour

D. 2 teaspoons baking powder

E. ¾ cup sugar

F. ¼ cup margarine

G. 2 eggs

H. ⅓ cup milk

I. 1 teaspoon vanilla

PREPARATION:

I. Drain A and discard juice.

II. Grease a round cake pan, dust with B, and arrange A over bottom of pan.

III. Sift together C, D, E.

IV. Melt F.

V. Beat G.

VI. Beat together F, G. Add H or enough of H to make 1 cup. Mix well, add B, and mix again.

VII. Combine C–E with F–H, mix until smooth.

VIII. Add I, mix well.

IX. Pour over A.

COOKING:

1. Steam 1 hour in steamer over boiling water.

2. Let cool, then turn pudding over onto a plate. Serve hot or cold.

PINEAPPLE CHERRY PUDDING
Bo Lo Ying To Tseng Go: Canton

Substitute 1-lb. can sliced pineapple for A and place a cherry in the center of each pineapple slice.

APRICOT PUDDING
Hung Tseng Go: Canton

Substitute 1-lb. can apricots for A.

BANANA PANCAKES
Heong Jiao Bang: Canton

A. butter for frying

B. ¼ cup plus 1 tablespoon flour

C. ¼ cup milk

D. dash salt

E. 2 ripe bananas, mashed

F. 1 egg

G. 2 tablespoons sugar

PREPARATION:

I. Mix B, C, D.

II. Add E, F, G to B–D, beat thoroughly.

COOKING:

1. Place 1 teaspoon A in hot frying pan. Add ¼ cup B–G batter for 8 to 10 small pancakes, pan-fry until both sides are golden brown (1 to 2 minutes each side).

2. Repeat process, using ¼ cup batter and adding 1 teaspoon A when necessary.

3. Serve pancakes hot or cold.

PRUNE PANCAKES
Tjo Bang: Canton

A. 10 prunes   C. 1 tablespoon butter   E. 1 cup flour   G. oil for frying

B. ¼ cup sugar   D. 1 egg   F. ¾ cup water

PREPARATION:

I. Pit A, steam over boiling water until soft (about 30 minutes).

II. Mash A, mix thoroughly with B, C into a very smooth paste. Set aside.

III. Beat D; add E, F alternately, beating until batter is smooth.

COOKING:

1. Put ⅙ of D–F into well-greased 8-inch frying pan. On low heat, turn pan so that batter spreads into a thin pancake.

2. Place ⅙ of A–C paste in center of D–F pancake. Using a fork, spread paste into a rectangle 2½ by 5 inches. Fold pancake edges over paste while batter is still moist.

3. Adding a little G, fry pancake until both sides are golden brown. Remove from pan, set aside, and keep warm until ready to serve.

4. Repeat procedure for remaining 5 pancakes and fillings.

BEAN PASTE PANCAKES
Dow Sha Bang: Canton

Substitute sweet bean filling for A.

CASHEW NUT COOKIES
Yauw Gu Bing Gahn: General

A. ¼ cup lard   F. ½ teaspoon salt

B. ½ cup sugar   G. 2 teaspoons milk

C. 2 eggs   H. 1 teaspoon vanilla extract

D. 1 cup flour   I. ¼ cup chopped cashew nuts

E. 2 teaspoons baking powder

PREPARATION:

I. Cream A, B together thoroughly.

II. Add C, 1 at a time, beating well until light and fluffy.

III. Sift together D, E, F, add to A–C, mix well.

IV. Add G, H, and beat thoroughly.

V. Drop from a teaspoon onto greased cooky sheet. Top each cooky with I, press each down lightly.

COOKING:

1. Bake in 350° oven 15 to 17 minutes. Makes 3 dozen cookies.

PEANUT COOKIES
Hwa Sun Bing: General

Substitute ¼ cup chopped peanuts for I, and 1 teaspoon lemon extract for H.

WALNUT COOKIES
Ha Tao So: Canton

A. ¼ cup lard   C. 2 tablespoons peanut oil

B. 1 cup sugar   D. 1 egg

E. 1 cup rice flour

F. 1 teaspoon baking powder

G. ½ teaspoon salt

PREPARATION:

I. Cream A, B together thoroughly. Add C, D, beat until light and fluffy.

II. Sift together E, F, G, add to A–D, mix well.

H. ⅔ cup finely chopped walnuts

I. 1 teaspoon vanilla or lemon extract

III. Add H, I (saving enough H to top cookies); mix thoroughly.

IV. Roll dough into balls 1 inch in diameter. Top each with a bit of H.

COOKING:

1. Place balls 2 inches apart on greased cooky sheet.

2. Bake 15 minutes in 350° oven. Makes 2 dozen cookies.

ALMOND COOKIES
Shing Ren Bing: General

A. ¼ cup lard

B. 1 cup sugar

C. 2 tablespoons vegetable oil

D. ¼ teaspoon sesame oil

E. 1 egg

PREPARATION:

I. Cream A, B together thoroughly. Add C, D, E, beat until fluffy.

II. Sift together F, G, H, add to A–E, mix well.

F. 1 cup rice flour

G. 1 teaspoon baking powder

H. ½ teaspoon salt

I. ⅓ cup finely chopped almonds

J. 1 teaspoon almond extract

III. Add I, J (reserving half of I for topping); mix well.

IV. Form dough into balls 1 inch in diameter. Top each with a bit of I.

COOKING:

1. Place balls 2 inches apart on greased cooky sheet.

2. Bake 20 minutes in 350° oven. Makes 2 dozen cookies.

STEAMED SPONGE CAKE
Gai Don Goh: Canton

A. 4 eggs

B. 1 cup sugar

C. ½ teaspoon lemon extract

D. ½ teaspoon vanilla extract

E. 1 cup flour

F. ½ teaspoon baking powder

G. ¼ teaspoon salt

PREPARATION:

I. Separate A.

II. In large bowl with electric mixer, beat A whites until fluffy. Add B, 2 tablespoons at a time, then beat until A whites are very stiff.

III. Beat A yolks with a fork, add C, D, mix well.

IV. Combine A, B, C, D, beat until blended.

V. Sift E–G.

VI. Add E–G to A–D gradually. Mix thoroughly.

COOKING:

1. Line two 8-inch round pans with waxed paper.

2. Pour in batter, steam over boiling water 30 minutes.

3. Serve hot or cold, sliced.

STEAMED CHINESE CAKE
Tsen Don Gow: General

A. 7 eggs
B. 1½ cups sugar
C. ¾ cup peanut oil

D. 3 cups self-rising flour
E. 1 cup milk
F. 1 teaspoon vanilla extract

PREPARATION:

I. Separate A whites from yolks.
II. Beat yolks and add B gradually.
III. Add C and mix well.
IV. Mix in D alternately with E; beat well.
V. Add F.
VI. Beat A whites until very stiff peaks are formed.

VII. Slowly pour B yolk mixture over whites, folding in mixture gently with rubber spatula until yolk mixture is just blended.
VIII. Line bottom of steam basket with cheesecloth, pour cake mixture in.

COOKING:

1. Steam over boiling water 45 minutes. Cake may be served hot or cold, and may be frozen.

FOUR COLOR RICE PUDDING
Sih Seh Ba Bao Fan: Adapted

A. 1 cup glutinous rice
B. 1½ cups cold water
C. 1 tablespoon dried seedless longans
D. 2 dried pears
E. butter or margarine
F. ½ cup sweet bean filling

G. 20 maraschino cherries
H. ¼ cup sugar
I. ½ cup water
J. 2 teaspoons cornstarch
K. ¼ cup milk
L. ¼ teaspoon almond extract

PREPARATION:

I. Wash A well and drain, add B, bring to a boil over high heat and cook 2 to 3 minutes. Lower heat and simmer 15 minutes; cool.
II. Dice D.
III. Grease shallow bowl well with E.
IV. Arrange C in a small circle at bottom of bowl.

V. Cover C with ⅙ of cooked A.
VI. Place D in bowl with A. Spread ¼ of A evenly over D.
VII. Place F on top of mixture and cover with ½ of A.
VIII. Arrange G on top, spread remaining A evenly on top.

COOKING:

1. Place bowl in steamer over boiling water and steam 45 minutes.
2. Remove bowl from steamer; run knife around edges of bowl to loosen pudding; invert bowl over serving dish.
3. Place H, I in saucepan, stir over medium heat until H has dissolved.
4. Mix J, K and stir until sauce thickens.
5. Add L, stir well and pour over pudding. Also goes well with Peach Fruit Pudding (see Index) but vanilla extract should be substituted for L.

EIGHT PRECIOUS RICE PUDDING I
Ba Bao Fan: General

A. 2 cups glutinous rice
B. 2 tablespoons pure lard
C. 1 cup sugar
D. 2 to 4 tablespoons pure lard
E. 4 maraschino cherries

F. 2 tablespoons mixed Chinese preserved fruit
G. 1 teaspoon raspberry or strawberry jelly (or jam)
H. 1 teaspoon peach preserves

PREPARATION:

I. Wash A well and drain.
II. Cut E in half.
III. Cut F into ½-inch pieces.

COOKING:

1. Place A in pot with 3 cups water.
2. Bring A to boil over high heat and cook 15 minutes.
3. Remove from heat. Add B, C. Mix well. Set aside to cool.
4. Liberally grease inside of deep heatproof bowl with D.
5. Distribute E, F evenly over bottom of bowl.
6. Place G, H in uncovered areas of bowl bottom.
7. Pour cooled A–C into bowl and press down firmly.
8. Place bowl in steaming utensil and steam over boiling water 45 minutes.
9. Remove bowl from steamer. Run knife around edges of bowl. Invert bowl on serving dish. Serve.

EIGHT PRECIOUS RICE PUDDING II
Ba Bao Fan: General

A. 1½ cups glutinous rice
B. 5 tablespoons sugar
C. butter or margarine for greasing
D. ¼ cup mixed candied fruit
E. ¼ cup raisins
F. ¼ cup pitted dates

G. ¼ cup candied lotus seeds or walnuts
H. 1 cup sweet bean filling
I. ¼ cup sugar
J. 1 tablespoon cornstarch
K. 1¼ cups water
L. 1 teaspoon almond extract

PREPARATION:

I. Wash A well and drain. Place A in pot with 2¼ cups water. Bring to boil, letting water boil down a little. Lower heat, cover, and simmer until soft (about 15 minutes).
II. Add B, mix well. Turn off heat.
III. Grease a 7-inch bowl with C. Place half of D in center. Then arrange E, F, G and rest of D in a flower pattern. This is done by starting from bowl's center, and spreading out ingredients in 8 directions toward outer edge of bowl.
IV. Place half of A over D–G. Add H.
V. Cover H with remaining A; spread evenly.

COOKING:

1. Place bowl in steamer; steam 30 minutes.
2. Turn pudding upside down on platter.
3. Mix I, J, K in pot and bring to boil, stirring constantly until thickened. Add L, stir well, and serve with pudding.

CANDIED FRUIT COCONUT RICE PUDDING
Tong Gwo Yeh Tze Noh Mi Fan: General

A. 7-oz. package coconut flakes
B. 2½ cups hot water
C. 1½ cups glutinous rice

D. ½ lb. mixed candied fruit
E. ½ cup sweet bean filling

PREPARATION:

I. Mix A, B well and let stand 1 hour, occasionally squeezing coconut in water. Squeeze out coconut juice* through a colander. Discard A. Make enough for 2¼ cups of juice.

II. Wash C, drain off water, add coconut juice; bring to a boil and cook for 2 to 3 minutes. Steam over boiling water 15 minutes; cool.

III. Grease a 7-inch bowl well with lard or margarine.

IV. Arrange D in bottom of bowl. Then place ½ of C mixture over D. Make an indentation in mixture to hold filling better.

V. Spread E over indentation; spread remaining C over layer of E.

COOKING:

1. Steam in steamer over boiling water 30 to 45 minutes. Run knife around edges of bowl to loosen pudding. Invert bowl over serving dish. Serve hot.

ALMOND FLOAT
Hong Yen Dan Ta: Canton

Note: When preparing several courses for a meal, this should be the first dish prepared to allow for proper setting in refrigerator. Addition of 3 cubes of ice at Step 5 will hasten setting, if necessary. Almond Float may be served after any meal. Other canned fruits or fruit cocktail may be substituted for mandarin oranges, if necessary. This dish may be prepared the day before; leftovers, if refrigerated, can be enjoyed for several days.

A. 1½ cups evaporated milk
B. 2½ cups cold water
C. ¾ cup sugar
D. 2 envelopes unflavored gelatin
E. 2 teaspoons almond extract
F. 1 cup mandarin orange segments

G. 16 maraschino cherries
H. juice of canned mandarin oranges
I. ½ cup sugar
J. 4 cups warm water
K. 2 teaspoons almond extract

PREPARATION:

I. Dissolve D in 6 tablespoons water.

II. Dissolve I in J to form a syrup. Cool. Add H, K. Set aside.

III. Cut F segments in half.

---

* Coconut juice may be substituted by 1 cup sweetened cream of coconut plus ¼ cup water. It can be purchased at a Chinese grocery or health food shop by the pound can (from Puerto Rico).

COOKING:

1. Combine A, B, C and heat to just below boiling.
2. Add D (in water). Stir thoroughly. Cool.
3. Add E. Stir thoroughly.
4. Pour into shallow rectangular serving dish.
5. Refrigerate until mixture sets (preferably overnight).
6. Cut into bite-size cubes.
7. Float almond cubes together with F and G in syrup formed by mixture of H–K.
8. Serve ¼ cup per person in shallow saucer.

STEAMED CAKE WITH FRAGRANT ROSES
Mei Kwei Don Gow: Adapted

A. 3 large eggs
B. ¾ cup sugar
C. 6 tablespoons peanut oil
D. 1½ cups flour

E. 2 teaspoons baking powder
F. ½ teaspoon salt
G. ½ cup milk
H. 2 fragrant red roses from garden or florist

PREPARATION:

I. Separate A into yolks and whites in two bowls.
II. Beat yolks well, add B gradually.
III. Add C.
IV. Sift D, E, F together.

V. Add D–F and G to A–C alternately, beating until batter is smooth.
VI. Chop H petals very fine (discard rest), add about 2 tablespoons to A–G.
VII. Beat egg whites until they form peaks; fold into A–H with rubber spatula.

COOKING:

1. Line a steam basket with cheesecloth, pour in A–H batter and steam over boiling water 45 minutes. Serve hot or cold.

FRIENDSHIP SWEET CAKE
Yow Yee Bang: Adapted

A. 1 tablespoon peanut oil
B. 1 lotus root segment (about ½ lb.)
C. 1 cup flour

D. ½ cup water
E. ¼ teaspoon salt
F. ¼ cup sugar

PREPARATION:

I. Wash B, scraping off outer layer. Slice into thin diagonal pieces, then shred.
II. Sift C.

III. Mix C, D, E, F into a smooth paste.
IV. Add shredded B, mix well.

COOKING:

1. Heat A in frying pan. Add 1 to 2 tablespoons B–F, fry over medium heat until both sides are golden brown.
2. Continue frying 1 to 2 tablespoons of mixture at a time until batter is used up.

PAGODA CAKE
Bo Top Go: Canton

A. ¼ lb. lard
B. ¾ cup sugar
C. 2 eggs
D. ¼ cup milk

E. 1 cup flour
F. 1 teaspoon lemon juice
G. 2 teaspoons port wine

PREPARATION:

I. Cream A, B together thoroughly. Add C, 1 at a time, beat until fluffy.
II. Add D, E alternately.

III. Add F, G, beat until batter is smooth.
IV. Pour into greased round pan.

COOKING:

1. Steam 30 minutes over boiling water.

2. Slice, and serve hot or cold.

HAPPY SMILE NEW YEAR CAKE
Hoi How Sieu: Canton

A. 1 cup flour
B. ¼ cup sugar
C. 1 teaspoon baking powder
D. ½ teaspoon baking soda

E. ⅛ teaspoon ammonium bicarbonate*
F. ¼ cup water
G. sesame seeds

PREPARATION:

I. Sift together A, B, C, D, E.
II. Add F, mix well.

III. Make batter into balls 1 inch in diameter; roll each in G. Let stand 15 minutes.

COOKING:

1. Fry in deep fat at 230° until golden brown, about 10 to 15 minutes.

MANDARIN ORANGE TEA
Mi Ju Tsa: General

A. 1 cup water
B. 1 small can mandarin oranges including syrup
C. ¼ cup sugar

D. 1 cup water
E. 3 tablespoons water
F. 1 tablespoon cornstarch

PREPARATION:

I. Mix E, F. Set aside. Stir well before using.

COOKING:

1. Boil A.
2. Add B, C. Bring to boil again.
3. Add D. Bring to boil again.

4. Mix E, F and add very slowly, stirring continuously, and again bring to boil.
5. Serve hot in soup bowl or teacup.

* Obtainable at any bakery shop.

INSTANT DISHES

The purpose of this section is to provide foodstuffs without delay or fuss that are suitable for afternoon or late evening snacks, luncheon tidbits, or side dishes, to increase the variety of dishes served at dinner or to provide additional dishes when unexpected company drops in. Although in some instances time must be allowed for soaking certain ingredients, the actual time spent cooking and handling the food before serving may range from only one to five minutes. All ingredients are available in Chinese groceries, often in the "delicatessen" or precooked food section. A number may be obtained in American supermarkets, as noted in the comments.

COLD APPETIZERS	Form Available
Abalone (also Vegetarian Abalone)	In cans; should be served with a sauce prepared with equal parts of light soy sauce and smoked peanut oil (about 3 tablespoons of each). Also available in some American supermarkets.
Bamboo Shoots, Braised	In jars; serve hot or cold. Also comes in can with Chinese cabbage.
Tips	Available in cans, ready to serve.
Bean Curd, Cake	Sold loose by the piece; serve cold, diced and mixed with meat, mushrooms, vegetables, etc. These may also be cut into 9 pieces and served with a variety of sauces (oyster sauce, heavy soy sauce, light soy sauce, a combination of soy and vinegar sauce) or with chopped scallions.
Pressed	By the piece; cut into 9 pieces, serve with same sauces as fresh bean curd.
Cabbage, Preserved	In jars; serve and eat as is.

COLD APPETIZERS	Form Available
Chicken, Roast	One variety of cooked meats available in Chinese grocery. Purchase and serve in the quantity and size desired. Available in American groceries. Also available as vegetarian chicken in cans.
Chop Suey, Vegetarian	In cans, ready to serve.
Cucumber, Preserved Sweet	A relish, available in cans; serve as a pickle.
Salted	Packed in cans; eat as is.
Sweet, in Soy Sauce	In cans; serve mixed with soy sauce or sesame oil.
Duck, Roast	A cooked meat available in Chinese grocery in chunks, by the pound. Serve with duck, soy, or oyster sauce. Available in American groceries.
Fish, Smoked	Many varieties are available, packed in cans; eat as is. Also available are canned white fish balls in brine and fish balls with bean cake. Available in some American supermarkets.

COLD APPETIZERS	Form Available
Ginger, Preserved Mixed	In jars; serve cold as a relish.
Red	In jars; slice thin and serve as a relish. Available in American markets.
Ham, Vegetarian	In cans, ready to serve.
Mustard Greens, Pickled in the Barrel	From the barrel by the pound; slice on the diagonal into 1-inch segments and serve as a side dish.
Noodles, Cellophane	By the package; soak in warm water, then cook with soup or sauce 5 minutes. Add to any soup or gravy dish.
Pakut (Fish or Shrimp)	Sold by the package. These have their own instant flavoring packet of seasonings which should be added with the noodles to the specified amount of boiling water and cooked until the noodles are tender.
Onions, Pickled	In jars, serve as is. Available in American markets.
Pork, Roast	Another cooked meat available in Chinese grocery, in chunks or sliced thin, by the pound. Serve with duck, soy, or oyster sauce.
Radish, Pickled White	In jars; serve as is.
Rice, Sweet Flavored	In cans, ready to serve.
Scallions, Pickled	In jars; serve as is.
Shrimp Chips, Fried	In bags; eat as is.
Unfried	In packages; fry in hot deep fat until they "explode" or float to the surface. Remove at once, allow to cool, and serve.
Steak, Vegetarian, Deluxe	In cans, ready to serve.

COLD APPETIZERS	Form Available
Vegetables Braised Mixed	In cans, ready to serve.
Pickled Chinese	In cans, serve cold as a relish.
Won Tons, Fresh	Won ton skins are sold by the pound package. Pull tips together and pinch so that they retain the shape of a nurse's cap. Boil until tender or fry until golden brown.

FLAVORINGS	Form Available
Bean, Black, Salted	In plastic bags, cans or bottles. Saturate in peanut oil and serve.
Bean Cake, Fermented	Cubed, in bottles. Has the same uses as Bean Curd Cheese, Red (below), but is more delicately flavored and, perhaps, more appealing to American tastes.
Bean Curd Cheese, Red	Cubed, in bottles. Mash into a paste and add very sparingly as a seasoning for meat or vegetable dishes.
Curry	Obtain and use as in Indian or American curry dishes.
Fish Gravy	In bottles; add to foods to taste.
Ginger, Minced	Loose bulbs by the pound. Slice from the main root and then mince for serving as a seasoning. Available in American markets.
Mustard, Hot	Packaged. Sold in most markets. Mix with water to desired thickness and amount.
Oil, Peanut (Smoking Hot)	Bottled and canned. Heat 3 tablespoons (or more, if desired) to smoking and pour over rice, noodles, or other fresh or warmed-up dish. Available in American markets.

FLAVORINGS	*Form Available*
Sesame	In bottles. Several drops impart a characteristic Peking flavor to any dish. Available in American markets.
Scallions	Fresh by the bunch in any market. They are excellent topping for most Chinese dishes.

DESSERTS	*Form Available*
Boston Fruit Jelly, Sweet: Assorted, Litchis, Orange, or Banana	By the box; eat as is.
Cookies: Almond, Fortune, Rice	By the pound, in packages, or in boxes; also available in American markets.
Ginger, Candied, Crystallized	Either in packages or loose by the pound; hot and spicy, whitish; eat as is.
Kumquats, Crystallized	Loose by the pound; eat as is.
Preserved in Ginger Syrup	In jars; also available in American supermarkets or gourmet shops. Chill and serve as snack or dessert.
Litchis, Canned	With a sweetened syrup. Chill and serve as a dessert or snack. The juice, served with ice, is a refreshing beverage. Also an excellent flavoring in dessert dishes.

DESSERTS	*Form Available*
Dried	Either in bags or boxes; occasionally in American markets. Shell; meat is eaten from around the pits.
Fresh	Loose by the pound. Refrigerate and shell before serving.
Longans, Canned	With a sweetened syrup. Chill and serve as a dessert or snack; juice may be served as a beverage.
Dried, Preserved	In packages; eat as is.
Loquats	Canned with a sweetened syrup. Serve same as litchis for dessert or snack; juice may be used same way.
Mixed Preserved Fruit	In jars. Serve chilled or over crushed ice.
Preserved Dried Slices: Apricot, Plum	In packages; eat as is.
Peels, Crystallized: Orange, Grapefruit, or Lemon	By the pound; also available in American confectionary stores; eat as is.
Sesame Seed Candy	In pound packages; eat as is.
Watermelon Seeds	In cellophane bags. Crack gently with the back teeth, remove meat from shell, and eat.

MENUS

The menus suggested below have been designed for family dining, for from two to six persons, and for banquets, which are, of course, for larger parties (and constitute an entertainment), in this case, for from eight to ten persons. In general, a meal consists of soup, one entree per person, and a dessert, each dish served as a separate course. Rice is served with every meal, as is tea. Some of the recipes, particularly the banquet hors d'oeuvres and soups, may require doubling.

Because duplication has been avoided in these menus, it should be noted that dishes that have become familiar and most pleasing may still be substituted for any others. Indeed, a more familiar dish should be easier to prepare and may be more to the family's liking. Also, familiar dishes might be matched with unfamiliar dishes, increasing the likelihood of pleasing everyone with at least one dish.

FAMILY MEALS

Serves Two
Squid in Hot and Sour Soup
Salad à la Chang
Lemon Chicken
Longans

Seaweed Soup
Sweet and Pungent Spareribs
Ding How Scrambled Eggs
Fresh Litchis (in June and July)

Egg Drop Soup
Curried Chicken
Stir-Fried Green Beans with Garlic
Bean Curd Tossed with Peanut Butter
Walnut Cookies

Beef of Tomato Soup
King Crab Salad
Stir-Fried Chicken with Mushrooms and Peas
Apple Fritters

Spareribs Soybean Sprout Soup
Onion Spareribs
Braised Chicken Wings I
Sweet and Sour Cucumbers I
Almond Cookies

Won Ton Sea Cucumber Soup
Stir-Fried Lamb
Salt-Cured Chicken I
Beef Stir-Fried with Bean Sprouts
Boiled Rice
Canned Litchis

Mustard Green and Bean Curd Soup
Pineapple Chicken Delight II
Stir-Fried Beef with Bean Sprouts
Mushrooms and Bamboo Shoots
Walnut Cookies

Chicken, Mushroom, and Bamboo Shoot Soup
Stir-Fried Veal Steak with Vegetables
Chicken and Mushroom Casserole
Boiled Rice
Chilled Canned Litchis

Pork Chops with Cucumber Soup
Stir-Fried Veal Cutlet with Walnuts
Simple Spicy Chicken
Boiled Rice
Steamed Chinese Cake

Celery Cabbage and Shrimp Ball Soup
Steamed Hot and Spiced Fish
Chicken Livers with Quail Eggs
Boiled Rice
Silver Ears with Tangerines

Bitter Melon and Pork Soup
Pork with Almond Beer Sauce
Chicken in Plum Sauce II
Boiled Rice
Steamed Cake with Fragrant Roses

Serves Three to Four
Chicken Giblets with Cucumber Soup
Stir-Fried Steak with Green Peppers and Tomatoes
Chicken Breasts with Cashew Nuts
Pork Rolls on Spinach
Sweet and Sour Shrimp
Banana Pancake

Ginger Beef Tea
Red and White Chicken with Almonds
Crab Meat Lion's Head
Lobster Egg Fu Yong (see Crabmeat Egg Fu Yong)
Roast Pork
Almond Bean Curd with Loquats

Stuffed Chicken Wing Soup
Lobster Cantonese
Curried Beef
Sweet and Sour Pork Cubes
Chicken Velvet and Peas
Whipped Cream Bean Paste Delight

Sub Gum Won Ton Soup
Litchi Snow Ball Chicken
Beef with Fresh Mushrooms
Crabmeat Egg Fu Yong
Baked Spareribs with Hoisin Sauce
Almond Cookies with Ice Cream

Bean Curd Hot and Sour Soup
Sliced Pork with Vegetables
Bean Sprout Salad I
Chicken Breasts with Cashew Nuts II
West Lake Boiled Sweet and Sour Fish
Happy Smile New Year Cake

Hot and Sour Soup I
Freckled Ma Po Bean Curd
Paper-Wrapped Beef I
Shrimp Roll
Bong Bong Chicken
Canned Litchis

Barbecued Chicken
Agar Agar Salad
Fried Rice
Vegetarian Chop Suey
Steamed Cake with Fragrant Roses

Chicken with Cucumber Soup
Stir-Fried Veal Cutlet with Tomato and Peppers
Broiled Bacon with Shrimp
Stir-Fried Pork with Cauliflower (see Stir-Fried Pork with Bean Curd)
Shrimp Lo Mein
Almond Cookies

Curried Beef Soup
Savory Steamed Lobster with Pork and Salted Egg
Crispy Duck
Stir-Fried String Beans with Fermented Bean Cake
Boiled Rice
Almond Bean Curd with Mandarin Oranges

Crab Meat Corn Soup
Tomato Sauce Steak
Broccoli with Mushrooms
Cubed Sub Gum Chicken
Boiled Rice
Fried Fruit Puffs

Egg Drop Soup
Steamed Pork Balls
Plain Egg Fu Yong
Cantonese Sweet and Sour Pork Cubes
Boiled Rice
Prune Pancakes

Hairy Melon Soup
Pineapple Chicken Delight
Peas with Ground Beef
Golden Shrimp Patties
Steamed Mushrooms
Boiled Rice
Almond Cookies

Vegetarian Triple Soup
Fried Rice III
Broccoli with Mushrooms
Marinated Broccoli Stems
Broiled Steak, Mandarin Style
Fried Almond Custard

Family Style Hot and Sour Soup
Stir-Fried Rice Sticks I
Phoenix Tail Shrimp
Fukien Snow White Minced Meat
Agar Agar Salad
Litchis

Preserved Kohlrabi Soup with Pork
Beef with Tomatoes and Onion
Chicken Breast with Cashew Nuts I
Stir-Fried Shrimp with Bean Curd I
Boiled Rice
Almond Gel with Peaches

Ham and Melon Patty Soup
Chicken Livers with Oyster Sauce
Pepper Steak
Pork Lo Mein
Bean Sprout Salad
Almond Bean Curd with Mandarin Oranges

Hot and Sour Soup III
Steamed Chicken with Ham and Bamboo Shoots
Szechuan Yu Siang Shredded Pork
Fish Maw in Crab Sauce
Stir-Fried Bean Green
Pineapple Cherry Pudding

(Shanghai Night)
Triple Soup II
Stir-Fried Shrimp (Shanghai)
Red-Cooked Fresh Ham I
Litchi Snowball Chicken
Cooked Rice
Tea, Dragon Eye, or Litchi Dessert

(Peking Night)
Hot and Sour Soup IV
Peking Crispy Duck
The Dowager's Favorite
Stir-Fried Shrimp with Vegetables
Boiled Rice
Steamed Fruit Nut Mix

(Canton Night)
Winter Melon Soup
Braised Sliced Abalone
Litchi Snowball Pork
Fried Triple Bean Curd
Boiled Rice
Almond Bean Curd with Loquats

(Szechuan Night)
Preserved Kohlrabi Soup with Sliced Chicken
Chicken Ding
Boiled Fish with Szechuan Sauce
Bean Curd with Beef
Boiled Rice
Kumquats in Syrup

(Vegetarian Night)
Vegetarian Triple Soup
Vegetarian Sweet and Sour Meat Balls
Buddha's Delight
Vegetarian Chop Suey with Fu Yu
Boiled Rice
Fruit

Serves Five to Six
Yang Chow Triple Soup
Grilled Steak with Oyster Sauce
Drunken Chicken I
Shrimp with Plum Sauce
Frog Legs with Frozen Peas
Braised Eggplant I
Steamed Chinese Cake

Chicken Soup with Asparagus Shoots and Bean Curd
Beef with Preserved Kohlrabi
Chicken in Sherry
Five Spices Pigeon
Stir-Fried Frogs' Legs
Haddock Fillet with Szechuan Sauce
Dragon Eye and Litchi Dessert

(Peking Night)
Watercress Pork Soup II
Peking Duck
Peking Salad
Chinese Bread
Pork Balls Glutinous Rice
Beef with Preserved Kohlrabi
Cashew Nut Cookies

Preserved Mustard Green Oyster Soup
Steamed Sweet and Sour West Lake Fish
Simple Scallion Egg Fried Rice
Chicken Velvet and Peas
Grilled Steak with Oyster Sauce
Pressed Bean Curd Spinach Salad
Pineapple Cherry Pudding

Velvet Mushroom Soup
Stir-Fried Celery Hearts with Beef
Soy Sauce Chicken Wings and Legs
Braised Soft-Shelled Crab
Stir-Fried Mixed Chinese Vegetables
Hundred-Year-Old Egg Salad
Peach Fruit Pudding

Chicken Giblets with Cucumber Soup
Squab Pekinese
Cellophane Noodles with Steamed Eggs
Stewed Duck with Chestnuts
Clear Steamed Trout
Braised Eggplant I
Pagoda Cake

Chicken Soup with Parts
Oyster Sauce Noodles
Fried Butternut Squash
Chicken Roasted in Salt
Steamed Minced Pork with Water Chestnuts
Fish Balls
Eight Precious Rice Pudding II

Mustard Green and Bean Curd Soup
Shrimp with Water Chestnuts
Roasted Duck with Orange Peel
Bean Curd Potpourri
Calf Brain Stir-Fried with Eggs
Red Bean Curd Cheese Pork
Almond Bean Curd with Loquats

Calf Brain Soup
Fried Fresh Oysters
Sweet Green Pepper Stuffed with Meat
Sweet and Sour Chicken Livers
Pork with Broccoli
Braised Chestnuts with Celery Cabbage
Golden Puff with Sweet Bean Paste

Hairy Melon Soup
Red-Cooked Blackfish
Steamed Spinach Cake
Litchi Duck
Stir-Fried Snow Peas with Pork
Veal with Szechuan Sauce
Cashew Nut Cookies

BANQUETS

Serves Eight to Ten

Hors d'oeuvres
Dem Sem (appetizers)
Paper-Wrapped Chicken I
Stuffed Cucumber
Pork Shu Mai

Soup
Bird's Nest Soup

Entrees
Red-Cooked Snails
Stir-Fried Squab with Oyster Sauce
Chicken Velvet I
Braised Bean Curd
Barbecued Pork
Peking Crispy Duck
Lotus Root Cake
Steamed Chicken with Wine

Dessert
Eight Precious Rice Pudding with Sauce

Hors d'oeuvres
Fried Spicy Chicken Nuggets
Shrimp Dumplings with Water Chestnuts
Crab Meat Shu Mai
Spareribs Steamed with Salted Black Beans

Soup
Special Shark Fin Soup

Entrees
Abalone with Chinese Cabbage Hearts
Braised Chicken Wings II
Stir-Fried Veal Cutlet with Walnuts
Beef Cubes with Green Peppers

Bong Bong Chicken
Crispy Bass
Sweet and Sour Pork
Lion's Head

Dessert
Happy Smile New Year Cake

Hors d'oeuvres
Braised Spareribs I
Fried Shrimp
Beef and Water Chestnut Fun Goh
Paper-Wrapped Beef

Soup
Floating Lotus Soup

Entrees
Stir-Fried Bean Sprouts with Pork
Bean Curd with Beef
Stir-Fried Duck with Spring Ginger
Asparagus with Almonds
Crabmeat Casserole
Pork Roast, Peking Style
Stewed Chicken with Chestnuts
Spiced Leg of Lamb

Dessert
Fried Fruit Puffs

Hors d'oeuvres
Pork Stuffed Steamed Bread with Oyster Sauce
Mushroom Shu Mai
Fried Walnuts
Caul Fat Shrimp Rolls

Soup
Sub Gum Won Ton Soup

Entrees
Curried Lamb
Pork Steamed with Water Chestnuts and Salt Eggs
Fried Chicken Wings with Hoisin Sauce
Mixed Vegetable Salad
Shark Fins with Shredded Chicken
Steamed Mushroom Cornish Hen
Red-Cooked Carp with Bean Curd Skin
Silver Sprout with Shredded Roast Duck

Dessert
Prune Pancakes

NUTRITION GUIDE
FOR CHINESE INGREDIENTS

Source of data: Leung, Woot-Tsuen Wu; Pecot, R. T.; and Watt, B. K.: Agriculture Handbook No. 34, Bureau of Human Nutrition and Home Economics, United States Department of Agriculture, Washington, D.C. A blank on the chart indicates that there is no basis available for a reliable value, although there is some reason to believe that a measurable amount is present.

100 grams of an edible portion	Calories	Proteins	Fats	Carbohydrates	Vitamin A	Thiamine (B_1)	Riboflavin (B_2)	Niacin	Ascorbic acid (C)
CEREALS AND GRAINS									
Flour, arrowroot	355	0.7	0.2	85.2%					
Rice, polished (highly milled)	360	6.8	0.7	78.9	0	.12	.03	1.5	0
glutinous	362	6.7	0.7	79.4	0	.16			0
Starch (corn, etc.)	362	0.5	0.2	87.0	0	0	0	0	0
FRUITS									
Jujube, fresh	105	1.2	0.2	27.6	40	.02	.04	.9	69
Kumquat	65	0.9	0.1	17.1	600	.08	.10		36
Longan, dried	286	4.9	0.4	74.0		.04			28
fresh	61	1.0	0.1	15.8					6
Litchi, dried	277	3.8	1.2	70.7					
fresh	64	0.9	0.3	16.4			0.05		42
Loquat	48	0.4	0.2	12.4	670				trace
Mango	66	0.7	0.2	17.2	6,350	.06	.06	.9	41
Papaya	39	0.6	0.1	10.0	1,750	.03	.04	.3	56
Persimmon	78	0.8	0.4	20.0	2,710	.05	.05	trace	11
Pomegranate	63	0.5	0.3	16.4	0	.02	.01	.3	10
Pummelo	48	0.6	0.2	12.4	20	.04	.02	.3	43
SEEDS AND NUTS									
Almond	597	18.6	54.1	19.6	0	.25	.67	4.6	trace
Chestnut	377	6.7	4.1	78.6		.34	.39	.8	

100 grams of an edible portion	Calories	Proteins	Fats	Carbohydrates	Vitamin A	Thiamine (B₁)	Riboflavin (B₂)	Niacin	Ascorbic acid (C)
Coconut, dried	636	6.0	61.4	24.8					
fresh	359	3.4	34.7	14.0	0	.10	.01	.2	2
Ginkgo seeds	349	12.2	2.7	69.9					
Lotus seeds	351	17.2	2.4	66.6					
Sesame seeds, whole	568	19.3	51.1	18.1		.93	.22	4.5	0

VEGETABLES

100 grams of an edible portion	Calories	Proteins	Fats	Carbohydrates	Vitamin A	Thiamine (B₁)	Riboflavin (B₂)	Niacin	Ascorbic acid (C)
Agar		0	0.2	0					
Arrowroot	126	1.7	0.2	29.6					
Balsam pear	29	1.1	0.3	6.6	180	.08	.03	.4	52
Bamboo shoot	27	2.6	0.3	5.2	20	.15	.07	.6	4
Broccoli, Chinese	29	3.3	0.2	5.5	3,500	.10	.21	1.1	118
Cabbage, celery (Petsai)	14	1.2	0.3	2.4	260	.03	.04	.4	31
Chinese	14	1.5	0.2	2.3	2,800	0.06	.17	.9	45
Chrysanthemum	17	1.8	0.2	3.0	70				20
Coriander	36	2.5	0.4	7.3	5,940	.10	.12	1.0	83
Green pods, young	44	3.4	0.3	9.2	1,670	.16	.10	1.1	34
Garlic	95	4.5	0.2	23.1	trace	.22	.08	.4	15
Ginger root	51	1.5	1.0	10.1	30	.02		.8	4
Kohlrabi	30	2.1	0.1	6.7	trace	.06	.05	.2	61
Laver		0	0.6	0					
Leek	45	2.2	0.3	10.3	40	.11	.06	.5	17
Lotus root	49	1.7	0.1	11.3		.05			22
Matai	78	1.4	0.2	19.0					4
Mung bean sprouts	23	2.9	0.2	4.1	10	.07	.09	.5	15
Mung beans (mature seeds)	339	24.4	1.4	59.7	40	.68	.21	2.0	3
Mushrooms	16	2.4	0.3	4.0	0	.10	.44	4.9	5
Mustard greens	22	2.3	0.3	4.0	6,460	.09	.20	.8	102
Radish	19	0.9	0.1	4.2	10	.03	.02	.4	32
Soybean, immature seeds	119	12.5	6.5	2/12.5	700	.37	.15	1.4	30
Soybean curd	71	7.0	4.1	3.0		.06	.05	.4	0
Soybean Miso (soy paste)	166	10.4	4.9	24.1		.05			
Soybean Natto or fermented beans	147	18.4	7.5	11.9					
Soybean sauce	46	5.7	1.3	9.0	0				0
Soybean sprouts	46	6.2	1.4	5.3	180	.23	.20	.8	13
Taro, corms and tubers	82	1.6	0.2	19.9	20	.13	.04	1.1	4
Watercress	18	1.7	0.3	3.3	4,720	.08	.16	.8	77

100 grams of an edible portion	Calories	Proteins	Fats	Carbohydrates	Vitamin A	Thiamine (B₁)	Riboflavin (B₂)	Niacin	Ascorbic acid (C)
POULTRY									
Bird's nest		54.3	0.3		0				0
Duck, dried, salted	413	20.3	36.2	0		.10	.27	6.1	0
FISH AND SHELLFISH									
Abalone, canned	80	16.0	0.3	2.3		.12	.12	1.2	
dried	309	40.6	1.9	28.8		.41	.37	3.6	
raw	107	21.7	0.5	2.4		.18	.14	1.4	
Oyster, dried	352	41.2	8.8	23.6	1,350	.47	.76	4.2	
Scallop, dried	341	64.6	1.8	12.0	0	.13	.40	5.2	
Shark's fin, dried	384	89.4	0.2	0.1					
Shrimp, dried	295	62.4	2.3		210	.14	.43	6.5	0
Squid, dried	305	62.3	4.3			.06	.42	4.7	
raw	78	16.4	0.9			.02	.12	1.4	
EGGS									
Duck, limed	201	13.9	15.2	0.9					
raw	189	13.1	14.3	0.8	1,230	.18	.29	.1	0
MILK AND MILK PRODUCTS									
Soybean milk	33	3.4	1.5	2.1		.09	.04	.3	0

DIETETIC INGREDIENTS GUIDES AND RECIPES

The following ingredients guides to food restrictions for diabetics, ulcer sufferers, and those restricted to a low-salt food intake are the work of Dr. Hsi-chin Tsai, M.D., Chairman and Professor of the Department of Internal Medicine, National Taiwan University, Taipei, Taiwan. The dietetic recipes that follow have been drawn to conform with the requirements of these guides, including approximate permissible amounts.

DIABETIC DIET GUIDE

	Absolutely Not Allowed	Should Not Be Taken	Allowed But Amount Kept to a Minimum	Allowed at Will
Abalone				X
Agar Agar				X
Dessert (black, sweet)		X		
Algae				X
Anise, Star			X	
Bamboo Shoots, pickled (salty, sour)			X	
simmered in oil		X		
simmered with soy		X		
spring			X	
winter			X	
Bean, Black			X	
salted			X	
Filling		X		
Bean, Mung			X	
Bean Cake, fermented			X	
Bean Curd (in liquid, barrel or can)		X		
dried, refrigerated			X	
fried, refrigerated			X	
Bean Curd, Cheese, red			X	
Milk			X	
Roll			X	
Sheet (sweet)		X		
soft precipitate; custard			X	
Stick			X	
Bean Paste (red sauce)			X	
Bean Sauce (Soy), brown or yellow			X	

	Absolutely Not Allowed	Should Not Be Taken	Allowed But Amount Kept to a Minimum	Allowed at Will
Bean Sprouts, Mung (pea sprouts)			X	
Soy (larger, harder)			X	
Beans, Green, Chinese (long)			X	
Bêche-de-Mer			X	
Bird's Nest			X	
Bombay "Duck" (dried, salted fish)		X		
Broccoli, Chinese			X	
Bun, Pork (large)		X		
roast		X		
Cabbage, Chinese				X
Chinese, dried		X		
Cabbage Hearts (young)				X
Caul Fat			X	
Celery Cabbage				X
Chestnut, Water (well-cooked only)			X	
flour			X	
large			X	
Cloud Ears (Wood Ears)		X		
Congee		X		
Cookies, Almond		X		
Fortune		X		
Crab Apple Strip		X		
Curry Powder				X
Dates, Red		X		
Duck Liver (gizzard)			X	
Sauce (dark brown, in can)		X		
Dumplings, boiled		X		
fried, then steamed		X		
Egg (duck), preserved			X	
salted			X	
Egg Roll Skins			X	
Fennel, sweet		X		
Fish, dry, wet (oil)		X		
salted		X		
Fish Gravy		X		
Maw			X	
Flour, Rice, fine			X	
glutinous			X	
Flower Spice				X
Fruit, candied		X		
preserved		X		
preserved with ginger		X		
Ginger, crystallized		X		
dried slices		X		

	Absolutely Not Allowed	Should Not Be Taken	Allowed But Amount Kept to a Minimum	Allowed at Will
new shoot			X	
pickled			X	
preserved in syrup		X		
red new root			X	
regular, old shoot			X	
Gingko Nuts		X		
Golden Needles (Lily Flowers)			X	
Hoisin Sauce		X		
Jam, Soy, red		X		
sweet flour (Plum Sauce), green		X		
Jellyfish, dried		X		
Kohlrabi, fresh			X	
Leek			X	
Lemon Peel (salty)		X		
Licorice		X		
Lily Flowers (Golden Needles)			X	
Lily Petals, dry			X	
Litchis		X		
Longans		X		
Loquats			X	
Lotus Root			X	
powder			X	
Lotus Seeds			X	
Meat, crumbs, diced			X	
dried, smoked			X	
minced			X	
salted			X	
Melon, Bitter				X
Candied, slices		X		
Hairy			X	
Tea (in honey)		X		
Tea (in ginger and honey)		X		
Winter, Candied		X		
Moon Cake		X		
Mushrooms			X	
Winter			X	
Mustard Greens, Preserved (with peppers or onion and garlic)			X	
Noodles, Rice (fine sticks)			X	
(wide)			X	
Oil, Peanut			X	
Sesame			X	
Okra (Silk Squash), Chinese			X	
Olives, fermented		X		

	Absolutely Not Allowed	Should Not Be Taken	Allowed But Amount Kept to a Minimum	Allowed at Will
salty			X	
sweet		X		
Oyster Sauce			X	
Oysters, dried with soy sauce			X	
Pancakes (rice flour)		X		
Parsley, Chinese				X
Peas, Snow			X	
Pepper, Anise		X		
Pickles			X	
Pork, Liver (gizzard), roasted			X	
preserved, smoked			X	
suckling, roast			X	
Prunes, black			X	
Red-in-Snow			X	
Salted (jar or barrel)			X	
small			X	
Red Pepper Sauce or Paste (chili)				X
Rice, Glutinous			X	
Rice Cake (New Year)			X	
sweet		X		
Rose Petal Syrup		X		
Sage			X	
Sausage, preserved			X	
Sea Vegetable (kelp)			X	
Seaweed, Hair			X	
Purple			X	
Shark Fin			X	
Shrimp, dried			X	
Paste (salty)			X	
Snails		X		
Snow Fungus			X	
Soy Sauce, dark			X	
heavy			X	
light			X	
pearl			X	
table			X	
Squash, Silk (Okra), Chinese			X	
Squid, dried (small)			X	
Sugar, white (cake, sticky)		X		
Tangerine Peel, dried		X		
Taro Root			X	
Tea, Chrysanthemum				X
Cool (bitter herb)				X
Jasmine				X

	Absolutely Not Allowed	Should Not Be Taken	Allowed But Amount Kept to a Minimum	Allowed at Will
Turnip, dried			X	
Pressed, salted			X	
sweetened, pickled (salted)			X	
white			X	
Vegetable Steak			X	
Vinegar, Rice, black (sweet)			X	
red			X	
white			X	
Watermelon Seeds, black			X	
red			X	
Wheat Germ Syrup		X		
Wine, Chinese (gin, vodka)		X		
Rice, sweet		X		
Wood Ears (Cloud Ears)		X		

DIABETIC DIET RECIPES (See Index)

WRAPPING SKIN FOR EGG ROLLS AND WON TONS

WON TONS

FRIED WON TONS

EGG ROLLS

WON TONS WITH CHICKEN SOUP

HOT AND SOUR SOUP

TRIPLE SOUP

CRAB MEAT EGG FU YONG

STEAMED EGG CUSTARD WITH MINCED MEAT

ABALONE WITH OYSTER SAUCE

ABALONE WITH MUSHROOMS AND BAMBOO SHOOTS

BOILED FISH WITH SAUCE

FRIED FISH

SALT-CURED CHICKEN

SPICED CHICKEN WINGS

STIR-FRIED CHICKEN LIVERS

SPICED CHICKEN GIZZARDS

STEAMED CHICKEN WITH CHINESE PRESERVED SAUSAGE

DICED CHICKEN WITH PEPPER

CURRIED CHICKEN

GLUTINOUS RICE CHICKEN ROLLS

RED-COOKED DUCK
SALT-CURED DUCK

JADE GREEN MEAT DING
STEAMED PORK
STEAMED SPARERIBS

PAPER-WRAPPED BEEF
CURRIED BEEF
STIR-FRIED BEEF WITH BROCCOLI
STIR-FRIED BEEF WITH CHINESE CABBAGE, CABBAGE HEART,
   OR CHINESE CELERY CABBAGE

STIR-FRIED LAMB WITH BROCCOLI
STIR-FRIED BEEF, LAMB, OR CHICKEN WITH KOHLRABI
CURRIED LAMB
SHREDDED LAMB WITH VEGETABLES

BROCCOLI WITH MUSHROOMS
CABBAGE OR CABBAGE HEART WITH MUSHROOMS
STIR-FRIED GREEN BEANS WITH FERMENTED BEAN CAKE
KOHLRABI OR CABBAGE PICKLES
LOTUS ROOT CAKES
LOTUS ROOT CAKES WITH BEEF
BEAN SPROUT SALAD
BEAN SPROUT AND PICKLED GINGER SALAD

ULCER DIET GUIDE

	Absolutely Not Allowed	Should Not Be Taken	Allowed But Amount Kept to a Minimum	Allowed at Will
Abalone (well cooked)				X
Agar Agar				X
Dessert (black, sweet)				X
Algae				X
Anise, Star		X		
Bamboo Shoots, pickled (salty, sour)	X			
simmered in oil	X			
simmered with soy	X			
spring	X			
winter	X			
Bean, Black		X		
salted		X		
Filling				X

	Absolutely Not Allowed	Should Not Be Taken	Allowed But Amount Kept to a Minimum	Allowed at Will
Bean, Mung			X	
Bean Cake, fermented				X
Bean Curd (in liquid, barrel or can)				X
dried, refrigerated				X
fried, refrigerated		X		
Bean Curd Cheese, red				X
Milk				X
Roll				X
Sheet (sweet)			X	
soft precipitate; custard				X
Stick			X	
Bean Paste (red sauce)				X
Bean Sauce (Soy), brown or yellow				X
Bean Sprouts, Mung (pea sprouts)		X		
Soy (larger, harder)		X		
Beans, Green, Chinese (long)			X	
Bêche-de-Mer				X
Bird's Nest			X	
Bombay "Duck" (dried, salted fish)			X	
Broccoli, Chinese				X
Bun, Pork (large)			X	
roast			X	
Cabbage, Chinese			X	
Chinese, dried		X		
Cabbage Hearts (young)				X
Caul Fat			X	
Celery Cabbage				X
Chestnut, Water (well-cooked only)				X
flour				X
large			X	
Cloud Ears (Wood Ears)				X
Congee				X
Cookies, Almond				X
Fortune			X	
Crab Apple Strip	X			
Curry Powder	X			
Dates, Red			X	
Duck Liver			X	
Sauce (dark brown, in can)		X		
Dumplings, boiled	X			
fried, then steamed	X			
Egg (duck), preserved				X
salted				X

	Absolutely Not Allowed	Should Not Be Taken	Allowed But Amount Kept to a Minimum	Allowed at Will
Egg Roll Skins			X	
Fennel, sweet		X		
Fish, dry, wet (oil)		X		
salted				X
Fish Gravy				X
Maw			X	
Flour, Rice, fine				X
glutinous				X
Flower Spice			X	
Fruit, Candied				X
Preserved				X
Preserved with ginger		X		
Ginger, crystallized		X		
dried slices		X		
new shoot		X		
pickled		X		
preserved in syrup		X		
red new root		X		
regular, old shoot		X		
Ginkgo Nuts			X	
Golden Needles (Lily Flowers)			X	
Hoisin Sauce		X		
Jam, Soy, red		X		
sweet flour (Plum Sauce), green			X	
Jellyfish, dried		X		
Kohlrabi, fresh			X	
Leek		X		
Lemon Peel (salty)		X		
Licorice				X
Lily Flowers (Golden Needles)			X	
Lily Petals, dry		X		
Litchis				X
Longans				X
Loquats				X
Lotus Root			X	
powder				X
Lotus Seeds				X
Meat, crumbs, diced			X	
dried, smoked			X	
minced				X
salted			X	
Melon, Bitter			X	
Candied, slices				X

	Absolutely Not Allowed	Should Not Be Taken	Allowed But Amount Kept to a Minimum	Allowed at Will
Hairy				X
Tea (in honey)		X		
Tea (in ginger and honey)		X		
Winter, Candied				X
Moon Cake			X	
Mushrooms				X
Winter				X
Mustard Greens, Preserved (with peppers or onion and garlic)		X		
Noodles, Rice (fine sticks)		X		
(wide)				X
Oil, Peanut				X
Sesame		X		
Okra (Silk Squash), Chinese			X	
Olives, fermented		X		
salty		X		
sweet		X		
Oyster Sauce			X	
Oysters, dried with soy sauce			X	
Pancakes (rice flour)				X
Parsley, Chinese			X	
Peas, Snow			X	
Pepper, Anise		X		
Pickles		X		
Pork, liver (gizzard), roasted				X
Preserved, smoked			X	
suckling, roast				X
Prunes, black		X		
Red-in-Snow		X		
Salted (jar or barrel)		X		
small		X		
Red Pepper Sauce or Paste (chili)		X		
Rice, Glutinous		X		
Rice Cake (New Year)		X		
Sweet		X		
Rose Petal Syrup				X
Sage				X
Sausage, preserved			X	
Sea Vegetable (kelp)			X	
Seaweed, Hair				X
Purple				X

	Absolutely Not Allowed	Should Not Be Taken	Allowed But Amount Kept to a Minimum	Allowed at Will
Shark Fin				X
Shrimp, dried		X		
Paste (salty)				X
Snails				X
Snow Fungus				X
Soy Sauce, dark				X
heavy				X
light				X
pearl				X
table				X
Squash, Silk (Okra), Chinese			X	
Squid, dried (small)		X		
Sugar, white (cake, sticky)				X
Tangerine Peel, dried			X	
Taro Root				X
Tea, Chrysanthemum				X
Cool (bitter herb)	X			
Jasmine		X		
Turnip, dried		X		
Pressed, salted		X		
sweetened, pickled (salted)		X		
white				X
Vegetable Steak			X	
Vinegar, Rice, black (sweet)		X		
red		X		
white		X		
Watermelon Seeds, black		X		
red		X		
Wheat Germ Syrup				X
Wine, Chinese (gin, vodka)	X			
Rice, sweet	X			
Wood Ears (Cloud Ears)		X		

ULCER DIET RECIPES (See Index)

SHRIMP WON TONS

EGG DROP SOUP

BIRD'S NEST SOUP

BEAN CURD CHICKEN SOUP

MEATBALL SOUP

CELLOPHANE NOODLES AND MEATBALL SOUP

LAMB CHOP CUCUMBER SOUP

PORK NOODLE SOUP

CONGEE

CHICKEN FU YONG

STEAMED EGG CUSTARD

PEKING CUSTARD

PRESERVED (100-YEAR-OLD) EGGS

RED-COOKED CARP WITH BEAN CURD SKIN

CARP WITH BEAN CURD CAKE

STEAMED SHAD

SHRIMP ROLL

SHRIMP ROLL WITH CELLOPHANE NOODLES

SHRIMP LO MEIN

LOBSTER CASSEROLE

KING CRAB MEAT EGG FU YONG

CRAB MEAT WITH CARROTS

CRAB MEAT CASSEROLE

STEAMED CHICKEN WITH SOUP

CHICKEN CREAM OF RICE

MUSHROOM CREAMED CHICKEN

STEAMED CHICKEN BREASTS WITH RICE FLOUR

COLD SAVORY NOODLES WITH CHICKEN

SCALLION STEAMED CHICKEN

CLOUD EAR CHICKEN

CHICKEN LO MEIN

PORK CARROT BAO

PORK MUSHROOM BAO

PORK LO MEIN

PEARL MEATBALLS

STIR-FRIED BEEF WITH SPINACH

MUTTON GELATIN

LAMB STEW

CELERY CABBAGE HEARTS IN CREAM SAUCE

EGGPLANT BUTTER

CHOPPED SPINACH IN CREAM SAUCE

CHINESE BREAD

BEAN CURD WITH SOY SAUCE

BEAN CURD WITH OYSTER SAUCE

SHREDDED BEAN CURD WITH CHICKEN

STUFFED BEAN CURD

ALMOND GEL WITH PEACHES

LOW SALT DIET GUIDE

	Absolutely Not Allowed	Should Not Be Taken	Allowed But Amount Kept to a Minimum	Allowed at Will
Abalone		X		
Agar Agar				X
Dessert (black, sweet)				X
Algae	X			
Anise, Star		X		
Bamboo Shoots, pickled (salty, sour)	X			
simmered in oil		X		
simmered with soy		X		
spring			X	
winter			X	
Bean, Black				X
salted	X			
Filling	X			
Bean, Mung				X
Bean Cake, fermented	X			
Bean Curd (in liquid, barrel or can)	X			
dried, refrigerated	X			
fried, refrigerated	X			
Bean Curd Cheese, red	X			
Milk				X
Roll	X			
Sheet (sweet)	X			
soft precipitate; custard	X			
Stick	X			
Bean Paste (red sauce)	X			
Bean Sauce (Soy), brown or yellow	X			
Bean Sprouts, Mung (pea sprouts)				X
Soy (larger, harder)				X
Beans, Green, Chinese (long)				X
Bêche-de-Mer	X			
Bird's Nest				X
Bombay "Duck" (dried, salted fish)	X			
Broccoli, Chinese				X
Bun, Pork (large)		X		
roast		X		
Cabbage, Chinese				X
Chinese, dried	X			
Cabbage Hearts (young)				X
Caul Fat				X
Celery Cabbage				X
Chestnut, Water (well-cooked only)				X

	Absolutely Not Allowed	Should Not Be Taken	Allowed But Amount Kept to a Minimum	Allowed at Will
flour				X
large				X
Cloud Ears (Wood Ears)				X
Congee (plain)				X
Cookies				
Almond		X		
Fortune		X		
Crab Apple Strip				X
Curry Powder		X		
Dates, red (dried only)				X
Duck Liver (gizzard)			X	
Sauce (dark brown, in can)	X			
Dumplings, boiled				X
fried, then steamed		X		
Egg (duck), preserved	X			
salted	X			
Egg Roll Skins	X			
Fennel, sweet		X		
Fish, dry, wet (oil)	X			
salted	X			
Fish Gravy		X		
Maw			X	
Flour, Rice fine				X
glutinous				X
Flower Spice		X		
Fruit, Candied		X		
preserved		X		
preserved with ginger		X		
Ginger, crystallized		X		
dried slices		X		
new shoot			X	
pickled		X		
preserved in syrup			X	
red new root			X	
regular, old shoot			X	
Ginkgo Nuts				X
Golden Needles (Lily Flowers)				X
Hoisin Sauce	X			
Jam, Soy, red		X		
sweet flour (Plum Sauce), green		X		
Jellyfish, dried	X			
Kohlrabi, fresh				X
Leek				X
Lemon Peel, salty	X			

	Absolutely Not Allowed	Should Not Be Taken	Allowed But Amount Kept to a Minimum	Allowed at Will
Licorice				X
Lily Flowers (Golden Needles)				X
Lily Petals, dry		X		
Litchis				X
Longans			X	
Loquats				X
Lotus Root				X
powder				X
Lotus Seeds				X
Meat, crumbs, diced		X		
dried, smoked		X		
minced		X		
salted	X			
Melon, Bitter		X		
Candied, slices	X			
Hairy				X
Tea (in honey)			X	
Tea (in ginger and honey)		X		
Winter, Candied	X			
Moon Cake		X		
Mushrooms				X
Winter				X
Mustard Greens, Preserved (with peppers or onion and garlic)		X		
Noodles, Rice (fine sticks)				X
(wide)				X
Oil, Peanut				X
Sesame				X
Okra (Silk Squash), Chinese				X
Olives, fermented		X		
salty	X			
sweet	X			
Oyster Sauce	X			
Oysters, dried with soy sauce				
Pancakes (rice flour)			X	
Parsley, Chinese		X		
Peas, Snow				X
Pepper, Anise			X	
Pickles	X			
Pork, liver (gizzard), roasted		X		
preserved, smoked		X		
suckling, roast		X		
Prunes, black		X		
Red-in-Snow			X	

	Absolutely Not Allowed	Should Not Be Taken	Allowed But Amount Kept to a Minimum	Allowed at Will
Salted (jar or barrel)	X			
small	X			
Red Pepper Sauce or Paste (chili)		X		
Rice, Glutinous				X
Rice Cake (New Year)		X		
sweet				X
Rose Petal Syrup				X
Sage				X
Sausage, preserved		X		
Sea Vegetable (kelp)	X			
Seaweed, Hair	X			
Purple	X			
Shark Fin			X	
Shrimp, dried	X			
Paste (salty)	X			
Snails	X			
Snow Fungus				X
Soy Sauce, dark	X			
heavy	X			
light	X			
pearl	X			
table	X			
Squash, Silk (Okra), Chinese				X
Squid, dried (small)		X		
Sugar, white (cake, sticky)				X
Tangerine Peel, dried		X		
Taro Root				X
Tea, Chrysanthemum				X
Cool (bitter herb)				X
Jasmine				X
Turnip, dried	X			
Pressed, salted	X			
sweetened, pickled (salted)	X			
white	X			
Vegetable Steak		X		
Vinegar, Rice, black (sweet)				X
red				X
white				X
Watermelon Seeds, black	X			
red	X			
Wheat Germ Syrup				
Wine, Chinese (gin, vodka)			X	
Rice, sweet			X	
Wood Ears (Cloud Ears)				X

TEA

OVER 250 DIFFERENT VARIETIES OF CHINESE TEA EXIST (OF ALL THOSE MEN-tioned here many can be obtained from Taipei), most from the same kind of shrub, differing in taste by area in which grown, time picked, and position of the leaves on the shrub, preparation before packing, and finally, method of infusion, brewing, etc.

The three main classifications, which indicate the method of leaf processing, are unfermented green, fermented black, and semifermented red tea, which are then divided into two grades: whole and broken; the latter normally gives darker and stronger tea. (A dark color does not always denote strength.)

To enrich fragrance, sometimes certain flowers are added; orange-flower buds, chrysanthemums, and jasmine go with green tea, while roses go with black. Oolong tea is smoked.

Outstanding tea is clear and pale gold in color, not brisk, with a delicate bouquet, and without a trace of bitterness. Poor quality tea is too light or too dark, with a bitter, crude taste, which many people attempt to disguise with sugar and lemon.

Five rules should be followed for making good tea: (1) the tea leaves should be of good quality, (2) the water should be freshly drawn and boiled, (3) the water should not be boiled beyond the boiling point or the oxygen will be expelled from the water and cause the tea to taste flat, (4) the water should be at boiling point when poured on the tea leaves, and the teapot kept hot enough so as not to lower this temperature, and (5) the tea should be brewed 5 minutes.

The shape and material of the teapot is quite important. A china pot is preferable to a metal one because the latter often adds unwanted flavors.

A good method for brewing tea is to use 2 tablespoons of tea for every four cups of water, or ½ to 1 teaspoon for each cup, depending upon the quality of the tea and one's taste. However, when a large quantity of tea is to be brewed, the amount of tea leaves per cup can be reduced somewhat. Tea that is correctly brewed, in the beginning, will have about ⅔ of its leaves floating, which then sink to the bottom. Tea that is incorrectly brewed will have about half of its leaves floating. Strong tea can always be altered by diluting it, but nothing can be done to strengthen weak tea. Most tea leaves can be used again. In fact, the second brewing is better than the first; however, a third brewing retains only partial flavor.

Tea should be kept in a tight-lidded can in a cool, dry place since the leaves have a definite tendency to absorb moisture and odors. Unlike some wines, good tea does not improve with age but a tight container will preserve its fragrance and flavor longer.

Tea for table use is like everyday wine—good but not superior. (Tea can cost as much as $300 a pound.) Freshness, purity, and lightness are the characteristics valued in a table tea, which must also harmonize unobtrusively with the flavors of the food while cooling and refreshing the palate and aiding the digestion. Between those who gulp their tea, strong, as a restorative, and the connoisseur who sips his, slowly, is the average drinker who derives simple refreshment and an opportunity for pleasant relaxation and conversation.

In China, the teahouse traditionally has been sought for amusement as well as refreshment, the most luxurious of these being set in a cool spot of natural beauty or historic interest. Many Peking teahouses are scattered along the lakes and in the parks; one famous teahouse is located on a marble boat at the Summer Palace, sometimes called "China's Navy" because the Empress had built it with money allocated for the establishment of a navy. At home and in the office, tea is kept hot all day in large porcelain pots set into baskets lined with thick cotton insulation.

However, tea is not always the beverage served with a meal in China; rather, rice wine is often served, while tea is included as a demitasse. A guest is always offered tea upon arrival, no matter what the time of day or night. The leaves are placed in individual cups and the tea is brewed right in the cup, with each cup equipped with a cover for the purpose. In the afternoon, almond or rice cakes and preserved ginger or shrimp chips are often served as well.

TEA GUIDE

TEA	PROVINCE	DESCRIPTION
Green		
Black Dragon Oolong	Formosa	A cross between green and black tea; long, daintily tipped leaves; served at any time.
Cloud Mist Wun Mo	Kiangsi	Generally served in the afternoon or at teatime. It is grown on high mountain cliffs and plucked and gathered by trained monkeys.
Dragon Beard Loong So	Canton	Also known as Dragon's Whiskers.

TEA	PROVINCE	DESCRIPTION
Dragon Well Jun Jing	Chinkiang	One of the finest green teas; light in color, fresh in flavor.
Eyes of Longevity Sho May	Canton	Served as a between-meal beverage.
Fragrant Petals Heung Peen	Chinkiang	Unusually fragrant; served at small parties for relatives or close friends.
Green Tea Lu An Dow Chow	Anhwei	Has the smell of new-mown hay.
Mulberry Swong Yuck	Hangchow	Made from young mulberry leaves.
Silver Needle Ngun Jum	Canton	Served as a banquet tea.
Water Nymph Swei Shien Hwa	Canton	A light tea, generally served in the midmorning.

Black

Clear Distance Ching Yuen	Canton	Preferable with late-night snacks.
Iron Goddess of Mercy Te Kwan Yin	Fukien	Quite thin; like a fine brandy; served in small cups. Grown on steep cliffs, gathered by monkeys.
Lapsang Souchong	Yunan	Very smoky and strong.
Poo Nay	Yunan	Regarded as a powerful tonic.
Su Tang	Fukien	Generally served as a late-evening beverage.
Wing Chow	Canton	Breakfast tea.
Woo Lung	Chinkiang	Served at public teahouses with talk of the day; smoky flavor.
Wu I	Yunan	Medicine for colds; very bitter.

Red

Hung Cha	Fukien	Served at teahouses and restaurants in the United States; dumped at the Boston Tea Party.
Keemun	Kiansi, Anhwei	Very popular; spicy, smooth, delicate; most famous.

Flowered

Chrysanthemum Chiu Hwa	Chekiang	Sweetened with rock candy and served with Chinese pastry after meals.
Jasmine Mook Lay Fa	Formosa, Fukien	Combination of Dragon Well leaves and flowers; aromatic, delicious.
Lichee	Formosa	Black tea with litchi leaf flavoring; faintly sweet.
Lo Cha	Formosa	Combination of Oolong and litchi flowers; served to renew friendship.
Rose Mei Kwei	Formosa	Black tea with dried rosebuds.

WINE

MILLENNIUMS BEFORE CHRIST, "WINE" WAS DRUNK IN CHINA. HOWEVER, because it was made from grain, not grapes, technically, it is not wine. Nevertheless, Marco Polo knew of Chinese wines.

Many sources accept the origin of wine found in an ancient Chinese classic, *The Country's Policy.* According to its tale, Yi Dick, a chef of the Imperial Palace, placed some rice in an earthen jug to soak and then completely forgot about it. Several days later he discovered the brew, tasted it, and found it to be delicious. As he continued to drink he became gay and soon broke into joyous song. When he brought a large sample to Emperor Yu, who tasted it, he, too, was stimulated and delighted and immediately ordered a large supply for a very special feast he was then celebrating. He quickly realized its value during the feast: after a few drinks, formerly stubborn opponents became amenable to his views. However, on the next morning, he learned of the wine's adverse effects—none of his officials were fit for work, upon which he issued the following regulations: (1) wine was to be served in very small cups instead of in soup bowls; (2) no one could drink on an empty stomach; and (3) one had to eat while drinking, as well as engage in some form of physical and mental exercise, which is one explanation for the popularity of such games as "guessing fingers."

A traditional source of pride among Chinese poets and writers is a large capacity for alcohol. Notwithstanding, the Chinese are very temperate; wine is used to augment good fellowship, nearly always imbibed with ample food, and intoxication is rare. Other applications of wine besides convivial drinking and cooking include its ceremonial use, in marriages, for example.

China's most popular wine is made from rice. The climate that enables provinces to produce the cereal is also suitable for the brewing of wine, of which there are two main kinds—white and yellow. Ordinary yellow rice wine tastes like sherry, and is used equally for cooking and drinking, at ceremonies, and at various other special occasions. It is usually warmed before serving, and then placed in a small, delicate wine pot, either of shining brass, floral porcelain, or pewter, and poured into miniscule thin cups. If the ordinary yellow (*shaosing*) wine is not readily obtainable for cooking, Japanese sake may be used, or regular dry sherry, the kind that can be served at the table (and never cream sherry or cooking sherry, which are not good for Chinese cooking). Gin is a very acceptable substitute and is actually more akin to rice wine than sherry; it cuts down on any fishy or gamy flavor. Other yellow wines include some very strong types, some flavored with spices, others believed to aid the circulation, and of therapeutic value.

The principal white wine is a distillation of a purple-topped variety of sorghum grain found in Northern China. It resembles vodka in flavor and strength (it may even be stronger) but with a major difference: it is much smoother. Also, it is as clear as water. This white wine is added to many vegetable dishes and is the one most used to replace the yellow wine when that does not come up to strength. Other white wines include tiger tendon and quince wine; rose petal wine, which is of a high alcoholic content and flavored with rose petals as fragrant as a bouquet; and the two mild orange and pear wines. Among this group are, of course, various natural fragrances.

Wine is a prominent feature of Chinese cooking. A small amount is always added to meat and seafood, especially, not as a flavoring but rather to neutralize any strong odor. However, many dishes require a great deal of wine for marinating, when a stronger wine is desired, such as in wine chicken, "drunken" chicken, "drunken" pork, and Peking duck. As for "abstainers," there need be no concern: in cooking, the alcohol evaporates and only the flavor remains.

Drinking or cooking wines may be purchased in any Chinese liquor store. They are quite expensive and, at first, probably will not be as pleasing to American palates as native, French, and Italian wines.

MAIL ORDER SOURCES FOR CHINESE FOODSTUFFS

BOSTON

Sun Sun Company
34 Oxford Street
Boston, Mass.
HA 6–6494

CHICAGO

Man Sun Wing Company
2229 Wentworth Avenue
Chicago, Ill. 60616

CLEVELAND

Sun Lee Yuen Company
1726 Payne Avenue
Cleveland, Ohio

DALLAS

Jung's
Oriental Food & Gifts
2519 North Fitzhugh
Dallas, Texas

HOUSTON

Oriental Import and Export Company
2009 Polk Street
Houston, Tex.
FA 3-5621

LOS ANGELES

Hismoco (American Co.), Inc.
Suite 1402
9000 Sunset Boulevard
Los Angeles, Calif. 90069
213-272-5158-9; 213 272-5150

NEW YORK

Eastern Ken's, Inc.
10 West 56 Street
New York, N.Y. 10019
LT 2-1159

Mon Fong Wo Company
36 Pell Street
New York, N.Y. 10013
WO 2-5418-9

Oriental Food Shop
1302 Amsterdam Avenue
New York, N.Y. 10027
AC 2-3100

Wo Fat Co., Inc.
16 Bowery
New York, N.Y. 10013
WO 2-9980

PHILADELPHIA

Wing On Company
1005 Race Street
Philadelphia, Pa. 10107

SAN FRANCISCO

*Chong Imports
Chong Kee Jan Co., Inc.
855 Grant Avenue
San Francisco, Calif.
YU 2-1433

Dupont Market
1100 Grant Avenue
San Francisco, Calif.
YU 2-2999, YU 2-1447

*Ginn Wall Company
1016 Grant Avenue
San Francisco, Calif.
YU 2-6307

Kwong Hang Company
918 Grant Avenue
San Francisco, Calif.
YU 2-5617

Ping Yuen Market
1109 Grant Avenue
San Francisco, Calif.
YU 2-1613

Tai Cheong Company
1143 Grant Avenue
San Francisco, Calif.
EX 2-1142

Wing Hing Chong Company
911 Grant Avenue
San Francisco, Calif.
YU 2-5994

Wing Sing Chong Company
1076 Stockton Street
San Francisco, Calif.
YU 2-4171

Wo Kee Company
644 Kearney Street
San Francisco, Calif.
GA 1-7764

Frank H. Yick & Company
772 Pacific Avenue
San Francisco, Calif.
YU 2-6411

SEATTLE

House of Rice
4132 University Way N.E.
Seattle, Wash.

WASHINGTON, D.C.

Mee Wah Lung
608 H Street N.W.
Washington, D.C.
RE 7-0968

Tuck Cheong & Company
Chinese Merchandise
617 H Street, N.W.
Washington, D.C.

*Catalog sent on request

BIBLIOGRAPHY

Au, M. Sing. *The Chinese Cook Book*. Reading, Pa.: Culinary Arts Press, 1936.

Beilenson, Edna. *Simple Oriental Cookery*. Mount Vernon, N.Y.: Peter Pauper Press, 1960.

Benedictine Sisters of Peking. *The Art of Chinese Cooking*. Rutland, Vt.: Charles E. Tuttle Co., Inc., 1959.

Caleva. *Chinese Cookbook for Quantity Service*. New York: Ahrens Book Co., Inc., 1958.

Chan, Esther. *Chinese Cookery Secrets*. Chungtai Press, 1960.

Chan, Sou. *The House of Chan Cookbook*, Garden City, N.Y.: Doubleday & Co., Inc., 1952.

Chang, Isabelle. *What's Cooking at Chang's*. New York: Liveright Publishing Corp., 1959.

———. *Chinese Cooking Made Easy*. New York: Paperback Library, Inc., 1961.

Chao, Buwei Yang. *How to Cook and Eat in Chinese*. New York: John Day Co., 1945 and 1949.

Chen, Joyce. *Joyce Chen Cookbook*. Philadelphia: J. B. Lippincott Co., 1963.

Cheng, F. T. *Musings of a Chinese Gourmet*. London: Hutchinson & Co., 1962.

Chow, Dolly (Mrs. C. T. Wang). *Chow!*. Rutland, Vt.: Charles E. Tuttle Co., 1960.

Chu, Grace Zia. *Pleasure of Chinese Cooking*. New York: Simon & Schuster, Inc., 1962.

Fang, John T. C. *Chinatown Handy Guide*. New York: Chinese Publishing House, 1958.

Feng, Doreen Yen Hung. *The Joy of Chinese Cooking*. New York: Grosset & Dunlap, Inc., 1954.

Froud, Nina. *Cooking the Chinese Way*. New York: Spring Books, 1960.

Grossman, Ruth and Bob. *Kosher Chinese Cooking*. New York: Paul S. Eriksson, Inc., 1963.

Hee, Yep Yung. *Chinese Recipes for Home Cooking*. Sydney, Australia: Associated General Publications, 1955.

Hiang, Lie Sek. *Indonesian Cookery*. New York: Crown Publishers, Inc., 1963.

Hong, Wallace Yee. *The Chinese Cook Book*. New York: Crown Publishers, Inc., 1952.

Hong Kong Y.W.C.A. *Noodles and Rice*. Hong Kong: *South China Morning Post*, 1960.

Huxley, Gervas. *Talking of Tea*. London: Thames and Hudson, Ltd., 1956.

Jan, Dr. Lee Su. *The Fine Art of Chinese Cooking*. Indianapolis: The Bobbs-Merrill Co., Inc., 1962.

Kan, Johnny. *Eight Immortal Flavors*. Berkeley, Calif.: Howell-North Books, 1963.

Keys, John D. *Food for the Emperor*. San Francisco: The Ward Ritchie Press, 1963.

Kuang-teh, Yang. *50 Chinese Recipes*. Peking: China Reconstructs, 1958.

La Choy Food Products. *The Art and Secrets of Chinese Cookery*. Archbold, Ohio: Beatrice Foods Co., 1959.

Lau, Margaret. *Chinese Cooking*. Hilo, Hawaii: Hilo Tribune-Herald, Ltd., 1962.

Lee, Beverly. *The Easy Way to Chinese Cooking*. Garden City, New York: Doubleday & Co., Inc., 1963.

Lee, Calvin. *Chinese Cooking for American Kitchens*. New York: G. P. Putnam's Sons (in Toronto, Canada, by Longmans, Green & Co., Inc.), 1959.

Lee, Helen Chiang. *A Chinese Cookbook for Everyone*. New York: Exposition Press, 1962.

Lee, M. P. *Chinese Cookery*. New York: Transatlantic Arts, Inc., 1945.

Lin, Chan Sow. *Chinese Restaurant Dishes*. Kuala Lumpur, Malaya: Chan Sow Lin, 1963.

————. *Hong Kong, Shanghai and Peking Restaurant Dishes*. Kuala Lumpur, Malaya: Chan Sow Lin, 1961.

Lin, Tsuifeng. *Cooking with the Chinese Flavor*. Englewood Cliffs, N.J.: Prentice Hall, Inc., 1956.

Lon, Shen Mei. *The Ancestral Recipes*. New York: Richards Rosen Press, Inc., 1954.

Ma, Nancy Chih. *Mrs. Ma's Chinese Cookbook*. Rutland, Vermont, and Tokyo, Japan: Charles E. Tuttle Co., Inc., 1960.

Mei, Yu Wen, and Adams, Charlotte. *100 Most Honorable Chinese Recipes*. New York: Thomas Y. Crowell Company, 1963.

Mitchell, Alice Miller. *Oriental Cookbook*. Chicago, New York, San Francisco: Rand McNally & Co., 1954.

Oliver, Frank. *Chinese Cooking*. New York: The Citadel Press, 1957.

Ouei, Mimie. *The Art of Chinese Cooking*. Toronto: Random House, 1960.

Renwick, Ethel Hulbert. *A World of Good Cooking*. New York: Macfadden-Bartell Corp., 1964.

Rosen, Ruth Chier. *Nippon These: The Fine Art of Oriental Cooking*. New York: Richards Rosen Press, 1961.

Searle, Townley. *Strange News from China: A First Chinese Cookery Book*. London: Ouseley Co., Inc., 1932.

Sia, Mary. *Mary Sia's Chinese Cookbook*. Honolulu: University of Hawaii Press, 1956.

Toupin, Elizabeth. *Restaurant of the Five Volcanos Cook Book*. Copies available by writing Elizabeth Toupin, Clearwater Lane, Pound Ridge, N.Y.

Tseng, Rosey. *Chinese Cooking Made Easy*. Rutland, Vt.: Charles E. Tuttle Co., Inc., 1963.

Waldo, Myra. *The Round-the-World Cookbook*. New York: Bantam Books, Inc., 1954.

————. *The Complete Book of Oriental Cooking*. New York: Bantam Books, Inc., 1960.

Wing, Fred. *New Chinese Recipes*. New York: Edelmuth Co., 1951.

Wong, Richard. *Enjoy Chinese Cooking at Home*. New York: Mong Fong Wo Co., 1949.

Young, Myrtle Lum. *Fun with Chinese Recipes*. New York: Vantage Press, Inc., 1958.

INDEX